About the Author

Sam Crompton, holding a powder horn, poses by the Soldier's Memorial in Northampton, Massachusetts (*photo: Dieu Etinde*).

Samuel Willard Crompton is the author or editor of many books written for a variety of publishers. Though he has written for children, teenagers, and adults, one of the constants of his career is that military topics have often played a major role. He has been a National Endowment for the Humanities Fellow on several occasions, the most recent of which was "The Civil War in Trans-National Perspective," held at New York University. Crompton teaches history at Holyoke Community College in his native Massachusetts.

Also from Visible Ink Press

The Handy African American History Answer Book
by Jessie Carnie Smith
ISBN: 978-1-57859-452-8

The Handy American History Answer Book
by David Hudson
ISBN: 978-1-57859-471-9

The Handy Anatomy Answer Book
by James Bobick and Naomi Balaban
ISBN: 978-1-57859-190-9

The Handy Answer Book for Kids (and Parents), 2nd edition
by Gina Misiroglu
ISBN: 978-1-57859-219-7

The Handy Art History Answer Book
by Madelynn Dickerson
ISBN: 978-1-57859-417-7

The Handy Astronomy Answer Book, 3rd edition
by Charles Liu
ISBN: 978-1-57859-190-9

The Handy Bible Answer Book
by Jennifer Rebecca Prince
ISBN: 978-1-57859-478-8

The Handy Biology Answer Book, 2nd edition
by Patricia Barnes Svarney and Thomas E. Svarney
ISBN: 978-1-57859-490-0

The Handy Civil War Answer Book
by Samuel Willard Crompton
ISBN: 978-1-57859-476-4

The Handy Dinosaur Answer Book, 2nd edition
by Patricia Barnes-Svarney and Thomas E. Svarney
ISBN: 978-1-57859-218-0

Handy English Grammar Answer Book
by Christine Hult, Ph.D.
ISBN: 978-1-57859-520-4

The Handy Geography Answer Book, 2nd edition
by Paul A. Tucci
ISBN: 978-1-57859-215-9

The Handy Geology Answer Book
by Patricia Barnes-Svarney and Thomas E. Svarney
ISBN: 978-1-57859-156-5

The Handy History Answer Book, 3rd edition
by David L. Hudson, Jr.
ISBN: 978-1-57859-372-9

The Handy Hockey Answer Book
by Stanley Fischler
ISBN: 978-1-57859-513-6

The Handy Islam Answer Book
by John Renard Ph.D.
ISBN: 978-1-57859-510-5

The Handy Law Answer Book
by David L. Hudson Jr.
ISBN: 978-1-57859-217-3

The Handy Math Answer Book, 2nd edition
by Patricia Barnes-Svarney and Thomas E. Svarney
ISBN: 978-1-57859-373-6

The Handy Mythology Answer Book,
by David A. Leeming, Ph.D.
ISBN: 978-1-57859-475-7

The Handy Nutrition Answer Book
by Patricia Barnes-Svarney and Thomas E. Svarney
ISBN: 978-1-57859-484-9

The Handy Ocean Answer Book
by Patricia Barnes-Svarney and Thomas E. Svarney
ISBN: 978-1-57859-063-6

The Handy Personal Finance Answer Book
by Paul A. Tucci
ISBN: 978-1-57859-322-4

The Handy Philosophy Answer Book
by Naomi Zack
ISBN: 978-1-57859-226-5

The Handy Physics Answer Book, 2nd edition
By Paul W. Zitzewitz, Ph.D.
ISBN: 978-1-57859-305-7

The Handy Politics Answer Book
by Gina Misiroglu
ISBN: 978-1-57859-139-8

The Handy Presidents Answer Book, 2nd edition
by David L. Hudson
ISB N: 978-1-57859-317-0

The Handy Psychology Answer Book
by Lisa J. Cohen
ISBN: 978-1-57859-223-4

The Handy Religion Answer Book, 2nd edition
by John Renard
ISBN: 978-1-57859-379-8

The Handy Science Answer Book®, 4th edition
by The Carnegie Library of Pittsburgh
ISBN: 978-1-57859-321-7

The Handy Sports Answer Book
by Kevin Hillstrom, Laurie Hillstrom, and Roger Matuz
ISBN: 978-1-57859-075-9

The Handy Supreme Court Answer Book
by David L Hudson, Jr.
ISBN: 978-1-57859-196-1

The Handy Weather Answer Book, 2nd edition
by Kevin S. Hile
ISBN: 978-1-57859-221-0

Please visit us at www.handyanswers.com

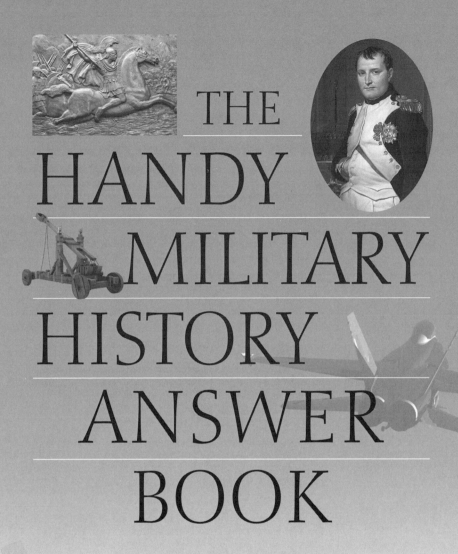

THE
HANDY
MILITARY
HISTORY
ANSWER
BOOK

Samuel Willard Crompton

VISIBLE
INK
PRESS

Detroit

THE HANDY MILITARY HISTORY ANSWER BOOK

Visible Ink Press®
43311 Joy Rd., #414
Canton, MI 48187–2075

Visible Ink Press is a registered trademark of Visible Ink Press LLC.

Most Visible Ink Press books are available at special quantity discounts when purchased in bulk by corporations, organizations, or groups. Customized printings, special imprints, messages, and excerpts can be produced to meet your needs. For more information, contact Special Markets Director, Visible Ink Press, www.visibleink.com, or 734–667–3211.

Managing Editor: Kevin S. Hile
Art Director: Mary Claire Krzewinski
Typesetting: Marco Di Vita
Proofreaders: Aarti Stephens, Shoshana Hurwitz
Indexer: Larry Baker

Front cover images: Catapult, fighter jets, and Alexander the Great from Shutterstock; Napoleon image is public domain.

Back cover images: Genghis Khan, "The Death of General Wolfe," and "U.S. Marines" poster are public domain; Vietnam War memorial, Shutterstock.

Library of Congress Cataloging–in–Publication Data

Crompton, Samuel Willard.
  The handy military history answer book / Samuel Willard Crompton.
    pages cm. – (The handy answer book series)
  ISBN 978-1-57859-509-9 (pbk.)
  1.   Military history–Miscellanea. I. Title.
  D25.C967 2015
  355.009–dc23   2014036927

Printed in the United States of America

10 9 8 7 6 5 4 3 2 1

Contents

Photo Credits

Ad Meskens: p. 242.
Bollweevil: p. 46.
Adam Cuerdon: p. 276.
Daderot: p. 288.
Das Bundesarchiv: pp. 369, 379, 389, 391, 423.
David Stanley from Nanaimo, Canada: p. 72.
Fanghong: p. 59.
Gautier Poupeau from Paris, France: p. 35.
Georges Jansoone (JoJan): p. 37.
Hans Jørn Storgaard Andersen: p. 477.
Ilya Schurov: p. 506.
Library of Congress: pp. 309, 315, 321, 335, 340, 371, 373, 378, 417, 433, 437.
Louis le Grand: p. 42.
Margaret Thatcher Foundation: p. 476.
Mike Peel (www.mikepeel.net): p. 16.
Moonik: p. 6.
National Archives USA: p. 405.
Nick-D: p. 410.
Pavel Kazachkov: p. 118 (top).
Pete Souza: p. 503.
Project Gutenberg: p. 248.

RIA Novosti archive: pp. 380, 383.
TheMachineStops: p. 492.
uncle.capung: p. 445.
U.S. Air Force: p. 488.
U.S. Army: pp. 414, 419, 431, 470, 494.
U.S. Army Signal Corps: p. 393.
U.S. Department of Defense: pp. 8, 484, 496, 509.
U.S. Marine Corps: p. 501.
U.S. National Archives and Records Administration: pp. 297, 475.
U.S. Navy: pp. 386, 400, 421, 435.
U.S. public domain: pp. 27, 99, 110, 112, 114, 120, 125, 127, 131, 134, 136, 139, 144, 146, 149, 151, 158, 163, 168, 182, 189, 198, 207, 234, 251, 255, 259, 260, 264, 267, 270, 272, 284, 293, 296, 304, 306, 330, 332, 345, 350.
Vassil: p. 80.
Welcome Trust: p. 121.
Witia: p. 250.
Zhang Zhenshi: p. 362.
All others images are in the public domain.

Dedication

This is for my beloved Charlotte, she who threaded her way through isolation, relocation, and single motherhood on the way toward peace, happiness, and the enjoyment of grandchildren.

Introduction

Hans, Tommy, Ivan, and Joe gather round the table to discuss their memories of the Second World War. For men who are often talkative at home, they are rather quiet, humble even, as they begin to talk with others who had incredibly important experiences at the same time they did, albeit in the service of different nations.

Hans, who still has the long, lean lines of a German athlete, declares that his people never supported the idea of war with the rest of Europe; they voted for Hitler because this seemed the only way out of the Great Depression, which, in 1932, was pretty awful. Hans admits that he signed up too quickly for the German infantry, and that he might have done better to hold off. War fever in 1939 was powerful, however, and he says that he had the wish to accomplish what his father—and millions of other Germans—had failed to do in the First World War.

Everyone nods. They understand the power of parental influence quite well.

Tommy speaks next. Life has not been as good to him as it was to Hans: he moves slowly from the effects of both war wounds and arthritis. He shows no bitterness, however. Like Hans, he was very young when the Second Great War—as many Brits call it— began, and he had no hesitation about signing up. Early on, he had no bad feelings about the Germans, he says; it was only when he helped in the liberation of one of the death camps, in the spring of 1945, that he experienced incredible revulsion. For a long time he blamed Hitler and the Germans, he says, but viewing the world for the last fifty years, some thirty of them spent in retirement, has shown him that people everywhere are capable of cruelty and terrible deeds. The important thing, Tommy says, is to prevent them from having the means to accomplish such deeds.

This speech is not as universally acknowledged as the previous one, but everyone is very polite as they turn to Ivan to ask if he can comment. There's a quiet respect in their voices, because they know that he—as a Russian—very likely witnessed unspeakable horrors to a great degree.

Ivan has bad words for Hitler and Mussolini, but he doesn't think much better of Churchill and FDR. To him, all these leaders were savages who allowed the beast within humans to emerge and paved the way for the deaths of millions. He never had personal feelings against the Germans, he declares; rather, it was their system that he objected to. Everyone hums and nods their heads a little, and then Joe asks what Ivan thinks or feels about Josef Stalin.

The worst! Hitler was a raving lunatic, Ivan declares, and Mussolini and Churchill were cravens who let other people do their dirty work. FDR was a bit of a cold-blooded fellow, but Ivan would choose him over "Uncle Joe"—as Americans used to call Stalin—any day of the week. Ivan surprises his fellows by saying that when the Germans first invaded his country in June 1941 he welcomed them as liberators. That sentiment lasted about forty-eight hours and was destroyed by his witnessing acts of cruelty by the invaders. Thereafter, he fought valiantly for Mother Russia, he says, but never for Uncle Joe.

At this point the conversation turns in the direction of another Joe who sits at the table. The other three men ask him to express some of his thoughts, feelings, or beliefs.

Joe explains that he is reluctant to comment because he knows darned well that he's a lucky fellow who escaped World War II without injury, living in what may just be the luckiest country in the world. He does have a question for his fellow veterans, however.

Given that Germany, Britain, and Russia were all so badly pounded during the Second World War, how is it that they look so darned well today, Joe asks? He remembers the end of the war rather well and can still close his eyes to see the wreckage. England, he says, looked like a large waste dump to the Allied armies, and Germany had hardly any houses left standing. He's never been to Russia, Joe admits, but he's seen photographs of the Ukraine and western Russia, both of which look as if they're doing all right. What did his fellows and their societies do right in the years that followed World War II, Joe asks?

The other three almost trip over each other, so eager are they to answer the question.

* * *

Military history is a fascinating and complex topic, not least because there are so many angles of approach. When one examines D-Day, for instance, he or she can look at the battle from the viewpoint of the German defenders, viewing the enemy coming over the roaring surf, or from the vantage point of the Allied assailants, who beheld the solid land of Normandy, complete with the hedgerows that would give them so much trouble in the days ahead. And, thanks to modern technology, one can also "see" or imagine D-Day from above, using the photographs taken by Allied bombers and planes. And, of course, even when all this is accomplished, there is yet one more angle to consider: that of the civilians whose lives were altered on that day in June 1944.

So it has been through most of human history. The soldiers, warriors, and desperadoes do their work, prompted by generals, commodores, and chiefs of staff, and then we—those lucky enough to still be here—get to examine what took place. A mere 150 miles from Normandy lies another battlefield that produces all sorts of memories of Waterloo. Here, too, the modern observer can "see" the day through the eyes of the French assailants, the British defenders, or the Prussian latecomers. In each case, a certain choice is involved, and that choice inevitably colors what modern-day people see. Are we with Marshal Ney, as he leads those nine battalions of the Old Guard up the long, sloping hill? Are we with General Peregrine Maitland, whose 3,000 men have lain concealed in the grass for hours? Or are we at one with Marshal Blucher and his Prussians?

Two hundred miles west of Waterloo and one hundred miles north of the Normandy beaches exists another of the great clashes that made human history: the Spanish Armada. No battlefield exists because the Armada and its English opponents tossed and turned on the waves of the English Channel. This is one reason that naval history has never quite drawn as much attention as land-based battles. But when we think of the consequences of the Spanish Armada—and its failure—we are taken aback. That autumn of 1588 was one of the great hinge moments in human history, a time when everything seemed at stake.

No one planned it this way: that three of the greatest contests of the last 400 years should be in such close proximity to each other. Equally, no human brain devised a scheme by which the battles of the Old Testament should be so aligned, geographically speaking, with the modern-day wars between Arabs and Israelis. If any hand can be said to have "plotted" or "planned" it, this would be the hand of natural geography, which made the English Channel and the coasts of Holland, Belgium, and northern France such key strategic points. Land, water, and the vicissitudes of weather have played huge roles in many of the great contests of human history. Imagine, for example, if there had not been such a heavy fog over Manhattan Island in 1776, and George Washington had been unable to evacuate the Continental Army from Brooklyn. Imagine if an enormous flood in the Mississippi River delta had prevented the arrival of Admiral Farragut's fleet? And, of course, the most significant of all: what if the weather report handed to General Dwight D. Eisenhower, on the afternoon of June 5, 1944, had been in error. One shudders at the potential consequences.

Because we need a handle for the frying pan that we call military history, let us set out a short number of words, each beginning with a consonant. Let these serve as the opener—not the conclusion!—to our discussion of how men—and sometimes women—have fought each other for thousands of years.

Men, Monarchs, Means, and Maneuver

At first glance this list may seem too short, but the human mind works better with short, punchy declarations than long lists. Let us use these words as the springboard into the topic.

Men, of course, are the great element of human warfare; they are perennially needed and often in short supply. Men make the difference, whether on the battlefield or in the strategy room. No matter how many computer simulations are used, or how many tactical schemes are created or abandoned, it still—nearly always—comes down to the men and women on the ground.

In our modern era, no one practices this human element better than the Israelis, whose defense force is second to none. Whether in the gathering of intelligence or the unleashing of an armored column, the Israelis know that 98 percent of everything depends on the people on the ground. Is he or she ready? Will he or she make the sacrifice, take the direct hit in order to gain time for his or her fellow soldiers? Successful modern states know that people cannot be removed from the formula; that, regardless of how many technical gadgets are deployed, the human mind, heart, and spirit always play the most significant role. It is as true in our time as in the era of the Vikings, when a few thousand Scandinavians terrorized much of Northern Europe by means of skill, intention, and will.

Monarchs are not much in the conversation these days. The only monarchy that is regularly in the news is that of Great Britain, and it often appears in the tabloids rather than the traditional news magazines. When we scan the entirety of human history, however, it is apparent that monarchs have sent more men into battle and war than any other type of leader. Presidents, prime ministers, and premiers may issue declarations of war, but they do not have the joint spiritual/political power of a king, queen, or emperor. Whether we consider the Great Khans of Mongolia, the kings and queens of the European nations, or David, Saul, and Jonathan of the Old Testament, we arrive repeatedly upon the importance of monarchs to military history. If one still has any doubts, he or she can simply whistle that marvelous tune "God Save the King."

Means refers to virtually everything necessary to put the soldier or warrior on the field. This can be as routine as buttons for his outer coat, or as involved as special glasses and goggles for night fighting. Too often we forget the thousands of sacrifices made behind the lines in order that soldiers can accomplish their tasks. Means are surely one of the most important of all aspects of military history, but they can sometimes be overridden by a powerful will. Who, for example, believed that the American revolutionaries of 1776 had the means to combat the British Army and the Royal Navy? Who could have imagined that a few thousand English knights and longbowmen could bring down so many knights at the Battle of Agincourt? And, in perhaps the single greatest example, who would have dreamed that Mao Tse-Tung would outlast the Nationalist Chinese? Most true soldiers—as opposed to armchair generals—will readily say that they like the equipment, just so long as it does not get in the way of the experience.

Maneuver may sound basic, prosaic even, but a company or regiment that does not learn to march—and to do so in the most effective manner—will swiftly be beaten. From the first moments of what we in America call "Basic Training," the soldier is trained to let his muscles react first and to let the mind catch up later. Maneuver, therefore, involves every kind of movement, from the humblest private soldier to the loftiest five-star general. The latter issues orders; the former executes them.

Who knows how many battles have been decided by the smallest maneuver? Who knows how many profound miscalculations have been made because they were based on things such as "turn and march 40 steps to the right" or "turn and march 40 steps to the left"?

The Emperor Napoleon is not always the favorite of the modern reader. We learn, for example, that he was profligate with the lives of his men and that he abandoned them in Egypt. When it comes to compressing several of the important maxims into one brief sentence, however, Napoleon does it best: "An army marches on its stomach."

And there we have it. An army, composed of people, performs maneuvers that often include long marches, and it does so at the command of its monarch, who was, in this case, Napoleon.

* * *

"We rebuilt from scratch," Hans declares.

"We were determined to remake Old England, and make her better," Tommy declares.

"Russia has been pounded many times, and she always comes back," says Ivan.

Joe—who once was called GI Joe by his coworkers—shuts his eyes in admiration. He remembers the America of 1945, the incredible enthusiasm that existed, and the belief that Americans were the best at almost everything, whether the making of automobiles, the election of leaders, or the creation of the new suburbs that sprang up after 1946.

Deep down, Joe envies his three fellow veterans. The Second World War was a horrible experience for them and their societies, but they survived, endured, and—thanks in part to U.S. economic assistance—they eventually thrived. But it's their incredible optimism about the future, their belief that their efforts will come to fruition—that a better world will be established—that's what really compels Joe's envy, as well as his admiration. It's an odd thing for an American, a nation that was only established in 1776, but he feels strangely older, more mature than Hans, Tommy, and Ivan, and he's not sure he really likes the feeling.

Joe thinks a few moments, and remembers a book he saw recently that directly challenged its readers, asking them if there were not some good things that came out of war. Though he's not inclined to switch places with Hans, Tommy, or Ivan, he thinks it quite possible that his grandchildren—of whom he's very fond—just might be willing to exchange places with the grandchildren of these men.

And then one of the best quotes he ever recalled comes back to Joe. He does not speak it aloud, but smiles gently, as he ponders Thomas Jefferson's words, written in 1786: "The tree of liberty must be refreshed, now and again, with the blood of tyrants. It is their natural manure." How odd that the Europeans, who've experienced so much tyranny over so many centuries, seem to know this better than his fellow Americans.

IRON, STONE, AND BRONZE: 3000 TO 320 B.C.E.

PREHISTORY

Who cast the first stone (of human history)?

How historians wish they knew! They could, then, cast all the blame and attribute all the subsequent mayhem to that person. But he remains anonymous to us.

Are we quite sure that it was a "he" or "him"?

Historians are not one hundred percent certain, but it seems very likely. Women are not inherently more moral or altruistic than men, but throughout human history they have shown much less propensity for settling matters by means of armed combat.

This does not mean women have not figured in the history of war, however. Far from it. Our best surmise is that many ancient battles and skirmishes—those which took place before the development of writing—may have been fought over who possessed the land, animals, and not so incidentally, women.

Can historians assign any sort of date to the beginning of armed combat?

They really can't. Archeologists examine Stone Age tools, such as the Acheulan Axe, for clues, but we cannot be certain whether they were used in human-on-human combat or for scraping the skin from animals. What we can say, with some confidence, is that nearly all the things—or aspects—that we today identify with being human had evolved around 50,000 years ago and that it is quite likely that there was some armed combat by that time.

As to the age-old question of whether humans are naturally competitive or naturally cooperative, we cannot render any firm assessment. Both traits clearly exist within the great majority of humans, and it may be a matter of circumstance which trait is dominant at any place or time.

1

Is there any truth to the belief that precivilized warfare was largely ritual in nature?

Much of it probably was. Chiefs and shamans may well have organized the first battles of human history and done so in a way that minimized casualties. That does not lessen the impact of conflict in the lives of our ancestors, however. Some of them survived, and quite a few died in a time that has been accurately characterized as "red in tooth and claw" (the expression was coined by the nineteenth-century English poet Alfred Lord Tennyson).

What tools, or weapons, did ancient peoples use?

Between about 50,000 years ago and about 10,000 years ago, weapons were limited to the bone knife, the stone axe, and the throwing spear, known as the *atlatal*. By the time humans began settling into farming communities, however, roughly 10,000 years ago, their capacity for building larger, more effective weapons was apparent. At the same time, early farmers may have had fewer conflicts than nomadic peoples.

FIRST SETTLEMENTS

Where did humans first settle on the land?

There may have been some early human settlements in China and Meso-America, but the first truly successful settlements seem to have been in the Middle East. The area was cooler and drier than it is today, and a proliferation of plants and seeds made it an attractive place to settle. To the best of our knowledge, the area historians call the Fertile Crescent, ranging from southern Iraq to southern Turkey and northern Syria, was the first place where long-term human settlement succeeded.

Is there any truth to the biblical stories of a Great Flood and the disappearance of most of the human race?

That there was a Great Flood seems undeniable, because stories of the inundation appear in many tribal and national histories. It seems unlikely that it wiped out all the humans because if it did, we would not, today, possess the rich variety of DNA samples that geneticists use to trace human lineage. The idea that a God or gods would wipe out the "other" humans, leaving the more virtuous ones in control of the earth, is as old as civilization itself.

On balance, it seems that many—if not most—human groups have asserted that "God is on my side," and that he or she is against the enemy. The trouble with this thought, is, of course, that the enemy is saying and thinking the same thing. Given that one contestant usually prevails, God or gods cannot answer the prayers of both.

Is there anything to the Homeric tales of Greece and Troy?

For a very long time, scholars believed that Homer—a blind, Greek poet who composed poetry in the eighth century B.C.E.—had invented the Trojan War. In 1871, however, the

A seventeenth-century painting by Anton Mozart depicts what one of the battles of the Trojan War might have looked like.

German archaeologist Heinrich Schliemann (1822–1890) unearthed not one but seven levels of civilization on a Turkish hillside near the Aegean Sea. Although no single piece of evidence has ever emerged with the name "Troy" or "Trojan," scholars generally believe that there is some truth to the Homeric tales.

Where Homer lets us—his modern readers—down, time and again, is in his lack of detail concerning the average soldier; and civilian. To Homer, war was about the heroes, men like Achilles, Ajax, Hector, Paris, and even old King Priam. Homer tells us almost nothing about the struggles of the average soldier; historians do not even know what he looked like. Even so, most people who read Homer—whether in the original Greek or in translation—agree that he had a magnificent bird's eye view of war, that he "saw" the battlefield better than any of his contemporaries.

Does archaeology tell us anything about the Greeks from that time?

It was, again, Heinrich Schliemann who did much of the work. Schliemann is often called the man that modern-day archaeologists love to hate, because his digs were so sloppy. He was in far too much of a hurry to get beneath the soil, and once there he dug so ferociously that thousands of artifacts were destroyed or lost. But we can thank

3

Schliemann, first for discovering Hissarlik—the hillside in modern-day Turkey—and then for unearthing much of the Mycenaean civilization on the Greek mainland.

At Mycenae, Schliemann unearthed enormous tombs, a throne room, and a suggestion of just how impressive the Mycenaean civilization was. His discoveries, naturally, led to another question: What happened to Mycenae and its people? To the best of our knowledge, they were overthrown by wild men from distant places: the barbaric folk that we often call the Sea Peoples.

What these men—and perhaps a score of others from that time—had in common was a classical education and a lot of time. Some were men of leisure and others had acquired their wealth the hard way, but they all believed the ancient world more fascinating than their own and were determined to ferret out its most remarkable ruins. Today there are far more archaeologists in the field, but few of them get to experience the amazing discoveries available to nineteenth-century amateurs, who literally turned studies of the ancient world on their heads.

THE LATE BRONZE AGE

How was bronze superior to copper, which was previously the preferred material for the making of weapons?

Bronze was much tougher. Perhaps around 7,000 years ago—or 5000 B.C.E.—people in the Middle East began to forge bronze by adding small amounts of tin to copper. The new technology spread slowly, but about 5,000 years ago, practically all the new civilizations—especially those along the river Nile and in the region we now call Iraq—were using bronze. As a result, the weapons of the new civilized peoples were quite impressive. The Egyptian army even had some early form of uniforms with the shafts of their spears being forged alike, displaying the same colors on their banners. For a time, the use of bronze gave the settled peoples an edge over their nomadic foes. This changed, however, when the nomads began using chariots.

How long have chariots been around?

Both chariots and the use of horses in battle are relative newcomers to the stage. The earliest horses of whom we have certain knowledge were too small—and weak in the back—to support human riders. Horses were "bred," however, and by about 2000 B.C.E. they appeared on battlefields, usually on the side of the nomads.

The civilized people in these battles—the Egyptians, Babylonians, and so forth—were able to capture horses and learn the equestrian arts, but it took them a long time to catch up to the nomads in terms of the use of chariots. Chariot warfare came naturally to nomadic folk, who sent down rains of arrows against their more civilized foes. Even Egypt, which is often credited with pioneering the chariot, borrowed the original idea from a nomadic group.

How large were the armies of the Late Bronze Age?

They were quite small by modern standards. Egypt may have possessed an army of 50,000, but it is unlikely that any Pharaoh could mobilize, much less feed, one-fifth of that number at any one time. Sumer, and later Babylonia, possessed around the same average range of numbers.

What we would call modern-day methods of military conscription and large-scale armies had to wait until the turn of the first millennium B.C.E. Even then, feeding the men remained a large problem.

What happened to the Late Bronze Age societies?

Nearly all of them either perished or were greatly reduced in importance and strength. Around 1175 B.C.E., a series of invasions took place which brought low the Assyrian kingdom, the Hittites, and quite possibly the Mycenaeans too. Lacking any records from the other side, we have to use the expression "the Sea Peoples" to describe the impact of these invaders on the civilized part of the eastern Mediterranean.

The Sea Peoples may have come from Sicily and Sardinia; it's equally possible that they came from the Black Sea and some of the Greek islands. In either case, the Sea Peoples came like a rush against the Hittites, Minoans, Assyrians, and even Egypt. The only remaining visual record of these peoples is contained in a bas-relief in Egypt.

Who was Ramses and why do we remember his reign so well?

The Pharaoh Ramses III (1186–1155 B.C.E.)—not to be confused with his more famous grandfather, Ramses II—left a telling set of inscriptions on a bas-relief in Egypt, including both an account of the invasion of the Sea Peoples and a pictorial representation of them. They seem "otherworldly" in the sense that aliens (in our movies and books) do today. Ramses III shows the Sea Peoples humbled by a valiant defense in the Nile River Delta. What he does not show is equally interesting: it may have been a close, near-run thing.

5

That the Sea Peoples nearly conquered Egypt demonstrates their strength and ferocity. On the bas-relief, Ramses III describes how the various Sea Peoples—he names six of their groups—attacked practically all the civilizations and how all except Egypt were laid low. Even in the case of Egypt, historians believe that the kingdom was badly damaged by their attacks and would not be strong again for several centuries.

Were the Sea Peoples alone responsible for all the devastation of the Late Bronze Age?

We think not. Ferocious as they were, the Sea Peoples were a passing phenomenon. Their actions, and the subsequent destruction, may have taken place over one or two generations. By contrast, the eastern Mediterranean was wracked by natural

The ruins of the Grand Staircase at King Minos' palace in Crete stands as a reminder of a once-great civilization that likely collapsed, in part, because of climate changes.

disaster and a fair amount of climate change, both of which likely contributed to the general breakdown of that part of the civilized world.

The Minoan civilization on Crete—named for the legendary King Minos—had already suffered cataclysmic destruction following the eruption of the volcano of Santorini on the Island of Thera. Scholars believe that this eruption, which happened around 1627 B.C.E., was so destructive that the tsunami which followed may have given rise to various tales of the Great Flood.

How low did the various civilizations fall?

Israel—or the twin kingdoms of Israel and Judah—survived the destruction fairly well. Egypt was staggered by the changes, but it remained the most stable place in the Middle East. Other areas—such as central Turkey and inland Greece—may have been set back by as much as 300 years.

Greece, perhaps most notably, fell into a period we now call a Dark Age. Very likely, good things were happening under the surface, but they were not visible. When Homer sang and played on his lyre, he did so about the heroes of the Mycenaean Age, a time which had come and gone. He did not expect that Greece would soon rise again.

HEBREWS AND JEWS

Why do we sometimes call them the Hebrews and sometimes the Jews?

There is yet another name: the Israelites. Each of the names refers to the same people at different times in their history. What unites the three names is the religious element.

By around 1800 B.C.E., the Hebrews were one of the smaller, less warlike peoples of the Middle East, occupying sections of the land that is now the State of Israel. By around 1000 B.C.E., they called themselves Hebrews or Israelites with equal certainty, because they had established the Kingdom of Israel. The name Jews came a bit later.

Who represented the greatest threat to the Kingdom of Israel?

The Assyrians, who originated in what is now northern Iraq, were the most violent and bloodthirsty of all ancient world peoples. Their kingdom was known to its neighbors by about 1300 B.C.E., but their army became the terror of the Middle East during the ninth century B.C.E. Our knowledge of this comes not from their oppressed neighbors, but from the Assyrians themselves.

A team of French archaeologists unearthed the ruins of Nineveh in the 1830s. Astonished as they were by the massive walls and magnificent palace paintings—many of which depict kings, horses, and hunting—the archaeologists were even more impressed by the inscriptions. Translated, these inscriptions brag that the Assyrians had leveled one civilization after another, sometimes committing unspeakable atrocities, such as when they boast of having cut off 11,000 pairs of ears and 8,000 noses.

Are claims such as these to be taken seriously?

Historians have pondered that question ever since. Some have labeled the Assyrians the "Nazis" of the ancient world. In retrospect, however, it does not seem likely that the Assyrians could kill, decapitate, and mutilate so many people.

Killing large numbers of people—as Adolf Hitler found out—is hard work. It is much easier to make captives of them and have them produce something useful for the conqueror. Just as important, however, are the population figures. If the Assyrians really killed tens of thousands of people as they claim, the Middle East would—over time—have been depopulated.

Was there any limit to the Assyrian reach?

Yes. Like most ancient world conquerors, Assyrians faced a perennial problem of supplies. It was one thing to field an army of 50,000 men—as we believe they did—and quite another to keep those men in food and water. Therefore, although the Assyrians eventually conquered most of the Middle East, their hold on certain regions was quite fragile.

The high point of Assyrian conquest came during the late eighth and the early part of the seventh centuries B.C.E. The Kingdom of Israel was destroyed by Assyria around 732 B.C.E., while the Kingdom of Judah—the southern part of the Hebrew domain—survived.

Even as they approached the peak of success, however, the Assyrians began to experience stresses and strains within their empire. They had acquired too many enemies, and toward the end of the seventh century B.C.E., the various peoples turned on them.

How and when did the Kingdom of Assyria fall?

In 615 B.C.E., the Kingdom of Babylonia, 200 miles south of Assyria, established a firm alliance with three or four other peoples—some settlers and some nomadic—to combat Assyria. The fighting was fierce, but the allies overcame the Assyrians and burned their major cities. This was accomplished with such thoroughness that 300 years later, the Greek General Xenephon passed through the region and marveled at the ruins, saying he had no idea who those people had been.

Assyria's downfall paved the way for a second rise of the Babylonian kingdom. Led by King Nebuchadnezzar II, the Babylonians attacked the Kingdom of Judah in 587 B.C.E. After a hard campaign, they knocked down the walls of Jerusalem and took many of the Hebrews as captives to Babylon. This was the beginning of what the Old Testament describes as the worst of times for the Hebrews and what commentators ever since have referred to as the "Babylonian Captivity."

How long did the Hebrews stay as captives in Babylon?

They were in captivity for nearly seventy years. Most Old Testament scholars believe this was a pivotal time for the Hebrew people, during which they refined and defined their monotheistic beliefs. Just as important, however, were the military changes that took place in the Middle East.

This view of ancient Babylon as it looks today reveals a stark contrast to how it must have looked in the days of King Nebuchadnezzar II. On this very spot stood the famous Hanging Gardens that were one of the Seven Wonders of the World.

Assyria had been on top for about 300 years. Babylon held that position only for about seventy years before two newcomers—the Persians and Medes—swept aside all rivals to become the new super-kingdom.

Who were the Persians and Medes?

They were Aryan peoples—not Semitic—who arrived on the high plateau of what is now Iran sometime around 1000 B.C.E. For some time, they made little impact on the area, largely because they were nomadic peoples cast adrift among groups of settled and civilized folk. In or around 550 B.C.E., however, the Persians and Medes joined hands and carried out a series of conquests that took them to Turkey, the northern part of Arabia, and even to the western part of Afghanistan.

By 550 B.C.E., the Persians and Medes were led by King Cyrus (circa 585-529 B.C.E.), later known as Cyrus the Great. No reliable illustration of his physique exists, and we have to use our imagination to picture the King of Kings. Starting from modest beginnings, Cyrus became king of the Persians and Medes and then led his peoples to conquest. Time and again, he defeated more seasoned, practiced foes by using what we would call guerrilla tactics. Cyrus was more than a warlord, however. He had a vision of universal empire, and to that end, he practiced mercy toward many of the people he defeated.

When and how did Cyrus capture Babylon?

The year was 539 B.C.E., but the means have been debated ever since. Did Cyrus actually dam a section of the Euphrates River so his men could practically walk through a dry river bed? Was there a wholesale massacre of the Babylonian aristocracy? Cyrus, who was perhaps the most clever manager of public relations of his time, prevented the answers from becoming common knowledge.

One thing of which we are certain is that Cyrus announced that all the captives of Babylon—Hebrews, Semites, Assyrians, Aryans, and others—were henceforth free. This action alone makes Cyrus stand out from nearly all other conquerors of his time, and he went out of his way to cultivate that very image: that of the benevolent conqueror.

Where did the Hebrews go?

The only place that made sense. As soon as they were released, Hebrews began the long trudge back to the Kingdom of Judah, which King Nebuchadnezzar had destroyed fifty years earlier. On arriving in their homeland, the Hebrews found most of their cities and towns in wreckage. They began the long, difficult task of rebuilding, and in the process they renamed themselves the Jews.

The name clearly derives from the Kingdom of Judah, which was now rebuilt, but the precise intention of the word is unclear. Did the change from Hebrew to Jew signify that these were the same people who had now returned? Or did it mean they had been transformed by the Babylonian Captivity and would forever look on themselves as a different people? Scholars remain divided on this point, but the nomenclature was now permanent. They were henceforth known as the Jews.

Could Cyrus have conquered the entire Middle East?

He came close. But in around 529 B.C.E., he went on a campaign against the Massegete people in Central Asia and was killed, tradition has it, while engaged in battle against a tribal group led by a woman. Cyrus' body was brought back to Babylon and then to the desert of southern Iran, where his tomb remains today. In a manner that is somewhat surprising, Cyrus had his epitaph carved above the door to the tomb.

"O Man, wherever thou comes from, and whoever thou art! Know that I was Cyrus and that I conquered the world. Grudge me not, therefore, my monument."

GREEKS AND PERSIANS

What were the major city-states of sixth-century Greece?

There were about a dozen, ranging from Thebes in the north to Sparta in the south. Though they all spoke the same language, these peoples were intensely competitive with each other, seeking the glory and well-being of their individual city-states. At the same time, they were quite conscious of being different from all outsiders.

Language defined a Greek, but so did culture, and we might say "culture with an attitude." The modern word barbarian comes to us from the Greeks, who thought that less civilized people had poor diction and that their conversation resembled the bleating of sheep. By about 500 B.C.E., the Greeks felt a conscious superiority to all their neighbors. Of course it made things easier that, being a peninsular nation with the city-states stretching from north to south, they had rather few neighbors. That was about to change with the arrival of the Persians.

How far had Persia progressed since the death of Cyrus the Great?

In only thirty years (530–500 B.C.E.) Persia had become the super state of the Middle East, the first true world superpower. The Persians knew nothing of China, and their sway ended at the Oxus River in Central Asia, but practically all the other nations and peoples had fallen under their banner. Even Egypt was conquered during the reign of Cyrus' son, King Cambyses II.

Persians called their leader the "King of Kings" because he received tribute from the former kings of Assyria, Babylon, Israel, Egypt, and elsewhere. The Persians often left the bureaucracy of the former peoples in place, with a thin layer of Persians and Medes at the top. Given all this success, one wonders why Persia needed to conquer Greece, and the answer is simple: it did not. Greece had no precious raw materials, nothing that Persia required. Instead, the campaigns against Greece were all about mastery and dominion. The Persian leaders were bothered, sometimes incensed, that this small people, to the far west of their empire, managed to remain independent.

How did the Graeco-Persian Wars begin?

In 498 B.C.E., the Greek city-states on the west coast of modern-day Turkey rose against their Persian overlords in the so-called Ionian Revolt. The mainland Greeks naturally supported the revolt, and when it was stamped out, the Persians decided to teach them a lesson. The first Persian offensive was in 493 B.C.E., but their ships were wrecked off the northern Greek coast, and the main challenge, therefore, had to wait another few years.

In 490 B.C.E., the Greeks learned that the Persians were back, with a much larger fleet and army. The Persians were not natural sailors; they appropriated their ships and seamen from the Phoenicians, who they had conquered a generation earlier. With such a formidable combination of land and sea power, it seemed only a question of time before Greece was overwhelmed.

Which of the Greeks were first on the scene?

Athens, located on the southern side of the peninsula of Attica, was a natural target, but so was Corinth, located right at the junction between mainland and peninsular Greece. The Athenians learned, just in time, that the Persians were indeed coming to land in their area, and the runner Pheideippides was sent—with all haste—to alert the Spartans.

Examples of how Greek soldiers dressed during the time of the Graeco-Persian Wars. At left is a soldier using a sling, and at right are "hoplites," or foot soldiers.

Arriving in Sparta after a run of 140 miles, Pheideippides was told that a religious festival was underway, and the Spartans could not depart until it was over. Declaring that Athens and Corinth might be laid waste, he ran the 140 miles back to Athens, where, presumably, he had a few days' rest before heading out with the army.

Where does the modern Marathon—exemplified by the Boston Marathon—get its name?

Pheideippides and the Athenian army marched twenty-six miles to a set of hills overlooking the beach called Marathon. The Persians were drawn up on that beach, with archers, cavalry, and the support of their ships. The Athenian leaders conferred and decided to make a headlong attack and to come on the run. They rightly figured that the Persians were unused to this type of attack.

The Persians were strongest in their center, but the Athenians attacked on their wings, driving all before them. The Greek historian Herodotus claims that 6,000 Persians died, while only 192 Greeks perished. Even if this is an exaggeration, there is no doubt that the Persians were stunned by the attack. Those who survived got onto their ships, and it was at that moment that the Athenian leaders recognized the danger. Though they had been mauled, the Persians could surely sail around the peninsula faster than the Greeks could march; it was imperative, therefore, to warn the city of the danger. Pheideippides was asked to make one more, supreme effort.

How did Athens escape the danger?

Pheideippides ran the entire twenty-six miles back to the city. He had run 140 miles to Sparta, 140 miles back. He had marched with his comrades to the beach and fought in an intense battle. Now he was asked to run once more, and he performed admirably. Tradition has it that Pheideippides reached the northern gates and shouted that the battle had been won but that danger still remained. At that moment, he died.

Historians and athletes alike have long raised their eyebrows when first told the Pheideippides story. Could one person really do all that running, and fighting, and still have enough gas in the tank—figuratively speaking—to go the last twenty-six miles? Many of these doubts were put to rest in the first decade of the twenty-first century, when Californian Menares ran 262 miles without stopping, over a period of three days. Subsequent investigations turned up a small tribe of Mexican Apaches who routinely run over one hundred miles, and do so with the skimpiest of footwear.

Who gained the most over the next decade?

Athens, for certain. The other Greek city-states participated in the joyous celebrations, but the greatest glory, by far, went to Athens and its people. A new leader, too, emerged during that decade. His name was Themistocles, and he became the primary spokesman for Athens. When the Athenians stumbled on a silver strike in 483 B.C.E., Themistocles

> ## What does Thermopylae mean?
>
> The word has since come to stand for freedom and an inspired fight against great odds, but its original meaning was "hot gates." There were some warm water springs close by.
>
> Leonidas and his 300—who had been joined by roughly 7,000 Greeks from other city-states—took up a defensive position at Thermopylae, with the mountains on their left flank and the sea on their right. This was a good strategy, but when the Persians arrived, it seemed utterly hopeless. Even though he had lost men to sickness and disease, Xerxes could still throw at least ten times as many as the defenders.

persuaded them to spend the treasure on building more warships rather than beautifying the city. He rightly suspected that the Persians would return.

Why did the Persians make such a grand appearance in 480 B.C.E.?

This time, the King of Kings, Xerxes I, led the Persian army. The historian Herodotus claims that there were three million Persians, but even a figure one-tenth that large would still be an exaggeration; there simply wasn't enough food to supply that many.

Angered by the Persian repulse at Marathon, Xerxes planned a grand campaign, bringing almost 1,000 Phoenician ships, as well as his host. The Persians crossed the Hellespont and entered Thrace on their way to Greece. The Greeks knew they were coming, and appeals again went out from Athens to all the other city-states. This time, Sparta claimed it was not ready to field its army, but King Leonidas declared he would bring 300 of his best fighting men to northern Greece. That seemed like a mere drop in the bucket, but the Spartans were great warriors.

What was the fighting like?

We have no eyewitness accounts but can surmise that it was extremely thick and heavy. Three times, Xerxes threw Persian troops at the Greeks, and each time they were repulsed. The last attempt was made by The Immortals, Xerxes' hand-picked bodyguards, but they, too, were turned back. Xerxes knew he could prevail over time, but he was in a hurry. His enormous army required food supplies, and the land just beyond Thermopylae was ripe for the picking. And then, just when everything was at its most difficult, the Persian monarch received a break. A traitor came forth.

Ephialtes, a goat herder, offered to lead the Persians through a mountain trail that would position them behind the Greek position. A large section of Xerxes' army set out on that way, while the rest stood and glared at the Greeks, with neither side making any attack. Just when the trap was about to be sprung, King Leonidas learned of the Persian

13

maneuver. He asked, and then commanded, the 7,000 Greek allies to make haste and escape, while he and his 300 Spartans remained and fought to the last man.

Where did the Persians go after their victory at Thermopylae?

It was a very expensive victory: 10,000 Persians were killed, wounded, or went missing. The slaughter of the Spartans opened the way to Attica, however, and within a month, Xerxes and his generals were in Athens. The King of Kings was astonished to find almost no Greeks in the city: they had been evacuated, by boats, to the nearby island of Salamis. Xerxes did the best he could, burning what parts of the city were flammable. He also released his army to burn and sack the countryside. The incomplete nature of his victory nagged at him, however, because he still had not faced the main body of the Spartans.

Themistocles, the primary leader of the Athenians, played a double game, sending messages to Xerxes, pretending to be a traitor. Themistocles informed Xerxes that the Greeks were divided because of the rivalries between the city-states (this was at least half-true) and that this was the opportune moment to send in Phoenician ships and sailors to crush the Greeks. Xerxes took the bait.

What was the Battle of Salamis like?

The 480 B.C.E. naval battle was a raging, swirling confrontation between about 600 Persian ships and 500 Greek ones. The Persians—actually manned by Phoenician sailors—had the numerical advantage, but the narrow waters in the Bay of Salamis prevented them from using this to its full extent. The Greeks and Persians exchanged ramming

The Battle of Salamis by nineteenth-century artist Wilhelm von Kaulbach. Although the Persians had more ships than the Greeks, it didn't matter because the narrow Bay of Salamis made it impossible to maneuver around the Greeks, who would be victorious that day.

techniques, but the Greeks used something fairly new in naval combat: they stripped the oars of their opponent's vessels. This was accomplished by coming close alongside the enemy ship, and, at a crucial moment, making a sharp right-hand turn. The Greek vessel, from prow to stern, would then pass by the Persian one, ripping or stripping all of its oars. The Greeks would then leave their opponent—who could no longer maneuver—and come back later, at an opportune time, to capture him.

How decisive was the Battle of Salamis?

It was even more earth-shaking than Marathon. The Greeks captured or destroyed 300 Persian ships, meaning that Xerxes' victory at Thermopylae was useless. Lacking an effective fleet to supply and transport his troops, the King of Kings feared being trapped in Greece. Soon after the Battle of Salamis, he led three-quarters of his army in a forced march to the pontoon bridge he had built across the Hellespont. One-quarter of the Persian army remained to sustain an active threat to Greece, but it was thoroughly defeated in 479 B.C.E. at the Battle of Plataea.

Put together, the Greek victories at Marathon, Salamis, and Plataea ended the Greco-Persian Wars. Any doubt as to Greece's continued independence disappeared with remarkable, long-lasting effects. Historians often name Marathon and Salamis among the most important battles of world history because if the Persians triumphed, Greece would have become a province of the great empire, and the Greek contributions to science, literature, drama, and the visual arts might well have been lost.

Why did the Greeks win so often, even when they were heavily outnumbered?

The answer is threefold. First and foremost, the Greeks fought in defense of their homeland and were much more familiar with the terrain. Second, Greek troops had a strong spirit of individuality and fought with greater cleverness—as well as desperation—than their opponents. The third, often overlooked, aspect is the Greeks' athleticism. Greek soldiers were—on average—faster and nimbler than the Persians, a quality derived in part from their interest in the science of the body.

GREEK VERSUS GREEK

Why did the Peloponnesian War begin? Was it inevitable?

According to the great historian Thucydides, it was the growing power of Athens, and the resultant envy of this power among Spartans, that brought on the Peloponnesian War in 432 B.C.E.

Whether the war was inevitable remains debatable. The Athenians demonstrated arrogance during the Greek Golden Age, and they certainly made other Greeks feel "less than." Even so, negotiations, and a better understanding of what each city-state had to offer, might have staved off the war. Instead the war came, with a league of city-states led by Athens arrayed against a league led by Sparta.

Was the Peloponnesian War what we call the battle between the elephant and the whale?

By 432 B.C.E., Athens had definitely become whalelike, a great maritime power whose ships ranged over the eastern and central Mediterranean. By 432 B.C.E., Sparta was still the great land power, but the numbers of its fighting men had declined, thanks to a loss of population to other, more exciting Greek city-states. When the war commenced, most observers believed that Athens would prevail within a few years because of its fleet, its trade, and above all its treasury, which had grown in recent years.

Pericles led the Athenians with a combination of military and political skill. This is a bust of the Athenian kept at the British Museum.

Pericles, leader of the Athenians, expressed his war policy in the following way. Athens and its allies would surely win, he asserted, so long as they did not fight Sparta on land. When the Spartans came north, the Athenians—their countrymen included—huddled within the famous "Long Walls" of Athens. The Spartans could ravage the countryside all they wanted, but Athens was still supplied by sea. Using this defensive posture at home, Athens would go on the offense against Sparta's allies, and in the end, wear them down. It was an excellent strategy, but it overlooked the law of unintended consequences.

What kind of plague visited Athens in the third year of the war?

Quite possibly it was the bubonic plague, which would later become a byword for horror in medieval times. One third of all the Athenians died because they were packed in the city for reasons of defense. Pericles was among those who perished.

The loss of so many people meant that Athens could not attack Sparta's allies, and the war dragged on for a number of years, with Sparta giving better than it received. In 415 B.C.E., however, Athens found a new, charismatic leader. A kinsman of Pericles, handsome and well spoken, Alcibiades seemed like the perfect new general. Most important of all, he was vouched for by none other than Socrates, whose life he had saved in an earlier battle.

What went wrong with Alcibiades' new plan for Athens?

Alcibiades violated a key aspect of Pericles' former policy: to avoid unnecessary entanglements or adventures. Because the Greek city-state of Syracuse on the eastern side of the island of Sicily was a Spartan ally, Alcibiades decided to strike there. Nearly half of the Athenian fleet sailed, with 10,000 troops aboard, but Alcibiades did not go; he was deprived of his command by the city fathers almost at the last moment. Not only did the Siege of Syracuse fail, resulting in the loss of nearly all the soldiers, but Alcibiades soon turned traitor, offering his services to Sparta. In one of the most circular movements of any military leader, Alcibiades went from being an Athenian admiral to a Spartan general, but he then defected from Sparta to Persia. While considering yet another defection—this time back to Athens!—Alcibiades suffered a defeat at sea and committed suicide.

How did Sparta finally win the Peloponnesian War?

Though Alcibiades was a major disappointment to Sparta, the Spartans used his strategy, which was to seek a naval alliance with Persia. This resulted in the creation of a Persian-built fleet, manned by Spartan sailors. In 405 B.C.E., Sparta won the naval Battle of Aegospotami. As a result, Athens lost the ability to resupply its population with grain from the Black Sea, via the Sea of Marmara and the Hellespont.

Athens sued for peace, and the terms were harsh. Sparta required that the Long Walls—running from the city proper to the naval port—be pulled down. Athens had to yield practically all its war-making capacity, and at the end of the war, only one-third of the population of the city survived. Sparta's allies wanted to go even further. They urged Sparta to kill all adult Athenian males, but that was too much, even for the elephant which had finally conquered the whale.

THE PHALANX

Given their success against the Persians, why did the Greeks need a new fighting style?

They probably didn't. It was their own set of civil wars (Sparta versus Athens and Thebes versus Sparta) that made the rise of the phalanx necessary.

By about 350 B.C.E., the Greeks fought in this new formation, which was quite different from any which had before been seen. The phalanx was an oddly shaped, irregular rectangle, with about 300 men packed into tight ranks. Men in the outer ring carried spears, some as long as twenty-two feet. Men in the second, inner row carried shorter spears and deadly swords. The innermost part of the phalanx was composed of men who hurled rocks at the foe. All together, the phalanx formation resembled a hedgehog or a porcupine, lurching toward the foe, but in modern terms we would probably associate it with a tank.

Where was the phalanx developed?

The phalanx formation was first deployed during a set of wars between Sparta and Thebes, but it reached the peak of its development under the leadership of Philip II, king of Macedon. Philip had been a hostage at Thebes during his teenage years; there, he saw and learned the best that Thebes had to offer. Returning to Macedon, Philip developed a new phalanx, adding a new dimension, that of cavalry on both wings. As a result, the Macedonian phalanx combined speed and strength, power and flexibility.

By the time of his death in 336 B.C.E., King Philip was the master of all of Greece except Sparta. He had begun to turn his attention east, with plans to invade the Persian Empire. However, Philip was assassinated at the age of fifty-six, and his plans were carried out by his son, the remarkable person known as Alexander the Great.

Was Alexander's childhood as tortured as we have sometimes heard?

Yes, indeed. Though he was prince and heir to the throne, Alexander lived a precarious life, alternating between the wishes and desires of his father—King Philip II—and his mother, Olympias of Epirus. These strong-willed personalities gave much to their son, particularly in terms of ambition, but his childhood was a dangerous time as he sought to adjust to their conflicting demands.

King Philip divorced his wife when Alexander was about fifteen, and there was concern that the son by his new marriage might replace Alexander as heir to the throne. Whether or not Alexander had a hand in his father's assassination (the full truth has never come out), he doubtless suffered some guilt after his father's death and his own elevation to the throne. Olympias was, naturally, thrilled with the developments, especially when it became clear that she would be the real power in Macedonia when her son went to invade Persia. First, however, Alexander had to deal with a rebellion in Greece.

What happened to Thebes?

At its height, Thebes was a city-state with a population of around 70,000. Today, all that remains of the city is a series of corn fields and olive groves, with almost no trace of its former glory. The culprit was the brief Theban Revolt of 335 B.C.E.

Believing that Alexander was an easier target than his deceased father, the people of Thebes rose in revolt and asked the other city-states to join them. While the issue hung in the balance, Alexander came south with his Macedonian army and utterly defeated the Thebans. He then proceeded to destroy the city, brick by brick. Tradition has it that he left exactly one house standing, which belonged to a poet whose work he admired. This display of ruthlessness was sufficient: there were no further revolts or rebellions against Macedonian rule.

ALEXANDER

How many men were in Alexander's army?

Alexander left Macedonia in the spring of 334 B.C.E., with 35,000 infantry and 5,000 cavalry. This seems like a preposterously small number with which to commence an invasion, but Alexander—whose spies kept him informed about Persian weakness—was supremely confident. Tradition has it that he slept with a copy of Homer's *Iliad* under his pillow and that he regarded himself as the new Achilles.

At twenty, Alexander was a superb combination of lean, athletic grace and razor-sharp intelligence. He had been tutored for a time by the philosopher Aristotle. Alexander had no doubt that Greeks and Macedonians were superior to all other peoples and that they were meant to govern the world. At the same time, he had some rather advanced ideas about ethnic and racial harmony, believing that he would one day create a blended society of Greeks and the people they conquered.

Where was Alexander's first battle?

Alexander performed the same passage of the Hellespont as Xerxes, but in reverse (he performed sacrifices on the Asian side, vowing to avenge Greece for the Persian invasion of 480 B.C.E.). The first three months saw only skirmishes, but the Persians gathered an army of roughly equal strength and the two sides clashed at the Battle of the Granicus (River).

The battle was fought on a dry riverbed during a time of drought, with the Greeks on the west side and the Persians to the east. Both sides struggled for possession of the

A painting by Sebastiano Conca (1680–1764) depicts Alexander the Great visiting the Temple of Jerusalem. Alexander conquered lands from Greece to Judea to Egypt to the edge of the Indian subcontinent before dying at the young age of thirty-two.

riverbed, and the outcome was doubtful for hours. Then Alexander took a fall from his horse—the famed Buchephalus—and lay on the ground for several minutes (very likely, his staff performed mouth-to-mouth resuscitation). The Greeks and Macedonians lost heart when Alexander went down, but when the commander rose and mounted his horse, it restored their confidence. The battle was won an hour later, with the Persians in a dignified retreat.

Meanwhile, where was the King of Kings?

Darius III was not a warrior like his ancestors. He had a reputation to defend, however, and an empire to preserve. Hearing that the Greeks and Macedonians were a tough group, Darius assembled a large army, perhaps as many as 100,000. When Alexander and his men descended from the last of the Turkish mountains onto the broad plain that lies at the northeast corner of the Mediterranean, they found Darius' Persians waiting for them.

We employ terms like "the Persians," but Darius' army was actually made up of Persians, Egyptians, Bactrians, Phoenicians, and others; this was almost inevitable, given the size of the Persian Empire. One reason Alexander would win so decisively is that his men nearly all spoke the same language, while Darius' may have spoken as many as six!

Who won the Battle of Issus?

The battle is celebrated in art with a mosaic that depicts Alexander on Buchephalus, driving straight at Darius, who is ready to turn and flee. Although the mosaic clearly intends to glorify Alexander, there is truth in this depiction.

The battle was about evenly matched, with the phalanx proving unbeatable, but with the Persians doing well on the two wings. At a critical moment, Alexander and the King's Companions—his chosen group of horsemen—drove straight into a gap in the Persian lines, coming close to Darius. The King of Kings fled, and his staff of interpreters—those who made coordination between his various ethnic groups possible—surrendered. As a result, the Persian army disintegrated, with the Macedonians and Greeks in hot pursuit. Approximately 20,000 Persians were killed, and many more were captured. That evening, Alexander also captured Darius' tent, with two of his wives, several of his children, and an immense amount of silver and gold.

Was there any chance Alexander could be stopped?

Darius III did not think so. On hearing of the loss of part of his family, Darius sent a letter, asking Alexander to return them. Alexander could keep the treasure, Darius said, and he was welcome to the western third of the Persian Empire if only he would make peace. Holding the letter aloft, Alexander brought the matter to his top generals.

Parmenion was eldest of the group. He had served King Philip II loyally and well. Parmenion now said, "If I were Alexander, I would accept this offer." It seemed almost too good to be true, to win all that territory after only two battles. Alexander, however, smirked, and said, "I would do so, if I were Parmenion!"

Where did Alexander go after the Battle of Issus?

He progressed down the Mediterranean coast—the part we often call "The Levant"—with all the towns and cities submitting to him. Only one chose to resist, the Phoenician city of Tyre, in modern-day Lebanon.

Located on an island half a mile from land, Tyre had resisted many would-be conquerors over the years, and to its people, Alexander seemed no different from his predecessors. They sank his quickly built fleet and defied him with flaming arrows and catapults. After some weeks of desultory, failed attacks, Alexander decided that if the city would not come to him, he must reach it. The only possible way was to build a causeway, of stone and earth, to turn part of the sea into land!

Was this the greatest of Alexander's accomplishments?

Because it involved the change of geography, as well as sheer doggedness, his victory over the people of Tyre stands very high on the list of Alexander's achievements. After seven months, the "mole" or artificial extension of the land was complete, and the Greeks and Macedonians stormed Tyre. All 8,000 inhabitants were either killed or sold into slavery. Today, Tyre is firmly connected to the mainland, because drifting sand, as well as wood, filled in Alexander's mole.

When did Alexander begin to think he was semidivine?

The idea may have been there from the beginning, planted by his ambitious mother, Olympias. But the turning point was clearly when Alexander reached Egypt in 333 B.C.E. Not only did the population submit to him, but the high temple priests took him into the desert to confer all sorts of honors and blessings upon him. During these ceremonies, they told Alexander he was the son of Amun, the sun god.

Egypt had languished for centuries after being conquered first by Assyria and then Persia. Egypt was searching for a heroic leader, and had Alexander been willing to remain, he might very well have been crowned Pharaoh. Alexander was always in a hurry, however, and soon after directing that a city be built in his honor—on the western side of the Nile delta—he led his men out of Egypt and toward modern-day Iraq, where he knew Darius III was waiting.

How large a force did Darius bring to his second battle against Alexander?

The chroniclers do not tell us the exact number, but we surmise that it was at least three times as large as Alexander's. Just as important, Darius got to pick the battle site. Arriving on the plain of Arbela weeks before Alexander, Darius had his men sweep the battlefield clean of anything that might impede the movement of his chariots. His men, too, had plenty of time to drill and prepare. Amid all the preparations, however, was a deep-seated pessimism. Many of Darius' men simply did not believe that Alexander could be beaten.

As Alexander's army approached, the Greeks and Macedonians were excited by a spectacular lunar eclipse. Alexander made the most of it, saying that the eclipse forecast the collapse of Persia. The Persians, by contrast, tried to ignore the eclipse. Thinking Alexander would launch a night attack, Darius kept his men at their posts all night, and they were exhausted when daylight came.

How did Alexander win the Battle of Gaugamela?

Fought on October 1, 331 B.C.E., the Battle of Gaugamela (also known as the Battle of Arbela) featured the Macedonian phalanx, especially Alexander's use of cavalry. Two hours into the battle, the situation looked good for the Persians, who were outflanking some Greek units and overrunning others. Alexander and the King's Companions, again, provided the decisive punch, driving straight into what looked like a solid wall of Persians and finding a weak spot.

Darius turned to run. He knew quite well that this was the end: there would be no comeback. Alexander did not pursue right away. He stayed at the battlefield, mopping up and accepting the surrender of thousands of Persians. He knew—as did everyone on the battlefield that day—that the struggle was over. He had won it all.

Why did Alexander burn the Palace of Persepolis?

Soon after winning the Battle of Gaugamela, Alexander entered Babylon in triumph. He found less silver and gold than expected, and soon he learned that the real treasure trove was at Persepolis, in southern Iran. After a few fierce fights with some last Persian holdouts, Alexander arrived at Persepolis. A few days after his arrival, he held a big celebration and then told his men to put the place to the torch in retribution for what Xerxes had done to Athens in 480 B.C.E.

An immense treasure was, indeed, discovered, and Alexander became—in one stroke—the world's richest man. Had he paid off his veterans, each one could have gone home to Macedonia with the equivalent of a million dollars—perhaps even more—in today's currency, but he chose not to do so. Rather than turn back, Alexander planned to go much farther. His tutor, Aristotle, had told him of a great ocean to the east, and Alexander wanted to be the first leader to see it.

Who did Alexander leave in charge while he headed east?

He already had a regent back in Macedon, and he now appointed Parmenion and other generals to command in his name in Babylon. Alexander paid little attention to those who warned him about endangering his empire due to his absence. In 329 B.C.E., he set out with about 20,000 men.

How far did Alexander travel?

Because it was not in a straight line, he and his men may well have covered 12,000 miles over the next four years. They ascended the high Pamir Mountains of Afghanistan, and may well have been the first people from any Western nation to see India. Alexander crossed the Indus in 325 B.C.E., and fought one of his last—and most desperate—battles against Porus, king of a northwestern part of India. Porus had many elephants, and they made the battle much harder, but, as usual, Alexander prevailed. Soon after this victory, Alexander prepared to move farther into India, but at this point his men rebelled. They had been on the march for over a decade, they said, and wished to get home to Macedon, if only to see their families one more time before they died.

Alexander was furious, but the "sit-down" strike of his men succeeded in stopping him where the attempts of all his opponents had failed. By 323 B.C.E., Alexander and his men were back in Babylon after a grueling cross of the Gedrosian Desert in southern Iran.

Could Alexander have gone even farther? Did anything remain for him to conquer?

Yes and no. Very likely he wished to cover more ground, but there were no foes to speak of. Alexander knew little, if anything, about the city-state of Rome, but even if he'd seen the Romans at work, he would not have feared them, and he would probably have beaten them as well. One reason for Alexander's early death (there are, of course, several) is that he lamented the notion that he had nothing more to do.

Alexander died in Babylon, a few days after he turned thirty-two. His record of conquest has to rank at the very top of anyone's list, especially given that it was accomplished in such a short time.

ALEXANDER'S SUCCESSORS

To whom did Alexander leave his vast empire?

Alexander was, at least in this regard, a realist, and when his generals raised the question of succession on his deathbed, Alexander replied, "To the strongest." He knew there would be a struggle for the succession, and he did not make things easier by declining to name an heir.

No one—it turned out—could rule so large an empire; perhaps even Alexander would have failed had he lived longer. The empire broke into four competing sections, which often made war against each other. The most prominent of the new sections was Ptolemaic Egypt, named for General Ptolemy. Using the brand-new city

After the death of Alexander the Great, the empire he built split into four pieces. Ptolemy I—a bust kept at the Louvre Museum is shown here—founded the Ptolemaic empire in Egypt.

23

of Alexandria as his base, General Ptolemy inaugurated a new chapter of Egyptian history, which by this point was nearly 3,000 years old.

In cultural terms, the Greeks brought their religion and philosophy to many areas. How about in military terms?

The Greeks brought the Western way of war—as described by historian Victor Davis Hanson—to the Middle East and beyond. Though the Greeks regarded all other peoples as barbarians, it is fair to say that Alexander and his successors introduced a much more barbaric method of warfare to many lands.

As Victor Davis Hanson describes it, the Western way of war involves a subtle but profound relationship between the individual and his society. A man raised in a democratic society is more likely to care about his country in a time of peril; he is also, according to Hanson, capable of far greater acts of violence against any foes. Hanson's theory is not without critics, but may help to explain how Alexander and his Greeks and Macedonians conquered such a vast amount of territory in little more than one decade.

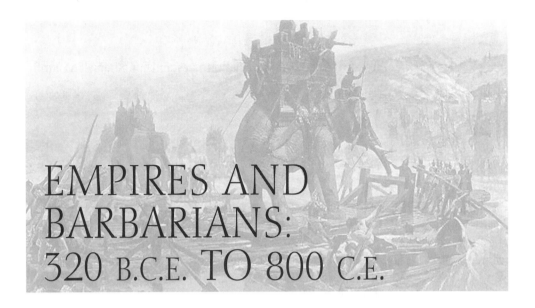

EMPIRES AND BARBARIANS: 320 B.C.E. TO 800 C.E.

EARLY ROME

What was so different about that one city, located on the Tiber River?

Historians, ethnologists, and archaeologists have attempted to answer this question for centuries. The best they have come up with is that early Rome experienced some success, built upon it and that the intense challenge later presented by Hannibal of Carthage forged Rome into the greatest warrior-society the world has ever known.

The traditional date for Rome's founding was in 753 B.C.E., and the Roman Republic, as distinguished from the Etruscan monarchy, commenced in 509 B.C.E. Rome, therefore, was a contemporary of Sparta and Athens, even though it received little attention in those early centuries.

Who did the Romans fight against in the early years of the republic?

Virtually all of their Italian neighbors. Rome possessed a genius for incorporation, for bringing other people into the fold, but lengthy wars took place beforehand. Rome fought and defeated the Etruscans, the Samnites, the Lamnites, and numerous other peoples. Though this was not planned, Rome moved north, south, and east, eventually taking over the entire Italian peninsula. The process required nearly two centuries of off-again, on-again warfare, and when it ended, the Romans were a much more militaristic people than before.

How close is Italy to the island of Sicily?

The "toe" of Italy's "boot" is only three miles from the northeastern point of Sicily. It was, and is, natural for the Italians and Sicilians to trade and exchange ideas. In 264 B.C.E., Rome intervened on behalf of a Sicilian city seeking independence from the North African city-state of Carthage. This was the beginning of the so-called Punic Wars, which marked the rise of Rome from a medium-sized nation to establishing herself as a military superpower.

PUNIC WARS

What and where was Carthage?

Carthage was a city-state rather like Rome, except that it was located on the North African coast (its ruins lie, today, under the city of Tunis). Carthage and Rome were about the same size—half a million people—and both were led by merchants who wanted control of the island of Sicily for their wares. This was the reason the First Punic War began, but, over time, the Punic Wars became a truly homicidal affair, with each city-state wishing to obliterate the other.

The First Punic War began with notable Roman successes on land, but also with Roman failures at sea. This is because the Carthaginians were a maritime people, who had far more experience in naval matters. Within a few years, however, Rome developed the *corvus*, a gangplank that came thundering down, embedding into the deck of the Carthaginian ship. Roman soldiers then charged across the bridge, fighting as if they were on land. In this type of man-on-man contest, the Romans nearly always won, thanks to their combination of patriotism and individual initiative.

How long did the First Punic War last?

The reason we might ask this question is because the First Punic War was a truly murderous conflict. It lasted twenty-four years, and many thousands of men died on both sides, including thousands of sailors who died in shipwrecks. The First Punic War ended when Carthage sued for peace. Rome imposed harsh terms that limited Carthage's potential for future war, and Sicily became part of the Roman republic. A few years later, while Carthage was embroiled in war with its own mercenary army, Rome also seized the island of Sardinia. The former acquisition could be justified under the rules of war and conquest; the latter could not.

Who was Hamilcar Barca?

Hamilcar Barca was a young Carthaginian general during the First Punic War. When the war ended, he and his men descended from Mount Aetna, which had been their stronghold for several years. In the aftermath of the First Punic War, Hamilcar fought and defeated Carthage's former mercenaries in a series of battles in North Africa. Distrusting the political leaders of his city-state, Hamilcar decided to establish a new Carthaginian colony in Spain. Tradition has it that he brought his nine-year-old son, Hannibal Barca, to a temple just before departure.

Hamilcar asked his son to swear—before all the gods—that he would never be a friend to Rome in any way. The nine-year-old did as he was asked; Hannibal's words have often been changed to make it sound as though he swore to be Rome's eternal enemy, while in fact he swore only never to be Rome's friend. In either case, this particular nine-year-old would make good on his vow.

How long did it take for Hannibal to emerge as Carthage's new military leader?

Hannibal learned at his father's side, in Spain, but he also learned much from his brother-in-law Hasdrubal. When both were killed in the fighting against the native Iberians, Hannibal became the leader of the Barca family, for which Barcelona is named. He showed himself a capable young man, but few people expected him to turn into a military giant.

In 218 B.C.E., Hannibal laid siege to the city of Saguntum, in southeastern Spain. Saguntum asked Rome for protection, and the Roman republic sent envoys to Carthage, demanding that Hannibal cease and desist. Even if they wanted, the city fathers of Carthage could not control Hannibal, because he was too far away. They, therefore, dared Rome to do its worst, and the Second Punic War began.

Where did Hannibal get the idea to march his men—and elephants!—over the Alps?

It was an inspired decision, but there was also little choice. If Hannibal remained in Spain, he would be forced to fight an entirely defensive war, and there was a good chance that the mother city of Carthage would be overwhelmed. If, on the other hand, he could reach

One of the most memorable chapters in the Punic Wars was when Hannibal of Carthage took elephants across land and water to attack the Romans. This 1878 illustration by Henri Mote shows the general crossing the Rhone River in southern France.

Italian soil, he could threaten Rome itself. However, since Rome controlled nine-tenths of the waterways, Hannibal, if he wanted to hit the Eternal City, had to go by land.

In 218 B.C.E., Hannibal brought about 40,000 men, and perhaps forty elephants, along the southern shore of the Mediterranean. His army forded, or even swam, across the Rhone River, in southern France, and then commenced the long climb through the Alps. The men and beasts climbed from about a hundred feet above sea level to almost 12,000 feet and kept going. Along the way, Hannibal recruited many Gallic tribesmen and incorporated them into his army.

What did the Romans think, and say, when Hannibal appeared?

Hannibal and his multiethnic army, composed of Greeks, Gauls, Spaniards, and Carthaginians, appeared in northern Italy during the spring of 217 B.C.E. The Romans were astonished he had made it so far, but they predicted his defeat. The First Punic War had clearly demonstrated Rome's superiority in warfare on land.

Hannibal astonished the Romans, however, by winning the Battle of the Tinicus River. One Roman consul barely escaped with his life, and about 10,000 of the rank and file perished. Consul Publius Cornelius Scipio became the first of numerous Roman generals to attest to Hannibal's military brilliance, and his eighteen-year-old son, Scipio junior, made the first of many notations about the skill of Hannibal's army.

What was so different about Hannibal's strategy?

First and foremost, Hannibal was a person of great charm, able to influence and persuade the various ethnic groups under his leadership. Second, Hannibal was one of the first of all generals—at least of those who we know—who planned an entire battle ahead of time. To be sure, he had to improvise at times, but on the whole, Hannibal had a well-designed battle plan on the morning of the event.

Third, Hannibal was likely the first military commander to exploit the technique of double envelopment. This meant creating an intentional weakness in the center of his infantry line and luring the enemy to charge straight ahead. Given that his North African and Spanish cavalry were superior to the Roman horsemen, Hannibal then brought his cavalry around the flanks and even into the back of his foe. This technique was certainly tricky and required excellent timing, but Hannibal pulled it off time and again.

What do we mean by "Fabian" tactics?

After suffering two crushing defeats, the Romans put all power, temporarily, in the hands of Quintus Fabius Maximus (c. 280–203 B.C.E.), giving him the official title of Dictator. Fabius chose not to meet Hannibal in the field; rather, he kept his forces secure in Rome and other Italian cities. Hannibal had the run of the countryside, but he lacked siege weapons, and the Romans were safe behind their walls.

When did the Romans go on the offensive?

By the spring of 216 B.C.E., the Roman public was weary of Fabian, or delaying, tactics. Fabius Maximus stepped down, and two new consuls raised the largest army Rome had ever seen: perhaps 85,000 men in all. Many were new recruits, but they had magnificent armor, and they looked far more impressive than their Punic foes. In the hot summer of 216 B.C.E., the two consuls brought their force south to encounter Hannibal in the province of Apulia (the modern-day tourist knows how hot the summer sun is in that area).

Hannibal planned yet another battle based on double envelopment. He had, perhaps, 55,000 men, but nearly all of them were battle-hardened, which could not be said of the Romans. On the morning of August 2, 216 B.C.E., Hannibal lured the Romans into an attack, and—as had happened so often in the past—they took the bait. Hannibal's center seemed weak, and the Romans pressed forward, not realizing that the ground and landscape became narrower with each passing minute. When Hannibal's cavalry sprang the trap, the Romans were jammed so tightly onto the corn field that they could not use their lances.

How great was Hannibal's victory at Cannae?

It was one of the greatest victories ever achieved in the ancient world, and it was, quite likely, the single bloodiest day of that historical epoch. Roughly 48,000 Romans perished that day, compared to perhaps 10,000 of Hannibal's force. All night long, Carthaginians searched the field, finding and hacking the gold rings off former Roman aristocrats' hands (the rings were placed in baskets and shipped to Carthage as evidence of the remarkable victory). When morning came, Hannibal's cavalry commander arrived to say that the victory was complete and that Hannibal would sup in the Roman Capitol five days hence (it actually would have taken two weeks to make that march).

Hannibal demurred, saying he lacked siege weapons and an understanding of Rome's defenses. Muharbal, astonished, declared: "Truly, the gods do not give all their gifts to one man. You, Hannibal, know how to create a great victory, but not how to use it!"

Was Muharbal right?

Yes. Throughout his career, Hannibal had dared the odds and prevailed. A siege of Rome may have been the greatest risk of all, but this was clearly the right moment, and Hannibal should have seized it.

What happened to Hannibal's invasion of Italy?

Hannibal had come a long way and achieved great things, but with each month that passed without a march on Rome, his reputation suffered. Rome was prostrate after the Battle of Cannae, but by the next spring, the government and people were breathing defiance once more. Hannibal laid siege to two or three southern Italian cities over the next few years, but with very few exceptions, the Italian allies proved loyal to Rome. Just as important, Carthage now had a new foe.

Publius Cornelius Scipio junior (236–184 B.C.E.) was son of the consul who fought Hannibal in 218 B.C.E. After his father's death, Scipio became leader of the family and the new military hope of Rome. That he possessed a genius cannot be denied, but some of his methods were clearly based on Hannibal's. Even so, many military commanders never learn this lesson: they fail to profit from watching their enemy.

Whom did Scipio defeat in Spain?

Over the next five years, Scipio met and defeated practically every Carthaginian commander in Spain. He captured the city of New Carthage and gained for Rome the silver and iron mines of the Iberian Peninsula.

Only one member of the Barca family—Hannibal's younger brother Hasdrubal—escaped from Spain. Leading about 30,000 men, Hasdrubal imitated his brother by crossing the Alps and reaching the broad plains of northern Italy. Had he effected a junction with Hannibal, they would have had about 90,000 men. Just enough, perhaps, to bring Rome to its knees. Hasdrubal sent six mounted messengers by different routes, but all were captured by the Romans, who therefore learned of his approach. Hannibal, meanwhile, knew nothing.

Why do historians label the Battle of Metaurus as among the most decisive in history?

Knowing that Hannibal was still in southern Italy, a Roman consul hastened north with 7,000 picked men. He effected a junction with the army of the north just days before Hasdrubal approached. On the morning of the battle (in 207 B.C.E.), Hasdrubal heard *two* trumpets rather than one, meaning that he faced two Roman armies instead of one.

The battle was short and sweet (from the Romans' point of view). The Romans had profited from the previous ten years' experience. Though they had not yet adopted all the characteristics of what was later referred to as a "legion," they were much closer than before. Ten thousand Carthaginians and their allies were killed, and another 10,000 taken prisoner. The first that Hannibal knew of this defeat was when a Roman horseman galloped near his camp and hurled the head of his brother over a wall. Tradition has it that Hannibal bowed his head, saying that at last he saw the destiny of Carthage.

Where did Scipio the Younger go after the Battle of Metaurus?

Scipio continued to win victories in Spain, and in 205 B.C.E., he received permission from the Senate to carry the war into Africa. His first campaign in North Africa was a desultory affair until he won the alliance of Massinissa, leader of a group of Numidian horsemen. These were the same African tribesmen who had been so instrumental in Hannibal's earlier victories, and Scipio used the advantage to its maximum extent. Threatened by a possible siege, Carthage summoned Hannibal, and in 203 B.C.E., he had 40,000 of his veterans land on home soil.

Hannibal knew the situation was dangerous, even desperate. In 202 B.C.E., he marched southeast, toward where Scipio and his soldiers waited. Upon reaching his destination on a wind-swept plain called Zama, Hannibal asked for a peace conference. Neither he nor Scipio got anywhere in the discussion: it was apparent that only a major battle would settle the issue.

How did Scipio win the Battle of Zama?

In what way did he not? Early that morning, Hannibal rode to reconnoiter his enemy's positions, and what he saw filled him with despair. Scipio had learned everything that Hannibal had to teach. But there was no remedy: the battle began around 10 A.M.

Hannibal began by launching a charge of elephants, but Scipio had trained his men to break into highly maneuverable cohorts which evaded the animals' charge; one section of elephants even turned and crashed into a Carthaginian line. Scipio then advanced and cut his way through Hannibal's first and second lines, only to meet the battle-hardened veterans of the Italian campaigns. This was when Hannibal should have launched a counterattack, but he was listless at Zama, not his usual self. When Scipio's men regained their breath, they made the final attack, and after a hard battle, won.

After Scipio defeated the Carthaginians at the Battle of Zama, instead of wreaking revenge and destroying his opponents completely, he spared Carthage. This became known as the "Continence of Scipio," which became the subject of numerous later artworks, such as this 1788 oil painting by Nicolas-Guy Brenet.

How complete was the Carthaginian defeat?

It was total. Perhaps 20,000 Carthaginians were killed at Zama, but the rest simply melted away. Hannibal galloped all the seventy-five miles to Carthage and told the city fathers to sue for peace. When Scipio and his army arrived, Carthage practically begged for terms.

Scipio exacted revenge for all of Rome's difficulties, but he did not destroy Carthage. The city had to pay a large indemnity and surrender all but twenty of its warships. Carthage was also forbidden from waging war without Rome's consent. The end of the Second Punic War left no doubt as to who was the number-one power in the Mediterranean world.

Who was Cato the Elder?

His full name was Marcus Porcius Cato (234–149 B.C.E.). He was a vigorous defender of traditional Roman values, which means that he was dead-set against the Greek influence in Roman life. Cato argued long and hard against the employment of Greek tutors, for example, saying they would bring about a decline in Roman virtues, especially military ones. It was toward Carthage, however, that Cato directed most of his anger.

Time and again, during a particular speech in the Roman Senate, Cato held aloft fresh figs, saying that they were still fresh because they had come from Carthage, only four days' sail. He went on, each time, to say that for this reason he believed that Carthage must be destroyed! Cato kept alive a vengeful spirit toward the city-state, which had been thoroughly defeated already.

Why was the Third Punic War necessary?

It wasn't. By all accounts, the Third Punic War (149–146 B.C.E.) was forced by Rome. When the Roman army first landed in North Africa, the Carthaginians tamely surrendered nearly all their weapons, including 2,000 catapults. But when they were told they would have to assist the Romans in the destruction of their city before being removed to the interior, the people of Carthage fought with all the energy of despair.

The Siege of Carthage lasted nearly three years, but the last ten days were, by far, the worst. The citadel finally fell, and the Romans sold nearly 100,000 people into slavery. They then sewed salt in the soil for miles around the city, intending to prevent—or at least discourage—anyone from ever settling there again. It is the height of irony that Rome herself would later settle some of its veterans in that region.

What did Scipio say as he watched the final destruction of Carthage?

Scipio Amelianus, a grandson of Scipio Africanus, wept quiet tears as he saw his men conquer the last ramparts, overwhelming the final Carthaginian defenders. The historian Polybius, who was standing next to him, asked why he cried, to which Scipio replied that he did so because he had realized that all cities—and civilizations, including his beloved Rome—would one day meet their doom.

How many casualties resulted from the three Punic Wars?

Some historians believe that Rome lost 400,000 men in the first and perhaps 150,000 in the second Punic War. Carthaginian losses are much more difficult to determine, but if they were comparable to the Romans, then it is possible that roughly one million people died. When we consider that later conflicts, including World Wars I and II, saw the use of much more effective weaponry, we can only shudder about the intensity of violence during the Punic Wars.

Historians often cheer for Rome, saying that its civilization was more advanced and that it has given us—her modern descendants—much more than Carthage ever could. We have to remember, however, that these words are written by the victors and their descendants. In truth, we know rather little about Carthaginian civilization, not least because it was so thoroughly destroyed.

"OUR SEA," THE MEDITERRANEAN

How quickly did Rome rise to become the greatest power in the entire Mediterranean?

Rome's progress was achingly slow during the fifth and fourth centuries B.C.E., but things really picked up after the double conquest of Carthage and Corinth, both accomplished in 146 B.C.E. By that time, the Roman legion was essentially developed and Roman generals could rely on the smoothest-running military machine the world had ever seen.

What was so different about the legion?

It combined power with flexibility and ease of maneuver in a way that was truly unprecedented. The Macedonian phalanx, as we have seen, was incredibly powerful, but rather bulky and slow on the battlefield; the Romans developed the legion to bring out the best in speed as well as strength.

Roughly 6,000 men strong, a legion was composed of centuries—of one hundred men apiece—and maniples, which averaged about 300. Any one of these groups or sections could swiftly change direction or go from offense to defense. The Roman legion-naire was highly alert to the trumpet calls that directed the action and to the centu-rion—the commander of the group of one hundred—who acted much like today's master sergeant. If the legion had any weakness, it was in cavalry, which the Romans did not form into a cohesive group. Each legion had its separate section of cavalry, and the Romans often lost when a battle was fought strictly in terms of horsemen.

Napoleon famously declared that an army marches on its stomach. Was this true of the Romans?

They had an excellent commissary system and better delivery of supplies than any of their opponents; even so, the Romans sometimes lived off the land. They did so in a highly dis-ciplined manner, however, with sections of each legion specifically detailed to the task. This means that looting—in the truly wild, undisciplined sense of the word—was a rarity.

Rome went one step beyond what Napoleon later prescribed, however: its men marched on their stomachs, but they also slept well because of the use of their shovels. Every legionnaire carried a shovel as part of his basic equipment, and each night on the march, the Romans dug a major trench around their perimeter. They adopted this prac-tice after being surprised by foes at night, but once learned, the lesson of digging trenches was never forgotten. The typical Roman legionnaire was as skilled with the shovel as with the sword, and there were times when the former was just as important as the latter.

Were the Roman legions composed entirely of Italians?

In the first four centuries of the existence of the Roman Republic, this was the case. By about 100 B.C.E., however, Italy ran short of manpower. Rome, therefore, began the prac-tice of recruiting in the provinces, and many of the soldiers who later accomplished great victories under the leadership of Julius Caesar were Spaniards, Sicilians, and even North Africans and Greeks by descent.

Rome was so skilled in making citizenship a desirable thing that many, if not most, legionnaires from foreign countries later settled in Italy, greatly benefitting the Roman motherland. Some retired legionnaires rose to political positions and thereby added an-other aspect of value to the Roman state.

It sounds as if everything was just about perfect. Did the Romans ever lose?

They lost plenty of battles and skirmishes along the way, but they nearly always won when it counted the most. By about 60 B.C.E., there was a sense of inevitability about Roman triumphs. Of course, it helped that Rome was led during this time by its great-est military genius, Julius Caesar.

Born in Rome in 100 B.C.E., Caesar was the epitome of the high-born Roman aris-tocrat, and by the age of thirty-nine he had everything—wealth, fame, and family—ex-cept military glory. His rivals in the Roman leadership scoffed, believing that Caesar was too old to launch a military career, but he quickly showed they were mistaken.

How did Caesar commence his rise to military fame?

He asked his two fellow Triumvirs for a five-year appointment in the province of Gaul. Pompey and Crassus were both suspicious: to them it seemed that Caesar was asking for too much. But the more they deliberated on it, the more Pompey and Crassus became convinced that it would be a good thing to have Caesar somewhere other than the capital city, if only because he had become too popular with the masses. They agreed to send Caesar north on a five-year-appointment.

This did not mean Caesar's path would be easy, not by any means. Rome claimed all of Gaul, but in 61 B.C.E. it controlled only the southernmost part. The Romans called it simply The Province, and that name has stuck to modern times: we call it Provence.

Marcus Licinius Crassus was a Roman general who defeated the slave rebellion led by Spartacus and then joined Gaius Pompey and Julius Caesar to form the First Triumvirate.

Whom did Caesar fight?

Immediately upon arriving in The Province—which equates to modern-day Provence in southern France—Caesar faced a huge migration movement by the Helvetti tribe. They lived in central Switzerland but were on the move toward The Province. Caesar challenged them, saying that Rome controlled who moved through these lands. Caesar's written report declares that 280,000 Helvetians came against him and that only one-third of that number returned. He forced them into mountainside skirmishes and battles along rivers whose banks were swollen from the spring rains. He outmaneuvered them, beat them consistently, and when all the strategic moves were accomplished, he left the field to his subordinate generals, knowing that the high efficiency of the Roman legion would prevail. He was correct.

After the Helvetian threat was neutralized, Caesar faced an invasion by Germanic tribes from the east side of the River Rhine. Caesar consistently beat the Germans in battle, employing the same mixture of tactics that worked against the Swiss tribes.

How about the Gauls themselves? Did they welcome Roman rule?

Far from it. From the little documentary evidence that survives, we gather that the Gauls—who proudly proclaimed themselves Celts—detested the rectangular, square-shaped organization of the Romans and that the highest compliment one Gaul could pay another was to declare, "I greet you as a free person."

Gaul was still semi-independent from Rome, but Caesar's numerous battles and campaigns threatened its autonomy. Caesar negotiated with, and sometimes bribed, leading Gallic chieftains, allowing him to pit one against another and to keep Rome's interests in the advance. It was through this type of clever diplomacy that Caesar was able to bring legions through sections of Gaul on his way north, where he fought the Belgae tribes, ancestors to modern-day Dutch and Belgian peoples.

What happened to the Belgae and the Britons?

The Belgae were subdued and nearly destroyed in an enormous campaign that lasted two years. Caesar claimed to have killed or sold into slavery a total of 800,000 Belgae, but this figures seems inflated: at that rate, he would have depopulated most of Northern Europe. But there is no doubt he succeeded or that he then crossed the English Channel to fight the tribes of Britain.

The British tribes—who were known for painting their faces blue before going into battle—had lived completely free from outside influence for hundreds of years, and they fought fiercely. They met Caesar's men on the beaches near the mouth of the River Thames and fought them all along the southern coast. Roman discipline, as usual, prevailed, but even Caesar could see that the time was not right for the complete conquest of Britain. He left that for a later date, and it was his collateral relative Claudius who carried out the conquest, eighty years later.

When was the first bridge across the River Rhine built?

There may have been some makeshift bridges earlier in human history, but the first solid bridge of which we have certain knowledge was built by Roman engineers in 55 B.C.E. across the River Rhine. Caesar marched three legions across this bridge and defeated the Germans in a number of skirmishes without engaging in a major battle. Withdrawing to the west side of the Rhine, he ordered the bridge destroyed. He rightly believed that he had chastised the Germans; what he did not know was that their descendants would later return as one of the barbarian groups that helped bring down Rome.

How good a general had Caesar become by this point?

Even if his career had ended in 55 B.C.E., we would recognize Caesar as one of the greats, both for his decisiveness and speed. Once Caesar made a decision, he never wavered but pursued his goal to the utmost, never failing to follow up a victory. But his greatest days were still to come.

In 53 B.C.E., the Gauls united behind one leader, Vercingetorix, chief of the Arvernii. He seems to have been a person of great personal magnetism, as well as a careful strategist, who correctly decided that the only way to beat the Romans was by denying satisfaction to their stomachs. In 53–52 B.C.E., Vercingetorix ordered the burning of one Gallic town after another to prevent the Romans from getting food, and after six months of this strategy, the Romans were on the brink of mutiny. Luck favored Caesar, however, when one town—Avaricum—was spared, and the Romans captured it. Flush with success and new food supplies, the Romans continued the campaign. Even though Vercingetorix achieved a signal success at the Siege of Gergovia—where the Romans lost 700 men—he made the mistake of retreating to another hilltop-fortified city—Alesia—where he was cornered by Caesar.

How did Caesar manage the conquest of Alesia?

The city, which was unearthed by French archaeologists in the 1860s, was built on a sloping hillside and possessed deep wells: there was no way it would fall under ordinary circumstances. Caesar, however, committed to the siege and had his men dig a series of walls which wrapped eleven miles around Alesia, completely boxing in the Gauls. When he learned that an enormous relief army was being summoned from all across Gaul, Caesar had his men build a second set of ditches and walls: this one was thirteen miles around. When the relief army appeared, its men attacked the outer walls, while Vercingetorix and his garrison attacked the inner ring. Numerous times a breakthrough seemed possible, but Caesar kept bringing reinforcements to just the right place, and after a two-day battle everyone was exhausted. The relief army melted away, and Vercingetorix came down the hill to surrender in person (Caesar kept him a prisoner but had him beheaded during a major celebration in Rome, three years later).

How great—and how ruthless—was Caesar?

He was both great and ruthless to the same very high degree. Caesar could be merci-

A bronze statue of Julius Caesar stands in Rimini, Italy. Many statues and busts of the great Roman leader may be found throughout Europe.

ful, but only when it was to his advantage. He employed bribery and flattery as effectively as threats and intimidation. He was, quite simply, one of the great talents of human history, and his *Gallic Commentaries*, the book he wrote about his campaigns in Gaul, reveals a truly masterful mind through writing that is sharp, fresh, and clear.

ROMAN CIVIL WAR

What does it mean to "cross the Rubicon"?

In 49 B.C.E., Caesar and his battle-hardened legions were on the north bank of the River Rubicon, in northern Italy. To cross that river was to break the law, and Caesar knew this quite well. He had just received letters from the Roman Senate, telling him to lay down his command and return to Rome, where he could have possibly been put on trial.

Caesar pondered the matter for a day or so and then ordered his men to cross the Rubicon. He told his generals that "the die is cast," and—ever since—we have employed that expression, as well as the phrase "crossing the Rubicon" to refer to a major life decision, one from which there is no turning back.

Why was the Roman Civil War fought in Spain and Greece, rather than Italy?

It happened by chance, because Caesar's foe, Gaius Pompey, fled to Greece, while two of his sons, with their armies, went to Spain. This formed a precedent, however, and for hundreds of years to come, Romans showed a marked tendency to fight civil wars in the provinces rather than the Italian homeland.

Caesar followed Pompey to Greece, and after months of maneuvering, the two armies clashed at the Battle of Pharsalus. Pompey had perhaps twice as many men (55,000) as Caesar, but his troops were not as battle tested. In one of the worst Roman-on-Roman collisions, Caesar prevailed, in part because he ordered his men to thrust their javelins at the faces of Pompey's cavalrymen rather than the horses. A Roman aristocrat could bear many difficulties and indignities, Caesar declared, but he was much too proud of his face to risk injury to it. Following his defeat, Pompey fled the field, and thousands of his men went over to Caesar.

How did Caesar wind up in control of Egypt?

In 47 B.C.E., Egypt was one of the few parts of the Mediterranean world that still was independent of Rome. Its ruler, King Ptolemy XI, was wedded to his sister Queen Cleopatra. Soon after his arrival at the city of Alexandria—named for the great Macedonian conqueror—Caesar was handed a basket in which he found the head of his Roman rival Pompey. The Egyptians had done this in order to please Caesar and to persuade him to leave Egypt alone.

Caesar, however, allied with Cleopatra to fight against King Ptolemy. Though the fighting was touch and go, Caesar prevailed as usual, and King Ptolemy and many of his men died in the Battle of the Nile. Caesar then chose to remain in Egypt for several months, during which time Cleopatra became his lover as well as his political ally. By the time Caesar departed, Cleopatra was pregnant with his son, and Egypt had moved at least halfway into the Roman camp.

What happened to all the rest of Caesar's foes: Pompey's sons, the king of Numidia, the Spanish tribesmen?

They were all beaten. Caesar came close to defeat only once, in southern Spain, and he recovered in time. By the time he returned to Rome in 46 B.C.E., he was *the* world conqueror, and everyone realized it.

Caesar had proved himself a fine administrator as well as a great general. He established new overseas colonies for his veterans, altered the Roman calendar to the one that was the basis for the Western world until the 1580s, and seemed on the verge of making himself king or emperor. He, very likely, knew that there was no need to do so: he already possessed more power than any person prior to his time. His political foes, however, insisted that he was on the cusp of destroying the Roman Republic and creating a new Roman Empire. They, therefore, assassinated him on March 15, 44 B.C.E.

THE ROMAN EMPIRE

Who were the candidates to succeed Caesar as leader of the Roman world?

At the moment of Caesar's death, it was obvious that there were only two men who could possibly succeed him. Marc Antony was his best subordinate general, and Octavian was both his nephew and his adopted son. One of these two men would clearly be the new leader.

Which of these two possessed the initial advantage?

Because he was so well known to the legionnaires, Marc Antony had the advantage at the beginning of the rivalry. Over time, however, Antony became identified with the concerns of the Eastern Mediterranean, and when he joined forces with Cleopatra (she bore him several children), Antony sealed his doom. Octavian was very young—only eighteen when Julius Caesar died—but he proved an able statesman and was successful in portraying Antony as a fallen man to the Roman public. When the two clashed in battle in 31 B.C.E., Octavian had most of the advantage.

How decisive was the Battle of Actium?

Fought in and just outside the harbor of Actium on the west coast of Greece, this was one of the most significant battles of that century. Both sides entered with roughly 175 galleys and transport vessels; by late afternoon, Antony and Cleopatra had lost all but twenty. Roman discipline was one reason for Octavian's victory; the rest of the cause can be assigned to his admiral, Agrippa.

The 1754 painting *Le repas de Cléoptre et de Marc-Antoine* by Charles-Joseph Natoire has Marc Antony and Cleopatra dining in luxury. Lovers and political allies, Antony and Cleopatra would lose the battle against Octavian and, consequently, both committed suicide.

Antony and Cleopatra fled to Egypt, which had become something of a haven for runaway Romans. Octavian took his time in pursuit, but the day he landed in Egypt, Marc Antony committed suicide. Cleopatra stayed alive long enough to look upon Octavian's face; he gave her the stark choice of suicide or execution (she chose to have a servant bring a poisonous snake to her chamber). Actium was not terribly exciting in its presentation, but it was an extremely important battle. Rome had—by virtue of Octavian's victory—completely eclipsed Alexandria, and from that point on Rome was *the* city of the Mediterranean world, with no rival or even close second.

How did Augustus reorganize the legions?

In 27 B.C.E., four years after winning at Actium, Octavian took the new name of Augustus, meaning the revered one. He never put a crown on his head or called himself king or emperor, but those symbols were unnecessary: he was the emperor, whether anyone said so or not.

Augustus was primarily a political leader rather than a military one, but he saw the need to reorganize the legions. He limited, or capped, their number at thirty and worked to bring all of them up to full strength: until his reign, many legions numbered between

4,000 and 5,000 rather than the expected 6,000. Augustus saw, too, that the frontiers of the empire needed defining, and he worked many years to create a defensible line of borders. He made only one major military mistake, but it haunted him until the end of his days.

What did Augustus mean by "Quintus Varrus, give me back my legions"?

In 9 c.e., Augustus sent General Varrus with three legions across the Rhine to chastise the Germanic tribes. Varrus knew the way quite well, and he and his men did fine for the first fifty miles or so, but when they entered the Teutoburger Forest they lost their way and were ambushed by Germans. A three-day battle ended in the destruction of all three legions. Varrus died, as did the great majority of his officers. For Augustus, this was the greatest disaster of his reign and a distressing indication that the empire needed to remain on the defensive on its northern frontiers.

What was the military situation like at the time of Augustus' death?

Much as he desired, the Roman Empire had taken on the configuration that would last for centuries. Rome and the towns of northern Italy were the heart of the empire, from which the legions were mobilized and dispatched. The entire rim of the Mediterranean Sea was now Roman, with Roman warships controlling the waterways. The empire extended north to the English Channel and west to the River Rhine. From the Rhine, the imperial boundaries made a sharp right-hand turn to the Danube and then to the Black Sea.

This was a truly enormous amount of land to govern and defend, but it was possible just so long as the emperors attended to business and the legions responded to trouble areas. There would be times, however, when the emperors were completely off the job—or out to lunch—and when the governors of the various provinces had to handle things themselves.

AUGUSTUS' HEIRS

Why do we call them "heirs" rather than "descendants"?

Augustus had several children by his two marriages, but none of his sons survived. The throne, therefore, passed to his stepson, Tiberius, who was the first man to call himself emperor. In his youth, Tiberius had been an active and courageous military leader, fighting the German tribes, but in late middle age he was weary. He paid little attention either to military or political affairs, and imperial governance suffered accordingly. It is worth noting, however, that the military situation stayed very much in control and that there were few, if any, revolts during Tiberius' reign.

One of the few civil disturbances was a minor matter in the Province of Judaea. Rome had been in Judaea—which equates to modern-day Israel—for almost a century, but it was during Tiberius' reign that many Jews expressed their discontent. Some gathered together behind a popular preacher named Jesus of Nazareth, and the Roman authorities found the situation dangerous enough that they had Jesus crucified. This event seemed insignificant at the time, but it led to the birth of a whole new religion, and the Christians—or "Christ followers"—would provide the Roman Empire with many headaches.

Who was truly the worst of all Roman emperors?

Beyond doubt this was Caligula (ruled 37–41 C.E.). Named by Tiberius shortly before his death, Caligula was about thirty-two when he became emperor. A psychopathic individual with a heart that seemed incapable of empathy, Caligula may have suffered brain damage in youth; then again, he may simply have never experienced true human kindness. In either case, he was a terrible emperor, tending entirely to his own caprice and whim, bending all

Emperor Caligula is regarded by many historians as the worst ruler of Rome, abusing his power to extremes that would have been considered absurd had they not been matched by his cold-hearted ruthlessness.

the rules in order to create pleasure or amusement. Surely one of the greatest set of laughs—as well as sighs—came when Caligula brought his favorite horse into the Roman Senate and nominated it for consul (high executive) for the coming year.

Again, it is worth noting that the external boundaries of the empire did not suffer during Caligula's reign. The imperial system was young and fresh, and there were many highly skilled and devoted leaders of the Roman provinces as well as the legions. As a result, the empire seemed to do quite well during Caligula's depraved rule, but had he lived another decade, things might have broken down. As it was, everyone expressed relief when Caligula was killed by a member of the Praetorian Guard and the throne passed to his uncle, Claudius.

Who conquered Britain and made it Roman?

The Emperor Claudius (reigned 41–54 B.C.E.) came to the throne at the age of sixty, but he knew it was necessary to establish a military reputation; no emperor could call his reign complete if he lacked a major conquest. Claudius, therefore, led the invasion of Britain that commenced around the year 60 B.C.E.

The Britons fought just as fiercely as their great-grandparents had in the time of Julius Caesar, but the Roman military was now so formidable that it could prevail even

What was the Praetorian Guard?

Established during the reign of Augustus, the Guard was a special legion unto itself, composed of about 4,000 highly skilled soldiers. Augustus created it as the imperial bodyguard, but he did not foresee the many troubles it would later cause. The assassination of Caligula was the first of many instances when the Guard took matters into its own hands and its leaders believed that they had to preserve the imperial dignity: without an emperor, they had no jobs.

when not led by a military genius. Claudius was a bit of a plodder, so far as military matters went, but he engineered the crossing of the Channel and watched as his generals won the battles on British (or English) soil. By about 63 C.E., the conquest of lower England was complete.

Which one emperor nearly brought down the imperial system?

The Emperor Nero (ruled 54–68 C.E.) was almost as great a disaster as the Emperor Caligula. During his short time on the throne, Nero focused all his attention to affairs in Italy and Greece—including entering himself in the chariot races of the Olympic Games—and far too little on the external parts of the empire.

No major threat from outside the empire emerged; rather, it was the threat posed by ambitious generals from within. Since the death of Augustus, they had never seen a truly effective emperor, and Nero was so weak—and personally conflicted—that it seemed a god-sent opportunity for revolt. When Nero died by his own hand in 69 C.E., a series of revolts and counter-revolts were set off, with the potential to destroy the center of the empire.

How did the Romans found a new dynasty?

All of Augustus' relatives—collateral or direct—were now deceased, and a struggle for the Roman throne ensued between prominent Roman noblemen. Whoever commanded or had the allegiance of the Praetorian Guard had a major advantage in this power struggle, which resulted in no fewer than four emperors over the period of eighteen months. Nero was followed by Galba, who was overcome by Otho, who lost to Vitellius, who was then overthrown by Vespasian. Things finally began to settle down when Vespasian won battles in Italy and ascended the throne. He had no special mandate or familial connection to Augustus, but the people of Rome were desperate for peace and they soon settled down under Vespasian's rule.

Were life and death as intricately connected in the Coliseum as we suppose?

It was a place of tremendous danger for those who provided entertainment for the imperial elite. When the Coliseum opened in the year 80 C.E., the event was commemorated by festivities that resulted in the death of 5,000 animals, many of them from North Africa. This was but the beginning, however, of the Coliseum's long rule as the place for blood, death, and imperial circuses.

THE PAX ROMANA

What did the Mediterranean world look like between about 100 and 160 C.E.?

Many historians have followed the lead of Edward Gibbon—author of the *Rise and Fall of the Roman Empire*—in declaring that this half century was the most prosperous and secure period of recorded Roman history. In some ways this is true: there were no major wars in this period. The Roman legions were so powerful that any revolts were quickly stamped out. One can, however, discover the roots of future weakness even in this time of great success.

By 160 C.E., the legions were mostly composed of non-Italians; very few natives of the Italian soil wished to serve in the provinces. The leaders of those legions, too, were increasingly foreign. This was not a terrible thing, but Roman patriotism—based on allegiance to the city-state and Italian peninsula—began to wither and was replaced by a much broader loyalty to the empire as a whole, represented by the emperor. As long as the emperor was a good and practical leader, the legions would accomplish their tasks; if he was a weakling, things could go downhill quite rapidly. As it turned out, there was to be one more truly great emperor, followed by a long series of mediocre or poor ones.

How do we know so much about the Emperor Marcus Aurelius?

We know a great deal, both from what was written about him at the time and because he was a true philosopher-emperor who composed the *Meditations*. A lesser known fact, however, is that Aurelius—who was a secondary character in the 2000 film *Gladiator*—was a true warrior-emperor. From the start of his reign, the empire was attacked on its eastern and northeastern frontiers. The Parthians attacked Syria while various Germanic tribes attacked in the Danube River Basin.

Aurelius spent most of the last ten years of his reign in the Danube Basin, responding to one crisis after another. On one occasion, in a battle against the Quadi

By the time Marcus Aurelius became emperor of Rome in the second century C.E., the empire was struggling to defend its borders in the east and north.

tribe, he was nearly defeated, but a thunderstorm—which all observers treated as a miracle—rescued his parched men, who rebounded to win the day. By the time of Aurelius' death in 180 C.E., the empire was largely victorious, but it required the constant attention of a vigorous emperor.

When did the decline of Rome really become apparent?

The reign of the Emperor Commodus (180–193) was bad enough in that Commodus was far more interested in gladiatorial events than anything to do with real military matters, but things only became worse with the turn of the century. One emperor after another deposed his predecessor, usually with the help of the Praetorian Guard, and none of them were men of great ability. There was a very surprising period of seven months when the empire was ruled by a man whose father had been a slave—this was a true anomaly—but this entire time was marked, in general, by mediocre leaders and an increasing sense of hopelessness.

THE MID-CENTURY CRISIS

Was there any time prior to the fifth century when Rome could have collapsed?

Yes. In the middle part of the third century, both the city of Rome and the empire showed severe signs of strain. Perhaps the worst moment was when the Roman Emperor Valerian (ruled 250–260) was captured by Shapur, king of the Sassanid dynasty in Iran. The event was commemorated in a number of sculptures and monuments in Iran (some of them exist today), and the shame felt by the Roman public was very great.

The Sassanids were a formidable foe, but they could never have threatened the integrity of the Roman Empire on their own; it was the simultaneous attack of tribal peoples along the vulnerable Danube River frontier that really accelerated the danger. Even then, had Rome in 260 been the Rome of two centuries earlier, it could have responded to all threats. As it was, currency devaluation combined with a weakness in the legions led to conditions that made a general collapse possible.

How did Rome make it through the crisis of the third century?

Neither the Sassanids nor the northern tribal peoples pushed their advantage strongly enough, and by about 275 Rome had steadied herself. A new emperor, Aurelian, was the first to appreciate that the city of Rome needed new defenses, and the Aurelian Wall was completed by 280. Other Italian cities were fortified, and by about 290 the empire had taken on a stronger, though highly defensive, look.

Then, too, a new emperor, Dicoletian, set a new set of rules and regulations. To us today, they seem extreme, as when he decreed that men must practice the trade of their fathers and that men and women must live in the towns of their birth. But to an empire

The Column of Constantine was erected in 330 C.E. when the name of the city was changed from Byzantium to Constantinople, the new heart of the Roman Empire.

that was on the verge of disintegration, these reforms made sense. Dicoletian, too, was the first emperor to acknowledge that the empire was too large for one person to manage; during his reign, there were two Augustuses and two Caesars, making for a total of four men who ruled.

What else was distinctive about Rome at the beginning of the fourth century?

Many people, including Diocletian, recognized that the city of Rome was no longer the heart of the Roman Empire. People still spoke of Rome with veneration, but the major public business had languished and quite a few merchants had picked up and moved. Dicoletian spent little time in Rome, but it was left to his successor to make the true break and establish a new imperial capital.

Constantine I (ruled 306–337) emerged from a four-way contest to become the new emperor. Born in Britain, he was the son of a pagan father and a Christian mother, and he carried that tension throughout life. We have no doubt that he won the Battle of the Milvan Bridge (in 306) and that his men carried some Christian symbols into that battle; whether he actually dreamed that "In this sign shall you conquer" is another matter. Constantine did become the new leader, however, and he declared that there had to be a second capital.

How soon did Constantinople rival Rome?

Constantine took a fishing village of 800 inhabitants and turned it into a city of 50,000 people. A century later, there may have been as many as a quarter million people in Constantinople, and the number just continued to rise. There were people, however, who insisted that Rome would always be the center of the Roman Empire, and the contest between the two cities lasted for many years. The single most important advantage enjoyed by Constantinople was that the emperors—almost to a man—preferred to live there or at Ravenna, a city on the northeast Italian coast, rather than Rome.

Constantine was not—to the best of our knowledge—a likeable or admirable person, but few of the Roman emperors were. What matters is that he gave new life to an empire which had almost died and that his efforts prolonged its life for another 150 years in the western section and almost 1,000 years in the eastern.

BARBARIAN TRIBES
AND THE FALL OF ROME

Doesn't everyone come from a distant place at some point in their development?

Yes. It is only in retrospect that some people can call themselves "civilized" and others "barbarians." If you trace the history of almost any people on earth far enough, you will eventually discover a time when they were the wild men, the outlanders, or the barbarians. For example, the French and Germans, who are considered among the most civilized of today's peoples, were wandering tribal peoples at the time when the Roman Empire fell. Similarly, the proud Manchu rulers of China, in the eighteenth and nineteenth centuries, had previously been among the far-farers on the outside of the Wall of China. There is something especially "wild" about the centuries that followed the fall of Rome, however, a time when the barbarians outnumbered civilized peoples by a large margin.

Who were the first of the "wild people from far off"?

Although the Visigoths, Ostrogoths, Vandals, and Burgundians can all lay a claim, the first truly wild folk to emerge were the Huns, who came to northeastern Europe in the first decades of the fifth century C.E. Very little is known about the early Huns, other than the fact that they were a Central Asian people who migrated westward, most likely in search of better pastures for their animals.

As soon as they arrived in the Danube Basin, the Huns sowed panic among the other tribal peoples of that region. Whether it was actual warfare or just rumors of conflict, the Huns seemed so fierce that the Ostrogoths practically begged the Roman Empire for protection. Quite a few Ostrogoths even entered the empire, with some joining the faltering legions. But the Huns became truly terrifying following the rise of Attila.

Who was Attila, and how did he become so powerful?

He was one of the two primary sons of the chief of the Huns, and he fought a long, protracted conflict with his brother to become "King." Once he did so, however, Attila truly lived up to that title. He led the Huns in increasingly ambitious and daring raids, even threatening the city of Constantinople. Attila did not really wish to conquer the Byzantine capital; it was far more profitable to extract tribute from the Byzantines.

By 440 C.E., Attila had turned his attention to the Western Roman Empire. The farther he drove into its confines, the more weakness he detected. Attila was not as successful in extracting tribute from Rome, but he possessed excellent intelligence about the city and its people. He was even in contact with General Aeitius, who had been a hostage among the Huns during his youth.

Could Attila have captured Rome, and if so, would that have been the summit of his ambition?

Very likely, Attila would have been disappointed because Rome, in 450, was not what it had been a century or two before. Then, too, he had lost the chance of being the "first" man to sack Rome: that distinction went to Alaric, who led his Goths there in 410. But even when we put in these qualifiers, we know that Attila wished to conquer Rome. In 451, he led a large army of Huns due west, to central France, in what may be viewed as preparation for his assault on Rome. His plans were detected, however, and Aeitius brought a Roman-Germanic-Frankish army to challenge the Huns.

The Battle of Charlons-sur-Marne, fought in the summer of 451, may be one of the most decisive of the entire Middle Ages. It was not a spectacular victory for the Romans and their allies, but they fought the Huns to a draw, and Attila withdrew from the area. Given that the entire Western Roman Empire could have collapsed, the battle is regarded as a decisive victory even though it was fought from a defensive position.

Did Attila try again?

Yes. He returned in 453 C.E., crossed the Alps, and marched across northern Italy with frightening ease. Not until he was within one hundred miles of Rome was there any significant resistance, and it came—in this instance—not from military men but the papacy. Pope Gregory the Great left Rome with a tiny bodyguard, and upon arriving at the Huns' camp asked to see Attila. The two men spent several hours in Attila's tent, and soon after the Pope departed, the Huns began to break camp. Clearly, the Pope had said something of great importance.

No one knows what words were spoken, but we suspect that the Pope threatened Attila, saying that the Christian God was more powerful than the pagan ones and that the Huns would all contract a disease if they remained in Italy. There was a virulent pestilence at the time, and Attila may have feared it more than anything else, but according to Catholic tradition, the Pope saved Rome.

What happened to Attila and the Huns?

Attila died a year later, on the evening of his wedding to a Bulgarian princess. Soon after his death, the Huns began breaking up, evidence of the fact that their clannish and tribal ties were not as powerful as one thought. A generation later, it was hard to find anyone that called himself a Hun.

Was that the end of the barbarian migrations?

By no means. The Vandals had just gotten started on a remarkable odyssey that would take them to North Africa, and the Franks, Lombards, and Burgundians were still on the move. All of these tribes were headed toward settling down, but there was still some wildness within them.

Each of these tribes, and quite a few others in Western Europe, were on the verge of the greatest challenge they had ever met. Time and again, they had defeated their enemies in battle, but they had never come against a force as powerful as the Christian missionaries. Over the next one hundred years—between 450 and 550 C.E.—many of the barbarian peoples became Christians, thanks to the efforts of some truly dedicated and heroic monks and priests.

THE BYZANTINE EMPIRE

What was the high point for the Byzantines?

The Byzantines—who called themselves Romans—hit their high point sometime in the sixth century C.E. This was partly due to a rigid social and political system that allowed the military leaders to establish stronger armies than any seen in the previous three centuries.

The Emperor Justinian and his wife, the Empress Theodora, presided over the Byzantine Empire at the time of its greatest strength. Not only did they beautify Constantinople, building the famous Hagia Sophia, but they commissioned General Belisarius to reconquer large parts of the Western Roman Empire. During the 530s and 540s, Belisarius conquered parts of North Africa, all of Sicily, and parts of Italy. He did not attempt to reestablish a Roman presence in Rome, however; he, like everyone else, believed the city was too far gone. The fruit of Belisarius' campaigns can, therefore, be seen in the magnificent Byzantine churches in northern Italy, especially the city of Ravenna.

Did the Byzantines hang on to what they had won?

Not for long. The pressure from the barbarian groups, who, by this time, can be considered semicivilized, was too strong. By 600 C.E., the Byzantines had lost nearly every-

Once a Greek Orthodox church and later a mosque and museum, the Hagia Sophia in present-day Istanbul, Turkey, was built at the height of the Byzantine Empire as part of Emperor Justinian's efforts to beautify Constantinople.

thing they had gained in the central and western Mediterranean. Part of the reason is that they were distracted by a newly resurgent Persian Empire.

How many times did the peoples of Iran and Iraq change their names?

So many times that one can spend hours trying to puzzle them out. Originally, the people in present-day Iran were known as Persians, but during the third century C.E., following a dynastic change, they came to be known as the Parthians. Later they became known as the Sassanids, another dynasty, and still later they reverted back to being Persians. During all these centuries and dynasties, one thing remained fairly constant: the Persians, Parthians, Sassanids, and others were aggressive and eager to combat the Byzantines.

Which Byzantine emperor pushed the Persians right to the brink?

The Emperor Heraclius (reigned about 600) fought the Persians relentlessly, driving them from Asia Minor and large parts of the Middle East. During his reign, the Byzantines gained definitive control of the city of Jerusalem and claimed to be defenders of the faith (this was, of course, disputed by the popes in the West). But just as he neared complete victory, Heraclius realized that his empire was overextended. He began a withdrawal that seemed like an excellent strategic move. Heraclius and his successors did not envision the new danger that was about to appear, however.

How important is the life of the Prophet Mohammed?

To those who believe he was the final prophet, Mohammed is the single most important person of human history. But even those who do not recognize Mohammed acknowledge him as one of the great change agents of the first millennium, whose impact lasted well into the third. Mohammed started a new monotheistic religion, with the faithful expressing their belief with a brief but poignant saying: "There is no God but God, and Mohammed is his Messenger."

One can dispute aspects and parts of the Prophet's teachings, but when it comes to war, there can be no mistake. Mohammed stands out among all the great religious figures as the one leader who believed force was sometimes necessary to accomplish the will of heaven. To be sure, some of his beliefs have been exaggerated or distorted by his followers, but the popular image of Mohammed holding the Koran in one hand and a curved sword in the other is not inaccurate.

To this point in military history—about 630—the Arabian Peninsula had not figured largely in the events or campaigns of any of the major powers. The Arabs, who numbered perhaps one million, were a people standing on the outskirts of history. No one—Byzantine, Persian, or Roman—expected them to make the sudden, swift appearance that occured in the 640s.

THE ARAB EXPLOSION

When did the Arabs leave their peninsula?

The Prophet Mohammed died in 632, and Arab military moves began within a handful of years following his death. No one person—civilian or military—lays claim as the leader of the Arab explosion; this is perhaps because Muslim writers wish to give all the credit to the Prophet. He had certainly established the path by creating a new religion, but even he would have been astonished at the speed and success of the Arab conquests.

Within ten years of the Prophet's death, the Arabs had conquered Jerusalem and were on their way to taking Damascus and Cairo. Baghdad and the Libyan Desert were conquered next, followed by Arab movements into Spain and Central Asia. There were times, quite likely, when their opponents cursed and raved about the Arabs. How could a rather primitive people, equipped only with camels and horses, beat so many other peoples and advance so far?

Who led the way for the Arabs?

During his lifetime 'Ali, the son-in-law of the Prophet, was the leader of most of the Arab forces. By the time the Arabs fought the Byzantines and the Persians, however, they were on the verge of the great split that remains today: that between Sunni and Shi'ite.

Those who claimed that the leader of the Arabs must be connected by blood to the Prophet followed 'Ali, and his name remains, in that Shi'ite means "follower of 'Ali." Those who claimed that majority ruled and whoever was designated by the majority would serve as the caliph became known as Sunnis, meaning majority. By the time 'Ali died in 664 the split was apparent, but the Arabs kept on winning battles and wars.

What was the farthest westward extent of Arab conquest?

In 711, the Muslim leader al-Tariq led a group of Arabs and Berbers across what the Greeks called the Pillars of Hercules and what we know as the Strait of Gibraltar. Little known is the fact that the very word Gibraltar comes from Arabic: it is a corruption of Tariq's Rock.

The Muslims soon occupied the southern two-thirds of Spain. They seemed destined to take over much of Western Europe, but they suffered a defeat at the hands of the Frankish cavalry at the Battle of Tours in 732. The defeat was not large, by Arab

Charles Martel, king of the Franks, defended Europe from the further advance of the Muslims at the Battle of Tours in 732 (painting by Charles de Steuben, c. 1835).

standards, but it prevented any further crossings of the Pyrenees, which became the unofficial division between Muslim and Christian Europe.

What was the farthest eastward extent of Arab conquest?

In 751, an Arab army clashed with a Chinese one at the Battle of Talas, in Central Asia. This battle was a standoff, but, like Tours, it was enough to stop the Arab momentum. No one can minimize the terrific extent of the Arab conquests, though; in the century that followed the Prophet's death, the Arabs took over ninety percent of all the urban centers in the Western world, and their conquests equaled those of ancient Rome.

CHARLEMAGNE

Why is Charlemagne's name still so well known today?

He lived in a time—the eighth century—when the population of Europe was much smaller than today, and he lived such a dramatic and full life that he is one of the few Europeans from that time we know much about. In addition, no fewer than five countries—France, Belgium, Holland, Germany, and Luxembourg—claim him as their founding father. Even more significant, many people around the world today like to claim they are descended from Charlemagne.

While we are on the subject of genetics, it is worth pointing out that if one traces his or her lineage a long way, he often finds that he is related—in one way or another—to almost all the people who were alive at any given time. Roughly fifty generations separate our time from that of Charlemagne, and if we really have as many ancestors as mathematics suggests, then we would be right to claim descent from him, but also from the fellow who held his horse!

What advantages did Charlemagne have in his early life?

He was one of the two sons of the king of the Franks, and given that his elder brother was a halfwit, it was obvious that Charlemagne would inherit the throne. He did corule

---

How do we know so much about Charlemagne's appearance?

One of the scholars at his court—in present-day Holland—wrote a biography, and when Charlemagne's bones were exhumed in 1862, they confirmed many things which had been written. We know, for example, that Charlemagne was about six foot two, very impressive for that time, and that he suffered a number of wounds over the years. Whether he actually spoke in a high, light voice is impossible to say.

with his brother, Carloman, for a time, but he deposed him and established his own one-man rule.

Charlemagne—whose name means "Charles the Great"—was obsessed with the idea of rebuilding Rome, rebuilding what the Roman Empire had once been. He was not the only person to have this vision, but he was, perhaps, the person equipped with more tools than anyone else. Even so, he knew many years of struggle.

How many campaigns did Charlemagne undertake?

In the neighborhood of forty. He typically spent the winter and spring at his capital city of Aachen and campaigned in the summer and fall. Charlemagne was an ardent Christian who wished to convert all the peoples of Europe, and he certainly was willing to employ the sword to do so.

Charlemagne fought the Saxons—from whom many today derive the ethnic name of Anglo-Saxons—in north-central Germany for many years. Upon finally defeating them, he looked further to the east and commenced a series of campaigns against the Avars, a tribe of Central Asia nomads who had moved into what are now Hungary and Czechoslovakia. Tradition has it that when Charlemagne finally defeated the Avars, he came away with wagonloads of gold, which were used to finance the cultural changes he had underway at Aachen.

Did Charlemagne fail in any of his campaigns?

Only once. In 778, he invaded Muslim Spain and besieged the towns which are now the major cities of Barcelona and Pamplona. Thwarted in his attempts, Charlemagne headed for home and to his chagrin, the Basque tribesmen of northern Spain—who were fellow Christians—ambushed his rear guard. Count Roland, one of Charlemagne's most dedicated knights, was killed in the battle. For centuries afterward, French children were raised on stories of Roland's bravery in the same manner as English children who delighted in tales of King Arthur.

What was the highest point of Charlemagne's long reign?

Having fought the Lombards and thereby made life easier for Pope Leo III, Charle-

Charlemagne, or Charles the Great, unified much of Europe in an attempt to restore some of the former glory of Rome. In 800 he was crowned emperor of the Romans by Pope Leo.

magne wished to cement his alliance with the papacy. In the autumn of 800, Charlemagne and several thousand of his countrymen journeyed south and crossed the Alps (this was one of the few times they were not traveling to a military destination). Arriving in Rome, Charlemagne made his last backstage deals, and on Christmas Day, Pope Leo crowned him emperor of the Romans in full view of thousands of people.

This was obviously a great moment for Charlemagne: it proved the cap or crowning moment of his long career. But it was also a major step forward for the Northern European peoples. Three hundred years had passed since Rome fell, and during most of that time, there had been little hope for a recovery. Charlemagne's coronation meant that the Pope and the king of the Franks were now political and military allies and that they intended to rebuild the glory of Rome, no matter how long it might take.

THE WORLD ISLAND: 801 TO 1405

What is meant by "The World Island"?

Halford MacKinder (1861–1947), a British geographer and historian, coined the term in his essay "The Geographical Pivot of History," delivered to the Royal Geographical Society in 1904. By "The World Island," MacKinder was referencing the great Eurasian landmass which runs from the west side of the Pacific Ocean to the eastern edge of the Atlantic. To MacKinder, it was apparent that The World Island was key to military and strategic dominance of the globe. He rightly pointed out that the Eurasian landmass was far larger than either Africa on its own or the two Americas jointed together. In more recent times, the historian Jared Diamond has proposed something similar, pointing out that both trade and people migrated more naturally across the Eurasian landmass—much of which is parallel in latitude to North, South, and Central America.

MacKinder's thesis was studied by many people over the next forty years; even Adolf Hitler appears to have been influenced by it. Hitler, however, reduced a complicated, even fascinating, thesis to a short lesson in the geopolitics of his region. To Hitler, it was apparent that he who controlled the Eurasian heartland—roughly defined as the lands between Poland and the Urals—would also control the globe.

How strong, or weak, did the empires look around the year 600?

The Western Roman Empire was no more, and the Chinese Han Empire had fallen, only to be replaced by the Tang dynasty. Africa had numerous peoples and kingdoms, but none of them were strong enough to speak to the needs of that continent, much less the Middle East and beyond. About the only viable empire at that moment was the Byzantine, which had been established 300 years earlier.

The Byzantines—they called themselves "Romans"—were well aware of being the only centripetal force in their world, but they had a great foe in the Parthians, who had replaced the Persians a few centuries earlier. The Byzantines and Parthians fought many battles and wars, with the former finally gaining an ascendancy under the Emperor Heraclius in the 620s. Just as he secured military success in the Middle East, Heraclius received a rather threatening message from the Arabian Peninsula. A man named Mohammed, who claimed to be the Prophet of God, urged Heraclius to abandon Christianity and to serve Allah. What Heraclius thought of this message is unknown, but his subjects and his descendants would wrestle with this force for a very long time.

THE MONGOLS

Which one person—more than any other—perceived the value of holding the heartland of Asia as the way to dominating the World Island?

This, beyond doubt, was Genghis Khan. When we speak or write of great military leaders, Genghis is among the top five of anyone's list, but when we examine what he accomplished with the rather crude means and methods of his time, it is tempting to say that he truly was the greatest military leader in human history and one heck of a strategist as well.

What was his boyhood like?

We call him Genghis Khan, meaning "Great Ruler" or "Universal Emperor," but his birth name was Temujin, and he came from a family of minor nobles within the Mongol tribe. His parents betrothed him to Borte, a girl from a family higher up the social ladder, but both he and she underwent enormous trials before their wedding. Genghis' father died when the boy was seven, and he had to struggle for many years, seeking the patronage of various tribal leaders. There was a heartrending period in which his mother and younger brothers practically starved, but Genghis survived these trials and took vengeance of all his enemies over time.

Genghis was, indeed, as cruel and vengeful as he sounds, but he also possessed tremendous talent, both social and military. While he may have lacked charm, he had enormous powers of persuasion, and he had the patience to wait to achieve his objective. By about the year 1195 he turned against his major sponsor, and after defeating him in battle, Genghis became leader of the Kerait subgroup of Mongols. From there, Genghis went from strength to strength, acquiring more peoples and groups as time went on.

Did Genghis know that he was destined for greatness?

He was a rather practical person, and when asked that very question, he replied that he knew he had been chosen by "the Sky" (as Mongols referred to the divine) when, as a boy of sixteen, he escaped an ambush by almost fifteen men and ended up killing or capturing them all. From that moment forward, he experienced little to no doubt.

Numerous victories came in his early forties, and in the summer of 1206—the year that Mongols called "Year of the Leopard"—Genghis was chosen as Great Khan or Great

Do we know what Genghis looked like?

We really don't. We have as many as a dozen eyewitness reports, but they differ from each other to such a degree that it is difficult to reach a consensus. One of the few things on which most accounts agree is that he was neither tall nor short and that his face was deeply marked, perhaps because of the many deprivations he experienced in youth.

Leader of all the Mongol tribes. This was a heady achievement for anyone, but to Genghis it was but the enormous first step in his quest for world dominance.

Was Genghis ever beaten in battle?

By our Western, standard of military technique, Genghis was beaten on numerous occasions, meaning that he ended up yielding the battlefield to his opponent. To him, a man of the great Eurasian steppe, this meant next to nothing. The enormous sea of grass, as many people call it, was too large for any person or army to occupy; what mattered was winning the final battle and putting one's enemies to the sword. And at these tasks, Genghis was unparalleled.

Which enemy, or neighbor, did he turn against first?

China was, at that time, divided in three sections: the Xi Xia in the northwest, the

A statue of Genghis Khan stands by his mausoleum in Ordos, China.

Chin in the northeast and center, and the Song Empire in the south. Had these three sections been fully unified, there was no way Genghis, or any other power, could ever have defeated them, but the social and political divisions opened the way to Mongol conquest. One should not minimize the difficulties involved, however.

Genghis had once been an ally of the Xi Xia Empire, but in 1211 he turned on that section of China, and he may have been one of the first of all military leaders to ride through the Great Wall (whether he had to fight his way past a Chinese garrison is not known). The civilians of Xi Xia fought fiercely, and Genghis became progressively more brutal during this conquest. He captured Zanadu—which we today know as Beijing—in 1215.

59

Were the Mongol slaughters compressive?

Noncombatants were usually spared, and Genghis had enough of a hold on his warriors to ensure this, but if a city or fortified place held out too long—in the eyes of the Mongols—then it was subjected to a terrible sack, and everyone's lives were forfeit. Genghis had an uncanny sense of knowing when to use mercy as a tool and when to withhold it; as a result, many towns and cities capitulated immediately upon his arrival.

At the same time, the Mongols increased their knowledge of urban warfare. They learned a great deal from the Chinese about gunpowder explosions and whirling mechanisms that released dozens, even scores, of darts. Whether they gained their knowledge of the counterweighted trebuchet from the Chinese or from the Middle East is difficult to say, but they soon became masters of its use.

Whom did Genghis turn on after the subjection of the Xi Xia?

He wanted to take a breather and consolidate his conquests, but the Muslim ruler of Khawramzeen infuriated him unnecessarily. Genghis sent emissaries and merchants to the capital of the Khawaramzeen; on the first occasion they were rebuffed, on their second visit many were killed. Genghis—who could not abide the breaking of an oath or guarantee—therefore prepared for war. Nearly three years passed before he crossed the Gobi Desert, but the size of his force—perhaps 150,000—indicated his resolve.

Where were the major battles of this campaign?

The first skirmish was fought in the open, and the Mongols won handily even though they were outnumbered. As a result, the emperor of the Khawramzeen moved well back from the frontier to a fortified city, and from that point on the war was one of sieges. Bukhara fell in 1219 and the glorious city of Samarkand—one of the truly great merchant cities of the ancient world—in 1220. Samarkand's fall was followed by an enormous slaughter; one Muslim tourist passing by thirty years later counted almost twenty mounds of skulls, clearly packed by the Mongols after the sack.

Did this campaign have a religious aspect? Was Genghis against the Muslims?

Not to our knowledge. Genghis seems to have been completely convinced that "the Sky," as he called his deity, was supreme and that nothing could stand against him. Genghis,

---

How large was the Mongol army at its peak?

Population statistics are lacking, but we think there were roughly one million Mongolians, of whom no more than 120,000 could be sent to war. Genghis, however, incorporated many other peoples into the growing empire, and he could—by 1219—perhaps send 200,000 men into battle. Far more important than the numbers was the terror he induced, however; Genghis proved an expert at spreading his ferocious reputation, and many people chose not to fight at all.

therefore, was much more interested in spreading his own glory and increasing his own power, and there were times when he seemed rather like a god—or a devil—himself!

Many religious persons attempted to convert Genghis, and the same held true for his descendants. Virtually all of these efforts failed, because to the Mongolians it was patently obvious that the Sky was supreme and all other powers were lesser ones. The Mongol leaders, however, were skillful at listening to various religious leaders and acting as if they might convert.

Could Genghis have stopped at this point?

No. He had unleashed such vital energy that the movement could no longer be contained. He was the supreme leader, but his battle-hardened warriors would not have stayed in one place even had he commanded this. Instead, he put them to use in the pursuit of the fallen Khawramzeen emperor, who died of disease on an island in the Caspian Sea. Genghis then pursued what remained of the Khawramzeen forces into northern India, where they escaped just in time. Tradition has it that Genghis—observing the bold leap of a ravine by the son of the emperor on horseback—called out "Happy the man who has such a son!"

Genghis and his Mongols pursued this man into northern India and carried out many sieges, but the lands south of the Himalayan mountains were of less interest to Genghis than the northern countries. He, therefore, returned to Mongolia and began a series of attacks on the Xi Xia, which still existed, though in a weakened state.

To this point, how many people had been killed, captured, or just plain murdered by the Mongols?

The number must have been at least half a million, but it does not include those who were displaced, and that number may well have exceeded half a million. In truth, given their own population size, the Mongols disrupted, disturbed, or outright destroyed the lives of more people—on a pound for pound basis—than any people before or since.

Genghis' initial probes into the Xi Xia and Chin empires revealed their relative weakness, but he knew these campaigns would be filled with sieges, which were not the Mongols' preferred type of warfare. Genghis was now old—for a Mongol—and it would have behooved him to turn over control of the battles and sieges to any one of his four sons by Borte, his principal wife. He chose to lead from the front, however, and in the late summer of 1227, he died shortly after he fell from his horse.

How successful was Genghis in his lifetime? How much remained to be accomplished?

Given that he became supreme leader of the Mongols in 1206 and that he died in 1227, Genghis has to rank—on anyone's list—among the most successful men of all human history. In those twenty-one years, he conquered more territory and felled more empires and kingdoms than any person before or since.

The Christian West heard its first stories of the Mongols in the 1230s, but these were fragmentary. The Mongols, on the other hand, once they learned of Europe, used their first-rate intelligence service to find out more about the West. By the time they entered Eastern Europe in 1238, the Mongols knew a great deal about medieval Christian society.

To the Mongols as a whole, however, it was evident that much still remained to be done. Southern China had not even been invaded, and the Muslim kingdoms and potentates in the Middle East were still untouched. The Mongols, at this point, knew little of Eastern or Western Europe, but their spies would eventually inform them that there was yet another area which could be conquered.

Who succeeded Genghis as leader of the Mongols?

Jochi, his eldest son, died in battle about the same time as Genghis, and the throne passed to Ogedai (ruled 1229–1241). He was never as well known—either to the conquered peoples or the Mongols themselves—as his father, but Ogedai seems to have been a clever and careful ruler. More than his father, he appreciated the need for consolidation, and he worked on this while maintaining a stately life in his tent city in Mongolia.

Meanwhile, Genghis' grandson, Batu Khan (ruled 1227–1255)—a son of Jochi—carved out a nearly separate and independent kingdom in southern Russia. Batu may have been angry at the death of his father and the loss of dignity to his part of the Mongol dynasty; then, too, he may simply have seized an opportunity as it appeared. Tensions built between him and his uncle Ogedai, however, and there might well have been an armed clash had events not moved in another direction.

When did the Mongols first invade Europe?

They came in the winter of 1238, attacking what is now the heartland of Russia. The kingdoms and principalities they attacked were a mixture of Christian in religion and Scandinavian in descent, with numerous Viking names among the rulers.

Moscow—which was still but a village—was sacked in 1239, and the much more important capital of Kiev in 1240. By now it was apparent that the Mongolian ponies were much more adept than their Russian counterparts and could cover longer distances. The Mongols, too, had refined their techniques; they were almost as good at siege warfare as they were at fighting in the open. They, therefore, decided to press on, and in the winter of 1241–1242 they attacked Eastern Europe. Polish and Hungarian knights met them but were crushed at the Battle of Leignitz, and the Mongols moved on into Hungary. They reached what is now Budapest and were ready to cross the Danube a second time— in a northward direction this time—when they learned of the death of Ogedai Khan.

How did Ogedai die, and how was his successor chosen?

Ogedai died of natural causes, although excessive drink may have contributed to his demise. He had no natural successor, and the Mongols held a great camp meeting, or election, at which it was decided that the throne would pass to his younger brother Kuyuk (ruled 1246–1248). It is important to remember that when we say "throne" we mean it in the European sense, but to the Mongols it was a much more mobile thing: to them, the great leader was more like "master of the horses and master of the camps."

Kuyuk's reign was short but eventful. He received the first embassy from the West, sent by none other than Pope Innocent IV. Kuyuk's reply is worth quoting here.

"You have said that supplication and prayer have been offered by you, that I might find a good entry into baptism. This prayer of thine I have not understood. Other words which thou hast sent me: 'I am surprised that thou hast seized all the lands of the Magyar and the Christians. Tell us what fault theirs is.' These words of thine I have also not understood. The eternal God has slain and annihilated these lands and peoples, because they have neither adhered to Chinghis Kgan, nor to the Khagan.... How could anybody seize or kill by his own power contrary to the command of God?"

Which nation—or people—was next on the Mongol list?

The Mongols had, by now, penetrated through the northern part of the Eurasian landmass and had found only the Southern Chinese empire—known as the Song—capable of withstanding them. They intended to take down the Song, but higher on the list were the Muslim states and kingdoms in the Middle East, with Baghdad at the very top of the list.

The Muslim Middle Eastern leaders understood their peril and sent numerous embassies to the tent city of Karakorum, which was the Mongol capital during the reigns of Kuyuk and then his younger brother, Mongke Khan (ruled 1251–1259). We know of these embassies because of another pair of Franciscan monks who went east, this time representing the Pope. Numerous religious debates were held, with the Franciscan friar speaking for Christianity against the Nestorian Christians and the Muslims. Mongke Khan listened to all but reached his own conclusion, saying that just as there were five

---

Could the Mongols have defeated all the major nations and conquered Western Europe?

One hesitates to be too bold, but this is one of the few times when something seems 99 percent likely. Yes. If they could take down the Russians, Poles, and Hungarians in such short order, the Mongols could surely have defeated the German, French, and English knights. Sections of Spain and Italy—shielded by mountain ranges—might have held out, but the broad heartland of Northern Europe would have been conquered.

fingers to the human hand, so had God created different ways for humans to reach, or commune with, him.

Did any people really call themselves the Assassins?

No. Their name for themselves was in Arabic, and it referred to their status as dissenters from the mainstream of Islam. Over time, however, they became known as the Assassins to millions of other people.

The Assassins were major users of the drug hashish, which is where their nickname derived. By 1250, they were a major force in the Middle East. Ruling from a series of mountain castles in Syria and Iraq, they sent out small bands of highly skilled men who did, indeed, carry out assassinations. The reason the Mongols wanted to subdue them was for the prestige of eliminating such a powerful force.

A 1307 manuscript by the author Rashid ad-Din shows a Middle Eastern city under siege by the Mongols.

Who carried out the Mongol campaign against the Assassins?

Hulegu was a brother of Mongke Khan. In 1253, he began a very slow march to the west, arriving in the Middle East two years later. Hulegu pointedly avoided Baghdad because he wanted to take down the Assassins first. Several sieges ensued, with both sides using all sorts of creative weaponry. The Assassins employed trebuchets and flaming arrows; the Mongols promptly seized the trebuchets and used them in return. All the castles were taken and the Grand Master of the Assassins killed.

Hulegu then turned his attention on Baghdad. The caliph of that city resented the Mongol belief—often expressed—that they were the instruments of God. Baghdad held out for weeks, and when the Mongols entered, they carried out a truly hideous sack. Not only was the caliph killed—the Mongols placed him in blankets and shook him to death—but many thousands of people, civilians and combatants alike. During the entire Mongol rule, no city suffered a worse fate than Baghdad.

Could anyone defeat the Mongols?

Not when they were at their best. As long as they had faith in their leader and plenty of hay for their ponies, the Mongols were generally unbeatable. The Middle East did not provide a lot of fodder for the ponies, however, and in 1260 the Mongols received their first check (to call it a defeat would be going too far).

Did these Franciscan friars travel as great a distance as Marco Polo?

Father John del Carpine and Friar William of Rubruck arrived almost a half century before Marco Polo, and if the Mongols controlled all of China at that time, their travels would have been just as extensive. At the time, however, it was sufficient to reach the tent city of Karakorum. There, Friar William of Rubruck found a Parisian goldsmith who had been captured during the Mongol attack on Hungary and who was now in the service of Mongke Khan.

While at Karakorum, the Franciscan friars observed enormous military preparations. They rightly suspected that these were directed at the Muslim-controlled Middle East but did not know that the first place selected for destruction was the Kingdom of the Assassins, in present-day Syria and Iraq.

Moving south from Aleppo, which they captured, the Mongols passed by Jerusalem on their way to the Sinai Desert. Just before entering the Sinai, they met an army of Mamelukes, sent from Cairo.

Was there much difference between a Mameluke and a Mongol?

Ethnically, there was not very much. The Mamelukes had been in the Middle East for well over a century, however, and they had adopted many of the Western approaches to fighting. They were composed of a mixture of cavalry and infantry, and they were regarded as "slaves" of their sultan, to whom they had tremendous loyalty. In this, they were rather similar to the Mongols.

The Battle of Ain Jalut was a small thing when compared to many others. Roughly 20,000 men on each side jostled for a few days, each side attempting to get the upper hand through maneuver. When there were direct, head-on confrontations, the Mamelukes gave as good as they got. This, in itself, was rather astonishing, and the Mongols withdrew. The situation in 1260 was similar to that of 1242: in both cases, the Mongol leaders were preoccupied with concerns about who would rule at home—in Mongolia—as well as who would triumph in battle.

THE MONGOLS IN CHINA

Who emerged triumphant in the struggle for the succession?

Mongke Khan died in 1258, at about the time Baghdad was sacked by his brother Hulegu. Mongke's death set off a succession crisis that lasted for nearly five years. The youngest son in the family, Kublai, had the best claim to the throne, but many Mongols suspected he was not tough—or battle-ready—enough to fill the shoes of Mongke, Kuyuk, and

65

Ogedai (no one ever compared any of these leaders to Genghis, who was rightly perceived as the founding father of them all).

Kublai proved better at warfare than anyone expected, however. He defeated his brother Ariq Boge several times, and by 1265 he was the undisputed leader of the Mongols. His uncle, Batu, had now died, and leadership of the Golden Horde—in southern Russia—was nominally in Kublai's name. Kublai, however, made a clear decision to concentrate on the eastern end of the Mongol Empire. The heartland already belonged to the Mongols; neither the Europeans nor the Muslims posed any threat; and Kublai, therefore, decided to bring down the Song Dynasty in southern China. This proved much tougher than anyone expected.

Kublai Khan, a grandson of Genghis, was the founder of the Yuan Dynasty and ruled over much of present-day China, Korea, and Mongolia.

What was different about the Song Dynasty?

Genghis had, of course, defeated the Xi Xia and the Chin empires, but neither of these was the real heartland of China. Ethnic differences between these two northern peoples and the Song Dynasty led to an abundance of confidence on the part of the latter. Perhaps the northern Chinese had succumbed to the Mongols: the Southerners never would.

The people of the Song Empire resisted as stoutly as their rulers. The cities of southern China were far larger than anything the Mongols had ever encountered, and all manner of techniques and tricks were employed by both sides. As a result, the slaughter of the innocents increased in scale as well, and Kublai's long, ten-year campaign to subdue the Song was filled with atrocities. Not until 1275 was the conquest complete.

Was Kublai the first member of his family to be Chinese?

He was, of course, ethnically as Mongolian as they come. But Kublai recognized, soon after the conquest of the Song, that the Chinese would never remain under the leadership of a monarch they perceived as foreign. He therefore became, in appearance, almost as Chinese as the Chinese themselves. This attempt at assimilation worked quite well for Kublai and his Chinese subjects; the Mongols, however, were displeased that their ruler—the grandson of Genghis—became a rather sedentary monarch, living in the cities of northern China during much of the calendar year.

Who provides us with our best "look" at Kublai?

This person is none other than Marco Polo (1252–1306), one of the best-known names from all of history. Though it has become fashionable to dismiss aspects of Marco Polo's writing—and there is no doubt that he exaggerated—it is foolish to throw away the good parts. He spent a number of years in China and met Kublai many times.

"The personal appearance of the Great Khan, Lord of Lords," Marco Polo wrote, "is such as I shall now tell you. He is of a good stature, neither tall nor short, but of a middle height. He has a becoming amount of flesh and is very shapely in all his limbs. His complexion is white and red, the eyes black and fine, the nose well formed and well set on." Kublai was in middle age when he first met Marco Polo: the Khan later became corpulent. But he was, when Marco Polo arrived in northern China, the greatest king or lord that the world had ever known. Genghis and his generals had done much of the work, but Kublai enjoyed the peak of Mongol success.

How do we account for "missing" parts of Marco Polo's work. He does not, for example, even mention the Great Wall of China?

This omission is indeed curious, but chances are good that Marco Polo never saw it. The Wall was already in disrepair when the Mongols invaded in 1211, and they had probably let it decay even further in the half century since. The modern Great Wall was mostly the work of the Ching dynasty in the seventeenth century.

How long did Marco Polo and his father and uncle remain in China?

Tradition has it that they departed in 1292 and were back in Venice by 1295. Their relatives did not recognize them at first, and the stories they told were so wild and fantastic that many people chose not to believe them. Marco Polo had a rare opportunity, however. Fighting for his native city of Venice, he was taken prisoner in a naval battle and thrown into a Genoese prison. There, he met a cellmate, Rustichello, who was an accomplished writer.

That Marco Polo and Rustichello exaggerated in their book is undisputed. If one chops a "zero" or two off each significant number, the truth begins to emerge, however. Of course, the Great Khan did not have 12,000 falconers, as Marco Polo declares, but he may well have had 1,200.

Meanwhile, what had Kublai accomplished?

Kublai was not the ruthless warrior his grandfather had been, but by 1280 he ruled over the largest and greatest empire the

The Italian explorer Marco Polo wrote of his meetings with Kublai Khan and his travels in China, providing historians with a helpful—though sometimes exaggerated—view of Asia in the thirteenth century.

67

world had ever seen; at its height, the Mongol Empire was more than twice as large as imperial Rome. Equally impressive, Kublai was able to enforce Mongol law throughout the vast empire; it was said—perhaps in exaggeration—that an unmarried woman could travel over the Mongol roads in safety.

Kublai had achieved all this by consolidating the conquests of Genghis and Mongke. His only failure came in Japan.

Why was Japan able to keep the Mongols at bay?

The Mongols were still primarily horse-warriors; the very thought of traveling at sea filled them with some anxiety. When Japan would not acknowledge Mongol supremacy, Kublai ordered the Koreans, who were among his subject peoples, to build ships for an invasion of Japan.

In 1274, a Korean fleet brought perhaps 10,000 Mongols to Japan's east coast. A storm blew up at sea, and the Mongols were quickly re-embarked. The Japanese marked the very spot where the Mongols had come ashore, and they built a massive sea wall so as to prepare for the next coming of their foes. When a much larger Korean fleet, carrying perhaps 20,000 troops, arrived in 1281, the Mongols encountered stiff Japanese resistance behind that sea wall. Given the Mongols' ability at maneuver, this seems like a relatively easy obstacle for them to manage.

On land, that would certainly be the case. But the Mongols showed much less imagination when traveling at sea. While the Japanese dug in their heels to resist, the Mongols noticed yet another major storm on its way. They re-embarked and sailed away, never to return.

Was it a genuine typhoon that kept the Mongols away from Japan?

Historians believe so, and many of the Korean-built ships may have sunk on the way home. This was, in some ways, an equivalent to the Spanish Armada of 1588 (see chapter six), but Mongol histories—not surprisingly—made little of it. The Japanese, on the other hand, built it into their mythology, claiming that the weather had worked on their behalf and that a typhoon would rescue them if anyone else attempted to invade. For this reason, the word kamikaze (meaning "divine wind") became part of the Japanese belief system, as the Americans discovered when they invaded the Philippines in 1944.

TAMERLANE AND BAYEZID

Who was Tamerlane, and how did he get that name?

He was born in Central Asia, not far from the city of Samarkand, around the year 1336. Due to a wound he received early in life, Timur walked with a limp, and a corruption of his Turkic name became known in the West as Tamerlane: "Timur the Lame." His career was anything but lame, however.

Timur grew up at a time when the great Mongol kingdoms and subkingdoms of Central Asia were in disarray. About the only exception to the rule was the Golden Horde, based out of the city of Sarai on the Volga River. The descendants of Jochi and Batu still ruled the Golden Horde, and it controlled much of what we now label as European Russia, or Russia east of the Ural Mountains. Timur left no diary—he could neither read nor write—but we suspect that from his earliest days he aspired to become the new Great Khan, the one who would restore the Mongols and Turks to their former glory.

A sixteenth-century illustration shows Tamerlane besieging the city of Urganj (now in Turkmenistan).

Was there—and is there—much difference between a Mongol and a Turk?

In the time of Genghis, and even in that of Tamerlane, there was little racial or ethnic difference: the two peoples were cousins. They have spent enough time out of each other's company, however, that today we would assert there is a considerable difference.

What was the richest city of Central Asia?

It was Samarkand, located southeast of the Aral Sea and directly west of the Tien Shan Desert, the traditional route to China. To say that Samarkand was a merchant city is not going far enough; Samarkand was the great merchant city along what we call the Silk Road, extending from western China to the Mediterranean Sea. Tamerlane understood the importance of trade, and during his rule he made Samarkand much more beautiful, but he was—from his teenage years—devoted to war.

Tamerlane started life as the eldest son of a chief of the far-flung Barlas tribe. This did not mean he was destined for leadership, however; like Genghis Khan— whom he clearly admired and sought to emulate—Tamerlane had to ascend, rung by rung. He started life as a small-time brigand, stealing sheep (the same can be said for many men who later became great leaders), and worked his way up to lead a small army of nomadic people in the Samarkand region. Very likely, he persuaded them to follow him by saying he would lead them as Genghis had previously done, but Tamerlane had to appeal to a more mixed audience: he led Mongols, Turks, Iranians, and all sorts of half-breeds.

Was Tamerlane's style of warfare different from that of his competitors in Central Asia?

Not at the outset. Tamerlane seemed on his way to becoming one of the major leaders of Central Asia, but not the predominant one. It was only when he began fighting against the Mongols to the north—the so-called Golden Horde—that he demonstrated the savagery that made him feared throughout the world. We do not really know how many mounds of skulls were created during his many conquests, but at least one neutral witness—who traveled to the region fifty years later—testified that he saw at least thirty piles of skulls outside one central Asian city.

How can one person inflict so much destruction, yet remain safe and secure himself?

Tamerlane scorned safety: throughout life, he prized the hunt and warfare more than rest and ease. Even during the few times that he was at rest, he engaged in heated discussions, especially on theological matters, and the modern-day reader is struck by Tamerlane's intelligence. He was a child of the Eurasian steppe, an unlettered nomad, but he understood great matters of war and peace, life and death, very well. This was testified to by an ambassador who came all the way from Spain to Samarkand shortly before Tamerlane's death.

But as to physical danger, Tamerlane commanded such respect, veneration even, from his men that it was unlikely anyone could get close enough to thrust a sword or dagger in his direction. He was a pious Muslim, who added the words "Timur, servant of God" to every letter that was sent by his secretaries. The combination of ferocious military skill and devout religious practice made him feared by all.

What happened to the Golden Horde?

For more than a century and a half, the Mongol leaders of the Golden Horde had lived magnificent lives, split between the rigors of the trail and their wonderful city of Sarai on the lower Volga River. It was their misfortune that Toktamish—who had known Tamerlane from his earliest days—became their leader around the year 1380. Whether Toktamish betrayed Tamerlane or the other way around will forever remain in doubt; all that is known is that the two men hated and feared each other.

Tamerlane was in the western part of his domain when Toktamish invaded and briefly occupied the city of Samarkand. Toktamish departed as Tamerlane returned, and perhaps he believed that would be all. Tamerlane pursued him, however, over a distance of 800 miles, and he finally sacked the city of Sarai. For more than a century, Sarai and Samarkand had been rivals in the merchant trade: Tamerlane put an end to that.

Could Tamerlane have taken and sacked Moscow?

He was within 250 miles, and to him that was a relatively short distance. The people of Moscow implored God to save them from the terrible Turks. But Tamerlane had no special interest in Moscow. Its 50,000 people would not have been any benefit to his Central Asian-based empire, and he, therefore, headed for home.

Is Tamerlane, then, one of the few leaders ever to invade Russia and succeed?

Yes. King Charles XII of Sweden failed in 1709, Napoleon failed in 1812, and Hitler failed in the truest sense of that word during World War II. About the only successful invasions of Russia have come from the south and the east, and most have been led either by Mongols or Turks.

The Golden Horde never recovered. Though some descendants of Jochi and Batu continued to call themselves "Khan" for some generations, there was no more reality to the claim. This was not the only kingdom or principality that Tamerlane would destroy, however.

How did Tamerlane find himself in India?

Tamerlane grew up within sight of some of the northernmost mountains of Afghanistan, and he had great curiosity about what lay beyond. In 1398, he brought an immense army, of perhaps 150,000, over the mountains and into northwest India. He encountered little opposition, and, from a religious point of view, he had little reason to fight because so many of those he encountered were fellow Muslims. But when he reached the city of Delhi, capital of the sultanate of the same name, a series of misunderstandings led to a terrible sack.

Whether the people of Delhi disrespected a banner of truce or some of Tamerlane's men stole some sheep and then blamed it on their foes is not certain; what we can say is that Delhi was captured and put to the worst sack of Tamerlane's reign. Mounds of skulls were placed near the city walls, and the death toll may have been as much as 100,000. Tamerlane never commented publicly on the matter, but there are indications that he regretted it.

Was there any force on earth that could stop, or defeat, Tamerlane?

At his peak, no. When Tamerlane set out on campaign, which was most of the time, he marched with a virtual city of soldiers, cavalrymen, and camp followers. These people lived off the land and did so in a rather grand style. They, therefore, destroyed their enemies' sustenance even before meeting them in battle, and once battle was joined, Tamerlane's incredible skill and ruthlessness always prevailed.

The best example of this came in 1402, when the Ottoman Turkish sultan Bayezid, known as "Bayezid the Thunderbolt," challenged Tamerlane. The Ottoman Turks were cousins to Tamerlane's people, but that did not matter; leadership of the Turkic-Mongol world was at stake. Tamerlane marched west and inflicted a terrible defeat on Bayezid at the Battle of Ankara, where the capital of modern-day Turkey is located. Tamerlane's

The Bibi-Khanym Mosque in Samarkand, Uzbekistan, is one of the few tangible legacies built by the conqueror Tamerlane. Completed a year before his death in 1405, it is named after his wife.

army captured Bayezid; Tamerlane kept him a prisoner until Bayezid died, a year later. Whether Tamerlane actually caged Bayezid or made him perform degrading tasks is unknown, but the rivalry between the two men has been fodder for poets and dramatists for centuries.

What did Western Christians think of Tamerlane?

To them, he was the bogeyman, the enemy that might appear at any time but would do so under the cover of night. Europeans knew more about Tamerlane than they ever did about Genghis Khan, and he was, in some ways, more frightful to them. Numerous European monarchs sent letters to Tamerlane, assuring him of their friendship. They were careful to observe his protocol, which meant that the letters were addressed to the "Lord of Asia."

How old was Tamerlane when he defeated Bayezid?

He was about sixty-five and in poor health. Two years later, when he set out for his intended conquest of China, Tamerlane was so lame that he had to be carried in a litter. No one doubted he would accomplish his goal, however, until he died of natural causes in February 1405.

Tamerlane is still, even in our time, the destroyer *par excellence*. Not even Genghis Khan killed so many people or ruined so many cities. A major difference between the two is that Genghis left a viable legacy to be enjoyed by his sons, grandsons, and great-grandsons, while Tamerlane left almost nothing. His army broke up soon after his death, and what he called his empire was revealed to be held together by his personality and nothing else. One of the few exceptions to the general rule is the magnificent mosque in Samarkand, built soon after his return from India. Tamerlane is buried there.

When was his body exhumed?

A legend long existed that if the grave of Tamerlane was ever disturbed, an even greater menace than him would come to destroy the world. That was enough to keep away most grave robbers, and it was not until the first half of 1941, when a serious, modern-day scientific team arrived in Samarkand, that Tamerlane's body was exhumed. Led by a Russian scholar, the team recovered the body and was able—based on forensics—to recreate Tamerlane's face. Many of the particulars conform closely to the chronicles. Tamerlane was tall, lean, and exceptionally fit. His face was a mixture of intelligence and ferocity, much as we might imagine. The single biggest coincidence, however, was that the German invasion of the Soviet Union—a terrible conflict that claimed more than twenty million lives—began on the very day—June 22, 1941—that Tamerlane's body was exhumed.

HOLY WARS: 1095 TO 1453

THE NORMANS

Why do we sometimes call the Normans the "supermen" of the eleventh and twelfth centuries?

It is because they seemed to be here, there, and everywhere. The Normans originated from a rather small population base in the peninsula of northern France, which later became famous due to the D-Day Invasion. Norman, in its original meaning, meant "North-man's-land." Some, though not all, of the early Normans had Viking blood in their veins, and they certainly acted the part, marauding far and wide. The great and important difference is that they did so with the blessing of the Roman Catholic Church.

In the middle of the eleventh century, the Normans began invading the Island of Sicily. They soon saw its great strategic potential, and within thirty years they had taken the island and established a Norman kingdom in the south. Their actions were just as important as those of William the Conqueror, though they are less known.

Who was William the Conqueror?

It helps to start with his original name, which was William the Bastard. This is because although his father was Duke Robert of Normandy, his mother was the daughter of a tanner in the market town of Rouen. As an illegitimate son, he was referred to as William the Bastard. Over time, as he defeated his legitimate brothers and became the leader of Normandy, he was known as William, Duke of Normandy. Only later did he become King William of England, and, of course, William the Conqueror (ruled 1066–1087).

Although William's case is an extreme example, it is helpful to remember that most people of the eleventh and twelfth centuries only used first names. Other examples include "Joan of Paris," "Robert of Avignon," or "James of Berlin." Only later, when there was a large population, did it become necessary to have a surname.

Why was William so keen to become king of England?

It made perfect sense because that kingdom (it is too early to call it a nation) lay just across the English Channel and because Normandy was better organized. Duke William had a more sovereign command over Normandy than the Anglo-Saxon monarchy possessed in England. It was one thing to desire the kingdom of England, another matter to have an actual reason, however.

In January 1066, King Edward the Confessor died. He had no living children and the Anglo-Saxon nobles gathered to elect Harold of Wessex, one of the leading men of the kingdom, as their new monarch. This satisfied many, though not all, people. Certainly it did not satisfy William of Normandy, who declared that Harold owed him the crown.

Why on earth would an English nobleman who had just become king owe his crown to a Norman?

It was the type of circumstance that could only happen in the Middle Ages. William, Duke of Normandy, had a blood relationship (albeit not a very close one) to the English monarchy, while Harold of Wessex did not. But beyond that, William of Normandy claimed that Harold of Wessex owed him the crown because he had saved his life a decade earlier. William's claim—that he rescued Harold after a shipwreck—is best demonstrated in the Bayeux Tapestry, an embroidered cloth sewn many years after the events of 1066. As strange as all this sounds to us today, it made sense to William's followers, and he soon had them at work building ships to prepare for an invasion of southern England.

Was there any way that the situation could become even more complicated?

There was! At about the same time that William of Normandy declared that England was his—by blood and by reason of his having saved Harald III from drowning—Harald

Does the Bayeux Tapestry still exist?

Yes. It is housed in a special museum in the town of Bayeux, where it wraps around the inner walls. The Tapestry (a small section is shown at left) is a marvelous, and curious, piece of history, and it is almost miraculous that it has survived for nearly a thousand years. It depicts the comet of 1066, the quarrel between William of Normandy and Harold of Wessex, and the Battle of Hastings.

of Norway (c.1015–1066) declared that England belonged to him. The way to keep these two men straight is to remember that Harold of England is spelled with an "o" and Harald of Norway is spelled with an "a."

Harald of Norway's claim was much less impressive than Duke William's, and few people took him seriously. Harold of England kept a close eye on the southern coast of his nation throughout the summer, and he was just about to send his militia home when he learned, to his dismay, that Harald of Norway had landed in northern England. Harald had brought perhaps 15,000 men, the largest Norwegian force ever sent overseas.

What did Harold of England—Harold with an "o"—do at this point?

He did something truly remarkable. Abandoning all his fortifications and preparations in the south, he marched his men over land, covering perhaps 400 miles in less than ten days. It was one of the great forced marches of the Middle Ages, and Harold and his men arrived at a time when the Norwegians were feasting.

Harald and his men got into battle array very quickly, and the two armies squared off. Tradition has it that there was one last parley before the Battle of Stamford Bridge began and that Harald's messenger asked what his leader would be given. "Six feet of English soil" was the answer, and the battle was soon joined. Given the odds, and the temperament, of the two peoples, one would almost surely choose the Norwegians, but the Anglo-Saxons carved them to bits. Harald died on the field, and those of his men who survived got to their ships and never returned. This was the last time a Viking, or Scandinavian, force ever threatened England.

What had happened with Duke William and the Normans?

They embarked on September 12, 1066, and had a stormy passage through the English Channel, but most of the men—and their horses—landed the following day at Pevensey, on England's southeast coast. The Normans were about 7,000 in number and had perhaps 1,000 horses, giving them far more equestrian power than the Anglo-Saxons. Duke William did not progress very far. He was satisfied with getting his men ashore and establishing a secure beachhead. He did not know what had happened in the north.

For his part, Harold of England got the bad news soon enough. Learning that William and the Normans had landed, Harold brought his men—by a much more restful trail—back to London. Upon arriving, Harold found that William and the Normans had remained pretty much where they had landed. To this point, Harold had performed extremely well, routing a force much larger than his own and persuading his men to undertake truly heroic endeavors. This was the moment when things went wrong, however.

Why did Harold not stay where he was, forcing William of Normandy to come closer?

This is the question that perplexes nearly all students of the campaign. Harold of England did almost everything "right" until about October 10, 1066, and from that day he did almost everything "wrong." Common sense dictated that the time had come to rest on the defensive, but Harold decided that a quick, surgical strike had worked against the Norwegians and that he do the same against the Normans. On the morning of October 11, he departed London with about 7,000 men.

The relatively small size of both forces can be attributed to the difficulties involved with supply. Neither Harold nor William could keep a large force in the field for any length of time because they could not feed them. Therefore, one of the most decisive battles of the Middle Ages was fought between two forces that were—each—slightly larger than a Roman legion.

Does the Bayeux Tapestry depict the men of both armies on the march?

Because it was sewn by Normans two decades after the event, the Tapestry naturally gives more attention to the Normans, and we see them in all their battle array. The men wore short armor that covered the chest but not the legs, and the horses were magnificent creatures, clearly bred over several generations.

How did the Battle of Hastings progress?

The Anglo-Saxons held the high ground, on a sloping hill, and the Normans possessed the initiative, thanks to their greater number of horses. The Normans attacked all day and several times came within a hair's breadth of breaking the line, but on each occasion the housecarls—or bodyguards—of King Harold made all the difference, driving the enemy back. The Anglo-Saxons made their own mistakes, however. When they came down the hill at around 2 P.M. to chase a retreating body of Normans, the Norman cavalry turned on them with a vengeance, wiping the Anglo-Saxons out almost entirely.

Late in the day, the battle still hung in the balance. If King Harold could fight the Normans to a draw, he would be able to gain reinforcements. Knowing this, the Normans made their supreme effort at around 4:30 P.M. Breaking sections of the line, the Normans were on the verge of victory, but it was not complete until Harold fell, with an arrow in his eye. Minutes later, the foremost Norman horsemen killed all three of Harold's brothers. Seeing this, the Anglo-Saxons broke, and the Normans pursued them on horseback.

A thirteenth-century French chronicle illustration of William the Conqueror stabbing King Harold of England during the Battle of Hastings. History tells us, however, that Harold was killed by an Norman archer.

How decisive was the Battle of Hastings?

Hastings is generally rated as one of the most decisive battles of the past 1,000 years. First and foremost, it meant that William of Normandy became king of England. Second, he and his Norman knights established a new regime, one distinguished by its tough tax laws and rigid enforcement. Third, England and France became loosely joined for the next two centuries, with the English nobles speaking French and Latin rather than English.

THE FIRST CRUSADE

How important was Pope Urban II's speech?

Without this speech, there would have been no First Crusade. In 1095, Pope Urban II (c.1042–1099) traveled to Clermont, in south-central France, to speak to a gathering of almost 10,000 men, most of them French and German knights. The Pope spoke outdoors, and, very likely, there were "relay" men who shouted his words to those in the far back. His message was that a "new accursed group" of infidels had taken over the Holy Land, preventing pilgrims from visiting to holy sites in Jerusalem. Using every rhetorical trick available, the Pope called on the knights to go east and recapture the Holy Land. Pope Urban had never been to the Holy Land, but he called it a land of "milk and honey," suggesting that there would be economic as well as spiritual rewards. When he had finished, there was a moment or two of silence; then a slow-building chorus began as the knights chanted "Deus Volt! Deus Volt!" ("God wills it!")

Did the knights realize the enormous task it would be to accomplish what the Pope asked?

They did. They, therefore, spent nearly the entire next year in preparation. Food was gathered, wagons were built, and the knights drafted horses. All this took time, and while the knights were engaged in these preparations, some of the lower-class Europeans decided to take matters into their own hands. Incredible as it seems, one preacher seems to have accomplished most of the work. His name was Peter the Hermit.

No one knew whether he was French or German or where he had spent his time as a hermit. He was not, to anyone's knowledge, an ordained leader in the Roman Catholic Church; rather, he was a self-proclaimed holy man (there were quite a few of these at the time). Within just three months of preaching to crowds, Peter had gathered an army—or really a large group of armed men—and set off for the Holy Land. This is called the Peasants' Crusade.

Did the average person really have time in his life for ventures such as this?

Generally speaking, he did not. Crops had to be planted, guarded, and then harvested. Shelters had to be built. Something about the Crusade movement, however, had the power to jolt people out of their mundane lives and persuade them to do something extraordinary. So it was with the roughly 30,000 men who joined the Peasants' Crusade in 1095–1096.

Peter was acknowledged as the spiritual leader of the crusade; military matters were handled by a council of leaders. This democratic spirit enthused the men of the Peasants' Crusade, but we cannot let some of their less admirable qualities pass by without comment. On their way to the Holy Land, the peasant crusaders attacked and even destroyed numerous houses and villages belonging to Jews. The rationale was that the Jews had killed Christ and that the crusaders, who were on their way to liberate the Holy Land, should take vengeance on the Jews. Of course, it did not hurt the cause that the Jews often had extra supplies of food, which were promptly confiscated.

What happened to the Peasant Crusaders?

The Peasant Crusaders had neither the organization nor the military skill for what awaited them. The Seljuk Turks ambushed them in the mountains of Turkey, killing perhaps a third. The others fled, some by way of Constantinople and others by way of the Gallipoli Peninsula. Peter the Hermit, rather miraculously, survived and became one of the midlevel tier of leaders of the Knights' Crusade.

How long did it take the Knights' Crusade to get moving?

Not until the summer of 1196 were the Knights ready, and it was somewhere along the way to Constantinople that they learned of the disaster which had befallen the Peasant Crusaders. Arriving at Constantinople, the Knights were impressed by the architecture and beauty of the place, and the Emperor Alexius was deeply frightened of what the Knights might do to his beloved city. Just how he managed it remains a mystery, but Alexius persuaded all the major leaders of the Knights' Crusade to bend the knee and swear that all their land conquests in the Holy Land would be held in fief to him.

The Knights were ferried across the Bosporus and commenced the long, hard march through the mountains of Turkey. Plenty of ambushes and traps were set by the Turks, but the Knights either evaded these or triumphed over them, and in the early summer of 1097, the Knights' Crusaders arrived in the city of Antioch, close to the border between modern-day Turkey and

A statue of St. Peter the Hermit stands near the cathedral of Amiens, France.

> ## Did they use modern-day nomenclature, calling each other Europeans and Turks?
>
> **N**o. Because the Turks encountered French knights most often, they generally labeled all Christian crusaders "Franks." Equally, because there were so many ethnic and racial groups in the Middle East fighting under the banner of Islam, the Christian Crusaders called all of them "Saracens," meaning descendants of the biblical Sara.

Syria. This was a natural stopping place, and the Knights were pleased, even delighted, to find it mostly empty. They were in Antioch for only a few days before a large army of Turks, comprised primarily of cavalry, arrived to block them in. Antioch was a strongly fortified city, but it looked as if it had the capacity to be the death of the Knights' Crusade.

Is there any truth to the story of the "Holy Lance"?

The veneration, indeed worship, of relics was particularly strong during the Middle Ages, and many people on both sides of the conflict regarded them as inordinately valuable. While the Turks besieged the Knights in Antioch, a rumor spread that the "Holy Lance"—which had pierced Christ's side while he was on the Cross—was somewhere in Antioch. A major search was launched, and eventually a wooden lance was brought forth. To say that this encouraged the Knights is to diminish the truth: they were ecstatic. A few days later, when they issued forth from Antioch, they beat the Turks in open battle, and as long as someone held the "Holy Lance," the Christian crusaders would not be defeated.

Peter the Hermit played a major role in this episode, and he later claimed that he had found the "True Cross," composed of fragments of wood from the cross on which Christ died at Calvary. Whether one gives any credence to these claims is not very important because the Crusaders did.

How long did it take the Crusaders to get from Antioch to the outskirts of Jerusalem?

It took nearly another whole year, and it was in June 1099 that the Crusaders arrived outside the Holy City. They were weary from their journey, but they also saw the need for haste because the Turks had poisoned many of the wells within a ten-mile radius. Once more, the holy men were asked for advice, and the leaders learned that it was necessary for the army to be purified in order to enter the Holy City. Three days were spent in fasting and prayer before the attack commenced on July 15, 1099.

The fighting was intense, with the heat making things worse. By the time the Knight Crusaders got inside the city—having burrowed under one of the gates—they were in a furious mood, and a wholesale massacre ensued. No one can say how many men, women, and perhaps children died that day, but some estimates run as high as 20,000.

The heat of the battle led to the Crusaders making no social or ethnic distinctions: Christians, Jews, and of course Arabs and Turks perished that day.

Did this massacre throw a cloud over the whole crusading movement?

It should have, but it did not. The reports sent back to Europe sanitized the worst of what had happened, and most Christians learned only that the four-year-long crusade had ended in a glorious victory. Pope Urban lived just long enough to learn of Jerusalem's capture: he died soon afterward.

If the city and its holy sites had been the only consideration, Jerusalem might have remained Christian for only a short time and then been transferred to Arab or Turkish rule. Commerce, however, became nearly as important as religion and many victorious Christian knights settled in Jerusalem, becoming merchants in spice, carpets, oil, and the like. As a result, the First Crusade—while tainted with the blood of many innocents—was viewed as a shining success in the eyes of the Christian West.

JIHAD

Does jihad, indeed, mean "Holy War"?

The meaning is close, but there are enough differences that we should not gloss over them. In its original use in the Koran, *jihad* is closer, in strict translation, to "struggle or conflict," and it may reference an inner conflict as well as an external one. Therefore, although many Muslims use the word "jihad" in the context of "Holy War," it is important for us to realize that this is not entirely accurate.

In 1185, Saladin (1138–1193), the emir of Cairo and the lord of Damascus, proclaimed a jihad against the Christians in the Kingdom of Jerusalem. Saladin was worldly enough to recognize the differences that existed between the Christians of Antioch and those of Jerusalem, but his army—which was composed of Arabs, Turks, and Kurds—probably did not: the men quite likely thought that all Christians came from the devil and should be put to death. Much the same, however, can be said of the Christian Crusaders, some of whom were quite sophisticated while others were not.

Who was defending Jerusalem?

The Knights Templar and the Knights Hospitaller—who later became the Knights of Saint John—were more than sufficient to defend Jerusalem. Nearly a century of Middle Eastern warfare had revealed that the average mounted Christian knight could defeat his Arab or Turkish counterpart nine times out of ten (this was thanks to the size of his horse and the thickness of his armor). But in order for the knights to retain this advantage, they needed to remain on the defensive and allow Saladin to waste his resources attacking the city. Instead, they chose to go out and meet him.

Even so, the Christians could have won, had they attempted to maneuver. Instead, they went straight at Saladin's host, which was arranged with the Sea of Galilee at its back. Saladin allowed the crusaders to come close, but he contained them at two old hillsides known as the Horns of Hattin. The hills appeared to offer the Christians a good position, but Saladin knew the land better, and he had arranged it so the Christians had no wells nearby. Over the next ten hours, the Arabs and Turks pelted the Christians with arrows, many of them flame-tipped. What little shrubbery existed was soon set aflame, and quite a few Christians choked to death in the smoke-filled area.

THE THIRD CRUSADE

First of all, why do we hear so little about the Second Crusade?

Because so little was accomplished. In 1147, the Second Crusade was launched with the goal of retaking the Kingdom of Edessa from the Arabs and Turks. Many important European leaders, including King Louis VII of France and Queen Eleanor—better known as Eleanor of Aquitaine—went on the Second Crusade. They did not retake Edessa, however, and the entire crusade is better known for its parties and festivals than for any substantive accomplishments.

Who was the first European leader to take up the Crusader cross?

Immediately upon learning of the Battle of Hattin, Richard the Lion-Heart, Prince of England and Duke of Normandy, announced his intention to go to the Holy Land. Richard was the fiercest and most feared of Europe's young leaders, but he was soon followed by two of the elder generation. His father, King Henry II of England, declared his intention to go on Crusade, as did Frederick II, Holy Roman Emperor, best known as Frederick Barbarossa (meaning "Frederick of the Red Beard"). King Philip Augustus of France, who was a bit younger than Richard, also announced that he would serve on the Crusade.

Troubles and disagreements between the major monarchs would haunt the Crusade, however. Richard and Philip had once been close friends; they now disliked each other. Frederick Barbarossa and King Henry II were battle-tested warriors, but it was unlikely that two so contentious personalities could work well together.

Who made the first move?

King Henry II (ruled 1154–1189) was in the midst of preparing to go to the Holy Land when he, rather suddenly, faced a rebellion by Richard and two of his brothers. Instead of traveling 2,000 miles to fight the Muslims, the Christians were at war with each other, even within family lines. Richard defeated his father in battle on July 4, 1189, and Henry II died just two days later. Tradition has it that his last words were: "shame, shame, on a conquered king."

Why was Aquitaine so important?

Located on the southwest side of France, Aquitaine was the major wine-producing section of the country (Cognac, Burgundy, and Chardonet had not yet come into their own). Beyond that, Aquitaine was the most civilized, or courtly, section of the kingdom. Life in Aquitaine, for the upper class at least, was a good deal more pleasant and refined than elsewhere.

Richard became king of England immediately following his father's death, but the actual coronation ceremony had to wait until September; by that time, Richard and his mother—the redoubtable Eleanor of Aquitaine—had taken possession of the kingdom as well as Henry II's continental possessions. It would have made sense for Richard to remain in England and consolidate his position, but he was eager to be off on crusade, and within two months he was back in Aquitaine.

How old and powerful was Frederick Barbarossa (ruled 1155–1190)?

At sixty-nine, he was far older than the other monarchs, and he clearly looked down on the "boys," as he considered Richard the Lion-Heart and Philip Augustus. Barbarossa was old enough to be their father, and he had been a young German noble on the Second Crusade, many years earlier. Barbarossa also fielded the largest force. Though records are scanty, he may have had 80,000 men in all—ranging from leading knights to launderers—and the German host was the scariest, so far as the Muslim foes were concerned.

Barbarossa sent threatening letters to Saladin, who returned them in kind, and the Muslims braced for the German onslaught. Barbarossa intentionally avoided Constantinople. His men crossed the Hellespont at Gallipoli and pushed into Turkey. They there encountered many of the difficulties which had beset earlier invasion forces: hunger, thirst, and the seemingly endless number of mountains to cross. By the summer of 1190, Barbarossa's Germans had come out of Turkey, however, and were close to the city of Antioch. They had taken some losses from disease and desertion, but the army was still imposing. Disaster struck before they could reach the Holy Land, however.

How did Frederick Barbarossa die?

Even though there were several eyewitnesses, Barbarossa's death remains one of the most interesting and disputed of questions. Did the bridge he used collapse, throwing him into the water below? Or did he and a handful of his knights jump in for a swim after a morning ride? In either case, there is no doubt, however, that Barbarossa drowned.

Kings, queens, and emperors often came to surprising ends, but drowning was not common. Barbarossa's sudden death—probably caused by a sudden drop in blood pressure—panicked the Germans. Thousands of them took off right away, and many others deserted in the following days and weeks. By the time the Germans reached Antioch, they were reduced to about one-quarter of their original number. Led by Duke Henry of Swabia, these pushed on, vowing to bury Barbarossa's bones in Jerusalem.

Meanwhile, where were Richard and Philip?

Richard and Philip rendezvoused in central France in the summer of 1190 and proceeded to the Mediterranean coast. Tensions between the French on one side and the English and Normans on the other surfaced almost at once, and the leaders did not do a great job of keeping the men together. It was small surprise, therefore, that the armies parted ways as they approached the Mediterranean. Philip and his Frenchmen embarked at Genoa, while Richard and his men worked their way slowly down the Italian coast. The two armies met again, at Messina, on the northeast corner of Sicily, and decided to winter there.

Some truly comic-opera events followed. Richard's mother, Eleanor of Aquitaine, arrived, bringing a Spanish princess whom Richard had promised to marry. Richard and Philip spent most of the winter quarreling, and their men did the same. Not until spring did the Franco-Norman-English forces depart, and even then they traveled in separate fleets. Richard took some time out from the crusade to attack—and conquer—the Island of Cyprus: it was there that he married Berengaria of Navarre. Not until June of 1191 did the entire army reach the Holy Land.

What was unique about the Siege of Acre?

Located on the coast of modern-day Israel, Acre was one of the last Christian cities to hold out against the Muslims. Saladin had placed it under siege, only to find that the arrival of Richard and Philip placed him in a state of near siege. Not only were the numbers of men the largest that had ever been seen in a siege, but the tools and weapons had grown in size and power. Richard and Philip had both brought mangonels with them: stone-throwers that could, over time, crush the battlements of most cities.

Saladin saw that the situation was hopeless, and he allowed the Muslim garrison to surrender. One of the provisions of the capitulation was that Saladin would provide food for the men who surrendered; when this was not done, Richard had 2,000 men summarily executed on the beaches near Acre. As this blood-curdling episode unfolded, Richard's reputation—for power and cruelty—spread. When the Christian force moved down the coast, in the direc-

Artist Gustave Doré's illustration of Saladin fighting King Richard at the Battle of Arsuf during the Third Crusade.

How did it so quickly become Richard's crusade?

It was Richard and Philip's crusade until the siege of Acre ended. Just days later, King Philip asked permission to return to France, pleasing illness. Richard required Philip to swear, in the presence of his knights, that he would neither harm nor distress Richard's castles in Normandy and Aquitaine. The two kings then parted, leaving Richard the clear leader of the crusade.

tion of modern-day Tel Aviv, the Muslims paralleled their movements, but did not attempt to stop Richard from advancing.

How did the crusaders gain the upper hand on the Muslims?

In terms of sheer courage or willpower, there was little difference between the two armies, with plenty of heroism displayed on both sides. But the Europeans—or the Franks, as they were called—had an undeniable advantage in horses and horsemanship. The European horses were bred to be larger and heavier than the Arab steeds, and the European armor was considerably thicker and heavier. This, to be sure, was not always an advantage. In the heat of a Middle Eastern summer, the crusaders sometimes wished to have the light armor of their Arab and Turkish foes.

Richard, too, was a figure too large to be overlooked. Perhaps we exaggerate his importance on the battlefield, but he was a commanding presence and his mere appearance would lift the spirits of his men and depress those of his foes. This was evident at the Battle of Arstul, fought in September 1191.

Was there any attempt to resolve the situation through negotiation?

There were, in fact, a number of parleys, with Richard and Saladin each acting like the gallant knight: they sent each other fruit, delicacies, and even horses. But the most promising negotiation by far fell through when Richard declared he needed to seek the Pope's permission before allowing his sister to marry a Muslim. One of Saladin's emissaries proposed, perhaps in jest, that Richard's sister Joan should marry Saladin's brother Yusuf and that they should reign as king and queen of a multiethnic, multireligious Jerusalem. As unlikely as this seems, it was an appealing proposition.

Richard and Saladin conducted numerous parleys, all the while seeking to learn of the other's troop dispositions. When the battles and skirmishes resumed, it became clear that the Europeans had the advantage, and they pressed the Arabs and Turks nearly all the way to Jerusalem. In July 1192, Richard and his men were a mere eight miles from the city, close enough that they could see the morning sunlight reflect off the Dome of the Rock. Inexplicably Richard chose this moment to hold back, saying that the army was not ready to capture the Holy City.

Why did Richard refuse to lead the attack on the Holy City?

No one ever accused Richard the Lion-Heart of cowardice; rather, it appears that he felt guilty about some conduct in his past and genuinely believed God would not allow him to capture Jerusalem. When his knights and advisors pressed the matter, Richard refused. He would resign his position and serve as a private in the army, he declared, but he would not lead it in an attack on Jerusalem.

In September 1192, Richard and Saladin came to an agreement. They signed a three-year truce under which fighting ceased, and the pilgrims of both faiths—Christian and Muslim—could visit the holy sites. Richard then turned and headed for home. The Third Crusade was an abject failure.

After refusing to invade Jerusalem, Richard the Lion-Heart came to an agreement with Saladin to allow pilgrims into the city. The English king then returned home, ending the Third Crusade.

What happened to Richard the Lion-Heart on his way home to England?

When we relate the story, it sounds unreal, but it is, in truth, fully factual. Richard and about fifty of his officers attempted to cross Eastern Europe incognito, riding through the countryside. They were detected, and arrested, in Vienna, where the duke of Austria held them prisoner for a brief time before handing them over to Henry VI, Holy Roman Emperor. Both the Austrians and the Germans resented Richard's high-handed actions on the crusade, but this was by no means enough grounds on which to arrest and imprison a leader of that enterprise. The Germans held Richard for almost two years before his mother—Eleanor of Aquitaine—raised an enormous ransom and delivered it to the Holy Roman Emperor. Tradition has it that the price was 100,000 marks (or pieces) of silver. If so, this was probably at least three times the value of the annual budget of the Kingdom of England.

Was nothing accomplished by the Third Crusade?

The Third Crusade was one of the grandest of adventures (so long as one survived), but it accomplished virtually nothing.

THE FOURTH CRUSADE

Why did Richard not lead the Fourth Crusade?

Oh, how he wanted to! As soon as he returned to England, following his captivity in Germany, Richard set about raising men and money, intending to return to the Holy Land. Both his English and his Norman subjects were more suspicious, however, because they knew he had come so close (within eight miles) and turned back in 1192.

Richard died in battle against the French in 1199, and the throne passed to his younger brother, John. Leadership of the Fourth Crusade, which commenced in 1202, went not to any of the monarchs, but to a group of top nobles. And when they looked for the best way to reach the Holy Land, these men decided to sail from Venice.

What were the two wealthiest and most competitive merchant cities?

Venice and Genoa, located on opposite sides of the Italian peninsula, became wealthy in the years following the success of the First Crusade. By 1202, these cities had become the richest in the Mediterranean. Venetian shipmasters were pleased to take the men of the Fourth Crusade aboard—for a handsome price—but not long after embarkation, they began to speak of how much easier, and more profitable, it would be to capture Constantinople.

The city on the Bosporus was in a weak condition in 1204. The Byzantines had fought among themselves for years, and the willpower of the Byzantine leaders was at an all-time low. Even so, when the men of the Fourth Crusade came ashore to commence a siege, the Byzantines resisted fiercely. The western Europeans defeated their eastern cousins, capturing the city in August 1204. A puppet state was created, with Venice ruling the affairs of Constantinople for the next fifty years. Today's tourist who admires sculptures in downtown Venice often does not realize that some of the finest of these came from Constantinople after the siege of 1204.

PHILIP VERSUS JOHN

We know so much about Richard. Why do we hear so little of Philip II of France?

When one looks at the two kings side by side, Richard was far more impressive. He was bigger, more intimidating, and more of a presence, all-around, than Philip II. Had Richard lived another decade, the two kings would have continued to fight, and the chances are good that Richard would have been victorious. But he died from a crossbow shot in 1199, while Philip lived another twenty years. And during that score of years, Philip was able to accomplish much of what had previously been denied him.

Who was King John?

John (ruled 1199–1216) was the youngest son of King Henry II and Eleanor of Aquitaine, and no one—except perhaps his father—ever suspected he would become king. John had

> ## Was it confusing to the people at the time that England and France seemed to have been joined at the hip?
>
> To them it made sense. A peasant owed allegiance to the local strongman, who owed his allegiance to the local lord. If that lord declared his allegiance to England, for example, then so did all of the people in the village, even the county. True nationalism had not yet developed, and local, provincial loyalties were far stronger than they are today.

three elder brothers, but two of them died and the third was a high churchman: the throne, therefore, went to John after Richard's death.

John has a bad press—almost everyone agrees on this—but he does seem to have been something of a coward. Perhaps it was the overwhelming presence of his brother Richard that made this so; in any case, John cut a poor figure, both on the battlefield and off. Philip II, meanwhile, had had plenty of time to develop his strategy, which was to dispossess the English king of his domains in present-day France.

How badly did King John stumble?

He stumbled to the point that Pope Innocent III placed all England under interdict, declaring that none of the seven sacraments of the Roman Catholic faith could be performed in that country. This was enough to bring King John to heel, and in 1206 he signed a remarkable document—which still exists—declaring that he was a vassal of the Pope and owed him political, as well as spiritual, allegiance.

John recovered from this disaster, only to stumble into military action against the French. John believed he would prevail because he had enlisted the aid of many German knights and nobles, but when Philip won the Battle of Bouvines in 1214, the poverty of John's cause became extreme. He evacuated his men from nearly all their posts in France and practically signed away both Normandy and Aquitaine. His final humiliation was yet to come, however.

How important was the Magna Carta ("Great Charter")?

The Middle Ages was an era practically teeming with charters. Towns chartered their independence from local lords, and villages established charters—written agreements—with their local knights. Many of these charters still survive and can be seen in major institutions such as the British Library and British Museum, but the most famous of all, beyond doubt, was the Great Charter of 1215.

Under its provisions, King John agreed that certain rights and privileges were beyond his royal power to remove. He could not, for example, seize a nobleman or distress him without the agreement of a council of the barons, and he could not have a man locked up in prison without allowing some sort of trial. To be sure, there were social gradients built into the Great Charter. Peasants had lesser rights; serfs had almost none. But the principle, the very idea that some people had specific rights which could not be removed, was little short of revolutionary. By forcing King John to sign this document, the barons, in 1215, asserted a powerful new trend, one that eventually led in the direction of greater personal liberties.

What is the difference between a baron, a knight, and a lord?

In the High Middle Ages, there were many knights and rather few barons (who might also be called "lord"). The barons usually came from longer lineages and could claim descent from the first knights of a given area. In 1215, the leading barons of England declared war on King John. They never aimed to overthrow him or to take him prisoner, but they asserted their right to defend their baronial privileges, which included near-absolute sovereignty over their lands. King John did not fight the barons—he knew that he would lose—but he came to an agreement with them in June 1215.

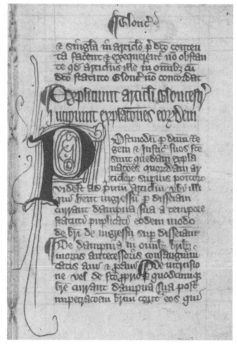

The first page of the Magna Carta. Signed by King John, this 1215 charter is one of the most important documents in the history of legal rights. It acknowledged that citizens have certain rights that cannot be taken away, even by a king.

BORDER WARS

When did the military revolution take place?

Between about 1150 and 1300, a quiet and subtle economic revolution took place, which consequently gave birth to a military one. In that century and a half, the lower-income folk of medieval society began an economic rise that established not what we would call a middle class but rather what we would label a significant, effective working class. Men who previously worked as day laborers now had regular employment, and numerous guilds were established to protect the rights of artisans. As a result, many truly lower-class people moved up to become wealthier and more respectable. It was these people, engaged in a social and economic revolution, who brought about a military one.

Not surprisingly, the countries that enjoyed the most success during this period, roughly 1300–1425, were those that emphasized upward mobility. Little Switzerland exerted a power beyond its borders, thanks to its mercenary soldiers, and medium-sized Scotland, which had so long been bullied by its large southern neighbor, won its independence. Then, too, the Flemings of present-day Belgium gained quasi-independence from both the Holy Roman Empire and the French monarchy. And most of this was accomplished by spears, rather than swords, and by common soldiers in the ranks rather than glittering knights on horseback.

What was the first battle that indicated the success of the new techniques?

The Flemings revolted against French rule at the beginning of the fourteenth century, and a major army of French knights rode north to punish the rebels. At the Battle of Courtrai in 1302, the Flemings met the French with infantry massed in blocks, carrying pikes. Some of the pikes were metal, but far more were of wood, spliced and then hacked from trees. The French made a typical, medieval attack, expecting to rout the rebels, and instead were routed themselves, both by the speed and ferocity of the Flemish infantry. Had the French possessed archers, they might have succeeded; instead, they sustained a bloody defeat. France did make an adjustment, having some of its men train with the Genoese crossbow, but even this weapon was "heavy" and slow: it released perhaps one round every two minutes. What they really needed was something "lighter" and faster, and they did not find it for a long time to come.

Where was the second place the military revolution showed itself?

The people of that time, of course, did not call it a revolution. They were interested in survival and in fending off the attacks of their foes. And the Scots, who had a long history of military failure, were among the first to seize on the new opportunities.

Scotland was a kingdom, but it had been subject to England for almost half a century. English suzerainty had been established by winning over many of the Scottish nobles, men who owned land on both sides of the border. England's King Edward I (ruled 1272–1307)—sometimes known as "Longshanks"— was the architect of the English policy, which resulted in Scotland being a vassal country. Edward I pressed his gains so strongly, however, that a backlash resulted, leading to the Anglo-Scottish Wars.

Who was William Wallace? Was he as important as he is portrayed in the movie *Braveheart*?

Released to the cinema in 1995, *Braveheart* was an outstanding film in terms of dramatic tension; it also contains some of the best scenes of medieval warfare ever filmed. William Wallace was indeed real, but his origins were not as humble as those shown in the film. He was a "hedge knight," meaning he possessed little land, and he was outraged over the brutal means England used to subdue Scotland. Wallace, therefore, started the rebellion that escalated in the middle part of the last decade of the thirteenth century.

What *Braveheart* shows very well is the discrepancy between the English and Scottish military forces. England had a powerful combination of heavy cavalry, solid infantry, and mobile archers, all of which had gained in strength and knowledge during the English wars with Wales. Scotland, by contrast, had a sprinkling of nobles—whose horses lacked armor—atop a ragged combination of individual fighters. Everything suggested England would win, and that was how the wars began, with solid English victories. Motivation and morale—which are not precisely the same—always play roles in military actions, however, and the Scots found their inspiration in William Wallace.

Was there ever a scene quite as amazing—and terrifying—as the one shown in *Braveheart,* where the Scots used wooden pikes to impale the enemy's horses?

The element of surprise that day was not nearly as dramatic as is shown in the film, but yes, the Scots—lacking heavy cavalry of their own—formed solid groups of men known as shiltrons. Resembling the ancient Greek phalanx, the shiltron was a blocklike group of pikemen that could repel its foes.

William Wallace was the Scottish hero *par excellence*, but it was Robert the Bruce who won the final battle for Scottish independence. In 1314, Robert and his Scots won the Battle of Bannockburn over King Edward II, ensuring that Scotland would be free.

Did William Wallace end up "dead," as he was warned in the film *Braveheart*?

Yes. Wallace won an outstanding victory at the Battle of Falkirk in 1296, but he was bested the next year at Falkirk. Resigning his post as defender of Scotland, Wallace played a hit-and-run, hide-and-seek war against the English for several years before being captured. He was brought to London, given a show trial, and then executed in the most gruesome method imaginable. His head was stuck atop London Bridge as a warning to other traitors. The movement that began with Wallace continued, however, under the leadership of Robert the Bruce.

Was Robert the Bruce as conflicted, and sometimes as cowardly, a figure as depicted in *Braveheart*?

Some of the scenes in *Braveheart* have seldom been surpassed in their depiction of medieval warcraft. One of these takes place when William Wallace, badly defeated at Falkirk, pursues King Edward I's party from the battlefield. One knight turns back to fight Wallace, and in the ensuing scrape, Wallace prevails and eventually pulls off the other man's helmet to find that he is a Scot in disguise, none other than Robert the Bruce. The epic treachery of Robert the Bruce should be rewarded with a swift death—this is what nearly all the viewers declare—but Wallace spares his life and staggers away from the battlefield, marveling that Scots could fight and betray each other in this manner.

Robert the Bruce was a slippery character. He *did* fight with King Edward I at Falkirk and only later was he converted completely to the idea of full Scottish independence. Several years later, the Bruce was involved in an assassination, and he struck the final, deadly blow. There is little to love in the man who later came to stand for Scottish free-

"The Trial of William Wallace" as depicted in the 1909 edition of *Cassell's History of England*. The trial was just for show; there was no way the rebellious Scotsman was going to escape his execution.

dom. But there was strength in the man, as well, as he showed a real capacity for growth. Crowned by the Scottish nobles, he fought the English long after both William Wallace and Edward I were dead.

How did the final struggle come about?

King Edward II—son of the one called "Longshanks"—was not a military man in the tradition of his father, but he was a wily, even cunning, opponent. In the spring of 1314, Edward II summoned all the English lords to provide a muster for the king's advance into Scotland; this was to be the single largest of all the border invasions.

Robert the Bruce knew that the English were coming, and by mid-June, he had about 7,000 men in position on the north side of the River Forth, hidden and protected by a rugged section of land called the Bannock, sometimes referred to as the Bannockburn. The Bruce knew he was outnumbered by more than two to one; even worse was the fact that the English had perhaps 2,500 heavy horses. The Scots had perhaps 500 horsemen, but almost none of them possessed the equipage—or even the sheer weight—of their cavalry opponents. In archers, too, the English had a marked superiority. The Bruce had to rely, therefore, on native skill and a measure of luck.

What was the most dramatic moment of the Battle of Bannockburn?

On June 23, 1314, the Bruce was directing and assembling a group of his pikemen when an English noble, just 500 yards away, began to charge. Sir Henry de Bohun espied the crown atop the Bruce's helmet and hoping to score a great coup, he charged alone on horseback. Even though the Bruce could have fled to a cover of trees, to do so would be to lose face in front of hundreds of his men. Therefore, though he was mounted on a pony rather than a real war horse, the Bruce waited.

As Sir Henry de Bohun came close, he leveled his lance and charged straight for the Scottish king, but the Bruce was a master at guerrilla tactics; he evaded the lance and, allowing the Englishman's horse to continue its charge, he came from behind and split de Bohun's head with his axe. Though the Scots chastised their king for exposing himself to such danger, they quietly applauded his bravery. The battle itself, however, did not take place until the following morning.

What were the results of Bannockburn?

Six thousand English troops were killed and wounded, and the list of men taken prisoner was enough to give any loyal Englishman pains. One earl, forty-two barons and bannerets, and scores of knights were taken prisoner.

King Edward II (ruled 1307–1327) was almost captured, but he escaped to fight another day. His ambitions remained strong, but the English attempt to take over Scotland had ground to a halt. Further battles would be fought, and the English would win their share of them, but it would never again be close to annexing Scotland. Between them, William Wallace and Robert the Bruce had accomplished what seemed impossible: winning complete political independence.

How did Switzerland win its independence from Austria?

The Battle of Morgarten, fought in November 1315, was one of the decisive battles toward the end of Swiss independence. Several thousand Austrians invaded Shwyz, one of the federations of the Swiss republic, and found perhaps 5,000 men of Schwyz opposing them. In the battle, fought near the mountain pass of Morgarten, the Swiss proved their superiority in mountain fighting. Using spears made of wood, the Swiss killed nearly 1,500 Austrians (many others drowned in Lake Ageri). As the Austrians retreated, it became plain that Switzerland was on its way to political independence.

Did the Dutch, too, fight for their independence?

They did not need to. Holland and the other Dutch provinces had won their independence from the Holy Roman Empire without any battles, and by the early fourteenth century those provinces were on the way to establishing themselves as solid political units. The major reason no one—such as England or France—claimed Holland is that there seemed to be nothing much of value there. No incentive existed for any of the great powers to invade Holland, and the area slowly evolved in a direction that involved fishing, farming, and a growing maritime presence.

What happened to the crusading movement?

It died in the half century following the year 1204. Three more crusades were formed, but very little was accomplished. Something had gone out of the soul of the crusading movement, and it could not be regained.

Christian Europeans had never been shy about fighting each other, but the number of conflicts and wars began to increase as the crusades wound down. One of the most persistent of conflicts was the series of border wars between England and Scotland. The cause of these border wars was the desire of England—its noble class especially—to add Scotland to the Kingdom of England.

Where else were "border wars" being fought?

They took place throughout much of Europe during the fourteenth century. It almost seems as if the common people realized that the mounted knights were vulnerable for the first time in almost two centuries. Border skirmishes and battles took place in Belgium, in Czechoslovakia, Poland, and Lithuania. A common theme was that foot soldiers employed new methods to bring down mounted knights and that they often succeeded.

THE HUNDRED YEARS' WAR

Can any people, or set of peoples, really sustain the motivation to fight each other for a century?

No. There have to be breaks in the action and time for people to forget—or at least put from their minds—the mayhem and destruction of the last set of episodes. But England and France, which had long experienced uneasy relations, did go to war in 1334, and the conflict lasted—off and on—for *more* than one hundred years.

What was the proximate cause of the Hundred Years' War?

King Edward III of England (ruled 1327–1377) claimed the throne of France because of the Salic Law, which declared that only male descendants and relatives could sit on the throne of Charlemagne. King Philip IV of France, best known as Philip the Fair, naturally disagreed, and the two kingdoms went to war in 1334. Neither side expected anything like what happened after that.

When the war began, France had a large advantage in population—about three to one—and resources. England, by contrast, had the better fleet and could therefore control the English Channel, deciding when and where to strike. The biggest surprises were in the area of military technology, however.

When did gunpowder first arrive in Christian Europe?

The precise date is unknown, but by the early fourteenth century some Europeans had experimented with gunpowder, and by about 1430, the first cannon were being forged. These were clumsy, heavy things, with almost no capacity for mobility; the sheer noise they created, however, could frighten a foe half to death. King Edward III of England brought a handful of ugly looking cannon to the Siege of Calais in 1336, but they did not succeed in battering down the walls. Cannon would have to wait nearly another century before becoming the "destroyers of castles." The longbow, on the other hand, was primed and ready.

The Welsh pioneered the longbow, and the English adapted this new technology during the reign of King Edward I. As long as the archer was tall, the longbow was made of yew, an especially supple wood. Through long practice, a long bowman could release six arrows per minute, and the best of these marksmen were able to pierce the separation points between a knight's armor. The longbow was costly to make and the practice sessions time consuming, but the weapon itself was extraordinarily light, and its ease of transportation made it the best weapon of the Hundred Years' War.

When was the longbow first used?

It had been in use in the British Isles for many years, but the longbow first appeared in a European battlefield at Crecy in 1346. King Edward III invaded France and was set upon by a French force that outnumbered his own. In the Battle of Crecy, the English knights beat the French ones by a narrow margin, but it was the English commoners, using the longbow, who really won the day. Raining down arrows on their opponents, the longbow men then charged, and often caught, French knights either flat-footed or on their backs (because their horses had thrown them off). Captured knights were held for ransom, meaning that the English won a victory that was both tactical and monetary.

Edward III continued to the coast of what is now Belgium and besieged the city of Calais. He captured the city after a long siege and then returned to England. As far as Edward was concerned, the war was won. He did not realize that things were just beginning to warm up.

Why did the French fail to change their own tactics?

It is easy to poke fun at the French, who continued to believe that the armored knights would, eventually, simply ride over the peasants carrying longbows. It is important to remember that people are—in general—resistant to change and continue to believe that the method which worked in the past will do so again. The French, there-

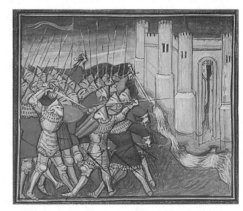

Illustration of Edward III defeating the French at Calais from Jean Froissart's *Chroniques,* c. 1410.

fore, kept making excuses to themselves, blaming the rain on the day before the Battle of Crecy and the difficult terrain as reasons for their defeat. They simply could not fathom the painful fact that military technology had changed and that he who possessed the lighter weapon—the bow—would now prevail over heavier means of transport: the horse.

There must have been more to this war than dynastic struggle, or else people would never have stayed with the conflict. Is that correct?

Yes. The dynastic conflict between the English and French was the initial reason for the Hundred Years' War, but to sustain the bad feeling and desire for blood, there had to be more. By about 1350, England and France were locked in a struggle that was economic, social, and dynastic.

How severe did the Hundred Years' War become?

The major armies were bad enough, but the mercenary forces that attended them were even worse. On both sides, the monarchs employed thousands of mercenary soldiers who preyed on the civilians. France suffered much the worst of this, as so much of the fighting was on its side of the English Channel.

By the 1370s, both England and France were on the verge of bankruptcy, and social disturbances began in earnest. In France, a rebellion known as the Jaquerie nearly toppled King Charles V; in England, the major disturbance came in the form of Wat Tyler's Revolt. In both instances, the established order eventually prevailed, albeit at an enormous cost in money, arms, and men.

Did anyone see that the time had come to end this fratricidal conflict?

Various Popes mentioned the fact, and numerous churchmen waxed indignant about how the two nations should combine to fight the Ottoman Turks. England and France were locked in a life-or-death struggle, however, and things only became worse when Burgundy exerted all of its power on behalf of the former.

The dukes of Burgundy had long been uneasy subjects of the French crown. Many of their subjects identified with Germany, or the Holy Roman Empire. By the 1420s, Burgundy was firmly in the English camp, with disastrous results for France. The single worst day of the Hundred Years' War had already come and gone, however.

Why did King Henry V (ruled 1413–1422) invade France in 1415?

He did so for all the usual reasons: to compel the French to come to terms and to extort treasure from the French nobles. Something about Henry V appealed to his men, however, and he was depicted as a hero in Shakespeare's play of that name. Henry V was young and a risk taker. He came to France with fewer than 8,000 men, and after the Siege of Harfleur, his force was reduced to fewer than 5,000 troops. Rather than be evacuated by ships, however, Henry chose to march over land, across Northern France, to one of the Channel Ports.

The French knew all about their previous failures at Crecy, Poitiers, and elsewhere. What they never believed, however, was that the humble English longbow man could have caused all this destruction. In each case, the French argued that something else was the reason for their failure. Therefore, on hearing that Henry V was marching with a small army, King Charles VI (ruled 1380–1422) summoned all the noblemen of France and commanded them to strike the English while they were en route to Calais.

How did France lose the Battle of Agincourt?

Saint Crispin's Day—October 25—dawned muggy and overcast, with rain showers threatening. This would have been the perfect time for the French to wait and slowly starve out the English. The French knights were impatient—to say the least—and their leader, the Constable of France, ordered an attack at around 9 A.M. Just then the skies opened up, making for terrible visibility and lots of mud.

The French attack progressed along a narrow front, too narrow, as it turned out. The English longbow men did not have to see special targets; they simply poured one volley after another into the mass of French knights. By the time a handful of knights got close to the English lines, their foes were ready for them: these were either killed or captured on the spot. The French made one last attempt, circling around to get at the English supply wagons, but this, too, was foiled. By noon, the French had pulled back, and the English were able to assess their victory, which, in every term imaginable, was simply stunning.

Couldn't the French have tried again, on another day, to defeat the English?

Not really. When an army is pummeled to that extent—roughly 10,000 men killed, wounded, and missing out of a total of 25,000—the fighting spirit shrivels. Besides, if the English had contrived some special magic on Saint Crispin's Day—as many believed—doubtless they would do so again. The French army returned home, and King Henry V headed for the safety of English-held Calais.

To say that Agincourt was a French disaster is to minimize its importance: both sides remembered the battle for centuries. Equally important, Henry V now held the whip hand in any negotiations with the French. Two years later, under the Treaty of Troyes, he married the French king's daughter and when their son—the future Henry VI—was born in 1421, it seemed likely that there would, indeed, be one solid realm of England and France combined.

Was the Hundred Years' War finally over after the Battle of Agincourt?

It should have been. We would, therefore, have called it the Ninety Years' War. But the tide still had one or two cycles to go through.

In 1429, the English pressed their campaign relentlessly. King Henry V was now dead—from natural causes—and the English nobles fought on behalf of his nine-year-old son, King Henry VI. The English had an overwhelming sense of moral superiority by this point: one had to look a long way back to find, or see, any battle they had lost.

The French, at this point, had no king; King Charles VI had died a few years earlier. They had a crown prince—the dauphin—who was in residence at the fortified town of Chinon on the Loire. The English, meanwhile, had invested the city of Orleans on the Loire. It was perhaps the third most important town in France, and if it fell, it was easy to see the English taking the heartland of the Loire River valley. But in the very days and weeks when it seemed that Orleans would fall, the French gained new, sudden inspiration from a most unlikely source: a seventeen-year-old girl.

Who was Joan, before she became famous?

Born around 1411, Joan was called Joan of Arc because of her family. She was from the little village of Domremy, in the province of Lorraine, close to the border of the Holy Roman Empire. Her father was a successful innkeeper, and it is a mistake to call her a peasant; rather, she belonged to the rather small middle class of that time. Even so, she was young and *female*, both of which argued against her becoming a factor in the Hundred Years' War.

Joan was an exceptionally religious girl, even by the standards of that time, and at the age of fourteen she began to have visions of the Catholic saints Michael, Margaret, and Catherine. These visions—or apparitions—told her to be a good girl, to stay close to God, and to be ready when she was called upon. During the winter of 1428–1429, Joan's visions increased in number and intensity. Joan was told that it was her task to rescue Charles, the dauphin, and to bring him to the cathedral city of Rheims to be crowned and anointed with holy oil.

How on earth was a seventeen-year-old supposed to accomplish this?

We must say—right at the outset—that Joan had an enormous amount of faith. Without telling her parents, she went to the local fortress commander—Robert de Baudricourt—and asked him to give her a cavalry escort to take her to the dauphin. De Baudricourt thought her crazy and bothersome, but when she came back for the third time, he did just as she asked. Tradition has it that she spoke some secret to him, something which neither she nor anyone else would have known. All we know for certain is that he gave her an escort of six men and that they headed off for Chinon, arriving there ten days later (they traveled at night to avoid the English).

This romanticized painting of Joan of Arc at the Battle of Orleans erroneously shows her wearing plate mail (*Siege de Orléans* by Jules Lenepveu, c. 1890).

The Dauphin Charles learned of Joan well before she came, and he set a trap so he might ensnare her (he feared she was a sorceress). When Joan entered the audience chamber at the castle of Chinon, she found dozens of men standing around a throne and a middle-aged man sitting there. She looked at that man, shook her head, went around the room slowly, and when she came to the dauphin—who wore clothing much like all the others—she sank to her knees and told him that it was her task to have him crowned and to liberate France from the English.

It sounds as if she was rather like a witch. Did Charles continue to fear this?

Charles had her examined by a group of priests and nuns for the next ten days. At the end of their investigation, they pronounced her of sound—if overenthusiastic—mind and testified that she was a virgin. The concern was that she might have lain with the Devil to gain satanic powers. Charles and his leading commanders continued to have their doubts—can anyone blame them?—but he chose to give her leadership of a section of his army. Joan was to be watched day and night, however, and the male commanders were to remove her if things went ill. Then again, one can ask whether things could get any worse than they already were?

Knowing that Orleans was the key to the Loire River countryside and that its fall would be devastating to French morale, Joan brought 4,000 men to relieve that town. By the time her counter of the English siege had begun, some of the men were already devoted to her. Wearing male attire and armor and carrying an immense white flag with the name of Jesus embroidered upon it, Joan was a striking sight.

How did Joan of Arc succeed where so many others failed?

That was, and remains, one of the great questions associated with Joan of Arc. Immediately upon arriving outside of Orleans, she sent letters to the English commander, imploring him, in the name of heaven—these were her words—to depart. When he scoffed, Joan started her own set of attacks.

Difficulties and dangers were everywhere during the siege, and Joan was wounded in the breast on the second day of battle. She had the wound dressed and appeared on the third day, much to the disgust and anger of the English. Her tactics were nothing unusual, but her adolescent excitement inspired the French, who broke into the strongly built fortress that was the key to the English siege. After a week of battle, the English lifted the siege and withdrew to the north.

Could anyone else have accomplished this?

Historians generally think not. Joan was the essential change element, the factor that allowed for the French victory at Orleans. When Charles the Dauphin arrived, he got off his horse and walked over to Joan and publicly embraced her (this was, sadly, the only occasion on which he fully expressed his gratitude). She told him that it was wonderful, but that God's plan was not yet complete. She was to take him to Rheims for his coronation.

Charles' military advisers spoke against this, saying it was better to consolidate what had already been accomplished. By now, Joan had a wave of confidence behind her, however, and many of the soldiers would not do their duty unless she led the army. Charles, therefore, went with Joan and within six weeks they reached Rheims, where he was crowned on July 17, 1429.

Was she real, this amazing girl called Joan?

She was the real thing, a person of great piety and devotion who turned her religious inspiration into military accomplishment. But her story, which is fabulous, quickly begins to go downhill. Once he was King Charles VII, duly anointed and crowned, the monarch showed less interest in Joan. In fact, he practically asked her to go home. In gratitude, he made her town of Domremy free from all royal taxes (it remained that way until 1789). But Joan had other ideas. The king did not have her services for long, she said, and he should make use of her now. She wanted to attack and capture Paris.

Charles VII held back from this. He wanted to negotiate, to win over the Burgundians who had caused so much havoc in the war, and then to eject the English slowly. It must be said that Charles VII's idea was strategically sound, while Joan's was tactically superior. Charles VII withheld support, and when Joan finally did attack Paris, she was defeated. Months later, she was captured by the Burgundians, who sold her to the English.

What happened to Joan?

After a two-month trial, at which she testified with great fervor and strength, Joan was found guilty of being a witch. The English burned her in the market town of Rouen on May 31, 1431. She was only about nineteen years old.

Joan of Arc's story is one of the most remarkable, and sad, of all connected with military history. That she was a fine, inspiring leader is beyond doubt, and that she accomplished unusual, even great, things cannot be argued. Most observers comment that she was ill-served by her monarch, who, very likely, could have done much more to save her after she fell into the hands of the English. Charles VII continued on his slow way, negotiating here, fighting there, and by the beginning of the year 1453, he and his Frenchmen were on the verge of expelling the English from their soil. The final battle was at Castillon on July 17, 1453.

Who won the final battle of the Hundred Years' War after more than a century of war?

The English performed quite well at the battle's beginning, and there were moments when it seemed that this might turn into another Agincourt or Crecy. The French had nearly 300 pieces of artillery, however, and they used these to turn the tide. By late afternoon, the English were routed, and France had the final victory it needed to claim that the province of Gascony was free of the English. Just a few months later, the war finally ended, with the English holding the city of Calais on the French side of the Channel, but nothing else.

END OF THE BYZANTINE EMPIRE

How large was the Byzantine Empire in the fifteenth century?

One can almost ask how *small* it had become. The empire had once encompassed all of Turkey and much of the Balkans, as well as sections of the African coast. In 1453, it was reduced to a tiny strip of land—perhaps 200 square miles—centered around the city of Constantinople.

One century earlier—almost to the month—the Ottoman Turks had crossed the Dardanelles to establish a presence in mainland Europe; since then, they had slowly strangled what remained of the Byzantine Empire. No scorn was shown, however, because the Ottoman Turks, most of whom had never been within the walls of Constantinople, revered the city nearly as much as their opponents. The Turks referred to the center of downtown Constantinople as the "big red apple."

How many times had Constantinople been besieged?

Perhaps twenty-two times in all, and on only one occasion had the city fallen. That was in 1204, when it succumbed to the Fourth Crusade. For perhaps fifty years thereafter, Constantinople had been under Venetian rule, but the Byzantines had ejected the Venetians by 1260. Now, in 1453, Constantinople faced its final test.

In April 1453, as the Turks approached, a feeling of fate and doom fell over the Byzantine capital. Constantinople had once housed 750,000 inhabitants; the number was now around 100,000, and of these only 7,000 had agreed to defend the walls. The Turks, by contrast, had well over 100,000 men, and their horses and oxen were dragging dozens of immensely heavy cannon. The largest artillery piece cast a bullet that weighed 750 pounds, and the gun itself required over 50 oxen to move.

The walls of Constantinople were no match for Mehmet the Conqueror's siege guns. He took the city for the Turks in 1453. (*L'Entrée du sultan Mehmet II à Constantinople le vingt-neuf mai 1453* by Jean-Joseph Benjamin-Constant, 1876)

When did the siege commence?

In mid-April, the sultan Mehmet—known as "The Conqueror"—invaded Constantinople. Many, if not most, of his predecessors had broken their forces helplessly against the walls of this city, but Mehmet had already determined that cannon and ships would do most of the work. Within days, his enormous siege guns were bringing down sections of the walls—some of which were over 1,000 years old—and his fleet had broken the iron chain that had, for centuries, defied each set of ships entrance to the Golden Horn.

The scene was something out of a movie, in that there were no trees or physical obstacles: one could see the entire panorama. Centuries of tradition endured within the walls, while centuries of aggression were arrayed against them. And on May 28, 1453, the Turks succeeded not only in breaching the walls but pouring into the city.

What happened to the emperor?

Constantine XI (ruled 1449–1453), the last Byzantine emperor, died that day, but whether he was killed on the steps of the great cathedral or in front of one of the broken set of walls is unknown. Thousands of civilians were killed as the Turks came into the city. The ceremony of victory, however, was reserved for the following day.

On May 29, 1453, Sultan Mehmet the Conqueror rode slowly through the ruined walls, passed through dozens of streets, and arrived at the building the Byzantines called Hagia Sophia, meaning church of divine wisdom. It had been built during the reign of the Emperor Justinian, roughly 920 years earlier. The sultan rode his horse up the steps and into the cathedral. Seeing beautiful Christian paintings on its inner walls, he decreed that these be covered over. He then declared that the building was now a mosque and that its name was Aiya Sophia, meaning "pride of the sultans."

What was so important about the year 1453?

It is easier to reverse the question, to ask what was not important about that year. France finally expelled England from Gascony, ending the Hundred Years' War. The Ottoman Turks finally captured Constantinople—"the big red apple"—which had been their goal for centuries. And, in a medium-sized German city, Johannes Gutenberg put the finishing touches on what would soon be known as the printing press, a technology that would change the lives of millions of people.

When did the Renaissance begin?

No one can put a true date for the precise beginning because the Renaissance was a social and artistic movement, rather than a primarily political one. If one poses this question to a group of scholars, however, chances are good that a majority would nod at the year 1453. In that calendar year, the Hundred Years' War ended and Constantinople fell to the Ottoman Turks. Then, too, Johannes Gutenberg's printing press began running off some of its first bibles around that time.

Is there any way to know, and to say, that one has passed the medieval type of warfare and entered the Renaissance?

Many of the weapons were quite similar. The crossbow, longbow, and lance were all still in use, but the early cannon and early muskets—known as harqubeses—had appeared.   103

Also, when examining paintings of Renaissance warfare, one is struck by the greater amount of color. Italian artists, especially, put many shades of red and blue into their paintings, and the deep grimness—and perhaps griminess—of the Hundred Years' War seems to dissipate.

To be sure, this does not mean that Renaissance warfare was less deadly; rather, it implies that the men involved had more of a sense of humor—and indeed of color—in their lives. The Italian mercenary bands, and the Swiss mercenary soldiers, especially, seem to have taken their warfare very seriously and their humor very lightly.

Which nation was furthest along the road to creating a modern-style army?

Spain had come the farthest distance in pursuit of that goal. The kingdoms of Aragon and Castile were united in the persons of King Ferdinand and Queen Isabella in 1469. Spain, too, had been at war with the Muslim population in its southern half for centuries, leading to the creation of a warrior culture. By 1485, only one Muslim enclave survived, the tiny Kingdom of Granada. Ferdinand and Isabella set their sights on Granada, knowing that a victory in Spain would do much to lift the spirits of men and women throughout Christendom.

Their Majesties attacked Granada in 1489 and following a three-year siege, the city capitulated. The siege went on so long that the Spanish forces built what amounted to another city—of the same size—in which they housed their troops and maintained their stores. To Ferdinand and Isabella the fall of Granada was the culmination of centuries of Christian Spain fighting against the Muslims, but to an Italian adventurer—from Genoa—it also represented a great opportunity. He was Christopher Columbus, and he staked nearly everything on persuading the Spanish king and queen to back his venture.

Which nation was furthest along the in the creation of a modern-style navy?

England. The English had long been among the world's best fishermen because of their long, indented coastline and because the hinterland did not support enough wheat for everyone. Starting in the High Middle Ages, however, and accelerating as they reached the Renaissance, the English pioneered the establishment of a real navy.

When did the term Christendom come into use?

We cannot date the precise year, but the expression was widely used throughout the fifteenth and sixteenth centuries. Rather than refer to Europe or to Western Europe, as we do today, the Europeans of that time spoke of Christendom, meaning all the peoples and nations who lived under the law of Christianity. It was a beautiful concept, and a far more appealing word than simply Europe, but it did not long survive once the Reformation took hold.

During the reign of King Henry VII (1485–1509), the English Navy became a professional organization with a table of ranks and schedules (still no pensions as yet). The English, too, decided to militarize several towns along their southern and southeastern coast. Naming these the Cinque Ports, the English monarchy established special laws for governance of these towns, and it is worth noting that hardly any of them ever fell to a foreign foe.

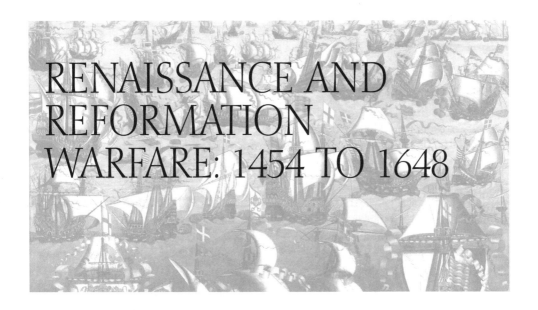

RENAISSANCE AND REFORMATION WARFARE: 1454 TO 1648

LUTHER AND POPE LEO X

When did the Reformation begin?

This is one of the few times when we can date something with great precision. The Protestant Reformation began on October 31, 1517, when Martin Luther (1483–1546)—a German monk and priest—tacked up a series of statements for debate on the door of the church at Wittenberg.

Luther did not, originally, wish to destroy or divide the Roman Catholic Church. His entire life had been devoted to the church, and he loved it with great intensity. Luther's goal was to reform the Roman Catholic Church by putting an end to the selling of indulgences. These documents, either handwritten or struck off a printing press, explained to the purchaser that his deceased relative was released from a certain number of years in Purgatory. To Luther, and many others, this amounted to spiritual fraud and encouraged materialism within the Church. He, therefore, posed his Ninety-Five statements—or Theses—for debate.

How many religious reformers were there?

The big three were Martin Luther (1483–1546), John Calvin (1509–1564), and Stefan Zwingli (1484–1531). What they had in common was the belief that one must read the Bible, preferably in one's native tongue rather than Latin. From that point, their beliefs diverged, but in sum, they brought about the Protestant revolution, guided by the idea that a Protestant is "one who protests."

Could the Roman Catholic Church have reformed, and would that have ended the protests?

Yes and yes. Luther was the foremost among many critics of the Church, but the great majority of them would have backed off if Pope Leo X (ruled 1513–1521) had withdrawn the sale of indulgences. The Pope was concerned with raising funds for the building of the new St. Peter's Cathedral in Rome, however, and he was not greatly concerned by the stipulations laid down by a German monk.

Pope Leo misjudged both the character of his critic and the sharp focus that would soon shine on the corruption and abuses within the Church. Luther was the first great reformer, but he was followed by many others.

How did Emperor Charles V become involved in the religious controversy?

Charles V was king of Spain from 1516 and Holy Roman Emperor from 1519. With the grandson of Ferdinand and Isabella on one side, he was the grandson of Emperor Maximilian I on the other, and overall he possessed a dynastic grandeur unsurpassed since the time of Charlemagne. Emperor Charles V was involved in many conflicts and struggles, but the religious one would be the defining aspect of his career.

In April 1521, Martin Luther appeared before Charles V at the Diet (or Council) of Worms. Charles' lawyers made numerous efforts to persuade Luther to recant his heretical beliefs, most notably that the Pope was merely a high churchman, not the vicar of God. After many hours of wrangling, Luther had the question put to him one last time. He replied, "I can do none other than to obey Scripture. Here I stand. I can do no other." Charles V, therefore, outlawed Luther, making it a crime for the people of the Holy Roman Empire to aid or comfort him. Not everyone accepted this, however, and Luther was hidden by a high German nobleman.

CORTÉS AND MONTEZUMA

Who was Hernán Cortés, and how did he get his grand idea of Mexican conquest?

Cortés (1485–1547) was a member of the minor Spanish nobility. He emigrated to Cuba by 1512, and in 1519 he led roughly 600 Spaniards to the coast of Mexico. Cortés, at that time, knew little of the Aztecs or their empire: he knew only that stories of silver and gold often originated from Mexico. While on the coast, Cortés won over some of the native peoples, who were not fond of the Aztecs.

Did any of the Indians actually think Cortés was a God?

Yes. Roughly 400 years earlier, a folk legend had developed about Quetzalcoatl, an Aztec leader who departed in the direction of the rising sun, saying that he would one day return. Over time, Quetzalcoatl developed from a folk hero into a god, and when Cortés and his men appeared from the east—the direction of the rising sun—carrying weapons that performed previously unheard-of wonders, many Indians concluded that Cortés was Quetzalcoatl.

Cortés would not have known all about this, or been able to take such advantage of it, were it not for Malinali. She was a sixteen-year-old Mayan girl who, along with nineteen others, was handed to Cortés as a gift soon upon his arrival on the coast. Malinali, whose Indian name meant "sharp blade of grass," was very skillful with languages: she knew both the coastal Indian languages and the Aztec tongue. Learning Spanish quite rapidly, she became Cortés' go-between, his chief interpreter. She also became his lover, and they had a son.

Spanish nobleman Hernán Cortés knew nothing about the Aztecs when he stumbled upon their empire and, eventually, decimated their civilization.

Which impressed the Indians more: guns, cannon, or horses?

All three were impressive, actually downright frightening. But the horses, very likely, had the biggest impact. Cortés came with fewer than twenty horses, but to people who had never beheld a horse of any kind, the massive war horses—bred in Andalusia, Spain—were a terrifying sight. In battle, the horses provided the Spaniards with their winning card on many occasions.

The Spaniards had no muskets or even matchlocks: their guns were clumsy harquebuses which had to be set upon a tripod just to control them. But the barking sound of these guns, plus the occasional roar of a cannon, was enough to persuade the Indians that these were no ordinary newcomers. Over time, the Indians realized that neither Cortés nor his men were gods (this realization may have occurred when they first witnessed a Spaniard bleeding), but they continued to fear the newcomers, who had powerful magic, to say the very least.

When did Cortés and Montezuma first meet?

On November 8, 1519, Cortés and 600 Spaniards, joined by perhaps 10,000 Indian allies, descended from the mountains into the Valley of Mexico. Approaching the magnificent city built on two islands on the Lake of Mexico, Cortés met Montezuma at the gateway to Tenochtitlan. All records concur that this first meeting was peaceful, with Malinali serving as the interpreter, but a mere two weeks later Cortés seized Montezuma and held him as a hostage. This was the beginning of the conquest of Mexico.

At nearly every stage of the conquest, Cortés proved bolder than Montezuma and those who followed him. Realizing that some of the Indians thought him a god, Cortés used it to its fullest potential. When the governor of Cuba sent 900 men to stop and arrest him, Cortés defeated these men and then turned them into his followers. On every occasion, he gained Indian allies among those who disliked Aztec rule. Very few people of our time admire or like Cortés—he is in some ways the archetypical Western conqueror of native peoples—but his audacity and skill were, at times, simply breathtaking.

Is it true that the Aztecs practiced human sacrifice?

Yes. The Spaniards may have exaggerated the numbers, but there is no doubt that the Aztec priests regularly killed hostages—young people especially—on the steps of the magnificent temple in the center of Tenochtitlan. The Aztecs believed that the world was on a fifty-two-year calendar (not fifty-two weeks) and that these sacrifices were necessary to persuade the gods and goddesses "to "renew" the world at the end of each of these cycles.

What was the "Night of Sorrows"?

In June 1520, the Aztecs rose in fury against the Spaniards and their allies. Montezuma was dead by this time: whether by the hand of the Spaniards or by his own people remains uncertain. Cortés led his army out of Tenochtitlan on the evening of June 30, 1520, fighting the Aztecs all along the causeway that bridged the two islands. The fighting was fierce, and much of the treasure he had obtained fell into the water. Beyond this, however, Cortés suffered more than 1,000 men killed and wounded during the Night of Sorrows.

If the Aztecs believed that this was it, they were sadly mistaken. Recruiting still more Indian allies, Cortés spent the next nine months in the mountains on the east side of the Lake of Mexico, and when he returned in the spring of 1521, he had small ships. Mounted on rollers, these ships slid down the mountains and into the lake. What followed was an intense, extremely bloody fight for the city itself.

How many people died during the Siege of Tenochtitlan?

The seventy-five-day siege lasted through much of the summer of 1521, and when it was over both the city and the Aztec nation lay in ruins. Cortés did not attempt an accurate account of the killed and wounded, but we suspect it was close to 100,000.

Montezuma II was the leader of the Aztecs at the time of Cortés' arrival. He died of uncertain causes before the Siege of Tenochtitlan.

How much treasure did Cortés and his friends find?

Much to their surprise, the Spaniards found that the Aztec valued gold less than they valued turquoise, the most prized of all their possessions. Over time, Cortés and those who followed him discovered that Mexico possessed vast quantities of silver. Indian laborers dug in the earth and brought out the raw silver, which Spaniards refined and then sent across the ocean.

Spanish steel was so superior to the obsidian in Aztec knives that a well-armed Spaniard could, indeed, kill up to ten of his enemies without taking a serious wound himself.

One hundred thousand people killed and wounded meant that the cream of the Aztec nation was gone. Cortés soon established a new Spanish colony, which he called New Spain. His cause was assisted by the fact that Roman Catholicism—especially the veneration of the Virgin Mary—was both liked and applauded by many Native Americans. Within a generation or two, the conquest was complete. Mexico had become part of Spain.

What happened to Cortés and Malinali?

She bore him a son, and they seemed like a good couple. Whenever native people condoled Malinali on the change in her circumstances, she resolutely told them that it was all God's will, that it was a great blessing to have converted to Roman Catholicism. Whether she and Cortés would have stayed together is unknown because she contracted smallpox and died at the age of twenty-four or twenty-five. Their son moved to Spain, where he lived the life of a nobleman.

MAGELLAN AND ELCANO

Who was the first person to go completely around the globe?

Magellan (c. 1480–1521) usually gets the credit because he conceived the idea and led the expedition until his death in 1521. The Spaniard Juan Sebastián Elcano (1476–1526) actually completed the voyage, however, arriving in Spain in September 1522.

What type of frustrations and delays did Magellan experience?

The list is very long. Not only did many of the Spanish sailors distrust him because he was Portuguese, but several of the ship captains wanted to overthrow him and return to Spain. Magellan put down not one but two mutinies even before he located the famous strait that now bears his name. Emerging from that strait, he crossed the Pacific, landing in Guam during the spring of 1521. To this point, Magellan had done nearly everything "right," but he overreached himself by joining one Philippine tribe to fight another. In the battle that ensued, Magellan died on a lonely beach, with many of his men fleeing to the ships.

Magellan had started the voyage with five ships, but these were reduced to two by the time of his death. Juan Sebastian Elcano was elected the new leader of the expedition. He brought the two remaining ships to the Spice Islands, where the Spaniards crammed them with cinnamon, nutmeg, and ginger, the spices that had been the motivation for the voyage in the first place. Elcano then led two ships from the Spice Islands, but one was captured by the Portuguese. Elcano and seventeen other ragged survivors arrived in Spain in September 1522. They were the first people to go completely around the world and to prove, beyond a doubt, that Columbus had been correct. The way to reach the spices of the East was to sail west, but it took much longer than Columbus—or anyone else—had anticipated.

Although Magellan did not complete his voyage around the globe (he was killed by native people in the Philippines in 1521), he is credited with the first circumnavigation of the globe.

HENRY, CHARLES, AND FRANCIS

What was the great monarchical rivalry of the early sixteenth century?

One can point to several intense rivalries, including that between the king of England and the king of Scotland, but the largest and greatest of them was the rivalry between Emperor Charles V of Spain and King Francis I of France.

Charles V was Holy Roman Emperor and king of Spain. Thanks to Cortés' efforts, he was now ruler, as well, of Spanish Mexico. The present was bright, and the future looked even brighter. Charles V had one great foe, however. King Francis I of France (ruled 1515–1547) was raised, from his earliest days, to look on Charles V as a deadly foe, and the two kings spent many years fighting one another, sometimes clandestinely and sometimes in the open. Both monarchs made occasional use of the king of England—who had his own reasons and motivations—as an ally.

Why do we usually think of King Henry VIII as a buffoon?

Because during the course of his long reign, he became one. Early in his reign, however, Henry VIII was athletic, skillful, and passably good looking (this changed over the years, thanks to his enormous appetite).

In watching the rivalry between Emperor Charles V and King Francis I, Henry VIII usually sided with the emperor, who was the nephew of his first wife, Queen Catherine of Aragon (1485–1536). Henry was eager to play a larger role in Continental politics, and in the spring of 1520, he planned to meet Francis I at a special extravaganza in what is now Belgium, the Field of Cloth of Gold. Before he could do so, however, Henry learned that the Emperor Charles also wished to meet with him. The "summit" meetings between these three men, therefore, became the talk of Europe in 1520.

Who met at Canterbury in June 1520?

Henry VIII waited anxiously along the coast, while Charles V's ships made their way from Spain. When Charles came ashore, he and Henry rode together on the short but memorable way to Canterbury Cathedral, where they celebrated Pentecost Sunday (known in England as Whitsun Sunday). Henry and Charles kept these conversations to marital and familial matters, but both were well aware that Henry was soon to meet Francis.

Just how much money was spent on the festivities at Dover and Canterbury is hard to say, but we know that nearly 1,000 knights and lords gathered that spring. Henry VIII never spared any expense where celebration was concerned; he was also quite anxious to ensure that Charles would remain his good friend.

What was the Field of Cloth of Gold?

Cloth of gold was a relatively new way to embroider one's garments, and the knights and retainers of England and France both spent small fortunes to make sure they were properly decorated when they met in Belgium. The actual field was about six miles from Calais, on neutral ground. This is where Henry VIII and Francis I met in June 1520.

The meeting had been planned for years, and both sides emptied their treasuries, seeking to outdo the other. Roughly 6,000 men and women met for the festivities, which included tournaments, hawking, and endless feasting. Henry and Francis engaged in a good-natured wrestling match, while their courtiers and knights attempted pleasant conversation. England and France had long been enemies, but it seemed, just for a few weeks, as if they might now become friends.

It seems as if peace was breaking out everywhere. What happened to spoil the general mood?

England and France managed to remain at peace another two years. France and Spain remained wary, suspecting foes. But the really bad news came not from Western Europe but from the East.

Selim the Grim (which translates better as Selim the Awesome) died in 1520, leaving leadership of the Ottoman Empire to his son Suleiman, who was soon known as Suleiman the Magnificent. Each newcomer to the Ottoman throne had to demonstrate military prowess, and it was no surprise that Suleiman chose the Christian West—also known as Christendom—as his foe of choice. In 1521, Suleiman brought a large army from Constantinople to capture Belgrade. This was the first of many times he would threaten the West.

Given that there was now a threat from the East, did the European monarchs come closer together?

On the contrary, they split even further apart. Henry and Francis went to war in 1522, and Francis and Charles V declared war against each other in 1523. Even though Henry and Charles were both fighting Francis, they both maintained secret feelings about each other. The really big upshot, however, was that Francis was captured by Charles' Spanish soldiers in 1525.

The Battle of Pavia, in northern Italy, was typical of the battles of that time. Mounted knights jostled with mercenary infantry. What was unusual was the number of harque-

Holy Roman Emperor Charles V ruled over Italy, Germany, and the Spanish Empire, among other lands, at the

time when the Spanish were first colonizing the New World.

buses, and most of them were held by the Spaniards. At a critical moment in the battle, Francis I galloped into the action, and before long he was surrounded by dozens of Spaniards. He wielded his magnificent sword as long as he could before being captured and led off into captivity. Many monarchs knew the taste of defeat, but rather few experienced captivity as Francis did for the next year.

How did Francis ever persuade Charles V to release him?

It was a rare thing for one Christian monarch to hold another captive. It was even stranger when we realize that the Ottoman Turks were practically knocking on the doors of Eastern Europe. Charles V held Francis I in captivity until the latter promised to be his good friend and ally, to pay for past transgressions, and to provide two of his sons as hostages. In a truly moving, even heartbreaking, event, Francis was released on the south bank of the river dividing France and Spain, while his two eldest sons were placed in captivity on the north bank. The two boats passed each other in midstream, and Francis was allowed a few minutes with his sons. The moment he reached French soil, he leaped on a horse, shouting, "Now I am king again!" For the rest of his life, Francis maintained that the oaths he had sworn had been taken under duress. He and Charles were soon at war again.

THE TERRIBLE TURK

How frightening were the Ottoman Turks, so far as Christian Europeans were concerned?

The Ottoman Turks played a role quite similar to the Russian Communists of the 1950s and 1960s; almost any time that someone needed a scapegoat, or to assign some blame, one said that "the terrible Turk" had done this or that.

Suleiman the Magnificent (ruled 1520–1566) was indeed a frightening character. Unlike his European counterparts, Suleiman was *owner*, as well as ruler, of all that he surveyed. The culture, law code, and language of the Turks was very different from anything known to the Europeans. If the Ottomans did conquer Europe, it would become yet another province of the domains of the Muslim faith, and Allah, rather than Jesus Christ, would be glorified.

What was the closest that Suleiman, and the Turks, came to taking Europe?

In the autumn of 1529, Suleiman brought roughly 80,000 men from Constantinople as well as a fleet that came up the Danube. Upon arriving outside Vienna, he demanded to know where "King Charles" (as opposed to Charles the Emperor) was because he perceived that Charles V was his greatest foe. On learning that a mere duke had been assigned the defense of Vienna, Suleiman settled down for what might have been a routine siege. His men were masters of siege craft, and they had by far the superior artillery.

In Emperor Charles V's absence, the Vienna garrison was capably led by Wilhelm von Roggendorf (1481–1541), the Hoffmeister of Austria. His men dumped endless barrels of water to flood the Ottoman Turks' siege lines, and he sent out sorties at just the right time. On one occasion, nearly 2,000 Turks were killed under Suleiman's eyes. By mid-October, the Turkish sultan had had enough. He headed back to Constantinople to announce what he called a major victory, but which almost everyone realized was his first real defeat. Suleiman had by no means given up, but he was blocked for the time being from invading the heart of Europe.

CATHOLIC VERSUS PROTESTANT

When did the religious wars of the sixteenth century begin?

Martin Luther and John Calvin laid down the doctrinal differences, and beliefs, between Catholic and Protestant, but the major battles and wars began in the 1540s. By that time, Emperor Charles V was the defender of Roman Catholic orthodoxy, while King Francis I was the heretic, who allowed Protestant reformers at his court and who even flirted with an alliance with Suleiman the Magnificent.

Though Charles V and Francis I were the great foes, the biggest battles and the longest campaigns were fought within the boundaries of the Holy Roman Empire. The Catholics won the larger number of battles, and after his victory at Muhlberg in 1547, Charles V seemed destined to rule over all. Charles knew how fragile his victory was,

Why is it so hard for men of great power to step away from it?

Human psychology suggests that we become accustomed to whatever is presented, and he or she who possesses great political and military power often has difficult relinquishing it. We do have a handful of remarkable examples, however, the foremost of which is the abdication of Emperor Charles V. In 1556, he renounced his title as Holy Roman Emperor, as king of Spain, and as lord of the Dutch Netherlands. Charles stepped down in favor of his son King Philip II, who gained Spain and the Netherlands, and his younger brother Ferdinand, who became Holy Roman Emperor and leader of Austria. This established the difference between the Spanish and Austrian Hapsburgs.

Charles V retired to Yuste, a Roman Catholic monastery in the Spanish countryside. He was weary of politics, of war, and of government, he said, and wished to live like a simple monk. No doubt, he enjoyed greater privilege and prestige than the average monk, but he did take that station and was there at the time of his death in 1558.

however. Spain was being bled dry of its best men, and his finances were in terrible shape. Even though he received enormous amounts of silver and gold from the New World, these were not sufficient to pay all his debts.

Fortune seemed to smile on Charles V when both of his great enemies died in the same year. Henry VIII died in January 1547 and Francis I followed in March, leaving Charles very much the master of the European scene. He declined to exult in his victories, and a few years later he took the unprecedented step of abdicating his major titles.

Might the Habsburgs have been wiser to keep all the leadership in one house and dynasty?

It certainly seems so, from our modern perspective. But Emperor Charles V had attempted that very thing and found it too much. Given that some of his descendants were less conscientious about duty than him, it seems that he made the right choice.

THE RISE OF RUSSIA

Is there a difference between "Russia" and "Muscovy"?

The latter term was used for decades, even centuries before the first, but they both refer to the same political block: the region that straddles European Russia, all the way to the Ural Mountains. Much of this area had once been ruled by the Mongol leaders of the Golden Horde, but by about 1500, the princes of Moscow had exerted their influence and pushed out the Mongols.

The leaders of Moscow did not yet call themselves "Czar," but that term came into usage soon after the fall of the Byzantine Empire. Numerous Muscovites referred to their city as the "third Rome," in succession after Rome itself and then Constantinople. Over time, the Muscovites also adopted the idea that they were an imperial people, bound or fated to carry on the mission of Rome and Constantinople.

Was there something different about Muscovy, or Russia, right from the beginning?

There was. Russia received a triple inheritance, which made it spiritually rich but materially confused. First and foremost was the Greek Orthodox Church, which came north and east at about the same time that the Roman Catholic Church went north and west. Second, Russia was overrun by the Mongols and held captive, so to speak, for nearly two centuries. Russia, therefore, missed both the Renaissance and the Reformation. Third, perhaps most important, was the Byzantine inheritance, which persuaded the Russian czars that they were on an equal level with the emperors of ancient Rome.

Much of this was good, excellent even. The triple inheritance made it difficult for the rulers of Muscovy to understand the Christian West, however, and the feeling was reci-

When was the Kremlin built?

The Kremlin, which is one of the world's true wonders, is a series of buildings and palaces built around an inner core that was established during the time of Czar Ivan III. Each successive czar saw it as his responsibility to glorify and beautify the Kremlin, giving it a greater significance, than, say, the White House in the United States. When Russians, therefore, speak of the Kremlin, they do so in terms that are both secular and spiritual: they see it as a fusion of the two.

procated in full measure. The first real trade contacts between Russia and the West did not occur until the 1550s, and for a full century after that, many Western Christians continued to think of Russia as a strange, far-off place that could never be understood. In the ultimate expression of this belief, Prime Minister Winston Churchill declared, centuries later, that Russia was "a riddle wrapped in an enigma."

Was there anything especially different about the Russian military?

It followed much the same lines as those of the Christian West, but it lagged two centuries behind. As a result, during the reign of Czar Ivan the Terrible, the monarch acted very much like a feudal king from the time of the Crusades, and even during the reign of Peter the Great, the czar still acted as if his subjects' bodies—their very persons—"belonged" to him in a sense that had disappeared in the West.

Then, too, Muscovy, or Russia, was thoroughly landlocked. Muscovy was a large state with immense potential, but its merchants, or potential ones, had little access to the goods of other nations. As a result, Russians discovered the use of gunpowder much later than the French, Italians, or other Western Europeans, and their wars against the Ottoman Turks were much closer than would otherwise have been the case.

Was Czar "Ivan the Terrible" really as bad as he sounds?

Like many other men in similar positions—one thinks of King Henry VIII, for example—Czar Ivan (ruled 1547–1584)

A seventeenth-century illustration of Ivan the Terrible.

was a much better leader in youth and early adulthood than in later life. He started his reign reasonably well and showed himself a person of shrewd strategic insight, but with each passing decade he became stranger, even outlandish. Like Henry VIII, Ivan the Terrible had many wives. We believe that he had a total of eight, of whom at least four were poisoned. Who poisoned them remains a mystery. Like Henry VIII, Ivan the Terrible grew much worse in later years, and by the time of his death in 1582, he was far gone in superstitions and paranoia.

Where was Russia toward the end of the sixteenth century?

Russia was experiencing one of her lowest periods in modern times. Known as the "Time of Troubles," the late sixteenth and early seventeenth centuries were a period of revolving czars, pretenders to the throne, and peasant revolts. On numerous occasions, the entire state of Muscovy stood on the brink of collapse, but in 1613 a new dynasty—the Romanov—was proclaimed, and Russia entered a time of greater stability. This does not mean its ties to the Christian West were any firmer, however; on the contrary, the Russians had a great dislike and fear of the Poles, against whom they fought during the Time of Troubles. Another eighty years would pass before Russia made firm contact with the Western powers.

THE RISE OF ENGLAND

Why did it take so long for England to become a player in the religious wars?

The great thing—so far as England was concerned—is that it did not have to. Protected by its island status, England could, usually, afford to watch the Continental powers waste their money and soldiery while England conserved them. But the rise of Philip II to the throne of Spain changed the situation somewhat.

Philip II (reigned 1558–1598) struggled throughout life to be a dutiful son and faithful follower of his father, who had been such an overwhelming presence. Unlike Charles V, Philip II was a religious bigot, who wished to crush the Protestants rather than win them back to the Roman Catholic Church. Philip's first concern was with the Dutch Netherlands, but few people doubted that he also intended to bring England and Scotland back into the fold.

How did Elizabeth, the middle child of King Henry VIII, become queen of England?

Even in death, Henry VIII attempted to control everything. His long and complicated will provided that Edward—his youngest child and only son—would inherit the throne, but that if Edward were to die without issue, the throne would pass to Mary, his eldest child. By off circumstance this happened, and when Mary died without issue, the throne passed to Elizabeth.

Queen Elizabeth I (reigned 1558–1603) was the shrewdest, most calculating monarch of the century. She listened to her advisers at length, pondered all the options, and then made her own choice. Perhaps for show, she sometimes attempted to go back on her original decision(s). That she was the most intelligent ruler of the time cannot be doubted. The Pope wrote that she was an amazing woman and that if she were on the side of Roman Catholicism, that faith would surely prevail.

Who did Elizabeth help first?

When the Dutch rose against Philip II in 1567, England was inclined to help. The Dutch were Protestants, and they were fighting against Spain, the great Continental power of the day. Elizabeth never aided the Dutch openly; she funneled money to them and sent English adventurers to fight in their long war for political independence. This infuriated Philip II, and he gradually became Elizabeth's sworn enemy.

ELISABETHA DEI GRATIA
ANGLIÆ FRANCIÆ ET
HIBERNIÆ REGINA.

A daughter of Henry VIII, Queen Elizabeth I proved to be one of England's finest rulers, bringing about a period of prosperity and growth unprecedented in her nation's history.

Complicating the situation even more was the issue of Mary, Queen of Scots. Born in France, she came to the Scottish throne in her twenties and did her best to bring her subjects back to Roman Catholicism. They threw her out, and she crossed the border to England and asked Elizabeth, who was her first cousin once removed, for help. Not only did Elizabeth deny her assistance, but she had Mary locked up in a castle and kept her away from all observers, friendly and otherwise. Elizabeth was correct in that Mary represented a political danger, but her treatment was cruel.

When did Elizabeth, and England, first become involved in the Caribbean?

England had watched with open envy as Portugal and Spain established maritime empires in the early sixteenth century. According to a papal decree, the eastern hemisphere belonged to Portugal and the western to Spain. England, France, and Holland disagreed, and all three nations wanted their part of the colonization game. England did not race to enter the business of actual colonization; she, rather, sought to despoil Spain.

In the 1560s, Elizabeth licensed a handful of privateers with authority to prey on Spanish commerce. John Hawkins and Francis Drake, cousins, led the way. They found it much easier to attack the Spanish overseas possessions than to establish new ones of their own. Philip II was outraged by these attacks, but Elizabeth was a master at giving calm, misleading answers to the Spanish ambassador.

How close did Philip II come to conquering the Dutch Netherlands?

The southern part of the Netherlands—that which we now call Belgium—was under Spanish control by 1570, and Philip continued to press to win back the northern Netherlands. His armies, led by the Duke of Parma, were the best organized of the time, and the Spaniards slowly conquered one Dutch fortress and town after another. The closer they came to success, however, the more that the Dutch resisted, and when William the Silent was assassinated in 1578, it only fueled the flames of Dutch anger.

When did Elizabeth send Francis Drake on his most famous voyage?

Drake, who was the most ambitious and ruthless of the queen's privateers, asked permission to attack Spain's South American settlements, which were rumored to be extremely wealthy. Elizabeth took her time, hemmed and hawed, but she finally gave Drake his commission, and he sailed—with five ships—in 1577.

Drake told almost no one all of his plans, but his captains thought him too ambitious just the same. He faced a minor revolt in Patagonia—the same place where Magellan had faced one—and he sentenced one of his captains to death. Moving further south, Drake found his way through the Strait of Magellan: he was the first non-Spaniard or Portuguese to do so. Coming out into the Pacific, Drake moved his way up the coast of Chile and Peru, attacking Spanish settlements and ships. Virtually every Spanish place was caught unawares because no hostile ships had ever sailed these waters.

What was Drake's biggest coup?

He found and captured an enormous Spanish treasure galleon that sailed from Manila in the Philippines to Acapulco every year. The loot from that one ship more than equaled everything else Drake acquired on his epic voyage. Drake put in on the North American coast, likely just north of modern-day San Francisco. After some encounters with the local population, he sailed again, this time right across the Pacific.

After obtaining much spice in the Malaccan Islands, Drake sailed for home. He was more fortunate than Ferdinand Magellan, who had died along the way. On his arrival in Plymouth, England, Drake

Sir Francis Drake was a privateer whom Queen Elizabeth I employed to lead attacks against Spanish ships, looting their cargos and sending the money back to England.

found himself the toast of the town and then the nation. In 1581, Queen Elizabeth visited his flagship—which he had renamed the *Golden Hind*—and knighted him on the quarterdeck. This public approval suggested that Elizabeth was ready to duel with Philip II. He, however, had already stolen a march on her.

How did Spain come to possess Portugal?

In 1578, King Sebastian I of Portugal (ruled 1557–1578) was killed while leading his army against the Moors in North Africa. Philip II had a blood relationship to the Portuguese monarchy, and he pressed his claim, first in legal documents and then by sending his army across the border. The Spaniards conquered mainland Portugal rather easily, but the Portuguese islands, the Azores especially, held out for two or three years. During that time, Philip II increased the size of the Spanish navy, both by adding the Portuguese ships to his fleet and by employing new methods of bombardment.

Philip II felt ready to attempt what he called the Enterprise of England. Elizabeth I and her subjects felt ready to contest any landing. What was needed was a spark to ignite the contest, which came in the form of the execution of Mary, Queen of Scots.

MALTA AND LEPANTO

Why was Philip II so preoccupied with the Mediterranean Sea?

Philip was so occupied as to feel beleaguered. He faced the Dutch Revolt to his northeast, the English freebooters to the west, and he faced the Ottoman Turks to the east. His father, Emperor Charles V, had been the great standard bearer against the Turks, and that task now fell to Philip.

In 1565, when Philip was still relatively new to the throne, the sultan Suleiman the Magnificent sent an enormous fleet and army to capture Malta. Back in 1522, Suleiman had forced the Knights of Saint John to evacuate the Island of Rhodes in the eastern Mediterranean; they had promptly found a new home on the Island of Malta. The Ottoman Turkish Empire had grown in the meantime, and the Turks found the Knights of Saint John a perpetual thorn in their side. Therefore, Suleiman sent over 200 ships carrying more than 30,000 men. There were fewer than 600 knights present on Malta, and when one counted their men-at-arms and volunteers, the entire defense force did not exceed 5,000.

What did the Turks find when they arrived?

They came in May 1566 and were astonished at how busy the Knights of Saint John had been. Malta was, and is, a natural harbor, but it can be fortified to a much greater degree when one controls the two promontories. Not only had the Knights done so, but they had erected a string of forts, from which bristled cannon.

The Turks landed on the island's southwest side and were able to progress to within a few hundred yards of the defenses before encountering much resistance; once they arrived, however, they found the defenders resolute. One Turkish charge after another was beaten back, and after a week, the Turks settled down to a regular siege. Their labor force was large, and they were able to build siege parallels and forts of their own; within three weeks, they were right up against the edge of the Christians' defenses. That was where the progress stopped, however.

What was it about the Knights of Saint John that made them special?

A combination of grit, fatalism, and the belief that they were defending all of Christian Europe against the infidel made the knights special. Even so, logic suggests that the Turks should have prevailed, when, in fact, each of their attacks was beaten back. On one of the closest of all these occasions, the Turks surged over the battlements of Fort Saint Elmo, and just for a few moments, the Ottoman crescent flag waved over the ramparts. Minutes later, the Knights retook it in a counterattack.

How great were the Turkish losses?

Neither the naval commander nor Suleiman the Magnificent was eager to release casualty figures, but we believe that at least 10,000 Turks died and just as many others were wounded in the six-week siege. The Christian loss was perhaps one-fifth as large.

The Turks might still have taken Malta, but they were too weak to use it for anything that year. They sailed away in September, leaving mounds of dead and giving the Knights of Saint John a reputation for invincibility. Suleiman, predictably, was furious, and he blamed the commanders for their folly.

Was that it for the Mediterranean naval wars?

By no means. The Ottoman Turks never gave up on their dream of turning the Mediterranean into a Turkish lake, filled with Muslim ships and sailors. Knowing this, King Philip II of Spain attempted to organize a crusade against the Turks, and in 1571, his illegitimate half-brother Don John of Austria sailed with a huge fleet from Venice.

When did Suleiman die?

He died in his tent in 1566, while besieging the Christian town of Sizget in Hungary. He had ruled for forty-six years, but, unlike Emperor Charles V, he never seemed to have thought of retirement. For Suleiman, it was perfectly appropriate that he die "with his boots on," meaning in the throes of yet another campaign. He was succeeded by his son Selim, who soon became known as Selim the Sot because of his love of alcohol.

The avowed Christian aim was to defend the Island of Cyprus from Turkish invasion, but there was another, underlying goal: to rout out and destroy the Ottoman fleet. The Turks, too, sailed, with grand ambitions. They wanted Cyprus as the first stage of a naval campaign to take over the entire eastern Mediterranean. The two fleets clashed at Lepanto, off the Gulf of Corinth, on October 10, 1571.

The Christians—who were drawn from nearly all the nations of Western Europe—numbered about 20,000 men aboard 220 oared warships; the Turks—who may have had 30,000 men—had 280 vessels. The Christians had the wind and the tide at their backs, however, and this allowed them to plow into the enemy.

Who was the great hero of the Battle of Lepanto?

Don John of Austria was a terrific commander, assisted by all manner of subordinates, one of whom was the Marquis de Santa Cruz. At the level of the rank and file, one of the notable heroes was Miguel de Cervantes, a Spanish poet and playwright, who later composed *Man of La Mancha: The Story of Don Quixote*. In truth, however, there were heroes all around, and the six-hour battle produced, perhaps, more dead and wounded than any other from the Age of Oars. When the Turks finally broke and fled, they left behind over 200 ships that either sank or were captured; even more importantly, they lost perhaps 10,000 archers, the mainstay of their naval efforts.

THE SPANISH ARMADA

When was Mary executed?

Elizabeth's leading advisers had asked, nearly begged, her to execute her cousin for years, but she always held back from the final step: it was not a good precedent, she declared. When Mary was put on trial at the end of 1586, Elizabeth still demurred, and it took a great deal of arm-twisting by her counselors to persuade her to sign the death

Who was one of the victuallers of the Spanish Armada?

Miguel Cervantes (1547–1616) was a brave, romantic Spanish hero who had been wounded in the head and lost one hand at the Battle of Lepanto; in 1587, he was one of hundreds of men assigned to rounding up food, supplies, even wine for the Armada. It was, quite likely, during his travels across the Spanish heartland that Cervantes developed the ideas that later bore fruit in *Don Quixote*. Cervantes did not fill all his rosters, and he was in prison when the Armada finally sailed in June 1588. Given what happened to many of the soldiers and sailors, he was, perhaps, fortunate to have been left behind.

warrant. On February 18, 1587, Mary, Queen of Scots, was executed (her head was chopped off) at Fotheringay, in central England.

The news spread rapidly, and Pope Sixtus V (ruled 1585–1590) pledged one million ducats to King Philip II for the day on which the first Spanish soldier would land on English soil. Philip had already made his own plans, and Queen Mary's execution was but the final pretext required. Philip made a great show of extolling the dead queen's virtues, but he was most interested in obtaining England and forcing its people to convert to Roman Catholicism.

How many ships and men were proposed for the Spanish Armada?

Spain's greatest admiral, Santa Cruz (1526–1588), was asked to estimate what was required. He came up with a simply fantastic set of numbers; had his recommendation been followed, virtually all the ships from Portugal and Spain would have sailed, carrying most of the coastal population. Philip II rejected this plan as unworkable and came up with an alteration. A large but not enormous Armada would carry many soldiers, perhaps even 20,000, and it would be joined in the English Channel by the Duke of Parma, who had as many as 50,000 under his command. To be sure, the Armada could not carry any more men; Parma's men, therefore, would come out in shallow-draft boats and cross the Channel under the protection of the Armada's guns.

In 1571 a fleet organized by a coalition of European maritime states called the Holy League confronted the sea power of the Ottoman Empire, defeating the Turks and preventing an invasion into Western Europe. (*Combate Naval de Lepanto (7 de octubre de 1571)* by Juan Luna, 1887.

Where did Drake attack?

In the spring of 1587, having won Queen Elizabeth's permission, Drake sailed from Plymouth. He went straight into the big Spanish harbor at Cadiz, attacking fireships, storeships, even some of the great galleons. After destroying roughly fourteen vessels, Drake sailed off to seize Sagres, the promontory on the extreme southwest part of Portugal. Using this as his base, Drake interposed himself between the Spanish and Portuguese fleets, striking terror into the captains of both. His reputation was already significant, but it was around this time that the Spaniards began speaking of the "magic mirror" possessed by Drake, which allowed him to see around the corners of the globe. There were times, it must be said, when he seemed to know it all and to baffle the Spaniards on every front.

Returning to England, Drake expressed his belief that the Armada would not sail in 1587: he had inflicted too much damage. Queen Elizabeth did not do a great deal during the respite Drake afforded her; she knew that in the coming year England's main, and best, defense would continue to be the sailors of the fleet.

Why did the Duke of Medina-Sedonia try to avoid leading the Armada?

As soon as Philip II appointed him, the duke wrote the king, saying that he was a poor sailor and inevitably became seasick. More to the point, he knew little of how to run a fleet. King Philip brushed these objections aside. To him, it was more important that the duke was of a high and noble family and that his organizational skills were well known.

The duke lamented his fate, but soon took up the business of leadership. He arrived in Lisbon to find the so-called Armada a mass of confusion. Whatever his nautical abilities, the duke was, indeed, a true organizer, and within two months he imposed order on the chaos. By May 1588, when the fleet intended to sail, the duke had an actual roster. It showed 134 ships, 19,000 soldiers, 8,500 sailors, 2,400 cannon, and 128,000 cannon balls. Food supplies were not abundant, but they seemed sufficient for the voyage.

When did the Armada set sail?

One delay after another occurred, but the Armada finally departed Lisbon in June 1588. Almost immediately, the difficulties of managing so many ships—ranging from galleons to galleys and from storeships to galleases—became apparent. Because it kept a tight formation, the Armada could not sail any faster than the speed of its slowest-sailing vessel. It took three weeks to get the Armada from Lisbon to the northwest corner of Spain, and by then supplies of fresh water were so low that Medina-Sidonia put the entire fleet into the port at Corunna. The duke sent urgent messages to Philip II, practically begging him to call off the entire enterprise, but the king was adamant. This was the year; this was the time. The entire Armada sailed from Corunna on July 15, 1588.

Is there any truth to the story that Drake was playing a game of bowls?

He may well have been doing something amusing to pass the time, and he may well have said something to the effect that there was enough time to finish the game and beat the Spaniards, too! But even if Drake said this, he knew that the circumstances were dangerous. If the Armada moved into Plymouth Harbor, where the English fleet was at anchor, it could attack them just as severely as Drake had attacked the Spaniards at Cadiz, one year earlier. Luckily for Drake and the English, Medina-Sidonia brought the Armada to anchor that night.

The duke believed he would be able to dictate the terms of battle the next day because he had the weather gauge (meaning that the wind was at his back) but overnight, the English slipped behind him, giving them the weather gauge. Drake and Lord Charles Howard, therefore, began the battle on their terms.

What did the two opposing fleets look like?

The Armada—130 ships strong—was drawn up in a crescent formation, almost as if it was composed of regiments on land. The center of the Armada was immensely strong. The English fleet, composed of about 110 ships, was arrayed much more unevenly, but this was an indication of its ability to maneuver.

Lord Charles Howard began the battle by sending a tiny ship—one of his smallest—out front to fire one cannon shot, an indication of what was to come. The Spaniards

The defeat of the Spanish Armada by the English navy marked a turning point in power. From that year, 1588, the Spanish sun began to set while the English empire would rise for the next three centuries.

hoisted all their battle flags, and the two immense fleets drifted close to each other. Cannonading began. Right from the beginning, there was an audible difference: the English fired almost three times as many rounds as the Spaniards. Not only did they have more cannon balls, but their gunners were far better trained.

Could the Spaniards have won even a partial victory?

Yes. If the Duke of Medina-Sidonia had brushed aside the many orders and commands of King Philip II and acted on what he observed rather than what the orders declared, he could have attempted a landing somewhere on the southwest coast of England. Even if he had lost many ships, he could have gotten about 20,000 men ashore, with little possibility of opposition from that part of England. The duke, who was not trained in naval warfare, stuck resolutely to the battle plan, which was to move slowly toward the English Channel and rendezvous with the Duke of Parma.

For his part, the Duke of Parma was deeply pessimistic; in one letter to Philip II, he declared that "God will grow weary of working miracles for us." Parma had about 30,000 men ready to move, but they were watched, day and night, by the Dutch rebels, who had the only large warships in that area.

What was the first Spanish ship to fall?

A large galleon became separated from the Armada on the first day of battle. Drake pursued it into shoal water and captured it. The fight for that one ship epitomized the Spaniards' problems. They had plenty of men aboard, and most of them were eager to fight, but they could not get at the English, who prudently stayed away and pelted the Spaniards with long- and medium-range cannon balls.

The Armada continued on its path, however slowly, and the English lit beacons all along the coast to warn of its approach. Many English feared that the Armada would attempt to land its men somewhere on the Isle of Wight. Some of Medina-Sidonia's advisers counseled just that, but the duke held to his orders and the Armada sailed past the isle on August 1, 1588. From there on, the Spaniards were in unfamiliar waters while the English captains knew the area extremely well.

Where was Queen Elizabeth at this point?

She was in London, receiving frequent updates. The Armada was near the English Channel, about one hundred miles away, and a series of horsemen, equipped with relay mounts, speedily relayed the news to the queen. Unlike Philip II, she left most of the naval matters to her captains and admirals.

The Duke of Medina-Sidonia sent one urgent message after another to the Duke of Parma, asking if the 30,000 men were ready to move into their shallow-draft boats. Parma received some of the messages, but every time he attempted to send a message of his own, it was intercepted. The Armada was on its own.

What city did the Armada reach?

On August 3, 1588 the Armada staggered into the harbor of Calais, the French city on the coast, just twenty-one miles from Dover. Medina-Sidonia asked the French governor for sanctuary in the inner harbor, but this was refused; the most that the duke could obtain were compliments and baskets of fresh fruit.

Once he was at anchor, the duke sent desperate messages to Parma, but nothing he received gave him any hope. Parma's men could not move until Medina-Sidonia's ships could clear the lower part of the Channel of English ships. As the two dukes attempted to develop a new strategy, the English came up with one of their own. They would use fireships to panic the Armada and break its magnificent formation.

How many fireships were sent into the harbor at Calais?

Calais was actually an open roadstead, affording the Armada no protection from high tides or sudden squalls; even so, it was the closest thing that the Spaniards had to a haven. On the night of August 5, 1588, seven midsized, leaky old English ships were packed with combustibles, including gunpowder, old sails, and all sorts of furniture dried from years at sea and sent in the direction of the Spaniards. To the Spanish lookouts, it seemed as if all hell were breaking loose and headed in their direction.

None of the Spanish ships were actually burned; the crews did a great job getting out of Calais and onto the open sea. To do so, they had to cut their anchors, however, and as many as 200 of these probably still lie at the bottom of the water near Calais. Cutting their lines meant that the Spanish ships could not reform or even hold a strategic position. When dawn came, the English came in for the kill.

How many Spanish ships were lost that day?

Perhaps a dozen were damaged so badly that they later sank. At least twenty more were so badly hurt that they would never sail again. The Spaniards fought heroically, but everything was against them. The English ships were much faster and more maneuverable, and their gunners had really taken the range of the Spaniards. Both sides were low on powder and cannon balls, but the English could—over the course of a few days—replenish their stores while the Spaniards could not.

The Duke of Medina-Sidonia knew that he could not succeed; at this point, he only wanted to save what was left. On the next day—August 7—he dreaded a resumption of the English attack, but the wind carried the Spaniards north. The English, still waiting to replenish their ammunition supply, followed closely but did not attack.

Did Elizabeth make the most of her victory?

She had long been a master at public relations, and on August 23, 1588 she rode to her army camp at Tillbury and delivered one of the best-known speeches of her reign. Speaking directly to the troops, Elizabeth uttered memorable words. She was a woman, she declared, but she had the heart of a king, scorning the idea that Parma, or any other Continental prince, would attempt to invade her realm. The speech was a major success.

What happened to the Armada?

What happened after the battles of July 29 to August 5, 1588 was one terrible event after another. Roughly half of the 130 ships that approached England eventually returned to Spain, but most of them were battered beyond repair. Many others were wrecked on the coasts of northern Scotland and Ireland, with terrible results for the men who came ashore. Even in Catholic Ireland, the Spaniards were, generally, butchered immediately upon arrival. The complete death toll for the Armada came close to 20,000, and these men—the sailors especially—were irreplaceable. When we pose the follow-up question—was the Armada really the disaster that is so often described?—the answer is an unequivocal yes.

Spain—and Portugal, which provided many of the ships—took years to recover from the Armada, but the interesting point is that they did. By about the year 1595, Spanish sea power was back to its pre-Armada strength, and Philip II actually sent a smaller fleet to probe England's defenses in 1596 (this fleet was driven off by autumnal storms). So while there is no doubt that the Armada was a tipping point—with the tip going to England—it is worth remembering that Spain made a strong recovery.

What happened to Sir Francis Drake?

He was lionized in the aftermath of the Armada's defeat, as was his superior officer, Thomas Howard of Effingham. Drake was, by then, the most famous of all Englishmen, and he had become quite wealthy as a result of his numerous privateering voyages. In 1596, Drake and his cousin, John Hawkins, made one last trip to the Caribbean. On this occasion, the Spanish defenses proved tougher than expected. Drake came down with the sweating sickness, and after a short illness he died and was buried at sea.

Many other Elizabethan adventurers died in circumstances like Drake's. They probably preferred it that way: part of their social code was that death in battle was preferable to a slow death by illness or old age. With Drake's death, the greatest of the Elizabethan leaders was gone, and the new generation—while full of fight and vigor—did not have the same opportunities to cause mayhem. The major reasons for this were the peace treaty that was signed with Spain and the death of Queen Elizabeth in 1603.

Was Elizabeth truly the great monarch that her public relations men took such pains to establish?

In many ways she was. Smarter than her father—Henry VIII—and much more clever than her elder half-sister—Mary I—Elizabeth set an enviable standard for kings and queens who followed. On a personal level, she was much less successful. Her vanity and intemperance only grew with the length of her reign, and toward the end she was an irascible, yet feeble, monarch. Elizabeth's great accomplishment was to keep England at peace during the decades of its weakness—roughly 1560–1580—and then to employ England in war when her strength had risen, from 1580 to 1603.

What happened to Philip II?

He died of natural causes in 1598. He had long been secretive and withdrawn; toward the end of his reign, these traits were even more apparent. Philip had striven mightily on behalf of the Spanish Empire, but he—like his father, Emperor Charles V—was pulled in too many directions. Had he addressed the Dutch Revolt and nothing else, he might well have succeeded; had he dropped everything else and addressed only the needs of the Armada, he might have succeeded in 1588.

With the exception of the defeat of his Armada, Philip II of Spain was a successful ruler who led his nation to the greatest extent of its worldwide empire (1556 portrait by Sofonisba Anguissola).

Like Elizabeth, Philip died alone and lonely. It can also be said that, like her, he left Spain much stronger than he found it. It was Spain's misfortune that his successors—Philip III and Philip IV—were less capable and less interested in truly governing the realm.

RELIGIOUS WARS IN FRANCE

We've heard little about France since the time of King Francis I (reigned 1515–1547). Did any major developments take place in that nation after 1547?

Ever since the regency of Queen Catherine de Medici, France had been torn apart by religious wars. Some of this can be laid at the queen's feet, but there were other factors, some of them beyond her control.

The Huguenots (Protestants) were ardent followers of John Calvin rather than Martin Luther, and they exemplified the type of hard-working, upwardly mobile people to whom his doctrines were especially attractive. The Huguenots were, by and large, very useful subjects to the French monarch; they contributed to the economic growth of the kingdom. Unfortunately, religious bigotry, as well as just plain stupidity, led three of Queen Catherine de Medici's sons to oppose them.

Does any one moment, or event, stand out as the worst among many bad ones?

In 1572, thousands of Huguenots left their country estates to celebrate the wedding of Princess Margaret and Prince Henry of Navarre. The former was from the Medici family, and the latter was a Huguenot prince from the south of France. The festivities were well along when Queen Catherine de Medici—influenced by some truly evil advisers—pressured her young son, King Charles IX, to attack the Huguenots. Her decision was based on rumors that the Huguenots intended to attack the royal family, and Catherine argued to reverse the situation. Charles IX set the forces in motion, and on August 24, 1572—Saint Bartholomew's Day—roughly 10,000 Huguenots, many of them from the midlevel nobility, were massacred. This terrible event set the stage of two decades of subsequent religious warfare and was disastrous for France.

What was the War of the Three Henrys?

Henry III, King of France (ruled 1573–1589), was the youngest son of Catherine de Medici and the last French monarch to pursue a policy of extermination of the Huguenots. He was not a bad person, but he suffered from mental illness for many years and was easily led.

Henry, the Duke of Guise (1550–1588), was a prominent Catholic nobleman who organized the Catholic League, whose goal was to stamp out the Huguenots once and for all. The Duke of Guise was a man of great sophistication and charm, but these qualities counted for little if one was on his bad side.

Henry of Navarre (1553–1610), the prince whose wedding had been ruined by the Saint Bartholomew's Day Massacre, was a colorful, charismatic man who fought ardently for the Huguenot cause. Like George Washington—with whom several parallels can be drawn—Henry of Navarre fought a long, sometimes desperate, battle against much greater forces. Unlike George Washington, Henry of Navarre had to make a key, even vital, change in order to triumph in the War of the Three Henrys.

What did Henry of Navarre mean when he said "Paris is worth a mass"?

In 1594, Henry of Navarre publicly abjured his Huguenot faith and became a Roman Catholic. At least half of the countrymen who had previously opposed him now sided with him, but it took another four years before Henry occupied Paris and became King Henry IV (ruled 1598–1610). Whether he ever declared that "Paris is worth a [celebration of the] Mass" is not known, but it has a ring of truth to it: Henry was a worldly man and by this point in his life, rather cynical about matters of faith.

Meanwhile, what had taken place in France?

France had been rent asunder by the Wars of Religion for almost three decades, with Huguenots (Protestants) fighting the Roman Catholic majority. France was on the verge of complete disunion in the early 1590s, but in 1594 Henry of Navarre made a dramatic conversion to Roman Catholicism and was accepted as King Henry IV.

When did Holland achieve political independence from Spain?

Some historians call the entire struggle for Holland's independence the Eighty Years' War, ranging from 1568 to 1648. There were plenty of breaks in the fighting, however, most notably the Twelve Years' Truce, which was instituted in 1609. During the long struggle for independence, the Dutch gained a self-reliance that served them well as they expanded their overseas empire.

What did the political situation look like in 1603, the year of Elizabeth's death?

Spain remained the most powerful of all European nations, but its power was more dependent on New World treasure than ever before. France was, potentially, the strongest of the land powers, but it was in a period of rebuilding and consolidation, under Henry IV. Austria was on the rise, and with each successive ladder that it climbed, the old Holy Roman Empire sank one step further into the dust. Holland was on the rise, especially in a mercantile sense, but it was unlikely that her small population and land base would ever provide a real counterweight to France. And England, though it had become the largest of the maritime and commercial powers, had a very small army.

Virtually all of the major European nations looked to the New World, not for fresh political ideas or utopian communities, but rather for precious raw materials that might provide the answer to the continuing struggles in the Old World.

THE THIRTY YEARS' WAR

Could anyone really fight for that long? Could they even remember why the war started in the first place?

It's an excellent question. Had the war remained strictly between Catholic Austria and Protestant Bohemia—the two powers that began fighting in 1618—the conflict would not have lasted that long. The war lasted much longer, however, and it eventually involved almost every single European national and principality except Russia.

The war started in southeast Europe, broadened to encompass most of the Holy Roman Empire and then expanded to include a naval war between Holland and Spain. Just to make things even more complicated—and slightly absurd!—England and France fought a short war of their own, followed by a separate war between Denmark and Sweden. France held its hand until 1635, but when it finally entered the lists, against Spain, it could be said that almost no one in Eastern *or* Western Europe was unaffected by the Thirty Years' War.

Where did it all begin?

On May 23, 1618, two bureaucrat-diplomats—both serving the interests of the House of Habsburg—stood with their backs to the wall in the high castle overlooking the city of Prague. They served the Holy Roman Emperor, who was a Habsburg, but they were now cornered by an angry mob that included some of the best-known merchants and bureaucrats of Prague. After a short exchange of words, men in the crowd lifted the two diplomats and hurled them out the castle windows (the secretary to one of the men soon followed). All three men survived, in part because they fell into a huge pile of human dung (this episode has been employed by many comics and filmmakers). But the event—known as the Defenestration of Prague—launched the Bohemian Revolt against Catholic Austria and was the beginning of the conflict that lasted for thirty years.

How important was religion in bringing on this titanic war?

Religion was very important, but it was not the whole story or motivation. Economic differences, as well as religious ones, characterized the division between Catholic and Protestant, which was made even worse by the division of Protestants into Calvinist and Lutheran camps. Dynastic rivalries—as between the Habsburgs and Bourbons—also played their roles. It is very difficult to say what lay beneath it all, but it likely that the enormous religious and social revolution begun by Martin Luther in 1517 had its most terrible and dramatic results during the wars of 1618–1648.

Who won the opening phase of the Thirty Years' War?

In the autumn of 1620 the Catholic armies led by Count Tilly defeated the Protestant ones at the Battle of White Mountain, fought in the present-day Czech Republic. King

A 1620 painting by Pieter Snayers of the Battle of White Mountain, the opening salvo of the Thirty Years' War pitting Protestants against Catholics.

Ferdinand of Bohemia had to flee his country (he went into exile in Holland). The Catholic cause seemed triumphant, especially when its armies occupied the southern half of the Holy Roman Empire. That type of success, naturally, inflamed Protestant angers and fears, and a backlash began. Most important, however, was the addition of the Dutch–Spanish War, which commenced in 1621.

Hadn't the Dutch and Spaniards been at each others' throats since 1568?

They had indeed, but a twelve-year truce had been negotiated in 1609. Spain and Holland watched each other nervously during those years, and in the spring of 1621—the same season that King Philip III died and was succeeded by his son, King Philip IV—the two countries went to war with each other again.

Which of these two countries was more ready for a resumption of war?

The Spaniards still held all the external advantages: more men, more ships, and potentially more wealth. Spain was weary from war and deprivation, however, and the Dutch were fast catching up in certain regards. During the 1590s, the Dutch army was reorganized under the leadership of Prince Maurice of Nassau. The Dutch were the first to center their forces around large bodies of musketeers and to make effective use of both the pike and sword.

When the war began, the Spaniards pressed the initiative against the United Provinces of the Netherlands (usually known as Holland). Their forces were already in modern-day Belgium, and they were steadily reinforced by forces that marched north along the so-called Spanish Road. By 1625, the Spaniards had the advantage, and when the fortified city of Breda capitulated (an event depicted in a major painting by the Spanish artist Velasquez) it seemed that Spain might eventually reconquer the Netherlands.

Where, meanwhile, was England? Did its people care about the contest between Spain and Holland?

They certainly did. Not only were the majority of them Protestants, but Princess Elizabeth—often called the "Winter Queen"—was married to King Frederick of Bohemia. King James I had given his daughter's hand to this Continental price before the war began. King James wanted to keep out of the war while funneling economic aid to his son-in-law. To be sure, some Englishmen crossed the Channel to serve as volunteers for the Protestant cause. The single most surprising event, however, had to do with love, rather than war.

In the winter of 1623, Prince Charles of England (1600–1649) and his bosom friend George Villiers, the Duke of Buckingham (1592–1628), dressed up as Jack and Tom Smith and crossed the Channel to get to Spain. They arrived in Madrid, unannounced, and declared their desire to see the Spanish princess, whom Charles wished to marry. The Spanish court, which was much more concerned with protocol than its England counterpart, was both astonished and put out by the sudden appearance of these Englishmen. After almost four months, Jack and Tom Smith were sent home. They went laden with gifts, but Prince Charles long remembered their reception in Spain as an insult, and both he and the Duke of Buckingham oriented English policy against Spain.

How did the Danes and Swedes become involved in the Thirty Years' War?

Both were predominantly Lutheran nations, and their kings watched with alarm as the Catholic cause—led by the Austrian Habsburgs—threatened to take over all of the Holy Roman Empire. In 1625, King Christian IV of Denmark invaded the northern part of the empire, turning what had been a relatively quiet season into one of great storms (figuratively speaking). The Spanish army was not large, but it arrived at just the moment where it could tip the balance, and Emperor Ferdinand II, therefore, turned to someone he had previously held at arm's length.

Who was Count von Wallenstein?

Count Albrecht von Wallenstein (1583–1634) remains the single most controversial figure from the entire Thirty Years' War. Born to a family of minor Bohemian nobles, Wallenstein was raised Protestant, but religion does not seem to have figured very much in his calculations. He was, above all, a soldier, but he was also a military organizer of the highest capacity. When Emperor Ferdinand summoned him, Count Wallenstein pledged to field 40,000 men and keep them in the field as long as necessary. Given the conditions of warfare in Germany, this was an enormous commitment.

Wallenstein was not the first general to have his men wear uniforms, but he regulated the practice more thoroughly than his predecessors. He was also not the first to employ mercenaries, but he kept them in combat and on the march much longer than any of his contemporaries. Many German nobles complained to emperor Ferdinand, saying that Wallenstein intended to dethrone him and become a dictator, but the emperor kept him for much the same reason that U.S. President Abraham Lincoln would later keep General Grant in command: the man was relentless, and he succeeded where others had failed.

Is it true that Wallenstein had his astrological horoscope made and that he took it seriously?

Not only did Wallenstein have his astrological chart made, but it was prepared by the greatest astronomer of the day. Tycho

Portrait of Count Albrecht Wenzel Eusebius von Wallenstein, the supreme commander of the Habsburg armies during the Thirty Years' War.

> ## Was there still a Holy Roman Empire at the time of the Thirty Years' War?
>
> The name had been altered to the *Holy Roman Empire of the German Nation*, which, at least, acknowledged that the Germans had something to do with the matter. The empire still figured on all the maps and in the calculations. It is true, however, that many of the noblemen and leading clergy of the empire acted rather as they pleased. Some of them feared that Wallenstein would deliver victory to Emperor Ferdinand and that he in turn would change the loose structure of the empire.

Brahe was a brilliant scientist who had a wonderful laboratory, thanks to the king of Denmark. Shortly before the Thirty Years' War began, Tycho Brahe worked up Wallenstein's horoscope, and while we may not wish to give great credence to the chart, it did contain words and phrases of interest. The subject was "of restless and military character," the chart declared, and he would never stay in one place for long.

If the Austrians, Germans, Dutch, and Spaniards were now involved, who had managed—so far—to stay out of the Thirty Years' War?

Russia had stayed out, and would continue to do so, but the Republic of Poland-Lithuania was about to be drawn in. France had stayed out so far, but it was about to fight the English along the Atlantic coast. Switzerland was not officially involved, but many of its men were mercenaries, serving one of the different sides in the contest. Only England and Russia, the nations at the two extremities of Europe, stayed out of the conflict completely.

What was the peak of Wallenstein's success?

By 1629 Wallenstein had practically cleared southern and central Germany of Protestant forces. He was not a religious bigot, and the Protestant peoples of Germany were not harmed, at least not on account of their religion. The fear existed, however, that Emperor Ferdinand would now use Wallenstein as a cleansing agent, to sweep all Protestants out of the Holy Roman Empire.

Emperor Ferdinand had troubles of his own, especially complaints from his leading nobles. At their insistence, he dismissed Wallenstein in 1629, at precisely the wrong moment. Emperor Ferdinand did not realize that a new phase of the Thirty Years' War was about to begin.

How large a figure was King Gustavus Adolphus?

He was one of those people who seem larger than life. He was tall, blond, and passably good looking, but it was his sheer physical energy that really drew people to him. In

July 1630, King Gustavus landed in northern Germany. He had fewer than 10,000 Swedish soldiers, but they were among the best troops of their time: battle-hardened and far better equipped than their foes. Like the Austrian soldiers, the Swedes used the matchlock musket, but their flints were better. Like the Dutch, they fought in formations that emphasized the use of cannon, foot soldiers, and cavalry, but the Swedes far excelled the Dutch in the use of artillery. And, unlike every other nation in the Thirty Years' War, the Swedes had their monarch to lead them in person.

Gustavus Adolphus won a handful of skirmishes and proceeded south. He met the army of the Austrian Habsburgs in October 1631 and smashed them at the Battle of Breitenfeld, in central Germany. The Austrians lost 7,000 killed and almost 10,000 taken prisoner. Gustavus Adolphus was now the champion of the Protestant cause, and money was sent to him by all the Protestant powers. He seemed ready to sweep all the way to Vienna.

The war has such a zigzag feel. What did the Austrians do at this point?

Emperor Ferdinand recalled Count von Wallenstein. Ferdinand had no choice. Wallenstein was the only man with a military reputation equal to Gustavus Adolphus. For the next six months, the Catholic and Lutheran armies maneuvered and countermaneuvered, with the Lutherans generally gaining the advantage. And when the two armies met in battle, at Lutzen, the Lutherans again prevailed. Their victory was impressive, if not as shattering at that of Breitenfeld, but in the very hour of victory, King Gustavus Adolphus fell from a musket ball. The impact of their victory was blunted, and, without their monarch to inspire them, the Swedes soon began to lose heart.

What happened to Wallenstein?

He was recognized for his good services. Even though he had lost at Lutzen, Wallenstein had fought well enough that the Swedes did not advance on Vienna. In 1634, however, Wallenstein was assassinated. Whether Emperor Ferdinand II had anything to do with his death remains a mystery.

Meanwhile, what had happened with the Spanish–Dutch War?

1625 was the "miracle year" so far as the Spaniards were concerned. They captured Breda in the Netherland, turned back a Dutch invasion force, and made headway in sending troops up the "Spanish Road." If it were strictly a matter of men and ships, the Spaniards would have prevailed, but money played a significant role throughout the Thirty Years' War. And the Dutch, knowing this, carried out one of the major coups of the century when they captured the Spanish silver fleet.

What was the single biggest haul, from a privateer's point of view, of the entire seventeenth century?

In the summer of 1628, the Spanish silver fleet sailed from Mexico. The annual fleet was always very important to Spain, but this year's "flota" carried even more silver for the Spanish mint than usual, and the precious metal was desperately needed. Dutch admiral Piet Heyn (1577–1629) had long planned for this moment, and he descended on the silver fleet as it lay in harbor at Matanzaz Bay in Cuba. Von Piet captured all the Spanish treasure ships, and the silver benefitted the Dutch, rather than Spanish, economy. Nor was that all. The Spaniards fell behind in their payments to international banking houses, and the Spanish monarchy went bankrupt.

It seems as if everyone was fighting, but no one was benefitting. Is this true?

On the level of soldiers, peasants, and workers, this was most certainly the case. Ninety percent or more of all the common folk of all the nations involved in the war would have gladly given up the contest. Among the European elites, there were just enough people, perhaps less than five percent of the total population, who did benefit from the war, and it was to their advantage to see the thing continue. Among them were families involved in international banking, such as the Fuggers and Medici, but there were also families involved in the forging of arms. Among them was the Krupp family of Germany, whose reputations as arms-makers would continue well into the twentieth century.

When did France enter the war?

Cardinal Richelieu, who was the real power behind the throne of King Louis XIII, made that decision in the spring of 1635. France entered the war as a belligerent against Spain, but by doing so it incurred the wrath of the Austrian Habsburgs as well. France was not as well prepared as Cardinal Richelieu believed, and the ensuing five years saw numerous Spanish victories over the French forces. Even so, the sheer weight of the nations and peoples was not tipped against the Austrian and Spanish Habsburgs.

If a cardinal was the main force in France, then who was the big power in Spain?

King Philip IV was a well-intentioned man who was more interested in pretty women, good songs, and magnificent art—as shown by his sponsorship of Diego de Velazquez—than in governing the nation. During the late stages of the Thirty Years' War, Spain was effectively ruled by the

Armand Jean du Plessis, Cardinal-Duke of Richelieu and of Fronsac, was a formidable figure in the Catholic Church. He served as chief minister under King Louis XIII of France. When it came to policy, Richelieu was the power behind the throne (portrait by Philippe de Champaigne).

Count-Duke Olivares. A shrewd, aggressive person, Olivares bet that Spain could outfight its enemies and force them to the peace table; as a realist, he knew it was essential to do so before Spain ran out of money entirely. He, therefore, began planning the launch of yet another Armada, this time directed against Holland rather than England.

How large was the Spanish Armada of 1638?

Vice Admiral Antonio de Oquendo had about thirty warships and forty transport vessels. He had 6,000 sailors, 8,000 maries, and 9,000 soldiers to bring to the Army of Flanders. That he was able to marshal all these forces and bring them to the English Channel attests to how well Spain had recovered from the Armada of 1588. But he was opposed to the Dutch, who knew the waters better, and to an admiral who was relentless.

What was the fighting like?

In mid-September 1638, the Spanish Armada entered the Channel and encountered the Dutch fleet. In number of ships, the Dutch had the advantage; in number of cannon aboard those ships, the Spanish were ahead. A furious cannonade ensued, with Oquendo showing great personal bravery, but he was not good at communicating with his subordinates. As a result, Oquendo's flagship was nearly forced onto a group of rocks. He fended off his attackers that day, and the following day he led the whole Armada into English waters, off the coast of Kent. The English showed up in record time, but they were interested only in maintaining their own neutrality.

After nearly a month in English waters, the Spanish fleet came out, but in the cannonades that followed it was obvious that the Dutch were winning. The Spanish ships fled to the coast of Flanders. Most of them reached it in safety, but there was no invasion of Holland that year. The Dutch had effectively made themselves masters of the Channel.

Where, by this point, was the conflict in the Holy Roman Empire?

It had degenerated in the worst sense of the word. Rather than real armies marching back and forth, trying to obtain real objectives, the Lutheran, Calvinist, and Catholic forces simply marched throughout the empire, living off the land. It was at this time that the growing of potatoes became more popular in Germany because the underground plants were not readily observable to the soldiers, who acted ever more like scavengers.

This last, sad, part of the conflict within Germany has been aptly described in *Simpliccisum*. Penned by a young man who was forced into one army, which he then deserted to join another, *Simpliccisum* is one of the most accurate depictions of war at its worst. Many Germans, indeed, believe that the horrors of the Thirty Years' War have not been equaled since, not even during World War II of 1939–1945.

Where was the conflict by the 1640s?

Forces still threatened each other within the Holy Roman Empire, but the main battles were now between Catholic France and Catholic Spain. There were endless maneuvers and countermaneuvers with each side trying to control the mountain passes of the Pyrenees, but the final, decisive battle took place in Flanders. The Battle of Rocroi, fought in May 1643, showed the passing of the military torch from Spain to France.

Until that day (May 12, 1643) the Spanish infantry had seldom, if ever, been decisively beaten. The famed *tercios*—the equivalent of modern-day regiments—were known for their staying power and cohesiveness. The French won the Battle of Rocroi with a major cavalry sweep to one side, demonstrating the weaknesses of the Spanish tercios in the light of new technologies. Spain had kept roughly the same military setup for more than a century, and as a result, everything came crashing down around its ears in the weeks and months following the Battle of Rocroi.

Where else had Spanish power failed?

Spain lost at sea in the Battle of the Downs in 1638. It lost on land at the Battle of Rocroi in 1643. In between those two disasters was yet another setback: the Portuguese revolt that began in 1640.

Portugal had been independent until 1580, when Spain took over in the wake of the death of King Sebastian I. Portugal had, ever since, been part of the Spanish Empire, the part that provided many of the galleons and merchant vessels for Spain's overseas enterprises. Weary of the Thirty Years' War and the many sacrifices, Portugal revolted in 1640 and had won de facto independence by 1643.

What did people of that time say about the decline of Spain?

It was like the fall of a giant tree, many people said. Spain had soared during the sixteenth century and had come close—at certain moments—to taking over much of Europe. Ultimately it failed because of an inability to combine economic and military strength. Some of this was beyond the control of any leader; no one knew, for example, that the practice of sheepherding would—over time—lead to deforestation until it was too late.

Then, too, a fatalism prevailed at the highest levels of the Spanish government. With the notable exception of Count-Duke Olivares, the Spanish leaders shrugged off painful defeats, saying that they were the will of God. Had Olivares been leader of the Spanish court two generations earlier, he might have made all the difference.

When did the Thirty Years' War finally come to an end?

Delegates from the various nations met at the free city of Westphalia, within the Holy Roman Empire, as early as 1645, but they got nowhere for a long time. Almost none of the contestants who had started the war back in 1618 were still in power, and almost no one could trace the labyrinth of causes and aftereffects that turned a war between Bohemia and Austria into a calamitous disaster for the entire Holy Roman Empire.

When a series of treaties were finally signed in the summer and autumn of 1648, the war finally ended. Almost no one inside of Germany could be called a winner. Estimates of the death toll range from six to eight million. The great majority of these were civilians, who had been manhandled or stolen from by marauding groups of mercenary soldiers. The death toll on the various battlefields was small compared to the number who died from illness, disease, and downright starvation.

Did anyone benefit from this terrible war?

Perhaps the Dutch. Holland had fought a total of nearly eighty years for its political independence, and this was finally assured by the Peace of Munster. Almost all of the other nations and peoples would—if questioned—have admitted that the war was a terrible disaster.

What did it mean for the Renaissance and Reformation?

As noted earlier, it is difficult to "pin" major movements like the Renaissance and Reformation to specific dates. But if we take Martin Luther's declarations in 1517 as the beginning of the Reformation, then we might say that its energies had petered out by 1648. All too many people had witnessed the horrible things which could be done in the name of following the "right" religion.

And for the Renaissance, if we take the placement of Michelangelo's statue of David in the center of the city of Florence as one of the high points of the Renaissance, then we have to say that its energies, too, had practically disappeared by 1648. One specific place, or spot, we can point to as a meeting ground between the Renaissance and Reformation is the building of St. Peter's Basilica in Rome. It was to raise funds for this construction that indulgences began to be sold in Germany, infuriating Martin Luther, who then posted his Ninety-Five Theses on the church door. St. Peter's was finally finished in 1633, marking the end of yet another great architectural achievement. That the completion took place during the Thirty Years' War only adds to the irony.

THE ENLIGHTENMENT: 1648 TO 1763

What is meant by the name "The Enlightenment"?

It means many things to many people but when we look back at the period from 1650 to 1750, we generally say that a new belief in human reason appeared and that the philosophers and scientists of that time cast a new "light" on the human experience. In England, the Enlightenment was personified by the great scientist Sir Isaac Newton; in Germany it was represented by the scientist Gottfried Leibniz and in France, the philosopher Voltaire. America had few philosophers at that time—life was too demanding!—but Benjamin Franklin qualified, by the end of his long life, as the foremost American representative of the Enlightenment.

The Enlightenment found a place in the annals of war as well as the halls of academia. More military treatises were penned and published than ever before, and a new belief that there was a science to war developed. In Europe, this led to smaller standing armies, composed of better-trained soldiers; in America, it led to the creation of citizen militias that could be summoned with great speed. One thing that really stands out, however, is the new literary quality of the soldier. Whether he was in Flanders, Austria, or North America, the soldier had more reading material and was more conversant with literary types.

Which country was the first to witness the "Enlightenment style" of warfare?

France, under Louis XIV (ruled 1643–1715), built its armies to new heights. France also found a magnificent military engineer, Sebestre de Vauban (1633–1707), who believed that the building of fortifications was the way to ensure success in war. England, however, pulled ahead of France and all other rivals, thanks to the enormous bloodbath known as the English Civil War of 1642–1649. Not for the last time did a nation suffer great internal agony only to emerge stronger at the conclusion.

King Charles I (ruled 1625–1649) was a true believer in the doctrine of Divine Right. He believed he was chosen by God to be king of Great Britain and that no power on earth

143

could gainsay him. Numerous other European monarchs believed the same, but they were smart enough not to talk about it as much. Then, too, King Charles had, in his English people, a rather literate population, composed of contentious people who cared both about the affairs of the political day *and* its effect on their pocketbooks.

Why was "Ship Money" so important?

King Charles had a devil of a time trying to raise money. He sent Parliament home in 1629, but found that lacking the House of Commons' consent, he could not raise taxes. King Charles, therefore, tried something new: he called for "Ship Money" toward the construction of new ships and extended the tax beyond the coastal communities of England. Previous Ship Money collections had been restricted to towns that bordered the coast.

Louis XIV of France led his country into a halcyon period of art, culture, and political power (1701 painting by Hyacinthe Rigaud).

King Charles' revenue enhancement was challenged in court. The Ship Money tax survived the legal challenge, but the English people became distrustful of their monarch. When King Charles finally summoned a new Parliament in 1641, he found its leaders obdurate: they would agree to no new taxes until he committed, in writing, to their rights and privileges. In a desperate measure, the king came before the House of Commons and attempted to arrest five members of that body. They had already fled, and King Charles stood, red-faced, while his royal authority was more imperiled than ever. The Civil War began a few weeks later.

Where do we get the names "Roundheads" and "Cavaliers"?

To be a Cavalier meant that one was a horseman, and, presumably, a member of the upper class. As such, a Cavalier would usually support King Charles. The Cavaliers became known for the length of their hair, and many block prints and newsletters showcased them as daring cavalrymen who supported the king. The Parliamentary opposition was represented by soldiers, more often on foot, who purposely chose to cut their hair short. The "Roundheads" became the bulwark of the Parliamentary cause.

There was, as well, a religious component to the war and clothing styles. The King's men tended to be members of the High Church, the one established by King Henry VIII a century earlier. The Parliamentary armies had plenty of High Church men in the ranks, but the leaders tended to be stiff-necked Puritans, personified by none other than Oliver

> ## How did the American colonists feel about the civil war back "home" in England?
>
> **M**ost of them lamented that it ever came to pass. To them, it seemed a terrible shame that the English motherland went through such political and military turmoil. At the same time, however, there were American Puritans who claimed that the English Civil War was just the beginning and that the apocalypse, foreseen by their parents and grandparents, was now in full swing. This idea remained strong on both sides of the Atlantic until 1666—the year identified with the Devil—came and went.

Cromwell (1599–1658). Over time, the close-cropped head of the Parliamentary foot soldier became identified with the dissenters who had established the Puritan church on both sides of the Atlantic Ocean.

Who won the major battles?

The Battle of Edgehill, where the war kicked off, was a draw, but the strengths and limitations of both sides were shown. When there were cavalry clashes, the King's Cavaliers, led by Prince Rupert of the Rhine, usually prevailed; in a straightforward slugfest of infantry, the Parliamentary forces won almost every time. Edgehill also confirmed Parliamentary control of the City of London. King Charles' forces made Oxford the center of their military camps.

In 1644, Oliver Cromwell, who had recently become a general, trained a group of Parliamentary cavalry so intensively that they became the equal, perhaps the superior, of the King's Cavaliers. Cromwell took these men north where they won the Battle of Marston Moor, defeating Prince Rupert in the field. By then, General Thomas Fairfax, commander-in-chief of the Parliamentary forces, had drilled and trained the infantry to a state of perfection, and he and Cromwell won the climactic Battle of Naseby in 1645.

What happened to King Charles after he lost the Civil War?

Taken prisoner in 1645, the king remained defiant. He even tried to persuade Scotland to intervene on his behalf, smuggling money north and across the border. Not until the beginning of 1649 did Oliver Cromwell and a handful of other Parliamentary leaders come to the painful conclusion that the king must die. Had they expressed it in those words, the people would surely have said "no," but Cromwell cleverly put the king on trial, and he was found guilty of crimes against the state.

To King Charles, this was absurd. He was the state: he embodied the kingdom of Great Britain. Enough Parliament men agreed with the notion of divine kingship that Cromwell became nervous. He hurried the proceedings, and, with the use of much arm-twisting, he

145

Charles I (left) was an arrogant ruler, feeling he could do no wrong as King of England; his policies led to the English Civil War, led by Oliver Cromwell (right).

got fifty-nine men to sign the king's death warrant. On January 30, 1649, King Charles I had his head cut off in front of the Banqueting House in downtown London.

Had this ever been done before? It doesn't sound very "enlightened"?

No, the action had no precedent. There were plenty of revolts and rebellions during the Middle Ages, but never had a solemn body of representatives sentenced a king to death, much less had the sentence carried out. King Charles' death shook the entire European community, and it can be said that it influenced many revolutionaries, or would-be revolutionaries, of the next century.

Did Parliament then become the supreme power in the land?

Technically it was, but Oliver Cromwell was well on the way to becoming England's dictator. In 1653, he sent the last members of Parliament home and took the title of Lord Protector. It must be said that Cromwell was a rather good chief executive, especially where military affairs were concerned. During his short period as Lord Protector, England seized Jamaica from Spain and began a series of military actions that led to the British Army being more respected in other nations.

When Cromwell died of natural causes in 1658, people tried to make his son Richard into his successor, but the son was nothing like the father. Richard Cromwell was, therefore, allowed to retire quietly to his farm, while the son of the man who had so recently been executed was invited to return. Prince Charles became King Charles II.

Was there a general exhaustion throughout the kingdom?

There was indeed an exhaustion with military matters. King Charles II realized this, and he made no sudden or aggressive moves against other nations. The King was keen to build up his military, however, and the English port at Tangiers, Morocco became the training ground for his officer corps. Many of the governors and lieutenant-governors who went to the American colonies over the next two generations were either Tangier-trained officers or their sons. At about the same time, the crimson colors of the British soldier became better known.

At some point either in Cromwell's time as Lord Protector or early in the reign of King Charles II—it is difficult to say in which—the red coat became synonymous with the British soldier. This had not previously been the case; there had been no standard uniform, and perhaps it was the tumult of the English Civil War that brought about the change. There is no doubt, however, that the scarlet uniform of the British officer and his regiment became well near identical with the power of Old England *and* the growing British Empire.

Did other nations adopt similarly clear signs of identification?

Never quite as successfully. The French had long employed a mixture of blue and white, but it never became as thoroughly recognized as the British scarlet. The Austrian soldier typically dressed in gray, but so did the Prussian, leading to a lot of confusion when those two nations went to war. Spain and Holland had finally ceased fighting each other with the Peace of Westphalia in 1648, but both nations used orange and yellow, emphasizing sometimes one color and sometimes another. Therefore, the red coats of the British forces were the easiest to identify.

Were there other changes in the works or in the regiments?

The regiment itself was fairly new: it had been popularized by the Spanish armies of King Philip II. The idea that a captain commanded a company and that a colonel commanded the regiment, with a brigadier-general being responsible for the operations of the brigade, were all ideas that were established during the seventeenth century. The weapons, too, were in the process of change.

Was there yet what we today would call a "military-industrial complex"?

No. Gun-making and the forging of swords and cannon were still in the hands of private enterprise, and there were no massive subsidies such as the ones enjoyed by arms-makers of our world today. A new set of wars, however, including the War of the Spanish Succession and the War of the Austrian Succession, would push some of the gun-makers into producing larger quantities of weapons.

Right up through the English Civil War, the sword and pike were at least as important as the musket and bayonet. One reason is that the blunderbuss musket, lit by a slow-burning fuse, was both slow and unreliable. Once gun-makers turned out flintlock muskets, where the flint struck the powder in the pan to ignite the explosion, the gun and bayonet began to replace the pike and sword. These changes nearly all took place in Europe, but it was in North America that they were put to the test. The change from the harquebus to the flintlock practically doomed most of the Indian tribes of America's east coast.

THE RISE OF FRANCE

How much more populous was France than its neighbors?

France had been held back by many matters—including the sixteenth-century Wars of Religion—but by the mid-seventeenth century, it was nearing a new height, especially as far as military power was concerned. There were about twenty million French, compared to seven million Spaniards, six million English, and about fifteen million Germans. Only Russia, which was too distant to influence events, could compare to France in terms of manpower.

How did Louis XIV become the preeminent monarch of the late seventeenth century?

Louis XIV (reigned 1643–1715) and France had the largest population, the biggest national treasury, and plenty of ambition. Louis had a penchant for war, but his was not the kind of overwhelming ambition that knew no bounds: his real desire was to round off what he considered the "natural boundaries" of France: the Alps, the Rhine, and the Rhone rivers.

The first of Louis' wars was against the Dutch. He started the war in 1672 and came close to taking the whole province, but was thwarted when William of Orange (1650–1701), the hereditary *stadholder* (magistrate), opened the dykes and flooded the countryside rather than see it conquered. The War of Devolution, as it was called, ended in 1678 with France gaining ground, but falling far short of the goal of taking the United Provinces of the Netherlands.

What was different about the French army of the 1670s and 1680s?

Perhaps most important, it was a truly national army. During the late seventeenth century, nearly all the major European nations hired mercenaries out of necessity. Because of France's large population, Louis XIV was able to develop a national army, dominated by Frenchmen and the use of the French language.

When did the Indian wars in America begin?

The Pequot War (1636–1637) assured that the white English people would take over in southern New England, while King Philip's War (1675–1676) assured that the towns

The Pequot War between English settlers and Native Americans was the first major conflict in what would be a long string of wars between Europeans and native peoples. The fighting from 1636 to 1637 forced the Indians to retreat into French-Canadian territory.

and settlements in Massachusetts and Maine would endure. The Indian threat, from the white settlers' point of view, did not disappear, however, because many of the Indians sought refuge with the French in Canada.

Even so, peace might have been maintained were it not for the introduction of war from Europe. In 1688, Prince William of Orange and Princess Mary, his English-born wife, overthrew her father, King James II. The English people were dismayed by King James' Roman Catholicism, and when his Italian-born wife, the very Catholic Mary of Modena, gave birth to a son, Old England practically begged Prince William of Orange to invade. In November 1688, William landed 14,000 Dutch and German troops in England's West Country and began a slow, nearly bloodless, procession to London.

Why would this European conflict bring about war in North America?

The answer is complex. William was Dutch, and many Dutch men and women lived in the New York colony. Queen Mary II was English, decidedly so, and the English people welcomed her and her Dutch husband to become the new king and queen. Finally, perhaps most importantly, King Louis XIV gave aid and sanctuary to the deposed King James II. Putting all these together, it was nearly inevitable that there would be war in North America.

The French struck the first blow. In the winter of 1690, war parties from Quebec and Montreal came south to devastate three communities: Schenectady, New York; Salmon Falls, New Hampshire; and Portland, Maine. Schenectady suffered the worst, but all three towns suffered the loss of many people, who were taken captive to French Canada.

Were the American colonies able to work together at this early stage of their development?

They nearly pulled it off. In May 1690, the first intercolonial congress was held in Manhattan, and it was decided to invade French Canada from both "ends," geographically speaking. The New York contingent, with some Mohawk Indian allies, never made it past the head of Lake Champlain because of smallpox in the ranks. The Massachusetts force, which sailed from Boston in August, reached the outskirts of Quebec City but was rebuffed in a one-week series of brush fights. The colonists had come tantalizingly close, however, and they had done so without any help from the English motherland.

Did much else happen during what we call "King William's War"?

The American colonists named the war thus in honor of the Dutch prince who had conquered England and thereby insured the continuation of the Protestant religion in that nation. The Europeans called it the War of the League of Augsburg, or sometimes the Nine Years' War. When all was said and the last musket had been fired, the two sides agreed to return to each other all the territories which had been seized or conquered.

King William's War was hardly the end of the matter, though. Britain and France continued to vie for the top position in Europe, while their colonists and the Native American tribes jockeyed for dominance on the other side of the ocean. And when Spain's King Carlos II died in 1700, the road was paved for another transatlantic war.

How about the war in Europe?

The casualties were far larger than in America, with France and England contesting for forts in the Dutch Netherlands. Neither side accomplished very much, but given that the war lasted nine years, it is quite possible that 100,000 people were killed or dislocated. The single most important action, however, was seen as a small one at the time. This was the Battle of the Boyne, fought on July 1, 1690.

James II—who had been ejected from the throne of England—was in Ireland with an army of about 12,000, a mixture of French and Irish. William of Orange, who had rejected his father-in-law, arrived in Ireland with about 15,000 men, a mixture of English, Irish, Dutch, and Germans. William won the Battle of the Boyne, named for the river that flowed between the two armies at the engagement's beginning, and James II soon fled Ireland. As a result, William of Orange extended English rule to all of Ireland and made certain that the northernmost towns—known today as Ulster—were thoroughly Protestant.

What did the Peace of Ryswick decide?

Virtually all the nations involved were exhausted, and the Peace of Ryswick, signed in the Dutch town of that name, simply returned all territories to the nation which had possessed them before the war began in 1689.

Why was the death of the Spanish king such a large affair?

King Carlos II had been in poor health for many years, but the critical point was that he had no heir: no children of either sex. Spain, and all its overseas possessions, therefore, were very much up for grabs, and both Britain and France wished to claim the prize.

William of Orange—King William III of England— deposed King James II, the last of the Catholic kings to rule over England, in what is called the Glorious Revolution of 1688. William also battled Louis XIV of France.

Louis XIV, the King of France, had a claim based on marriages: he was a brother-in-law of the deceased Carlos II. Leopold VI, Austrian monarch and Holy Roman Emperor, had an even better claim, based on the relationship of cousins. England, however, which had no dynastic claim, was very much involved. William of Orange—who was now King William III of England—gathered a coalition of European nations with the express purpose of denying the Spanish throne to Louis XIV.

When did the War of the Spanish Succession commence?

A compromise seemed to have been reached. Philip of Anjou, the grandson of King Louis XIV, would become king of Spain under the condition that the two thrones of France and Spain would never be united in the same person (monarch). The agreement fell through, however, when Louis XIV seized forts in the Spanish Netherlands. William of Orange

151

died after a fall from his horse and was unable to lead the Grand Alliance, but his efforts bore fruit, nevertheless.

England, Holland, Bavaria, and Austria were soon allied against France and Spain. The early battles ranged all across Western Europe, with smaller events taking place in North America. One major difference from the previous conflict—King William's War— is that the northernmost parts of Europe became involved in a war of their own.

What, meanwhile, happened in the War of the Spanish Succession?

England captured Gibraltar from Spain in 1703, meaning that British ships would control the entrance to the Mediterranean Sea. One year later, John Churchill, the first Duke of Marlborough (1650–1722), won a stunning victory over the French at the Battle of Blenheim, in Austria. These victories meant that England had the upper hand, and it soon pushed this advantage further, threatening to invade France.

Not only did France suffer defeats on the battlefield, but its finances, even its supplies, were in a desperate condition. The winter of 1709, perhaps the worst of the eighteenth century, created havoc with the French food supply, and the kingdom was in very bad shape. Louis XIV therefore negotiated with the Allies, only to be told that he must drive his grandson, Philip of Anjou, off the throne of France. That was too much by far: Louis resolved to fight on.

We often hear of John Churchill—an ancestor of Winston Churchill—and his great victories. What was so different about the battles in the War of the Spanish Succession?

The casualty lists were much longer than in earlier wars. The flintlock musket and the use of the bayonet had a lot to do with it. So did the stakes involved. Unlike earlier wars, which were created by monarchs and prime ministers, the War of the Spanish Succession devolved into a truly national war, with Frenchmen and Englishmen hating each other. Dutchmen and Spaniards had long detested each other, and Austrians and French now had a profound animosity. When one adds the volatile mix generated by the Great Northern War (Russians and Swedes hating each other), it becomes obvious that the War of the Spanish Succession had as much to do with feeling on the local level as with decisions made by the monarchs involved.

Did the fighting in North America parallel the savagery shown in Europe?

In some ways it was even worse. In February 1704, a French and Indian war party attacked Deerfield, Massachusetts. They took 110 white, English captives, many of whom were later ransomed by their families. The Anglo-American settlers struck back with raids of their own and encouraged the Six Nations of Iroquois to do the same.

In 1709, the governor of New York colony and the mayor of Albany decided to ask Old England for help. Given that the English crown had turned down earlier requests, the colonial Americans buttressed this one by sending four Mohawk chieftains to London. Known to Londoners as the "Four American Kings," these woodland chieftains became the rage of the metropolis. They had a formal audience with Queen Anne, who favored their petition to send an army and fleet to join with them and wipe out French Canada for once and all.

How much was Old England willing to do to help the colonists and their Indian allies?

In 1711, Rear Admiral Sir Hovenden Walker sailed from England with a large fleet and about 5,000 red-coated British soldiers. He picked up roughly 3,000 colonial soldiers in Boston, and the Anglo-American force sailed for Quebec City. The overland expedition, meanwhile, fell apart, much as had happened in 1690.

In August 1711, the Anglo-American fleet ran on reefs on the north side of the St. Lawrence River. Seven ships sank, and over 700 men were drowned. Plenty of others were there to take their places, but Admiral Walker had seen enough. Returning to Boston, he disembarked the colonial troops and then sailed for Old England. Shortly after his arrival, his flagship, the HMS *Edgar*, blew up in Portsmouth Harbor. It was a fitting culmination to an expedition where nearly everything had gone wrong.

Was there any energy left for a final campaign?

No, the English, French, Spaniards, Dutch, and Austrians were thoroughly played out, as were the English and French colonists in North America. The War of the Spanish Succession ended in 1711, with a peace treaty that granted Newfoundland to England, which also kept possession of the fortress of Gibraltar. England also received the much-coveted *Asiento*, which allowed for limited trade contacts between the British Isles and the Spanish Caribbean colonies. Not surprisingly, the single largest item of concern, and profitability, was the trade in slaves.

For how long had the slave trade been in existence? How much money was made from it?

We often attempt to "finger" or blame one nation or group for the African slave trade, but, in truth, almost all nations which had ships in the Atlantic participated to some degree. Portugal was, almost certainly, the first country to enter the business, and Spain and Holland both got into it with enthusiasm, but Britain may have provided the largest number of ships and sailors involved in the selling of human cargo. At the same time, we have to remember that England was the first European nation to outlaw slavery on its own soil (1772) and the first to forbid its captains to participate in the trade as a whole (1806).

THE SHORT PEACE

For how long did peace prevail on both sides of the Atlantic?

Everyone—from all the European nations—was utterly weary of war in 1713. Peace generally prevailed for the next twenty-six years.

During that time, England moved decidedly in the direction of true Parliamentary government. Though he did not have the precise title, Sir Robert Walpole is often considered the first real prime minister of England. Walpole's task was made easier by the fact that King George I (reigned 1714–1727) spoke no English and that his son King George II (ruled 1727–1760) spoke English with a thick German accent. These essentially German monarchs were content to allow Walpole to direct most of the policies of the nation. One thing that neither Walpole nor the kings he served did anything about was the problem of piracy.

Was there ever a "Golden Age of Piracy"?

If so, it ran from about 1675 to about 1730. During that time, pirates captured an untold number of ships, primarily in the Caribbean but also some in the Indian Ocean. No one really knows how much silver and gold was taken, but if it had ever been assembled in one spot, it might have surpassed the annual revenue of many of the smaller nations.

Providence Island, in the Bahamas, was the capital of the pirate world. Hundreds of ships came in and went out each year. Though we, naturally, think of the pirates as a semisuicidal bunch of desperadoes, they were often rather intelligent, especially when it came to picking their targets. If France was at war with Spain, then the pirates chose the weaker of the two as their target and asked for help from the other nation. If the American colonies were disjointed and weak, then the pirates took advantage of them. Perhaps the most spectacular pirate successes took place in the Indian Ocean, where they preyed on the treasure ships of the Mogul Empire.

Did the Spaniards really do terrible things, such as cutting off the ears and noses of pirates?

They did. One of the lesser-known cases is of a pirate ship which arrived off the coast of New Jersey around the year 1723, with *all* of the sailors lacking either noses or ears. The most infamous case, however, involved Captain Robert Jenkins.

Jenkins appeared before the House of Commons, perhaps in 1737, to display a jar of brandy, in which—he said—was his missing ear. Spanish revenue officers had done this to him, Jenkins said, and he asked for retribution. The House was outraged, and a drumbeat for war began. Sir Robert Walpole, leader of His Majesty's party in the House, replied that the bells were ringing for war in 1737 but that the merchants would be "wringing" their hands before long. The War of Jenkins' Ear began in 1739.

Who were the most notorious of all the pirates?

John Avery, Bartholomew, William Kidd, Edward Teach (better known as Black-beard) … there is a long list from which to choose. Few of these men ever got to enjoy their fortune in comfort or leisure; most of them had to keep fighting, despoiling, and capturing ships just to keep their crews happy. One of the few exceptions was the pirate Thomas Paine of Rhode Island (not to be confused with Thomas Paine who later wrote *Common Sense*). After many years of pirating in the Caribbean, he settled into a normal life in rural Rhode Island.

When did piracy—as opposed to privateering—begin to diminish?

A pirate sailed under his captain and followed no other rules than those of the ship-deck. A privateer sailed with a commission from a king, queen, or prince, allowing him to commit depredations against the ships and merchants of other nations. It was not always easy to distinguish between a privateer and a pirate because men—notably Captain William Kidd—sometimes straddled the line.

What we can say, however, is that piracy—in the fullest, most genuine sense—began to slow down after about the year 1730. More revenue agents, as well as navy captains seeking retribution, were active in the Caribbean, and even Providence Is-

Edward Teach, a.k.a. Blackbeard, was one of the most famous pirates during the Golden Age of Piracy. He was killed in 1718 by the English Lieutenant Robert Maynard.

land began to lose some of its luster. And when the European wars resumed in 1739, privateering became just as lucrative as piracy, perhaps even more.

WAR OF THE AUSTRIAN SUCCESSION

We know that the War of the Spanish Succession was caused by a major monarch; was it also the case with this conflict?

It was. Charles VI, King of Hungary and Holy Roman Emperor, died in 1740. His daughter Maria Theresa, was much admired for her strong stance; the Hungarian nobles, especially, rallied to her cause. Her neighbors, Prussia most especially, saw this as a marvelous opportunity to invade, however.

Frederick II, King of Prussia, had recently inherited, from his father, the best-disciplined, most organized army in Europe. Some people liked to quip that many countries had armies but that Prussia was an army which possessed a county. In the autumn of 1740, King Frederick, soon to be called "Frederick the Great," invaded and seized the mineral-rich province of Silesia. Marie-Therese protested, to no avail. Soon, other nations declared war on Austria, hoping to obtain spoils.

It sounds like there was an Eastern European war and a war in the Atlantic, between England and Spain. How did this broaden to become a truly Atlantic conflict?

It's true that England and Spain were already at war. To this was joined the Eastern European conflict that eventually dragged in every nation except Russia. But, just to complete the scenario and round out the list of possible disasters, England and France declared war on each other in 1744. By the end of that year, there was—truly—no place to hide.

Who were the major opposing monarchs?

Frederick the Great (ruled 1738–1786) was both the youngest and most enterprising of the monarchs. Louis XV (ruled 1715–1774) was a decade older than Frederick but ambitious for his name and fame. Marie-Theresa simply wanted to hold on to the territories she had received from her late father, Philip V, king of Spain, was the same man who had arrived in 1700, at the beginning of the War of the Spanish Succession. Out of all the monarchs and other leaders, however, the one who stood out the most was King George II of Great Britain.

He spoke English reasonably well, but when excited he would lapse into his native German. He sponsored George Frideric Handel, surely one of the greatest musicians of all time, but was himself both coarse and inelegant. He presided over England, which was becoming the richest nation in the world, so far as its merchants went, but he counted pennies and loved to hear the clank of coins, one rolled atop the other.

Who took the first major action?

Bonnie Prince Charlie—whose full name was Prince Charles Edward Stuart—was the grandson of King James II, who had been dethroned in 1688. Prince Charlie now lived in Rome in exile, but he left there in 1744 and made his way to France. Louis XV received the prince graciously and promised him assistance for an invasion of England. But to the surprise of most people in Europe, it was the colonial Americans who took the first major step of the war.

In March 1745, 4,000 New England men—farmers and fishermen, primarily—sailed from Boston in a great number of transport vessels, headed for Nova Scotia. The New England forces rendezvoused with a British naval squadron commanded by Sir Peter

Warren, and in April they appeared off Fortress Louisburg, on the east side of Cape Breton Island. This daring action was planned in Boston—not London—and the colonists took a major risk, because if the effort failed, they would be the ones blamed.

How did these amateur New Englanders learn the art of a European-style siege?

They did it with the sheer daring and gusto of amateurs: men who trained themselves. The colonial American commander was William Pepperell of Maine (1696–1759)—a prosperous merchant—and the head of the artillery was Seth Pomeroy of Northampton, Massachusetts, a self-taught gunner. They, and scores of other New Englanders, learned the tricks of their new trade in a very short time, and by May they had established a true siege of Louisburg.

The French defenders were first surprised and then appalled. The New England men kept the pressure on, building siege parallels and bringing their lines closer to the city walls, while Commodore Warren snapped up every merchant ship that came close to Louisburg. The French fought on for a total of seven weeks, but on June 17, 1745, the garrison capitulated. Louisburg, sometimes called the Gibraltar of America, had fallen to the New Englanders.

Who got the glory and the prize money?

Commodore Warren and the British squadron received more than their fair share and when he sailed to England, the commodore indulged in a good deal of self-promotion. The New Englanders believed he ignored their efforts. Old England did not need to be convinced of the value of the American efforts, however; William Pepperrell was made a baronet (hereditary knight), and all sorts of medals and coins were struck in honor of Louisburg's fall. The irony, however, was that Pepperrell lost far more men to smallpox in the two years that followed than he ever did during the actual conflict.

As for the French, they could scarcely believe what the New Englanders had done. A major war fleet was fitted out with the intention of retaking Louisburg, but it was driven off by gales, thunderstorms, and the like. As a result, New England held Louisburg to the very end of the war and enjoyed its first taste of foreign conquest.

Meanwhile, what happened in Europe?

The only major clash between the English and French occured at the Battle of Fontenoy in May 1745. In this classic, Enlightenment-style battle in an open field, the French got the better of their opponents. England, however, was much more concerned with the possibility of an invasion by Bonnie Prince Charlie, and when he landed in Scotland in the summer of 1745, something like panic gripped many supporters of the Hanoverian dynasty.

Prince Charlie had been let down by the French, who provided him with only three ships, but when he came ashore in northern Scotland, the Highland clans rallied to him. The irony of the very Protestant clansmen supporting the very Catholic Prince Charlie was overlooked, and the Highlanders won skirmishes, then battles, and pressed all the way to the border with England. This was, of course, the border which had seen a whole series of battles and wars, going all the way back to the time of William Wallace and Robert the Bruce.

Was Prince Charlie as romantic as he sounds?

Later in life, after the failure of his effort, Bonnie Prince Charlie became old, careworn, and a bit of a drunk, but he cut a romantic figure at the age of twenty-five. Also, he was truly daring in his tactics, bringing his men across the border into England. There was a run on the banks in London, and some supporters of King George II threw up their hands, saying that all was lost. The red-coated soldiers of King George did not give up, however, and their actions were the ones that really counted.

Prince Charles Edward Stuart led an unsuccessful campaign to restore his Stuart family to the throne of England.

In the early spring of 1746, George, the Duke of Cumberland—second eldest son of King George II—led the British forces north and engaged with Prince Charlie's Highlanders at the Battle of Culloden. A furious cannon bombardment preceded the clash, and the Highlanders got the worst of it on both counts. That day, and for weeks after, the English pursued the Scots, killing, capturing, and putting the rebellion to an end. Bonnie Prince Charlie, dressed as a servant girl at one point, aided by the MacDonald clan, escaped to France. Although many great songs would be composed about the "king over the water," Bonnie Prince Charlie never came back.

With the Scottish rebellion crushed, how did King George's government prosecute the war?

There was not that much left to accomplish. As long as the home islands were safe from invasion, Great Britain could ride out any storm. And so the fighting was left pretty much to the French, who took town after town in Holland, and to the Prussians, who fended off every attempt by Maria Theresa and others to reconquer the province of Silesia. As a result, when the peace treaty was signed in 1748, all territories, towns, and forts which had been taken were returned to their previous owners.

The return of Louisburg to France did cause something of an uproar in New England. The newspapers lamented the loss of so many good men—both in the siege and in holding the place—all for naught. Some relief existed with the outrage, however. It had been a serious strain on Massachusetts' finances to keep Louisburg, and the war's end meant that the men could come home.

Did Frederick the Great keep Silesia? Was Prussia made to suffer for having started the war in the first place?

Although it cost him many men and a great deal of money, King Frederick held on to Silesia during the war and managed to keep it in the peace treaty as well. His actions had long-lasting effects. Maria Theresa of Hungary and Austria would never rest until she could regain Silesia, and both Russia and France were alarmed by Prussia's sudden appearance as a major military power. Although all the powers swore to the peace of 1748, some of the monarchs seem to have crossed their fingers while signing the treaty of Aix-la-Chapelle.

FRENCH, INDIANS, ENGLISH, AND AMERICANS

Who broke the short peace that commenced with the treaty of 1748?

Of all people, we would not expect the miscreant to be George Washington (1732–1799). The twenty-two-year-old Virginian was sent by the governor of that colony to warn the French out of the Ohio Country in 1753. His mission having failed, Washington was made a colonel in the Virginia militia, and he brought about 300 men to southern Pennsylvania. On learning that the French had seized the vital "Forks," the area where the Allegheny and Monongahela rivers come together to form the Ohio River, Washington chose to ambush a column of Frenchmen.

The skirmish, fought on the morning of May 29, 1754, was tiny in size, but it led—over the next two years—to a truly worldwide war which involved the peoples of Europe, North America, and the Caribbean, with repercussions as far away as India. Washington had no way of knowing this. He was just a rash and inexperienced officer who took a risk in attacking a group of Frenchmen, and when their leader, Ensign Coulon de Jumonville, fell in the skirmish, the wilderness affair resulted in greater consequences.

Where was "Fort Necessity"?

Six weeks after the wilderness fight, Washington was forced to go on the defensive when the French and Indians chased him to a blockhouse and entrenchment that he called Fort Necessity (in southwest Pennsylvania). During a day of tremendous rainstorms, Washington and his men held out against ceaseless musket fire, but the next morning—which just happened to be July 4, 1754—Washington and his men capitulated. The document that confirmed the surrender was written in French, and Washington did not realize that it contained an admission on his part for the "assassination" of Ensign Jumonville. The document was later reprinted on both sides of the Atlantic, and Washington became much better known as a result.

Paroled on his honor not to fight the French for the next twelve months, Washington marched back to Virginia. There he found himself something of a hero because of his defense of Fort Necessity against a much larger force.

How long did it take for England and France to go to war once more?

They—and the other great powers—did not make the formal declarations of war until the spring of 1756, but nearly everyone could see what was in the making. In 1755, France and Austria, which had been perennial foes since the time of King Francis I, and Emperor Charles V signed a treaty of alliance, whereupon Britain and Prussia did the same. This, the so-called Diplomatic Revolution, fundamentally shifted the balance of power in Europe and made the ensuing conflict even more deadly.

If any two people can be blamed for the start of war, they were George Washington and King Frederick the Great of Prussia. They were, to be sure, very different men with very different goals, but they had one thing in common: they were both rash. Frederick had started the War of the Austrian Succession in 1740, and his stubborn determination to hang on to Silesia—regardless of the cost—helped bring about the Seven Years' War. Washington was a very small player in a very big game, but his sudden, surprise attack on the French in the Pennsylvania wilderness made the war a likelihood.

What is the correct, or appropriate, name for this new conflict?

The Europeans call it the Seven Years' War, and the Americans label it the French and Indian War. The problem with the first name is that it is so nondescript, and the trouble with the second label is that there had been three previous conflicts—King William's War, Queen Anne's War, and King George's War—all of which could also be titled the "French and Indian War." Some historians—most notably Lawrence Gibson—have therefore chosen to call it the "Great War for Empire."

Where did the action kick off, on which side of the Atlantic?

In the winter of 1755, British General Edward Braddock (1695–1755) arrived in Virginia with two British regiments. His orders were to capture French Fort Duquesne, which had recently been built where Pittsburgh, Pennsylvania now stands.

Braddock was about sixty, and he had seen little warfare during his long career. He was a fine logistics man, however, and there seemed to be no reason for him to fail. He was joined by quite a few young American colonists; among them were Daniel Morgan, Horatio Gates, and of course, the twenty-three-year-old George Washington. Though no one knew it in 1755, these men—and quite a few others—would become officers in the Continental Army during the American Revolution. Even in 1755, however, there were tensions between the British soldiers and the American militia; the men of both sides seemed to detest the other.

Why did George Washington *always* rise to the top— and get there so quickly?

About one-third of it was character—of which he had tons—and about one-third was sheer good luck. The remaining third can only be attributed to his remarkable physique and physical presence. He stood about six foot two and was as fine a specimen of lean muscle as one can imagine (no movie actor of our generation—not even Daniel Day-Lewis—can pull off a physical reproduction of Washington for the movie screen). It was as if trumpets sounded when Washington entered a room.

What happened to Braddock's expedition?

The Anglo-American force set out in May 1755 and got within ten miles of Fort Duquesne before being ambushed by about 800 French and Indians. In the wilderness fight that ensued, the British were not at their best: they fired ceaseless volleys that mostly hit the trees and bushes. The French and Indians, surprised by their own success, attempted to kill George Washington—one of the few men on a horse—but it seemed as if he was specially guarded by Providence that day (he claimed so, in a letter to his brother). General Braddock was mortally wounded, and Washington and a small group of men brought him back to Fort Dunbar, where he died a few days later. Of the 2,200 men who had started out, roughly fifty percent were killed, wounded, or missing in the action of July 9, 1755. In the long history of Anglo-American military cooperation, this was probably the single worst—or most costly—day.

What happened on the Virginia and Pennsylvania frontier?

The French and Indians were not strong, or numerous, enough to take full advantage of their victory, but in the months that followed, many American frontier settlements were attacked, and some were wiped out entirely. Washington, who was now a full colonel, had the difficult task of defending sections of that frontier, and from his letters we gather that he found it the most wearisome and vexing part of his military career. Even so, things were not as bad as they might have been; had the French in Canada been able to send a real army to the Ohio Country, they would have accomplished a great deal more.

Why do we always remember George Washington and forget Sir William Johnson?

The two men actually had some things in common. William Johnson (1714–1774) was an Anglo-Irishman who came to the Mohawk River valley at the age of thirty. Like Washington, Johnson was a fine specimen of raw-boned, lean strength; unlike Washington, Johnson had a real gift for dealing with the Native Americans, and, over time, he became King

161

George II's special commissary and diplomat to the Six Nations. In 1755, at about the same time that General Braddock commenced his ill-fated campaign, William Johnson brought about 4,000 American colonists and Mohawk warriors to the foot of Lake George.

While he prepared to cross Lake George and seize Fort Crown Point, Johnson and his men were attacked by about 3,000 French and Indians, led by Baron Ludwig von Dieskau (1701–1767), a German in the service of France. On this occasion it was the French and Indians who stumbled, allowing themselves to be tricked into a headlong attack on the American encampment. The fight was furious, with plenty of men dying on both sides, but the French were driven off, and General Dieskau was captured. As a result, William Johnson won the biggest victory of any Anglo or American leader in 1755 and was rewarded with the dignity of a baronet of Great Britain. (We forget Sir William Johnson because he died in 1774, just before the start of the American Revolution.)

Meanwhile, when did the action in Europe commence?

It began in 1755 but really accelerated in 1756. King Frederick the Great had only one ally, and that was Great Britain. King George II and the British Parliament sent Frederick the Great men and money to assist in his fight against France, Austria, and Russia.

Even with British assistance, it seems impossible that Frederick the Great was able to fight off so many foes, but that is part of why he deserves the title "Great." In the early fighting, Frederick went on the offensive at times, but the enormous numerical superiority of his foes meant he had to shift to the defense. The credit for Prussia holding on in the midst of such odds is due both to Frederick and to the staying power of the Prussian soldier.

What did Frederick the Great mean when he spoke contemptuously of female rulers?

Decades, even centuries, had passed since there had been such a plethora of women rulers. In Austria and Hungary, Queen Maria Theresa held the reins. In Moscow, the Czarina Elizabeth heartily hated Frederick the Great, who reciprocated her hatred with contempt. And in France, Louis XV looked like the great leader, but those in the know snickered that the kingdom was really run by Madame de Pompadour, his mistress.

We say "Prussian," but were these men actually Germans?

The Kingdom of Prussia lay in the northeast part of what is now Germany, and Berlin—which was still quite small—was its capital. Frederick the Great, therefore, can be seen as the earliest embodiment of the warrior ethic that made the Germans such formidable opponents in World War I and World War II. There was, as well, a certain recklessness about Frederick the Great that prompts some comparison to Adolf Hitler's many gambles. Unlike Hitler, Frederick the Great never really had to pay, or suffer, for his errors of judgment.

The cartoon and caricatures of the time often showed a masculine combination of Great Britain and Prussia contesting the female wiles of France, Austria, and Russia. What these playful portraits omit, however, is the incredibly large number of men who were killed or wounded in the endless battles between these nations. The historian Francis Parkman estimated that 860,000 men died in Europe during the Seven Years' War.

Speaking of cartoons and caricatures, what was the relationship between Voltaire and Frederick the Great?

Frederick the Great was King of Prussia from 1740 to 1786. He was known both for his championing of arts and culture and for being a great military leader.

It was, perhaps, the oddest and most poignant public relationship of the mid-eighteenth century. On the surface of it, there appears to be nothing in common between the young Prussian king and the middle-aged French philosopher. They formed a bond, nevertheless.

In between the War of the Austrian Succession and the Seven Years' War, Voltaire visited Potsdam—Frederick's palace—and spent some months in the king's company. They delighted in satire, laughter, and such oddities as Frederick playing the flute. When Voltaire returned to France, he continued to sing Frederick's praises. Even when the Seven Years' War began, pitting France versus Prussia, Voltaire could not restrain himself from the occasional expression of approval when he heard of yet another Prussian victory. As strange as this sounds, the relationship very much belonged to the context of the Enlightenment, a time when poets were—sometimes!—as important as politicians.

Who was the Marquis de Montcalm?

In 1756, France sent several veteran regiments to North America. The Marquis de Montcalm (1712–1759) was selected to be their commander.

Montcalm was a clear-thinking strategist, who participated in many battles in Europe. He took to the wilderness of French Canada more rapidly than many of his peers and was soon discussing how to prevent the Anglo-Americans from ever moving farther west. Montcalm had two great handicaps, however. First, French Canada had less than 80,000 souls, while the Anglo-American colonists now numbered about 1.5 million. Second, and almost as important, Montcalm was perennially at odds with the Marquis de Vaudreuil, the governor-general of Canada. The two men clashed so many times, over so many matters, that they agreed Montcalm should command the regiments from Old

France and that Vaudreuil would command the native-born French-Canadians. This division in the command structure had many results, nearly all of them negative.

What were the plans, on either side, for the year 1756?

The British planned a joint Anglo-American attack on the Fortress of Louisburg, on Cape Breton Island. The French, for their part, planned a strike somewhere in the New York colony.

Montcalm's plans paid higher dividends than his opponents. In the summer of 1756, he brought a French force across Lake Ontario and captured Fort Oswego. Montcalm subsequently destroyed the fort and village and returned to Canada. If not a great victory, it was something substantial. The British, by contrast, could not get their fleet and land forces to work together, and the entire plan against Louisburg had to be scrapped.

What did both sides plan for 1757?

Montcalm planned for an invasion of New York that would involve the French, the French-Canadians, and the largest group of Native Americans ever to join a European-style army. In the summer of 1757, Montcalm brought 8,000 men—or roughly 10 percent of the entire French-Canadian population—by way of Lake Champlain and Lake George to attack Fort William Henry.

The fort was at the foot of Lake George, right where the battle between Sir William Johnson and Baron Dieskau had been fought in 1755. Montcalm was well aware of the symbolic as well as strategic importance of the place. His opponent was Colonel Munro, a lowland Scot who had been loyal to King George during the rebellion of 1745. When Montcalm's mixed force appeared, Colonel Munro had about 2,000 men to defend against a force that was four times larger.

Montcalm's strength here is obvious. Was there weakness as well?

There was indeed. Montcalm's Native American warriors were likely to desert if he did not provide them with a swift victory. His French-Canadians had to get back to bring in the crops. If Colonel George Munro was under pressure, so was Montcalm.

The French and their Native American allies moved closer and closer, digging siege parallels and launching a seemingly endless number of cannon balls against the fort. Finally, having learned that the British garrison at Fort Edward was not coming to his aid, Colonel Munro agreed to terms. The ones Montcalm offered were quite generous. The British garrison could march out with its arms and its flags flying.

When did the Massacre at Fort William Henry take place?

The massacre took place on the very afternoon that the garrison departed. The Native American allies of the French were angry that the British garrison was allowed to leave, and when someone broke in the barrel heads of kegs of rum, the Native American troops went wild. Perhaps two hours later, they attacked the column of men headed to Fort Edward, killing perhaps 200.

The Massacre at Fort William Henry was not that unusual: employing Native American allies was tricky both for the British and the French. The size and scale of the massacre was unprecedented, however, and the news doubtless brought many thousands of young Americans into the militia forces. Montcalm withdrew to Canada, knowing full well that the massacre had undone most of the positive effects of his campaign.

What was the high point of the war, so far as the French and Native Americans were concerned?

The autumn of 1757 was the high point of the war. Up until this point, Montcalm and his forces had fended off every assault on Canada and had made two strong indentations into New York. Not only that, but the news from Europe was also good. Frederick the Great continued to win battlefield victories, but it was hard to replace the men he lost, and Britain was faltering. The attempt to capture Minorca in 1756 had failed, and in 1757 France seemed close to its goal of isolating Great Britain.

Just then, however, came the appointment of a new minister, the person who would undo much of what had transpired. This was William Pitt, a longtime member of the

Fort William Henry as it looks today after being restored in the 1950s and becoming a tourist attraction. The French seized it from the British in 1757 during the French and Indian War.

House of Commons, who now became secretary of state in the government of King George II. Unlike his predecessors, Pitt believed that the Seven Years' War would be won or lost on the Atlantic Ocean and in the wilderness of North America. Pitt, therefore, dispatched far greater numbers of men and supplies to America in preparation for the campaigns of 1758.

What was the three-pronged plan of attack for the year 1758?

One British army was to march along the Hudson–Lake George–Lake Champlain route. Another was to march from Virginia to the Ohio River and capture French Fort Duquesne. Still a third was to be transported by ship to Cape Breton, there to seize French Fort Louisburg. If this seems like an ambitious set of plans, it truly was, and only the directing guidance of William Pitt—who was willing to spend enormous sums to obtain results—made it possible.

Who was the tortoise and who was the hare in the Louisburg campaign?

General Jeffrey Amherst was a traditional British military man: calm, unflappable, methodical. His second-in-command, Brigadier-General James Wolfe (1727–1759), was a new style of British officer: rash, impetuous, and often brilliant in execution. Wolfe had been a young officer at the Battle of Culloden and had earned the hatred of many Scots for his energetic pursuit of the defeated.

Amherst and Wolfe made a curious combination, but they worked well together. In July 1758, they landed on Cape Breton and soon instituted a naval blockade that would reduce Louisburg by starvation, if nothing else. Wolfe, meanwhile, began a series of rapid advances that brought the British right to the walls of Louisburg, while Amherst juggled the supply lines and balance sheets. By the time the two men were ready for a wholesale attack, the population of Louisburg had had enough and the white flag was displayed over its walls. This was the second time Louisburg had fallen: there would not be a third siege.

Meanwhile, what happened at Fort Ticonderoga?

The French called it Fort Carillon because of the musical sound of the local waterfall. The fort was built in 1755 and 1756, and it overlooked Lake Champlain at its narrowest point, allowing Ticonderoga, or Carillon, to dominate the surroundings. The Marquis de Montcalm was there to command the defense, but he had only about 4,000 men.

The Anglo-Americans, who numbered about 15,000, came north over Lake George on whaleboats and then disembarked to file through the forest on their way to Ticonderoga. There were red-coated British soldiers but also black-shirted Highlanders, members of the Night's Watch, New Yorkers and New England men, and a few Iroquois as well. Taken in all, this was the largest and most impressive force yet assembled on the mainland of North America, and it was more than enough to overwhelm the French defenders.

How, then, could the attack possibly have failed?

As the old saying goes: "For the want of a nail the shoe was lost, and for the want of a shoe the horse was lost, and for the want of a horse the rider was lost, and for the want of the rider the message was lost, and for the want of the message the battle was lost." So it was with the attack on Fort Ticonderoga in July 1758.

Brigadier-General George Howe was shot and killed in the woods even before the battle began. Born in England, Howe was the soul of the army, the person most able to deal with the arrogant British and the difficult Americans. He was so well loved that the Province of Massachusetts later spent 500 pounds sterling to erect a monument for him in Westminster Abbey (it still stands today). Howe's death cast a pall over the Anglo-American army, and the result was a true calamity.

How badly did the Anglo-American army fare?

Major-General James Abercromby was a solid military man, but he lacked both the charm and the skill of Brigadier-General Howe. Perhaps Abercromby, too, was paralyzed by grief in the wake of Howe's death. In any case, Abercromby ordered a full-scale, head-on assault, even though he had plenty of time to reconnoiter.

Hoping that the Anglo-Americans might make this mistake, Montcalm had erected a cheveau-de-frise, constructed of wooden stakes, about 300 yards outside of Fort Ticonderoga. On July 8, 1758, the Anglo-Americans made one frontal assault after another, each of which failed in turn. They never came close to making a breakthrough but the dead and wounded were heaped up by nightfall. At a cost of about 400 to his force, Montcalm inflicted nearly 2,000 casualties on the Anglo-Americans.

What happened to the third of the three prongs aimed at French Canada?

General Abercromby and the Anglo-American force retired to Fort William Henry and made no further moves that year. General James Forbes brought several British regiments to Virginia, where he was joined by Colonel George Washington and a few hun-

How could anyone—much less a major-general —commit this kind of error?

It is easy to blame Major-General Abercromby, but it would be more accurate to condemn the system under which men rose to become major-generals in the army. Someone like General George Howe was quite rare. Far more common were men like Abercromby, whose commissions were purchased by their fathers, making them lieutenants and captains at a young age. Quite a few of these men rose to become majors and colonels without ever seeing a day of truly hard fighting.

dred Virginia militiamen. The joint British-American force took a very long time getting its carts of supplies over the Allegheny Mountains, but when they arrived at Fort Duquesne late in November, they found the fort both abandoned and blown up. Forbes had succeeded where General Edward Braddock failed.

That was the end of George Washington's career, at least as far as his service under the British flag. Weeks after returning home to Virginia, he married Martha Dandridge Custis, a woman of his own age who had recently been widowed. She brought 18,000 acres of land to the marriage, and Washington declared, in letters to friends, that he was finished with military life and desired nothing more than domestic harmony.

Was there any attempt to broker a truce between Great Britain and France?

No. Great Britain could feel that this was the moment at which it could break through to supremacy. France, too, had one last card to play. Even if the British triumphed in North America, India, and on the sea, all of these losses could be redeemed by a successful invasion of the British Isles. The government of Louis XV decided, therefore, to risk everything on a cross-Channel invasion in 1759.

William Pitt and the government of George II knew the danger all too well, but they were determined to persevere in the overseas war. Even more troops and sailors were sent to America, therefore, with the intention of seizing both Quebec and Montreal. General Jeffrey Amherst, the conqueror of Louisburg, was assigned the task of going over Lake George and Lake Champlain, while General James Wolfe—now promoted to major-general—was tasked with the capture of Quebec City.

William Pitt, 1st Earl of Chatham, for whom the city of Pittsburgh is named, led the British Parliament during the French and Indian (Seven Years') War.

How far is Louisburg from Quebec City?

As the crow flies, it is a difficult 650 miles, but going by way of the St. Lawrence River makes it closer to 1,000. No previous British expedition had ever made it past the mouth of the St. Lawrence; only the colonial expedition of 1690 had reached the outskirts of the French-Canadian capital.

Rear Admiral Thomas Saunders had his hands full during the difficult passage up the St. Lawrence, but the Royal Navy had great confidence in its sailors and pilots. By the end of June, Admiral Saunders had landed General Wolfe and 9,000 men on the Island of Orleans, right smack in the middle of the St. Lawrence and less than three miles from Quebec. The sights they saw were daunting, however. Quebec City overlooks the river, frowning from a height of 300 feet. The St. Charles River runs down to empty into the St. Lawrence, and Quebec's other side is guarded by the fortifications on Cape Diamond. It is no exaggeration to say that Quebec was one of the best-defended places, by nature, to be found.

What was Wolfe's first move?

Early in July, he crossed from the Island of Orleans to Point Levis, on the south side of the St. Lawrence River. Chasing off the few French defenders, Wolfe set up batteries, and cannon balls began cascading into the Lower Town of Quebec. When Montcalm sent a flag of truce to point out that this was a violation of civilized warfare, Wolfe responded that the French—and their Native American allies—were equally guilty of transgressions. More to the point, however, Wolfe asked Admiral Saunders to run part of the fleet past Quebec City so he could threaten the city from the other side. The British sailors again performed what other people believed impossible, and by mid-July the British were both above and below the city, threatening an attack from almost every angle.

What was Wolfe's first big mistake?

On July 31, 1759, Wolfe sent his best troops, the British grenadiers, into action against the French camps at Beauport, three miles above the city. The spot chosen for the attack was not ideal, but the execution was much worse. Hit by a rainstorm at just the wrong moment—from the British point of view—the grenadiers were swamped by their own heavy equipment as they came ashore. The French defenders poured volley after volley into the attackers; about 450 men were killed or wounded that afternoon.

Had Montcalm counterattacked, he might have driven the British away completely, but throughout the Quebec campaign he was hamstrung by the prevalence of militia forces in his army. Only about one-quarter of his men were regular soldiers, from Old France, and Montcalm viewed them with about the same disdain which General Edward Braddock had shown the Virginia militia. Wolfe, therefore, had one last chance, just as long as winter did not arrive first.

Can climate change be observed in the Canadian winters as well as our American ones?

Absolutely. The Canadian winters of the 1700s were severe, but the same can be said of the Canadian winters of the 1960s and 1970s. Since those two decades, however, Canada has seen just about as much climate change as the United States, with the overwhelming trend toward greater warmth. To General Wolfe, in 1759, it was of paramount importance to make his move before October, when ice would begin to form in the St. Lawrence River.

Meanwhile, what had happened on the southern front as General Amherst tried to cross the lakes?

Amherst collected a very large army around Albany and cautiously made his way north to Ticonderoga. None of the previous year's mistakes were repeated, and the French evacuated first Ticonderoga and then Crown Point (of the two, the former is more visited these days, while the latter lies in a state that truly resembles its condition in 1759).

Amherst then settled into a routine, building a road from Crown Point to Ticonderoga and generally acting as if the campaign season were over. In a way it was. The French had a small fleet of gunboats on Lake Champlain, and so long as those boats patrolled, the Anglo-American forces could not continue to Canada. Sensing the discontent among his troops, Amherst made a token gesture; he dispatched Major Robert Rogers and his Rangers to attack the Native American village of St. Francis, in Quebec.

Were Amherst and Wolfe in contact?

Only by the most hazardous paths could messengers get through, but by September 1, 1759, Wolfe realized that Amherst would not come further north and that he was, essentially, on his own. Many armchair historians have criticized Wolfe for acting too quickly, for grasping at straws in the Quebec campaign, but he knew that he could not afford to waste the immense expense of money and men at his disposal. He would either conquer Quebec in 1759, or it would not be taken. Equally, there was the condition of his own health.

Wolfe was tubercular. People of that time called it consumption, but they understood that the disease slowly killed the person by destroying the lungs. Wolfe did not have long to live, and this, quite likely, made him keen to take big chances. And so he did.

How did Wolfe and his men get to the top of the Plains of Abraham?

On the night of September 12–13, 1759, dozens of British vessels snuck past French outlook points to land at the little cove called *Anse de Foulon*, about two miles south of

---

Is Robert Rogers (1731–1795) really the founder— in a distant sense—of today's Special Forces?

He is. Born in New Hampshire in 1731, Rogers accomplished little in his early life (he was once jailed for counterfeiting), but the French and Indian War brought his latent talents to the fore. Establishing the Rangers—known for their green uniforms—Rogers became as good, perhaps even better, than the French and Native American wilderness fighters. The sad part of the story is that Rogers went bankrupt later in life and that he attempted to recoup his fortunes by joining the British during the Revolutionary War. This is, perhaps, why he does not receive the honor that should be his due.

the city. The night was spent getting the men and their equipment, including four small cannon up the steep cliff, and when morning came, 5,000 red-coated British soldiers greeted the dawn. They were on the Plains, named for a farmer named Abraham. Although historians sometimes romanticize the Quebec campaign excessively, there is no doubt that this was a skillful and daring maneuver.

The Marquis de Montcalm discovered his bad fortune at 8 A.M. In no time, he had troops converging from different directions, and by 11 A.M., he had a roughly equal number of men—about 5,000—on the hilly land just south of the city. If anyone can be criticized for moving too fast, it is Montcalm. Had he waited perhaps six more hours, he would have had almost twice as many men. His blood was up, however, and he feared that his men would begin to lose heart if he did not act.

How long did the decisive battle last?

About twenty-five minutes. For the first ten minutes, the French force moved ahead, with skirmishers hiding in the grass to take shots at the British. Mounted on a black horse, Montcalm stood out, encouraging his men as they moved. Not until they came within one hundred yards did Montcalm allow the main body of his men to fire; not until they were within forty yards did the British return fire. That first British volley was devastating, however.

The death of British General James Wolfe during the 1759 Battle of Quebec was immortalized in this romanticized 1770 painting by Benjamin West.

Nearly 5,000 muskets fired at once, and even though at least half missed their marks, it was enough to hollow out the first French line. Before there was time to recover, the British loaded and fired again, and this second volley was enough to send the French running.

How did Wolfe die?

In what is perhaps the most romantic but also truthful description, Wolfe, hit by three different musket balls, fell to the ground. Coming back to consciousness, he heard one of his aides declare that "they run, egad, they run everywhere!" Wolfe asked simply "who," and was told that it was the enemy that was in flight. Wolfe then closed his eyes, saying, "Now, God be praised, I can die in peace."

The scene of Wolfe's death was later commemorated in a magnificent painting by Benjamin West. It shows the red color of the British uniforms, the dying general, and a Native American as well as a Ranger from Robert Rogers' force, all on the scene. Although the painting takes artistic liberty, it is magnificently conceived, and it became, perhaps, the best-known and most-loved of all military paintings from the Age of the Enlightenment.

How did Montcalm die?

He was wounded as his force was swept from the field. On arriving at the gates, he found his surgeon, who pronounced that Montcalm's wound was mortal. Montcalm's famous reply, according to tradition, was "So much the better; I will not live to see the fall of Quebec."

Was that the end of the campaigns of 1759?

Not quite. Quebec did capitulate, on September 16, 1759, but by then Robert Rogers and his Rangers had struck the last blow of the year. Evading enemy outposts, they made their way over the Canadian border and attacked and destroyed the Abnaki village of St. Francis. On their return, the Rangers were harassed and attacked by all manner of militia and Native Americans, but Rogers lived to tell the tale. He arrived at Fort Number Four in New Hampshire and awoke to find himself a great hero.

Did anything more to the war remain?

In the summer of 1760, General Jeffrey Amherst brought three major forces to converge on Montreal, which capitulated in September. With that action, the war in North America was over. The same cannot be said of the European war, however.

France had staked everything on a cross-Channel invasion in 1759, but its troops were not ready until autumn, and the gales of that season boded ill for the attempt. Something had to be done, however, and Admiral Conflans brought out twenty ships of the line from the French port of Brest. He was immediately pursued by Rear Admiral Thomas Hawke, and as the weather grew progressively worse, Conflans led his ships into Quiberon Bay. He believed the wind and tides would prevent the British pursuit, but Admiral Hawke acted in the same manner as General Wolfe: the time was now or never. Bringing his own ships into Quiberon Bay, Hawke won a huge victory, capturing or destroying nearly half the French fleet. The Battle of Quiberon Bay put an end to any idea of invading the British Isles for the remainder of the war.

The war in America ended in 1760, but how long did it last in Europe?

For another three years. Frederick the Great had, remarkably, been able to fight off his many foes, and Prussia was still standing, but this came at an immense sacrifice. The allied powers of France, Russia, and Austria were equally exhausted, and the only new action, therefore, came from Spain.

In 1762, Spain entered the war as an ally of France, and it ran—immediately—into a very bad situation. The British already held Gibraltar; they now attacked both Havana, Cuba, and Manila in the Philippines. It seemed that no one in any part of the world could hold their own against the British.

When did the Seven Years' War finally come to an end?

The Peace of Paris, signed in 1763, confirmed the great victories Britain had won in so many places around the globe. Havana was restored to Spain, but Florida passed to Britain. All of French Canada, including Nova Scotia, now came under the British Union Jack, which flew from Florida to Newfoundland and from New York to Hudson's Bay. India was a more complex matter—France did not have the right or the power to cede to the British there—but it was increasingly evident that the British East India Company would one day rule the subcontinent. Sugar islands in the Caribbean, which some statesmen valued more highly than entire continents, passed from one side to another.

In 1763, Britain became the world's first true superpower. Imperial Rome had governed just as much territory, but it had not been as far-flung. The British merchants, too, were the envy of almost all others because of the riches that passed through London.

AGE OF REVOLUTION: 1763 TO 1799

Did the educated observer anticipate that the last third of the eighteenth century would be the "Age of Revolution"?

No. The midcentury wars had been so costly—in human and monetary terms—that most observers believed the last part of the century would be one marked by peace. Then, too, the major issues between Britain and France as well as Prussia and its foes seemed to have been settled.

What the educated observer expected instead was that the "revolutions" of the late eighteenth century would focus on the furthering of the Enlightenment, that knowledge would continue to spread, and that life would become better for millions of everyday folk. There would, indeed, be a significant expansion of knowledge, with consequential results, but the wars would resume with a whole new ferocity, and they would sometimes be even bloodier as a result of the new technologies.

Was there any country, or nation, that exemplified the trend toward knowledge and financial expansion better than the others?

Historians usually point to England, which underwent an enormous expansion of its economy as well as its human resources in the late eighteenth century, but when one looks on a "pound for pound" basis, the answer is to be found in Scotland. A mere thirty years after the failure of the 1745 rebellion—and the defeat of Bonnie Prince Charlie—the Scots put aside dreams of individual glory and concentrated on making the Enlightenment "work" or "pay" as far as their nation was concerned.

More scientists, philosophers, and humanists—as well as humanitarians—lived or studied in Edinburgh than any other European capital, and this at a time when Edinburgh, and Scotland, had very small populations. One can point to any number of great philosophical and technical treatises written in Scotland during this period, but there were also the technical changes that assisted in the rise in the level of warfare. It was in Scotland that the "carronade," a new type of short-barreled cannon, was invented, with enormous consequences for naval warfare.

Was there a downside to the increase in knowledge, in financial speculation, and so forth?

There was indeed. The biggest downside was that the national debt of nearly all the major European nations ballooned during the mid- and late-eighteenth century. The British, who were the most successful at handling their debt, estimated that theirs amounted to 167 million pounds sterling at the end of the Seven Years' War. This, more than any other factor, helped to bring on the Age of Revolution(s).

In 1763, King George III—who had succeeded his father three years earlier—agreed with his ministers that the American colonists needed to pay more in taxes: they had escaped very lightly so far. A good portion of the British national debt was incurred while making the American colonies safe from invasion by French Canada, and it was only fair that the Americans should pay their share.

What was the first direct tax laid on the American colonists?

One can argue about the difference between a "duty" and a "tax," but both of them brought more revenue to the British crown. There is no doubt, however, that Americans were angry and appalled with the passage of the Stamp Act in 1764. For the first time, newspapers, magazines, wills, contracts, and a host of other documents would have to bear the king's "stamp," for which the colonists would have to pay royal officials. Compared to the tax burden of the average Englishman, the Stamp Act was far from onerous, but for the Americans it was a violation of the concept of "no taxation without representation." This idea was, in part, born of the Enlightenment, but it was also based on direct experience. Everything in the colonies—houses, barns, boats, and churches—had been built by the hands of the colonists themselves; why, therefore, should they pay taxes to Old England?

If the crown had contributed next to nothing, how had the colonies become so successful?

This was one of the marvels of the age: that the colonists had grown from a few hundred people to two million and that the colonies had become prosperous. The answer is short and simple, however: the ready availability of land. In Old England, a husband and wife might labor for a lifetime and still be renters of their cottage; in America, most families would end up—with hard work and a bit of luck—with dozens, perhaps hundreds, of acres of land.

How many people were harmed—on either side—during the Stamp Act controversy?

To the best of our knowledge, no one was killed, but quite a few were "tarred and feathered," a truly barbaric practice that dated to the Middle Ages. Many others were run out of town, never to return. Britons were as angry and appalled by American resistance to the Stamp Act as the Americans were to the act itself.

Liberty Poles suddenly replaced May Poles throughout twelve of the thirteen colonies (Georgia did not participate in the resistance). Royal officials were scorned, spat upon, and sometimes beaten up. Just as it seemed that the conflict would truly get out of hand came the news that King George III and Parliament had rescinded the Stamp Act. In what seemed like a very quick turnaround, thousands of Americans praised the king's name and set off fireworks in his honor.

A 1773 portrait of King George III of England by Nathaniel Dance-Holland. George III reigned from 1760 until his death in 1820. His later years were plagued by mental illness.

Did King George III ever understand his American subjects?

No. The king knew and understood his English and Scot subjects rather well (the same cannot be said for his relations with the Irish). When it came to the Americans, however, the king had a huge blind spot: he never realized that they had become—after more than a century of colonization—quite different from their Old World cousins. Things such as taxes, that an Old Englishman could countenance, were simply beyond the pale in North America.

When was the first blood between British and Americans shed?

On the evening of March 5, 1770, a crowd of 200 Bostonians arrived outside the Customs House to taunt and intimidate seven British guardsmen and their captain. The crowd started with insults but moved to snowballs and finally to ice balls (these last really hurt!). Captain Thomas Preston repeatedly told his men not to fire, but on one occasion they did not hear the world "not," and they emptied their muskets into the crowd. When the smoke cleared, five Bostonians lay dead or dying in the snow.

The Boston Massacre was a bad scene, but it could have been much worse. Lieutenant-Governor Thomas Hutchinson and Samuel Adams—one of the Patriot leaders—

intervened between the soldiers and the crowd, preventing what could have been a real massacre. Within forty-eight hours, most of the British garrison had been evacuated to the islands of Boston Harbor. Months passed before the trial, in which two British soldiers were found guilty of manslaughter (not murder) and had their thumbs branded as punishment. Remarkably, things between England and the colonies smoothed over for a time, and it seemed as if relations were almost normal again, until the summer of 1772.

What was the *Gaspée* Affair?

HMS *Gaspée* was a revenue cutter, or sloop, which chased smugglers off the Rhode Island and New York coasts. Its captain, Joseph Duddington, was known for extreme views where the Americans were concerned, and his sentiments were returned in equal measure. In August 1772, after the *Gaspée* ran aground in Naraganssett Bay, nearly a dozen boats filled with Rhode Island men rowed out to attack her. Captain Duddington was slightly wounded in the scuffle, and the *Gaspée* was first captured, then burned to the waterline. This was the first direct attack on the royal flag—the Union Jack—in North America.

In some ways, the *Gaspée* Affair was even worse than the Boston Massacre, but when the king's agents and lawyers investigated, they could not even find anyone to interview. The *Gaspée* Affair, therefore, was another marker on the road to the American Revolution.

Why was the Boston Tea Party so important?

It seems so harmless in retrospect—no one was killed or even injured as Bostonians dumped 342 chests of tea into the harbor. To King George III's government, however, the Tea Party—which took place on December 16, 1773—was a flagrant violation of British law. The colonists had protested a three penny tax per pound of tea, which seemed a very small amount to the average British taxpayer. The protestors in Boston had gone much further, however, taking over the three ships that night and hurling a cargo worth perhaps 20,000 pounds sterling into the harbor.

As significant as the Tea Party was, the repercussions were even more important. A furious George III and Parliament set forth the so-called Coercive Acts, which closed the port of Boston, moved the Massachusetts government from Boston to Salem, and ended the Massachusetts tradition of town meetings. These acts inflamed most New Englanders, but, almost for the first time, hundreds of thousands of Americans from the other colonies agreed with the people of Boston. Fast days were held in Virginia, and the First Continental Congress was called for the autumn of 1774.

Was the Revolution inevitable by the autumn of 1774?

No. It was highly likely, but conciliatory sentiments on either side of the Atlantic could have slowed things down, or even stopped them. Instead, however, the "hotter" heads prevailed on both sides of the ocean. More British troops were sent to Boston, and General Thomas Gage (1719–1787) was ordered to confiscate the powder and musket balls of the colonists.

General Gage—who was married to an American—knew this would be difficult, but he was a British soldier and followed his orders. On the evening of April 18, 1775, he sent nearly 2,000 British soldiers out of Boston, by way of the Charles River to Cambridge. Gage did not know that one of the most flamboyant, and successful, of the Boston Patriots—Paul Revere (1735–1818)—was already in Charlestown, waiting for a signal light to appear in the belfry of the Old North Church. Revere and his co-conspirators had decided to watch the movements of the British, where one signal light would mean that the British were leaving by "The Neck" (a narrow strip of land connecting Boston to the mainland) and two lights would mean they were departing by way of the Charles River. Once he saw two signal lights, Revere galloped off into the night, shouting "The Regulars are out!" (Tradition later altered this to "The British are coming!")

What happened at Lexington Green on the morning of April 19, 1775?

The long files of British troops came to a halt when their commanders saw about seventy American militiamen drawn up on the town green. British Major John Pitcairn (1722–1775) rode out in front of his men to shout, "Disperse! I say disperse, ye rebels!"

For a moment or two, it seemed that Pitcairn's order had taken hold. The militiamen on the green began to disperse to different sides of the common, taking their muskets with them. And then, perhaps sixty seconds after Pitcairn's shout, came a solitary explosion and musket ball. Who fired it—British or American, Loyalist or Patriot—and from which direction was never ascertained. The result was immediate, however. The British leveled their muskets and began blazing away. When the smoke cleared, about twenty Americans were killed or wounded.

After a short rest, the British gave three cheers and moved on toward Concord.

How well (or poorly) had Paul Revere done his job?

Revere sometimes gets more credit than he deserves: there were at least three dispatch riders that night. But the sum total of his efforts and theirs—as well as of unnamed people who did similar work—resulted in alerting most of Middlesex County. The alarm came too late for Lexington, where only seventy men stood against the British, but when the British columns reached Concord, there were already a few thousand militiamen on the other side of the Concord River. Samuel Adams and John Adams had, by this time, already slipped out of town. Tradition has it that they heard the opening shots on Lexington Green and that Samuel Adams rejoiced that his countrymen had taken the bold road of defiance.

What was the Battle of Concord Bridge?

At around noon, the American militiamen saw smoke arising from the town and guessed, incorrectly, that the British were about to burn the entire town. A lead column of Americans, therefore, advanced on Concord Bridge, where they were met by about one hundred British regulars. The fight at the bridge was inconclusive, but enough British redcoats fell that their commanders decided it was time to turn for home, meaning Boston. The men had marched since midnight, they had done much good work, and there was no reason to push the fight any further.

To the Americans, the situation was almost completely the opposite. Many of them were weary from their long marches, but they were angry about the deaths at Lexington and Concord. The British had made the mistake of entering the countryside: let them pay for their error. As the British headed for Charlestown and the safety provided by the guns of the Royal Navy ships in Boston Harbor, they were harassed continually by American militiamen. Roughly 280 British soldiers were killed, wounded, or went missing that day.

How was the news of Lexington and Concord received?

Twelve of the thirteen colonies—Georgia being the lone exception—greeted the news with enthusiasm. Many colonists had suspected that war was possible and that it required just one major spark. That did not mean all the colonists wanted to participate, however. Quite a few wanted to sit on the fence and observe which side came out ahead.

An engraving showing Colonel Ethan Allen demanding the surrender of Fort Ticonderoga.

Of course there were some exceptions, and in May 1775, roughly one hundred men from Vermont, under the command of Colonel Ethan Allen (1738–1789), arrived in the wooded area just outside of Fort Ticonderoga. Their goal was to capture the fort and its cannon for the Continental cause. Just by chance, another column, of perhaps one hundred men, arrived from Connecticut and western Massachusetts. Led by Colonel Benedict Arnold (1741–1803) of Norwich, these men had the same objective. Some hours were spent in wrangling over who should lead, and in the end it was agreed that Ethan Allen and Benedict Arnold would be co-commanders. They surprised Fort Ticonderoga at dawn and captured it without shedding any blood. Tradition has it that the British commander demanded to know who gave these men their authority and that Ethan Allen shouted back, "By the order of Jehovah and the Continental Congress!"

Which regiment made it to Boston the fastest?

Many New England men reached the outskirts of Boston within days, and there soon formed into new regiments. The regiment that came the farthest the fastest, however, was a Virginia rifle regiment. Led by Colonel Daniel Morgan, these riflemen marched from western Virginia to Cambridge in thirty-some days.

COMMANDER IN CHIEF

How did George Washington become leader of the Continental Army?

Washington (1732–1799) had been in retirement from military service for roughly sixteen years, and he had very much enjoyed the domestic scene at Mount Vernon. When the news of Lexington and Concord arrived, however, Washington was one of the first Virginians to declare for liberty. Chosen a member of the Second Continental Congress, he arrived in Philadelphia in June 1775, wearing a brand-new uniform. Though he declared to some people—including his wife—that he did not seek the job of commander-in-chief, Washington was far too ambitious to let this opportunity pass by. He wanted the job.

Washington's only significant opposition came from John Hancock (1737–1793), a Bostonian who also wanted to be commander-in-chief. Hancock possessed no military experience, however, and it was no surprise that the Continental Congress decided, on June 17, to invest George Washington with the power and authority to lead the Continental Army. He and the delegates who chose him did not know that a major battle was being fought that same day.

Who "won" the Battle of Bunker Hill?

Technically the British did because they pushed the Americans off Bunker Hill and Breeds Hill, both on the Charlestown peninsula. This was a Pyrrhic victory, however, because 1,054 British were killed, wounded, or went missing in one afternoon.

On the night of June 16–17, 1775, 1,000 American militiamen snuck onto the peninsula and began to dig in. At daylight, the British detected the Americans' new position, and General Thomas Gage sent General Sir William Howe (1729–1814) and about 2,000 men to dislodge them. Not until afternoon did the British start their march up Bunker Hill, and not until they were within forty yards did the Americans begin to ply them with powder and ball. The Americans were first-rate sharpshooters, and they gave far better than they took. Only on the third try did the British seize the hill, and General Howe—as well as many others—concurred that if this was what it took to capture two hills and one peninsula, the conquest of America would be a very tough undertaking.

When did Washington arrive, and what change did he bring?

Washington arrived at Cambridge and took command of the Continental Army on July 3, 1775. His first set of orders indicated that he was not a permissive kind of person and that he expected the men of the newly formed regiments to act like gentlemen and soldiers. This was very much in keeping with Washington's character, but he did not fully realize who he was dealing with.

Washington was accustomed to deference from family members and obedience from slaves. This was not what he received in New England, and one of his longstanding complaints was that the New England men did not understand discipline. Had he been fully honest, however, Washington would have admitted that the New Englanders made up—in dash and vigor—for what they lacked in compliance and obedience. These were the sons of the men who had taken Fortress Louisburg in 1745, and a few of them were at both places. Colonel Seth Pomeroy, who became one of Washington's brigadier-generals, had directed the Yankee artillery at the Siege of Louisburg.

What did Washington—and the Continental Army—need the most?

Their greatest need was for artillery. The American militiamen had plenty of muskets, powder horns, and musket balls, but they lacked the heavy siege guns that could make or break the situation in and around Boston. Washington, therefore, turned to a self-educated Bostonian, asking him to bring cannon from Fort Ticonderoga all the way to Cambridge.

Colonel Henry Knox (1750–1796) was a Boston bookseller who had read all he could find on the subject of military history. Pleased to accept the assignment from

An 1855 illustration of Colonel Henry Knox entering Fort Ticonderoga with his troops.

Washington, Knox traveled west to Fort Ticonderoga that autumn and began the incredibly arduous task of dragging, pushing, and sledging nearly one hundred pieces of artillery all the way to eastern Massachusetts. Today, the "Knox Trail" shows the walker how difficult it was to get those cannon over the Berkshire Hills and across Massachusetts. Knox accomplished the task, however, and had his cannon to Cambridge by February.

Could anyone else have done it?

Historians often ask that question for various circumstances and leaders throughout the book. This is one of the rare occasions, however, when we flatly declare that no one else that we know of could have done it as well as Knox. Blessed with a cheerful disposition and a hearty approach to problem solving, Knox was the right man at the right time.

Washington had the cannon placed on Dorchester Heights, just south of the city of Boston. When General Sir William Howe saw those cannon in their emplacements, his first thought was of the terrible losses he had suffered when capturing Bunker Hill. Howe, therefore, agreed to a truce under which his British forces and their Loyalist friends would evacuate Boston in return for assurances that the Americans would not molest them. March 17 is still celebrated as Evacuation Day in Massachusetts.

How was Benedict Arnold—America's most infamous traitor—perceived at this point?

In 1775–1776, Arnold, a native of Norwich, Connecticut, was a big hero. He led 2,000 men by an incredibly difficult combination of land and water, through northern Maine, on the way to Quebec City. On December 31, 1775, Arnold and his co-commander General Robert Montgomery failed, by a hairsbreadth, to capture Quebec. Montgomery was killed in action, and Arnold suffered a bad leg wound. Arnold held the ragged American forces together through the winter of 1776, however, and began an orderly retreat in the spring.

Arnold's negative aspects—his mercenary quality especially—were already apparent to some observers, but his battlefield heroism made up for everything in the first three years of the war. Not only did Arnold nearly take Quebec, but in the autumn of 1776, he—with a makeshift American flotilla—kept the British off Lake Champlain until late in the season. Overall, it can be said that Arnold performed invaluable services for the American cause in the first half of the Revolutionary War.

THE TIMES THAT TRY MENS' SOULS

What forces were backing up the British as the revolution began?

Following their evacuation of Boston, the British fleet and army went to Halifax, Nova Scotia, where they were pleased to learn that King George III had decided to go for broke. Even though he knew about the Battle of Bunker Hill and the American skill in defensive fighting, the king arranged for British, German, Loyalist, and Native American forces to assault the colonies then in rebellion.

The British were, of course, red-coated soldiers who had become so well known during the campaigns of the Seven Years' War. The Germans were Hessians, so called because the ruler of Hesse-Canau sold their services to the British king. The Loyalists, also known as Tories, were American colonists who remained loyal to the king. A large number of Native Americans were also ready to assist the British because King George III's Proclamation Line ended at the crest of the Appalachian Mountains.

Who was to command this rather overwhelming force?

General Sir Guy Carleton (1724–1808) was already in Canada and planning to move south, until his advance was slowed by Benedict Arnold. General Sir William Howe would command the 35,000 men sent to capture Manhattan. His brother, Admiral Richard Howe (1726–1799), commanded the Royal Navy warships and transports. General Sir Henry Clinton was to create a diversion by attacking Charleston, South Carolina. And the Native American allies were to be led, rather loosely, by Sir John Johnson, son of the man who had won the Battle of Lake George in 1755.

When did the British make their first major assault?

In August 1776, General Sir William Howe brought almost 35,000 men from Staten Island to the eastern end of Long island, which George Washington defended with about 20,000 men. The Battle of Long Island—also known as the Battle of Brooklyn or Brooklyn Heights—was a classic case in which a man who understood sound tactics went up against, and beat, a gifted amateur. To be sure, Washington labored under some difficulties, including the propensity of his men to leave when they liked. Even so, General Howe completely outmaneuvered and then beat Washington at the Battle of Long Island: about 1,100 Americans were killed or captured. The (much) larger danger was that Howe might then bag the entire Continental Army.

Was anyone surprised when the Johnson family turned out to be Loyalists, or Tories?

Sir William Johnson, who had been knighted after winning the Battle of Lake George, died in 1774, but there is little doubt he would have supported the royal cause. His son, Sir John Johnson, was, if anything, even more of a Tory. The Johnson family's stance makes sense when one considers how many hundreds of thousands of acres in up-colony New York were at stake. These lands belonged to the Johnsons because of various grants by King George II and King George III, and to go against the royal cause would imperil these holdings and the family's titles.

Not for the last time, Howe waited too long. In the forty hours he delayed, Washington got his entire army off Brooklyn Heights and into the city of Manhattan. This was accomplished by the regiment of fishermen from Marblehead, Massachusetts, and has to rank as among the most inspired escapes of the Revolutionary War. General Howe was unperturbed, however; he had tested Washington's battle strength and found it wanting.

Why did Washington wait so long in Manhattan?

This mistake was clearly due to Washington's lack of experience. He waited in Manhattan too long, and when the British attacked on September 15, 1776, he was caught completely flat-footed. Many of his men simply turned and ran, leading Washington to exclaim: "Is it with these men that I am to save America?"

Through luck, Washington managed to get most of his men out of Lower Manhattan before the British pincer movement came together; even so, his retreat was disastrous. Not only had Washington lost the biggest battle of his career to date, but he had been chased out of North America's biggest merchant city.

Could anything more go wrong at this point?

Yes, indeed. The British moved north to capture Fort Washington, on the east side of the Hudson River, and Fort Lee, on the west side. Washington was not present at either occasion, but he learned the full extent of the loss, more than 3,000 men taken prisoner. By now, his men were deserting in droves, and as he headed across New Jersey, Washington saw his overall troop strength fall to around 5,000. The British, meanwhile, only increased in strength because of the Loyalists who now declared for King George.

General Howe was a slow and cautious man, but the man he sent in pursuit of Washington, General Charles Cornwallis (1738–1805), was fast and aggressive. Washington barely made it to the south side of the Delaware River before winter began, and his situation was so desperate that he wrote his brother that "the game is pretty well up."

How important was Thomas Paine to the Revolutionary cause?

It is difficult to overestimate his importance. Thomas Paine (1737–1809) may well have been the second most important to the cause, coming behind George Washington.

Was George Washington a writer of letters?

Yes, and equally important, he saved those that he received. We, therefore, have a rather good idea of his state of mind through the dark, desperate days at the end of 1776. Washington was not going to submit tamely, however; he had one last trick up his sleeve.

Born in England, Thomas Paine came to America in 1774, just in time to witness the beginning of the Revolution. An impulsive person, he quickly joined the Continental Army and was in service during the retreat across New Jersey. Paine had already written a number of well-received pamphlets, but the one he penned in December 1776, "The Crisis," took first place. He began with the stirring words: "These are the times that try mens' souls." Paine went on to contrast the actions of the summer soldier and the sunshine patriot with the man who would stand and give his all in a time of crisis. The pamphlet was read aloud to the remaining soldiers of the Continental Army, and there is little doubt that it had a powerful impact.

Philosopher and practical revolutionary Thomas Paine did much to inspire the American cause of independence with his political pamphlets.

When did Washington finally make his long-desired counterattack?

He had waited so long that many people had despaired of the American cause. Washington, however, never really gave up hope: he knew that a major blow on his part would give a boost to American morale, and he planned to strike the Hessian encampment at Trenton, near the north side of the Delaware River.

The 3,000 Hessians—who had been detailed by General Cornwallis to keep an eye on Washington—were roughly equal in number to the hungry and despairing Americans, but their food and equipment were vastly superior. The Hessians enjoyed good winter fires and plenty of rum on Christmas Day and had no sense that Washington was about to attack. Toward evening on December 25, 1776, Washington led his men to the Delaware River, which they crossed in shallow boats. The cold was bad enough, but the ice drifting through the river was both more dangerous and dismaying; even so, the Americans got to the other side to begin the eight-mile-long march to Trenton. They got there before dawn and at about 6:30 A.M., Washington initiated his surprise attack.

How successful were the Americans at the Battle of Trenton?

It scarcely deserves the name of "battle" because the Americans simply romped through the town. Within minutes, they had artillery at the head of the street, cannon which raked any Hessian who dared come out. Those Hessians who could rally from their post-Christmas stupor fought bravely, but to no avail. At the cost of less than twenty men—killed, wounded, and missing—Washington bagged nearly 3,000 prisoners and an enormous cache of clothing and winter gear. When one compares it on the balance sheet

Had no one warned the Hessians?

Tradition has it that a message was brought to Colonel Rall at suppertime and that he folded the paper, stuck it in his breast pocket and forgot all about it. Given that the Hessians were 3,000 miles from home and that Christmas was their biggest celebration of the calendar year, his neglect of the situation is not all that surprising.

to Washington's losses in and around New York City, the Battle of Trenton seems small but it had all the power of a massive counterpunch. The American spirit began to revive, while the British and Hessians were jolted out of the winter complacency.

Who came after Washington and the Continentals?

General Charles Cornwallis came in a hurry, with Hessian and British troops who amounted to about 7,000. Washington, by now, had received reinforcements, but he had no more than 5,000 to oppose the British and Hessians. General Cornwallis moved with great speed, and by January 2, 1776, he had Washington and his men backed up to the Delaware River, with no means of retreat. This was yet another example of the consummate skill that the British commanders demonstrated in maneuver, and the end for Washington looked very near. The Americans—by this time—had become minor experts in the art of withdrawal, however, and overnight they escaped around Cornwallis' left flank, while leaving their camp fires burning. Early on the morning of January 3, 1776, Cornwallis awoke to hear cannon in his rear, and he realized that Washington had both outmarched and outfought him.

Was the Battle of Princeton as important as the Battle of Trenton?

Not in terms of American morale, which had already been lifted. But by escaping General Cornwallis' trap and getting to his rear—where he defeated Cornwallis' men at the town of Princeton—Washington demonstrated a one-two punch that was seldom equaled during the Revolutionary War. It is no accident that many of the finest, and most stirring, paintings from the Revolution executed by Jonathan Trumbull, Gilbert Stuart, and others concentrate on the dark, desperate days before Trenton and Princeton. The American cause would never again be brought so low.

Was that it for the campaigns of that winter?

Yes. Washington went into winter quarters at Morristown, New Jersey, while the British and Hessians retired to Manhattan for the winter.

YEAR OF THE HANGMAN

What did the British plan for the year 1777?

Numerous wits commented that the three "sevens" contained in the date resembled a hangman or noose and suggested that 1777 would be a negative year all around. The British planners paid no attention to this; they envisioned a massive, three-pronged invasion of the Hudson River valley to culminate with three armies converging on Albany. By holding the line of the Hudson River, the British and their allies would cut off the rebellious New England states from their less contentious southern neighbors, or so the British reasoned.

The plan had much to recommend it, but it required excellent timing, with all three armies sticking to the plan. The season began with British General John Burgoyne (1722–1792) leading 8,000 men—British, Hessians, Loyalists, and Native Americans—south from Montreal. A charming, witty man who had written several plays, Burgoyne seemed a good choice to command the northern invading force: his major foible was a reluctance to let go of things that most military men considered luxuries. Throughout the campaign, Burgoyne and his staff drank large quantities of fine liquor. This meant that the baggage train of his army was much heavier than was ideal and that his force took longer to pass through the Champlain and Hudson river valleys than one might expect.

What was the first major action of 1777?

Late in June 1777, Burgoyne's force approached Fort Ticonderoga, which the Americans had seized at the opening of the war. Burgoyne had a healthy respect for the American gunners, but he pulled a surprise on them; his engineers and quartermasters somehow managed to get cannon of their own atop Mount Defiance, overlooking the fort and the lake. This, one of the best strategic moves of the war, forced the Americans to evacuate Fort Ticonderoga and, seeing them on the run, Burgoyne committed his army to the pursuit.

The skirmishes and battles over the next day or so seemed to indicate both that the British had pulled off a real coup and that the Americans had plenty of fight remaining. When Burgoyne pulled in all his men from the pursuit, he found more casualties than expected, and his daring began to wane. Indeed, over the next three weeks, he showed little interest in pursuing the Americans, choosing instead to hack his way through a near wilderness between Fort William Henry and Fort Edward. Even so, Burgoyne had come close to success all on his own, and he eagerly awaited news from the other two commanders.

Where was the Battle of Oriskany?

Colonel Barry St. Leger (1733–1789) had about 3,000 British, Loyalist, and Native American troops, and he crossed Lake Ontario without incident. Moving quickly, General St. Leger reached the walls of American Fort Stanwix, in upstate New York, and commenced a siege.

To this point, St. Leger had done very well, but the approach of his Native American allies led the settlers of the Mohawk River valley to rise in force; perhaps 2,000 men left their farms and marched to the aid of Fort Stanwix. St. Leger met them halfway, and his ambush led to the Battle of Oriskany, considered perhaps the single most desperate fight of the Revolutionary War. Both sides were mauled in the fighting, which raged for seven hours, and when it was over, St. Leger's Native Americans had no fight left in them. The relief column had to turn back, but St. Leger's grip on Fort Stanwix was weakened, and when Benedict Arnold used a ruse, St. Leger had to give up the siege.

Was Benedict Arnold as colorful and creative as he appears?

He really was. Promoted to major-general, Arnold rushed to the Mohawk River valley, but he arrived too late to participate in the Battle of Oriskany. Arnold pulled off a magnificent ruse, however; he sent a half-witted half-breed by the name of Hon Yost Schuyler into the camp of General St. Leger's Native American allies. Native Americans often believed that mental illness was a sign of being visited by the gods, and they listened to Schuyler who babbled both about the smallpox—which he declared was on its way—and the Americans, who he claimed were as numerous as the leaves on the trees. St. Leger's Native American allies panicked and fled. When St. Leger discovered they had disappeared, he had no choice but to turn for Canada. One of the three British armies was taken out of the equation.

Where did that leave General Burgoyne?

He did not learn of General St. Leger's failure for some weeks, but even then, Burgoyne had pinned most of his hopes on General Howe. As long as Howe came north from Manhattan with a strong force, he would surely be able to rendezvous with Burgoyne in Albany. Unbeknownst to Burgoyne, however, Howe had moved in nearly a completely opposite direction. He had loaded 25,000 men on ships and sailed with them toward Philadelphia. Howe went by way of Delaware Bay.

Whether General Howe truly ignored his orders or merely misinterpreted them remains one of the great questions of Revolutionary-era warfare. But regardless of Howe's motivations, his move was disastrous for General Burgoyne who, to this point, had taken practically all the risks. About the only thing one can fault Burgoyne for is that he failed to retreat to Canada.

General John Burgoyne was responsible for planning the invasion into America during the Revolutionary War. After his defeat in 1777, he went back to England, serving in the House of Commons and also writing plays.

What happened at the Battle of Bennington?

Bennington, Vermont is a college town today, set in a truly scenic area near the border of Massachusetts, New York, and Vermont. In 1777, however, it was the scene of a bloody battle between two columns of Hessians—sent by Burgoyne to find cattle—and a large group of American militiamen, who seemed to spring from the very ground. What Burgoyne did not know was that the recent murder of a young Loyalist woman had set the frontier aflame.

The murder of Jane McCrae brought thousands of New York and Vermont farmers off the fence and into the conflict. Led by Colonel John Stark (1728–1822), these farmers routed Burgoyne's men in two skirmishes, which are collectively known as the Battle of Bennington. This does not mean that all of those men remained in the field, but rather that there was no chance of Burgoyne expanding anywhere to his left, or eastern, flank.

Could Burgoyne have escaped to Canada?

Very likely, it was too late. Throughout the campaign, Burgoyne had insisted on dragging the heavy baggage along, and all of it would have to be jettisoned if he were to make a run for Canada. This was also not Burgoyne's style and he marched bravely on, right into the trap planned by Generals Horatio Gates and Benedict Arnold.

Gates and Arnold knew that Burgoyne would have to travel by way of the Hudson River, and they had nearly 20,000 men—militia for the most part—waiting for him. Among the Americans were the sharpshooting Virginians led by Colonel Daniel Morgan. Burgoyne stumbled right into the trap at the Battle of Freeman's Farm, late in September 1777.

In what way had the Americans gained the upper hand?

From the Battle of Oriskany—which was a bloody draw—onward, the Americans won almost every wilderness fight, meaning any time there was shelter from trees, stone walls, and the like. This advantage had long been noticed, but after the summer of 1777 the Americans won almost every time. In part, this was because of their sharpshooting abilities, but it was also the result of having developed a peculiar kind of aggression, one which the Americans had learned by battling the Native Americans.

The Battle of Freeman's Farm cost Burgoyne well over 1,000 men killed, wounded, and missing, but most of all he lost Brigadier-General Simon Fraser, considered the most inspiring officer of the army. Burgoyne, by now, would have liked to retreat, but it was far too late.

Who won the Battle of Bemis Heights?

This has long been debated. General Horatio Gates (1727–1806), who was in overall command, clearly drew up the day's battle plan and set about executing it, but General Benedict Arnold was the person fighting on the ground. Late in the afternoon, when it was clear that the Americans would prevail, Arnold led a reckless but inspired attack in person: he galloped straight into one of the British redoubts. Arnold went down with a wound in the leg, the same leg that had been wounded during the assault on Quebec City, in December 1775.

General Gates received the honor for the victory, but many of the common soldiers believed that Benedict Arnold was *the man*, who had really done the work. The controversy between Gates and Arnold simmered for years.

How large a victory was Saratoga for the American cause?

The battles were fought at Bemis Heights and Freeman's Farm, but Burgoyne's surrender took place at the village of Saratoga. He handed his sword to General Gates and admitted that the 7,000 men who remained were now prisoners of war. There is no way to overdo the importance of the surrender at Saratoga. Anyone who had previously been skeptical of the Americans' ability to fight on an equal basis now changed their mind. Most important was the Court of King Louis XVI, which was watching closely. This was not the end of the battles of the Year of the Hangman, however.

Did Howe demonstrate his usual tactical brilliance at the Battle of the Brandywine River?

No. This time, Howe was in a hurry. He wanted to reach Philadelphia and winter quarters before the season changed. Howe, therefore, used his men in a full frontal assault at Brandywine. The British and Hessians came on strong, but the Americans—who had some foreign volunteers on their side—resisted stubbornly. Instead of Howe's usual precision tactics, the Battle of the Brandywine was a straight-ahead contest, with the side that showed more stubbornness likely to win.

The Marquis de Lafayette (Marie-Joseph Paul Yves Roch Gilbert du Motier de Lafayette; 1757–1834)—who had recently arrived to tender his sword to the Continental Congress— was wounded in the middle of battle. Other leaders, too, were in danger of being captured, and George Washington reluctantly broke off the engagement. He had yet to win a single battle from General Howe and had staked everything on attaining victory here.

Did the British reach Philadelphia that autumn?

They made it, early in November, and found that the Continental Congress had escaped eighty miles to the west, to the town of York. General Howe showed no dismay over this;

Born in central France in 1757, Lafayette was the eldest son of one of the great noblemen of that nation. His father died fighting the British when the boy was two, and Lafayette always wanted to strike at the people who had deprived him of his father. In 1777, Lafayette snuck out of France—there is no other way to express it—and arrived in South Carolina. Making his way northward, he observed the temper and resolution of the American people, and by the time he met George Washington, he was completely convinced that the American cause was worth all his effort. Many other foreign noblemen—including Friedrich Von Steuben and Casimir Pulaski—joined the Americans, but of them all, Lafayette made the deepest impact.

---

he was delighted to make Philadelphia his winter home. Many of his best officers, too, settled in for a winter of balls, parties, and masquerades. It was at one of these events that sixteen-year-old Peggy Shippen, the daughter of a prominent Loyalist, met Major John André of the British army. Their infatuation was mutual, and it led—over time—to the treason of Benedict Arnold.

In the meantime, Howe believed that the fighting for the year was done, but Washington was about to surprise him once again.

How close did Washington and his Continentals come to success at the Battle of Germantown?

They came within a smidgeon, as we say.

Germantown was the farthest of all Howe's garrisons, and Washington hit it

An 1834 portrait of General Lafayette by Joseph-Désiré Court. Lafayette was a French revolutionary who became a strong American ally and personal friend to George Washington.

early on the morning of October 27, 1777. Washington knew that victory depended on an early morning success, before Howe could bring up reinforcements, and the Continentals did their job well, driving in first the British pickets and then the vanguard. Success was nearly attained by 10 A.M., but two factors conspired to rob Washington of the victory he so deeply desired.

A heavy fog descended on Germantown by 9 A.M., causing some units on both sides to fire on each other rather than against the foe. Much worse was the British seizure of the

Chew House, a prominent landmark on the way to the center of town. By the time the Continentals arrived, the British had turned the house into a fort. Common sense is always easy to apply in retrospect, but it seems that the Americans should have bypassed the Chew House and moved on down the road to confront the main British force. Instead, they attempted to batter it down with cannon fire, and when this failed, they made repeated charges, all of which failed to take the house. By early afternoon, Washington knew he had failed yet again and withdrew his men. Germantown was a very close thing, however, and Washington took heart from the way his men had fought, toe-to-toe, against the British.

DIPLOMATS ABROAD

Who were the most important Americans in the effort to win assistance from abroad?

About two dozen people were directly involved, and their efforts were probably backed up by a few hundred others. Little doubt exists, however, that the two men most responsible for representing the American cause to Europe were Benjamin Franklin (1706–1790) and John Adams (1735–1826) (they, by the way, usually did not get along).

Franklin went to the court of King Louis XVI, where he purposely wore a coonskin cap and run-down clothing to make himself appear a rural man from America, albeit one who was in touch with the ideas and ideals of the Enlightenment. He and Voltaire never met in the flesh, as the French philosopher died in 1778, but Franklin cleverly built on the edifice that Voltaire had erected. Who better than the Americans to humble the British, Franklin implied? John Adams also spent some time in Paris, but he moved on to The Hague, the capital of the Dutch Netherlands. Adams secured several important loans for the American cause, and in 1780—for reasons of their own—the Dutch joined the naval war against the British.

When did Louis XVI come around to the alliance with the United States?

In March 1778, the French court signed two treaties with the Americans, one for military purposes and the other for commercial. France wanted to make the most of the alliance, most especially to deny trade to Great Britain; what America wanted, and needed, was French troops and ships as well as money. In the spring of 1778, it all seemed possible.

The Count d'Estaing sailed from France with about twenty warships and a large number of troop transports: his destination was North America. At the same time, France and Holland arranged for loans to the Continental Congress. The future looked bright.

When did Washington and the Congress learn of the new alliance with France?

They had the news of the French alliance by June, and they had the equally good news that the British were on the verge of departing Philadelphia. General Sir William Howe had never lost a battle in America, but he had failed—on numerous occasions—to polish off the rebels, and he was therefore replaced by General Sir Henry Clinton. Knowing that a French war fleet was on its way, General Clinton decided to evacuate Philadelphia and concentrate his forces in Manhattan.

Why did Washington fail at the Battle of Monmouth?

It was not a personal failure, in that Washington did his best, but it was deeply painful to see the British escape to New York City without taking a major loss. Early on the morning of June 29, 1778, the vanguard of the Continental Army attacked the rear guard of the retreating British at the village on Monmouth, New Jersey. Washington ached for victory on this spot to remove the stain of his previous defeats, but it was not to be.

First, American General Charles Lee proved a craven and attempted to withdraw. When Washington prevented this by galloping up and down the lines, the Americans fought like tigers, but like great animals they tired rapidly in the severe heat. We believe that the mercury reached 100 degrees that day, and many men on both sides suffered heatstroke. By early evening, the Americans were clearly victorious on the battlefield, but the British were making good their escape. By the next morning, Washington knew it was too late. His men were too fatigued to pursue, and the British reached Staten Island, to be ferried across to Manhattan. The failure to achieve victory at Monmouth was one of Washington's deepest personal disappointments.

THE FRENCH ALLIANCE

How deeply involved did France become in the Revolutionary War?

Nations only become involved when their own interests are at stake, and France very much wanted to punish Britain for the losses it had suffered during the Seven Years' War. In the summer of 1778, the Count d'Estaing appeared off Manhattan with a large French fleet, but he was unable to persuade his pilots to enter the harbor because they believed it was too treacherous. The count, therefore, sailed off for Rhode Island, where he attempted to attack the British at Newport.

George Washington gritted his teeth. So much had been expected, and so much hoped for, but here at the outset, the French alliance did not appear to be worthwhile. The British fleet pursued d'Estaing's fleet to Narragansett Bay, where the two fought a major naval battle. Thanks first to the pounding from the enemy's guns, and then from a major summer storm, the French fleet sailed off to Boston to refit.

What plans did Washington make for the year 1779?

Washington's single great desire was to recapture Manhattan and thereby end the war in a blaze of glory. The situation was not ripe, however, and all Washington could do in 1779 was to chip away at the British defenses.

The major move Washington made in 1779 was the capture of Stony Point, on the west bank of the Hudson River. This fortress had been in British hands for several years, and it had a garrison of about 600. Washington assigned the task to Colonel "Mad Anthony" Wayne, who captured Stony Point in a daring night attack.

What was the British plan for the year 1779?

For the first half of the year, the British were on the defensive. French Count d'Estaing returned from the Caribbean with his war fleet to make an attempt on Savannah, Georgia, which had fallen into British hands the previous year. This, the third attempt at Franco-American cooperation, failed miserably.

Like many naval commanders, d'Estaing was afraid of the impending hurricane season; he, therefore, insisted that the attack happen soon. Had he been willing to wait, the French and Americans would very likely have captured Savannah; instead, they suffered several hundred casualties while the British exulted in their good fortune. The allies' failure at Savannah emboldened the British to make their next attempt in the Southern theatre.

Who was Sir Henry Clinton, and what was his big moment?

General Sir Henry Clinton—who succeeded General Howe in 1776—was a very cautious person who weighed every situation and possibility before making any move. Clinton had almost 30,000 British troops in and around Manhattan and was very secure in his position, but he was finally persuaded—by some bolder subordinates—to take a chance on an attack on Charleston, South Carolina. The rationale was that there were more American Loyalists in the southern states than the northern ones (this was probably true, but difficult to prove).

Clinton, therefore, sailed from New York City with over 10,000 of his best troops, and early in the winter of 1780 he laid siege to Charleston (the same city that endured a very long siege during the American Civil War). American General Benjamin Lincoln fought ably and well, but the Royal Navy sealed off his escape

General Cornwallis' right-hand man, General Banastre Tarleton, was a brilliant leader of light cavalry. Americans declared he slaughtered surrendering troops at the Waxhaw Massacre and called him "The Butcher" or "Bloody Ban." He later became a Whig politician (*Portrait of Sir Banastre Tarleton*, 1782, by Sir Joshua Reynolds).

route, and in May 1780, Lincoln and 5,000 of his men surrendered, in the largest capitulation by American forces during the war. Clinton then returned to Manhattan, leaving his able subordinate, General Charles Cornwallis, to continue the British conquest of the Southern states.

We have all heard of Cornwallis because of his later actions at Yorktown. But who was Banastre Tarleton?

Banastre Tarleton (1754–1833) was a young British nobleman, intimately connected with the merchant trade of Liverpool, most especially with the slave-traders of that city. Tarleton was a colonel of dragoons—light cavalry—and he was General Cornwallis' right hand in the pursuit of the Americans. The fall of Charleston meant that Americans attempted to escape South Carolina, and Cornwallis sent Tarleton off to pursue.

Tarleton caught a group of Americans in The Waxhaws settlement, right on the border between North and South Carolina. As was his style, he initiated a furious, all-out attack immediately, giving neither the Americans nor his own men any time to rest. The move succeeded, and within minutes, the Americans attempted to surrender. Tarleton refused to accept this, however, and his men cut down their opponents. Perhaps one hundred Americans were killed that day.

What did Washington do in response to the loss of Charleston?

Washington and the Continental Congress were appalled by the loss of Charleston to the British. Under political pressure, Washington selected General Horatio Gates—the victor of Saratoga—to go south and recoup the American fortunes there. Gates had his doubts about the situation, but he accepted the job and took about 3,000 soldiers south. He recruited more soldiers along the way and had about 5,000 men when he encountered General Cornwallis and Colonel Tarleton at the Battle of Camden, in South Carolina.

Camden was a complete, unmitigated disaster for the American cause. Perhaps 2,000 men were killed, wounded, or captured, and those who escaped chose—for the most part—never to fight again. In part this was due to Cornwallis' carefully scripted battle plan; it was also the result of the savagery of Colonel Tarleton's dragoons, who sliced and diced their way all that afternoon. Colonel Baron von Kalb—a German soldier of fortune who had joined the Americans—was one of the few leaders to stand all the way, and he died late in the battle. General Horatio Gates, meanwhile, escaped from the battlefield and rode roughly seventy miles before reining in his horse. The flight of Gates from Camden became a staple in caricature, as well as poetry, for many years to come.

Did anything remain to the American cause in the South?

Not on paper or in the calculations of the generals of either side. To them it was obvious that the Americans were finished in the South. This was one of those times, however, when the men whose battle strength was not counted on paper emerged to make a big difference.

Where were rifles first made?

No one has ever identified the precise shop, or even the exact locality, but it seems to have been a race between a handful of German gun-makers in the old country and a group of their compatriots in Pennsylvania. Germans had long been skillful in the making of firearms and combustibles, and by about 1730, the first Pennsylvania Rifles—which were later, erroneously, called the Kentucky Rifles—appeared. A long series of grooves in the gun barrel created a new type of trajectory, which allowed for greater accuracy.

What was the Battle of King's Mountain?

King's Mountain stands very close to the border between North and South Carolina, and it was the temporary camping ground for Major Patrick Ferguson and about 1,400 Loyalist Americans. Many of these men had come out for King George III quite recently and were not battle-tested, but they had in their leader—and in his invention—something quite new: the breech-loading rifle.

What happened to Major Ferguson and his men?

Ferguson had invented and patented the world's first breech-loading rifle; in theory, this meant his men should have been able to fire three rounds to every one round fired by their foes. Ferguson did not have many of his breech-loaders with him, however, and when his unit was attacked on King's Mountain, it was nearly wiped out.

Ferguson had made the mistake of taunting the wilderness men who lived on either side of the Appalachian Mountains. He threatened to burn their homes and chase them from the land; they, in turn, rose up in a mass and cornered him on King's Mountain. The battle, fought in August 1780, was a complete wipeout of Ferguson and his command: those who survived yielded to the Americans. When General Cornwallis learned the news, he cancelled his invasion of North Carolina; it was too dangerous to invade the state when there were so many wilderness men hanging on his left, or west, flank.

BENEDICT ARNOLD'S TREASON

How much did George Washington depend on Benedict Arnold?

Washington relied on Arnold to a degree that was rivaled only by the confidence he reposed in two other men: Alexander Hamilton and the Marquis de Lafayette. It is no coincidence that all three of these men were younger than Washington; having no children of his own, the commander-in-chief "adopted" a number of young men during the Revolutionary War.

197

Benedict Arnold was heavier and slower than he had previously been; the two wounds to his left leg meant that he now walked with a cane. Arnold was still viewed as a gallant patriot, however, and when he asked George Washington for the command of the fortress of West Point—on the west bank of the Hudson—Washington agreed. What Washington did not know was that Benedict Arnold's young wife, Peggy Shippen (1760–1804), had strong connections to the British cause. She was one of the Philadelphia Shippens, a prominent merchant family.

America's most famous traitor, General Benedict Arnold, was a successful leader in the Continental Army before making plans to turn over West Point to the British.

Is it fair to say that Peggy Shippen made her husband into a traitor?

It is not. A spouse may cajole, threaten, or even intimidate, but a person—a military person most especially—is 100 percent responsible for keeping his or her oaths. Arnold had, until 1780, been one of the best American battlefield commanders, and no one had ever doubted his allegiance to the patriot cause. The sad truth is that Arnold betrayed the revolutionary cause for money.

Major John André (1750–1780) was a promising young British officer who, during the occupation of Philadelphia in 1777–1778, had been Peggy Shippen's friend and possibly her lover. André was the go-between and corresponded in code with Benedict Arnold, who promised to deliver the fortress of West Point for 20,000 pounds sterling and a command in the British army. Why any British soldiers would wish to serve under a traitor was never taken into consideration. John André had nearly consummated the deal when his superior, General Sir Henry Clinton, demanded a face-to-face meeting with the would-be traitor. André snuck through the American lines dressed as a civilian and obtained maps and plans of West Point. On his way back to Manhattan, he was surprised and detained by three American militiamen who found the plans of West Point carefully sewn into the soles of André's shoes.

Was what happened to John André fair?

Under the rules of war, it was perfectly fair that André was tried as a spy, sentenced, and then hanged. However, André was an especially youthful and charismatic British officer and many people—on both sides of the conflict—pleaded with George Washington to commute the sentence. Washington chose not to do so, and André was hanged. The

---

What happened to Benedict Arnold and Peggy Shippen after the war?

They went to live in London but never attained the kind of social distinction they desired. The British were, quite naturally, suspect of a traitor, and there are many stories about how much Arnold repented his actions and wished he had remained with the Americans. Whether these stories are true cannot be said. What we do know is that Arnold was—and remains—one of the most notorious traitors in American history.

British, to perpetuate his memory, had a statue designed, built, and placed in Westminster Abbey.

What, meanwhile, had happened to Benedict Arnold?

On the morning following John André's detention, Benedict Arnold and his wife were enjoying breakfast, awaiting the arrival of George Washington, who was making a routine inspection of West Point. Tradition has it that Arnold was in the middle of shaving when an aide handed him a note and that in one flash Arnold understood his peril. He had always been a man of rapid reflexes, and within seconds he was out the door and stumbling—thanks to his bad leg—down the hillside to a boat. Jumping in, he rowed himself several miles south and found refuge aboard a British warship on the Hudson River.

Peggy Shippen was definitely involved in the plot, but she acted innocent and persuaded George Washington that she did not know why her husband had fled. Washington suspected something terrible and when the news of Arnold's betrayal was confirmed a few hours later, he turned to one of his aides to say: "Arnold has betrayed us. Whom now can we trust?"

GREENE VERSUS CORNWALLIS

Who was the new American commander in the Southern theater?

Washington chose General Nathanael Greene as the new Southern commander. When Greene arrived and met General Horatio Gates, there was almost no army to speak of. The British had triumphed everywhere except at King's Mountain, and it seemed possible that the patriot cause might collapse. Greene soon proved himself a masterful tactician, however.

Even though Cornwallis and the British outnumbered him by at least three to one, Greene had the nerve to divide his outnumbered army and move in two different directions. Greene had the main body of about 4,000, and Brigadier-General Daniel Morgan—who had commanded the American sharpshooters at the Battle of Saratoga—had command of the second, numbering about 2,000.

How did Morgan achieve the "Miracle at Cowpens"?

Colonel Banastre Tarleton and his King's Legion set off in hot pursuit of General Morgan, who had been a wagoner during Braddock's ill-fated campaign in 1755 and understood speed and maneuver very well. Morgan moved his men at a moderate pace, allowing Tarleton to catch up. When Tarleton came within striking distance, he did what he always did: he ordered an immediate assault.

Certainly, there are moments when an immediate attack is a good idea. Tarleton's men had been pushed for days, however, and he sent them into battle without any breakfast. Morgan had already made his calculations, and as Tarleton's force charged, his initial two lines of militia fired two rounds—according to the plan—and then withdrew to the rear. Their movement persuaded Tarleton that the day was won, and he committed his entire force to the battle. This was a terrible mistake.

How bad was the wipeout, from the British point of view?

Colonel Tarleton started the Battle of Cowpens with about 1,300 men; he escaped with less than fifty. Cowpens was the most one-sided battle of the Revolutionary War, and the credit goes to Daniel Morgan. When Tarleton's weary men reached the center of the Continental line, they encountered stiffer resistance than expected, and suddenly the two lines of militia that had previously withdrawn rejoined the fight. At that moment, Greene's small cavalry force appeared, led by Colonel William Washington (no relation to the commander-in-chief). Morgan caught Tarleton in a classic double envelopment. (much as Hannibal did to the Romans at the Battle of Cannae). Tarleton's force was nearly wiped out.

How important was the Battle of Cowpens?

Cowpens did not end the Revolutionary War, but it made the end of the Revolutionary War possible. By eliminating Tarleton's force, Daniel Morgan prevented Cornwallis' invasion of North Carolina; he also ensured that General Greene would now have a fighting chance. Most of all, however, Cowpens demonstrated that the Americans could do more than hold their own: they could administer a true thrashing.

General Cornwallis made a terrible decision at this point: he burned his heavy baggage in order to move faster and catch up to Nathanael Greene. On hearing the news, Greene rejoiced: "Then he is ours!" Greene was correct. In a wilderness race, the Americans would always outdistance the British, who now would suffer because they had no heavy equipment. Greene led Cornwallis on a race to the Dan River, and when Greene's men got safely across the river, Cornwallis was left standing on the south bank, knowing that the game was over.

How close were the Americans to victory?

Very close indeed. A major component was still missing, however. The Americans could win numerous battles on land, but they could not prevent the British from evacuating their men by sea.

> ## What happened to Colonel Banastre Tarleton?
>
> Tarleton continued to fight, but never with the signal success he had previously enjoyed. When the war ended, he went home to England and soon became a leading member of the House of Commons. Sadly, Tarleton's major parliamentary efforts were made on behalf of the British slave trade. When the trade was abolished in 1806, Tarleton looked like the loser all around.

In the summer of 1781, French General Rochambeau brought 5,000 first-line troops from Newport—where they had spent the winter—to join Washington at Wethersfield, Connecticut. Rochambeau was second in command to Washington, who wanted very much to make a final attack on Manhattan and thereby end the war in a blaze of glory. Washington had to recalculate, however, when he learned that the French war fleet was headed not to Manhattan, but to Chesapeake Bay.

How many ships did Admiral de Grasse bring from the Caribbean?

Born in the little town of Grasse, in southern France, Admiral François-Joseph-Paul de Grasse was a veteran sailor. In the summer of 1781, he decided to take a big risk and bring his entire fleet of twenty-eight warships—as well as many transports—north to Chesapeake Bay. In one important way, Admiral de Grasse was very much like his predecessor, Admiral d'Estaing, however; he was very afraid of hurricanes. De Grasse's message to Washington, therefore, stated that he could only remain in the Virginia Capes area until the end of September.

Washington received this all-important message on August 14, 1781, and he immediately switched plans. Washington longed to recapture Manhattan, but this clearly was not to be, and he and Rochambeau swiftly agreed to march the Franco-American forces all the way to the Chesapeake to block in General Cornwallis. Even today, for an American equipped with an automobile, it is no small trip from the Hudson River to the Virginia Capes, but Washington and Rochambeau set their men in motion right away.

Were eighteenth-century men and women more athletic than us today?

They were not stronger—our fitness machines see to that—but they were capable of greater endurance. It was a rare person during that time who was not accustomed to doing hard physical labor or covering long distances by foot.

How did Washington pull the wool over General Clinton's eyes?

Perhaps 20 percent of the Continental Army was left behind, and these men dug trenches, lit bonfires at night, and did all sorts of shenanigans to persuade the British that the Americans still threatened New York City. So successful was the ruse that General Clinton did not suspect the Americans of being up to anything until Washington and his men had passed Philadelphia.

Although General Cornwallis was not actually present when the British surrendered at Yorktown to the joint American–French forces, the 1820 painting *Surrender of Lord Cornwallis* by John Trumbull paints for dramatic effect.

Even so, there was plenty of anxiety in the Continental ranks. Neither the men nor their commanders knew—for example—whether the French fleet had arrived or if the British had sent a fleet to oppose it. As the weary men neared the James Peninsula—a geographic region that would figure again in the American Civil War—they had the glad tidings that Count de Grasse and his twenty-eight warships had arrived, bringing 3,000 French regular soldiers with them.

When did Cornwallis realize that he was in a trap?

He never did, not until the first Franco-American columns arrived. By then it was too late, and Cornwallis hunkered down for the inevitable siege.

The British fleet did appear early in September, and a naval battle was fought just on the Atlantic side of the Virginia Capes. The British had their chances and opportunities, but this time the French prevailed. When the British fleet sailed away—having lost one ship-of-the-line—its leaders knew that Cornwallis was doomed to fail. Learning of the naval victory, the Franco-American forces worked even harder to get their siege guns in place, and they were in great luck, because French Admiral de Barras sailed in with eight more ships and a whole lot of artillery.

It seems as if everything went "right" from the Franco-American perspective. Is that true?

Yes. The Yorktown campaign was one of the few times that the French and Americans cooperated effectively and bagged their British opponents. The siege lasted nearly a month, but on October 19, 1781, the British came forward to surrender their arms. General Cornwallis managed to evade the surrender ceremony by pleading illness, and George Washington, therefore, declined to receive the surrender. He directed General Cornwallis' substitute to hand the general's sword instead to General Benjamin Lincoln, the American commander who had been so humiliated when he lost the city of Charleston about eighteen months earlier.

Was that it? Was the Revolutionary War truly over?

For all his stunning success, George Washington still wanted more. He asked, nearly begged, Admiral de Grasse to come north and attack Manhattan. Had de Grasse agreed, the war would have been over even sooner and perhaps with a far greater loss to the British. The French admiral was most concerned about his ships, however, and he did not wish to be off the American coast during hurricane season. The French, therefore, sailed for the Caribbean, and Washington and his men returned to the Hudson River valley.

The war was indeed over, however. Immediately on receiving the news, the British prime minister threw up his hands and declared, "It's all over!" King George III typically, showed more spunk and desire to continue the struggle, but neither the British military nor the British taxpayer would stand for it. America had won its independence, in fact, and it won the symbol as well, when the Peace of Paris in 1783 confirmed that the former colonies were now free and independent of the British crown.

Washington's Farewell to His Officers, 1783, by Alonzo Chappel.

Do historians make too big a deal of George Washington's farewell to his officers?

The ceremony took place at Fraunces Tavern in Manhattan on December 4, 1783, and no, historians exaggerate neither the symbolism nor the importance. Washington was, by this time, the most famous person in the Western world: he had accomplished what seemed impossible. Had he desired, he could easily have become the chief executive, perhaps even the king, of a newly reconstituted America. Washington had no wish for this, however. After an emotional leave-taking of his officers, he rode south for Mount Vernon, the home he had seen but once during eight years of service.

Washington, to be sure, was not a perfect man. He had his faults, a hot temper being foremost among them. It can be said, however, that his will to achieve a state of virtue exceeded the vices which could have brought him low. Most students of world history concur that Washington was the "greatest" (most virtuous) leader of the eighteenth century and that many people—ever since—have used him as a model.

Did the foreign observers and volunteers stay in America after the war ended? Or did they return home?

It was about a fifty-fifty proposition. Quite a few settled down to become American farmers and merchants. Those who returned, however, were nearly unanimous in declaring their belief that the United States was the best hope of the world. Precisely how many people's minds were changed by hearing these words is impossible to say, but we are confident that the American Revolution had an enormous impact on the French Revolution of 1789.

THE REVOLUTION OF 1789

Why did France suddenly rise up against Louis XVI and Queen Marie Antoinette?

The key factor, trumping all others, was the rise of the price of bread. In the two years prior to the French Revolution, bread rose in price almost constantly, and it is no coincidence that the price spiked shortly before the attack on the Bastille. To be sure, other factors were involved, not least of which was the tax exemption enjoyed by the clergy and the nobility. But the price of food was the immediate, pressing reason.

When did the Revolution commence?

The political revolution began in May 1789 when the members of the Estates-General disobeyed a royal command and grouped together as the new National Assembly. The violent revolution began in July 1789, however, and the attack on the Bastille on July 14 was the big benchmark.

The Bastille was a royal fortress which was now being used as a political prison. Only a handful of political prisoners were housed in the Bastille in 1789, but it had become a hated symbol of oppression. The Parisians rose on July 14, and after a bloody clash, they charged into the Bastille to free the prisoners. They cut off the governor's head and carried it out on a pike.

Is it fair, or accurate, to say that the French Revolution was quite violent, right from the start?

It is. Ninety percent of all the French people had never enjoyed any opportunity of self-government prior to 1789, and some of them went a little crazy with their new freedom. Many aristocratic homes in the countryside—the famous chateaux of the nobility—were attacked and plundered during the late summer of 1789. At the same time there was a strongly idealistic basis to the Revolution: a belief in liberty, fraternity, and equality.

The French aristocrats generally made matters worse by refusing to yield their age-old privileges. Some of the wiser aristocrats fled the country right away, suspecting that anything which began so quickly could turn into something even worse. Those who remained made things worse for the aristocracy by attempting to resist the tide of progress. The Marquis de Lafayette, who deeply desired to be the George Washington of France, was caught right in between the opposing impulses. He was a liberal and a revolutionary, but he was also born into one of the true-blue aristocratic families. His career during the Revolution evolved into a tragedy.

What was Lafayette's best day, or moment?

On October 5–6, 1789, about 10,000 Parisians, most of them female, left the city for the royal palace of Versailles. Along the way, they chanted that they had come to take the "baker, the baker's wife, and the baker's little boy," referencing, of course, King Louis XVI, Queen Marie-Antoinette, and the crown prince.

Learning that the women had departed Paris, Lafayette summoned the National Guard and hastened after them. He and the guards arrived at Versailles just in time to prevent a bloodbath, and Lafayette brokered the agreement under which the royal family returned to Paris. Versailles stayed empty for many years thereafter.

What was the high point of success for the constitutional movement?

In 1791, France received a new constitution, written by the men of the National Assembly. The new document provided for general male voting rights for a one-house (unicameral) legislature and for Louis XVI to remain as a constitutional monarch. Almost as the very words were being penned, however, Louis XVI and Marie-Antoinette were involved in what can only be described as treasonous discussions with her brother, the emperor of Austria.

When Louis and Marie-Antoinette attempted to escape Paris in the spring of 1792, it was the beginning of the end for them as well as the constitutional process. Even the common Frenchman in the provinces, who was usually not interested in Parisian affairs, now viewed the king and queen as dangerous to the nation. Louis and Marie-Antoinette were apprehended just ten miles shy of safety, in Belgium, and returned to Paris. The worst was still to come, however.

How did the Swiss Guards die?

Louis XVI had almost 1,500 red-clad Swiss Guards, the same group of men who have traditionally protected the Pope. On August 10, 1792, infuriated by stories of Prussia and Austria marching on France, the Parisian crowd rose again. The provocations were similar to those at the taking of the Bastille, but the fighting was much more savage. Nearly all of the Swiss Guards died while defending the royal family at the Tuileries, the downtown palace very close to the Louvre.

Twenty-three-year-old Napoleon Bonaparte was close at hand that day, though he did not choose either side. For years afterward, he commented that Louis XVI—had he appeared on horseback—would have won the day and perhaps brought prestige back to the monarchy. As it was, however, both the king and queen were in fear for their lives. In their view, it was fortunate that the crowd was contained by the National Guard and that a formal trial—rather than a summary execution—would be the result.

Where, at this point, was the Marquis de Lafayette?

His is one of the saddest stories connected to the failure of the moderate, or constitutional, part of the French Revolution. Lafayette yearned to be the George Washington of France, the great man who would calm the crowd, save the king and queen, and guide the revolution in a new direction. He never really had the chance, however, not least because France lacked a substantial middle class, which perhaps could have reined in the Parisian mob. Lafayette lost heart in 1792. He attempted to make his way to America, but was, instead, caught by the Austrians, who threw him in a dank prison at Olmutz. He remained there for five long years.

When did the French Revolution turn into a full-scale war?

It was well on the way to that stage when the revolutionaries executed King Louis XVI on the guillotine in January 1793. Tradition has it that one of the leading orators cried out, "We throw them the head of a king!"

Even if the Revolution had not been so bombastic, the monarchical powers of Europe had reached a breaking point. It was bad enough to see the clergy and aristocracy deprived of their privileges and much worse to see a king executed (Marie-Antoinette was guillotined a few months later). By spring of 1793, France was at war with Britain, Spain, Austria, and Prussia (Holland and Russia would later enter the fight).

This seems as if France was overmatched. How did the nation survive?

For some months it was questionable whether the Revolution would endure. By the autumn of 1793, however, the French Revolutionary leaders made a drastic decision: they

King Louis XVI was sent to the guillotine in 1793 after being charged with high treason; his queen, Marie-Antoinette, was executed a few months later. Their deaths marked the end of the French monarchy and the beginning of the First French Republic.

would mobilize the entire nation rather than submit. The *Levee en Masse*—proclaimed through every village and town—declared that young men would fight, middle-aged men and women would cast bullets and knit uniforms, and that old men and women would sing patriotic songs in the village squares.

No previous regime, or nation, had ever undertaken such a step, and by 1794 France had 800,000 men under arms. Not only did the French have great manpower, but their generals also employed creative ways of fighting the enemy. Taking a page from the American Revolution, the French Revolutionaries employed skirmishers to harass their enemies and then marched huge, rectangular columns to smash their lines. These tactics produced heavy casualties, but they often worked, and the French Revolutionary armies became feared throughout Europe.

When did Napoleon Bonaparte emerge?

Napoleon was only a captain of artillery under King Louis XVI, but he rose to colonel in the French Revolutionary armies, and in 1794 he used artillery to force the British to give up the city of Toulon, on France's Mediterranean coast. Bonaparte's military brilliance was in its early stages, but his charismatic personality was felt throughout the nation. Extremely handsome in youth, he also possessed great charm, when he wished to employ it.

How important was Napoleon Bonaparte in the year 1798?

He had, rather suddenly, become Revolutionary France's most successful general. Napoleon, as he is well known, was not French, at least in a technical sense; he was Corsican. Following a brief career in Louis XVI's army, Napoleon was in Paris to watch the fall of the monarchy and he endured some lean years, just getting by on bread, soup, and coffee (he could never get enough of the last of these). Napoleon's moment came when the Directory Government rose in 1795 and France became dedicated to the business of war.

One can say, of course, that France had been at war for centuries, but there was something special, nearly unique, about the concentration of energy within the French military during the 1790s. As the *Levée en Masse* declared, young men were to fight, middle-ages ones were to cast bullets, and old men were to sing patriotic songs in the village square. The explosion of human history allowed for great opportunities, and Napoleon was just the person to seize upon them.

Was Napoleon's mother a powerful presence?

Madame Mere—or Letizia Bonaparte—was quite young when she gave birth to Napoleon, her second eldest child. Over the years, she had six other children. In her youth, Letizia had been a revolutionary, a follower of General Pasquale Paoli the Corsican nationalist, but by the time her children came of age, she was a serene, but highly ambitious, matriarch, willing to use all tools at her disposal.

Napoleon's siblings, too, played a role in his career. Even though he was clearly the leader, Napoleon tried to be deferential to his elder brother Joseph; to his younger brothers, he was a commanding despot. His sisters, all younger, generally did as they were told, at least in his presence. With the exception of Napoleon, the Bonapartes were not a stand-out family; they were, in fact, quite normal for their place and time. But when Napoleon exerted his amazing powers and rose like a shooting star, they advanced as well.

How significant was Napoleon's marriage to Josephine?

On a personal level, it was everything: he simply adored her. But the marriage was advantageous on a political level, too. Like Napoleon, Josephine was what we would call "Island French." She came from the sugar colony on Martinique, not the French mainland. She had married above herself the first time, however, and she was identified both as the former French aristocracy and with the nouveau riche ("new rich") of the Directory Government. Finally, she was a woman of great charm.

Napoleon helped his own cause by marrying Josephine; he was good to her in that he helped raise her two children and provided for them handsomely. By the time he was ready to depart for Egypt, Napoleon was a major star in the French Revolutionary scene, and he was about to become even more famous.

Why Egypt? Did France not desire to conquer England and end the long war?

Napoleon, like so many great leaders, had his blind spots. When he had too much to do, too many battles to fight, he generally looked for yet another! There was some method to his madness, however. If France could conquer Egypt, it would control the communication and trade lines of the Eastern Mediterranean.

Napoleon's ambition for Egypt was not limited to military conquest. He wanted to be known as a sponsor and promoter of the arts and sciences, and no previous general—except perhaps Alexander the Great—brought as many men of learning along on a major military expedition. There were chroniclers, astronomers, and experts in Ancient Greece and Egypt. Napoleon wanted his conquest to be remembered for many things, and, as things turned out, he succeeded.

How did the French army reach Egypt?

It was no small feat since the British Royal Navy was, largely, in control of the Western waterways. Napoleon and a large fleet of nearly eighty ships slipped out of the Mediterranean port of Toulon, and, for the first half of the voyage, completely evaded the British ships. Modern shipmasters have examined the records of both fleets and found that they came very close—perhaps within two miles of each other—on a certain night, but Napoleon's luck held marvelously, and in July, he and his army disembarked on the left, or west, side of the Nile Delta. Thus far, it had been an extremely successful venture with Napoleon's famous luck (he often said that one of the major requirements of being a general was that one must be lucky) doing most of the work.

In what way was Admiral Horatio Nelson the British equivalent to Napoleon?

Both men were relatively short in a time when height was valued highly. Both men possessed obvious charisma, with which they inspired their men to fight harder and accomplish more.

The military geniuses of their day, Napoleon Bonaparte (left) and Admiral Horatio Nelson, who chased the French fleet across the Mediterranean to Egypt.

In 1798, Nelson led the British fleet that chased Napoleon across the eastern Mediterranean. In a spurt of bad luck, Nelson missed the French fleet not once but twice, with fogs concealing the French. But when he learned that Napoleon had landed his army, Nelson moved with stunning speed. By the first day of August, 1798, the British were on the open sea, headed for Aboukir Bay, where Admiral Brueys had his fleet drawn up in a defensive position.

At this point, how much difference was there between the two fleets?

In numbers of men and guns, as well as overall tonnage, they were roughly the same, with ten lines of battle ships on each side. Brueys, moreover, had secured his anchorage brilliantly by running cables through the aft and sterns of all his vessels, so that they were "tied together" in a line that ran very close to the shore. Brueys had learned this trick by observing British Admiral Sir Samuel Hood during the American Revolution. Given normal circumstances, Brueys had done everything right. He was not up against a normal commander, however.

Admiral Nelson also had a connection to Admiral Hood: he had served under him during the Revolutionary War. Nelson, quite likely, knew what Brueys had done, and he decided to do the most daring thing a naval commander could: to place his ships between those of the enemy and the land. To do so meant that the British would have to thread the needle; they had to get between that long line of French warships to get to the Egyptian coast. That is precisely what they did.

How did the British sailors manage to accomplish this?

They were, beyond doubt, the most skillful of all sailors during the Age of Sail. Even so, they had to work their way up to the French line and then slip around it to perform their maneuver, and this ranks as one of the trickiest endeavors in all of naval history. Amazingly, those sailors and captains did it, and when they came around the other—or landward—side, they found the French had no cannon mounted on those decks. All the French armament was pointed outward, to the open sea. From that moment, it was not a fair fight but a simple slaughter.

Admiral Brueys died when his eighty-gun flagship blew up. Seven other ships were captured or destroyed that night. Only two French vessels escaped to the open sea, and they were commanded by Rear Admiral Pierre Villeneuve who would face Nelson again.

How great a victory was the Battle of the Nile?

It was, technically speaking, the greatest victory won during the Age of Sail. Never before had two fleets of roughly comparable size engaged, with one side winning so lopsided a victory. Nelson basked in public praise for years afterward.

The Battle of the Nile also meant that Napoleon's army was marooned in Egypt. There was no escape by sea. Napoleon, therefore, campaigned in Palestine in 1799 and seemed ready to push on to Constantinople, but he stopped and returned to Egypt. In

August 1798, he abandoned his army and took a small ship across the Mediterranean. After evading the British blockaders, he slipped in to Corsica for what would be his final visit to his homeland. He then sailed to Frejus, on the southern coast of France.

How did Napoleon lift himself yet again?

Given that he had abandoned his position and most of the army he took to Egypt eventually surrendered to the British, it seems incredible that Napoleon was able to pull the wool over the eyes of the French people. That was his specialty, however; he never lingered long or lamented deeply over any of his mistakes.

Napoleon arrived in France in October, and in November he launched a military coup that brought the government into his hands. Very few shots were fired; the main action took place inside the legislative chamber, where Napoleon's younger brother, Lucien, did much of the work of persuasion and intimidation. In just a few hours, the Director Government was declared defunct, and the new Consulate government established. Under the terms of the agreement, there were three Consuls of the French republic, with Napoleon being named the lead or First Consul.

How remarkable was Napoleon's rise to power?

Two decades earlier, Napoleon had been an impoverished student of military tactics at one of the mainland academies. One decade earlier, he had been an impoverished captain on half-pay, watching as the French Revolution gathered steam. Now, at the end of 1799, he was the first man in the nation. If it was not the single most extraordinary rise, it certainly belongs among the top four or five.

Once in power, Napoleon did his utmost to make his rule personal, meaning that everything depended on him. He also sought to elevate his six siblings to the maximum possible extent. Amazingly, he had converted a revolutionary movement, one based on the idea of constitutional government and the rule of law and turned it into a personal dictatorship, the likes of which the Western world had not previously seen.

THE NAPOLEONIC ERA: 1800 TO 1815

Who was the great "disturber of the peace"?

Napoleon usually gets the rap, and there is much truth in the accusation, but it is not the whole truth. Napoleon was a powerful representation of the enormous amount of human energy released by the French Revolution, and he would carry its positives and negatives to their ultimate expression. Other troublemakers existed, however, not least of which were the Barbary Pirates, small city-states on the southern rim of the Mediterranean. These would be the first people to feel America's wrath.

In 1800, there seemed no special reason why Napoleon—or France, for that matter—should remain at war indefinitely. Here, however, Napoleon's vast ambition got the better of him: he never was able to remain still for very long.

BARBARY PIRATES

How did the peaceful United States come to be at war with the Barbary Pirates?

In 1801, the sultan of Tripoli declared war on the United States for failing to pay sufficient tribute to his city-state. It seems inconceivable today that the powerful United Sates would ever pay tribute, but this was the case in the 1800s. It was cheaper and easier to pay occasional tribute to the Barbary Pirates than to fight them. President Thomas Jefferson (president 1801–1809) broke this convention, however, and war commenced, with the Barbary pirates seizing many American merchant vessels.

The U.S. Navy was small but highly professional. President Jefferson dispatched a squadron to the eastern Mediterranean (it is from here that we get the Marine song words "to the shores of Tripoli"). Commodore Edward Preble was in overall command, but the largest heroics and glory went to Lieutenant Stephen Decatur (1782–1820).

What was it like, cutting out the U.S.S. *Philadelphia*?

The U.S.S. *Philadelphia,* one of six American frigates, had run aground and been captured by the Tripolitans. To lose the ship was bad enough; that the Tripolitans would subsequently copy it to make even larger and more dangerous warships was intolerable. Lieutenant Stephen Decatur volunteered to lead a mission into the harbor at Tripoli either to destroy the *Philadelphia* or to cut her loose and bring her back to the squadron.

On the night of August 10, 1803, Decatur and his men—in six longboats—entered the harbor, passing numerous Tripolitan vessels before reaching the *Philadelphia*. Coming aboard with stealth, they overpowered the crew and set their gunpowder explosives, managing to get away in time before the subsequent explosion. No less an authority than Admiral Horatio Nelson—the lion of the British Royal Navy—called it the boldest act of the age. Decatur was soon promoted, and he became the leading daredevil of the fledgling U.S. Navy.

How did the U.S. Marines become involved?

Although the Americans blockaded the port of Tripoli, harming the commerce of the Barbary Pirates, the sultan of Tripoli refused to negotiate. It was, therefore, left to a rather wild American adventurer, Colonel William Eaton (1764–1811), and a handful of U.S. Marines to engineer the fall of Tripoli. Landing in Egypt, Eaton and Sergeant O'Bannon recruited a group of Arab camel drivers, many of whom supported the sultan's younger brother's cause to replace the sultan of Tripoli.

After a truly romantic 500-mile march across the Libyan Desert, the colonel, the Marines, and their Arab allies won a battle and captured the port town of Derna. This was enough to bring the sultan of Tripoli to terms, and the treaty that was signed guaranteed that there would be no future tribute payments. Small as the Tripolitan War was, it set the American forces—the navy most especially—off on a winning foot that would turn into a winning tradition.

After the USS *Philadelphia* was disabled and captured in Tripoli Harbor, U.S. forces under the command of Lieutenant Stephen Decatur Jr. snuck aboard and burned the frigate to keep it out of the hands of the Tripolitans (*Burning of the Frigate Philadelphia in the Harbor of Tripoli,* 1897, by Stephen Moran).

FRANCE VERSUS EVERYONE

What, meanwhile, had happened with Napoleon and his ambitions?

Between 1800 and 1805, Napoleon went from strength to strength. In 1800, he was the First Consul of France; in December 1804, he became France's emperor. The French army, meanwhile, was transformed into the Napoleonic armies. Napoleon, naturally, built on much that was good in the Revolutionary forces, but he added twists and embellishments that were entirely his own. The Revolutionary forces had emphasized an egalitarian approach to leadership; Napoleon, by contrast, created the Marshals of France—twenty-six in all—to showcase a truly imperial approach to military leadership. The marshals often came from humble backgrounds, but when mounted on splendid Arabian horses and dressed to the nines in stupendous uniforms, they were even more imperial and grand than the French leaders of the time of King Louis XIV.

If Napoleon possessed a specialty, it was in the use of artillery, and this army became number one during his long and impressive time at the top. Napoleon had a fantastic mathematical brain, and he could calculate how much artillery fire was needed—and in what location—faster than anyone on his staff. In other areas, such as the deployment of cavalry, he assigned matters to his marshals.

Who was Napoleon's greatest, or most long-lasting, foe?

It was a tie between monarchical Britain and Czarist Russia. King George III was still on the British throne, but he was descending into madness, and it was actually the leaders of the House of Commons—William Pitt the Younger especially—who directed the British campaigns against Napoleon. On the other side, geographically, Napoleon faced the young Czar Alexander I, who had a special dislike for the revolutionary movements Napoleon had done so much to spread.

Over time, however, Napoleonic France would face other enemies. Austria, ruled by Emperor Francis I, was an important foe, as was Prussia, ruled by King Frederick William IV. Spain started out as an ally of Napoleonic France but turned into a foe after Napoleon invaded that nation in 1807. When one adds various Italian city-states to the mix, it becomes clear that Napoleon, and France, faced a vast coalition of foes for many years. Yet the French often prevailed on the battlefield.

Was Napoleon as good a leader—as quick and decisive—as we often hear?

At his best, he was extremely good: a daring swashbuckler of a military leader who was nearly as good as Julius Caesar. Napoleon had numerous bad days, however, owing to poor health, which accelerated after he took on so many responsibilities. One can, therefore, stand amazed at certain Napoleonic successes—such as when he squashed Prussia in 1806—and shake one's head in wonder at some of Napoleon's blunders, such as his invasion of Russia in 1812.

Napoleon was often his own worst enemy. He never realized that other people, too, could make daring and complicated maneuvers, and he never "got it" that Britain—because of its navy—was beyond his reach. Even so, there were times when the splendor of his reign seemed to put all other monarchs and leaders in the shade.

Did Napoleon ever attempt to invade Great Britain?

In the spring of 1804, Napoleon stationed more than 100,000 men in the port town of Boulogne, right on the English Channel, waiting for the right moment to invade. The English, naturally, recruited militia by the thousands, and an epic contest seemed in the making. Napoleon believed he only needed mastery of the Channel for twelve hours to ensure success, but in this he was very much mistaken. Even Duke William of Normandy—the last man to carry out a successful invasion in that direction—had needed more like three days to get his men across and secure a beachhead.

The possibility of a French invasion led to enormous speculation, however. Napoleon rightly judged that he needed a diversion; he therefore commanded Admiral Villeneuve to lead his fleet all the way to the Caribbean and lure Admiral Nelson to do the same. The French-British race to the Caribbean and back was a true feat of seamanship on both sides, but there never was any doubt that the British naval reserves could prevent any invasion during Lord Nelson's absence.

Was Nelson as great a naval leader as we have previously heard? Or was he one of those leaders who depended primarily on the skill of his men?

The answer is in the fifty-fifty realm. By 1805, the British Royal Navy had gained immense superiority over all its opponents: French, Spanish, Dutch, or other. The British sailor and gunner was simply used to winning. But the presence of Lord Horatio Nelson on the bridge of HMS *Victory*—a massive, one-hundred-gun warship—made a huge difference.

Like many great leaders, Nelson was relatively fearless, a fact testified to by many wounds. He had a relentless belief in his own destiny. But on top of this was a marvelous

How tall, or short, were these two great leaders?

Measurements were not often taken in those days, and the records that survive are conflicting, but we suspect that the Emperor Napoleon and Admiral Nelson were approximately five feet, four inches in height. This did not make them tiny, but they certainly were shorter than many of the big and brawny fellows they commanded. Of the two, Napoleon seems to have commanded more through intimidation and threat of force, while Nelson appears to have been a more egalitarian leader. We know, however, that images can be deceiving, and this will become clear when we examine some of World War II leaders, of whom so many photographs were taken.

common touch, an ability to relate with his sailors and gunners. Like Napoleon, Nelson was of relatively short height; like Napoleon, he never let this deter him from action or accomplishment.

What was the lead-up to the Battle of Trafalgar?

In the late summer of 1805, the British admiralty learned that the Combined Fleet of France and Spain would soon sail from the entrance to the Mediterranean. Very much like what happened in the days of Sir Francis Drake, the British decided to take the fight to the foe, and by September, Admiral Nelson had twenty-seven ships of the line off the coast of France. When the Combined Fleet of thirty-three ships ventured out from Cadiz, Nelson moved quickly to counter.

The sailors aboard the British ships were convinced that this was the moment. They had been fighting the French, Spaniards, Dutch, and Danes for many years, and if they could win an overpowering victory on this occasion, the naval war would be in Britain's pocket. Admiral Nelson, too, understood the importance, and the last flag he hoisted before going into battle read: "England expects every man to do his duty."

Could the Franco-Spanish fleet have won the Battle of Trafalgar?

No. The British Royal Navy crews were better sailors, and their gunnery was, by now, far superior. When one adds to this the impetuous but also sublime personality of Admiral

With victory at the Battle of Trafalgar, the British would decisively rule the seas; however, the great cost was the life of Admiral Nelson, who was shot through the spine and died that day in 1805 (art by J.M.W. Turner).

Nelson, one realizes that the French and Spaniards stood little to no chance of victory. They seem to have understood this, and they went into action with an admirable coolness as the battle commenced.

Nelson had many times shown himself the master of maneuver, but on this occasion he simply wanted to break through the enemy's line. With HMS *Victory* leading the way, the British pierced the line of the Combined Fleet, turning Trafalgar into a true melee. In that type of close-quarters action, British victory was assured. Late in the afternoon, Admiral Nelson fell on his quarterdeck, wounded by a French sharpshooter aloft. Nelson lived for a few hours more, long enough to know that many Combined-Fleet ships had struck their flags. The French and Spaniards lost about 5,000 men that day, the British about one-eighth of that number.

Did Napoleon ever try to rebuild his fleets?

He did. Napoleon did not give up after Trafalgar; he had many ships built. His biggest difficulty, however, was finding competent officers and men to staff them. So many naval officers had died in the many naval battles that France had very few experienced leaders left in their navy, and there was no opportunity to train new ones because the Royal Navy blockaded the French in port.

Many historians and novelists have attempted to solve the riddle: Why did the British win at sea so often? One of the simpler explanations—and of course it cannot cover the answer entirely—is that England, with its enormously long coastline, simply had more sailors on which to draw than any of its opponents. Only when the United States, with even longer coastlines, entered the naval equation did the British experience any chance of losing.

Did Napoleon grieve, or mourn, the loss of so many good men at Trafalgar?

One of the less attractive parts of Napoleon's personality was his profligacy with men's lives. It should be said, however, that in the autumn of 1805, he was very busy with another, and different, type of campaign. Even before the Battle of Trafalgar, Napoleon had broken his camp at Boulogne and headed his army toward Austria. Prussia, Russia, and Austria had all taken the field against him. Napoleon brought his force rapidly east, and on December 4, 1805, he fought one of the great battles of the age: the Battle of Austerlitz.

Napoleon was clearly better than his opponents at maneuver and the massing of artillery, but there was another factor he could not control: the weather. To avoid winter-related problems, Napoleon made his rapid march; even so, the heavy fog that enveloped the village on the morning of December 4 threatened his chances. Then, just as the battle began, the sun peeked through the clouds, and Napoleon—ever quick to seize an opportunity—proclaimed it the "Sun of Austerlitz."

What was the fighting at Austerlitz like?

Like many Napoleonic battles, it was on a very large and grand scale. Perhaps 70,000 French maneuvered and fought against perhaps 85,000 Russians, Austrians, and Prussians. The smoke from hundreds of cannon was overwhelming, as was the stench from so many dying men and beasts. Because photography was still thirty years in the future, the Napoleonic battlefields are not as immediately "available" to us as, say, the American Civil War. But the overwhelming impression we get is that of men clashing, fighting, seeking to gain the upper hand, and the brilliance of Napoleon directing most of it.

Austerlitz was Napoleon's greatest victory. He lost 12,000 men but 19,000 of his enemies were dead, and—for the moment—the King of Prussia, the Emperor of Austria, and the Russian czar were all keen to make peace. When Prime Minister William Pitt (the Younger) learned the news, he commented: "Roll up the map of Europe and put it away; it will not be needed these next ten years." Pitt was right.

Did Napoleon, then, have everything his way?

Not quite. Not until he thrashed the Prussians, in a lightning-swift campaign in the spring of 1806, was he really the master of the Continent. Of course, there were still dangers, and to prevent these from becoming larger, Napoleon tried to isolate Great Britain.

To isolate the people of an island who also control the waterways is a difficult thing, but Napoleon proposed the Continental System, under which all the peoples of Europe would refrain from trade with England. To an extent he succeeded, but it meant that his naval and customs men had to be on high alert at all times; France, too, suffered from lack of overseas trade. The one area where the Continental System had the potential to alter the scenario, however, was with the Americans.

How did the United States become a major commercial power so quickly?

Americans are natural at buying, selling, negotiating, and bartering: just ask any of them! This was already the case in the early 1800s, and, given that the Americans built so many ships, it was natural that they would become major carriers of oceanic trade. The rub, however, was that they had to get around both the British naval blockade of France and the French commercial blockade of Great Britain.

As they attempted to sell their goods and wares, the Americans faced a secondary threat. Not only did the British periodically stop American ships to inspect for violations of neutral status, but British naval captains frequently "impressed" American sailors, claiming that they had been born in Old England. Under the expression "once an Englishman, always an Englishman," the British pressed about 5,000 Americans into service between 1800 and 1812.

What did the United States do about this violation of its sailors' rights?

When the War of 1812 began, the rallying cry was "Free Trade and Sailors' Rights!" In 1806, however, when a British warship fired on an American one—the U.S.S. *Chesapeake*—the United States was too weak to do anything except register severe protests. A year later, President Thomas Jefferson announced an embargo on American commerce with all foreign nations. He intended to hurt Britain the most, but in fact it was the young United States—with its merchant-based East Coast—that suffered the worst. Jefferson finally admitted the failure of his embargo system in 1809.

Americans, in 1807 or thereabouts, were displeased both with Britain and France, but their anger burned more hotly against the former. Bad feelings predominated on both sides of the Atlantic, and it was not a complete surprise that America declared war on England in 1812.

NAPOLEON'S ZENITH

When did Napoleon, and his empire, peak?

In about the year 1807. That was the year when he defeated the Russians for what he hoped would be the last time, and it was also the year in which he met Czar Alexander I.

Soon after the Battle of Friedland—which he won narrowly—Napoleon met Czar Alexander in a handsome tent that floated on a raft in the middle of the River Niemen (it was one of the most colorful and also most secret of all big conferences of that time). No one ever reported what the French emperor and the Russian czar said, but we strongly suspect that they agreed to separate zones of influence, with France dominating in Western Europe and Russia in charge in Eastern Europe. Had the two monarchs stuck to this plan, Napoleon's empire would have lasted a good deal longer. He became frustrated with Alexander, however; the Russian czar did not enforce all aspects of the Continental System.

How and why did Napoleon get involved in Spain?

It was a terrible error. Later, when everything had collapsed, Napoleon admitted that it was the "Spanish ulcer" that ruined him. In 1807, however, it made sense for him to invade Spain in order to set up his elder brother Joseph as the new king of Spain.

Napoleon first ousted the hereditary Spanish monarch and then installed Joseph in Madrid. To this point, it was just another Napoleonic triumph, and it extended the Con-

---

Why had Spain, which gained so much gold and silver from the New World, fallen so far behind?

One could see it even during the reign of King Philip II—who sent the Armada against England. Spain had been relatively prosperous during the Middle Ages but suffered from deforestation by the seventeenth century. And the silver and gold from Mexico and Peru brought about price inflation more than anything else. Spain almost entirely missed the Enlightenment of the eighteenth century as a result of the religious wars of the sixteenth and seventeenth centuries. Its population was, therefore, less literate and less enterprising than that of its European rivals.

tinental System another 500 miles, depriving the British of even more trade. Napoleon overlooked some important factors, however, and one of his worst calculations had to do with roads (or the lack thereof).

Spain was about two centuries behind the rest of Europe in agricultural production and the unification of its economy. Railroads had not appeared yet, but they were only twenty years away, and the Spanish, by contrast, lived with roads straight out of the Middle Ages. This meant that Napoleon's men had to march longer distances and to live off a soil that was less productive than, say, Germany or Austria. Napoleon tended to be dismissive of factors like these, but this was one time when his disregard of the odds really came back to haunt him.

Who came to rescue the Portuguese and Spaniards?

In 1808, England—which had been very wary of Continental battles—sent a small force to Portugal to assist the people from being Napoleon's next conquest. Napoleon was back in Paris, but his armies were in Spain, and when they invaded Portugal, they found the British expeditionary force tougher than expected. The British assistance emboldened the Portuguese to resist, and before long, parts of rural Spain, too, rose against the French.

Napoleon hastened to the Iberian Peninsula in 1808, and he prevailed in a very fast campaign. This was to be the last of his lightning-swift conquests, however, and he never succeeded in chasing the British—"the leopards," he called them—into the sea. That failure emboldened the guerrilla resistance in both of the Iberian nations.

When did Arthur Wellesley, the first Duke of Wellington, enter the Napoleonic scene?

Arthur Wellesley (1769–1852) was a late bloomer. He came from a powerful and prominent Anglo-Irish family, but his elder brothers were the stars for a long time, while he was very much the junior. During six years in British India, however, Wellington came into his own as a military commander, and when he was sent to Portugal in 1809, he knew that much depended on him. He commanded England's only army-in-being and could not afford to lose men the way his French opponents could. Wellesley, therefore, determined to be a true husbandman: a careful conserver of men, resources, and supplies.

When did the word *guerrilla* enter the English language?

It entered around the year 1811 and can be traced directly to the rural fighting between the Spanish and Portuguese and the French. Europe had not seen this type of fighting, at least not since the Thirty Years' War. Guerrilla warfare became synonymous with desperate, dirty battles fought well off the beaten track, and the name has lasted right to our own time.

In 1811, Napoleon sent André Masséna one of the best of his marshals, south to chase Wellesley and the British into the sea. Massena made great progress and came within thirty miles of Lisbon before encountering a natural set of defenses which the British had turned into an impregnable fortress. Massena had no choice but to position his army just north of these lines, and many of his men went hungry that winter. By the spring, it was Wellesley's turn to attack, and he soon had the French on the run.

Portrait of Arthur Wellesley, 1st Duke of Wellington, 1814, by Sir Thomas Lawrence.

What was Wellington's special magic?

Wellington was a common-sense soldier, rather than a brilliant one. He took for granted that matters of supply and reinforcement were critical, and he put his attention on these relatively mundane matters. While his men did not love him—he was too cold for that—they respected him and knew that he worked unceasingly on their behalf.

On the battlefield, however, Wellington had two or three tweaks or twists that proved successful time and again. He allowed the French to move forward in their column formation, which had been so successful against the Prussians and Austrians; rather than meet them in force, he deployed the so-called "thin red line" of soldiers to slow them down and wear them out. The sharpshooting skills of his men made it possible for Wellington to keep his line thin, allowing him to nearly always have men waiting in reserve, usually on the reverse side of a slope, during critical moments in battle. There, out of danger, these troops preserved their energy and appeared at the most important moment.

When did it become apparent that Wellington would eventually liberate Portugal and Spain?

The Peninsular War was a seesaw struggle with the French sometimes coming close to victory, but they were constantly denied by the combination of Wellington's disciplined force and the Spanish guerrilla fighters. As one recent historian has pointed out, the French could beat Wellington's army or the guerrillas; they could not do both. The Siege of Badajoz, in the spring of 1812, was one of the major turning points.

Badajoz sits near the border between Portugal and Spain, and it had already changed hands several times during the war. In April 1812, Wellington assaulted it, and though his men took the heaviest casualties of the campaign, theirs was a signal achievement. The French had booby-trapped Badajoz to the greatest extent possible, but the British— led by the Light Division—captured the city.

What was the Light Division?

Wellington decided, early in the Peninsular War, that mobility was the key to success. Not only did his army move faster than the French, but the so-called Light Division, spearheaded by the Rifle Brigade, became famous for its ability to cover ground. The British Rifle Man—they always expressed it as two separate words—had learned much of his trade while fighting the Americans during the Revolutionary War. A series of novels and PBS films, including *Sharpe's Rifles* from the 1990s, are based on the real exploits of men in the Rifle Brigade.

How many attempts did it take for the British to eject the French from Spain?

There was something about the Peninsular War which required, even demanded, the stubbornness of fighters. When the French invaded initially, the Spaniards fought them like wildcats, and when the British and their allies attempted to throw the French out, they had to make one effort after another. Even after Wellington's great victory at the Battle of Salamanca in July 1812, the French fought fiercely.

By November of 1813, however, the British had the French on the run, and late in that year they crossed the Pyrenees to enter the French homeland. Some of the most difficult battles were fought in and around the cities of Toulouse and Bayonne, but Wellington's veterans, who now called themselves Wellington's Invincibles, continued to win.

THE MOMENTOUS YEAR

Why does 1812 last so long in our memories? Then, too, why are those memories so blurry?

It's a great question. The calendar year 1812 will last in the collective memory as long as people listen to Tchaikovsky's symphony of that same name. 1812 will also be forever an American memory because that is the year when the war of that title began! But as to the memories, they are—perhaps—so blurry because so much happened at one time. This is one of the few times when a strict chronology is necessary.

- May 11, 1812: The British prime minister was assassinated.
- June 1, 1812: President James Madison asked Congress for a declaration of war against Great Britain.
- June 18, 1812: Congress approved, and Madison signed, the declaration.
- June 22, 1812: Napoleon invaded Russia, with 600,000 men at his back.
- June 23, 1812: Great Britain rescinded the Orders-in-Council, maritime laws which brought about the war in the first place.

223

If the British government took back the maritime laws—and claims—why did the United States not rescind its declaration of war?

Countries and nations almost never do this. So much is at stake, not least of which is national pride. This is why nations are very careful, and slow, about declaring war, but once it is declared, they tend to go full throttle.

Did anyone have a complete, or full, view of what took place in 1812?

Not one. There were just too many events, and we have to remember there was no quick or swift way of sending the news. The average English man or woman, therefore, learned about Napoleon's Russian invasion and the American declaration of war at about the same time. Even though there was no connection between these two huge events, the average person cannot be blamed for thinking that there was.

Napoleon had the largest intelligence network, and he was a huge consumer of information, reading from all manner of sources. Even he had no idea of what the Americans would do, however, and once he commenced his epic invasion of Russia in June 1812, he was largely cut off from the most recent news.

Was Napoleon's army of 600,000 men all French?

Not even close. The Revolutionary and Napoleonic wars had bled France to the extent that Napoleon had to recruit among his subject nations; there were Germans, Italians, and Poles in his vast invasion force.

Napoleon had 600,000 men and 200,000 horses (we often forget the latter number), but almost one-third of them were out of action—from illness, fatigue, or death—within the first month. Crossing the enormous plains of the Ukraine was much more difficult than Napoleon expected, and all the while he had to keep one eye out for the British, who might raise trouble while he was gone.

Were the British able to take advantage of Napoleon's absence?

Not really. They might have been able to had the Americans not declared war on them in June of 1812. But once this happened, Britain had to rush troops to Canada as well as advisers to Russia. Though Napoleon had clearly overextended himself, his foes, too, were on the brink of maximum expansion.

One aspect of the Napoleonic Wars we often forget is the fighting between the various colonies of both sides. When Napoleon conquered Holland, he added its overseas colonies to his own, and there were lively fights between British, French, and Dutch as far off as the Caribbean, the Indian Ocean, and even Malaysia. From an American perspective, however, the single biggest news was the subjugation of the remaining Native North American tribes.

Who is the most important of all the Native American resistance leaders?

King Philip was perhaps the earliest of them, and Chief Pontiac later built a formidable confederacy. Chief Sitting Bull and Chief Crazy Horse later won the Battle of the Little Big Horn, and Chief Osceola won much admiration for his spirited defense in Florida. Of all the great Native American chiefs, however, the Shawnee Chief Tecumseh has the largest reputation, both in the United States and abroad. Generations of German boys, for instance, have grown up reading about Tecumseh's brave stand against the Anglo-Americans.

Did the average American—white, black, or red—understand how many forces were in motion in 1812?

Almost no one, European or American, red, black, or white, did. But the Native Americans realized that this might be their last chance to resist the Anglo-Americans. Chief Tecumseh created a confederacy among the northern tribes, and the Creek tribe, in the south, went to war against the white settlers of Georgia and Alabama.

Tecumseh crossed into British Canada in 1812, where he was made a brigadier-general of the British forces. The British needed all the Native American allies they could get because the Anglo-Americans outnumbered them by more than ten to one. Then, too, the British were appalled by the early American victories at sea.

Tecumseh was the leader of the Shawnee. He created a confederacy of native tribes that became a formidable force against the Americans when it allied with the British. Tecumseh helped capture Fort Detroit during the War of 1812, but when he was killed the next year the confederacy fell apart.

How did "Old Ironsides" obtain her nickname?

On August 19, 1812, U.S.S. *Constitution*, out of Boston, met and fought HMS *Guerriere*, off the coast of Nova Scotia. The *Constitution* was physically larger and carried a larger gun deck; even so, people were astonished to learn that the *Guerriere* was dismasted and that she later sank. The British captain and his crew were evacuated from the sinking ship.

American Captain Isaac Hull became an immediate hero, and Americans pointed to their small but growing navy as proof that they would one day surpass the British. For their part, the English people were both angry and distressed. Accustomed to naval victories over virtually everyone, the British looked for a way to contain, and perhaps destroy, the young American navy. The U.S.S. *Constitution* got her nickname "Old Ironsides" when one of her sailors looked over the side and saw British cannon balls bouncing off her heavy oak timbers.

Where was the Battle of Borodino?

It was fought seventy-five miles west of Moscow. The Russians had dug in, preparing to resist, and Napoleon gave them every opportunity. An eight-hour affair, the Battle of Borodino was the single costliest battle of the Napoleonic Wars. Dozens of French generals died on the field, and there were enormous casualties on both sides. As many as 30,000 men were killed, wounded, or went missing. Historians still debate whether Napoleon missed his great moment late in the battle, when one of his generals asked him to commit the Imperial Guard. Almost 10,000 men had gone the entire day without firing a shot, and by sending them in, they might have turned the Russian retreat into a rout. Napoleon's famous answer was, "And if I have to fight tomorrow, what will I fight with?"

Although few people knew it at the time, Napoleon was not himself during this war. He was only forty-three, but he suffered from a variety of ailments and was in intense physical pain during the battle. As anyone who has experienced sharp physical pain knows, it takes all one's will to concentrate on what is happening, leaving little energy for other matters.

At the same time, did Napoleon reach Moscow?

He did. We often forget that Napoleon succeeded where Hitler later failed. The French and their allies—much depleted from the summer campaign—entered Moscow in the second week of September 1812. One hundred miles shy of the city, they had fought the enormous Battle of Borodino against very stubborn Russian opponents (the guns sounding in Tchaikovsky's symphony are the cannon of Borodino).

Napoleon entered Moscow riding his favorite horse, an Arabian steed. He found the Russian capital strangely deserted, however. Just a day or two later, an enormous fire started; it raged for nearly a week, destroying about three-fifths of all the available housing. Just who started the fire and who fought the most to contain it—French soldiers or Russian civilians—is a question that has never been answered. What we can be quite certain of is that the fire wrecked Napoleon's chance to winter in the capital and that it threw off practically everything he had planned.

What role was played by Czar Alexander I?

The Russian czar had previously been something of a patsy to Napoleon, but in 1812 he found his stride, and it was one of defiance. The czar steadfastly refused to negotiate so long as a single foreign soldier—French or otherwise—remained on Russian soil.

Realizing that Moscow was more of a trap than a prize, Napoleon turned and headed for home on October 15, 1812. The weather had been unusually fine for weeks, and so it remained for the next three days, but after that, early winter began to set in. Unaccustomed to the severe cold, the French were soon in a rather bad way. Their opponents, meanwhile, had been reinforced by groups of Russian Cossacks, warriors for whom the word guerrilla seem to have been coined. Napoleon's position, meanwhile, had gone from decent to bad. He had thought his men could winter in Moscow and that the czar would come to terms. Instead, winter quarters were denied them.

How bad was Napoleon's retreat from Moscow?

It could scarcely have been worse. Up to that time, it was, perhaps, the worst of all military disasters in the Western world. Napoleon had entered Russia with 600,000 men; by the time he left Moscow he had only 115,000 effectives, and by the time the last Frenchmen crossed the border into Poland, there were less than 20,000 men in any sort of formation.

This does not mean that 580,000 men died. Many deserted; others settled down in Russian villages; and still others straggled home years later. But of the 600,000 who had crossed into Russia, probably no more than one-tenth—or 60,000—ever were able to contribute effectively to society. Though the phrase "post-traumatic stress disorder" had not yet been coined, it can readily be used to characterize the condition of the survivors of the Russian campaign.

Was there any outstanding hero of the Russian campaign?

Certainly it was not Napoleon, who took a fast-moving sleight to get home to Paris by Christmas time. The big hero, therefore, was Marshal Michel Ney. He had already earned the title "bravest of the brave," but the Russian campaign confirmed it. Ney was one of the last men to cross the Vistula River and one of those with the worst set of stories to tell.

On the Russian side, there were hundreds, perhaps thousands, of heroes. Cynics pointed to the uniforms of the Russian military, saying that every man seemed to have received the highest honors. It must be said that Czar Alexander I did not try to hog the glory, but that he spread it out among the full military.

Marshal Michel Ney, who was known as the "bravest of the brave," was the hero of the Russian campaign, even though it ended in disaster for the French.

Was there any chance Napoleon could have "bounced back" from his defeat in Russia?

There was—just the slimmest of chances. If Napoleon had realized the extent of his mistakes, and had he been willing to negotiate with his foes, he might have salvaged much of his empire. Napoleon, by now, was in the full grips of the type of delusion which takes over many great leaders, however; he had listened to no one else for so long that he could not alter his conduct. As a result, the Napoleonic Wars continued.

Numerous contestants that had previously been written off now re-emerged. Prussia had nearly been carved up by Napoleon in 1806; that nation now rose against him with a fury. Austria, which was led by Napoleon's father-in-law, was also in arms against him. The guerrilla war in Portugal and Spain continued, meaning that Napoleon's armies were stretched to the breaking point in almost every direction. This was the time, clearly, to remove his forces from Spain and to go on the defensive. Napoleon refused to do this, however.

THE AMERICAN WAR

What did the British call the War of 1812?

Even the Americans did not come up with that name until well after the conflict was over. For lack of a better title, the British simply labeled it the American War. To them, it was definitely a sideshow to the major Napoleonic events, but it had significance. Either the Americans would capture Canada, or the British would invade the United States.

In June 1813, the British struck back, gaining vengeance for the loss of HMS *Guerriere* the previous year. HMS *Shannon* met and captured U.S.S. *Chesapeake,* outside of Boston Harbor. The armament on both sides was roughly equal, but Captain Philip Broke had specially trained his gunnery crews. Broke came aboard the American ship and was wounded. American Captain James Lawrence fell mortally wounded. Tradition has it that his last words were: "Don't give up the ship!"

Why was a position on the Great Lakes so critical?

Right from the war's beginning, the Americans had tried to conquer British Canada. This made eminent sense, because whatever success the British had elsewhere would be more than balanced if the Americans took Montreal and Quebec City. The British-Canadians fought fiercely, however; part of the Canadian national identity is still based on that nation's resistance to the American invasions of 1813 to 1814.

During the summer of 1813, Commandant Oliver H. Perry took building crews from western Pennsylvania to what is now Erie, Pennsylvania. After blazing a woodlands trail to the water, Commandant Perry built an American squadron of ten vessels. Opposed to this was a roughly equal number of British ships, already on the Lakes. Given that the

Who killed Tecumseh?

His body was never found, and it is quite likely we never will know who gave him his death blow (or musket ball). Numerous frontier Americans over the next few decades, however, claimed to be Tecumseh's killer; the most prominent of these was Colonel Richard Mentor Johnson, who used the supposed death as one of the reasons he ran for vice president in 1844.

British were such masters of battles on the high seas, many people expected them also to prevail on the Lakes.

Where does it come from: "We have met the enemy, and they are ours"?

In September 1813, Commodore Perry took his fleet out on Lake Erie to confront the British squadron. The battle raged for nearly ten hours, and at one point, Perry's flagship was so badly damaged that he had to get in a boat and transfer to another. The Americans stuck to their guns all day, however, and when darkness fell, the British fleet was no more. As Perry expressed it in his victory dispatch: "We have met the enemy, and they are ours."

Perry's naval victory shook the British so badly that General Henry Procter evacuated Fort Detroit and retreated across Ontario. General William Henry Harrison pursued the British and their Native American allies so rapidly that General Procter turned to fight a defensive battle at the Thomas River. The Americans won in the opening hour of the battle, and the British turned to flee. Only Chief Tecumseh and his warriors hung on to the bitter end.

Did the Americans capture British Canada?

No. Two invasion forces entered Lower Canada, meaning the Province of Quebec, late in the year, but neither made much progress toward Montreal. By then, the Canadians had formed enough fighting resolve to repel almost any American assault. Then, too, the tide of the war in Europe had shifted rather dramatically.

Was the Creek War part of the War of 1812?

Yes, but in a tangential fashion. Chief Tecumseh had gone south in 1811, trying to stir up the Creeks and get them to join his confederacy. At that time, the young warriors were in favor, while the chiefs and sachems were largely against. This changed in 1813, and the Creeks started the war with a massacre of the civilian population at Fort Mims, in Alabama. The Creeks may have believed that the range of fighting—from Lake Erie to the Gulf of Mexico—would keep them safe, but they reckoned without Andrew Jackson.

Jackson (1767–1845) gathered a frontier fighting force to chastise the Creeks. In each wilderness battle, the Americans gave better than they got, and when Jackson cornered the major fighting force of the Creek nation, the result was the one-sided Battle of Horseshoe Bend. Roughly 750 Native Americans were killed in the one-day battle, after which Jackson imposed peace terms that stripped the Creeks of three-fifths of all their territory. Just when it seemed that the Americans had wrapped things up on their soil, however, came the astonishing news from France. Napoleon had abdicated his throne. The European wars were over.

EXILE TO ELBA

How did Napoleon fall so far so fast?

It's true that he fell nearly as fast as he had risen a decade and a half earlier. In the summer of 1813, Napoleon was down but not out; he still had a good-sized army and enjoyed

An 1814 cartoon shows Napoleon on a donkey, riding backwards, and carrying a broken sword as he is exiled to the island of Elba.

the loyalty of the famed Imperial Guards, his oldest and longest-serving veterans. By the spring of 1814, however, Napoleon was down to his last 50,000 men, and even they had no stomach to continue the fight.

Napoleon nearly won the three-day Battle of Leipzig, in Germany, but after that narrow defeat he, and Imperial France, went rapidly downhill. In January 1814, the Prussians entered eastern France, with the Russians and Austrians not far behind. Arthur Wellesley, who had by now become the Duke of Wellington, was pressing Napoleon's troops in southern France very hard. Napoleon, being Napoleon, made a final effort.

How close did Napoleon come to fending off the Allies in March 1814?

He did quite well in January and February, keeping his foes at bay. Some students of Napoleon's campaigns believe that he was at his most inspired during the late winter campaign of 1814. Late in March, however, at the insistence of Czar Alexander I, the Russian and Prussian armies took a major gamble, going straight past Napoleon on their way to Paris. At first, Napoleon could hardly believe his good luck (as he perceived it); by the time he realized the danger, it was too late.

Hastening back, Napoleon got to within twelve miles of Paris before learning that the capital had capitulated to the Allies, on March 31, 1814. For once, Napoleon had no return, no way to strike back. He went to Fontainebleau, his favorite palace, where, on April 2, he signed the declaration of abdication. He stepped down from the thrones of Italy and France, he said, and did so in favor of his three-year-old son.

Did the Allies honor Napoleon's wish?

By no means. Some of them—notably the Prussian generals—felt that Napoleon was getting off lightly by not being hanged. The Allies required Napoleon to make a second, unconditional, abdication and to agree to go into exile on the Mediterranean island of Elba. Located six miles off the coast of Tuscany, Elba was close enough that the Allies could keep a close watch, yet far enough so that Napoleon could not influence events on the Continent.

Napoleon arrived at Elba on May 4, 1814. By sheer coincidence, that was the same day that King Louis XVIII—the younger brother of the king who had lost his head to the guillotine in 1793—arrived in Paris to commence his reign. Louis XVIII was a poor substitute for Napoleon in that he lacked charisma, but the restoration of the Bourbon monarchy seemed a marvelous thing. The monarchical powers of Europe had not gotten over their desire to turn the clock back and re-experience the world that existed prior to 1789.

Who was the man of the hour? Who had done the most to defeat Napoleon?

That was the great question that all the Allied leaders wished to have answered. To Czar Alexander I, it was obvious that Russia—with its huge army—had accomplished the task, while to George, the Prince-Regent of Britain, it was patently obvious that the

Royal Navy as well as the Duke of Wellington's men had done it. To King Frederick William of Prussia, it was clear that the blue-coated Prussians had picked up where their grandfathers had left off, under King Frederick the Great. And to the Austrians, well, everyone knew they had been in the field against Napoleon the longest.

The great thing in the summer of 1814 was that the Allies stayed together and did not squander their advantage. With Napoleon safely exiled to Elba, the leading European monarchs gathered in Vienna to start a congress which would redraw the maps and, hopefully, bring things back to how they had been prior to the Revolution of 1789.

Was everyone at peace that summer?

Everyone except the British, who wanted to strike hard at the Americans.

ROCKETS' RED GLARE

When did the British come to strike at, and punish, the Americans?

Almost as soon as the news of Napoleon's fall from power was learned. The British war ministry was in tip-top shape, thanks to years of war, and within two months, two large forces were on their way across the Atlantic. The first was led by General Robert Ross, with the naval command entrusted to Admiral Alexander Cochrane.

Ross was a Peninsular (Iberian) War veteran, noted for gallantry and courage. Cochrane was a shrewd, rather elderly navy man who remembered the Americans in a very negative way from the Revolutionary War. After a rendezvous in Bermuda, the British expeditionary force arrived in Chesapeake Bay. Admiral Cochrane was undecided, wondering about whether to strike New York, Baltimore, or Washington, D.C., but the number-two naval man, Rear Admiral George Cockburn, was quite sure that Washington was the best target.

How did the British reach Washington, D.C.?

They did not come straight up the Potomac River, which might have been expected, but rather up the Patuxent River. Ross' 4,000 men went ashore on August 19, 1814, and commenced the long, hard trudge to the American capital. Several times along the way, Ross became unnerved, feeling that the move was too big a stretch; on each occasion, he was talked back into it by Rear Admiral Cockburn.

On August 24, 1814, the British came to the bridge at Bladensburg and found it defended by an American force slightly larger than theirs. General Ross ordered an immediate attack, and even though the British lost 150 men killed and wounded, they scattered the American militia. After a short rest, the British resumed their march, entering Washington that evening. One last firefight, in which Ross had his horse shot out from under him, was followed by an eerie quiet as the British entered the American capital.

How badly did the British damage Washington, D.C.?

They remained in Washington, D.C., for only about thirty-six hours, not long enough to do much damage. Their anger toward the Americans, however, was palpable. To many Britons, the Americans had stabbed them in the back during the long wars against Napoleon, and this merited special revenge. The British actually took some losses, however; a gunpowder explosion killed and wounded almost fifty men.

A tremendous tornado also came over Washington, D.C., and a rather shaken General Ross decided it was time to get out of the area. Over the next four days, the British force marched back to the Patuxent and reboarded their ships. This was the most successful British move during the American War and one of the best strikes the British pulled off during the entire Napoleonic era.

Meanwhile, where was the second British expeditionary force?

This one was much larger, composed of nearly 12,000 veterans of the Napoleonic Wars. The British disembarked at Montreal and immediately commenced a southern invasion, headed into Vermont. General George Prevost had already constructed a flotilla on Lake Champlain, and it seemed possible that this British force would burn New York City in the same way that General Ross had already done to Washington, D.C. It was not to be, however.

The British land forces advanced to the outskirts of Plattsburgh and won a skirmish. They were about to attack the town when Sir George Prevost learned that the naval battle had gone the Americans' way. Master Commandant Thomas McDonough pulled a page from the adventure book of Admiral Nelson. Like Nelson at the Battle of the Nile, McDonough ran cables through the line of his ships so they could rapidly be "jerked" or hauled around in order to present two sets of broadsides. This was enough to ensure the American victory, preventing the British from advancing down Lake Champlain.

How close did the British come to capturing Baltimore?

In the days following their heady success at Washington, the British commanders discussed and debated the merits of attacking Baltimore. That city had sent out more privateers to harass British commerce than any other on the East Coast, and the British desired revenge. They realized, however, that Baltimore Harbor was well defended, and would be a tougher nut to crack. Emboldened by their recent success, Admiral Cochrane and General Ross pushed on.

The British land forces went ashore on September 11, 1814, and made their initial probes on the evening of September 12. General Ross fell dead in the opening minutes (he had always been both a daring man and a conspicuous target), and the heart went out of the land forces. The naval force, meanwhile, entered Baltimore Harbor and rained cannon balls as well as mortar bombs and Congreve rockets on Fort McHenry.

How big was the American flag at Baltimore?

Weeks before the British attack, Major George Armistead, commander of Fort McHenry, asked the ladies of Baltimore to stitch the largest possible American flag, one that would be seen from far out to sea. They obliged, and that flag flew proudly during the night bombardment of September 12–13, 1814. Early that morning, Francis Scott Key, a Baltimorean who was aboard a British ship, effecting an exchange of prisoners, went up on deck to look and beheld the U.S. flag—it had eighteen stars at that time—flying over Fort McHenry. Key almost immediately penned the words that later became the American national anthem:

Artist Edward Percy Moran painted this dramatization in 1912 of Francis Scott Key happily gesturing at the still-standing Fort McHenry after it survived the British attack that inspired Key's famous poem.

> O, say can you see, by the dawn's early light?
>
> What so proudly we hailed, at the twilight's last gleaming....

Many people—then and now—have commented that "The Dawn's Early Light" is a difficult song to sing. As a description of patriotic efforts in the middle of war, however, it has seldom been surpassed.

Was that it for the British attacks on America?

Very nearly. The drive south from Canada had stopped at Plattsburgh, and the British success at Washington was followed by their failure at Baltimore. Admiral Cochrane had one last hope, however; he wished to capture New Orleans, the seventh largest of all American cities.

New Orleans, in 1814, was not as fabulously wealthy as the British believed, but it was the hinge on which American westward expansion depended. If the British took New Orleans, they might well possess the lower Louisiana area and be able to thwart American settlements west of the Mississippi River. There were, therefore, excellent strategic reasons for making the attack on New Orleans. By December, Admiral Cochrane and a new army commander, Major-General Sir Edward Pakenham, were in the Gulf of Mexico, probing for soft spots. They did not realize that they were up against one of the toughest, flintiest of all American commanders, however. Andrew Jackson, who had recently been promoted to major-general, was now commander of the Seventh U.S. Army District, including New Orleans.

> ## Was Jackson as much of a "he-man" or tough guy as he sounds?
>
> **V**ery much so. Jackson was on the thin side and ramrod straight in posture. He had a well-earned reputation for toughness and aggression: he fought his last duel in 1813. Where military matters were concerned, Jackson would endure just about any hardship. This endeared him to his men, but it also impaired his health, and he was never as vigorous again after 1815.

Wasn't New Orleans—then and now—a difficult target?

This is true. If New Orleans truly sat at the mouth of the Mississippi River, that would be one thing. But the Crescent City is 110 miles above the mouth, and it is protected by good-sized lakes to its east. This is not to say that New Orleans was impregnable, but it was a tough nut to crack.

Only the sailors of the British Royal Navy could have pulled off the seemingly endless labor of transporting 7,000 men across Lake Borgne. The lake was too shallow for the major vessels, so Admiral Cochrane's Jack Tars got out their longboats and literally rowed the British force across nearly fifty miles of shoal water. The boats were so crowded, and the labor so difficult, that each British soldier carried a cannon ball in addition to his knapsack. Amazingly, Admiral Cochrane's sailors got the army men to within ten miles of their destination, and when British scouts discovered the Bienvenue Bayou, entering into the Mississippi River, success seemed assured.

Why didn't those first 1,500 men make straight for New Orleans?

In retrospect, it is clear that they should have done so. These men had spent days crossing Lake Borgne, however, and Colonel John Keane, who commanded them, did not have good maps of the region. He, therefore, had his men bivouac and enjoy their first fire-cooked meal in days. During those vital three or four hours, Andrew Jackson got the news. Tradition has it that he swore: "By the Eternal! They shall not sleep on our soil!"

Even if the words were concocted later, Jackson went straight on the offensive. By late afternoon, he had 2,000 men ready, and he led them straight south. The American attack on the British encampment came at dusk, and it was started by a schooner drifting downstream and opening cannon fire. Caught entirely by surprise, the British fought stubbornly and well, but they took more casualties—including about fifty captured—than the Americans. After a three-hour slugfest, Jackson withdrew a mile or so and began to entrench his position.

Could the British have punched their way through and taken the city?

The odds were against them. Jackson's men knew the terrain better, and they were not averse to employing all sorts of odd tactics to lure the British into compromised posi-

235

> ### What was that Christmas for the British like?
>
> Christmas Day brought cheers, better food, and the arrival of Major-General Sir Edward Pakenham. The British cheered, believing that "Pak," as they called him, would lead them to victory. But Sir Edward was confronted by the same dismal situation as his predecessor, Colonel Keane. The British were packed into a narrow, confined position, and every day brought more reinforcements for General Jackson.

tions. British pickets complained of the ungentlemanly ways the Americans used to pick them off during the night.

Amazingly, the Royal Navy sailors were able to bring about twenty heavy cannon across the lake, and Sir Edward Pakenham had them in position for an early morning attack on New Year's Day. The British bombardment commenced as soon as the morning fog lifted, but the Americans—even when caught by surprise—turned out to be first-rate cannoneers. By midafternoon, all of the British guns had been silenced. Sir Edward Pakenham had to wait a full week before launching his full-on assault.

What was the situation on the morning of January 8, 1815?

The British were in position, ready to attack. The Americans were entrenched, waiting for what they believed might be an assault. Both sides had to wait until the fog burned off, however, and as that happened, Sir Edward ordered a rocket to be fired, the signal for the attack. Minutes later, thousands of brightly clad British and Scottish soldiers— some of them with bagpipes—moved toward the American lines. They marched, however, into a veritable rainstorm of bullets and cannon balls.

Seldom, if ever, had the British veterans experienced such a ferocious defense. Veterans of the Peninsula War claimed they had never heard so many guns—large and small—popping at once. The British—the Highlanders especially—continued to march and maneuver, but their efforts were doomed. Sir Edward Pakenham was killed early in the battle, and his second in command ordered a withdrawal after thirty minutes' contest. The British lost roughly 2,050 men killed, wounded, and missing. American losses came to about eighty, making this the most one-sided battle of the era.

Was that it? Was the War of 1812 over?

One last drama had to be played. As he evacuated his men from the debacle of New Orleans, Major-General Sir John Lambert wanted to accomplish something to salvage his name and the reputation of British arms. The British, therefore, attacked and captured Fort Bowyer, located near present-day Mobile, Alabama. This small victory was all the consolation the British got, because they—and the Americans—now learned that peace had been signed in Ghent, Belgium, on Christmas Eve of 1814.

We twenty-first-century readers are naturally appalled, because we perceive that so many men died unnecessarily. Neither the British nor the Americans talked about it much or presented it as a tragedy. They lived in a time when communications were slow, and everyone accepted that fact.

What did the Peace of Ghent, as it was called, resolve?

Almost nothing. Because the wars against Napoleon were over, the British had no further need to impress sailors, Americans or otherwise. Impressment, therefore, was not even mentioned in the peace treaty. What was clear at the peace conference was that many Britons and Americans regretted that their nations had gone to war and that they wanted to prevent any future ones. The biggest losers in the Peace of Ghent were the Native Americans. They had fought in the war, believing that King George and the British— though not wonderful—were better than the Anglo-Americans, meaning they would not seize as much land. In the negotiations leading to the Peace of Ghent, the British diplomats did their best but found that the Americans would not budge. They were sovereign over a large section of North America, they said, and would brook no interference from the British in any of their affairs, including their relationship with the Native Americans.

How did Americans greet the news of the peace treaty?

They were thrilled, nearly ecstatic. Because New Orleans was the last major action, Americans persuaded themselves that they had "won" when the war was, in fact, a draw or stalemate. But even as they cheered themselves hoarse, the Americans learned—to their great surprise—that Napoleon had escaped from exile and the European wars had resumed.

NAPOLEON'S LAST GAMBLE

How on earth did Napoleon ever get off the Island of Elba?

He snuck off in the middle of the night. The Allied monarchs had, foolishly, allowed Napoleon a bodyguard of 600 men, and when he raised this to 1,000, Napoleon decided to take a great gamble. He had his men get off in the middle of the night and landed, three days later, on the coast of southern France.

Napoleon posted proclamations, saying that he would rule as an enlightened monarch and that he had no desire to upset the peace which had arrived since his exile began. Many Frenchmen claimed that they did not believe the words, but when they saw Napoleon in person, they flocked to his banner. Without firing a shot, Napoleon made his way from Cannes, on the Mediterranean coast, to Paris, in a little less than three weeks.

Was there any chance that Napoleon's return would be peaceful?

Less than one in one hundred. The Allied leaders, at the Congress of Vienna, were appalled, but they showed great resolution, pledging to field one million soldiers in total, if that were necessary. The Duke of Wellington, also at Vienna, moved very quickly to take command of the small British forces in Belgium and Holland.

Napoleon, for his part, very much wanted and needed peace, but he could see that it was not possible. Within two months, he whipped together an army of about 220,000. The force was small compared to its foes but was composed of some of the best of the old regiments, the men who had triumphed on so many battlefields. Napoleon's greater difficulty was to obtain powder, muskets, and uniforms for the men.

How did the Waterloo campaign commence?

In mid-June, Napoleon stole a march on his foes. Knowing that the Russians and Austrians would soon invade eastern France, Napoleon decided to strike the British and Prussians in Belgium. The Duke of Wellington and many of his officers were at a ball—thrown by the Duke of Richmond—when he learned that Napoleon had crossed the Sambre River and was close to engaging with his foes. Wellington immediately put his own forces in motion, and the clash at Waterloo was made possible.

On June 16, 1815, the French approached from the south while the British came from the northwest and the Prussians from the northeast. There was not one but two battles that day. Napoleon narrowly defeated the Prussians in the early evening, at the Battle of Ligny, while Wellington held off another French force led by Marshal Ney. By midnight, the British were retreating in one direction and the Prussians another. Though he had suffered perhaps 8,000 casualties, Napoleon had achieved his objective, preventing a union between his foes.

How did all three armies spend the day of June 17, 1815?

Were it not for the rain, there would have been another battle that day. The rain was tremendous, however, slowing the movement of all three armies to a crawl. Arguably, this benefited the British the most because the Duke of Wellington had already determined where to make his stand, and his men reached the low hills of Mount St. Jean before nightfall. Two miles behind them was an eight-mile section of forest, and beyond that was the city of Brussels. As so often in his career, Wellington found the right spot of ground on which to fight.

The French pursued, but they were weighed down by their artillery: nearly 130 big guns. Another section of French, perhaps 40,000 men, was sent to pursue the Prussians and make sure they did not make a sharp turn to the west to effect a junction with the British. Napoleon, like Wellington, had laid his plans well, and everything now depended on the execution of the following day.

How did the Battle of Waterloo commence?

The ground was so wet and soggy that Napoleon had to wait until 1 A.M. even to start his artillery barrage, but when it came the roar was so great that some English farmers in the County of Kent heard the distant rumble. Napoleon had his artillery play for a full

The 1815 Battle of Waterloo pitted the French under Napoleon against English forces under the Duke of Wellington, Prussian troops under Gebhard von Blücher, and additional soldiers from the Netherlands, the Province of Hannover, the Duchy of Nassau, and the Principality of Brunswick-Wolfenbüttel (art by William Sadler II).

hour before launching his first assault. There was no special maneuver; Napoleon simply intended to pound his way through the British lines.

Right from the beginning, it was apparent that the Hougomont Farm, located a quarter mile in front of the British lines, was a key to the battle. The British garrison was continually reinforced, and the French lost nearly three hours in the seesaw battle to control the farm and its buildings. One can fault Napoleon for giving the farm so much attention, but as long as it stood, he could not make an attack all along the line.

Were there any special anecdotes concerning bravery?

There were so many that hundreds of books have been published on the subject. In general, it may be said that the English writers are generally taciturn, the French rather glum, and that the Scots Highlanders make the most of the day. To read some of the accounts, one would think that there were only sons of Scotland on the battlefield! In general, however, we tend to believe the memoirs and anecdotal accounts. Enough of them correspond to each other that we are confident that one tiny group of Scottish cavalry *did* seize two French eagles and that Marshal Michel Ney *did* have five horses shot out from under him that day.

Once the Battle of Waterloo was joined, both sides fought with ferocious intensity. There was a sense, on both sides, that this day would be decisive and that there was no need to conserve anything: all energy, all force, should be thrown at the enemy. In a pounding contest such as this, he who stands on the defense generally has the advantage because his men take less of a beating from marching all over the terrain, and so it was on June 18, 1815.

How important a role was played by Marshal Michel Ney?

He seemed to be everywhere that day: galloping up the hill at the British, directing cavalry charges, and sending hasty messages to Napoleon. Marshal Ney had not recovered from the post-traumatic stress he had experienced during the invasion of Russia, and he, therefore, was both unsteady and uncertain. But he was, undeniably, brave.

At 3 P.M., without consulting Napoleon, Ney led his cavalry, 5,000 strong, straight up Mount St. Jean because he believed the British were in retreat. They weren't. This was one of the many guises and feints the Duke of Wellington had learned over the years. But Ney and his cavalry rose right to the brow of the hill where they met thousands of British foot soldiers, massed in squares. This was, perhaps, the last time in Western history that so many horsemen made such a desperate attack on well-positioned infantry, and the results were just what one would expect. Ney suffered 2,000 men killed and wounded during his sequence of assaults and gained nothing.

Where, meanwhile, was Napoleon?

He was half a mile behind, surveying everything with his telescope. He saw, at once, that Ney's action was precipitate, but he made no move to alter it. Instead, Napoleon continued to watch, and then, rather suddenly, he detected a cloud of dust to the northeast. Some of his aides commented that it must be the Prussians, to which Napoleon replied, "Rubbish! It's [Marshal] Grouchy. At last!"

Over the next hour it became clear that the advancing column was, indeed, Prussian, putting Napoleon under more pressure than ever. He simply *had* to break through the British and get to Brussels. And at about the moment he made that realization, he received the welcome news that Hougomont Farm had at last fallen to his men. Perhaps 3,000 French were killed, wounded, or missing from that tremendous endeavor.

How much time—how many hours of sunlight—did Napoleon have?

Waterloo is situated at about 50 degrees north latitude, placing it well above the Canadian cities of Quebec, Montreal, Ottawa, and Vancouver. This means that the sun hung up in the sky until about 10:30 P.M., and then made a fast descent. Napoleon, therefore, had all the time in the world, except for the sudden advance of the Prussians on his right flank.

What happened to Napoleon?

He was taken to England and held on a British warship in the harbor at Plymouth. In August, he learned that Britain intended to send him to the Island of St. Helena, in the middle of the South Atlantic. Napoleon protested roundly—as did some of the people of Plymouth, who believed he should be allowed to live on a country estate—but to no avail. He arrived at St. Helena in October 1815 and spent the remaining six years of his life in that remote location.

At 6:30 P.M. Napoleon decided to employ the Imperial Guard—his oldest and longest-serving veterans—to break the center of the British line. Given that both sides had taken an enormous pounding over the day and that the Imperial Guard had not been used, this made eminent sense. Massing nine battalions of the Guard, Napoleon led them himself, on foot, to the halfway point, then turned over command to Marshal Michel Ney, who—amazingly—was still unhurt. Napoleon stopped to watch as his Imperial Guards slowly ascended the hill.

Was this the critical moment of Waterloo, even of the Napoleonic Wars?

It was. If Napoleon could punch his way through, he might as well split the British army and have a respite, after which he could defeat the Prussians. This was a sketchy scenario, but a real possibility. Everything depended on the Imperial Guard, which, in the forty major battles of Napoleon's career, had never failed him.

The Guards ascended to the first level without meeting any resistance. For the next 200 paces, they met nothing but the occasional musket ball, and success seemed within their grasp, when suddenly, 3,000 soldiers of Wellington's reserve leaped from the grass where they had lain for hours. The British Life Guards poured a devastating volley into the Imperial Guard; perhaps 400 Frenchmen fell in that volley. The Imperial Guard wavered, and when a second round of British musketry sounded, the French turned and ran. It was the first time this had ever happened to the Imperial Guard.

What did Wellington do at this point?

Seeing the Imperial Guard turn to run, Wellington rode to the highest point—where thousands of men could see him—to take off his hat and wave it in a southerly direction. This was his signal for the pursuit, which began immediately.

Seldom in recorded history has an army melted as fast as the French did after 8 P.M. on June 18, 1815. At 7:45, there were still thousands of French on the attack, and their overall lines looked nearly as solid as they had looked at 2 P.M. But by 8:30 P.M., the French were entirely on the run, and the British and Prussians were in full pursuit, cutting, hacking, and destroying what remained. Sections of the Imperial Guard formed infantry squares and repelled weaves of attacks before succumbing, but at least three-quarters of the French army simply fled. Napoleon was cut up in the disaster, and he barely made it back to his carriage, only to discover that it could not be made to move in the crush. He, therefore, cut out one of the horses and galloped off into the night.

How bad was the defeat for the French?

Roughly 40,000 Frenchmen were killed, wounded, or went missing that day, and thousands of others were captured. The British and Prussians, between them, suffered fewer than half as many casualties. But the results of Waterloo were more than material: on that day, Britain gained an ascendancy over France that would never completely go away. The long wars, which had begun in 1689—between Louis XIV and Prince William of Orange—were well and truly over.

The British and Prussians pursued for the next day, only to find that virtually no resistance remained. Napoleon, predictably, made his way to Paris, where he all too predictably spoke of raising another army: this time, the French Senate would have nothing of it. As the Allies approached, Napoleon fled for the coast, and on July 15, 1815, he surrendered to Captain William Maitland of the British Royal Navy.

Was there any last fighting?

Not this time. The Allied armies entered Paris in July 1815, and Louis XVIII returned to resume his rule a few weeks later. Allied forces continued to occupy Paris and sections of northern France for the next three years until it was evident that there would be no repeats or attempts to bring back Napoleon. The new peace treaty was, naturally, less generous than the one of 1814, but even so, France recovered in record time. What was over, for a long time, was the idea of France as the great military power of Western Europe.

What happened to the great heroes of Waterloo: Wellington and Marshal Michel Ney?

Ney, in one of the great tragedies, was shot by a firing squad. This was because he had sworn allegiance to King Louis XVIII, only to break his oath when Napoleon returned

The Duke of Wellington enjoyed honor and respect throughout his days until he passed away in 1852. Today, he is still remembered with statues such as this one by John Steell located on Princes Street in Edinburgh, Scotland.

from exile. Many observers claimed that Marshal Ney was weary of life and that his death was not tragic. Historians, with the advantage of hindsight, generally think otherwise.

Wellington was the man of the hour, the month, the decade. He was England's greatest hero, and so he remained until his death in 1852. That Napoleon was, over the course of his long career, the better general is a reasonable proposition; that Wellington was, on June 18, 1815, the better general is indisputable. To the end of his days Wellington remained a cautious, circumspect man. He never let fame get the better of him, and he was the most trusted man of the realm, beloved by King George IV, King William IV, and finally by Queen Victoria.

Could it all—the incredible drama of the Napoleonic Wars—have ended any other way?

Probably not. Even though France at its peak had terrific armies and morale, Britain had something better: sound finances and the Royal Navy. Over time, the British and their Continental allies would have prevailed. But had Napoleon not bungled so badly by invading Russia, and had he been willing to come to some sort of agreement with England, his rule might have lasted a long time.

Where are Napoleon's remains interred?

Napoleon died on St. Helena in 1821, but his remains were brought back to France in 1840. They are interred at Les Invalides, the golden-domed military hospital and museum on the south side of the Seine River, in present-day Paris.

NATIONALITIES AND GRIM PRACTICALITIES: 1815 TO 1860

CONSERVATIVES AND REACTIONARIES

It often seems as if European history comes to a sudden "stop" with the Battle of Waterloo. Is this true?

That feeling is very real, but it is based on the fact that the romance and excitement went out of many people's lives. As destructive as the Napoleonic Wars were, they lent purpose and meaning to millions of people, who felt bereft when they all were over. When Napoleon died, in sad and lonely exile on the Island of St. Helena, it seemed that something vital had gone out of European life.

The monarchs and military men of the post-Napoleonic era tended to be rather drab as well. They did institute changes which have lasted down to our present time, however. Some of these changes were administrative and economic, while others dealt directly with the military experience.

Who was the biggest disappointment in the post-Napoleonic era?

Beyond doubt, this had to be Czar Alexander I of Russia. During the Franco-Russian war that started in the summer of 1812, the czar seemed like the right person to lead a post-war world. He was still in his thirties, fairly handsome, and he expressed a liberal sentiment. To the best of our knowledge, Czar Alexander did not make up or invent these positive qualities; rather, he allowed his other or "dark" side more room to grow.

By the time of his death in 1825, Alexander had become a true reactionary, eager to contain the aftereffects of the French Revolution. In the weeks following his death, some of the key Russian regiments in St. Petersburg carried out a mini-coup, which called for "Constantine and Constitution." Prince Constantine was Czar Alexander's younger brother, but the throne went to Prince Nicholas, who proved just as conservative and reactionary as the regiments had feared. The coup was aborted, and Russia moved toward strict autocracy.

Who represented the greatest hope of the post-Napoleonic era?

To the liberals and nationalists, the greatest hope was expressed by Simon Bolívar the Colombian-born general who liberated several South American nations from Spanish rule. Bolívar was not without his own militaristic side, but he used it to push the Spaniards out of Colombia and Venezuela.

Mexico had already fought a long, ten-year war that culminated in the overthrow of Spanish rule. By 1823, Mexico was a federal republic, with a constitution loosely based on that of the United States. In that same year, American President James Monroe coined the doctrine that bears his name.

What did the Monroe Doctrine declare?

In 1823, President James Monroe, assisted by Secretary of State John Quincy Adams, drew up a lengthy document that declared North, South, and Central America free from further involvement by the great European powers. To Russia, Austria, Prussia, and France, this seemed like great effrontery, because the United States was not—in their eyes—a real military or naval power. But to Great Britain, which possessed the world's largest navy, the idea was a sound one. Britain wished to trade with the new South American republics, not to conquer or to govern them. Although the British, too, found the Americans presumptuous, they lent their support to the idea that no new colonies would be created in the New World.

What role did France play in the post-Napoleonic era?

France became downright conservative. King Louis XVIII wanted to avoid the mistakes of his ancestors, but he was drawn, in 1823, to support the Spanish government against a popular rebellion. In the height of irony, the French army—which, under Napoleon, had invaded Spain—now crossed the border to help King Ferdinand IV keep his crown.

The disaster at Waterloo had by no means persuaded France to give up on military affairs. The French army was the largest in Western Europe and second only to the Russians in Europe as a whole. Moreover, France began remaking its navy, doing so in novel ways.

President James Monroe championed what became the 1823 Monroe Doctrine, which asserted that the United States would consider any further attempts by European powers to colonize the Americas to be an act of aggression.

> ## Is the United States a nation blessed by God? Or just a very lucky one?
>
> Historians, as well as journalists, have wrestled with this question many times, and no one yet has composed a definitive reply to the question. When we examine American military history, we are struck—time and again—with how much luck seems to favor the Americans. No one else with a military of 10,000 could have issued the Monroe Doctrine and gotten away with it.

When did naval experts begin to discuss "iron-clad" ships and fleets?

To the average naval leader, the very words "iron" and "steam" seemed counterintuitive at the time. To them, it was obvious that sails, and men working those sails as well as the rudder, would forever be the major means for naval operations. We know, of course, that they were mistaken, but in their eyes, the new technologies seemed little short of heresy.

What was Britain's status at this time?

During the 1820s, Britain embarked on the largest—but also the quietest—of all its overseas expansion. The end of the Napoleonic Wars meant that Britain, for the moment, had no naval competition; its army, too, was beyond compare. As a result, Britain expanded in almost every area of the globe.

England had already taken South Africa from the Dutch during the Napoleonic Wars. It now proceeded to expand its colonial status in Southeast Asia with the acquisition of Singapore. England already possessed Canada; Australia was now on the verge of becoming the biggest agricultural producer for Great Britain. All these conquests and acquisitions were achieved with a minimum of bloodshed, and they positioned Britain as the world's true superpower.

Were there any exceptions to the general trend, which was one of conservative and reactionary powers in the lead?

One of the few promising areas was the eastern Mediterranean, where the old Ottoman Empire was clearly in danger of breaking up. Three hundred years earlier, the Ottomans had been number one in military technologies; by 1800, they had fallen nearly to the bottom of the heap. When the Greeks, who had been subjects of the Turks for centuries, started a revolt in the 1810s, few people believed they had a chance of success. But in 1827, Britain, France, and Russia—in one of their rare moments of cooperation—put together a joint fleet that destroyed the Turkish fleet at the Battle of Navarino. Unable to resupply their men in Greece, the Turks gave up the fight, and Greece became free.

Who was Lord Byron, and why was he so important?

Lord Byron was a truly gifted poet, whose words were informed by the Romantic Era. He traveled to Greece and Spain during the late Napoleonic era and wrote *Childe*

Harold's Pilgrimage, one of the first real "best sellers" in the English language. Later, Byron went to Greece and wrote magnificent poems about the need for the Greeks—who had established democracy in the first place—to be free from Turkish oppression. Byron was one of the greatest poets ever to hold a pen, and he was a poet-revolutionary who wanted to change the world. Like many of his kind, Byron endured a rather tortured personal life, and he died before the age of forty.

NEW TECHNOLOGIES

When did the steamship first appear?

Robert Fulton—the quintessential American inventor—designed the world's first successful steamboat in 1807, and the steamboat made its first appearance in Scotland as early as 1812. Anyone could see that a vessel which could move against the tide and even the wind was useful, but few naval authorities were ready to commission steam-built warships, at least not yet.

The steamboat was soon paralleled by the railroad, which made its first appearance in England in 1830. The novel idea soon crossed the Atlantic, and the first American railroads appeared by the late 1830s. As with the steamboat, many authorities discounted the new technology, saying that the horse and buggy were quite good enough. It was—and is—the way with Western culture, however, that once a more efficient design appears, men and women flock to it. And so it was with these steam-propelled machines.

What about the guns of the era? Were they still primarily muskets?

The musket had practically ruled the battlefield between 1680 and 1820, but the rifle became stronger over the next two decades. A Scottish clergyman—of all people—was instrumental in designing the percussion cap, making the loading and firing much easier. No machine guns had yet appeared, but one could envision the arrival of a new day in weapons technology.

The cannon remained much the same as before, but they loaded heavier balls than previously, and it was difficult to see how any castle or fortification could hold out in the future. The 1820s, therefore, was the first decade in which some futurists declared that war might have to become obsolete because of the possibility that it would become too destructive.

Robert Fulton's steamboat was a significant step forward in water transportation, not only for shipping but also for the navy.

Which countries were far behind the others in military technology?

Russia was so isolated—geographically and politically—that it lagged, but the powers which truly became dated in this period were China and Japan. The great distance between them and Europe had previously afforded them safety from the technological revolution(s), but by the 1830s, European merchants were all over eastern China and were looking for ways to penetrate Japan as well.

It is safe to say that these two decades, roughly 1820 to 1840, were when the West gained a lasting advantage over the Far East. China was immensely powerful in potential, but at this period it could not compete with the Europeans in the weapons of destruction.

Did the Native Americans suffer from the same "weapons" gap?

Yes. Native Americans generally liked guns, and they seized upon each new one that came their way. The trouble was that they had no gunsmiths to repair or replace them. The Native Americans, therefore, were outgunned as well as outnumbered. This did not seem that important in the 1830s, but once Anglo-Americans began taking new trails to the Far West—the Oregon Trail especially—the tribal peoples of the Great Plains met far more Americans than they wanted.

Were there many Indian Wars during the 1830s and 1840s?

This was one of the quieter times on the Western frontier, because the progress of white settlement had not yet surged across the Mississippi River. The last of the Indian Wars east of the Mississippi took place in 1832, when Chief Black Hawk led the Fox Native Americans in present-day Iowa and Illinois. Numerous Anglo-Americans who took part in the Black Hawk War—one of them being Abraham Lincoln—later rose to prominent positions in the U.S. government and military.

Black Hawk later went to Washington, D.C., and had his portrait painted. He was one of the first of a number of defeated Native American warriors who were romanticized in American portraiture and the newspapers. Given that the Native Americans east of the Mississippi presented so small a threat, it became easier for the Anglo-Americans to sympathize with their misfortunes.

REVOLUTIONS, AGAIN

France had been quiet during the reign of King Louis XVIII. Why was it different during the reign of King Charles X?

Both men were younger brothers of King Louis XVI, who had lost his head in 1793, but of the two, Louis XVIII learned the lesson and Charles X did not. When Louis XVIII died in 1826, the throne passed to Charles X, who acted, right away, as if he wished to eradicate all memories of the Revolution of 1789.

In July 1830, Charles X rather suddenly dismissed the Chamber of Deputies and announced a new set of highly restrictive laws. Parisians rose against this, and three days of intense fighting raged around the barricades set up in the middle of Paris' streets. The rebels emerged victorious, and Charles X fled into exile in England (London became the place of choice for many dethroned nineteenth-century monarchs).

Is there any accuracy to the street-fighting scenes in *Les Miserables*?

Les Miserables has been performed on Broadway for so long that most people refer to it as "Les Mis." Based on the play by French writer Victor Hugo, *Les Miserables* depicts the lives of the down and out in Paris in 1833, just three years after the July Revolution of 1830. *Les Miserables* does a good job showing the desperate nature of the fighting and of the intense patriotism that fueled it.

Why did France not become a republic right away?

One of the saddest parts of the revolutionary story in France is the slow downhill ride of the Marquis de Lafayette. He, who had crossed the Atlantic to assist the Americans in 1777, was still alive in 1830, and the Parisian revolutionaries looked to him for leadership. Lafayette knew he was far too old to be the new president or prime minister, and he also doubted whether his countrymen were ready for a new republic. Lafayette, therefore, persuaded the Parisian crowd to accept Prince Louis-Philippe, a second cousin of the departed King Charles X, as their new monarch.

Lafayette and Louis-Philippe stressed that this new "July Monarchy" would be different from the Bourbon one that preceded it. This would a monarchy for the people. Lafayette lived only three more years, but that was long enough for him to witness how the July Monarchy disappointed the people.

Was France unusually cursed in its leaders?

It often seems that it was. The Bourbons, who ruled from 1598 until 1830 with a break during the Revolutionary period, were often said to have "learned nothing and forgotten nothing." Louis-Philippe, leader of the brand-new July Monarchy, had spent time in America as an exile during the Revolution, and he appeared to have learned many lessons, but he soon began to rule in an arbitrary fashion.

A statue of King Albert stands in Brussels, Belgium. He was overthrown in 1831 as the Belgians pushed to become independent of Holland.

Who said, "When France gets a cold, all of Europe sneezes"?

This was Prince Klemmens von Metternich, the prime minister of Austria. Of all the monarchs and statesmen of that time, Metternich most identified with the principles of reaction and conservatism. In person, Metternich was charming, the soul of hospitality. But his policies were directed to one end: to return Europe to the way it had been before 1789.

Why did Belgium, too, go through a revolution?

The people of Belgium had long felt oppressed, both by their Protestant monarch (King Albert of Holland) and by the military situation which placed them smack in the middle of practically all the big European conflicts. In 1831, the Belgians rose against their king, and the leading European powers—eager to prevent further outbreaks—agreed that Belgium would be separated from Holland. Equally important, all the major nations swore to guarantee Belgian neutrality in any future military conflict.

FAR EASTERN WARS

Why was China suddenly so vulnerable to external threat?

For a long time, China had been almost impervious to outside forces. It had not experienced a major flow of immigration, and both its institutions and its military languished as a result. In the 1830s, China opened herself to greater trade with the West and was soon poisoned by the appearance of opium.

An 1860 image from the *Illustrated London News* shows the King's Dragoon Guards battling Tartar calvary in the Second Opium War.

The opium poppy flourishes only in small parts of the world, and at that time, northern India and northern Afghanistan were the major suppliers. British merchants and officers of the East India Company were the *de facto* rulers of India, and, as such, they began sending large amounts of opium to China. A cycle that was trade lucrative for the traders and detrimental to the people of China was established, with opiates traveling from India to China and tea going from thence to the British Isles. Not all of this was new: the East India Company's financial woes had led to the Boston Tea Party in 1773. The sheer size of the trade shipments was much greater, however, and even larger fortunes were being made. When the emperor of China forbade the introduction of any further opiates, Britain fought the First Opium War (1839–1842) to insure its products were brought ashore in Chinese cities. A Second Opium War lasted from 1856 to 1860 and was fought for the same reasons as before, with the British wanting to legalize the opium trade and opening up trade in general between Britain and China.

What, meanwhile, happened in Afghanistan?

Afghanistan is rightly known as the graveyard of empires, which the British also discovered in 1837 when a major British force departed northern India on its way to subdue the rebellious tribesmen of Afghanistan. Months later, a solitary horseman rode back to deliver to astonishing news that the column had been wiped out. This was one of the few great defeats the British military suffered during its nineteenth-century imperial wars.

Subsequent British expeditions were more successful, but the British decided, over time, only to occupy the "floor" of Afghanistan, leaving the more mountainous areas to the tribal peoples.

TAIPING REBELLION

Why is the Taiping Rebellion so little known when compared to other events of that time, including the American Civil War?

The Taiping Rebellion should, perhaps, be labeled the Taiping Revolution because it was an event of such great consequence. The event is little known, perhaps because it ended in the death of its leader and the failure of the moment. This should not obscure, however, the amazing human and material energies that were unleashed.

In 1850, China was still governed by the Manchu dynasty, which had been established in the 1640s. The Manchus had come as conquerors, and so they remained a population set apart from the mainstream of Chinese life. The common Chinese person accepted many things about the Manchus without complaint, but the Opium Wars revealed the weakness of the regime and opened the way for nationalistic movements. There may be smaller movements of which little is known, but the largest and most significant was the Taiping Rebellion, which began in 1850–1851.

Who led the Taiping Rebels?

The rebel leader's adopted title was Huang, which translates roughly as "water," or perhaps "life-giving force." He was from the Chinese peasant class but had studied the Confucian classics intensively to prepare for the examinations that determined who could, or could not, enter the bureaucracy. Failing these examinations, he returned home to his village about forty miles from Canton, where he had a sudden, dramatic vision. During the next few hours—in earthly time—he went to heaven, where he met God, the Father, and God's Eldest Son, meaning Jesus.

As to whether Huang was influenced by Christian missionaries, there is no doubt; precisely which books or pamphlets he read is also well understood. What is not so well established is precisely how he developed his own brand of Christianity, one that declared he was the younger son of God and that with the help of Jesus, his elder brother, he would free the people of China from foreign influence and oppression (by "foreign" he meant both the Manchu rulers who had come in the 1640s and the more recent arrivals, such as the British, French, and Americans).

China had been through many revolts and political takeovers. What was so different about the Taiping Rebellion?

The Taiping Rebellion was, quite likely, the first genuine popular revolution in Chinese history, meaning that major decisions were made and major actions undertaken by the will of many common people, acting in unison. In any nation or geographical setting, it is difficult to know what the will of the people is, but in the early 1850s, it was apparent that many lower-class Chinese genuinely supported the rebellion that took place in and around Canton.

The Taiping Rebels claimed that the wealth of the rich belonged to them, that they might distribute it according to need. Foreign devils, such as the merchants of the Western powers, were tolerated as long as their trade was useful to the rebel cause. It was essential, however, that foreign ship captains—whether merchant or naval—acknowledge the sovereignty of Huang, who was the younger son of God.

How did the foreigners respond to this claim?

They were, alternately, amused, offended, and appalled. British, French, and American naval captains were equally stunned by the effrontery of the claims and by the skill of the Taiping Rebels. Abandoning Canton in 1851, the rebels moved west. Here they proclaimed the "Great Taiping Peace," which included all people who submitted to the will of God's younger son.

Just to make the situation a little wilder, or more bizarre, Huang had associates who claimed to speak for Jesus, or for God, the Father. Through their mouths came proclamations, divinations, and prophecies. At the same time, the communal, or communistic, ideals of the Taiping Movement brought many people from their fields to the city, where they willingly followed Huang's edicts.

It sounds like this could have been an enormous disaster, leading to unprecedented suffering. Is that what took place?

For many upper- and middle-class Chinese, the Taiping Rebellion was nothing but misery. Those who attempted to hold on to their wealth were summarily dispatched. Those who refused to acknowledge Huang as the Son of Heaven were given a short time to change their minds. Those who believed any other religion—Buddhists and Confucianists especially—were often put to death.

At the same it must be said that millions of ordinary Chinese saw salvation in the edicts promulgated by the new Son of Heaven. They may or may not have believed all that Huang said about his divine mission, but they willingly accepted his decrees. No looting was permitted, and the men and women of the Taiping Revolt lived in separate quarters for years, with any sex—including conjugal—strictly forbidden.

How did the Taiping Rebels succeed so well on the battlefield?

In part, they succeeded because of sheer numbers, but there was a good deal of skill involved. The Taiping Rebels were simple farmers at the beginning, but they became experts at river warfare, building, finding, and then discarding vessels and exchanging them for new ones. They traveled from south to north, capturing several cities before arriving at Nanking, which Huang announced was their capital and the place where the Heavenly Peace would be fully established. In nearly all their movements and campaigns, the Taiping Rebels fought against Manchu forces, which possessed better firearms; one of the few areas in which the rebels had the upper hand was in the use of fireworks and explosives.

Could the Taiping Rebellion have succeeded completely to the point where Huang was the new ruler of China?

He came close to accomplishing that. Once he was established in Nanking, Huang set about trying to end the Manchu rule for once and for all; he sent armies north and west, trying to root out the last resistance. If his only opposition had been the Manchu regime, he might well have succeeded, but he overreached himself, especially with the people of the areas he had conquered. By about 1862, for example, Huang lived in truly palatial style in Nanking, while his followers barely got by and the general population—composed of those who had not accepted his reign—were on the edge of starvation. Precisely how many people perished in the rebellion is unknown, but some scholars venture that it could be as many as twenty million. The great majority of these were not killed in combat but were "collateral damage," meaning that they died in the disease and famines that accompanied the war.

How did the Taiping Rebellion come to an end?

The Manchus never gave up, and by enlisting the aid of a few thousand Western soldiers, they greatly assisted their cause. One group of about 4,000 mercenaries was led

The Taiping Army is ambushed by the Qing army at Wangjiakou during the Taiping Rebellion in this c. 1855 artwork.

by Colonel Frederick Townsend Ward, who hailed from Salem, Massachusetts; a second group, led by French officers, established itself as a rival to Ward, even though they both fought the same enemy. The Chinese labeled Ward's group the "Ever Victorious Army" and the French-led force as the "Ever Ambitious Army."

Historians sometimes overdo the importance of these two groups, but the materiel they used, cannon especially, were very important in helping the Manchu Chinese subdue the Taiping Rebels. Huang died in Nanking of natural causes, and his son, who was proclaimed as yet another son of the Heavenly Father, fled the city before being captured that year. By 1865, the same year that the American Civil War ended, the Taiping Rebellion came to its conclusion.

Was China ever the same again?

No. The combination of foreign influence, opium, religious change, and open rebellion meant that the Manchu dynasty was on its way out. The military victories of 1864 to 1865 glossed over the reality that the Manchus had no answer to China's social or economic problems. The Chinese, as a people, were deeply affected. Huang was a dirty name to the upper class, but many peasants remembered his bold approach to social conditions. He was, in some strange ways, a predecessor of Chairman Mao, who came a century later.

TEXAS REVOLUTION

Why does Texas, even today, act as if it is something quite different from the rest of the United States?

Partly it is a matter of geography. Texas is bigger than any other state in the union except Alaska, and it is a low-lying state, with great vistas. People who have moved to Texas over the decades have a different idea about themselves and what they want to establish (the enduring popularity of this idea can be seen in the success of the television series "Dallas"). Beyond that, however, is the fact that Texas was born from a combination of blood and sweat, and the Texans of today recall their revolution in 1835–1836 much more clearly than the New Englanders remember theirs from 1775–1776.

Who owned Texas first: the Americans or the Mexicans?

Probably the Native Americans—of whom there were several different tribes in Texas—had the first rights, but they, in general, did not establish titles to land. Native Americans believed that the land was owned by the Great Spirit and that men and women were merely passing through.

Mexicans first arrived in Texas in the late seventeenth century, and they were rather overwhelmed by the sheer size of the place. A handful of missions—where Franciscan priests and brothers sought to convert the Native Americans—were established, but at no time was the Mexican presence any larger than about 5,000 people. The Mexicans in Texas observed as their country won its independence from Spain. They had little time to rejoice over the change, however, because the North Americans—or gringos—began to arrive as early as 1821.

What did the North American settlers think about Texas? What conditions did they agree to?

In the entire history of the world, only three peoples have had access to vast areas of relatively unsettled land: the Russians, the Australians, and the Americans. All three of these groups were aggressive and sometimes unprincipled when it came to the native inhabitants, but it must be said that the Americans of the 1820s and 1830s were excep-

---

How many different flags have flown over Texas?

In the height of irony, the American rebels of 1835 originally flew the flag of the Mexican Republic, claiming states' rights against the power of the federal government. Over two centuries, Texas has seen the Mexican flag, the flag of the Texas revolt, the flag of the Lone Star Republic (1836–1845), and finally the Stars and Stripes.

tionally so. Many of them believed that it was "Manifest Destiny," God's design that the Anglo-Americans take over all of North America.

When they first crossed the Sabine River and thereby entered Mexican-held Texas, Anglo-Americans had to swear allegiance to the new Republic of Mexico and to promise they would become Roman Catholics. Most of the settlers took neither of these oaths seriously and continued to think of themselves as citizens of the United States who, almost by chance, had moved westward into Mexican-held areas.

Where was the other migration of this period, the 1820s and 1830s?

Numerous Americans went southwest to Mexico, while others trekked northwest to the so-called Oregon Country. The numbers were different—with more Americans going to Texas—but the impulse was the same: the desire to settle in large areas of relatively uncultivated land. By about 1835, the Americans in Texas and those in Oregon were endangering the rule of their respective hosts: the Republic of Mexico and the loosely organized Hudson's Bay Company.

When did the conflicts begin?

The first big-time settlers in Texas were the Austin family, for whom the state capital is named. Moses Austin led one of the first immigration groups, and his son Stephen Austin became the de facto leader of the Americans in Texas. The first major conflict had to do with slavery, because many of the recent American immigrants brought slaves with them. The new Mexican constitution specifically forbade slavery, and when Mexican officials attempted to enforce the law, they found trouble with the recent Anglo arrivals, many of whom were experts with the pistol and rifle. The Mexicans, by contrast, were more familiar with the sword and lance.

In 1833, Stephen Austin went to Mexico City for negotiations: he was thrown into a Mexican prison, where his health deteriorated. Upon his release and return to Texas, he became one of the leaders of the Texas Revolution, which raised its flag in the summer of 1835.

Who was General Antonio López de Santa Anna?

He was an unscrupulous politician who was very clever at manipulating the voters of Mexico, leading them to believe he was a savior of the Mexican Republic. During a long career, Santa Anna fought the Spaniards, the Native Americans, the United States, and sometimes groups of his fellow countrymen. In 1836, however, he was a relatively young hero, and he declared it was time to subdue the rebellious state of Texas (Mexicans called it the state of Texas-Coahilla).

Coming across the desert of northern Mexico, Santa Anna crossed into Texas with about 6,000 smartly uniformed soldiers. They arrived at the outskirts of The Alamo, an old mission post in present-day San Antonio, late in February, and Santa Anna imme-

The Alamo, where Mexican forces massacred a small Texan force, is a famous landmark and tourist attraction today.

diately demanded its surrender. The 170 defenders, who included famous men like Davy Crockett and James Bowie, immediately refused, and the Siege of the Alamo began.

How much do we know about the Battle of the Alamo?

None of the Americans survived, so most of our evidence comes from archaeology and from the Mexican records. Santa Anna seems to have been especially cruel and vindictive; when the Texans refused to yield, he promised to put them all to death. For the next week, the Mexicans made assaults, usually preceded by artillery bombardment, but the men inside the Alamo held out a long time, causing many casualties to the Mexican attackers. What the final scene was like is open to our imagination. Did David Crockett wield his rifle and bayonet to the very end? Did James Bowie leap over the walls, taking down three Mexican attackers? We don't know. But the imagination of the popular mind in 1836 was just as lively as our own, and Americans soon began to chant, "Remember the Alamo!"

What happened at Goliad?

Just three weeks after winning a costly victory at The Alamo, Santa Anna captured roughly 300 Texas revolutionaries at Goliad. Deciding it would be too costly and time-consuming to feed them, Santa Anna had his men lead the Texans down to the banks of the San Antonio River. Believing they were about to be fed, the Texans went willingly, and, at just the right moment (from Santa Anna's perspective), they were shot in the back. A few survivors spread the news, and "Remember Goliad!" became just as important a rallying cry as "Remember the Alamo!"

Who was Sam Houston, and why did he have such a hold over the people of Texas?

Sam Houston (1793–1863) was one of the most unusual of frontier Americans, that rare person who could really move back and forth across racial and ethnic lines. He grew up in a traditional Anglo-American household, but he spent several years living with the Cherokee and was almost as at home with their rituals as his own. He was a great friend of Andrew Jackson, but he did not share all of Jackson's ideas about Indian Removal. Houston lived in Texas by 1835, but he was not a typical Texan. When he heard about The Alamo and Goliad, however, he was incensed, and many Texans were glad to have him as their leader.

Sam Houston had an illustrious career as a state senator and governor of Tennessee, a U.S. senator, then president of the independent republic of Texas, and, finally, governor of Texas after it joined the Union.

How did Sam Houston win the Battle of San Jacinto?

Almost entirely by means of a surprise attack. Houston was outnumbered almost two to one, and the Mexicans had enjoyed one triumph after another since having entered Texas. They were within fifty miles of the Sabine River, which marked the separation between Mexico and the United States, when Houston's irregular force surprised them on April 15, 1836.

Houston attacked at 1 P.M., just as the Mexicans were digesting a rather heavy meal. His men swarmed into and through the Mexican camp, capturing Santa Anna within the first twenty minutes. Once their chief was captured, the Mexicans showed little stomach for a continued fight. Tradition has it that Houston dictated the terms of the treaty to Santa Anna, while the Mexican general sat underneath a cottonwood tree.

U.S.–MEXICAN WAR

Why did the United States get into a war with Mexico?

Numerous reasons were cited at the time, but most historians believe that the single biggest reason was that American President James K. Polk (in office 1845–1849) wanted access to the ports of California in order to turn the U.S.A. into a two-ocean country. Polk negotiated, at the same time, with the British, because he also wanted access to the magnificent natural harbors of Puget Sound.

The United States had already annexed Texas, which angered Mexico, but the sending of about 5,000 troops—almost half of the Regular U.S. Army total—to the north side of the Rio Grande really set off the Mexicans. General Zachary Taylor occupied the north bank of the river, and in April 1846, groups of Mexican cavalry crossed to attack American units. Getting the news by telegraph, President Polk informed Congress that Mexico had "shed American blood on American soil," and Congress approved his request for a formal declaration of war.

What were the first battles of the U.S.–Mexican War like?

They followed a rather painful pattern, from the Mexican point of view. In terms of bravery, the Mexicans were second to none, but their equipment was badly outdated. Just as important, many of the American officers were recent West Point graduates, and, as such, were trained in the most recent technical developments. The Americans proved especially adept at the use of "flying batteries," or artillery that was pulled by horses. Mexican gunpowder, by contrast, was so faulty that cannon balls often dropped to the ground and rolled harmlessly toward the American lines.

The Americans won two battles before moving into Mexico proper. They captured the city of Matamoros and occupied about one hundred miles of Mexican soil before the campaign came to a halt. At the same time, American troops—both regular army and militia—had overrun much of Mexican California. President Polk's vision of a two-ocean navy and merchant marine was well within the American grasp.

Why did Mexico not sue for peace?

The Mexican government was very much based on military strength, and to admit that they had failed against the United States would probably have resulted in the fall of the government. General Antonio López de Santa Anna, therefore, decided to beat the Americans at their own game; he led about 6,000 men on a daring forced march across the desert to confront General Zachary Taylor's Americans.

Taylor learned of Santa Anna's approach just in time to organize his defense. Not only were the Americans outnum-

Antonio de Padua Mar a Severino López de Santa Anna y Pérez de Lebrón (commonly called Santa Anna) was the most famous general of Mexico in his day and also served as its president for eleven non-consecutive terms.

bered, but many of Taylor's best regiments had been siphoned off to support General Winfield Scott's invasion of Mexico. Taylor, therefore, fought entirely on the defense that day. Wave after wave of Mexican assaults broke on the American lines; the Mississippi troops—led by Colonel Jefferson Davis—proved especially steady that afternoon. When morning came, Taylor found that the Mexicans had escaped in the night. He made no attempt to pursue: both armies had suffered badly during the Battle of Buena Vista.

Meanwhile, where were the Americans on the offensive?

One reason that General Taylor's force was weak is that General Winfield Scott had demanded the use of several of his regiments for the long-planned attack on Vera Cruz. Scott was a methodical general, sometimes called "Old Fuss and feathers" by subordinates, but he had the long-range vision necessary to make the invasion succeed. After landing near Vera Cruz and then taking the city, Scott planed an uphill movement, 150 miles against Mexico City.

Scott's Americans in 1847 took almost precisely the same route as Hernan Cortés' Spaniards three centuries earlier, but they encountered many more ambushes and traps. The closer to Mexico City that the Americans came, the fiercer the Mexican resistance was. As they entered the Valley of Mexico, the Americans looked on land which had not been conquered since the Spanish invasion of 1519–1521.

How did Scott capture the Mexican capital?

He did it with subtlety and intelligence, meaning that he did not throw his men straight at the walls of the city itself. Scott, instead, worked his way around Mexico City, capturing one fort or redoubt after another. By the time he was ready for the biggest attack of all—against the fortress of Chapultepec—the Mexicans were down on their luck.

The attack on Chapultepec—which was the Mexican equivalent to West Point—was fierce, and it produced numerous heroes who later won fame during the U.S. Civil War. By late afternoon on September 11, 1847, the Americans had the citadel. Tradition has it that a handful of young Mexican cadets—"the Lost Ones"—leaped to their deaths rather than surrender.

What kind of occupation followed?

It depends very much on who one asks. Some Mexicans declared that the Americans were marvelously law abiding, and a story continues to this day that a delegation asked Scott to change nationalities and serve as their temporary leader. Other sources note that plenty of violence followed the conquest, with the Texas Rangers foremost among those who wished to even old scores. In either case, however, the American occupation did not last very long. The Treaty of Guadalupe-Hidalgo, signed in February 1848, granted nearly everything that the United States wanted, and so the Yankees began going home.

REVOLUTIONS OF 1848

Was there really yet another group of revolutions?

Not only another, but this was the largest group of them yet seen. In February 1848, Parisians rose against King Louis-Philippe, with whom they were greatly disappointed. He had not proved to be an egalitarian leader, as he had promised.

Barricades went up in the streets of Paris, and after three days of bloody fighting, Louis-Philippe fled into exile (like King Charles X, he went to England). The Second French Republic was immediately proclaimed. But for the new French Revolution to succeed, it needed to see other peoples and nations overthrow their monarchical rulers, and this happened in short order. The people of Prussia rose against their king but did not send him into exile. The people of Vienna rose against their emperor, and he had to flee the city for a time. The Viennese also ejected Prince Klemmens von Metternich, who came close to holding the all-time longest tenure of power. Spain was one of the few countries not rocked by revolution. Russia also managed to evade trouble in that year. But even Great Britain, which boasted the world's most prosperous society, experienced social turbulence in 1848: a revolution, however, was avoided.

It sounds as if all of Europe was up in arms?

Not only was it up in arms, but for the first time since 1789, there was a genuine prospect of the liberal cause prevailing in most places. The incredible promise of the late winter and early spring did not last long, however, and by midsummer, the powers of reaction were gaining strength.

Perhaps the most painful loss—to the liberal cause—was in Prussia. The Prussian king promised the people a constitution, but the middle-class deputies summoned to a convention faltered, and while they hesitated, the king took action, sending them home. Emboldened by this, the Austrian emperor returned to Vienna after having his artillery bombard the outskirts. And by late summer, the revolutions were fading almost everywhere.

Where was the reaction, or push-back, the strongest?

Austria managed to suppress its own revolution with a minimum of casualties, but it found it impossible to accomplish this in the sister state of Hungary. The Hungarians, or

---

What is meant by the "Forty-Eighters"?

It is an American expression which refers to the many Europeans who fled the Old World for the United States in 1848 and 1849. Germany, which had seen the liberal cause flounder, sent the most people to America, but there were Italians, Irish, and French as well. Many of these new immigrants established strong ethnic communities in American cities, where they became known as the Forty-Eighters.

Magyars, rose against Austrian rule, but they suffered the heavy hand of Russian displeasure. Czar Nicholas I, who was known as the "gendarme of Europe," sent over 200,000 troops across the border to make sure that the Hungarian revolution was crushed.

About the only significant gain that could be seen—in 1849—was that serfdom was abolished in the Austro-Hungarian Empire. That was the only concession made by the ruling class, and it took a great deal of bloodshed and suffering to bring it about.

CRIMEAN WAR

How long had Russia and the Ottoman Empire—also known as Turkey—been at odds?

By the 1850s, these two powers had been in conflict, to greater or lesser degrees, for just about 300 years. One could look all the way back to the reign of Czar Ivan the Terrible and find roots of the Russian–Turkish animosity. The two powers had fought many times.

The Turks generally prevailed in the first two centuries of their wars against Russia. Even Czar Peter the Great had gone too far when he invaded the Sea of Azov. He'd been surrounded and forced to bargain his way out. But by about 1750, the Russian Empire was very much on the rise, with the Ottoman Turks headed in the opposite direction. The Turks, for example, had been the world's foremost artillerists in the sixteenth century, and they were still rather good in the seventeenth. By the mid-nineteenth century, Turkey was almost the bottom of the barrel where cannon and artillerists were concerned. When Russia picked a fight with Turkey in the early 1850s, it seemed a safe bet that the former would prevail.

What was the Crimean War about?

It is named for the peninsula where most of the fighting took place, but the war was actually over holy sites in the Holy Land and who should control access to them. The Russians claimed the right of first defense of the Christian holy sites, but this was disputed by the French, who referred back to the Crusades to claim that they were the rightful defenders. And both Christian nations looked on the Turks as interlopers.

France had recently experienced yet another change in government, with Louis-Napoleon—a nephew of Napoleon Bonaparte—taking over, first as president of the Second Republic and then as emperor, after he carried out a *coup d'état* in December 1851. Emperor Napoleon III was anxious to assert French territorial rights in the Middle East, and he engineered an alliance with Britain. Those two powers then agreed to defend Turkey from the Russian aggressor. If this sounds strange to historians now, it was certainly so to the people of the time. They said it was extraordinary that England and France—traditional foes—agreed to work together, in concert with the Ottoman Empire, to fight the Russians!

It sounds as if this was one of the few wars of that time which did not revolve around land and territorial possessions?

That is correct. The Crimean War was primarily about prestige and a new alignment of the major European powers. The balance of power swung hard against Russia, and the people of that nation resented it deeply.

How many men went from Western Europe to the Crimea?

The British and French contingents came to well over 400,000 men. Even two generations earlier, it would have been impossible to transport so many, but the advent of the steam engine and steam-powered ships made it feasible. Perhaps 50,000 Turks joined the expedition, but most of the Turkish army remained in and around Istanbul.

Russia had a vast population but was only able to mobilize about 250,000 men in time for the war. These, too, were less trained and less disciplined than their Western European foes. But the insults and degradations were not only between the Allies on one side and the Russians the other; the British and French exchanged continual pot shots against each other, each alleging that the men of the other nation shirked their duties.

How many men rode into the "Valley of Death"?

Because of Alfred Lord Tennyson's magnificent poem, the world is more aware of the charge of the Light Brigade than of almost any comparable action in human history. What

Russian artillery fire upon the British light brigade led by the Earl of Cardigan in the doomed charge during the Crimean War (artwork by William Simpson). The event was immortalized in a famous poem by Alfred Lord Tennyson.

stands out is the brazen folly of the British leaders and the absurd heroism of the men who charged along that dirt road with Russian cannon thundering in every direction.

What was decided at the peace congress in 1856?

Not surprisingly, the peace congress was held in Paris, where Emperor Napoleon III was all too pleased to preside. The treaty that ended the Crimean War guaranteed Turkey's independence and demilitarized the Black Sea.

GARIBALDI'S REVOLUTION

Why is Garibaldi's name so familiar? Was he reminiscent of someone like the Marquis de Lafayette?

Giuseppe Garibaldi (1807–1882) was, perhaps, the single greatest hero of the Western world during the nineteenth century. His career, in some ways, paralleled that of the Marquis de Lafayette, but Garibaldi was even more ubiquitous, meaning that you could find him almost anywhere.

Born in the town of Nice, in southern France, Garibaldi grew up speaking French and Italian, but he always identified himself as an Italian. It irked him, and many of his contemporaries, that there still was no unified Italy; rather, the Italian peninsula was carved up into small city-states and principalities. Garibaldi left home in his teens and spent years sailing the Mediterranean; by his thirties, however, he had become a revolutionary, or freedom fighter. Over the span of two decades, he fought in Argentina, Paraguay, Colombia, and elsewhere, always on the side of constitutional government and personal liberties.

How did Garibaldi ever come home?

In 1848, Garibaldi was on hand to witness the revolutions that took place throughout Western Europe. He and a few hundred desperate followers briefly took over the city of Rome, where he declared a republic. The end of the 1848 revolutions forced him to withdraw, however, and he went to the Mediterranean Island of Caprera. By then, he was the most famous freedom fighter in the Western world.

Early in life, Garibaldi had been inspired by Giuseppe Mazzini, the so-called "prophet" of revolutions and nationalism. The two were quite different, in that Mazzini was more intellectual and had a deeper understanding of populist movements, with both their positive and negative potentials. No populist movement could really take place in Italy without Garibaldi, however; he was the essential element.

How did the Kingdom of Sardinia-Piedmont figure in to the situation?

The union of the Island of Sardinia and a rugged section of mainland Italy was one of the many compromises brought about by the Congress of Vienna in the wake of

Napoleon I's downfall. The kingdom was not loved and the monarchy was too new to inspire much loyalty, but this was the only political structure on which a larger one might be built. Garibaldi recognized this and pledged to work with King Victor Emmanuel, even though he was, at heart, a republican who disliked all monarchies.

What was Garibaldi's shining moment?

In the summer of 1860, he sailed from Nice, France, with slightly more than 1,000 volunteers. Known as the "Red Shirts," these men vowed to liberate Sicily from Bourbon rule. When they landed, the Bourbon army of more than 25,000 tried to capture them, but Garibaldi evaded them for weeks, and when the two armies finally came to battle, he prevailed. Weeks later, Garibaldi led his men across the Straits of Messina into southern Italy and soon worked his way up the coast. At the same time, King Victor Emmanuel of Sardinia-Piedmont landed in northern Italy and began working his way down the coast. The two men met at Teano in October.

What were the battles like?

The Bourbon army looked like a modern one, with fine artillery and drawn-up regiments. Garibaldi's men did not look like an army; he often referred to them as the irregulars. Something about the man, however, and the movement inspired them, and they often performed daredevil feats that astonished their opponents. By this time, Garibaldi's trademark clothing was part of the situation. Clad in a red shirt with a sweater or overcoat, he invariably wore a light felt cap. Many people professed, on meeting him for the first time, that he was one of "nature's aristocrats," a man so clean and without artifice that they at once believed in him.

Garibaldi's volunteers won the Battle of Volturna, then entered Naples. In three months, he had accomplished more for the cause of Italian unification than any other leader, yet he held back from declaring a dictatorship. Perhaps he knew the Italians needed more than a military hero, that they would only come together if he provided them with a king. And when he met Victor-Emmanuel on the road between Naples and Rome, Garibaldi declared himself willing to turn all his powers—real and supposed—over to the king.

Was that all for Garibaldi?

It should have been. He retired to the Island of Caprera, just north of Sardinia, where he lived the life of a peasant-adventurer. He had never been interested in money or power for their own sake. Adventure, however, continued to call him, and in 1864 he led an insurrection against the government he had done so much to create. When this was suppressed, he accepted a pardon from King Victor-Emmanuel and once more retired to Caprera.

By this time, Garibaldi was the most famous freedom fighter in the entire world. He received congratulations and signs of admiration from peoples and governments from around the world. Abraham Lincoln offered him a major-general's commission in the

Northern armies during the Civil War, but Garibaldi turned Lincoln down on two points: he wanted to be leader of all the Union forces, *and* he wanted a firm commitment that the war would be fought to end slavery.

Was Garibaldi rather like Che Guevara?

In style, they were rather similar. Both men wore plain, unaffected dress, and both had an outsized effect on people they met. Internally, however, they were quite different. Garibaldi was a romantic dreamer, who occasionally managed to impose his views on a larger society. Che Guevara was a truly radical person, who believed almost no sacrifice—of himself or others—was too much to bring about a communist society.

As guerrilla fighters, Garibaldi and Che were very much alike. Both believed that armies were servants of the state and could not perform the important tasks of revolution. Both men, therefore, much preferred the wild and irrepressible style of the guerrilla fighter. We have much more evidence to work with in Garibaldi's case, because he was so often in the front lines, and there is so much testimony, including from newspaper reporters. We have to say, however, that Guevara was equally courageous.

What did Garibaldi have to say about guerrilla warfare?

"I believe that the theory of great regularity of masses and lines is generally carried too far and that the open order of battle is too much neglected, as it has become necessary through the perfection of firearms and through the obstacles that cultivation has rendered at every step." Garibaldi did not prescribe guerrilla warfare for every freedom fighter, but anyone who examines his career is impressed by what he managed to accomplish.

When did Garibaldi die?

He died on Caprera in 1882 and was immediately hailed as the greatest man of his time. The British press, most particularly, paid homage to him as a liberator and a man who could be counted on to resist temptation, meaning he was not in it for the money.

Many journalists and historians spent time with Garibaldi—either in his pres-

Giuseppe Garibaldi was one of the founding fathers of modern Italy. A brave general and politician, he unified the peninsula into one nation.

ence or by interviewing those who did—and most concur that he was a person of very simple habits who possessed a singular vision. Garibaldi did wish for a united Italy, but his grander, long-term goal was the diminishment of nationalism, so that men and women could live in a freer, more harmonious world. He was far ahead of his time in terms of racial and gender equality, and he embraced more causes than almost any other nineteenth-century leader. The twentieth century had no leader of his stature; it was not until Nelson Mandela (1918–2013) became president of Africa in 1994 that a person of such fame was in a powerful political office.

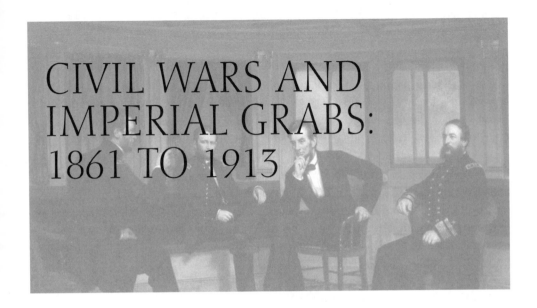

CIVIL WARS AND IMPERIAL GRABS: 1861 TO 1913

UNION VERSUS CONFEDERACY

Was the American Civil War (1861–1865) inevitable?

In a moral sense it was; lacking the Civil War, it is almost impossible to see how the four million African-American slaves would ever have been freed. But in material terms, the Civil War seems like a major blunder on the part of the North and South (which will be used synonymously with Union and Confederacy). Numerous opportunities existed for the North and South to come to an agreement, but heightened tensions and high emotion on both sides prevailed.

When did the Civil War begin?

There are those who point to the Confederates firing on a Union steamboat in January 1861 and others who suggest that the establishment of the Confederacy, in February 1861 was the key moment. In sheer military terms, however, there is no doubt that April 12, 1861, was the critical day; that was when Confederate batteries in Charleston, South Carolina opened fire on federal Fort Sumter.

The federal fort held out for thirty-six hours before capitulating on honorable terms. The garrison was taken by steamship to New York City, where its members were greeted as heroes. Most importantly, however, Abraham Lincoln, president of the Union, called for 75,000 volunteers. The war was on, or, as the *New York Times* expressed it, "the ball is opened."

Which side held the advantage(s) when the Civil War began?

Even though the South had a more robust military tradition and a larger number of cadets at the Military Academy at West Point, there is not the slightest doubt that the North (or

Union) held the advantage in almost every single area. There were about nineteen million whites in the North compared to eight million in the South, and the North had roughly ten times as many miles of railroad track. In industrial capacity, there was no comparison. About the only thing going for the South in 1861 was the possibility that foreign powers—notably Britain and France—might intervene on behalf of the Confederacy.

If the North had won one or two major victories in 1861, the Confederacy might have folded. Instead, it was the Southern men who demonstrated the greater energy and won more battles and skirmishes. Most important was the Battle of Bull Run, fought on July 21, 1861, about forty miles outside of Washington, D.C. Though the battle was hard-fought, the late afternoon surge won it for the Confederates, and many Northerners panicked. The result was that the Virginia, or the Eastern theater, would remain hotly contested for years to come.

How about the circumstances on the Western Front, or theater?

In that area, the North held a commanding advantage. Not only were more Northern soldiers available for duty right away, but the quality of the Northern commanders proved much more superior. Brigadier-General Ulysses Grant seized Cairo, Illinois, at the confluence of the Ohio and Mississippi Rivers, and the energetic actions of Brigadier-General Nathaniel Polk insured that St. Louis—and the vital federal arsenal there—would remain solid for the Union. Much to its dismay, the Confederacy had to fight on the defensive in the Western theater right from the beginning, and that never changed throughout the war.

What do we know about the relative level of morale on both sides?

It was high; that is certain. Historians generally emphasize the greater excitement shown by the Confederates, but in the spring of 1861, the North, exemplified by New

An 1865 photo of Fort Sumter after the Civil War. The extensive damage to the fort is still evident.

When did balloons first appear in war?

The Northern armies had the first one or two, as early as 1861. General George B. McClellan was probably the first officer of general rank ever to ascend in a balloon. When he brought the Army of the Potomac to the James Peninsula in 1862, the balloons were deployed more than ever. Generally speaking, however, balloons proved a disappointment. They often drifted to the "wrong" side of the battlefield. None were shot down by enemy fire, however, because of the angle.

York City, was practically afire for the war. The insult shown to the "Old Flag" by the attack on Fort Sumter prompted outrage in the North, and April 20, 1861, witnessed the single largest crowd—perhaps 200,000—ever seen on the North American continent.

When did the North gain control of the Cumberland and Tennessee rivers?

Brigadier-General Grant captured Confederate forts Donelson and Henry in the winter of 1862, insuring that the Union navy would control the inland river waterways passing those forts. By now, Grant had emerged as the most vigorous and aggressive of Northern leaders and was soon promoted to major-general. The South, appalled by Grant's victories, sent General Albert Sidney Johnston—not to be confused with Joseph E. Johnston—to attack the Northern lines in Tennessee. The clash came at the Battle of Shiloh, fought on April 6, 1862.

Shiloh—named for the little church at the middle of the battlefield—was a terrible exchange, with both sides fighting savagely. The Confederates had the advantage all day on April 6, but they narrowly missed breaking the Union center (General Johnston was killed in the fighting). That night, many Confederates believed they had won, but Union General Grant struck at them early on the morning of April 7. Before long, the Confederates were in full retreat. Shiloh was, by far, the deadliest battle to this point, and it pointed toward a bloodier war in total.

How did the North capture New Orleans so easily?

This, surely, has to rank as one of the South's greatest failures. In April 1862, the Northern flotilla, commanded by David Farragut, forced its way past the forts and hulks in the river and appeared off New Orleans on April 25. The city yielded a few days later, and the largest Confederate urban area and port therefore passed into Northern hands.

Not only had the South lost the Battle of Shiloh and New Orleans, but the Confederate capital, Richmond, Virginia, was now imperiled by a major move of the Army of the Potomac. Major-General McClellan brought 110,000 men by water to the James Peninsula, and they marched to within a dozen miles of Richmond (some Union men could hear the church bells of Richmond).

271

When did Robert E. Lee become commander of the Army of Northern Virginia?

Lee had been restricted to secondary commands until June 1862, but the crisis that threatened Richmond—and the wounding of Confederate General Joseph E. Johnston—brought him to the fore. Lee was an inspired battlefield commander, and in Thomas "Stonewall" Jackson he had a remarkable number-two man. Lee led a series of attacks against McClellan's force, and though nearly 20,000 Confederates went killed, wounded, or missing, it was the Northern commander who blinked first.

Mistakenly believing that Lee outnumbered him, McClellan brought his enormous army all the way back down the Peninsula (this caused guffaws among many observers). McClellan successfully got his army back to Washington, D.C., where he was, temporarily, sacked by President Abraham Lincoln. McClellan was soon needed again, however, because Lee and Stonewall Jackson now commenced their invasion of the North.

General Robert E. Lee, commander of the Confederate Army of Northern Virginia.

Given the disparity in sheer numbers, could the Confederates have achieved anything with their invasion?

Lee's great, quiet hope was that he would win a major victory on Northern soil, which would persuade the great powers of Western Europe to intervene for the Confederacy. Things seemed well as the Confederates crossed the Potomac River into Maryland, but on September 10, 1862, a series of Lee's maneuvers and organizational tactics fell into McClellan's hands (he had been reinstated as commander of the Army of Northern Virginia). Armed with this information, McClellan soon had the army moving and nearly trapped Lee and Jackson separately. The Confederates effected their junction just in time for the Battle of Antietam, fought on September 17, 1862.

How close did General McClellan come to winning the war at the Battle of Antietam?

He should have won the war that day. McClellan had roughly 80,000 to about 37,000 for Lee. But the fighting, which began at the crack of dawn, seesawed for several hours, giving Lee just enough time to reposition his units and keep his force together. There were massive infantry charges on both sides and enormous cannon exchanges; by day's end, both sides had lost about 11,000 killed and wounded. Antietam was, and remains, the single bloodiest day of American history.

It was in his failure to pursue Lee that McClellan really let the Union down. He made no attempt to prevent Lee from getting to the south side of the Potomac, and weeks passed before he made any attempt to follow. President Abraham Lincoln was appalled by McClellan, who, he told a friend, "has got the slows." Lincoln had to keep McClellan as commander of the Army of the Potomac until the midterm congressional elections; once they were past, he sacked McClellan for the second and final time.

VICKSBURG AND GETTYSBURG

What, meanwhile, had happened in the Western theater?

General Grant was pressing the Confederates hard. In December 1862, he came close to taking the fortified city of Vicksburg, but failing on the outskirts, he held back. Grant was now number one to a remarkable number two: General William Tecumseh Sherman. Between them, Grant and Sherman would become the scourge of the South.

In the spring of 1863, Grant finally took an enormous gamble, bypassing Vicksburg to march his force on the opposite side of the Mississippi River before recrossing. Showing his usual speed, Grant out marched his foes and captured Jackson, Mississippi. Grant then marched on Vicksburg; the Confederate garrison held out gallantly but could do little to prevent Grant from establishing his batteries and siege lines. The possibility that Vicksburg might fall prompted Robert E. Lee to take even greater chances in the Eastern Theater.

Who fooled who at the Battle of Chancellorsville?

In May 1863, Northern General Joseph Hooker brought 110,000 men, the entire Army of the Potomac, over the Rappahannock River into Virginia. Hooker was a fine leader of men and an even better battle commander, and he had everything in his favor. Lee knew the odds and decided to make them even greater. When General Stonewall Jackson pro-

Was Robert E. Lee a gambler?

Yes. Lee gambled not because he liked to, but because—as the leader of an outnumbered army—he had to. On several occasions, Lee divided his army in the face of superior numbers and managed to pull out a victory. Of course, the more times he played this trick, the more likely it was that a Northern general would finally see it for what it was and make Lee pay the price.

posed a daring twenty-mile march around Hooker's right flank—leaving Lee with but 30,000 men to face the enemy—Lee agreed.

Jackson and his men made the march and caught the Union right completely unawares late in the afternoon of May 5, 1863. If ever there was a high Confederate tide, this was the moment. As night fell, Jackson and Lee had scored a big victory, with every chance that they would do even better on the following day. But Jackson was wounded—shot by some of his own men by mistake—and the glory of the Battle of Chancellorsville faded in light of the fact that Jackson would soon die. As Lee expressed it: "He had lost his left arm, but I have lost my right."

Was there any Northern general who could beat Robert E. Lee?

This was the question President Lincoln asked himself when, in late June 1863, he replaced Hooker with General George Meade. By then, Lee and the Army of Northern Virginia had invaded Maryland, and some Confederate units had reached southern Pennsylvania. To be sure, Lee's move north had some desperation to it—he was trying to relieve pressure on the besieged fortress of Vicksburg—but to the Northern civilians who beheld the invading army, it seemed as if the Confederates had come to stay. For their part, the Confederate soldiers were amazed at the peace and prosperity of the North, Pennsylvania most especially. Here was a land without slave labor, yet the average white laborer seemed to live better than his Southern counterpart.

How did the opposing forces come to meet at the little town of Gettysburg?

Oddly enough, the Confederates, who ranged over an area of thirty miles, approached from the northern direction on the morning of July 1, only to run smack into some Union forces approaching from the southerly direction. Nothing was preordained; no commander determined that the village of 2,500 folk would be the place for the clash; instead, the forces of both armies were sucked into the skirmish, which became a confrontation and then turned into the single greatest battle ever fought in North America.

Lee arrived on the battlefield a little after twelve noon and immediately decided that he must support his forward units. General George Meade arrived that evening and learned that his men were drawn up in a defensive, horseshoe-like position, placed on

---

In what way(s) was the North richer than the South?

In almost every conceivable way. The best description of the difference between the two societies came from the pen of Alexis de Tocqueville, a Frenchman who toured America in 1831–1832. Floating along the Ohio River, de Tocqueville noted the progress and industry on the north bank and the slovenly habits on the south. A free people, he declared, would always make more of what they had than a people who depended on slave labor.

> ## How accurate—nor not—is the 1993 film *Gettysburg?*
>
> Filmed by the Turner Company, *Gettysburg* was one of the largest and most expensive of all military movies, and there are moments in the 3.5-hour film that are truly superb. The incredible adoration accorded Lee by the Confederate rank and file is shown, and the most convincing moments are those which depict the fight for Little Round Top. Of all the films ever made concerning military matters, *Gettysburg*, at its best, comes closest to showing both the horror of war and the irresistible attraction it has for many people, young men most especially.

favorable ground. Neither general had the luxury of choosing; both men had to deal with what lay in front of them. On that first day, July 1, the Confederates pushed the Union men out of the town of Gettysburg and onto the heights that lay just to the south and southwest.

What was Lee's first great mistake at Gettysburg?

Lee was, on most occasions, the master of feint, surprise, and maneuver. It was not his style, by any means, to be suckered into a massive attack. But he was weary, impatient, and he may have been suffering—at this time—from the first effects of the heart disease that would kill him seven years later. Lee made the decision for a massive onslaught on July 2, 1863, with the heaviest Confederate attack coming from the west, aimed at the heights that culminated at Little Round Top and Big Round Top.

Lee's usual gift for tactics deserted him on July 2; even so, his men nearly pulled it off. A ferocious battle raged all along the western side of the hills that afternoon, and the Confederates nearly seized Little Round Top. They were stopped by a regiment from Maine, whose colonel, Joshua Chamberlain, became one of the best-loved and most-admired heroes of the entire war.

What was Lee's second great mistake at Gettysburg?

On the morning of July 3, 1863, Lee learned that nearly 10,000 of his men, including several generals, had been killed or wounded the previous day. He had, however, administered plenty of losses to the enemy, and this—clearly—was the time to withdraw and fight another day. Lee became deeply stubborn, however, insisting that General James Longstreet's corps carry out a frontal assault on the center of the Union defenses at Cemetery Hill. Longstreet opined that it was an impossible mission, but Lee was adamant.

At roughly 4 P.M. on July 3, 1863, about 15,000 Confederates—most of them Virginians—stepped out of the shelter of the woods to commence a slow, dignified march to the top of the ridge. Lee was watching, as were General Longstreet and General George Pickett, whose men formed the center of the Confederate advance.

Pickett's tragic charge during the Battle of Gettysburg is portrayed in *Hancock at Gettysburg* by artist Thure de Thustrup, 1887.

What happened to those 15,000 men?

They came under a blistering, raking fire from muskets, rifles, and cannon. Never in the history of American warfare had an attacking force been met with such volleys. The Confederates kept moving, however, and made it two-thirds of the way before they reached a white picket fence that obstructed their movement. It only took ten seconds for each man in the forward ranks to get over or under the fence, but as they did so, the men presented a magnificent target for the Northern gunners.

Confederate General Lewis Armistead and about 300 men did reach the brow of the hill, but they were killed or captured almost immediately. Northern cannon fire continued to plough into the Confederate lines, and by the time the Confederates turned to run, their ranks were truly shattered. No one can say precisely where each Confederate lay or died, but within one hour of the commencement of the attack, roughly 7,000 men were lost, either because they were killed, wounded, or went missing.

Did Lee admit to his error?

He did. He galloped up and down the shattered lines, declaring that it was all his fault. He was correct.

How did the Army of Northern Virginia escape after its shattering defeat?

By all the rules of war, the Army of Northern Virginia should have been captured or destroyed. General George Meade was continually being reinforced, while Lee was completely on his own. Meade and other Union leaders often cited the tremendous

> ## No one can "afford" to lose 7,000 men.
> ## Why was it especially bad for the Confederates?
>
> When one takes the white population of the eleven Confederate States—eight million—and divides it by 7,000—he or she comes up with the painful fact that nearly one out of every 1,000 white Southerners was a casualty on that single day, July 3, 1863. This day was one of great tragedy for the South, which never recovered.

rainstorms of July 4, 1863, for making Lee's escape possible, but this overlooks the fact that the Confederates managed to move in that weather. The truth is that Meade—and the Army of the Potomac—was not sad to see Lee depart. Even though the Confederates had been drubbed, the knowledge of what they had accomplished, at Chancellorsville especially, was strong in the Northern mind.

President Lincoln, as so often, was furious at his commanding general, but he could not sack the victor of Gettysburg. Meade, therefore, remained in charge of the Army of the Potomac, while the North learned of yet another spectacular victory.

When did Ulysses Grant capture Vicksburg?

That Grant, by 1863, had become the Union's most successful general was impossible to argue. He had taken forts Donelson and Henry, recovered after the tough first day at Shiloh, and had completely outmaneuvered the Confederates in the Vicksburg campaign. Grant's finest moment, the one he longed for, came on July 4, 1863, when the Confederate garrison at Vicksburg capitulated. Nearly 14,000 men, along with cannon and rifles that were simply irreplaceable, were taken.

The Confederate hopes for victory were, with Gettysburg and Vicksburg, completely dashed. Their only hope now was that they could delay Union victory long enough that Abraham Lincoln might be denied a second term in the elections of 1864.

What was the final big campaign of the year 1863?

In September 1863, Confederate General Braxton Bragg won the Battle of Chickamauga and nearly captured the vital railroad town of Chattanooga, Tennessee. Bragg stayed on the heights overlooking the town too long, however, and President Lincoln did everything he could to rescue the situation. Regiments from the Army of the Potomac were dispatched west, and General Grant was called from Mississippi. Soon after arriving at Chattanooga, Grant took a series of risks that led to the supply lines being reopened. There was no chance, at this point, that Chattanooga would fall.

In November 1863, Grant unleashed a series of attacks that drove the Confederates from their mountaintop positions; once General Bragg's army was on the run, it proved impossible to stop. Grant laid the plans and issued the orders, but the Battle of Lookout Mountain was won by the daring of the men of the Army of the Cumberland. Though

277

it was too late in the year to proceed, the way to the center of Georgia, and the city of Atlanta, was now open.

THE LAST BATTLES OF THE U.S. CIVIL WAR

When did Grant become general-in-chief of all the Union armies?

No one had held this elevated rank since George Washington, but it was conferred on Grant by President Lincoln in March 1864. Grant was the most famous man in the Union, and it was believed that once he started the war in the Eastern Theater, the Confederates would quickly collapse. Grant came to Washington, D.C., in March, and by the first of May he was ready to begin his offensive. Though he was the supreme commander, Grant kept General George Meade as commander of the Army of the Potomac.

The Northern confidence was not misplaced. Lee and the Army of Northern Virginia were in a truly ragged state in the spring of 1864. Roughly 50 percent of the Confederacy was now in Union hands, and the Confederate supply system—which had always been suspect—had now failed completely. Even so, Lee and his men were ready for a last stand, and they vowed to make the North pay for its (eventual) victory.

If Grant was to go after Lee and his army, who was to pursue the Confederates in the West?

General William T. Sherman had that task. Like Grant, Sherman had an enormous numerical superiority over his foe. General Braxton Bragg had been replaced by General Joseph E. Johnston, and he and Sherman conducted a series of maneuvers in northern Georgia that looked more like a dance than a fight. Johnston continually moved to avoid a major clash, and Sherman was all too happy to oblige. The maneuvers brought Sherman and the Western forces close to Atlanta by the summer of 1864.

When did the fighting in the Eastern Theater resume?

In the first week of May 1864, Grant and the Army of the Potomac crossed the Rappahannock, very much as General Joseph Hooker had done a year earlier. The first serious fighting with the Army of Northern Virginia took place in "The Wilderness," very close to where the Battle of Chancellorsville had been fought. Many men—North and South

The Peacemakers by George Peter Alexander Healey, c. 1868, shows (left to right) General William Sherman, General Ulysses Grant, President Abraham Lincoln, and Admiral David Porter aboard the *River Queen* in 1865 during an unsuccessful attempt at a peace conference with the Confederates.

alike—claimed that The Wilderness was the worst of all battles they experienced. Fire spread in the thick brush, and smoke enveloped the men; not only was it hard to tell friend from foe, but many men died from smoke inhalation. That night, the screams of the wounded and dying echoed in the enclosed area.

Grant came quite close to breaking the Army of Northern Virginia, but at critical moments Robert E. Lee appeared, always bringing just enough reinforcements to prevent a critical breakthrough. After three days of fighting in The Wilderness, both armies had lost more than 10,000 men in some of the most brutal type of fighting. Some observers claimed that this was the moment when Grant would show himself to be another Joseph Hooker or George McClellan. He would turn around, the Army of the Potomac would retreat, and Robert E. Lee would continue to be the immovable object. None of this happened, however. Instead, Grant moved forward and to Lee's right flank, forcing the Army of Northern Virginia to move into yet another defensive position. As one Union soldier put it, "That Ulysses, he don't scare worth a damn."

Where did the two armies go after The Wilderness?

Grant and the Army of the Potomac kept moving to their left, imperiling Lee's right. Lee, consequently, had to keep moving backward and toward the coast. Every now and then, the two armies clashed, usually with large numbers of casualties on both sides.

First they fought at Spotsylvania Court House and then at Fredericksburg. Grant kept up the remorseless pressure, and by the first of June the Confederates were in their

279

trenches at Cold Harbor, only a dozen miles or so from Richmond. This was the closest a Union force had come since 1862, when McClellan had come up the James Peninsula. By now, Northern newspapers—having surveyed the casualty lists—were calling for Grant's head. President Lincoln listened to each and every appeal and answered them all the same way. He could not spare Grant, he said, because unlike every previous Union commander, "he fights."

What was the single costliest mistake of the war?

We have seen that Lee made a terrible mistake on the third day of Gettysburg, sending forth 15,000 men in a fruitless effort. Grant was to outdo him slightly at Cold Harbor.

On June 3–4, the Union forces attacked all along the line, which stretched more than five miles. The Confederates, secure in their trenches, brought down the Union men by the score and then by the hundreds. When the Battle (or massacre) of Cold Harbor was complete, the North had lost 8,000 men killed, wounded, and missing and had gained absolutely nothing. This was Grant's biggest mistake in the war, and many observers believed it would cost him his job. But President Lincoln remained rocklike in his defense of Grant; he believed that the informal man—who cared little for the spit-and-polish of military style—would pull it all together in the end.

Where, by this point, were Sherman and General Joseph Johnston?

Some people called it a dance; others labeled it a minuet. The two generals, so different in temperament and style, continued to feint and maneuver until the Northern men reached the outskirts of Atlanta. On June 26, 1864, General Sherman made one of his few and rare mistakes, sending thousands of men in a frontal assault against the Confederates on Kennesaw Mountain. The Union suffered nearly 2,000 men killed, wounded, and missing that day, but the elated Confederates did not realize they were up against a foe, in Sherman, just as relentless as Grant.

Was the Battle of the Crater really as vicious as we sometimes hear (and as was depicted in the film *Cold Mountain*)?

On July 30, 1864, explosives placed by Union sappers exploded underneath the Confederate lines at St. Petersburg, and nearly 5,000 Northern troops rushed in to take advantage. The explosion was, quite likely, the largest sound yet made by human hands in warfare, and the possibility for a breakthrough was real. The "crater" worked against the Union men, however, who ran into the opposite end, where they looked uphill at Confederate rifles and bayonets. The Battle of the Crater was a minor disaster for the Northern cause, but it anticipated what warfare would be like in World War I.

By mid-August, General Joseph Johnston was replaced by General John Bell Hood. This was one of the biggest mistakes President Jefferson Davis made, because Hood, while a brave and gallant man, was neither a strategist nor a tactician. He made several ill-timed attacks on Sherman's forces, and by the end of August he had completely run out of options. Hood evacuated Atlanta, and Sherman entered it in triumph that same day. He telegraphed President Lincoln: "Atlanta is ours and fairly won."

Did the Confederates stand any chance at this point?

No. Nothing less than a miracle could have saved the Confederacy at this point. Not only had Atlanta fallen, but Grant had brought his army—in a truly daring maneuver—right to the gates of Richmond.

In July 1864, Grant stole a march on his foe and got most of his army across the James River before Lee even knew they were in transit. Grant's vanguard nearly seized the all-important city of Petersburg, Virginia, but they were just barely stopped by about 3,000 Confederates. Petersburg was the vital rail link between Richmond and what remained of the Confederacy, so Grant settled into a siege where his lines kept wrapping around the Confederates, forcing them to extend as well.

Where did General Sherman go after the fall of Atlanta?

Sherman could, quite reasonably, have remained where he was: he had already accomplished great things. He was a true bulldog, however, and in November 1864, having obtained permission from Grant, Sherman began what is called the March to the Sea.

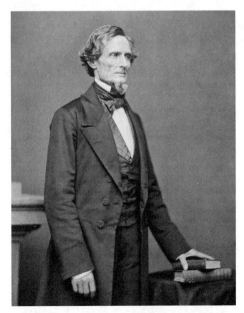

Cutting free from his own supply lines and even telegraphic communication, Sherman moved across Georgia in an enormous swathe, with his 60,000 men living off the land. His infamous prediction, that he would "make Georgia howl," came true.

Late in the year, Sherman approached Savannah, one of the last major cities of the Confederacy. Using feint and maneuver at least as much as brute force, Sherman pushed the Confederates out and entered Savannah. He captured large quantities of baled cotton, one of the few items the Confederacy was able to sell abroad.

How did the Confederates fare during that last season (the winter of 1865)?

The people—civilian and military—suffered terribly. Price inflation had ruined the Confederate economy, and even Pres-

During the siege of Richmond, Virginia, Confederacy President Jefferson Davis had to flee the city with his family to avoid capture.

ident Jefferson Davis and his family went without many things that in normal times would be considered standard. The strength of the Union, meanwhile, was more apparent than ever. As spring approached, the Army of the Potomac readied for its final set of battles, which, everyone was quite sure, would finish the war.

On the April 1, 1865, President Jefferson Davis and his Cabinet escaped Richmond just in time to evade a Union pursuit; General Lee and the Army of Northern Virginia, too, got out of town just in time. But if Lee believed that there was any mercy, or lassitude, among Grant and his generals, he was utterly mistaken. The Army of the Potomac was soon in hot pursuit.

Where was the last battle fought?

The Battle of Sayler's Creek, in rural Virginia, was not one of the big battles of the Civil War, but it was among the most vicious. Roughly 50,000 Union men clashed with less than half that number of Confederates for several hours, and when darkness came, almost 11,000 of the latter were taken prisoner. Numerous accounts suggest that the fighting was especially intense and that many men who under normal circumstances would have been allowed to surrender were, instead, bayoneted. Sayler's Creek was the final nail in the coffin of the Army of Northern Virginia, and when General Grant sent a letter to General Lee three days later, Lee indicated a willingness to discuss terms.

Lee and Grant met at Appomattox Court House on April 9, 1865, which just happened to be Palm Sunday. During the two-hour meeting, Lee agreed to surrender the Army of Northern Virginia, while Grant agreed that the men could take home their horses and mules and the officers could retain their side-arms. The surrender itself was performed the following day.

How was this news received in Washington, D.C.?

In Washington, indeed throughout the North, the news of Lee's surrender was met with widespread rejoicing. The North had won, and the South had bowed to the inevitability of the two sides coming together as one new nation. And, in the hour of triumph, the North extended its hero worship to a man who had long deserved it: President Lincoln.

Lincoln relished the victory as much as anyone, but he continually told his generals to "let 'em up easy." He wanted to be the man to bring the two sections back together, to "bind up the nation's wounds." Sadly, Lincoln did not have that opportunity. He was shot at Ford's Theatre in Washington, D.C., on April 14, 1865, and died of his wound the following morning.

Was Lincoln as great a leader as he seems?

He was indeed. Though he made mistakes, and though the sophisticated people of Washington, D.C., never took him into their hearts, Lincoln was the great American leader of the 1860s, perhaps even of the entire nineteenth century. In terms of military success and holding a country together, he can only be compared to two other men of the time: President Benito Juarez of Mexico and Chancellor Otto von Bismarck of Prussia.

Would the subsequent history of the United States have been different if Lincoln lived to complete his second term?

Very likely so. Lincoln was not perfect—he had his foibles and prejudices—but the chances are rather good that he would have effected some type of reconciliation between North and South. Instead, he was brought down by an assassin's bullet and the presidency passed to Andrew Johnson, a person of political skill but also of poor judgment, especially where issues of reconciliation and forgiveness were concerned.

THE RISE OF PRUSSIA

At what point in the nineteenth century did Prussia become the most militaristic of the German states?

The potential had always been there, thanks to an aggressive buildup of the Prussian military in the seventeenth century. We have seen, too, that King Frederick II, known as Frederick the Great, made much use of that army during the eighteenth century. Even so, Prussia made a marked turn to the right—politically speaking—in the mid-nineteenth century (this caused many of Prussia's most liberal citizens to pack up and move to the United States).

When Otto von Bismarck became Chancellor of Prussia in 1862, he flatly declared that the great issues of the day—by which he meant German unification—would be achieved by "blood and iron" rather than speeches, deliberations, and the writing of constitutions. Bismarck was very much in the Prussian military tradition, but it was not preordained that he would succeed; rather, he seized upon certain moments and opportunities and managed to confirm Prussia both as the leader of the German-speaking peoples and the most militaristic state in Europe.

FRANCO-PRUSSIAN WAR

Did the Europeans observe the American Civil War with interest?

The great powers of Europe took a lively interest in the Civil War, sending numerous observers. There were German nobles who fought for the North and French and British observers covering many of the major battles. Britain, France, Austria, and Prussia all recognized that the American conflict had the potential to alter the future of warfare; this was especially evident from the naval battles and the appearance of ironclad ships. Rather few Europeans realized, however, how soon their nations would be exposed to similar types of wars.

How did the Franco-Prussian War begin?

In 1870, both France and Prussia were relatively eager for war; the general population of both nations were keen for a clash. The same cannot be said of Emperor Napoleon III of France and King Wilhelm I of Prussia: both leaders hoped for peace and quiet. Prussian Chancellor Otto von Bismarck, however, enacted some clever diplomatic maneuvers to make it seem as if the Prussian king had offended the French ambassador. In the charged atmosphere that existed, it was relatively easy to move from this first step to outright war.

Many observers predicted a French victory, but their notions were based on the era of Napoleon I (reigned 1804–1814) rather than Napoleon III (reigned 1852–1870). The French military of 1870 looked rather like the one of 1810, while the Prussians had made every effort to modernize their forces. In particular, the Prussians had pioneered in the making of steel cannon and in the use of railroads to bring their troops rapidly to the front.

When did the war commence?

In the summer of 1870, Prussia initiated its invasion of eastern France. The Prussians moved much more rapidly than anticipated, and by August they had cornered a large

Kaiser Wilhelm I of Prussia (left) led his country to victory against the French in the Franco–Prussian War with considerable help from Chancellor Otto von Bismarck (right), who was the true architect behind unifying most of the German peoples.

section of the French army at Sedan. Emperor Napoleon III was with his men, and like them he was forced to surrender in September. There were moments, and even days, when the French fought well, sometimes inflicting heavy casualties on their opponents. The Prussian military was better organized, however, and Chancellor Otto von Bismarck had the timetables of the Prussian trains posted in all the offices of the Prussian General Staff. Then, too, the surrender of Napoleon III—who went off into exile in England—lowered the morale of the French.

Had this been a "normal" nineteenth-century war, that would have been all. But there was a citizen's component to the Franco–Prussian War which had not previously been seen. When the Prussians approached Paris, they found its inhabitants determined to resist, and a four-month siege ensued. The Parisians had no hope of success, but they fought on, and when the city finally capitulated in January 1871, the people were on the verge of eating rats and mice.

What was the single most momentous event of the late-nineteenth century from the monarchical and imperial viewpoint?

On January 18, 1871, King Wilhelm I of Prussia became Kaiser Wilhelm I of Prussia and Germany. This move, the culmination of Otto von Bismarck's policy, came as a result of victory in the Franco–Prussian War; the other members of the German confederacy agreed to Prussian leadership and to making the king into an emperor.

Plenty of other governmental and monarchical changes had taken place during the nineteenth century, but none had such long-lasting effects. In one bold stroke, Otto von Bismarck lifted the Hohenzollern monarchy into an imperial dignity and consolidated the status of the Prussian military within the German Empire. Although neither Bismarck nor the newly created emperor had any of the racist ideas of Adolf Hitler, their sudden rise to prominence made Hitler's—in the long run—possible. Meanwhile, however, the other monarchies and empires were on the move, attempting to consolidate or increase the size of their overseas colonies.

OVERSEAS EMPIRES

How had the British gained first place in the race for imperial possessions?

England, or, more properly, Great Britain, had a long head start over all its rivals. The first British Empire had been built on the American mainland, in Canada, and in the Caribbean. When roughly half of that empire disappeared at the conclusion of the Revolutionary War in 1783, the British expanded in other directions and accomplished great things.

The British were already in India by 1783, and they expanded their presence until the East India Company came to dominate about half of the subcontinent. When the Indian soldiers of the East India Company rebelled in 1857—starting the so-called "Sepoy

Mutiny"—the British Parliament decided that India would be better off governed by the nation than the Company. Most of India, therefore, became part of the British Empire during the 1860s and 1870s. This was not all, however; the British were on the move elsewhere.

How did the British become so important in South Africa and Malaysia?

Some of the British imperial possessions came by "accident," while others were the result of definite plans and strategies. During the Napoleonic Wars, Britain seized the South African colony first settled by the Dutch; twenty years later, many of the Dutch moved 700 miles northeast in the so-called "Great Boer Trek." Britain could have left them alone, but when news spread of the discovery of gold and diamonds, the British began pursuing the Dutch Boers into their internal possessions.

Malaysia, too, had been in Dutch hands for a long time, and the British used the Napoleonic Wars as a springboard to gaining entry. By 1880, the British had Singapore, which they turned into a great merchant city and naval base. On top of all of this, the British also had control of Australia and New Zealand, making the British Empire, by far, the greatest the world had ever seen. At its zenith, the British Empire encompassed about one-fourth of the world's land surface and about one-fifth of all the world's peoples.

Where did France turn to expand its empire?

France had already been in Algeria for decades, but France's loss to Prussia in the war of 1870–1871 made the need, and desire, for colonies even more urgent. During the last quarter of the nineteenth century, France's Algerian holdings, therefore, extended far beyond the current-day nation of Algeria; at one point, France's African holdings came to about seven times the size of France itself.

Even before the Franco–Prussian War, France had expanded on the other side of the globe, in what is now Vietnam. At the time it was known as Indochina, and France managed to obtain most of it in the 1860s and 1870s. When one remembers that France still had sugar islands in the Caribbean, it is evident that the Third French Republic—

How did the discovery of quinine assist in the European invasion of Africa?

Until the mid-nineteenth century, much, if not most, of Africa remained in the hands of the indigenous peoples. One reason was that the European explorers and military leaders were unable to handle malaria, the most common disease in central Africa. With the discovery of quinine and its use in the prevention of malaria, the European peoples became much more adventurous. Often the Europeans ran into poorly organized tribal resistance, but there were times when the resistance was ferocious.

while a far cry from the nation in the time of Napoleon III—had a very respectable colonial empire.

Why did it take France so long to conquer Algeria?

The modern-day nation of Algeria is much smaller on the map than colonial Algeria, which was conquered by the French over roughly a thirty-year period. During the long struggle, the French abandoned some of their traditional forms of warfare and adopted some of the tribal methods. The establishment of the French Foreign Legion, for example, stemmed directly from conflict with the Algerian tribes.

Where did Belgium turn to expand its power overseas?

Belgium had already been in what we now call the Democratic Republic of the Congo for some time, but the last third of the nineteenth century witnessed an incredible expansion of Belgian rule and power. At its height, Belgium controlled a vast section of Central Africa, roughly eighty times the size of Belgium itself. Just as important, Belgium extracted raw materials, rubber in particular, which allowed it to become wealthy on a per capita basis.

Holland, or the United Provinces of the Netherlands, had fallen a long way in terms of Great Power European politics, but it still possessed much of what we now call Indonesia: at the time it was called the Dutch East Indies. Between them, the British, French, Belgians, and Dutch controlled perhaps fifty percent of the world's merchant ships and transported at least that much of the world's goods.

Had any European nation been left out of the race for overseas empire?

Russia and Germany lamented their slow start and claimed that it was their right and prerogative to have overseas colonies. Germany, which only became unified in 1871 under the rule of Kaiser Wilhelm I, was late to the imperial game, but it took swift action. By the 1890s, there were small German colonies in Polynesia and a swathe of East

Who "opened" Japan to Western trade?

The United States. In 1853, a naval squadron composed of both wooden and ironclad vessels arrived on the coast of Japan. Its commander, Captain Matthew C. Peary (1794–1854)—brother of Commodore Oliver H. Perry—asked for an audience with the Shogun, the *de facto* ruler of Japan. The Japanese were appalled by the effrontery and the Shogun never agreed to meet in person, but a commercial agreement was hammered out, because the Japanese had no real choice. Those who marvel at Japan's economic success in the late twentieth century, in the auto industry especially, often point the finger at the United States, saying it was the Americans' fault in the first place.

Africa under German rule. Many Germans complained that all the really good places had been taken before they came to the table, but Germany—with its powerful army and a growing navy—was doing quite well for itself.

Russia, one can say, had been in the imperial game for a very long time, but it had not seen much in the way of reward. The state of Muscovy, in the time of Czar Ivan the Terrible, had expanded greatly to the east, and the Pacific was reached in the time of Czar Peter the Great. Many Russian leaders pointed out, however, that these vast sections of Siberia and coastal Pacific were of little use, or value, when compared to the holdings of, say, Britain or France. Then, too, the more that Russia pushed in that direction, the closer it came to a confrontation with Imperial Japan.

A veteran of the Mexican–American War and the War of 1812, Commodore Matthew Perry is credited with opening the trade door between Japan and the United States.

How is it that Japan was the only Far Eastern major power to start to catch up with the West?

When the American ships, under Commodore Perry, arrived in 1853, Japan was in a state that can only be described as medieval, and that was precisely how they wanted to remain. The pressure from the Western powers was irresistible, however, and by the 1870s, Japan made a clear choice to play the game on the Westerners' terms. Miniature railroads were imported, so Japanese engineers could begin building life-sized ones. Army manuals were borrowed from Britain, Germany, and France so the Japanese military could begin to organize along more modern lines. No one could be certain that Japan would come all the way to Western standards, but it must be said it had done remarkably well by about 1900.

THE AMERICAN EMPIRE

When did the first battles between the Far Western tribes and the United States take place?

In 1853, a small incident outside of Fort Laramie—having to do with ownership of a single cow—led to a confrontation between Native Americans and whites.

What was so different about the horse warriors of the Great Plains?

Many tribal peoples showed that their courage and willpower was equal to that of the imperialist invaders. The horse peoples of the Great Plains had something most of the others did not: horses.

Runaway horses from Spanish Mexico reached the Great Plains by about 1700, radically transforming the lives of the native peoples. Previously, their hunting range had been in the neighborhood of fifty square miles: the appearance of the horse increased that by a factor of almost ten. Of course, there were some negatives involved. Numerous Great Plains peoples who had previously lived in peace with each other—thanks to distance—now went to war. The wars between the Cheyenne and the Crow, and the Cheyenne and the Pawnee, are among the best known. But when the white Americans encroached west of the Mississippi, they found many well-mounted peoples who quickly obtained muskets and rifles. As a result, the Indian Wars of the Trans-Mississippi West had a different character from those of the East Coast.

Was George Armstrong Custer really as remarkable as he has been portrayed in books, films, and documentaries?

Yes. Custer does not appeal to our modern-day sensibilities, and if he were—by some miracle—to appear in our twenty-first-century world, he would have few admirers. That is because the Indian Wars are long over, and no one fears being tomahawked or scalped. To the majority of nineteenth-century white Americans, however, Custer was a fantastic hero: a fearless cavalryman and the protector of white American civilization.

Custer was a superlative military leader who rose to brigadier-general during the Civil War (thanks to his youth, he was known as the "Boy General"). In the decade that followed, he won an even larger reputation as the chastiser of the Native Americans on the Plains. Some of the tribal peoples even developed a grudging admiration for him, saying that "Yellow Hair" was the manliest of all the Americans. That Custer was a ruthless foe, no one can dispute: he pursued his foes to the nth degree, and did not always spare civilians.

Why was June of 1876 so important to the white Americans?

It represented the 100th birthday of the United States, and great ceremonies were scheduled in Philadelphia. As Centennial Day approached, Americans had little thought or concern for the frontier, but on Independence Day—July 4, 1876—they learned that Custer and 275 of his men had been wiped out at the Battle of the Little Bighorn.

This was not the first time Native Americans had done in a United States column; the forces under General Arthur St. Clair had sustained even worse losses in 1791. But the timing of this battle and the arrival of the news just as white Americans celebrated their 100th birthday could not have been worse. White Americans who usually expressed a sympathetic attitude toward Native Americans now declared they must be exterminated, and practically all the resources of the U.S. Army were devoted to that task.

What happened to Crazy Horse and Sitting Bull?

Chief Crazy Horse was captured by the whites and killed in a scuffle. Whether this was premeditated or not will never be known. Chief Sitting Bull, the best known of the medicine men of the Sioux tribe, crossed into Canada, seeking refuge and protection from the British government. When he returned a year later, he, too, was taken into custody. As important as these men were, their military accomplishments pale in comparison to those of Chief Joseph of the Nez Perce.

How did the Nez Perce hold out for so long?

They were a tribal people, living in what is now central Washington State, when the U.S. government decided to move them to another location, which was unfamiliar to them. Although Chief Joseph was an admirer of General Nelson Miles, the American military commander, he decided to escape with his people to Canada. The great trek of the Nez Perce began in1877 and lasted four months.

The Nez Perce always fought defensively, attempting to increase the distance between themselves and their pursuers. They inflicted several defeats on the pursuing American forces, however, and admiration for their fight began to grow, even among white Americans. In September 1877, the Nez Perce reached the rolling lands just shy of the Canadian border. They settled down for a night of good rest, and it proved fatal. The Americans, who had pursued from three different directions, opened fire the next morning.

Could the Nez Perce have escaped?

Not this time. There were almost 2,000 bluecoats surrounding them, and the Indians were down to their last one-hundred-odd warriors. On the morning of October 3, 1877, Chief Joseph emerged from his hiding place, presented himself to the white soldiers, and declared: "Tell General Miles that I know his heart.... From where the sun now stands, I shall fight no more forever."

Most American schoolchildren learn these famous words and admire both Chief Joseph and the men who captured him. The sad part of the story—and less known—is that Joseph and his Nez Perce band were eventually sent to a remote section of Idaho, as unfamiliar and distasteful to them as the earlier reservation had been.

Chief Geronimo was the leader of the Chiricahua Apaches.

Was that it for the Native Americans?

Not quite. The Cheyenne, who were divided into northern and southern groups, fought on for several more years. The Apaches fought both the Mexican military and the U.S. Army until the capture of their chief, Geronimo. But it is safe to say that none of these Indian groups really had a chance: they were all ground down, eventually, by the enormous power of the U.S. military.

The final indignity, for the Western tribes, took place at Wounded Knee, South Dakota in the winter of 1890. Native Americans from several different tribes had been influenced by the so-called "Ghost Dance" which harkened to earlier times, claiming that the whites would eventually be extinguished. Given the relative strength of the two peoples, this assertion seems ridiculous, but just enough men in the U.S. military took it seriously to bring about a bloodbath. The Battle of Wounded Knee, on December 23, 1890, was the last stand by the Plains tribes. From that point on, they either assimilated into the Anglo-American culture or lived separate lives from it: in neither case did they threaten it. Although they did not know it, the Native Americans had a parallel; at the same time they resisted the U.S. cavalry, a major native tribe fought Queen Victoria's soldiers in South Africa.

THE ZULU WARS

Who were the Zulus?

They were Bantu tribespeople of South Africa who had emigrated from Central Africa perhaps 500 years earlier. They had almost no knowledge of white, or European, peoples until the Dutch came to Cape Town, South Africa in 1652.

Something about the geography and natural beauty of South Africa makes it delightful both for those who have lived there for generations and newcomers. So it was with the Dutch, who fought a number of skirmishes with the Zulus. But in the 1830s, many of the Dutch Boers undertook a long 800-mile trek north to what is now Pretoria. In so doing, they left Cape Town to the British, who had arrived during the Napoleonic Wars. As a result, it was the British who would feel the wrath of the Zulus.

How warlike a people were the Zulus?

If one compares them to the Sioux and Cheyenne of the American West, there is little doubt that the Zulus were among the most ferocious of all native peoples to resist white Europeans. The Zulus employed a mass body of warriors, all of them armed with thrusting spears, and they relied on foot speed, not on horses or wagons.

The Zulus were a tribal group for hundreds of years, but they became a serious fighting force during the reign of King Cetawayo in the 1830s. They fought the British with great skill and intensity but were finally defeated in the 1880s.

END-OF-THE-CENTURY CONFLICTS

What was the general sentiment, at the end of the nineteenth century, about the future of war?

Many people in Western Europe and the United States declared that war would soon be obsolete. New international organizations had been established, and there was a general consensus that the major powers—of Europe especially—had gained so much in the preceding fifty years that nothing more was needed. Certainly it looked this way from the perspective of other peoples, who observed that the European imperialist powers had virtually doubled the size of their holdings since the Crimean War.

Along with this belief ran another: the idea that humans had become more rational and would not lightly choose to go to war. Many other mechanisms, economic ones especially, seemed to have the power to influence events. Then, too, it was believed that the level of education which had reached the "masses" was sufficient so that the average person did not look forward to, or think about, war as much.

Given the antiwar sentiment, or the notion that war had gone out of style, how do we explain the rash of wars at the end of the century?

Imperialism had a lot to do with it, both the imperialism that had already succeeded and the desire of major powers who felt they had been "left out" of the race for colonies. In this case, the United States led the way.

In February 1898, the battleship U.S.S. *Maine* arrived in the harbor of Havana, Cuba. The *Maine*, one of the state-of-the-art American battleships, had been sent by President William McKinley to protect U.S. nationals in Cuba, but also to provide firsthand intelligence on the state of the war on that island. For nearly three years, many Cubans had been in revolt against Spain, while a Cuban minority supported the continuation of the regime. The fighting had become ugly, with Spanish General Valeriano Weyler placing many civilians in detention camps, secured by the use of barbed wire.

Did little boys play with toy weapons in the way that our children do today?

No. Boys of the late Victorian Era had to make up their own play games where war was concerned, and they could often do so in brutal fashion; the hardness of life in the English private schools (which, oddly enough, are called "public") was well known. But in terms of toy weapons made out of plastic or wood, the children of that era had none.

A photo of the U.S.S. *Maine* entering Havana Harbor not long before explosives were set off that killed 250 sailors on board.

What led to the start of the Spanish–American War?

The sympathies of a majority of Americans were with the Cuban rebels, and their support increased dramatically when the U.S.S. *Maine* exploded in Havana Harbor. The explosion was dramatic enough, but the casualties—more than 250 sailors and marines—were much worse. And, almost from the outset, most Americans believed that the Spaniards had done the deed.

President William McKinley came under heavy pressure, both from the general public and from members of his own administration, to bring about a full-scale war. The president waited until two investigations—one Spanish, the other American—were conducted. Both were inconclusive, but the president could no longer hold back the clamor for war, which was declared on May 15, 1898. The United States had started a war with the object of freeing a people from colonial rule.

How large a role did Theodore Roosevelt play in the Spanish–American War?

He seemed to be here, there, and everywhere. As assistant secretary for the U.S. Navy, he pressured President McKinley. He dispatched Commodore George Dewey and his squadron to Manila Bay, in the Philippines. And, once the war was really underway, Roosevelt resigned his post in order to raise a regiment of volunteers. They were a special cavalry group which soon became known as the "Rough Riders."

The Rough Riders came from all walks of life, but Roosevelt had a special fondness for athletes and Wild West types, as well as Ivy League graduates. The Riders became, therefore, the single most colorful regiment in the U.S. military, and Roosevelt's subsequent fame was assured, just as long as the war went according to plan. And that it certainly did.

What was the first major action of the Spanish–American War?

On May 1, 1898, Commodore George Dewey brought his squadron of American ironclad vessels into Manila Bay. Dewey is believed to have said, "You may fire when ready, Gridley," and if the words are accurate, they show the calm and relative ease with which the squadron entered its contest. The Spanish ships were, by contrast, mostly built of wood, and their crews had not been at sea for months: they were, therefore, no match for the Americans. The two-hour gunfight left 273 Spaniards dead and most of their ships either sunk or beached. By contrast, Dewey had one man killed.

The Battle of Manila Bay was reported immediately, and Americans swarmed to the flag, both literally and figuratively. Dewey was hailed as a great hero; people began to speak of the possibility that he would run for president. The Battle of Manila also demonstrated, beyond any doubt, the superiority of the U.S. Navy to its Spanish counterpart and indicated that this would be a short and successful war.

When did the Americans invade Cuba?

They landed on the southeast side of the island in the summer of 1898 and placed a stranglehold on the supply lines leading to the city of Santiago (which means St. James). The Americans were joined by Cuban guerrilla fighters who showed them the best ways to come close to the city, but capturing it was another matter. Santiago was ringed by forts and by jungle areas; many American troops would have fallen prey to malaria if they settled down to a long siege. It was therefore decided to make a quick move.

On July 1, 1898, the Americans attacked the Spanish defensive positions on the northeast side of Santiago. The Spanish defenders ran the first half of the day, employing their Mauser rifles to great effect. Not until mid afternoon did the issue become close, and then it was Colonel Theodore Roosevelt who "took the bull by the horns" ("bully" was one of his favorite words). The Rough Riders were by no means the only American troops that surged up San Juan Hill that afternoon, but they were among the foremost, and, thanks to Roosevelt, they grabbed 99 percent of the publicity. Photos taken at the top showed a jaunty Roosevelt and his crew. Bravery and skill had indeed been involved, but the press made Roosevelt seem like a superhero.

What were the results of the Spanish–American War?

The Spanish fleet inside Santiago made a run for it on July 3, 1898. The American ships were waiting, and the contest was almost as unequal at the Battle for Manila Bay. Most of the Spanish ships were sunk, and it was clear that America had won the war. The negotiations that followed led to a peace treaty that granted the Philippines, Puerto Rico, and Guam to the United States, as well as what can be described as a protectorate over Cuba.

How did Americans feel about their new position in the world?

They were painfully divided on the subject. Many Americans applauded the Spanish–American War and were pleased that the Stars and Stripes now flew over foreign areas. Others were appalled, and a group of East Coast leaders—including Andrew Carnegie and Mark Twain—formed the Anti-Imperialist League.

The Anti-Imperialist League declared that America had been founded on principles opposite to those of the major European powers. What made the United States so different, they argued, was that it needed no serious navy and no permanent army. Bad enough, they declared, that the army and navy had risen in importance, but much worse was that America had now become a genuine imperialist power, with its flag flying in remote locations, over peoples with no connection to the United States.

What did Rudyard Kipling say to the Americans about their new status?

Take up the White Man's Burden—Send forth the best ye breed
Go bind your sons to exile, to serve your captives' need;
To wait in heavy harness, on fluttered folk and wild
Your new-caught, sullen peoples, Half devil and half child.

Kipling was a great poet who knew what he spoke of; he was the son of a British administrator and had been raised in India (he also lived in the United States briefly). Precisely what he meant in his poem has been debated ever since, however. Was Kipling, indeed, congratulating the Americans for joining the British and others in the imperialist game? Did he, rather, suggest that all empires were essentially "burdens" to those who possessed them? In either case—and one can perhaps venture other theories—Kipling could not let his own, British, people off the hook, for they were about to become embroiled in not one but two imperial adventures.

How did the Boer Wars begin?

There were two Boer Wars: the First Boer War lasted from December 1880 to March 1881, and the Second Boer War was from October 1899 to the end of May 1902. Great Britain had gained possession of the former Dutch colony in South Africa during the Napoleonic Wars and had never relinquished it. The Boers were descendants of the original Dutch settlers. Many of them moved 600 miles northeast to escape British rule in the 1830s. They had since formed two republics, both of which existed precariously on the borders of British South Africa.

Diamonds were discovered in the Transvaal region in the 1880s, and the European population of the area simply exploded. The Boers were already resentful of British influence in the area, and they knew that one of the greatest of British imperialists—Cecil Rhodes—envisioned what he called the "Cairo to Cape Town" railroad, one that would obviously be under British control. Fearing a takeover, the Boers started the war in October 1899. Superb guerrilla fighters, armed with Mausers, the Boers surprised the British in several locations and laid siege to Mafeking, Pretoria, and Ladysmith.

An English cavalryman attacks a Boer farmer in a 1900 painting by Richard Caton Woodville. While the British were successful in subduing the South African farmers, it came at the great cost of 25,000 casualties.

How did Britain respond to the Boers?

Queen Victoria's Gold Jubilee, just two years earlier, had celebrated the incredible, amazing success of the British Empire; it would not be dismantled under her watch. Therefore, Britain put together the largest expeditionary force since the Crimean War. Headed by a group of rather mediocre generals, this force descended on Cape Town in 1900 and began the long, slow march to the Transvaal region. It is from this march that the British obtained one of their best marching songs: "We are marching to Pretoria, Pre-toria, Pre-toria, We are marching to Pretoria, Pretoria, Hooray!"

The British found the Boers tough opponents. The latter were excellent defensive fighters, and they surprised British forces repeatedly. Over time, however, the British numerical superiority (there were only 87,000 Boers in total) prevailed. The cities and towns which had been besieged were relieved, and the British began to hunt the Boers, now in the countryside. Finding it difficult to hold all the prisoners they took, the British built concentration camps, secured by barbed wire.

What was the result of the Boer War?

The British won on all fronts, but they had over 25,000 men killed, wounded, and missing. This was much more serious than expected, and it led the British to allow the Boers a graduated state of semi-independence. Then, too, the Boer War persuaded many Britons that their empire had reached its natural limit. No major attempts at further conquest were attempted, and the death of Queen Victoria (in 1901) neatly coincided with the curtailment of further military adventures. By the time Queen Victoria died,

Where did barbed wire originate?

It was an American invention, developed shortly after the American Civil War. Barbed wire was extremely useful in the American West for the separation of livestock, but it began to be used for military purposes during the Spanish–American War and then the Boer War. By the time World War I began, barbed wire was an important war material.

Britain was also discouraged by yet another symbol of natives rising against the empire: this event took place in China.

Who were the Boxers?

We call them the Boxers because of their martial arts expertise; they called themselves the Righteous Society of Harmonious Fists. In 1899, the Boxers were a formidable grassroots organization in eastern China, and they hoped to push the Westerners out of their country. The expression "foreign devils" had been in use since the First Opium War, but never did it seem as appropriate to the Chinese as in 1899.

Roughly a dozen foreign nations, including Germany, Britain, and the United States had established both diplomatic relations and a flourishing merchant trade with China. The balance of trade was favorable to the foreigners, and negative toward China, but this was not the only reason the Boxers wished to eject the foreign devils; the Boxers believed that the foreigners corrupted Chinese morals and values, and they were at least half correct. The Empress Dowager favored the Boxers, even though she dared not make a public stand on their behalf. When the Boxers crashed into the foreign legations in the city of Beijing, it seemed that all the efforts of the Western powers had been in vain.

How long did the foreign legations hold out against the Boxers?

Western military power again asserted itself; the rifles of the soldiers of the legations kept the Boxers at bay for a siege of four months until a large relief army—composed of British, French, Germans,

The Chinese Boxers were people skilled in the martial arts who wished to expunge the Westerners from their homeland.

297

and Americans arrived. The Europeans routed the Boxers, and the Empress Dowager had to escape Beijing disguised as a peasant woman.

The foreign devils were now in control of Beijing and the surrounding area. The Europeans did not realize, however, that by revealing the weakness of the Ching (or Manchu) dynasty, they had opened a Pandora's box. The dynasty struggled on for just a few years before officially expiring in 1911.

What did the world situation look like on the first of January, 1900?

The seasoned observer was generally optimistic. There were lots of small conflicts, sometimes called brushfire wars, but the major powers were at peace. There was a rough economic parity between the United States and Great Britain and a rough military parity between Czarist Russia and Imperial Germany. France was most occupied with building its defenses for a possible war with Imperial Germany.

When one looked around the globe, which had recently reached 1.5 billion in population, the prospects for peace seemed to outnumber those of war. European diplomats, meeting in the Netherlands, drew up a series of codes and agreements concerning warfare. To many people, a great war between the major powers was unthinkable.

Was there a wild card in the situation?

To be sure. A century earlier, the wild card had been Belgium and Holland. If they had managed to take over France, it would have enabled an invasion of England. A century later, in 2001, the wild card was usually Israel and its Arab neighbors. But in 1900, the wild card was in the Balkans, the mountains that run from Eastern Europe down to Greece. As if to recognize this, the Eastern powers began to squabble and then fight for the Balkans.

Why did Imperial Germany challenge Imperial Britain at sea?

One could argue that there was no need for this competition. The Germans, however, saw it differently. They had been unified politically in 1871, and as the last of the European imperial powers, they had received only scraps at the international table. Britain now controlled roughly one-fifth of the entire globe, while France possessed large sections of Africa and Indonesia. The Americans, too, were a power on the rise. Imperial Germany, now led by Kaiser Wilhelm II, wanted its share of the international spoils.

RUSSO–JAPANESE WAR

How had Japan managed to enter the ranks of the Great Powers?

Japan had not quite made it, but by 1900 it was very close. Japan, after being forced to open to Western trade in 1853, had made a fabulous effort to modernize and Westernize its military, while keeping much of its society intact. The emperor remained a symbol of

Japan's long past and the samurai were still venerated, although they no longer enjoyed any real power. During the 1870s and 1880s, Japan made incredible leaps forward in the building of railroads, steamships, and the acquisition of rifles and cannon from the West. By 1900, Japan was—pound for pound—as strong as many of the Western nations.

Russia did not realize this. The czarist-ruled society was drifting ever closer to a cataclysmic revolution, and many leaders of that society remained oblivious to the dangers. When Japan insisted on its rights to a group of islands known as the Kurile, Russia naturally refused. Rather than prepare a declaration of war, Japan decided to strike first (this was a clear precedent, one which the Americans should have heeded in 1941).

Where and when was the first strike?

Imperial Japan hit Czarist Russia on April 12, 1904. The attack came from torpedoes launched from Japanese ships, and following that initial attack, Japanese warships came in for the kill. In one short day, they devastated the harbor at Port Arthur in present-day Manchuria.

The Russians fought back with everything they had, but all equipment and supplies had to be sent over the Trans-Siberian Railway, which, at this early stage, was single-tracked. This meant that each and every train had to stop and be removed from the tracks in order to let another, coming from the opposite direction, pass. The Russian high command was in Moscow and St. Petersburg, 5,500 miles from the action, while the Japanese leaders were about 800 miles off.

How could Russia strike at Japan?

The Russian Bear—as so many people called it—was immensely powerful but also unwieldy. Russia's troop strength was most concentrated along its western borders, not the eastern ones. The only recourse, therefore, was to send a major fleet against Japan, and to do so meant the ships would have to pass through thousands of miles of hostile waters. In October 1904, the Baltic Fleet—twenty major warships and many transports—steamed out of Russia, headed for Japan. Knowing that the British, who controlled most of the coaling stations en route, were sympathetic to Japan, the Russians carried what looked like mountains of black coal on their decks.

The voyage began with a near disaster, when the Russians fired on a few fishing boats in the English Channel. The trigger-happy Russians believed that these were Japanese torpedo boats, operating half a world away from home! Despite this incident, the Russian fleet made it almost all the way to Japan, only to learn that Port Arthur had already surrendered to the Japanese. To turn for home would be disastrous for Russian prestige; it was also impossible because of the lack of coal. The Russians, therefore, proceeded right into the trap laid for them by the Japanese.

Who won the Battle of Tsushima?

The Japanese were outnumbered in ships and guns, but their vessels were far more maneuverable. Their morale was also high. Admiral Togo Heihachiro issued orders at the

The Japanese Guboat *Maya* was an iron-hulled Imperial Navy ship launched in 1886 and saw action during the Russo–Japanese War.

battle's beginning which echoed those of Admiral Horatio Nelson at the Battle of Trafalgar a century earlier, except that this time it was *Japan* which expected all men to do their duty.

The Japanese gunners proved far superior, and by the end of the day the entire Baltic Sea Fleet was either captured or destroyed. In one memorable day, Admiral Togo put to rest the idea of European invincibility and announced that a new era—one in which the Asian powers were to be included—had arrived.

BALKAN WARS

How long had the Ottoman Empire been known as the "Sick Old Man of Europe"?

The expression first came about in the early nineteenth century, and it showed no signs of diminution in the early twentieth. The Ottoman state—at least to foreign eyes—had not altered since the time of Suleiman the Magnificent. The sultan still owned, at least in theory, the property and servitude of all his subjects. Ottoman industry was almost nonexistent, and even the trade routes that had once made Istanbul world famous had diminished (this was, in part, because the Suez Canal permitted European merchants to bypass the Ottomans).

The Ottoman Empire still looked impressive on paper, stretching from sections of the Balkans all the way to the Sinai Peninsula. The Ottomans' weakness was fully exposed in 1912, however, when Bulgaria, Romania, Serbia, and Greece formed the Balkan League. Declaring that the Ottomans had oppressed Christians for centuries, the Balkan League declared war, and the Christians won a number of important victories.

Who were the "Young Turks"?

Today we use this expression to describe almost any group of reformers, and we usually emphasize the word Young, meaning that reform usually comes from leaders in their twenties and thirties, not in their forties and fifties. But in the early twentieth century, the term was coined to refer to the would-be reformers of the Ottoman Empire. They did not get rid of the sultan—that would have been too severe a break with tradition—but they sought to modernize the army and to bring the Ottoman Empire into the twentieth century.

The Young Turks observed the defeat of the Ottoman armies in 1912, but they rejected the terms of the Treaty of London; as a result, the Second Balkan War began in 1913. The Turks did better in this second contest, and when World War I began a year later, the Ottoman Empire still looked like one of the impressive world powers.

THE GREAT WAR: 1914 TO 1918

Was the Great War inevitable?

By no means. One can declare that there were circumstances which pointed in the direction of a great conflict, but there were several days, or even moments, along the way when highly placed officials could have acted more wisely and possibly achieved different results. The populations of the various European nations, also, cannot escape censure; the peoples pretty much jumped at the opportunity to go to war. In retrospect, we can say that they did so because they did not know how horrible this war would be.

Have historians come to any consensus about what caused the Great War?

Each historian has his or her favorite subject to discuss, but there is a broad consensus that four major elements played their parts in bringing on the Great War. These were 1) nationalism; 2) an arms race; 3) dissension in the Balkans; and 4) interlocking or entangling alliances.

Why should nationalism be a problem? Don't we have it today?

Not in the same way that we had it one century ago. Today, one can proudly say that he is an American, an Australian, a Russian, or a German without feeling the need to prove or demonstrate that his national or ethnic group is superior. Of course there are some exceptions to this rule, and they tend to be in the trouble spots of our world today. But to our great-great-grandparents—the generation that fought the Great War—nationalism was much more intense a thing: when one claimed something in public, other people might respond that those were "fighting words."

It's important to remember, too, that nationalism, in 1914, was still a rather youthful phenomenon. The French had been around as a people for many centuries, but France had only become a nation during the Revolution of 1789. The Germans had been speaking the same language for at least 500 years, but Germany only became a nation in 1871 with the conclusion of the Franco–Prussian War. Much the same could be said for Italy, Austria, and other European countries.

What was the arms race?

No major European war had been fought since 1871, and in that time the inventors of the Western world had developed all sorts of new war materials. The airplane, the submarine, and the machine gun were all relatively new inventions, but there were also the hand grenade, the artillery that threw shells rather than cannon balls, and even barbed wire, which played so important a role in trench warfare. Even though the European powers had largely remained at peace since 1871, their governments had purchased a tremendous amount of new weaponry, and some were keen to see it used.

At sea, there was a naval race between Great Britain and Imperial Germany. Starting in 1890, the Germans built up their High Seas Fleet, seeking to achieve parity with England. Much of this was the result of Kaiser Wilhelm II's personal animosity toward England. The British pulled ahead when they completed HMS *Dreadnought* in 1906, but the Germans did not lag behind, expending an ever-larger part of their national budget on battleships and cruisers.

Speaking of the Kaiser, didn't he have some English blood in his veins?

Actually he did. He was the son of a German prince and an English mother, who was herself the eldest daughter of Queen Victoria (ruled 1837–1901). The Kaiser, therefore, grew up with an appreciation for England but never an understanding of its people. He mistakenly believed that they could be intimidated, and he had a terrible way of putting his foot in his mouth. Not only did he declare that Germany must have her "place in the sun," meaning colonies, but he had some rather ugly racial and ethnic beliefs. Consider what he said to an American reporter in 1908 (*Century Magazine* censored the interview until 1934).

Kaiser Wilhelm II was the leader of Germany during World War I.

"The future belongs to the Anglo-Teuton, the man who came from Northern Europe—where you to whom America belongs came from—the home of the Germans. It does not belong, the future, to the Yellow, nor to the Black, nor to the Olive-colored. It belongs to the Fair-skinned Man, and it belongs to Christianity and to Protestantism. We are the only people who can save it. There is no power in any other civilization or any other religion that can save humanity; and the future—belongs—to—us!"

Given that the Kaiser believed this so strongly, why did he help bring about a European war that eventually weakened the European powers, or what he called the "Fair-skinned Man"?

If we take the Kaiser at his word and give credence to what he said, then we have to conclude that his life—along with that of millions of his people—was a rather tragic story. By attempting to give Germany its "place in the sun" and by attempting to show that the future belonged only to white-skinned Protestants, he played his part in bringing on the Great War.

This does not mean the Kaiser was a monster: he was an intemperate, rash, and ultimately rather weak person who let his emotions get the better of him. Many other people of his time might have felt, or believed, much as he did; they were smart enough not to say so in public.

How did the alliance system help bring on the Great War?

In the two decades preceding 1914, virtually all the European powers scrambled to find new allies. Republican France joined hands with Czarist Russia; monarchical England established a loose understanding—the *Entente Cordiale*—with Republican France. Imperial Germany allied itself with the Austro-Hungarian Empire and sought better relations with the Ottoman Empire.

Not only were there many alliances, but some of these alliances were secret. It was entirely possible, therefore, for Country A to declare war on Country C without realizing that Country B had a prior alliance with Country C. And there were even some cases—Italy comes to mind—where the country had so many different alliances that it was quite possible it would be called upon as an ally by both sides! But the largest of all European conundrums lay in the Balkans, the southeastern section of Europe. This was where nationalism, ethnicity, religion, and the arms race all competed at the same time, and it is no coincidence that World War I began with an assassination in the Balkans.

Which country, or empire, experienced the greatest amount of ethnic tension?

It is safe to say that Eastern Europe, on the whole, experienced much greater tensions than Western Europe. Poland had disappeared from the map after the partitions of 1796, and its people lived, unhappily, under Russian rule. Millions of people in the Baltic Sea area were also under Russian control. But even Russia's sway paled when compared to that of the Austro-Hungarian empire. Serbs, Croats, Magyars, Czechs, Bulgarians, and others lived under the sway of the empire, centered in Vienna. In the early twentieth century, there were perhaps a dozen languages spoken in the empire and at least as many subject nationalities.

Emperor Franz-Josef knew that he sat atop a powder keg, but he was in his eighties and was weary both of his position and life itself. He knew that Otto von Bismarck had famously predicted that if a major war were to start, it would be with something happening in the Balkans, but there was little that Franz-Josef could do.

Which countries experienced the greatest level of anger or hatred toward each other?

France was furious at Germany for having taken the provinces of Alsace and Lorraine at the end of the Franco–Prussian War. Germany resented Britain's control of the seas and the superior attitude of its people. The Polish people generally loathed their Russian overlords but were no fonder of the Germans or Austrians. And within the Austro-Hungarian Empire, only two people—the Austrians and the Hungarians—also known as Magyars—really got along. The Russians generally feared the Germans and vice versa.

Czar Nicholas II was captured by Bolsheviks in 1917. Shown here in captivity, the czar and his family were executed in 1918.

In what way can World War I be labeled the "cousins' war"?

Kaiser Wilhelm II was first cousins with Czar Nicholas II of Russia and with King George V of England. All three men were grandsons of Queen Victoria. They were distantly related to Emperor Franz-Josef of Austria-Hungary.

The close blood ties did not mean that these men liked, or admired, each other. A long-simmering animosity had built between Czar Nicholas II and Kaiser Wilhelm II. The Kaiser and King George V were on relatively good terms, but the Kaiser could not forget that King George V's father, King Edward VII, had acted toward him in a patronizing manner. In better situations, the various monarchs might have overcome their personal differences, but as it was, the crisis came on much too quickly.

Given all these tensions and animosities, how did peace hold, even until 1914?

Several crises took place before 1914, any one of which might have been sufficient to lead the Great Powers into a great conflict. On each of these occasions, however, sanity prevailed, and there was just enough common sense at the top levels of diplomacy and government that a meltdown was prevented. The events of the summer of 1914, however, led Europe right to the brink.

THE ASSASSINATION OF
ARCHDUKE FRANZ–FERDINAND

Why was Archduke Franz-Ferdinand in the city of Sarajevo on June 28, 1914?

He and his wife had come on a goodwill tour: they had been asked to do this by his uncle, Emperor Franz-Josef. The twenty-eighth of June had both personal and historical connotations for the royal couple and the city of Sarajevo.

Franz-Ferdinand and his wife Sophie celebrated their fourteenth wedding anniversary on June 28, 1914. Theirs was a true love match; Franz-Ferdinand had gone ahead even when his uncle told him that neither his wife nor his children would enjoy royal status (this was deemed a morganatic marriage). June 28 was also the anniversary of the Battle of the Black Birds, a terrible contest fought in 1394 between the Serbs and the Ottoman Turks. Sarajevo was not a Serbian city, but a number of Serbs had snuck in overnight and about twenty of them were involved in a plot to kill the Archduke. Their reasons were ethnic and political, not personal. By killing the Archduke, they hoped to create chaos in the Austro-Hungarian Empire and win greater freedom for the Serbs who lived within its confines.

All went well for the first two hours. The Archduke and his wife sat in the third seat of a magnificent automobile that rumbled through the streets of Sarajevo. Then, at about 11 A.M., a Serbian nationalist heaved a bomb at the car. The Archduke took a trifling injury to his hand and shoulder and the car bomb went underneath the automobile, causing little damage. The Archduke was, naturally, infuriated, and when the car came to a stop, he lambasted the businessmen and mayor, accusing them of luring him to their city on false pretenses. They swore up and down this was not the case, and the automobile tour continued.

Who was Gavrilo Princip?

At seventeen, he was the youngest of a group of conspirators who had sworn to kill the Archduke or die in the attempt. Princip knew that the first attempt had failed and was in low spirits when the Archduke's driver took a wrong turn, bringing the automobile down the very street where Princip stood. When the automobile came close, Princip stepped forward and at almost point-blank range fired two pistol shots, wounding both the Archduke and his wife.

Most accounts agree that the Archduke, knowing the seriousness of his

This photo shows soldiers arresting Gavrila Prinzip after he killed Archduke Franz Ferdinand.

wound, shouted, "Live, Sophie, live for our children!" They were both dead within the hour, however. Meanwhile, Gavrilo Princip had attempted to kill himself but was restrained by the crowd which had seized him. To say that Sarajevo was in a state of confusion is an understatement, but that condition was about to spread to the rest of the Austro-Hungarian Empire.

How many ethnic or religious groups lived within the empire?

Roughly a dozen. There were Serbs and Croats as well as Bosnians and Bulgarians. There were Ottoman Turks who had been stranded by the fortunes of war, and Christians who had turned Muslim, only to be reconquered by a Christian power. All these various ethnic and religious groups were ruled by the Austrians and Hungarians, who stood atop the imperial structure. Though many people called the Ottoman Empire the "sick old man of Europe," something similar could have been said of Austria-Hungary.

Ruling this vast panoply of peoples was Emperor Franz-Josef. When he had come to the throne in 1848, he had been handsome, young, and relatively popular. Sixty-six years had passed, however, and he was now old and set in his ways. Franz-Josef was both lucid and competent, but thoroughly out of touch. Unlike his nephew who toured in an automobile, the emperor eschewed all twentieth-century inventions: he refused to ride in elevators, for example.

Was there any chance that the conflict could be limited to Eastern Europe?

Under normal circumstances, it could have been limited or "quarantined." The death of the Archduke, however, came at a time when all the Great Powers were well prepared militarily, while none of them were prepared psychologically. We often hear that the Cold War of 1946–1990 saw too much military power in the hands of people not equipped to manage it; this can be said even more clearly of the Great Powers on the eve of World War I.

Austria-Hungary feared that Czarist Russia would come to the aid of its "Slavic" kin in Serbia. Czarist Russia feared that Imperial Germany would come to rescue Austria-Hungary. Imperial Germany feared being strangled by Czarist Russia on one side and Republican France on the other. Great Britain was prepared to assist the French in a pinch and the Belgians out of obligation to a century-old agreement. When we add to all of this the enormous arms buildup which had taken place over the previous twenty years, it is difficult to see how the war could have been contained to one section of the Continent.

How did the war begin?

On August 28, 1914, precisely one month following the assassination of Archduke Ferdinand and his wife, Austria-Hungary declared war on the kingdom of Serbia. Austrian ships fired shells at Belgrade.

One day later, on August 29, Czar Nicholas II gave the order for full mobilization of the Russian armies. To the czar and his advisers, it seemed there was no choice. Russia was so vast a nation, and its people spread over such a large area, that it was imperative to get the orders out quickly. But as soon as Czarist Russia mobilized, so did Imperial Germany. The German Kaiser sent several telegrams to the Russian czar, but mutual suspicion led to a breakdown of relations, and on August 1, 1914, Germany declared war on Russia.

How did France enter the war?

Humiliated by its defeat in the Franco–Prussian War of 1870–1871, France had long since allied itself with Russia. Tourists today delight in the beauty of the Pont Alexandre-Trois in downtown Paris: it was built in honor of the Russian czar of that name. As soon as Germany declared war on Russia, France's leaders conferred and announced their declaration of war against Germany.

Virtually all the Great Powers in central and Western Europe had been drawn in, but Great Britain remained a question mark. Would it honor its loosely composed obligations to France or remain neutral? This was answered on August 3 when German troops invaded Belgium. The Germans asked for free, uninterrupted passage on their way to France, but the Belgians fought, and Britain—which had guaranteed the neutrality of Belgium back in 1832—entered the war.

How did the Allies become known by that name? And what about the Central Powers?

The second group is easier to define. By August 1914, Germany and Austria-Hungary were engaged in a great conflict with Serbia, Russia, France, Belgium, and Great Britain. Over

the next two months, the Ottoman Empire and Bulgaria entered the war as allies of Germany and Austria-Hungary. The name "The Central Powers" makes sense because these four nations had an unbroken section of territory, running from the Rhine to the Dardanelles, the narrow strait that separates European from Asiatic Turkey.

On almost any map, the Central Powers look blessed because their lines of internal communication were so secure. But this obscures the fact that the Allied Powers controlled a far larger territory and had more manpower. Because of Russia's entry, the Allied nations controlled all the area from the Ural Mountains to the North Atlantic, with the exception of Germany. Additionally, Britain and France's vast overseas empires, including India,

U.S. President Woodrow Wilson tried to remain neutral in the European conflict but he finally led his nation to war against Germany and its allies in 1917.

Australia, South Africa, and Algeria, as well as the Canadians and New Zealanders, would fight under the Union Jack.

Why was the United States not involved?

As soon as he learned of the European war, President Woodrow Wilson (1856–1924) asked Americans to remain neutral in word and action. Anyone who knew Wilson was aware that he admired the British system of government and that he wished the Allies to prevail. But there was a powerful mood of neutrality in the United States, and Wilson knew perfectly well that there were many Americans of German descent who would resent, and perhaps even fight against, American entry. From Wilson's point of view, it made more sense for America to remain powerful, but benevolently neutral, perhaps to assert its influence at the eventual peace conference. Of course, neither Wilson nor the other major leaders suspected just how long the war would last.

FIRST BATTLES OF WORLD WAR I

Who struck first?

Germany led the first military action. The German General Staff had a thick file in its archives, which detailed its plans in the event of a two-front war. Written by Count von Schlieffen (1883–1913), the plan called for a swift strike against France, to be followed by a long, but victorious, struggle against Russia.

The German planners knew that a two-front war would ultimately be disastrous. They intended, therefore, that the hammer blow fall on France in the first six weeks. Three German armies would move through the lowlands of Belgium, enter northern France, and capture Paris. The Germans assumed that France, minus its capital city, would quickly fall apart. At that point, massive numbers of German infantry would be transferred by rail to the East. The war against Russia might take a long time, but as long as there was no further trouble from France, the Germans felt confident of their ultimate victory.

Why was Belgium so important to the plans of both sides?

Belgium was a small European nation that controlled The Congo, eighty times larger in size than itself. The country was one of the keys to European diplomacy as well as geography. In 1831, all the major European nations had signed a treaty promising that Belgium would be allowed to remain neutral in any future conflicts. Named after General Alfred Von Schlieffen, the Von Schlieffen Plan, however, called for German infantry to march through Belgium on their way to Paris.

On August 3, 1914, Kaiser Wilhelm demanded that King Albert (1875–1934) allow his men free, unhindered passage through Belgium. King Albert refused, and the German invasion began later that day. Britain sent a telegram to Berlin, demanding the

Why do we have such an overpowering notion of the German General Staff?

Americans who fought the Germans in either World War I or II came away with a powerful impression of German combat skill. Those who later studied the German war efforts were equally impressed by the amount of planning that went into Germany's wars. Prior to the Franco–Prussian War, Germany sized up its opponent well, and this was also the case in 1914. Because of its long military heritage and a tradition of civilians being subservient to the military, German war planners were able to draw up plans that were more detailed than anyone else. But, and it was a large but, everything depended on the soldiers in the field being able to maintain the rigid timetable.

evacuation of Belgium within twenty-four hours; when the Germans refused to comply, Britain declared war on Germany.

Lord Edward Grey (1862–1933), the British foreign secretary, watched as the electric lights came on in London that evening. Turning to a staffer, he remarked that the lights were going out all across Europe and that they would not be rekindled in his lifetime.

Who mobilized the most rapidly?

Virtually all the major powers mobilized more rapidly than the experts had anticipated. France had three million men under arms within ten days, and the British Expeditionary Force (BEF) mobilized and crossed the Channel by August 25. Even the Russians, who were expected to take a long time getting into the field, did better than anticipated. It was in Russia, however, that the greatest resistance was experienced. Many peasant farmers lamented and even anguished over having to leave their families at a time when the autumn harvest was about to begin. Russia achieved 96 percent success, however, in getting its young men into the field.

What was the French plan at the war's beginning?

The French had analyzed their defeat in the war against Prussia (1870–1871) many times and concluded that they had erred in that war by fighting too much on the defensive. They planned a quick strike in 1914, straight into the Rhineland.

The French got off to a good start, but they ran into two German armies which had been transferred from near the Swiss border. In the fighting that followed, the French fought gallantly but hopelessly. They were, quite likely, the first soldiers in World War I to discover just how different this conflict would be. Each French assault was met by machine-gun fire, and the French 75 mm light artillery was not "heavy" enough to smash the enemy lines. As a result, France lost 260,000 men killed, wounded, and missing in what is called the Battle of the Frontiers.

Where, meanwhile, were the British?

The British Expeditionary Force (BEF) was in Belgium, where it encountered the Germans on August 26. The Germans had come straight through Belgium, but they had almost 200,000 men killed, wounded, and missing, and those who remained were footsore. The BEF was, therefore, in a position to inflict some heavy casualties and perhaps make the Germans think twice before advancing to France.

The Germans expressed great contempt for the British, calling the BEF the "contemptible little army," but when the two groups met, the British gave a good account of themselves. Under General Sir John French (1852–1925), the BEF delayed the Germans just long enough that the conquest of northern France became less certain. Meanwhile, the action on the Eastern Front was generally dictated by the Russians, who were coming on faster than expected.

If Sir John French commanded the BEF, who commanded the entire British army?

On August 7, 1914, just as he was about to depart on a pleasure cruise, Lord Horatio Kitchener (1850–1916; best known as "Kitchener of Khartoum") was stopped and asked if he would serve as field marshal and commander of all the armed forces. Kitchener agreed, and he soon stepped up efforts on many fronts: the most successful was in the area of recruiting.

What mistakes did the Germans make on the Western Front?

Most of the errors were completely understandable ones. No one had expected, for example, that the German armies would wear out three million pairs of shoes in Bel-

---

Is there any truth to the stories of the Taxicab Army?

It is the best loved of all French military stories. When the Battle of the Marne hung in the balance, Parisian taxicab drivers rounded up able-bodied men in the streets and drove them to the front, making all the difference in the critical battle.

The legend is built on reality. Perhaps 1,200 taxicab drivers did bring men from Paris to the front, and some taxicab drivers abandoned their vehicles to play a part in the fighting. As to the crucial aspect, it seems unlikely that the Taxicab Army, which would have mustered somewhere between five and 6,000 men, would have made the difference. In the desperate days of the autumn of 1914, French men and women fastened on to almost anything that would grant them the courage, and will, to believe they would eventually prevail.

gium and northern France. No one realized just how weary the soldiers would be or that the days of seemingly endless sunshine would make matters worse. But if there is one thing for which the German high command can be faulted, it is the switch away from aspects of the Von Schlieffen Plan.

On his deathbed, one of the leading German generals had muttered, "Only let the right be strong." He meant that it was essential for the German forces on the farthest right point—meaning those that were farthest to the west—have enough energy and traction to sweep through, and envelop, the city of Paris. Capture of the French capital was the *sine quae non* (es-

German soldiers prepare for action in a trench during the Battle of the Marne in 1914.

sential aspect) of the Von Schlieffen Plan; once the capital fell, the rest of the nation would follow. Failing to take Paris would be a disaster. But halfway through the invasion of Belgium, the German General Staff detached two army corps from the effort and sent them rapidly east by railroad. The German right wing would, therefore, not be as strong as Von Schlieffen intended.

What miracle saved Paris in 1914?

Officially it is known as the Miracle of the Battle of the Marne (River), but there were actually a handful of miracles, one piled atop the other. To realize this, one need only look at the progress of the German armies in August. Forcing their way through southern Belgium into northern France, the Germans took heavy casualties but advanced continually to where it seemed nothing could stop them. Morale in the German armies was high, but the men were exhausted after having traveled so far so fast. It is important to remember that this was World War I and that the men advanced on foot or horseback; there were no jeeps or personnel carriers.

The miracle that led to all the others came when a French airplane pilot, on reconnaissance, noted that the German right wing—which was on the east—had made a sharp-angled turn and was headed in a northerly direction *above* Paris. Thanks to a series of changes in the plan—and to the need to rush two army corps to the Eastern Front—this was not the case in 1914.

What did the French do with this intelligence?

Tradition has it that the French sprang immediately into action, but the truth is more prosaic. The French government was on the verge of abandoning Paris, and panic gripped the French, from the highest to the lowest levels. Only after three days of coun-

313

cils and anxiety-filled conversations did the French decide to attack, and the British Expeditionary Force was crucial to their plans.

By cutting too far to the north and failing to envelop Paris, the German advance left itself vulnerable to an attack on its exposed right flank. Here, the French hit the hardest, when the Battle of the Marne began on September 3, 1914. Meanwhile, the BEF was called from its central position to assist the Allied attack.

How long did the Battle of the Marne last?

Almost ten days. We call it a battle, but the struggle along the River Marne is better described as an entire campaign, with several sub-battles. The fighting ranged from just northeast of Paris all the way to the city of Verdun, seventy miles farther east.

Had the Germans been fresh, they would quite likely have prevailed and ended up in possession of Paris. They were footsore, however, and the strength of the Allied attacks took them by surprise. After ten days of on-again, off-again fighting, both sides settled down and everyone took a much-needed breather.

What was the situation in October and November?

For several weeks, the British, French, and Germans remained in place; all the men were thoroughly exhausted. Only in October did the Allies and the Germans engage in the so-called "Race to the Sea."

Remarkably, the British had not secured the channel ports in Belgium and northern France. Both sides raced to the Channel, fighting each other along the way. There were numerous skirmishes and one big battle, that of Ypres. By late November, the two opposing sides had reached the Channel, establishing what would be a semipermanent boundary. What escapes the power to describe is the number of men who had fallen. During the invasion of Belgium, the defense of France, and the Race to the Sea, roughly one million men had been killed and perhaps another million wounded. This was modern warfare at its most destructive.

Is there any truth to the stories of Christmas Day fraternization?

To be sure. On Christmas Day 1914, German, British, and French soldiers came out of their trenches and bomb shelters in various positions along the Western Front. The soldiers swapped gifts, stories, and even sang together. The heartwarming story is somewhat spoiled by the reaction of the generals. On both sides, the leaders declared there must be no repeat and no fraternization with the enemy. The Christmas Day experience was not repeated.

What did trench warfare look like?

From the English Channel to northern Switzerland, along a front that was 400 miles long with the Allies on one side and the Germans on the other, both sides dug trenches. These ranged between ten to thirty feet in depth.

Six hundred yards of no man's land lay between the opposing trenches. The troops—commanded to attack with the memorable words "Over the Top!"—charged across those yards, encountering land mines and barbed wire. What the desperate battles of 1914 had revealed was the power of the machine gun and of men fighting on the defense. With a handful of exceptions, he who fought on the defense would prevail on the Western Front until almost the end of the war.

THE EASTERN FRONT

How long, and broad, was the Eastern Front?

It ran half as long as the Western Front, roughly 600 miles from the Baltic Sea to the Carpathian Mountains in Hungary. The Eastern Front was broader, too, because the opposing sides did not settle into trench warfare. Therefore, the Austrian, German, or Russian soldier in the East often had to cover far more miles than his Western Front counterpart.

In the heady days of August 1914, this did not seem to matter. The Russian steamroller—as people described it—sent 650,000 men in two armies into East Prussia; opposing them were only 150,000 Germans. The terrain proved difficult for the invaders, however, and there was the nagging problem that the commanders of the two Russian armies detested each other. Lacking good communications, the Russians managed to turn almost certain victory into stunning defeat.

Field Marshal Paul von Hindenburg was one of Germany's most successful military leaders. After World War I, he served as his country's president from 1925 to 1934.

What was the "H-L" combination?

Paul von Hindenburg (1847–1934) was the quintessential German field marshal: dry, cynical, yet gifted with tactical skill. Erich von Ludendorff (1865–1937) was the image of a low-born staff officer, brilliant but

315

quirky and limited by his birth to the rank of colonel. In 1914, the two very different men met and planned the twin victories that saved Germany in the East.

Allowing the Russians to approach in two separate army groups, Hindenburg and Ludendorff met and defeated the first group of Russians at the Battle of Tannenburg, fought between September 3 and 10. Hindenburg then completed the sensational German autumn by smashing the second Russian army at the Masurian Lakes. Roughly 200,000 Russians were killed or taken prisoner. German casualties were also high, but no one thought much about that: had H-L failed, Germany would have lost the war. Hindenburg and Ludendorff, therefore, became the darlings of the German military establishment.

WAR AT SEA

What was the relative strength of the British and German navies?

When the war began, Britain had twenty-nine major warships—ranging from Dreadnoughts to battle cruisers—and Germany had seventeen. The difference between the two could also be calculated in terms of broadsides: the number of shells that could be hurled from the decks of all the ships combined. In this area, too, the British had a significant superiority. But in the war's early stages, several captains and commodores of the German navy showed more flair and risk taking than their British counterparts.

Maximilian Graf von Spee (1861–1914), commander of German Pacific naval forces, was at the Shantung Peninsula of China when the war began. Knowing that Japan would soon attack the peninsula, he steamed away with his battleships and cruisers and headed for Chile. One of his captains protested so vociferously that Spee allowed him to conduct a cruise of his own. Steaming into the Indian Ocean, this captain downed more than twenty British merchantmen before being surprised and sunk himself.

How did the British react to the Germans' acting so boldly on the high seas?

The British press made much of it, lamenting that the age of heroes seemed to have passed. The leaders of the British Admiralty—including Sir Winston Churchill—made a concerted effort to corner Spee before he could head for home. The British wireless operated more effectively than the German, and though Spee won a significant victory off the Chilean coast, he was cornered near the Falkland Islands in December 1914. The *Scharnhorst* and the *Gneisenau* both sank, and with them went the German hope for igniting trouble for Britain in other parts of the globe.

What was the British plan for the defense of its home waters?

Even before the war began, British naval planners believed that a "distant blockade" or a "secondary line" was better than a direct one. In other words, it would be too costly to bottle up the Germans in their ports; far better to maintain a cordon far out to sea that the enemy could not pass. Recognizing that the 150 miles between northern Scotland and Denmark was the best place for this blockade, the British Royal Navy concentrated their efforts there, with the center of the blockade at Scapa Flow, in the Orkney Islands. The British already possessed numerical superiority; they now employed the geography of the North Sea to their advantage.

The Germans were anxious to accomplish something that first year, and on December 16, 1914, two battleships shelled the towns of Hartlepool and Scarborough, killing more than one hundred civilians. Horrified at the potential of further loss, the Royal Navy sent several battleships and cruisers south. If ever there was a time when the German High Seas Fleet possessed the advantage, this was it. The German admiral, however, turned for home.

What were the admirals—on both sides—worried about the most?

They were worried about *torpedoes* delivered by *submarines*. When the war began, both sides had fewer than one hundred submarines, but the factories of Britain and Germany became ferociously busy, turning out one after another. On the whole, the German subs were better built, and their crews enjoyed higher morale. What set them back—time and again—was the British possession of several of their naval code books.

The Australians found one; the British found two more; and by the end of 1914, a special section of the British war office was routinely capturing German signals and translating them. It took some time for this office to transmit its findings, however, and throughout the war there were missed opportunities, especially at the Battle of Jutland. It is safe to say, however, that if the British had not possessed those code books, their naval and maritime losses would have been much larger.

GALLIPOLI

How did the situation stand at the end of the year?

Toward the end of 1914, the Eastern Front settled into a stalemate. Germany had done much better than expected, and Russia had taken some punishing hits, while Austria-Hungary fared the worst of all. One thing that the war planners did not anticipate was the speed with which Russia's supply system was falling apart. The most serious aspect of the deterioration was noticed by those on the ground: the lack of shoes.

Russia had at least three million men in arms, but perhaps one-third of them had no shoes. Russia could produce enough rifles and machine guns, but in the basics of military uniform and accoutrements, it was far behind all the other Great Powers. This became even more serious in the second year of the war. Early in 1915, however, many people turned their attention to what developed in Turkey and the Middle East rather than Russia and Poland.

Whose idea was it to attack the Ottoman Empire?

First Lord of the Admiralty, Sir Winston Churchill, was a leading advocate. So was First Sea Lord Jackie Fisher. Between them, these two men argued for an attack on Turkey and most particularly the capture of the Dardanelles, the narrow strait between Europe and Asia. Once the Royal Navy took the Dardanelles, Istanbul would fall and the Allies would be able to supply Russia by the southern route, via the Black Sea. All this made good sense, but it depended on the navy being able to force the passage.

The Turks knew an attack was coming; they fortified the Dardanelles, which was now guarded by nearly a hundred big guns. Churchill and Fisher were right on one score: the people of Istanbul were near panic when they learned of the British approach.

Who shipped out for Istanbul?

Nearly 50,000 troops were slated, but the majority were Australian and New Zealanders. Eager to make their presence known, these soldiers from "Down Under" had arrived in Egypt in 1914 and conducted their exercises in and around the city of Cairo. The New Zealanders were calm and obedient; the Australians, by contrast, were rowdy and disreputable. Even so, one guessed they would perform well in battle.

The British plan was for the big ships of the Royal Navy to force the Dardanelles and the troops to land at Istanbul. The narrow straits dividing Asia from Europe proved tougher than expected, however; three British battleships went down to enemy fire and mines in the water. Seeing this, the British high command altered its decision and decided to land enough troops to capture the Gallipoli Peninsula. With it in hand, the Turkish forts—and their formidable land guns—would fall in due course.

Was there any chance of success at Gallipoli?

There was, in fact, a rather good chance. The British, Australians, and New Zealanders who landed on April 25 secured their beachheads and advanced a mile or two inland. That was it, however. The Turks brought up reinforcements who established a line of trenches, and soon the ring of the Gallipoli Peninsula resembled, to some degree, the terrain on the Western Front.

Why does April 25 loom so large in the calendar "Down Under"?

Americans commemorate April 19 as the day their revolution began. The French celebrate July 14, when Parisians took the Bastille. But for Australians and New Zealanders, April 25 is by far the most important military date: that is when they landed at Anzacs Cove, on the west side of the Gallipoli Peninsula. ANZACS stands for Australian New Zealand Army Corps, and the heroics of the men who landed there during World War I have been celebrated by their nations ever since.

The Australian 4th Battalion, 1st Brigade, and the 26th Indian Mountain Battery land at Anzacs Cove during the Battle of Gallipoli.

The Turks also had more inspired leadership than the Allies. A young colonel, Mustapha Kemal (1880–1938), rallied his men at a crucial moment, telling them he did not expect them to win, but that he did expect them to die. This was one of those rare moments when one man made a profound difference. Ten years later, Kemal became the first president of the Republic of Turkey.

How many men became involved in the Gallipoli Campaign?

Roughly 300,000 Allied and an undetermined number of Turkish troops. The lines of trenches ran well over one hundred miles. The Allies had the tougher job of being on the offense, but they, at least, were well supplied. The Turks, by contrast, had to send supplies down the entire length of the peninsula, adding greatly to the cost—in men and materiel—of the campaign.

The French, meanwhile, had landed almost 50,000 men on the Asiatic side of the Dardanelles, upping the ante in the campaign. That the Allies wanted to capture Istanbul was obvious to anyone; less apparent was the fact that the British and French were already considering various ways of dividing up the spoils in the postwar world.

319

THE WESTERN FRONT IN 1915

Who opened the "season" of 1915?

The Germans. In April 1915, they began a series of concentrated attacks in central Belgium, trying to dislodge the French and the British Expeditionary Force. There were also 100,000 Belgians fighting. Led by King Albert (1875–1934), the Belgians proved excellent on the defense and rather ineffective on the offense. But the main story of the spring of 1915 had to do with the introduction of chemical warfare.

On April 22, 1915—just three days before the Allied landings at Gallipoli—the Germans released 150,000 tons of lethal gas at the Allied defenders, who happened to be French colonial troops. Completely unsuspecting, the colonial troops either died or fled. A major German breakthrough was narrowly averted when two Canadian divisions arrived to plug the gap. This was the first use of chemicals in modern warfare, and people on both sides of the Atlantic called it a dastardly new means of war. This was not the only technological surprise of that spring, however.

How did Britain fill the ranks of its depleted regiments?

By 1915, the British army was a shell of its former self. Throughout the nineteenth century, England had been able to avoid conscription, but in 1915, as that moment approached, the British war ministry ran a famous bulletin, or poster, which would be imitated by the Americans. The poster showed Lord Horatio Kitchener ("Kitchener of Khartoum"), who pointed one finger at the reader. "BRITONS," the poster declared, "want you." The poster did not use Lord Kitchener's name. It was unnecessary, because his face was, after that of King George V, the most recognized in the land.

Who was first, or foremost, in submarine warfare?

Practically all the maritime nations had started submarine research early in the twentieth century, but it was the Germans who were in the lead. When the war began, Germany had almost forty submarines, soon to be known as U-Boats.

Because the British Royal Navy was so dominant, controlling most of the seas, the Germans believed that submarine warfare was their only option. They had an excellent point in that their civilian population would slowly starve as a result of the effectiveness of the British naval blockade. But to carry out their mission, the U-Boats had to take on all passenger and military ships around the British Isles; only in that way could they compete with the Royal Navy blockade. Therefore, the German embassies in practically all North and South American countries warned the local populations not to sail aboard British ships or even to sail in the seas around England. This policy would soon be known as "unrestricted submarine warfare."

What was RMS *Lusitania*?

Launched by the Cunard Line in 1906, Royal Mail Steamer *Lusitania* was very similar to its more famous counterpart, RMS *Titanic*. Both ships carried the mail, a big cargo,

A German submarine sank the RMS *Lusitania* in 1915. Of the 1,960 passengers, 1,192 perished, including 128 Americans.

and many passengers. In the spring of 1915, the *Lusitania* was the most elegant means of transit between England and the United States. Though many German pamphlets warned Americans against travel to and from the British Isles, many Americans—upper-class ones especially—disdained the risk. On May 1, 1915, RMS *Lusitania* sailed from Manhattan with more than 1,000 passengers.

What kind of ruckus was stirred by the sinking of the *Lusitania*?

On May 7, 1915, a German U-Boat attacked the *Lusitania* in the Irish Sea. Of the 1,950 passengers on the mail steamer, 1,192 died, including 128 Americans, when it sank. A London newspaper headline called it the "World's Greatest and Foulest Crime." To the Germans, this was an act rendered necessary by Britain's naval blockade; to the British, Americans, and some other peoples, it was another step on the way toward barbarism. Germany was the first to use poison gas in war; now, it was the first to fire on civilian passenger ships. Of course, this was entirely true.

Only many years later, was it revealed that the *Lusitania* had also carried munitions for the Allies and that Germany had been correct in that supposition. In the immediate aftermath of her sinking, Germany was accused of war crimes, and there was a distinct possibility the United States might enter the war. President Wilson was against war, however, making his famous statement: "There is such a thing as a man too proud to fight." The American secretary of State, William Jennings Bryan, had to resign because

321

**Didn't the Germans realize the great risk
they ran in provoking the United States?**

Not really. While Theodore Roosevelt was president (1901–1909) the American military had been perceived as a growing threat to European power politics, but during the early presidency of Woodrow Wilson, America was seen as militarily impotent. The entire U.S. Army numbered less than 200,000 men, and the U.S. Navy was in slack condition. Most important, however, was the European perception that Americans were too pacifistic to become involved in the Great War.

of his neutral leanings, but it was clear that Germany could not risk another provocation of the United States.

Could anyone have broken the deadlock in 1915?

No. The trenches were too deep and well defended for either side to make an impression on the other. This does not mean there were no attempts, however; by the autumn of 1915, the expression "Over the Top" was known in any number of languages. To the average infantryman from Germany, France, Britain, Russia, or Turkey, those three words meant an intimate rendezvous with death.

When a captain or lieutenant shouted "Over the Top," his men scrambled out of their trenches and began moving, bayonets fixed, toward the enemy. A distance of 600 yards, known to all as "no man's land," existed between opposing trenches, and it was here that the great majority of men were killed. Machine-gun fire, pistol fire, detonation of explosives, and even death from the cuts of barbed wire all conspired to ensure that the defenders usually prevailed.

When did England enact its first wholesale conscription?

The British—from top officials to farmers—did not like the idea. To resort to a military draft meant betraying many of the principles, and attitudes, that made England different. As a last-gasp attempt to fill the armies, the British developed the world's most successful poster to date. By the midpoint of 1915, this was insufficient. Too many Britons had seen countrymen come home without limbs or not at all.

The Munitions Acts of June 23, 1915 paved the way to universal conscription. Approved by Parliament, the act allowed the government to regulate virtually every aspect of the British economy. While it did not announce conscription, it was a clear move in that direction.

What were the last campaigns of 1915?

The British and French had attempted several partial offensives, but the latter saved their biggest effort until autumn, when they attacked in the province of Champagne.

Were any Americans yet involved in the Great War?

A small number, somewhere between 500 and 1,000 had found a way to participate. Some went north to join the Royal Canadian Air Corps, while others joined the French Foreign Legion. One of the latter was the poet Alan Seeger.

Born in New York City in 1888, Seeger had an impressive intellectual heritage. After graduating from Harvard, he dabbled for a time, living a Bohemian lifestyle in Greenwich Village. The beginning of the Great War found him in Paris, where he quickly joined the French Foreign Legion. Seeger's poems, as well as letters to his parents, are classic examples of an exuberant young American involved in a great European struggle. He died on the Western Front in 1916. (His nephew was Pete Seeger, a poet, musician, and antiwar activist.)

General Joseph "Papa" Joffre directed the attacks, which went almost nowhere. To be sure, there was the occasional, exuberant feeling that a breakthrough might occur, but nothing of the sort was real. Roughly 150,000 French soldiers went killed, wounded, or missing in the campaign.

Almost at the other side of Europe, the British, Australians, and New Zealanders had given their all in the Gallipoli Campaign, but to no avail. Almost 250,000 men were killed, wounded, or missing with what the Australians considered a disproportionate number of their own. In December, plans were made to evacuate the force from Gallipoli. Remarkably, this was carried out without any attacks from the Turks.

What did the situation look like on December 31, 1915?

To the British, French, and their colonial troops, it had been a year of great sacrifice, made for minimal reward. One could imagine that the great supply of men, especially from British overseas possessions, would eventually get through the German defenses, but no one could be certain. Then, too, the Eastern Front looked even worse, with Russia in danger of collapse.

Only the Americans could rescue the Allies at this point. But the United States, sheltered by a great ocean and its navy, had almost nothing to say.

MEAT GRINDER

What was the German plan for 1916?

It is more accurate to call it General Erich von Falkyenhan's plan. In a lengthy letter to the Kaiser, Falkyenhan outlined the necessity of achieving a breakthrough. The meat-

323

grinding style of the war would catch up with Germany before the Allies, he declared, and it was imperative to break the French spirit and force the Franco-English alliance to collapse. To that end, Falkyenhan proposed a series of massive blows directed both for territorial and spiritual purposes, and he outlined either the city of Rheims or the city of Verdun as targets. The German high command selected the latter.

When did the Battle for Verdun begin?

On February 16, 1916, after an enormous artillery bombardment, the Germans attacked the outskirts of Verdun. They arrived with high morale and hopes but found the French defenders in an excellent position. The greatest battle of the war had begun.

87th Regiment, 6th Division of the French Army hunkered down in a trench by Hill 304 during the 1916 Battle of Verdun.

Did the French have to fight for Verdun?

The city was important for psychological reasons rather than strategic ones. The Germans had guessed correctly that France would fight like the devil for Verdun.

The fighting was day in and day out, over a course of four months. The soldiers on both sides declared it was the worst they had ever seen, with the weather—damp and foggy—paralleling the miseries of the siege. The Germans continually tried to gain a "right hook" around Verdun, and the French fought to keep them off. About a third of the way into the terrible siege, France found a new hero in Henri Philippe Pétain. A colonel when the war began, Pétain soon rose to the rank of general and now he directed the defense. Cautious, pessimistic by nature, Pétain was cast for the role of heroic defender.

Was there any time, or moment, when the Germans could have broken through?

They came close at least three times but never had the reserves in place to exploit the opportunity. Some critics of the German war effort assert that this was true to form: throughout the war, the Germans performed right on time and schedule, only to miss the final cue that would have produced victory. France also played true to form, recruiting men by the thousands.

When the Battle for Verdun ended in the late spring of 1916, France had lost roughly half a million men. Germany had lost about 400,000. Regardless of who might claim "victory," there was no true winner in a meat grinder such as this; France, in particular, suffered demographically for years to come.

Couldn't any of the generals see that offensives always failed?

Virtually none of the top generals—British, Russian, German, or French—ever admitted what the common soldier knew after only three months of combat: all offensives were doomed so long as the enemy held machine guns. Trench warfare had created something almost entirely new, a static military front where the human losses increased, rather than the reverse.

Who was General Sir Douglas Haig?

Haig (1861–1928) came from one of the richest of British families—connected with the liquor trade—and was a man of great self-confidence. The more he examined the situation, the more Haig was convinced that all the previous offensives had failed because of human failure, rather than technical reasons. One enormous push in the right direction would topple the German defenses, he asserted. But where should that push be made?

Haig settled on the River Somme, which meanders through Belgium on its way to the North Sea. The British and Germans had been locked in combat along the Somme for almost two solid years, with neither side making any progress, but Haig rightly surmised that a German collapse in this locality would produce a ripple effect. To that end, he assembled the largest BEF (British Expeditionary Force) ever seen with front-line British troops sharing the glory with colonials from India, Australia, Canada, and South Africa.

When did Britain finally go over to full conscription?

The measure passed the House of Commons in January 1916. All the recruiting posters in the world were no longer sufficient to fill the army ranks. This meant that the army General Haig sent into action was a splendid mix of true veterans—those who had joined in 1914—and a great mass of men who had participated in no previous offensives. On one matter Haig was surely correct: the German defenders were low in morale.

By the summer of 1916, the German people were on rations, allowing for the best food to be sent to the front. The so-called "Potato Winter" of 1915 had been followed by

What enabled the Germans of 1916 (and 1917) to make such extraordinary sacrifices?

One thing is certain: no democratic nation would have withstood the strain. Germany had only been a unified nation since 1871, and in the two generations virtually no democratic or popular institutions had been created. Imperial Germany was a true "top-down" society, with authority flowing from the Kaiser to his ministers, his generals, and then the common folk. When the Germans did begin to break under the strain, however, in 1918, they did not head toward a limited democracy or a middle-of-the-road republic. Many Germans, by 1918, were ready for communism.

the "Turnip Winter" of 1916. Behind the power and dash of the German army was a dispirited population that needed some good news from the front.

Why is it that we know so much about the first day of July of the year 1916?

First, because so much was at stake. Practically the entire British army was ready to go over the top.

Second, we know so much because so many future poets, essayists, and social commentators were in the trenches. British literature, for the next fifty years, would be filled with references to the worst day of all: the first of July 1916.

When did the Battle of the Somme begin?

At 7:28 A.M. on July 1, 1916, thousands of British soldiers went over the top. They did not dash for the enemy's trenches but moved at the traditional march of four paces a second. The men were extremely well equipped, their morale was good, and there was every reason—according to their leaders—that they would be successful. Instead they met a withering barrage of artillery and machine-gun fire, and those who made it to the barbed wire usually died there, sometimes with their bodies caught in the terrific snarls of light metal. This, naturally, leads us to a follow-up question: Could any army of that time have succeeded?

No. Regardless of whether it was British fusiliers, Russian life guards, or German Death Hussars, the attack would have failed. There was no military force that could have succeeded in the face of all the defensive equipment.

How bad were the results?

Slightly more than 60,000 British soldiers were killed, wounded, or missing on the opening day of the Battle of the Somme. To give that number its proper context, 60,000 men is more than Queen Victoria's armies had lost between 1837—the year of her accession to the throne—and 1899, the start of the Boer War. During those sixty years, the Queen's armies had policed something like one-fifth of the world at less cost than was suffered on one day in July 1916.

General Haig kept feeding troops into the meat grinder, mistakenly believing that the Germans would break. The Germans, however, knew precisely where the attacks were coming from and were ready for each one. Over the long summer of 1916, the British suffered at least a quarter of a million casualties, the Germans somewhat less. And the result, at its best, was an indentation of a few kilometers. Some of the poets accurately claimed that at this rate, the entire British Empire would be depopulated before they ever reached Berlin.

Were the British ever the same again?

As a fighting force, they were. The British Expeditionary Force went on to notable successes in 1918. For the British nation, and its many peoples, however, the Somme was the end of a very long, glorious era. From 1815 (the year the British fought in the Battle of Waterloo) until 1916 (the year of the Somme), Britain maintained a distinct sense of moral and physical superiority where all her foes were concerned. That feeling never returned.

When did the type and style of helmets change?

Many of us imagine the Kaiser's German soldiers marching to war with spiked helmets on this heads, and so it was during 1914 and 1915. Those thin helmets offered little protection, however, and the same was true of those issued to British and French soldiers. 1916, therefore, was the key date for the change.

A German helmet from World War I on display in a Kansas City museum. While the helmets were elaborate, they offered little actual protection.

The Germans went from the spiked helmet to the rounded one with flaps. The British went from cloth headgear to light steel, and the French did the same.

Was there a peace movement in England, or anywhere else, for that matter?

Peace movements were just beginning to gain momentum. In December 1915, the eccentric American automaker Henry Ford (1863–1947) chartered a ship to carry himself and a group of advisers to England, where he believed he could talk the various powers out of war and into peace. Ford failed, but other people—notably British and female—began to pick up where he left off.

In France, the population was so weary of the war that the generals feared mutinies in the trenches. In Russia, the people were disenchanted that Czar Nicholas II had taken personal control, mistakenly believing he was more needed at the front than in Petrograd. Only the Germans were still quiescent, and this was very likely because of the strict, hierarchical society that had developed since the time of Bismarck.

What shape were the Americans in?

The question was continually asked, and Europeans were beginning to shrug their shoulders, saying the American would never enter the war. While the Old World was bleeding to death, the New World seemed content to go about its (profitable) business.

Many Americans merchants were making fortunes from the war. They supplied everything from barbed wire to machine guns, and at this point the United States was the only country in the Western world—save perhaps Australia—with more food than its people could eat. Many of the Allies, especially the British, thought the Americans deeply selfish, but they did not say so loudly: they could not afford to offend the people they wished to become allies.

How did Woodrow Wilson win a second term in the White House?

Wilson said little about the international situation during 1916. He knew that things could pull him, and the country, in the direction of war, but he chose to concentrate on domestic affairs. Wilson had been relatively successful in promoting his so-called "New Freedom," and in 1916 Americans were more prosperous and confident than usual (a recent poll revealed there were almost ten times as many millionaires in the United States in 1900 than there were in the late twentieth and early twenty-first centuries). Whether Wilson coined it or it was the formation of a White House staffer is unknown, but the major campaign slogan became "He Kept Us Out Of War." The truth of this could not be denied.

Wilson won re-election by a narrow margin, with 49 percent of the popular vote to 46 percent for his Republican challenger.

BATTLE OF JUTLAND

Why had there been no major match-up between the British Royal Navy and the German High Seas Fleet?

The leaders on both sides were frightened by the potential threat of submarines. Nothing unnerved a naval commander, who had grown up before submarines were invented, than the idea of being lured into a contest on the open water, only to find that the enemy had a number of submarines in the depths. A torpedo could sink a Dreadnought as easily as it could a merchant liner.

Then, too, the German High Seas Fleet had never been intended to match the British pound for pound. The huge sums Germany expended on its fleet had been meant as a deterrent, a means to persuade Britain to go more softly in diplomatic channels. By 1916, however, the leaders of the German navy were convinced they must act before their men became "soft" through disuse. It was agreed to use part of the fleet to lure the British closer in to German waters.

What was the Battle of Jutland like?

It was on a scale that had never been seen before. Roughly 100,000 men—soldiers, sailors, and marines—were on more than 250 ships, many of them recently built and state-of-the-art. The sheer sound of the guns firing was enough to provoke intense feelings: some of them sublime, others suicidal.

The British opened the action at 4 P.M., sending enormous gun salvos toward the Germans. The latter had the better of it at first by endangering *Sea Lion,* Admiral Beatty's flagship. All the while, the commanders on both sides looked nervously for signs of submarines or torpedoes, but none appeared. By evening the British had more and better ships in position and were ready to "cross the T" of the Germans. The Germans sailed south-by-southwest, away from the enemy but also away from their home ports. The British pursued, and the last actions were fought around 10 P.M.

Did either side really win the Battle of Jutland?

Technically the Germans did. They sank fourteen British ships and caused 6,784 casualties to the Royal Navy. The British, by contrast, sank eleven German ships and caused 3,058 casualties. But for Germany, at this late stage of the naval war, to make a difference, it had to be decisive. German captains and admirals celebrated their "victory" at Jutland, knowing that they would not engage again anytime soon.

What were the last offensives of 1916?

During that terrible year, some armies had seen their strength cut in half. Some regiments had practically disappeared. But there was one last round of offensives.

The Russians had pressed the Austrians hard all summer, and in the autumn of 1916, the Brusilov Offensive (named for the commanding general) came close to success. German divisions had to be switched from the Polish front to Hungary: the Austro-Hungarian Empire was on the verge of collapse. But when the Brusilov Offensive finally lost strength, the Germans pushed the Russians back with relative ease, and by Christmas Day the Russians were right where they had started, minus half a million men. France, meanwhile, lost almost 200,000 men in the futile Neuville Offensives of the autumn of 1916.

T. E. LAWRENCE

Who was the most eccentric English leader of World War I?

The English have long been known for eccentricity, especially at the high, aristocratic levels. T. E. Lawrence (1888–1935; also known as Lawrence of Arabia) did not come from a rich or famous family, but he attended Oxford and was as offbeat as an English gentleman of his time could be. Lawrence was working on his dissertation on Crusader architecture when the war began; he and all four of his brothers were soon in the war. Two of his brothers died on the Western Front, but Lawrence had the good luck to be posted to the Middle East.

Arriving in Cairo late in 1914, Lawrence was a junior officer in a secondary or even tertiary theater of the war, but the importance of oil soon made the Middle East more

Thomas Edward Lawrence, better known as Lawrence of Arabia in the annals of history, was a British Army officer who united many of the Arab tribes in revolt against the Ottoman Turks during World War I.

important. The British feared that the Turks, assisted by Germany, would make a drive across the Sinai Peninsula to attack oil-rich Egypt (the larger oil fields in Saudi Arabia and Iraq had not yet been discovered).

Why did it fall to this junior officer to make contact with the Arabs?

Lawrence was a Romantic with a capital "R," meaning that he saw the world through glasses tinted by drama and excitement. To him, the idea of an Arab countercrusade, with the Ottoman Turks as the enemy, was a marvelous idea; the difficulty was in finding a group of Arabs who would cooperate. Lawrence was not the leader of the delegation that went to Arabia in 1915, but he had success meeting King Faisal of Mecca and his four sons, and Lawrence's superiors soon decided that this young man was just the ticket for getting along with the Arabs.

Lawrence was a dreamer and a mystic, but he possessed something denied to many people with those qualities: he had fantastic powers of physical endurance. Even his Arab friends were amazed by his ability to stay in the saddle, day after day, and to endure privations which they believed only men born to the desert could handle. This was part of the reason for his success; another was his command of Arabic. Lawrence did not always like the Arabs—or some of their behaviors—but he understood them better than any other Allied officer.

What was Lawrence's first objective?

The Arab Revolt became official in the spring of 1916, when Faisal declared himself king of Mecca and guardian of the sacred places at Mecca and Medina. T. E. Lawrence and Faisal's son planned a daring strike against Aquaba, a major port on the eastern side of the Red Sea. To get there, Lawrence and his Arab allies had to ride several hundred miles across blazing desert sands. They mostly traveled at night and arrived at their destination just in time to surprise the Turks. Most of Aquaba's guns were trained on the coast, but enough of them still pointed in the landward direction to make it a real fight. Lawrence and the Arabs conquered Aquaba in a one-day fight, and suddenly the Arab Revolt had strength to its legs.

What did the Regular British Army do upon learning the news?

Now that it could be resupplied by the Red Sea, the British army took more interest in the Middle Eastern theater. As Lawrence and his Arab irregulars continued to blow up Turkish bridges and disrupt their communications, the British forces in Cairo readied for a major push. They had a new commander, Major General Sir Edward Allenby (1861–1936). He had been transferred from the Western Front, where his talents were largely wasted, and sent to Cairo. Allenby was a bull of a man, a true army man, and he breathed new life into the British forces. By the time he departed Cairo in the summer of 1917, the British effort was rising, and the Turkish defenses were greatly weakened.

Why was Jerusalem so important to the Allied cause?

It was valuable both for strategic and religious reasons. No Christian army had entered Jerusalem for centuries: it had been under the Ottoman Turks since the 1520s. Then, too, Jerusalem, which faces a long set of mountains, was strategically important for control of Palestine. The British were lucky to enter Jerusalem without fighting a major battle.

The capture of Jerusalem was a "Christmas present" to the government of David Lloyd George.

How bad was the situation on New Year's Day of 1917?

It was truly appalling. Two and a half years of unrelenting warfare had achieved practically nothing for all the peoples and powers involved. Despite its defensive victory at Gallipoli, the Ottoman Empire was imploding from within. Regardless of its vast sacrifices, Czarist Russia had gained absolutely nothing from the war. The French were in a deep state of cynicism, approaching despair, and the British were simply stunned by the losses they had taken. The Germans were enduring their third winter of low rations, and the Austrians could see nothing but gloom. To put all this in its proper context, one has to imagine the capitals of these nations prior to the war: scenic Istanbul, beautiful Vienna, mercurial Paris, stunning Berlin, and of course London, capital of the English-speaking world.

One thing that most of the peoples did not know was that the evil genius of Russia had perished the night before.

How important was Rasputin?

Grigorii Rasputin (1872–1916) was a thoroughly unlikable person who had an outsized effect on Russian history. Thanks to genuine hypnotic powers, he was able to gain great influence over the Russian royal family.

Born in Siberia, Rasputin was a self-ordained holy man, a wanderer in the Russian tradition (such persons are usually called *starets*). By chance, he met the czarina just when her son, the Crown Prince, was discovered to be a hemophiliac, meaning his blood did not clot properly. Many physicians were consulted, but Rasputin, who possessed an undeniable power of hypnotism, was able to calm the prince and stop his bleeding through the power of autosuggestion. As a consequence, Rasputin became very influ-ential at court, to the extent that he addressed the czar as "papa" and the czarina as "momma."

How and when was Rasputin killed?

It must be admitted that Rasputin was no fan of the war; he argued long and hard against it. Over time, however, his sexual excesses and demonic presence at court led a handful of noblemen to associate him with all the ills besetting their country, and on New Year's Eve they invited him to dinner at one of their apartments.

Rasputin proved very difficult to kill. The conspirators put cyanide in his food, and he showed no ill effects. They shot him numerous times, kicked the body, and still he breathed. Finally they took him to the River Neva, held him beneath the ice, and he perished. Virtually no one outside the Russian royal family was sad at his death, but his tremendous powers, even in his last minutes, have become something of a symbol for Russian toughness.

Grigorii Rasputin was a Russian mystic who became influential in the Romanov court because he managed to help the Crown Prince Alexei's hemophilia symptoms.

RUSSIA AND AMERICA

Where was the major action at the beginning of 1917?

At sea. The U-Boat had truly come into its own. The Germans had designed and built new, stronger submarines that could stay subsurface for many hours. More, they had gathered crews who demonstrated a fanatical type of courage. By early 1917, the German U-Boat campaign threatened to put Great Britain, which was often called a nation of shopkeepers, out of business. Had the Kaiser kept his eye on England only, he might well have succeeded. But in January 1917, he upped the ante by announcing a policy of unrestricted submarine warfare.

Was there any logic, or justice, to the German policy?

Yes. The British played a double game, blockading Germany while insisting that a submarine blockade was illegal. In truth, international law had not caught up with the submarine's development, and even if it had, it is unlikely that the Germans could be talked out of using such a potent weapon. Having said that, however, it was rank folly for Germany to announce it would sink any merchant ship headed to England or any part of the British Isles.

On January 31, 1917, the German ambassador to the United States called at the office of the secretary of state and handed him the diplomatic note which announced the change in policy. The German diplomat offered his sincere regrets (he was against the policy), and the American offered his equally sincere wish that it had not been altered (he was actually in favor of American entry to the war). Three days later, on February 2, 1917, the United States severed all relations with Imperial Germany.

Where was Wilson by this point?

He loathed Imperial Germany and wished to strike it a blow, but he was still concerned about America's moral authority. Could the United States, having entered the war, still appear above it all as the disinterested party which could steer the peace? This dilemma was solved for Wilson by yet another German blunder: the Zimmermann Telegram.

Who was Zimmermann, and what did he say?

Arthur Zimmermann had recently become the German foreign secretary. His notorious telegram, intercepted by British intelligence, was sent to the chief German diplomat in Mexico. Zimmermann announced that the new policy of unrestricted submarine warfare might bring the United States into the war and that if this happened, Germany wished Mexico to become its ally. Assuming that all went well, Mexico would be rewarded by the repossession of all the Western areas it had lost to the United States during the war of 1846–1848.

To send the telegram was foolish; to make these assertions and promises was ridiculous. Mexico was emerging from a long civil struggle. It had no army worthy of the name, and to think it could harm the United States was absurd. However, the Zimmermann Telegram helped unite American public opinion in favor of war and because of this, it was the single worst blunder of the war.

Was Wilson ready to take the plunge?

He was terribly close. But even with all that had transpired, he might have stayed his hand if Czarist Russia had not melted down. For nearly three years, Wilson had maintained it was obnoxious for the Americans to join the Allied Powers as long as one of them was an absolute monarchy. That hurdle was now removed by the Russians themselves.

When did the Romanov dynasty come to an end?

Early in March 1917, Petrograd was rife with rioters, deserters, and ne'er-do-wells. Czar Nicholas was close to the front, attempting to direct a lost war, when he learned of the trouble in his capital city. The czar refused to believe at first, but his top military men practically forced him to abdicate, which he did on March 15, 1917. Czar Nicholas stepped down in favor of his brother, Grand-Duke Michael, but he was soon forced to abdicate as well. By March 17, the Romanov dynasty, which had ruled Russia since 1613, had ceased to exist.

What replaced the Romanov dynasty?

A provisional government was formed at once in Petrograd by leading military and civilian men. A cabinet of eighteen persons was formed, with Alexander Kerensky being the outsider (he would soon rise to become its leader). The new provisional government declared it was for peace in the long run but that it would not abrogate the agreements made by the czarist government. Russia would, therefore, remain in the war.

In the weeks that followed, numerous constituencies jockeyed for power in Petrograd (Moscow, meanwhile, was quiet). One of the leading groups was the Bolshevik Party, which had previously been outlawed. Led by Vladimir Illych Ulyanov (1870–1924)—known to the world as Lenin—the Bolsheviks demanded "Land, Bread, and Peace." The simplistic formula proved quite effective, and many of Petrograd's citizens began to favor the Bolsheviks. In the meantime, however, the United States finally entered World War I.

How and when did America finally join the Allies?

On April 2, 1917, President Wilson went before Congress to deliver a speech, asking both Houses to return a declaration of war against Imperial Germany. The speech was uneven, with some fine rhetorical points and many wasted asides. Wilson hit his best stride with the memorable words: "The world must be made safe for democracy." As he left the chamber, he was treated to the greatest applause of his long career.

The U.S. Senate approved the request by a vote of 82 to 6. The House of Representatives enjoyed a more spirited debate, and the final vote was 373 to 50. One of the 50 "nays" was a young congresswoman from Montana, Jeannette Rankin.

Who is the only person to have voted against America entering World Wars I and II?

Jeannette Rankin (1888–1976) bears this distinction. When, in 1917, the vote for war approached, she was a brand-new congresswoman from Montana. She gave her "nay" with a sign of fear, and she was correct in that her constituents bounced her from office two years later. But by a remarkable, some might say incredible, synchronicity, she was back in the House of Representatives in 1941, when she cast the only vote against U.S. entry into World War II.

Was America ready for war in 1917?

In technical terms, the United States was not ready. The Regular U.S. Army numbered about 140,000, and much of its equipment was outdated. There were still some Civil War cannon in its arsenal. The U.S. Navy was efficient but small.

In moral terms and sheer enthusiasm, America was ready for war. For three years and a distance of 3,000 miles, Americans had witnessed the death and destruction of the Great War. Many were weary of waiting and wished to play an active part. Even so, rather few suspected just how decisive President Wilson would become. After dragging his feet for three years, Wilson acted with a great deal of enthusiasm once the war began.

When did the U.S. resort to military conscription?

To make it more palatable, Wilson's administration called it the "Selective Service." Almost immediately upon declaring war, Wilson realized more men would be needed, and the first selective service draft looked for 560,000 soldiers. Even that proved insufficient, however, and soon the projection was for an army of 1.3 million men.

When it came to the top leadership, Wilson and Secretary of War Stimson had rather few choices. Most of the Spanish–American War leaders had left the service for more profitable opportunities. One leader merged: Brigadier-General John Pershing (1860–1948).

What was the Pershing mystique?

First, it should be said that Pershing did not cultivate it. The man was made of iron in most respects; he was not a play actor. Tall, ruggedly handsome, and as determined a soldier as the U.S. Army has ever fielded, Pershing was a close-to-perfect choice for American supreme commander. Tales soon developed of "Black Jack" Pershing, the indomitable taskmaster who was too severe for his troops; most of them were false. He was what he was: a magnificent figure of American manhood.

Right from the beginning, Pershing demanded that his men fight as one united American army, that they not be parceled among the various European allies. President Wilson had few thoughts on this subject, but his top military advisers completely concurred with Pershing.

Why was Pershing so grim of face and demeanor?

It would take a psychologist to answer the question completely, but it was surely related to the tragic deaths of his wife and daughters. In August 1915, while Pershing was away, a coal-induced fire swept through his two-story military house at the Presidio, in San Francisco. His beloved wife and his two daughters died almost instantly; only his five-year-old son escaped. If Pershing had been grim already, he now turned into a man of stone, iron, or marble (all three have been used to describe him).

General John "Black Jack" Pershing led American forces into Europe during World War I.

Who was Pershing's naval counterpart?

Rear Admiral William Sims (1858–1936) is less well known than Pershing, but he played a key role in making it possible for the U.S. Army to reach Europe. Reaching England soon after the declaration of war, Sims was appalled by the losses Britain was taking from U-Boat attacks; he accurately predicted that Britain would be forced from the war if something were not done. Sims established a convoy system under which U.S. warships escorted British and American merchantmen across the North Atlantic. He found the British more willing to cooperate than he expected, and Queenstown, Ireland was soon almost an American naval base.

When did the first American troops arrive in France?

Only a skeleton crew was available to move right away, but immediacy was necessary, because morale in the French army had reached such a low point. On July 4, 1917, Colonel Charles Stanton stood at the grave of the Marquis de Lafayette in Paris and declared: "Lafayette, we are here."

These were but the first of three million Americans who were to be deployed. It did become obvious to the Germans, however, that they must win the war quickly to prevent the Americans from tipping the balance in favor of the Allies.

AMERICANS IN
OTHER ARMIES

How did Americans who wished to get into the war do so early on?

Quite a few Americans wanted to participate and could not because of the long separation—July 1914 through April 1917—between the beginning of the war and the American engagement. Some of these men enlisted in foreign armies, with special preference often for the French Foreign Legion. One such fellow was Edwin Austin Abbey, who wrote home while serving in the Canadian Army:

> A soldier must live from day to day with no thought of the future, just a steadfast purpose of carrying out orders and being stronger and steadier than he naturally is, and faith and trust in God's purpose make it possible for me. Do you not think that the war is making people less selfish in the world and in the United States? Surely it must when in so many places people are sacrificing their dear ones and their money for a cause.... I often think of the rank and file of the German army.... They are suffering untold hardships and showing magnificent bravery in the face of heavy odds.

Was this kind of generous spirit typical of men in the trenches?

When Allied soldiers spoke of the Germans they used expressions like Kraut, Boche, and so forth, but when they wrote in their diaries, they often expressed generous thoughts toward their enemies. The longer the war lasted, the more commonality of feeling that developed between the soldiers of the various armies on the Western Front. The same cannot be said for the Eastern Front, where the Russians, Germans, and Austrians regarded each other with undiluted hatred.

THE NOVEMBER REVOLUTION

How did the Provisional Government in Russia fare?

Not well. Kerensky, its leader, believed Russia had to remain in the war because of the treaties and alliances it had previously signed. One last Russian offensive was planned, and when it came to a deal halt in the late summer of 1917, everyone realized that Russia would have to remain permanently on the defensive.

This failure was the sign, the green light, for Vladimir Illych Ulyanov. Better known as Lenin, he had planned for perhaps twenty years to lead a communist overthrow of the great industrial powers. Like Karl Marx, Lenin believed that the communist revolution would first raise its head in the industrialized West, but when the opportunity to establish a communist society presented itself in Russia, Lenin seized the moment.

When did the November Revolution begin?

On November 11, 1917, Lenin and perhaps 10,000 communist followers overthrew the Provisional Government. Lenin needed only the major cities of Moscow and St. Petersburg to bring about his coup; knowing this, he concentrated on the telegraph wires and railroad lines. Within forty-eight hours, the Bolsheviks, as they were known, had seized the downtown of both these big cities and were on their way to carrying out a very successful coup. Kerensky fled into exile: he spent much of the remainder of his life in the United States, declaring to anyone who would listen that the Russian people of 1917 had not wished for Lenin and the communists to prevail.

Vladimir Ilyich Ulyanov (Lenin) was the famous leader of the Bolsheviks who took over the Russian government in 1917, ushering in the communist era of the Union of Soviet Socialist Republics.

How did the November Revolution affect events on the battlefield?

Lenin and his closest associate, Leon Trotsky, agreed on a policy of "no war, no peace." This meant they would not negotiate with the Western powers—be they capitalist or otherwise—but that they would not continue with the war. This was a reasonable proposition because the Russian soldiers were so weary of war. To Imperial Germany, however, this proposition was a dream come true.

During the winter of 1917–1918, the Germans pressed the Russians hard, capturing up to 500,000 square miles of land in the Ukraine. Not until Trotsky met the top German diplomats did the fighting cease, and by then Germany had conquered much of Russia's best, most fertile soil. The Treaty of Brest-Litovsk was one of the most unfair ever concocted. Even though Germany had done more to start the war in the first place, it was Russia that suffered, losing much of the Ukraine and many of its best factories. Lenin and Trotsky were infuriated by the naked German greed, but they needed breathing room to consolidate their hold on Russia. They signed the treaty, and Russia finally departed the war.

SLEDGEHAMMER BLOWS

Who was Germany's unofficial dictator?

Eric von Ludendorff had become that person. In rank and title, he was still number two to Paul von Hindenburg, but Ludendorff, had, by the winter of 1917–1918, become the dictator of Germany in matters civil as well as military.

Ludendorff was a terrific army general but not a great strategist, and the plans he developed during the war's last winter were not unusual or surprising. He intended to smash the French lines in order to get at the British Expeditionary Force and make it evacuate to England. He then could take Paris and defy the newly arrived Americans to do their worst. It was not a brilliant plan, but it did have some potential for success. The missing element was the one million German soldiers holding sections of the Ukraine and Russia: had these been released and moved West, Ludendorff might well have succeeded.

What was the big day?

Ludendorff intended to make several massive assaults. The first commenced on the morning of March 21, 1918. Roughly 6,000 German guns carried out an intense bombardment, which was followed by thousands of German infantrymen infiltrating the British lines. For once in the war, a plan succeeded.

Operation Michael was a distinct success by noon, with Ludendorff gaining thousands of yards, but his men tired easily. The German soldier was known for his ability to get by in all sorts of weather, but many of these soldiers had not enjoyed good, hot food in weeks; they were asked to carry out little short of a miracle. From his post about twenty miles back, Ludendorff believed that all was well: penetration, after all, had been achieved. The British and French high commands were nervous enough that they called a joint conference, and on March 26, French General Ferdinand Foch (1851–1929) was selected as overall commander of the Allied forces (for the moment, however, he did not command the Americans).

How close did the Germans come to success?

They achieved a genuine breakthrough, one far more significant than anything in the previous three years, but were unable to follow it up. Had they possessed tanks, they might well have succeeded, but the common German infantryman—who by this point wore the rounded helmet rather than a spiked one—was simply too weary to press on.

How many times did Marshal Foch and General Pershing go at it?

Perhaps half a dozen. When the cameras were set up, the two men knew how to strike a pose and act like genial colleagues; behind the scenes, they were ready to tear each other apart. Foch wanted to employ sections of the American Expeditionary Force (AEF), placing American regiments and brigades in with French and British counterparts. Pershing, whose orders from Washington were quite clear, was adamant that the Americans would serve and fight as one army and not be used piecemeal.

When was Paris hit for the first time?

In four years of war, Paris had known hunger, deprivation, and low morale, but it was never attacked directly until the last week of March 1918. Ludendorff's men at the Krupp iron works had developed five gigantic guns capable of hurling shells seventy-five miles (the original estimate had been sixty). A battery of these guns was set up behind the German lines, and the first shells landed in Paris during Holy Week of 1918, causing consternation among civilians. As was so often true in World War I, the German gunners showed a strange combination of savagery and mercy. When a major Parisian church was shelled, causing many casualties, the gunners withheld the next day because they knew the funeral for the victims was in progress.

How eager were the Americans to get into this conflict?

They were chomping at the bit. One thing that most American soldiers—or Yanks—shared throughout the war was an overwhelming confidence that they would win. Caution and anxiety played a role among the Americans at all levels and ranks, but there was no pessimism, no sense of impending defeat. Whether he came from Missouri, Massachusetts, or California, the typical American infantryman believed that the Stars and Stripes would prevail.

What lay behind this confidence was the enormous amount of materiel that the United States provided for the Allied cause. Matters in the American war industry could be, and often were, chaotic, but a whole lot of things got done. By the end of the war, America was producing 10,000 airplanes a year, for example.

Why didn't the Germans transfer those one million men from the Eastern Front?

It was too late. Once the major battles of 1918 were joined, the Germans had to fight with what they possessed on the Western Front. The Allies, by contrast, had the BEF—

How did the nickname "Doughboys" come into general use?

U.S. Marines

Who used it first is unknown, but by the middle of 1918, the nickname was ubiquitous. British, French, Belgian, and even some Germans noted how much taller and better fed the Americans seemed in contrast to their own men. Much of this had to do with diet. The American soldier from the Midwest, for example, ate a hearty diet of corn, potatoes, and raw milk, all of which gave him a protein base that was at least 1.5 times as much as his European counterpart. There was something else to it, however: a jauntiness in the Americans that was noticed by almost everyone.

which was weary but unbowed—the French army, which was still shaky from the Neuvile Offensives, and the newly arrived Americans, who, almost everyone declared, were the finest looking fellows seen in the war.

Where were the Americans most needed?

Late in May 1918, the Germans broke through in the Argonne area and came within forty miles of Paris. A division of U.S. Marines was rushed to the area called Belleau Wood, and a fierce fight developed over who would control this one-square-mile area. The Marines were fresh and inexperienced, but some of that worked in their favor; they were not intimidated by the Germans. The fight went on for a full week, and when it was over, Ludendorff's third sledgehammer blow had failed.

Now, if ever, was the time for the Germans to seek peace, but Ludendorff would not permit it. The Kaiser was on the verge of a nervous breakdown, and no one else had the authority to put Ludendorff in his place. As a result, the war continued, with ever more disastrous results.

When did the tide finally turn in favor of the Allies?

By the beginning of July, the Germans were exhausted. Even Ludendorff conceded that nothing could be gained by further assaults. The Germans, therefore, went on the defensive while the Allies made their first major attacks.

Beginning on July 18, 1918, the French and Americans moved forward in the Aisne-Marne offensive. Their assault was preceded by a massive artillery barrage, and roughly 400 tanks slowly rumbled from their positions to attack the German lines. The Germans suffered 30,000 men killed, wounded, and missing on the first day of battle, and things only became worse, from their perspective. Another joint Allied offensive began on August 8. On that single day, the Allies liberated nineteen French villages and advanced nine miles; they also captured 16,000 Germans. Ludendorff later referred to August 8, 1918 as the "black day of the German army."

By this time, the summer of 1918, how many tanks were in the field?

British and French factories had labored since the spring of 1916, and now, two years later, they had manufactured a total of about 5,500 tanks. The best of these was the British Mark IV, but it was supplemented by the Renault-FT, made in France. By contrast, German factories had manufactured roughly twenty tanks in all.

It was not only the Germans who were skeptical, though. No less an authority than General Pershing declared that the fate of infantry battles would continue to rest with the rifle and bayonet. The German defenders ardently hoped that the Allies would not make any more tanks, because the mechanical monstrosities—as so many called them—could move into and then up out of trenches.

Where did the Germans make their last stand?

The Hindenburg Line—sometimes called the Siegfried Line—was the natural spot, but the German will to resist had practically disappeared. One of the most significant incidents to reveal Germany's low morale occured on October 8, 1918 when U.S. Corporal Alvin York came back to his post with 132 German prisoners and thirty-five machine guns. Incredibly, York had killed roughly twenty-five Germans with his sharpshooting and then compelled their comrades to yield. He was, indeed, a fine shot, who hailed from the backwoods of Tennessee.

The U.S. military, naturally, made a great deal of Corporal York, while the Germans hushed up the incident. That an American, of all people, was able to capture so many Germans was very bad for morale.

What was the last straw for the Germans?

It came from within, rather than without. On October 28, 1918, the naval high command of Imperial Germany ordered the battle fleet to sail from Keil and encounter the British Royal Navy. The German ships had been at anchor for more than two years, and morale, as well as material conditions, was at a low ebb. Knowing that theirs would be a suicidal mission, the majority of German sailors mutinied, and the ships stayed where they were.

By the end of October, both Turkey and Bulgaria had surrendered to the Allies. Austria-Hungary had also folded, meaning that Germany stood alone.

British troops in Brie, France, in 1917, pursuing the Germans as they retreated to the Hindenburg Line.

Was the kaiser the major obstacle to ending the war?

Not really. He was, in November 1918, a rather pathetic man, made old before his time. For the past two years, he had exercised little control over civilian or military affairs. Even so, it was a shock when one of his top subordinates informed him that he must abdicate in order to clear the path to an armistice with the Allies. The Kaiser blustered for hours, but finally signed his abdication statement on November 9, 1918. Even at that moment, he attempted to fudge, saying he abdicated as German emperor but not as king of Prussia. This was a fig leaf, and everyone realized it. The official statement was altered for the press, and when the news went out on radio, it was declared that the Kaiser had abdicated both posts.

Within hours, a civilian government was formed, and a major statement was made from the top of the government offices. As of November 9, 1918, Germany had become a republic.

When did the German and Allies representatives get together?

They first met at Compiegne on November 8, 1918. The German diplomats tried to play the Bolshevik card, saying that the Allies did not realize how dangerous Communism was. Field Marshal Ferdinand Foch rejected this, saying that all armies tended to see breakdown in order at the end of a war. He demanded to know if the Germans were ready to sign an armistice and he ticked off a long list of terms, all of which aimed to ensure that Germany would be completely disarmed and possibly even broken apart and no longer exist as a military power.

When did fighting cease?

The German and Allies representatives signed the armistice at 7 A.M., but the fighting was scheduled to cease at 11 A.M., meaning the eleventh hour of the eleventh day of the eleventh month of the year. The symbolic nature of that hour was well understood, but handfuls of men died between 7 and 11 that morning, and a few others died even after the last bell (metaphorical) had been rung. Fighting did not completely cease until later that afternoon.

No one had a clue, at that moment, just how great the human and material losses were. It took years to estimate that two million Germans, three million Russians, 1.3 million French, and 900,000 British had died during the Great War. Turkish losses are more difficult to estimate. The nations that came off the lightest, by far, were Japan and the United States. America suffered roughly 50,000 killed in battle, and many others that later died of their wounds, but given the huge role the United States played in the last three months of fighting, this was not a high toll. Japan, which seized several Pacific Islands from Germany, lost about 350 men in the war.

TOTALING THE LOSSES

Is it accurate to say that Germany lost World War I?

Very soon after the armistice and for many years thereafter, there were claims that Germany did not lose the war to the Allies but that it was "stabbed in the back." If there was a knife thrust, it came—the adherents declared—from the Jews, liberals, and Communists, and not necessarily in that order. About the only flimsy proof that these people could offer was that the Allies were not quite inside Germany when the war ended on November 11, 1918.

This sounds rather silly, but the theory provided a foothold for many unscrupulous politicians, including the young Adolf Hitler. Not only would Hitler assert that Germany had never been beaten, but he would also declare that the Treaty of Versailles, by imposing reparations on Germany, had turned the German people into "slaves until 1988" (because that is when the reparations payments were scheduled to be completed).

Is it fair to say that America won World War I?

Ever since 1918, it has raised the ire of British and French commentators when they hear that the United States won the war, because to them it is apparent that their nations sacrificed far more. They are half right.

Britain, France, and the other Allied nations gave and sacrificed far more of their manpower and material resources than did the United States, so in a way, their efforts "won" the war. However, technically speaking, especially looking at who delivered the most important punches and whose entry into the war tipped the balance in favor of the Allies, a good case can be made for the United States. And if one asks which country gained the most while expending the least, then it is a tie between the United States and Imperial Japan.

What persuaded President Wilson to go to Paris?

Wilson experienced a heady rush of optimism at the war's end, and he believed, perhaps rightly, that only the United States could exert the moral authority necessary to prevent this from being another "revenge of the victors." He, therefore, left America in December 1918 aboard an ocean liner and landed in France, where he was greeted by rapturous crowds who hailed him as a liberator.

Again, public demonstrations went to Wilson's head. He found his three counterparts—Prime Minister David Lloyd George, Vittorio Orlando, and Georges Georges Clemenceau—difficult to work with, and they found him impossible because of his idealism and naiveté, which worked together to make him an isolated figure. Wilson truly wished a "war without victors," but it was not possible given the enormous losses suffered by the Allied nations. Then, too, he proved naïve about the threat posed by Russia, which was now in Communist hands.

Who among the "Big Four" was most interested in vengeance?

George Clemenceau, the premier of France, was convinced that Germany must be broken. He had witnessed two invasions of his country—in 1870 and 1914—and was determined that there must never be another. Clemenceau also believed that he understood the Americans because he had been a foreign observer in the United States during its Civil War. In truth, however, Clemenceau and Wilson never understood each other: they were much too different.

David Lloyd George, prime minister of Great Britain, had England's international and overseas commitments uppermost in mind; he wanted to preserve the British Empire while allowing for some reforms. And Vittorio Orlando, the prime minister of Italy, was most interested in gaining land for his nation as recompense for its wartime sacrifices.

Did the "Big Four" pay any attention to the influenza epidemic?

On a human and personal level, they certainly knew that people were dying in droves. As professional politicians, however, they chose to ignore the reports and concentrate their efforts on redrawing the map of Europe and the various colonial zones around the globe.

The "Big Four" were (left to right) Prime Minster David Lloyd George of Great Britain, Italian Premier Vittorio Orlando, French Premier George Clemenceau, and U.S. President Woodrow Wilson, shown here at the Paris peace conference on May 27, 1919.

345

No one can blame the Big Four, or any other group of politicians, for the disaster which commenced in the summer of 1918 and accelerated rapidly thereafter. Roughly 650,000 Americans—many of them from military and naval towns and cities—died in the Influenza Epidemic of 1918–1919; worldwide, the total may have reached eight million.

When the Versailles Treaty was finally complete, how many nations had either been created or wiped off the map?

Four great empires—Czarist Russia, Imperial Germany, Ottoman Turkey, and Austria-Hungary—had all disappeared from the maps; Kaiser Wilhelm II, in one of his few perspicacious moments, had predicted this. Roughly nine new nations had been established, nearly all of them in Eastern Europe. From Latvia and Lithuania in the north to Yugoslavia in the south, the map had been profoundly altered. Wilson and his advisers had done most of this redistricting based on the concept of national self-determination, and many Poles, Czechs, and others were deeply grateful for the change (at least at first).

France looked much the same as in the past, but it would take decades to recover from the damage to its northern farms and factories. Britain, on the map, was much as before, but she, too, would go through many adjustments. The British and French colonial empires remained intact, but a mandate system was established, under which many colonial peoples would eventually gain their independence. About the only country that really did not have any changes in territory or composition was the United States.

What was the moment when the United States became the world's greatest, or strongest, power?

Some scholars delay that moment all the way to World War II, pointing out that the United States did not dominate international events in the 1920s and 1930s. While there is some truth to the assertion, the fact is that America became the *economic* superpower sometime in 1918. Prior to 1914, London had been the center of international banking, finance, and insurance; after 1917, New York City increasingly took over that role. Then, too, the United States emerged from World War I as the only major nation which had more than enough food to feed its people.

What happened to President Wilson after the Treaty of Versailles?

He returned home aboard a passenger liner and was greeted by rapturous crowds in the United States; popular feeling was very much with him. The same cannot be said for the U.S. Senate, which balked at the idea of a treaty that would commit U.S. troops to future causes, even if the cause was that of preserving international peace.

Wilson had never been good at compromise, and he was infuriated by the leaders of the Republican-dominated Senate. In September 1919, he embarked on a speaking tour, traveling by train in an effort get the American people behind him and force the Senate to approve the Versailles Treaty. Wilson made a number of first-rate speeches, and all was going well until he suddenly fell ill in Pueblo, Colorado. The next day he suffered a stroke and was brought back to the White House as an invalid.

Did Wilson ever recover? Did the United States ever join the League of Nations?

No and no. Wilson remained in the White House for the remainder of his term in office, but he was—for the most part—unable even to sit up in bed. His wife brought him documents, which he read and then signed, with a very shaky hand.

The U.S. Senate rejected the Versailles Treaty, and in so doing it ensured that America did not join the League of Nations. When the League convened in Geneva, it lacked the world's greatest military and economic power, the only nation capable of enforcing the League's decisions.

What did Americans of the next decade—the 1920s—think about the Great War?

They mostly tried to forget about it. The Great War had been a political disaster, they said, and it was followed by a health disaster, the Great Flu. Far better, most Americans said, to forget about the war and about European politics in general. From this sentiment arose the isolationist movement which would bedevil President Franklin D. Roosevelt when another great conflict began in 1939.

FROM COAL TO OIL: 1919 TO 1939

What did the Western world look like during the five years that followed the Great War?

Perhaps three-quarters of the areas involved in the war looked the same, but that look was deceptive. Roughly one-quarter of the areas involved looked like, and were, disaster zones. The hardest-hit areas were northern France and southern Belgium. Large portions of western Russia, too, looked as if they had been hit by tornadoes.

Even in places where no visible damage existed, many people were shell shocked: that term became prevalent in 1916. Rural England, for example, had only been hit in the most tangential ways, but its population was never quite the same again. Poets and essayists described the feeling of lassitude and defeatism that crept into many, if not most, of the Allied countries after 1919. One major exception to the rule was the United States, which suffered neither material destruction nor debilitating human losses. But even the Americans had their own peculiar form of retreat: they called it isolationism.

What were the material conditions—those of everyday life—for those who had survived the Great War?

In certain areas, Belgium, for example, deprivation was so severe that millions of people might have died if the United States had not formed food relief committees. In parts of the Soviet Union, the combination of death, disaster, and famine was so prevalent that millions of people *did* starve to death between 1918 and 1921.

The Russians had suffered the most during the Great War, and in the immediate aftermath they, once again, took it the worst. Not until 1921, when Lenin and Trotsky established control over the nation, did anything like normal life begin to resume. The Russians were not the only people that suffered, however.

What was the plight of the German middle class?

Prior to 1914, Germany's middle class had been among the most successful in Europe, with many people enjoying a high standard of living. That came to an abrupt halt with the war's commencement, and things only got worse. When the war ended, some parts of the German economy began to recover, only to run into the truly ruinous price inflation of 1923–1924. Millions of people lost all their savings, and just about everyone struggled to put food on the table.

The inflation was tamed by 1925, and some aspects of German life began to head in a better direction.

THE ADVENT OF OIL

For how long have we lived in the "Age of Oil"?

Not as long as we might think. Oil was first found in large quantities in the United States at the time of the Civil War. Pennsylvania was where the first oil was brought up and refined, but after about 1900, the center of action moved to Texas, which has, ever since, been the center of the American petroleum industry.

The potential for oil to change the basis on which the industrial world ran was seen rather early, but it took a long time to persuade the manufacturers. About nine-tenths of the Industrial Revolution, to that point, had been accomplished by the use of coal, and leaders of industry naturally wished to stay with what they knew. Therefore, coal con-

The HMS *Queen Elizabeth* (shown here in 1936) was the first battleship to be powered by oil.

tinued to be the source of industrial energy right up to the brink of World War I. The British, as ever, proved quick on the mark; HMS *Queen Elizabeth*, launched in 1912, was the world's first battleship to be powered by oil.

How much did the areas of energy—geographically speaking—effect the types of energy that were used?

England is rich in coal, and coal had allowed for the spread of the Industrial Revolution. Germany is rich in coal and steel, and it therefore gained a slight edge on England by about 1910. The United States is rich in copper, iron, and coal, and it had the capacity to overtake and surpass those powers, though it did not do so until the end of World War I. Russia—whether governed by the czar or the Soviets—had perhaps the greatest resources of all: it was rich in iron, coal, steel, and oil. But Russia's economy was a mystery to the Western powers during the 1920s, and intentionally so. Therefore, the person or the company that looked for future sources of oil tended to look first at Mexico, then at Venezuela, and finally at the Middle East.

Military leaders, like industrial ones, tend to work with proven entities. If the British Royal Navy leaders had their way, we would still be in the Age of Coal today. The Germans were adroit at many things, but the development of the tank passed them by almost completely, and they did not recognize the great need for petrol until the 1920s. Therefore, it tended to be outsiders, even wildcatters, who led the Western world from the Age of Coal and into the Age of Oil.

What was the situation in the Middle East when World War I ended?

T. E. Lawrence intended to hand over Syria, and perhaps Jordan too, to the Arabs who had fought so well against the Turks. When he brought King Faisal to Damascus, however, Lawrence found General Sir Edward Allenby adamant that Palestine and Egypt would be British "mandates" and that Syria would be a French one.

Established by the victors at the Versailles peace conference, the "mandate" system meant that areas that the British and French deemed unripe for self-government would learn the methods of constitutional government under the supervision of the great powers. The mandate system was intended to last for fifty years, but it was a rare place where it lasted that long.

How long did it take for the Arabs, as a whole, to recognize the wealth on which they sat?

A few may have gotten it right away, but as long as the Western world clung to the use of coal, oil remained a secondary source of energy. The British steel strike of 1926, however, revealed weakness in England's supply system, and by then a number of agents, many of them wildcatters, were already in the Middle East, probing for petroleum.

These outsiders were not interested in conferring benefits upon the various Arab nations or mandate countries; they wanted to earn profits for their companies and share-   351 holders back home. The early contracts between British and American companies and Arab governments, therefore, worked very much in favor of the so-called imperialistic nations. Many Americans were disgusted, even horrified, to hear that they were now included in that general category.

AIRCRAFT CARRIERS

What was the most noticeable change in arms and armaments after the end of World War I?

The battleship served very well during World War I, but by the war's end there were numerous captains and admirals—in most of the major nations—that asserted something new was necessary for maritime supremacy. Virtually all of the major leaders had witnessed the efficacy of the airplane, first for reconnaissance and then for the dropping of bombs, and they prodded the civilian leaders of their nations toward the development of a new weapon that would combine speed, maneuverability, and crushing power. The result was the aircraft carrier.

To say that it was an American invention is ninety percent accurate, but British, French, and Japanese engineers were also on the trail. It was an American, Eugene Ely, who made the first liftoff of an airplane from a warship (1910) and who accomplished the first successful landing on a warship (1911). World War I provided momentum to those who wished for an American carrier fleet, and the first real carriers were laid down in the early 1920s. The United States was in the lead, with the U.S.S. *Langley* (1923), U.S.S. *Saratoga* (1927), and U.S.S. *Lexington* (1927), but the British were not far behind.

The U.S.S. *Lexington,* one of the first aircraft carriers built by the Americans, is currently on display at its permanent dock in Corpus Christi, Texas.

Why was it so important to Japan to keep pace with the major European powers?

Japan had played a small, and very successful, role in World War I. It had seized a number of German islands in the Pacific for a minimum of men lost. Japan was aggravated, however, by the condescending attitude of the Great Powers at the Versailles peace conference. Even worse was the Washington Naval Agreement of 1923, which asserted that Japan was in the "three" range. This meant it could build three new major warships to every five that was built by Britain, France, and the United States.

To say that Japan already had in mind a war against the United States goes too far, but there were militant leaders in the Japanese Imperial Navy who war-gamed what such a conflict would be like. At the highest levels, including the emperor and his Cabinet, the United States was seen as an irritant because it could prevent Japan from taking over large parts of the Eastern Pacific. Then, too, Japan was, by 1925, thoroughly dependent on oil supplied by American companies. As a result, Japan found ways to "cheat," to get around the 5-5-5-3 agreement.

What were some of the first Japanese aircraft carriers?

Hosho, which translates as "Flying Phoenix," was launched in 1922. She displaced 7,470 tons and used Kanpon Turbines to achieve a speed of twenty-five knots. *Akagi* was completed in 1927 and retrofitted in 1938. She displaced 26,900 tons and had a maximum speed of thirty-one knots. The Japanese were first-rate builders of aircraft carriers, and if they had ever achieved the level of aircraft building later seen in the United States, World War II in the Pacific would have been a much more difficult proposition for their opponents.

For how long did the United States maintain the lead in the building of aircraft carriers?

Once America possessed that lead, it did not relinquish it. One of the few military appropriations that managed to get through the House of Representatives during the Great

What did Americans think of the Japanese during the 1920s and 1930s?

At the beginning of the 1920s, Americans knew little about Japan and perhaps cared even less. But the enormous Tokyo Earthquake of 1923 brought Japan to the attention of almost all nations, and a handful of dedicated American scholars sought to make Japan more comprehensible to the American public (one of the foremost of these was Hugh Borton). By about 1935, therefore, many Americans did have an image of Japan and the Japanese: this image tended to be of an exotic, peaceful, and perhaps childish people who would never amount to much in terms of warfare.

Depression was that for the building of carriers. Experiments were made, with airplanes employing folded wings in order to bring more onto the decks. A whole new section of the U.S. Navy emerged, with specialist personnel.

At the same time, however, America did not give up on the battleship. If the carrier was the wave of the future, the battleship was the sound and dependable instrument which had done so much in the past. More carriers than battleships were laid down in the 1930s, but the U.S. Navy maintained an almost equal number of the two.

Could coal ever have fueled these great warships, these floating platforms?

No. Coal is a much denser source of fuel than petroleum, and only the latter could flow and burn smoothly enough to provide the great power, and maneuverability, of the aircraft carriers. What made the aircraft carrier development possible was the relative cheapness of oil during the 1930s. American refineries, in Texas especially, were turning out vast quantities of oil, and there was the promise of even larger oil discoveries in the Arab world. As a result, American politicians and diplomats became more aware of the Arab peoples.

THE WORLD IN DEPRESSION

Where did the Great Depression begin?

It started in the United States, which, after about 1918, had become the world's center of banking, finance, and insurance. It began in the nation which had benefitted the most from World War I.

Between 1918 and about 1928, the United States upheld the economies of the Western world. The United States did not do this out of friendship or sympathy; it was the natural consequence of American firms expanding and the American consumer keeping pace. During the 1920s, American banks lent money to German ones, allowing the economy of that nation to begin to recover from the war. A new currency—the Rentenmark—replaced the old one, and Germany was stabilized by about 1928.

Did Americans like the fact that they subsidized the former Allied nations?

They did not. President Calvin Coolidge (1872–1934) demanded the repayment of

U.S. President Calvin Coolidge wanted the European Allies to pay back the money America spent fighting for them in Europe.

354

war debts by the Allied nations, saying, "They hired the money, didn't they?" And one could argue that the United States was doing fine in the mid-1920s, with enormous increases in consumer spending, especially for automobiles, radios, and refrigerators. There are economists today who declare that much of the world economy we now know came into being during the 1920s. Certainly, some of the economic techniques employed by many nations—most notably Keynesian economics—are the result of what America saw in the Great Depression.

When did the Great Depression begin?

It commenced with a major fall in stock prices on Wall Street. The end of October and the beginning of November 1929 witnessed the most dramatic falls, but over the next year the prices of major companies such as General Electric and Radio City America dropped by more than half. Very likely, the fall in prices was the result of overproduction in the previous year. There were only so many cars, radios, and refrigerators that the American people needed.

Many people—including Presidents Calvin Coolidge and Herbert Hoover—believed that the Depression would ease, but it only became worse. By 1932, roughly one-quarter of all working-age Americans were out of a job, and millions more had accepted half-pay in order to keep what they had.

What did the world look like, from a military point of view, in the year 1920?

It looked like a disaster, from a military, political, social, and economic viewpoint. Never had so much destruction occurred over so wide an area. But in terms of military strength, the only two nations that emerged stronger—not weaker—were the United States and Imperial Japan.

That America would come out well is no surprise: American arms merchants had made fortunes during the war. Then, too, the Americans had become a more military-minded people than before. But Imperial Japan, on the other side of the Pacific Ocean, was quite a surprise. Japan had joined the Allies in 1915 and had suffered little loss while it snapped up German colonies throughout the Far East. Having experienced victory against Russia in 1904–1905, and having done well in the Great War, Japan was in a strong position.

Did the British Empire still exist in 1920?

It did. On the map, it looked as big as ever. Anyone who spent time in the Dominions, however, knew that it was not the British Empire of 1910. The British and their colonial subjects were badly shaken by the Great War; on some levels, life in England was never the same again.

London was still a great powerhouse, but leadership of the financial and insurance industries was slowly passing to New York City. Some Britons continued to claim that the British Empire was the most powerful force on earth, but in sheer material terms that mantle had passed to the United States. Then, too, Communist Russia presented a greater threat than Czarist Russia ever had.

How did Russia fare in the immediate aftermath of the war?

The Great War was bad enough with four million Russians killed and wounded, but the aftermath was even worse. Perhaps another four million men and women starved to death in the three years that followed the war, and plenty more died on the battlefield as the "White" armies which wished to bring back the czar fought the "Red" armies that looked to a truly communistic future. By 1920, the Red Armies had prevailed, and Lenin was the undisputed leader of the new Union of Soviet Socialist Republics (U.S.S.R.).

Were any nations "on the march" in the early 1920s?

Of all those that participated in the Great War, only Japan and Italy were keen for new action. Japan was humiliated by the Great Power agreement of 1921, which limited its battleship fleet to three for every five of the European Great Powers. Italy, which was taken over in a bold coup by Benito Mussolini (1883–1945) in 1923, was keen to obtain the land its leaders had failed to gain in the aftermath of World War I.

NATURAL RESOURCES

When did the shift from coal to oil commence?

Coal had been the primary source of industrial energy for one hundred years and more. It had fueled the Industrial Revolution in England as early as 1820 and was the primary power behind the rise of the other industrial nations. Oil, however, began to emerge at the end of the nineteenth century, and by 1920, it posed a real competition to coal. Oil, or petroleum, provided a smoother release and longer-lasting energy.

The United States was far ahead of all the other major nations in petroleum production in 1920, but others had their eyes on the prize. The U.S.S.R. possessed vast petroleum reserves in Siberia and the Caucasus Mountains, and it soon became apparent that South America had a good deal as well. What was not immediately apparent in 1920 was how oil rich the Middle East was; the actions of a number of aggressive individuals and companies were required to make that reality known.

When did the major nations start to realize the importance of air power for any future conflicts?

Practically all the leaders of all the major nations swore that there would be no future wars, but the military staffs of all those nations were on the lookout for new weapons. Air power had made a small appearance in World War I, and the American military was keen to size up its chances. At the same time, any military leader who expressed too great an interest in air power—at this point—risked being ostracized by his fellows. This happened to William "Hap" Arnold of the U.S. Navy.

Almost no one spoke of the future of aircraft carriers; most naval experts continued to follow the thinking of Alfred Thayer Mahan, who in his majestic studies of naval warfare concluded that battleships would always form the heart of any nation's fleet.

What happened to England during the Great Steel Strike?

In 1926, Britain suffered from a long strike by its workers in the coal industry. Winston Churchill, who was back in the thick of politics, vowed to break the strike and even brought in armored cars, but the result was a disaster for the government and the country. Suddenly more aware of their importance—thanks to the incredible sacrifices they had endured in World War I—the common man and woman of England was much less willing to accept what the government decreed. Churchill, in particular, would find this to be increasingly true.

RISE OF THE DICTATORS

Which was the first postwar dictator to arise?

Benito Mussolini (1875–1945) was the son of an Italian blacksmith and was named, ironically, for Benito Juarez, the first president of a unified Mexico. Mussolini served in World War I and, like many of his countrymen, was disillusioned by the results. Italy suffered well over one million men killed and wounded, and the Versailles Treaty accorded it very little.

By 1923, Mussolini was leader of the so-called Black Shirts, a Fascist group which modeled its early behavior on the principles of Garibaldi, and the Red Shirts of 1859–1860. In the autumn of 1923, Mussolini led his "March on Rome."

When did Hitler first appear on the scene?

In November 1923, Hitler joined forces with Eric von Ludendorff, the brilliant and eccentric general who had become virtual dictator of Germany in 1916–1918. Hitler and

Ludendorff were odd allies, but they were united in their belief that Germany had been "stabbed in the back" in World War I and that only the military could restore Germany's national honor. Hitler, of course, was Austrian by birth, but by this point in his career he was quite able to gloss over that fact.

On November 18, 1923, Hitler and Ludendorff staged the Beer Hall Putsch in Munich, and they came within a hairbreadth of success. Only the providential arrival of some National Guardsmen prevented Hitler from success; he and Ludendorff were both captured and put on trial, while about twenty of their comrades died.

The 1920s and 1930s saw the rise of two great fascist dictators in Europe: Benito Mussolini of Italy (left) and Adolf Hitler of Germany.

How did Hitler parlay a five-year-prison sentence into celebrity and success?

This was his particular genius, or might even be called his magic: by defying logic and the traditional order of things, Hitler made himself look like a hero. In the trial, he appeared brave and resolute, refusing to compromise, while General Ludendorff tried to evade responsibility. Hitler received a five-year sentence, but he was released for good behavior after little more than six months. The day he walked out of that prison, he looked like a winner.

During his time in prison, Hitler wrote *Mein Kampf* ("My Struggle"). The book is a difficult read as one struggles over the turgid prose and endless recitations of personal sacrifice. However, *Mein Kampf* provides a road map for almost everything Hitler would subsequently attempt. He outlines in detail the need for more living space for the German people and the need to move eastward to eject the mindless barbarians of Russia. Little invective is employed against France, and Britain is, in some passages, held up as a model of modern-day society.

Did Hitler himself believe the racist supremacist ideas he espoused?

Almost certainly. His was a bizarre personality, shaped by odd twists and turns in the road of development, and by his thirties Hitler was completely convinced that the Germans were the best people in the world and that he had been chosen to lead them.

Hitler was on the rise by 1924, but he would not become Germany's leader until 1933. In the meantime, it seemed that the Western world would recover from World War I. This was the case until the Great Depression struck in 1932.

Where did the Great Depression begin?

It was an American phenomenon that slowly spread to other parts of the Western world. As early as the summer of 1932, financial analysts spoke of "overproduction" and "underconsumption" in the United States economy. These words would have meant little in the past, when all articles—clothing, food, transport—would quickly be snapped up. But the American consumer, in the summer of 1932, had enough. He had a car, a radio, a telephone, and perhaps a new home, and that seemed quite enough.

Political and social polling were in their infancy, and no one knew just when a major economic change would come, but it burst on the American stock market in the autumn of 1932. The first newspaper accounts were not too negative (one declared that "Wall Street lays an egg") but over the next few months, stock market investors kept pulling money out of the market, opting to keep what they possessed in cash. The market, therefore, lost more than two-thirds of its value, and the price-per-share of great corporations such as Radio City of America and General Motors declined dramatically. Had there been some other sort of crisis, something that required Americans to get moving again, the country would very likely have responded. But confronted by a shrinking economy, many Americans fell into a deep depression—both financially and otherwise.

How long did it take for the Great Depression to work its way to other countries?

The English had already been in an economic funk, made obvious by the Great Coal Strike of 1926. The Irish, who had recently attained nationhood, were in no mood to cooperate with the English or the Americans. The French, whose economy was a clever mixture of farming and manufacturing, took longer to be impacted by the Great Depression, but once there they remained mired. The Russians, who were no longer part of the capitalist Western world, rejoiced at that fact because their levels of employment and manufacturing output were not affected. But the country that suffered the worst was, predictably, Germany.

How long did it take the various nations to get out of the Great Depression?

The United States did not escape the Great Depression until a greater crisis—that of World War II—called on all its energies. Britain, Holland, Belgium, and Ireland mud-

Which generation of Germans was affected the most?

The German man or woman born around 1895. These people would have been nineteen when the Great War began, and, assuming they survived it, they would have been twenty-four when the Great Flu commenced. Assuming they survived the flu epidemic, they would have been twenty-nine when the runaway inflation of 1923 ruined their economy, and they would have been about forty when Hitler came into power. Given their experiences, it is quite likely that this generation of Germans and their children may have had a rather pessimistic view of the world.

dled through the 1930s, with many highly educated and skilled people going without jobs. Of all the major Western nations, however, it is clear that Hitler's Germany emerged from the depression the earliest and looked the best.

Hitler, who became the chancellor of Germany in 1933, correctly saw that the loss of war production materials hurt the German economy the most. He, therefore, brazenly defied the clauses of the Versailles Treaty, which prohibited Germany from rearming, and within two years of taking office, Hitler had the German economy well along the way to pre-1914 levels. The same could not be said of any of the Western democracies.

Was Hitler, then, really the kind of genius that many people often describe?

If so, it was a very limited type of genius, but he did have aspects of brilliance to him. Hitler possessed a fine intuitive mind, which, if coupled with sound logical thought, might have accounted for many successes. Early in his career, Hitler acted as if he were reasonable and could discuss matters, but the longer he was in power, the more wedded to one-man rule he became. If he had a kind of genius, it was the type that most leaders can do without.

Who played the bigger role during the 1930s: Hitler or Mussolini?

Both of these dictators were absolutely convinced that the other should follow his lead. In truth, Mussolini was in the lead until the year 1935, when he made the mistake of in-

vading Ethiopia. Though Italian tanks and flame-throwers crushed the Ethiopian resistance, the newsreels were, naturally, sympathetic to the latter, and as a result Mussolini's standing suffered. Hitler continued to consult with his Italian ally, but increasingly he made his own decisions. One of the few times the Germans and Italians cooperated effectively came in 1936, when the Spanish Civil War began.

We haven't heard much about Spain for a while. Had anything major taken place?

Spain had been on a downhill slope since the mid-eighteenth century. Following its defeat by the United States in 1898, Spain became insular. Its road system, factories, and commercial interests all languished during the first third of the twentieth century. Then, in 1936, a deadly civil war

Spanish dictator Francisco Franco was actually the most successful of the right-wing rulers in Europe, dominating his country until his death in 1975.

began, pitting Spanish nationalists against Spanish fascists, who were led by General Francisco Franco.

The Spanish Civil War appealed to people from all parts of the world. Young men in England and the United States were, generally speaking, firmly in favor of the nationalists, and perhaps 3,000 foreigners fought on that side. Germany and Italy both perceived that Franco would be very useful to them in future conflicts, so they backed him. It was thanks to German assistance that the Fascists were able to carry out the bombing of Guernica in 1937, the first city in the world to be bombed from the air.

The world seems to have been increasingly more dangerous. Who did Americans view as the number-one threat?

President Franklin D. Roosevelt—hereafter referred to as FDR—was convinced that Hitler represented the greatest danger, but the average American did not feel that way. There was some sympathy in America for the Germans, who were perceived as a gallant, though flawed, foe in World War I. If Hitler could bring the German economy back to its feet, that was well and good.

JAPAN AND CHINA

Why was Japan so eager to take on China?

Japan's relative strength in the 1930s was based on China's weakness, and the top Japanese leaders intended to keep things that way. In 1937, Japan provoked an incident at the Marco Polo Bridge between Manchuria and Japan and used it as a pretext for declaring war on China. Japan soon went much further, however, invading China and carrying out terrible outrages, such as the Sack of Nanking in 1938. It is estimated that 300,000 Chinese women may have been raped during that episode.

Japanese armies occupied much of the coastline of China, and some historians have labeled 1938—with the Marco Polo Bridge as the marker—as the beginning of World War II. To the observer at the time, however, it looked like an Asian war, with China and Japan battling for supremacy. Then, too, the average European observer was more worried about what Hitler and the Nazis were doing in Western Europe.

How did China respond to the "grab" by Imperial Japan?

Chinese, on the whole, loathed the Japanese, who they sometimes called the dwarf men. It was mystifying to China how such a small nation, with so few natural resources, could inflict so much punishment upon it. The answer, to be sure, was that Japan had jumped on the bandwagon of Western military technology and China had not.

Making matters worse, the Chinese were divided among themselves. The National Chinese Party called for unification and the preservation of a capitalist economy, while

It was a slow process. He was the son of traditional Chinese peasants who had become a school teacher. Nothing in his early background suggested he would become a revolutionary. By the mid-1920s, Mao had become a communist, however, and by 1933, he was leader of the Communist Party.

the Chinese Communist Party called for unification, ejection of the Japanese, and the overthrow of the capitalist economy. The issues were far larger than any personalities could encompass, but for many Chinese it came down to a choice between Chiang Kai-Shek, leader of the Nationalists, and Mao Zedong (1893–1976), leader of the Communists. To complicate matters even more, the two men were brothers-in-law, having married sisters.

When did Hitler make his first territorial grab?

In July 1936, German troops suddenly marched into the Rhineland, which had been established as a neutral zone, under French control. The French tamely withdrew, allowing German tanks and troops to occupy the vital industrial area known as the Ruhr. Through this one bloodless stroke, Hitler nearly doubled Germany's industrial capacity.

Mao Zedong was the leader of the Communists in China and would eventually oust the Nationalists, led by Chiang Kai-Shek.

The trauma of World War I remained strong in the French mind. They had lost 1.3 million men in the Great War from a population that was smaller than Germany's. Equally important, the French leaders of 1936 were obsessed with defensive thinking; they had already begun a massive building project intended to wall off any potential invasion. The so-called Maginot Line would eventually become a line of pillboxes and stationary defenses, but it would never extend all the way north to the Belgian border.

Could anyone have stopped Hitler at this point?

To do so required a joint British-French resolve, and this alliance simply did not exist at this time. France acted like a defeated country—instead of one of the victors of World

War I—and Britain was obsessed with keeping out of Continental wars. Franklin D. Roosevelt could have possibly led a concerted movement to block Hitler's aggressions, but to do so he needed a united country at his back, and that, too, simply did not exist.

We sometimes make too much of Hitler's tactical gifts, ascribing to him military skills that he possessed only in the vaguest sense. But as a strategist and a gambler, Hitler had few peers, and throughout the 1930s he outguessed his opponents time and again.

Where was Hitler's second territorial grab?

In 1937, Hitler announced that he would annex Austria, making it part of what he called "Greater Germany." To be sure, many Austrians—of whom German speakers predominated—welcomed the move; even so, it was a shock to see newsreels of German tanks moving rapidly through Austria to take over Vienna. Once again, however, Hitler guessed correctly. The former Allied nations were too weak—economically and otherwise—to interfere, and by the end of 1937, Austria had become part of what Hitler referred to as the "Third Reich."

Hitler had already accomplished more than anyone anticipated, but in 1938 he spoke of yet another acquisition. The western part of Czechoslovakia was German, he declared, by virtue of its many German speakers. He wished to add this territory to the Third Reich, saying that this was his "last territorial demand." As usual, Hitler mixed just enough truth in with the falsehood to make it palatable. There were some German-speaking Czechs who wished to join with Germany. But to add the Sudetenland to Germany would make the latter much too powerful, stripping the rest of Czechoslovakia of the natural defense provided by the mountainous areas located in the Sudetenland.

How did Hitler "shake down" British and French leaders?

He invited them to meet him in Munich, the capital of Bavaria. British Prime Minister Neville Chamberlain flew to the meeting (it was his first time in an airplane). Mussolini was also invited, but he played a minor role in the proceedings, which Hitler dominated through a combination of threats and theatricals.

Germany had suffered too much at the end of World War I, he argued, and the Allies owed it to Germany to allow it to regain its economic strength. Prime Minister Chamberlain actually agreed with this somewhat, because an economically weak Germany was very bad for the European economy as a whole. More important, however, was Chamberlain's view that the British people not be talked into a war over something that had happened in Eastern Europe. On this score, he was probably correct. Chamberlain, therefore, persuaded the French to abandon the Czechs, and, realizing that neither Britain nor France stood with them, the Czechs ceded the Sudetenland in the winter of 1938–1939.

Can this be labeled anything but a betrayal?

There is no other word to describe it. Britain and France both acted spinelessly through the 1930s, but this was their single worst performance. Making matters even worse,

Chamberlain attempted to sell the Munich agreement as a valuable diplomatic accord; landing in London, he held up a newspaper describing the event and declared, "I believe that this is peace in our time."

Chamberlain was not a fool, far from it. He was a typical English gentleman of that time, however, and as such he believed that a handshake with Adolf Hitler really meant something. He soon learned otherwise. In March 1939, Hitler seized the rest of Czechoslovakia, putting the lie to what he had said was his "last territorial demand." From that day forward, the British government acted differently, and when Hitler turned up the heat on Poland in the summer of 1939, Chamberlain was adamant that Britain stand behind the beleaguered nation.

Why did Hitler pick on Poland?

In a geographical sense, there was no one else left! Hitler had already absorbed the Rhineland, all of Austria, the Sudetenland, and then all the rest of Czechoslovakia. He had greatly expanded the size and power of Germany, but Poland remained a thorn in his side.

As usual, Hitler had to have a pretext, an excuse for invading his neighbor. He, therefore, declared that Poland had benefitted unfairly from the Versailles Treaty of 1919 and that there were German speakers within its borders (if there were some, they had long since become Poles). He also pointed to the infamous "Danzig Corridor," a stretch of Pol-

German soldiers reenact the removal of a Polish border crossing in this 1939 propaganda photo.

ish territory that blocked Germany's communications with East Prussia. There was just a smidgeon of truth, just enough that one could not dismiss Hitler's claims out of hand. But the British and French were very clear about their position: they guaranteed the security of Poland.

How many of Hitler's generals were with him in the summer of 1939?

Although many German generals survived World War II, rather few of them wrote comprehensive memoirs, which would illuminate our understanding. Our best guess is that most of the generals despised Hitler when he first won election as chancellor (they called him "the corporal" behind his back). Over time, however, many of the generals were persuaded by Hitler's remarkable run of success. Had he not been right about the British and French? Had he not almost doubled the size of Germany without the loss of a man? Those generals that still had doubts about Hitler knew, as well, that the SS was always on the lookout for traitors and disbelievers; even a general's rank did not make one immune to the SS.

How about the possibility of a two-front war?

That possibility was the one thing which might have prevented Hitler from taking the final step. He knew, all too well, that Imperial Germany had been exhausted in 1914–1917 by the strain of fighting simultaneously on two fronts. Hitler, typically, prepared a master-stroke to confound his foes.

On August 23, 1939, Hitler's top diplomatic aide arrived in Moscow to negotiate and then sign the "Non-Aggression Pact." It was hardly a statement of friendship; rather, Nazi Germany and the Soviet Union pledged not to fight each other, at least for the foreseeable future. Secret agreements were also reached concerning Poland. Stalin and the Soviet Union would stand by while Hitler attacked Poland, but Stalin reserved the right to invade Poland from the east. The two titanic powers, based on thoroughly different social and economic systems, therefore, planned the destruction of Poland.

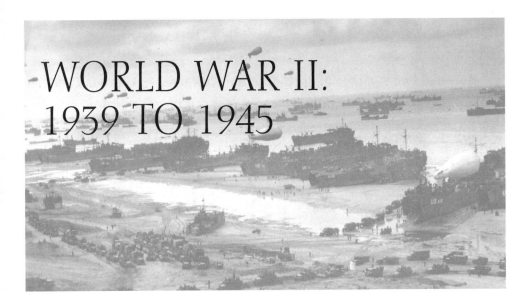

WORLD WAR II: 1939 TO 1945

When did World War II begin?

On September 1, 1939, when German planes strafed Polish infantry from the air. Hours later, German tanks crossed the border, invading Poland.

In spite of all the warnings and the anticipated invasion, the general sentiment was one of shock. French, Russians, Poles, Belgians, and even Germans were appalled by the beginning of another titanic war. That it would be widespread was universally expected, and the declarations of war started coming in shortly thereafter. France and Britain immediately declared war on Nazi Germany, which meant that peoples and nations as far off as Australia, New Zealand, Canada, Vietnam, and Algeria were also affected due to their colonial status.

How did Poland fare?

Very poorly. The Poles were ready for a resumption of World War I-type activities and were stunned when the Germans hit them with something completely different: lightning warfare (*blitzkrieg*). The Poles fought bravely and well, but they were outnumbered and outmaneuvered by the Nazis. Even Hitler was surprised by the speed and success of his early movements.

As the Nazis made great headway, Joseph Stalin grew nervous. He had anticipated a longer war, which would tie up the resources of both Poland and Germany. Seeing the way things were, Stalin sent Russian troops over Poland's other border. Worldwide opinion condemned this cynical move, but Stalin wanted to acquire territory. In a three-week campaign, his Russians took over the eastern third of Poland while Hitler's Nazis captured the western two-thirds. All was over in less than six weeks.

How had Hitler and his generals accomplished this?

Germany achieved extraordinary successes during the first couple of years of the war. Several factors account for the early victories.

First, the Germans were a highly cohesive, armed formation, men trained and dedicated to the idea that Germany was number one, and it was its destiny to rule (the famous song *Deutschland uber all* commemorates this idea). Second, and just as important, the Nazis were the first to use Lightning Warfare, which used a combination of tanks, jeeps, and fighter/bomber aircraft to attack the enemy. None of these weapons or techniques were extraordinary in themselves; rather, it was the combination of them, all at once, that overwhelmed the Poles. Third in importance was the leadership factor. Hitler was never as great a general, or commander, as he liked to think, but he did possess a keen intuition and often surmised where his enemies were weakest: both in military strength and morale. Even his generals, who called Hitler "the corporal" behind his back, were impressed with the easy victory over Poland.

How many men did the Allies have in the field?

In the autumn of 1939, France mobilized almost three million men, and Britain sent roughly 500,000 to France. Although there were lots of volunteers, both nations had to turn to conscription to mobilize these numbers. The 3.5 million Allied troops in France roughly equaled the Germans on the other side of the border. Given that the Allies were in a defensive position, it was likely they could hold out against any and all assaults.

The Germans, naturally, had other ideas. But in the autumn of 1939, they acted tamely. There were no offensives against France, and the Western Front roughly paralleled that of World War I, meaning that men dug deep trenches and awaited a change in circumstances. The Western Front was so peaceful that there was a football game between Germans and British on Christmas Day, 1939. Of course, this was the calm before the storm.

BATTLE OF FRANCE

Why did Hitler wait until the spring of 1940 to unleash his new onslaught?

His thinking was sound: it was better to attack when German tanks could move on solid ground rather than struggling through snow and mud. Then, too, Hitler was putting the finishing touches on what would be a remarkable set of plans and conquests.

Hitler was all too aware of what had happened to Imperial Germany in World War I, how it had been starved out by the Allied blockade and slowly worn down through attrition. He wanted to avoid any repetition of the mistakes made by Germany in World War I, partly by seizing so many extended territories that no one, not even the British Royal Navy, could possibly blockade them all. Therefore, in April 1940, Hitler set the Wehrmacht to work.

Which nation was first on the "hit list"?

Denmark, which bordered directly with Germany, had no strategic value or great resources, but Hitler wanted the Danes to become part of Germany's new European empire. The Danes collapsed in less than two days, and German forces took both the country and its borders with Norway. To the Danes' credit, however, this was one conquest that was not followed by a turnover of the Jews to the Nazis; throughout the entire war, Denmark successfully hid many Jews.

The conquest of Denmark was followed by a lightning strike to the north as German troops and transport vessels raced up the west coast of Norway. This was, and is, one of

German soldiers prepare two Panzer tanks during the 1940 Battle of France.

Were there any accepted "rules" for aerial war in 1940?

The League of Nations, whose task it was to assess these matters, had never addressed the issue of aerial bombing or the dangers posed to civilians. There were, quite literally, no rules of warfare regarding airstrikes or civilian casualties. And while Hitler took full advantage of the situation, the same can be argued for the British and Americans—who later pounded German cities to rubble—going much further than Hitler in the use of aerial bombings.

the world's most beautiful coastlines—known for its fjords—but in the spring of 1940 it was the scene of fierce battles between the Germans and Danes, with the British assisting the latter. Within six weeks, the Nazis had taken all of Norway, but the conquest came at a high price. Germany lost a number of destroyers and battle cruisers, some of which were never replaced. In terms of men and casualties, however, the conquest was well worth the price, so far as Hitler was concerned.

Was there any country in a position to stop the Nazis?

France seemed to be that nation. In the spring of 1940, the French had three million men under arms and more tanks—by a slight majority—than the Nazis. If France had moved quickly to threaten the German border while Germans went north to conquer Norway, the spring of 1940 might have taken on a very different complexion. But the French, as well as the British Expeditionary Force (BEF), stayed in their defensive positions, allowing Hitler to pick and choose his targets.

Late in April 1940, Hitler declared war on Holland and Belgium. Both nations had anticipated the attack and had done their best to prepare, but the Lowlands were an almost perfect geographic location for the Nazis; the rivers and trench systems which had been so effective in World War I presented few problems to the Nazis, who came with tanks and planes. Then, too, Hitler stepped up his brutality where civilians were concerned; he authorized a major Luftwaffe strike against the city of Rotterdam, which was nearly leveled. Holland's Queen Beatrix fled into exile in England.

Where did the Germans make their move against France?

France was protected by the Maginot Line, a series of walls, pillboxes, and bunkers that sheltered the nation's border with Germany. The Maginot Line was incomplete, however, and there was a major gap in its northeastern sector; then, too, it did not cover France's border with Belgium. Though much of the French army seemed secure within the Maginot Line, the same old danger that had bedeviled France in 1870 presented itself during the Battle of Sedan and in 1914 during the German march through Belgium. itself. Making matters worse, the French high command refused to believe that any significant

German attack would come from the Ardennes Forest, which was unsuitable for tanks. The French calculations were wrong on virtually every point.

Hitler did not know—nor could his generals—how relatively easy this conquest would be, but when the first German tanks poked their way through the Ardennes Forest, the German high command was elated. Hitler diverted practically all the Luftwaffe air attacks to one spot, the crossings of the River Meuse, with spectacular success. The first real penetration was on May 5, 1940; a week after that, the defenses in the north and northeast of France lay in ruins.

When did Winston Churchill come back into power?

On May 10, 1940, King George VI summoned Churchill to Buckingham Palace and asked him to form a new government. Churchill, who was sixty-seven, had been one of the few people to note Hitler's rise during the 1920s and understand the dangers he presented. Churchill accepted the great challenge before him, and in his first speech to the House of Commons he declared that "the struggle to defeat Hitler would be long and arduous." Churchill's honesty appealed to the British public. For years they had endured platitudes and rosy scenarios from their leaders; now they had a leader who told them to get ready to get their hands dirty. And in the very week that Churchill gave this speech, it became evident that the British Expeditionary Force (BEF) would have to come home.

What did Churchill say in his first speech for the House of Commons?

The Members of Parliament knew that the new prime minister would not take the situation lightly, but they did not anticipate the gravity with which he addressed them or the confidence he expressed that Britain, in the end, would prevail.

In this first speech to Parliament, Churchill declared: "I would say to the House, as I said to those who have joined this government, that I have nothing to offer but blood, toil, tears, and sweat. We have before us an ordeal of the most grievous kind."

How bad was the situation in Belgium in northern France?

It was so bad that the BEF was effectively cut off from its French ally. Holland and Belgium had nearly collapsed, and it was possible that the BEF would be forced to surrender. Churchill, clearly, would move heaven and earth to prevent this, but it

Great Britain's Prime Minister Winston Churchill is considered to be one of the finest leaders of the twentieth century.

was the actions of men and women on the water that really made the difference: they were the ones that made possible the Miracle of Dunkirk.

By May 25, 1940, British soldiers were streaming into the town of Dunkirk and setting up tents on the nearby beaches. Roughly 800 British vessels, ranging from battleships to pleasure yachts, became involved in a heroic effort to rescue these men and get them home before France fell, and the full weight of the Nazi forces turned against them. Just how many people traveled on those vessels to France is difficult to say, but we know that they rescued roughly 210,000 British and 105,000 French troops over ten days.

Why did Hitler not send in his tanks to destroy the BEF on the beaches?

He should have. This was one of the few moments when caution overrode risk taking, where Hitler was concerned. Even he was astonished at the success of his attacks on Belgium, Holland, and northern France, and he wished to consolidate the gains that had been made. Even so, Hitler made his biggest mistake listening to Air Marshal Hermann Goering, who declared that the Luftwaffe could finish off the British right where they stood, on the beaches. Not for the last time did Hitler make the mistake of listening too credulously to Goering, who was ever anxious to please.

The German bombers did kill a few hundred British at Dunkirk, but that was nothing compared to what the Nazis might have done if the tanks had been sent. The BEF left behind all its heavy guns, all its baggage and equipment. But when those first British soldiers got off the vessels and stood on English soil, they were hailed as conquerors. Churchill gave a memorable speech, declaring that wars were not won by retreats, but that this particular retreat was vital to the survival of the British Empire.

What, meanwhile, had happened in the Battle for France?

It was proceeding toward a lamentable conclusion. Some French units stood and fought bravely right up to the end, while others completely folded. The Germans entered Paris on June 14, 1940. A photograph of a Parisian watching with tears on his face as the Nazis march up the Champs Elysees is an iconic representation of this momentous event.

The French leaders asked for terms, and Hitler demanded that they meet with him at Compiegne in the same railroad car in which German representatives had been forced to sign the armistice on November 11, 1918. After the signing, Hitler performed a jig. He was clearly on top of the world.

What was agreed to in the surrender ceremony?

Some of the details were to be worked out later, but in essence, the northern half of France became part of the Nazi empire while most of the southern half became known as Vichy France, a collaborator state. To humiliate the French even further, the Germans chose Marshal Henri Pétain—the victor of the Battle of Verdun in 1916—to lead the puppet regime of Vichy.

Was de Gaulle truly as haughty as he appeared?

Yes. Two of the best historians of British–French relations—Robert and Isabelle Toombs—conclude that while Winston Churchill was an Englishman who often acted French (complete with a love of the good life), de Gaulle was a Frenchman who seemed to embody the worst aspects of British arrogance. Much of this had to do with de Gaulle's early life; he was raised in a strict Roman Catholic family which detested the Third Republic and looked back to earlier times as those which were good for France.

Petain was not pleased, but he had long believed that his country could not survive another war on the size and scale of 1914–1918. He agreed to serve as president of Vichy France and therefore became the most infamous of all collaborators. Hitler's success now seemed complete.

How did Charles de Gaulle suddenly become the face, and voice, of Free France?

De Gaulle (1890–1970) was a recently appointed brigadier-general in the French armored corps. He had been a young soldier during World War I, when, captured by the Germans at Verdun, he spent years as a prisoner of war (POW). He had no intention of repeating the experience, and when Prime Minister Paul Reynaud offered him

Charles de Gaulle served as military leader of the free French during World War II and would later serve as his country's president from 1958 to 1969.

the position of assistant secretary of state for military affairs, he jumped at the opportunity. De Gaulle had previously been a protégé of Marshal Petain, and it doubtless pained him greatly to see Petain extend the olive branch to the Germans. De Gaulle crossed the English Channel on June 17, 1940, and the following day he made a memorable address on the BBC (British Broadcasting Service).

"Has the last word been said? Must hope disappear? Is defeat final?" The answer to all three of these questions was a resounding "No!" France would fight on in the person of those that refused to collaborate, de Gaulle asserted, and he asked all Free French persons to meet with him in London. Quite remarkably, the reins of whatever government still existed had been seized by one man.

What did Churchill say in his radio broadcast?

On the same day—June 18, 1940—that de Gaulle spoke to the Free French community, Winston Churchill gave one of his most memorable broadcasts to the British people. "The battle of France is over. I expect that the battle of Britain is about to begin.... Let us therefore brace ourselves to our duty and so bear ourselves that if the British Commonwealth and Empire lasts for a thousand years, men will still say, 'This was their finest hour.'"

Churchill did not fully realize that the worst danger had already passed. The moment for a swift German cross-Channel invasion had been in the ten days or two weeks following the evacuation of Dunkirk.

Could Britain and France, which had so often been enemies, truly have come together?

Not in 1940. There was still too much mutual mistrust. The British frequently complained that the French made poor allies, and the French returned the favor, labeling England "perfidious Albion." As it turned out, the situation resolved in the worst way possible: with a defeatist French government collaborating with the Nazis and a Free French government feuding with Britain.

To what extent had Hitler succeeded in the summer of 1940?

The best way to express this is to compare his efforts with those of Kaiser Wilhelm II, the German leader in World War I.

From 1914 to 1918, Germany lost three million men, by a conservative estimate, and it never conquered France. In 1916–1918, Germany was under continuous naval blockade, now made impossible by the conquest of Norway. And, in 1917–1918, the German people suffered from low morale because of the lack of food and the news of Allied victories. By contrast, in 1939–1940, Hitler had conquered Poland, Denmark, Norway, the Netherlands, and France, accomplishing all this with a loss of about 200,000 Germans. No one would discount the loss of so many men, but his success stands in sharp contrast to that of the Kaiser.

Was Hitler ready to call it quits?

Yes. As much as he wanted to conquer England, Hitler did not believe it was the proper time. He, therefore, made a radio address, saying he saw no reason for the war to continue. This was but the opening salvo in a series of radio broadcasts, with Hitler and Churchill taunting and defying each other. Churchill spurned the Nazi effort to make peace.

When did Italy enter the war?

In June 1940. Benito Mussolini waited until it was obvious France would fall and then declared war on that nation. Italy made some gains on the northern Mediterranean coast and

Who was the better speaker: Hitler or Churchill?

It is actually a four-way contest between Churchill, Hitler, de Gaulle, and Franklin D. Roosevelt. All four men had terrific voices, tailor made for radio, but the effort to say which was "better" or "best" is generally futile. If one listens and thinks in German, then Hitler's shrill words seemed the best. If one likes to hear the king's English, pronounced in heavy, dramatic tones, then Churchill clearly comes off as number one. If one is accustomed to French, de Gaulle's words seemed the most apt. And if one listens and speaks in American English, it is perfectly clear that Franklin D. Roosevelt had the best radio voice.

became Nazi Germany's ally. Once again, the observer can only marvel at Hitler's success. In one short year he had dismantled all of Britain's allies, while gaining one for himself.

The only negative, from the Nazi point of view, was that the United States inched closer to entering the war. Franklin D. Roosevelt made the most of Italy's entry, declaring that a cynical aggressor had stuck his knife in the back of an unsuspecting nation. Many upper-class Americans, including FDR, had vacationed in France at some point in their lives; they grieved to learn that beloved spots such as Chamonix, Notre-Dame, and Chartres were now under Nazi or Italian control.

Could Hitler have conquered England?

That, of course, is the sixty-four-million-dollar question. By August 1940, when he set about doing so in earnest, it was already too late. Had he struck in June, immediately after the collapse of France, he might well have succeeded.

To this point, the late summer of 1940, Hitler had called it right about nine times out of ten. He had consistently outguessed, outmaneuvered, and outclassed his Allied foes. From this point forward, he would commit numerous errors, however, and one of the first was his belief that the German Air Force could conquer Britain. Air Marshal Hermann Goering assured Hitler that the Luftwaffe could pound the British into submission, and thus Operation Sea Lion involved relatively few naval or ground forces.

SO MANY, SO MUCH, SO FEW

Who won the opening rounds of the air war over southern England?

The Luftwaffe. When the struggle commenced in earnest in September 1940, the Germans had more planes and more well-trained pilots. In the first weeks, Goering directed his pilots to strike at the British air fields, which were often grassy rather than made of tar. Many British planes were destroyed on the ground, and it looked as if Hitler had once again guessed correctly. When a handful of British planes snuck though the German defenses to drop a handful of bombs on Berlin, Hitler altered his plans.

Vowing to reduce British cities to rubble, Hitler and Goering sent the Luftwaffe to attack London, as well as more remote places such as Coventry. The Germans achieved considerable success, killing many people and destroying many buildings, but each air strike raised the British morale. There was something intensely stubborn about a British person under fire, and the Londoners of 1940 would not submit, even if they had to take to the subway tunnels every night.

How close did the Germans come to success?

There was a three-week window in which they might have prevailed. Once they turned their attention to the British cities, however, the British Royal Air Force began to recover. First it trained more pilots, then it pioneered in the use of radar, and by November it was winning the dogfights in the skies.

Hitler was disappointed, but he was already thinking about his eventual attack on Russia. When he cancelled Operation Sea Lion in November 1940, he had suffered his first setback, but his power—on the map—still looked overwhelming.

FDR'S AMERICANS

What was so remarkable about Franklin D. Roosevelt?

He was a patrician to his fingertips, a person who had experienced much of the best that life had to offer: private schools, tutors, nannies, and many trips overseas. But he was also a cripple, a person who could not stand on his feet as a result of a bout with polio. This combination made him a most effective political leader: someone who knew the best and worst life had to offer.

By the autumn of 1940, FDR still had not persuaded his fellow Americans to enter the war. He inched a little closer all the time, but he had to win election to a third, unprecedented term as president. FDR won the election of 1940 in good style and immediately upped the pressure on his propagandists. He needed to bring the United States into the war to assist Great Britain.

How many Americans were drafted?

One thing FDR was able to persuade his fellow Americans of was the necessity for a new military draft (to make it more palatable, he called it the "Selective Service"). In 1939, the United States had a peacetime army of only about 130,000, many of whom had never seen combat. FDR worked hard to change this, and in October 1940, the first lottery numbers were drawn. FDR made it plain that his intention was to have two million men in uniform within a year's time.

Little resistance was offered either by the press or the draftees themselves. A majority of Americans by now, had quietly accepted that they would be needed in some capacity before the war was over. Just how many sacrifices would be required was not yet apparent.

What was Lend-Lease?

Even before winning the election of 1940, FDR announced the start of Lend-Lease, a program under which aging American naval ships were lent to the British and U.S. coal bases throughout the Atlantic were made available to British ships.

FDR also met Winston Churchill off the coast of Newfoundland in the summer of 1940. The two men who shared many things, including a love of the written word, composed the Atlantic Charter, an informal alliance of the peoples of the North Atlantic. FDR and Churchill made an interesting pair: the middle-aged American who looked strong but was actually an invalid, and the rather old, grumpy, and run-down British prime minister. No one would have expected in 1941 that Churchill would outlive FDR.

What was the American public attitude toward Japan?

FDR's attention was so concentrated on Hitler's Germany that he sometimes lost sight of the dangers posed by Imperial Japan. He did not share the rather ugly racism expressed by many Americans in 1941, but FDR may well have believed the Japanese too clumsy and backward to attempt anything serious against the United States. He and his fellow citizens were mistaken.

In the fifty years prior to World War II, Japan had made greater strides, proportionally speaking, than any other power in the world. Japan had progressed from a nation defended by the swords of samurai warriors into one that used tanks, jeeps, planes, and battleships. All this technological change had not altered an important Japanese calculation, however; they believed in striking the first blow and doing so with a vengeance.

What did FDR do about the threat from Japan?

By the spring of 1941, FDR acknowledged that Japan did present a threat, and in the summer of that year he unilaterally cut off all oil shipments from American companies to Japan. FDR had grown up in the age of coal, an item that was still quite abundant. He also governed a nation that, in 1941, possessed surpluses of both coal and oil. Japan, on the other hand, lived or died by oil and coal shipments from elsewhere. Very likely, the American oil embargo forced Japan to take the plunge to war. Before it could do so, however, Germany struck.

The thirty-second president of the United States, Franklin Delano Roosevelt, was also the only president elected four times to the nation's highest office.

HUNT FOR THE *BISMARCK*

What was Hitler's approach to war at sea?

He freely confessed to members of his staff that he was a hero on land and a coward at sea. Unlike Kaiser Wilhelm II, who had spent much time on yachts and warships, Hitler was very much a landsman, or what we might call a landlubber. Even so, he had built up Germany's navy in the years prior to the war, and he was especially proud of the *Bismarck*, an enormous battleship which had been laid down in the keel yards a few years earlier. The *Bismarck* was launched on February 14, 1939, meaning that she was just barely operational when the war began. The British Royal Navy quickly established defensive lines and an outer blockade, similar to what it had done in World War I, and Battleship *Bismarck* was locked in.

When did *Bismarck* venture into the North Sea?

On May 20, 1941, *Bismarck* and the battle cruiser *Prinz Eugene* both came out of Wilhelmenshaven looking for soft targets. Their commands came not from Hitler or anyone at army headquarters, but rather from navy personnel who were weary of seeing the German navy stay in port. Once Hitler learned of the sortie, he almost begged his navy men to bring the ships back.

The German battleship *Bismarck* was one of the largest ships of its day, carrying a crew of over 2,000 enlisted men and officers. It sank the Royal Navy's HMS *Hood* and in 1941 was destroyed in the North Atlantic by the British fleet.

On May 21, 1941, *Bismarck* fought an uneven half-hour battle against HMS *Hood*. Once the pride of the Royal Navy, the *Hood* was neither very seaworthy and nor was her gun deck at its best. A shell from *Bismarck* crashed into the forward deck of the *Hood*, seconds later there was a terrific explosion, and more than 1,000 British sailors practically disappeared in smoke.

Why didn't the *Bismarck* head straight home?

She had come so far into the North Sea that it made more sense, at this point, to stay in open waters and then head for any of the German-controlled ports of France. *Bismarck* cruised for the next six days without finding any other targets; what she and her men did not know was that the British Admiralty had dropped everything in a frantic attempt to locate and sink the *Bismarck*. More than sailors' lives were on the line; the Royal Navy had to demonstrate she was still mistress of the seas.

A true flotilla of British ships caught up with the *Bismarck* on the morning of May 28, 1941 (her rudder had been damaged in the battle with the *Hood*, causing her to lose speed). The British opened fire, and within thirty minutes, *Bismarck* was a smoking wreck. Many sailors jumped in the water before the explosion, which killed nearly 1,500 Germans. Perhaps 300 others were picked up by British boats and went into captivity. The sinking of the Bismarck was, for the British, one of the crucial moments of 1941; had the Royal Navy failed, the damage to British prestige would have been immense.

OPERATION BARBAROSSA

When did Hitler make the decision to attack the Soviet Union?

For those who have read *Mein Kampf* ("My Struggle"), it is apparent that Hitler had had this in mind for almost twenty years. Though he disliked the French and envied the

British, Hitler always saw the Russians—Czarist, Communist, or otherwise—as the great foes of his National Socialist state. His intention was to conquer all of Russia, establish control over the so-called "World Island," and make the surviving Russians into industrial slaves for the Nazi regime.

Perhaps it was for this reason that Hitler code-named his invasion "Operation Barbarossa." Perhaps he thought of the crusades of the Teutonic Knights and other operations against the Slavic peoples to the east. Even so, it was a terrible mistake to name the invasion after Frederick Barbarossa. Also known as Frederick II, Holy Roman Emperor, this German leader had *drowned* while on crusade in 1191.

When was the Nazi invasion of Russia supposed to begin?

Hitler wanted to move on April 15 or April 20, 1941, but the operations of his Italian ally slowed him down. Without informing Hitler beforehand, Mussolini sent Italian troops into northern Greece, where they became bogged down in a war to oust the king and native government. Hitler did not wish to see his ally fail; he, therefore, put off Operation Barbarossa for a few weeks while German airplanes and parachutists took over much of Greece. The campaign was yet another vindication of the Nazi war machine. The Greek government and its British advisers fled south, taking refuge on the island of Crete.

When did the Nazis pursue the British to Crete?

In May 1941, Hitler approved a major drop of paratroopers to seize the Island of Crete. Just seventy miles south of mainland Greece, Crete seemed invulnerable, until the Nazis sent in a great number of paratroops. The German invasion of Crete was a textbook study of how to conduct a campaign in every respect but one. A great many paratroopers lost their lives, depriving the Nazis of an important section of the army destined for Russia.

Even so, the record of Nazi victories was, by this point, very long. In 1941, Hitler had an impressive track record of victories that spanned over five years. He had taken the Rhineland, Austria, and Czechoslovakia without having to fire a shot. He had conquered Poland, Denmark, Norway, Holland, Belgium, and France for a total of less than 100,000 Germans killed. The time had come, Hitler decided, to strike the Soviet Union.

A Russian tank departs Leningrad for the front in this 1942 photograph.

When did the Nazi invasion of Russia commence?

On June 22, 1941, 129 years after Napoleon's invasion, the Nazis flooded across the border. They took the Russians by surprise, destroying many planes on the ground. By an odd coincidence, this was also the day that a group of Russian archaeologists exhumed the body of Tamerlane (*Timur the Lame*). They confirmed many aspects of his body and appearance, but their actions also gave new life to an old legend. It had often been claimed that if Tamerlane's body came out of the ground, a disaster even greater than those he had performed would befall the world.

Why was Stalin—as well as his people—so surprised?

There was every reason for him *not* to have been surprised. Stalin had plenty of intelligence—some from his own spies and some from British agents—that the Germans were up to something big. These pieces of intelligence did not persuade the Russian leader, however. In his self-imposed isolation, he seems to have believed Russia was too vast a nation to be threatened, even by Nazi Germany.

As a result, the Germans practiced their *blitzkrieg* (lightning warfare) with great success. They covered as much as forty miles a day, advancing rapidly into the Russian heartland. Thousands, even hundreds of thousands, of prisoners were taken in the opening weeks. And it was in their treatment of these prisoners that the Nazi invasion began to show its weakness.

How successful were the Nazis in the opening weeks of Operation Barbarossa?

Their success was simply stunning. Tanks advanced swiftly, while the Luftwaffe ruled the skies, eliminating one-quarter of the Soviet air force within the first week. By mid-July, Hitler exulted that the war was as good as won, and there was something like truth to the assertion.

Something like the truth, but not the whole truth. By mid-August, the top Nazi leaders detected a stiffening of the Russian resolve. One leading general gloomily noted in his diary that he had believed, at the outset, that the Russians had 240 infantry divisions. Now it seemed there were closer to 360. These misgivings were kept from the public, however; all that the average German citizen knew was that the Wermarcht was achieving wonders in Russia.

Why was Hitler so brutal to the Slavic peoples?

Regardless of whether they were Ukrainian, Bello-Russians, or pure Russians, Hitler wanted them dead. Had he been more generous in his treatment of these people, millions of Russians who were discontent with Stalin's rule might have joined him. Witnessing the murder that was routinely performed in the German prison camps, the Russians decided that the devil they knew (Stalin) was better than the one they did not.

Hitler had not behaved this way toward the conquered French, Dutch, or Norwegians. He seems to have held a special animus toward anyone who came from the east.

Was Hitler's loathing of Eastern European peoples the same as his hatred of the Jews?

The two were connected. Hitler had a mania where the mixing of blood was concerned. He held a mystical, and mistaken, belief that pure-blooded Germans descended from the ancient Aryans, who had overrun much of the Middle East and Central Asia in the twentieth century B.C.E. As to his sentiments regarding the Jews, the source still remains mysterious. There was plenty of anti-Semitism in the Austria of Hitler's youth, but most of it did not extend to the notion of killing all the Jews.

In the summer of 1941, his success was so spectacular that he could afford to ignore those Russians who wished to join him, but this would not always be the case.

How close did the Germans come to victory in the summer of 1941?

To the German tank commanders, it was apparent that they had won the war on the Eastern Front. On almost every occasion, the German tank columns defeated their Russian counterparts, and each move farther east resulted in the taking of more prisoners. Given that the Luftwaffe controlled most of the skies on the Eastern Front, the war seemed as good as won.

To the British, observing the situation from the outside, the outcome was not so clear-cut. That the Germans were winning in grand style was obvious, but no one knew whether they would reach Moscow in 1941. And to the American citizen, listening to the radio 5,000 miles away, the whole scene appeared barbaric: two great military titans bashing each other.

What was Stalin's morale like during the autumn of 1941?

He nearly broke under the pressure. He may even have suffered a mild heart attack. But once the crisis in October passed, Stalin buckled down to the immense task that lay before him. Where he had previously considered abandoning Moscow, he now forced thousands of Muscovites—many of them women—to dig enormous trenches for miles on the western side of the city as tank traps for the Germans.

Stalin and Churchill were in constant contact, but theirs was never a comfortable alliance. When Stalin made too many demands for materiel, Churchill replied that the Soviet Union had not, until June 1941, cared whether Great Britain lived or died. He could not rush everything to the Russians' disposal, at least not right away.

Who "blew it" in the autumn of 1941?

Hitler. His tank columns were within 150 miles of Moscow with little except hard, dry ground in between when he ordered most of them to turn around in order to capture the Russian city of Kiev. The operation was a huge success and 700,000 Russians were taken prisoner, but the weeks of excellent summer had disappeared.

Hitler also did not know that Stalin had relocated large sections of Soviet industry, including entire factories, to the eastern side of the Ural Mountains. This allowed the Russians to produce tanks and planes at a spectacular rate. At the same time, Stalin had called in reserves from as far off as Siberia. None of this was apparent to the Nazis, who only knew that every time they fought the Russians, they won.

How close did the Germans come to Moscow?

On December 5, 1941, a tiny group of German tanks made it to the suburb of Khimki, about eight miles shy of the central city. Opening the hoods of their tanks, the men could make out the spires of the Kremlin. They had done it!

That was as close as the Germans ever came to Moscow, however. Much as Richard the Lionheart had withdrawn from his Crusade within sight of Jerusalem, the Germans were about to be ejected from their farthest advance.

What was the weather like when the Nazis resumed their advance toward Moscow?

The dust of summer gave way to the chill of autumn, but Hitler's troops were not, like Napoleon's, vulnerable to every chance in the weather. Heavy autumnal rains did slow

Russians duck under fire near Moscow as the Germans came perilously close to taking the city. However, Hitler decided to withdraw and capture the city of Kiev instead.

up the advance, however, and by November the Germans were strained in every category. They also did not know that a group of top German war statisticians had already determined that the Third Reich had to achieve victory in 1941 or 1942, that a prolonged war of attrition would surely end in German defeat.

For a time, it seemed as if Hitler could have his cake and eat it too. The panzers threaded their way through the treacherous conditions, with the commanders claiming Moscow would be the last effort. Once the Russian capital fell, the communications and control would disappear. But the cold weather was the last part of the equation, and by early December, some German tank leaders claimed it was forty degrees below zero.

In what week was the war lost?

One can, of course, debate and discuss this claim. To this writer, however, the week of December 5–12, 1941, was clearly when the Germans lost the war.

On December 5, the Germans came close to downtown Moscow. That night, the weather took a decided turn for the worse, with many Germans suffering from the cold. The next day, December 6, the Russians counterattacked all along the line, causing thousands of casualties to their opponents. And the day after, December 7, the Japanese attacked Pearl Harbor. As if all this was not bad enough, on December 11, Hitler declared war on the United States, even though his alliance with Japan did not require him to do so. In one short week, Nazi Germany went from being inches from victory to being at war with three great powers: Imperial Britain, Communist Russia, *and* the United States. If December 7, 1941, was, as FDR declared, a date which shall live in infamy, then it was also the week that determined who had lost the war.

TORA, TORA, TORA!

When did Imperial Japan decide to attack the United States?

The Japanese were—and are—excellent at keeping their records private and secret. We can surmise that they were moving in the direction of war by the spring of 1941, but the American oil embargo likely pushed them further. Even so, it required both the plans of the military leaders and the final decision of the emperor.

Hirohito was not a pacifist; had he been one, the Japanese would never have invaded China in 1937. He was a student of *realpolitik*, however, and taking on the United States seemed an enormous endeavor. Hirohito was influenced by the top military leaders, including Tojo, but he would have done better to heed the advice of Admiral Isoroku Yamamoto. Having studied at Harvard and served as a naval attaché, Yamamoto understood the manufacturing power of the United States. When asked if he could win the war, the Japanese admiral told his superiors that he could make it "interesting" for a year or two, but he refused to comment beyond that point.

Didn't the Japanese understand the enormous gamble they were taking?

Most of them did. They believed they had no choice, however. FDR's embargo on the sale of oil to Japan was already cutting into their potential to wage war, and if they complied with the American demand to evacuate their army from China, Japan would have spent almost five years engaged in a conflict with nothing to show for it. The top Japanese leader, therefore, decided war with America was their best option.

One thing the Japanese leaders did not understand was the American character. Just as many Americans mistakenly believed the Japanese were "squint-eyed" people who could not handle modern technology, many Japanese believed the Americans were soft materialists who could not handle the rigors of war. Both peoples were mistaken about the other.

How did Japan achieve such complete surprise at Pearl Harbor?

By the most slender of margins: a matter of minutes. The Japanese task force sailed from the Kurile Islands on November 25, 1941, and maintained complete radio silence during its 2,500-mile trek across the eastern Pacific. Led by Admiral Chuichi Nagumo (1887–1944), the task force was supervised from a distance by Admiral Isoruku Yamamoto, architect of the audacious plan.

The Japanese naval leaders knew they had to maintain secrecy and to achieve a knockout blow for any of their hopes to mature. Japanese air pilots were trained down to the last detail; most of them had memorized the names and statistics of the fleet that lay in Battleship Row at Pearl Harbor. Even so, everything had to come off perfectly in the timing, or else it would all be for naught.

How alert were the Americans to a possible threat from Japan?

Ever since FDR had placed the embargo on oil supplies to Japan, leaders of the U.S. Army and Navy had been concerned that Japan might attack; few of those leaders suspected such an audacious Japanese plan, however. As to the Americans—soldiers, sailors, and Marines—they knew that they would one day fight the Japanese, but they were not much concerned by the prospect. A high level of ignorance about Japan and its people prevailed in the American public, who believed that the Japanese were incapable of mounting a major offensive. There were even jokes, current in the U.S. armed forces, that the Japanese were too "squinty-eyed" to pilot high-performance airplanes.

FDR was certainly concerned. He monitored events closely, and just days before the Japanese attack he sent a personal appeal to Emperor Hirohito; it went unanswered. Then, too, the U.S. State Department monitored the Japanese Embassy and had, unbeknownst to the Japanese, broken several of Japan's diplomatic codes. That "something was up" was obvious, but just what it might be remained unknown.

Where were the major U.S. leaders on the morning of December 7, 1941?

FDR was having brunch with Edward R. Murrow—the CBS broadcaster—and his wife. General George C. Marshall, chairman of the Joint Chief of Staff, was out for a long horseback ride, as was his Sunday custom. Admiral Ernest King was monitoring developments but did not know that one of the most important messages to the naval leaders at Pearl Harbor had been sent by Western Union rather than the traditional Navy teletype.

Had the Japanese attack come even three hours later, it might well have been beaten off by a resounding U.S. defense. The Japanese, however, had laid their plans carefully, and when their planes took off from the decks of five aircraft carriers at 5:20 A.M., they had the advantage of complete surprise. Even so, there was the possibility that a small U.S. Army radar station, at a northern point on Oahu, might detect the incoming Japanese planes.

Why did radar let the Americans down on December 7, 1941?

The technology did not do so. Two U.S. soldiers manning the radar location quickly radioed in to Pearl Harbor that blips had appeared on the screen. A junior lieutenant curtly informed them that a flight of B-17s was expected from California and that they should therefore pay no attention (amazingly, the lieutenant did not realize that those planes would have come from the southwest!). The detection was of no value, therefore, and when the first line of Japanese fighter and bomber planes descended, they caught the U.S. Navy completely off-guard.

One hundred and eighty Japanese planes descended from the sky, dropped low, and delivered their payloads two or three at a time. The devastation was almost universal, but the heaviest, and best-timed, bombs were dropped on the vessels of Battleship Row. The pride of the U.S. Pacific Fleet, seven heavy battleships, were lined up like sitting targets for the Japanese, who had planned every move.

How bad was the confusion and mayhem?

In all of American military history, there is no parallel to what happened at Pearl Harbor (the attacks of September 11, 2001 were primarily aimed at civilian targets). At least

The destroyed U.S.S. *Arizona* in Pearl Harbor three days after the Japanese attack on December 7, 1941.

> ## We all know that the Japanese scored "big" at Pearl Harbor. But what did they miss?
>
> Three U.S. aircraft carriers were out at sea, and the Japanese cannot be faulted for failing to hit them. The major Japanese mistake, however—and it was a big one—was in failing to hit the naval petroleum reserve, located in large storage tanks. Had the 4.5 million barrels of oil been hit and destroyed, it might have taken the U.S. Navy another six months, even a year possibly, to mount a comeback in the Pacific. War often turns on seemingly small decisions; in retrospect, the Japanese failure to launch that third wave of bombers seems like a very big error.

200 American aircraft were destroyed right on the ground; the Navy had chosen to park them wingtip to wingtip to prevent minor damage from hoodlums. A few American planes did scramble, and a handful of pilots fought the Japanese relentlessly, but it was a thoroughly unequal contest. By the time the second wave of Japanese bombers came forty minutes later, the attack was already a major success. The second wave of planes dropped their payloads, and as the Japanese planes turned for "home" (the decks of their carriers), Pearl Harbor was a smoking ruin.

The Americans were, for the most part, still too stunned to act. There were a handful of outstanding heroes that day, including the African-American messmate Dorie Miller, who valiantly manned an anti-aircraft gun, even though he had never been trained in the art. But for the most part, the Americans were simply crushed by the events of the day. And had the Japanese launched a third wave of bombers—as was within their power—the devastation might have been even worse.

What was the American death toll at Pearl Harbor?

Roughly 2,400 servicemen were killed outright and another 1,200 wounded. About 260 American planes were destroyed, and another one hundred or so were badly damaged. All seven battleships were either sunk or severely damaged. Japan had delivered an enormous, though not a knockout, blow.

What was the response to the attack on Pearl Harbor in Washington, D.C.?

FDR went before both Houses of Congress a day later and described December 7, 1941, as a "date which shall live in infamy." He asked for, and received, a declaration of war against Imperial Japan. The Senate vote was unanimous; in the House, there was one vote against, cast by Jeannette Rankin of Montana, who had previously voted against American entry to World War I.

The response in the American public was immediate and overwhelming. The great majority of Americans condemned the Japanese as "dirty bastards" and vowed revenge.

Though the war would go on for nearly four years, the Americans always saved their choicest epithets and greatest anger for the Japanese.

How did Hitler seal his own fate following the Japanese attack on Pearl Harbor?

Hitler's treaty of alliance with Japan was largely defensive in nature. It did not require him to go to war if Japan were the aggressor. Amazingly, however, on December 11, 1941, Hitler declared war on the United States.

Generation after generation of Americans have noted the immense error in Hitler's judgment. Given that he could not force the British to surrender, and given that he was now locked into an immense one-on-one contest with the Russians, why on earth did he declare war on the United States? The simple answer is that those whom the gods have decided to destroy, they first make insane. And so Hitler's decision was simply insane.

Could Japan have won the war in the Pacific?

No. The home islands of Japan simply did not have enough men and materiel to defeat the United States in a prolonged contest. But given the heroic, self-sacrificing attitude of many of their soldiers, sailors, and pilots, the Japanese could have made it a longer and harder war if they had pressed their advantage immediately after the victory at Pearl Harbor.

GERMANY FIRST

How well, or poorly, did America and Britain coordinate their efforts?

Even before Pearl Harbor, the United States and Great Britain had experimented with conducting joint war plans; this process now accelerated greatly. In the first major meetings between policymakers and strategists, it was agreed that the Allies—who now included America, Britain, and the Soviet Union—would concentrate on "Germany First."

Even though Japan had attacked at Pearl Harbor, FDR, Churchill, and others were convinced that Germany presented the greater threat. The Japanese could overrun large sections of the Pacific, but they did not—at least at the moment—have the capacity for making new types of weapons. Germany, by contrast, was feverishly involved in rocket experiments. Knowing this, the Allies agreed to concentrate on Germany. This did not mean that the going was easy, however.

How did the American public react, or respond, to the attack on Pearl Harbor?

One has only to put oneself in the shoes of the typical blue-collar American of that time. He, or she, had either been unemployed or underemployed for almost a decade, during which his savings—as well as his aspiration—had been reduced. Now, suddenly, there was both an unprovoked war—in which the enemy had struck first—and the opportunity for full-time employment, either in the U.S. military or any of the defense-related industries. It comes as no surprise, therefore, that the average American, who was enraged at the "Japs" and angry with the "Krauts," would jump at the opportunity.

BATTLE FOR NORTH AFRICA

Who was Rommel, and why does such a mystique surround him?

Field Marshal Erwin Rommel was a brilliant and slightly eccentric German panzer commander. During the Battle for France, he served with great distinction, driving far ahead in a Volkswagen to radio enemy positions back to his men.

In 1941, Rommel was sent with a small German force to back up the Italians, who were experiencing great difficulties. The British operating from bases in Egypt routinely defeated the Italians, but it was a different matter when they faced Rommel and his *Afrika Korps*. Perhaps it was Rommel's undeniably good looks (many movie stars have yearned to portray him); then again, it may have been his cavalier attitude toward death and danger. In any case, the British in North Africa viewed Rommel as one of their own, saying he was a British gentleman who, through force of nationality, had wound up on the wrong side.

What were the Germans after?

In a word, oil. In World War I, coal had been the primary provider of energy; in World War II, everyone needed petrol. Rommel and his *Afrika Korps* wanted to capture Egypt, primarily to deprive the British of one of their major sources of oil.

Of course, this raises a corollary question: Would the Germans have done better simply by capturing the Strait of Gibraltar and denying the British access to the Mediterranean Sea? Hitler was well aware of this possibility, and he spent several days with General Franco in Spain, trying to persuade him to allow free passage of German troops through Spain. Though he was a Fascist who preferred that the Germans and Italians win the war, Franco was too canny and shrewd to be lured into the war. Spain remained neutral throughout.

How did the Germans fare in the spring of 1942?

Rommel was a charismatic general whose appearance on the scene made a great difference. His *Afrika Korps* was plagued by a slow-running, ineffective supply system, however. The British controlled most of the Mediterranean shipping lanes, but the

Field Marshal Erwin Rommel—the "Desert Fox"—was a crafty tank commander who earned the respect of his men and his enemies. He was a co-conspirator in the unsuccessful plot to assassinate Hitler, after which the Führer forced Rommel to take a cyanide pill.

single greatest thorn in Rommel's side was their control of the small island of Malta (see chapter four). Using Malta as their base, the British harassed German shipping, sometimes meaning that supplies that should have arrived in a matter of days came in as many weeks, or not at all.

One of Rommel's great frustrations was his inability to persuade Hitler of the vital importance of the war in North Africa. The oil fields of Egypt lay just 500 miles off, ripe for the taking, he argued. Hitler was well aware of the importance of petrol, but he had his intention firmly set on a more distant supply: the oil fields in the Caucasus Mountains.

OFFENSIVE IN RUSSIA

How close had the Germans come to losing everything in Russia?

Perilously close. In the days and hours following the great Soviet counterattack on December 6, 1941, it seemed as if the Germans might lose everything they had gained from such hard fighting. Hitler, typically, refused to hear any talk of retreat: he insisted that every German soldier fight, and die if necessary, precisely where he stood. This was one of the few times in the entire war when Hitler's perverse refusal to yield ground probably made sense; had the Germans retreated to another perimeter, the blow to their morale might have been disastrous.

Despite his painful setbacks in December 1941, Hitler still retained the initiative. In the spring of 1942, he announced to his generals his plan for driving to, and past, the city of Stalingrad. The city was important, he declared, but the oil fields 400 miles beyond were much more so. At the same time, Hitler announced his intention to capture the city of Sevastopol on the Crimean Peninsula.

Were these goals attainable?

Just barely. If all force had been concentrated precisely in those spots, it is conceivable that the Germans might have won on the southern part of the Eastern Front. As so often, however, Hitler then began dividing his strength.

The drive to the Crimean Peninsula began with a bang, and soon Sevastopol was under siege. Meanwhile, the great city of Leningrad, in the northernmost part of the Eastern Front, was also under siege. Perhaps Hitler would succeed at the two ends where he had failed in the middle. What all the German plans overlooked, however, was the Soviet capacity for building more tanks and planes and for recruiting, or drafting, more men. Stalin was on the defensive, but he was a cagey fighter.

What was the German Sixth Army?

Commanded by Field Marshal Friedrich Von Paulus (1890–1957), the Sixth Army was the strike force of the entire German military machine. The Sixth had marched through

France, made detours into Norway, and had been prominent throughout the Russian campaign. The Poles remembered with tears the arrival of the Sixth in Warsaw in 1939. If the entire Germany military was one great killing machine—and many people said that it was—then the Sixth was the heaviest instrument in its arsenal.

Field Marshal Von Paulus drove toward Stalingrad during the summer of 1942. There were times when it seemed like a pleasure march because they met with such little resistance. The Luftwaffe, operating from bases hundreds of miles in the rear, was able to drop supplies right in the advancing men's way, and all seemed very well. Neither Paulus nor Hitler suspected that Stalin had laid an enormous trap, one big enough to catch a bear such as the Sixth Army.

Field Marshal Friendrich Von Paulus commanded Germany's Sixth Army and is best remembered for leading the fight in Stalingrad.

What made Stalingrad so important?

The city lay on the Volga and was the signpost to the Caucasus Mountains. If Moscow was the spiritual heart of Russia and Leningrad its intellectual center, then Stalingrad was the industrial and agricultural capital, somewhat akin to the role Chicago plays in the United States. Atop of all of this, however, was the simple fact that it bore Stalin's name.

There were times when Hitler truly lost his head where the Eastern Front was concerned: he could become completely obsessed with small details. In this case, he wanted to acquire and hold Stalingrad as compensation for his failure to take Moscow the year before.

When did Stalin spring the trap?

In November 1942, three different Soviet armies—all well-equipped and trained—crossed the Volga from the east and within a week accomplished their goal of effecting a rendezvous. They had completely encircled Von Paulus' Sixth Army, which was still fighting for the streets of Stalingrad.

Western histories naturally assert that D-Day was the greatest logistical feat of the war, and in terms of sheer materiel—planes, tanks, jeeps, etc.—this is true. But in human terms, in sheer number and mass of men, the Russian move in the early winter of 1942 was at least as difficult and just as well conceived.

Why did Von Paulus not turn and break out of the trap?

He wanted to. He pled with Hitler, asking permission to withdraw the Sixth Army. The Führer was in one of his "uncompromising" moods, however, and he refused. Instead, he told Von Paulus that the Luftwaffe would supply him by air until spring, and he would consider the options at that time. Hitler had erred several times in his trust of Goering, but this was the time when it counted the most. The Luftwaffe supplied Von Paulus for about a week before the Russian air force took charge of the skies around Stalingrad. For the first time in the war, Hitler's Nazis were in a position from which they could not escape, and the dangers became more obvious with each passing day.

TWIN DISASTERS

What had the Americans been doing all this time?

It has to be admitted that the United States was slow out of the gate. Even though FDR penned a policy of "Germany First," the Americans made no show of strength in Europe until the autumn of 1942, and by then the British had accomplished a good deal of the work.

In October 1942, thousands of Americans poured ashore in Tunisia, inaugurating "Operation Torch." They landed with little difficulty and were soon joined by thousands of Free French troops, recruited by Charles de Gaulle. The Americans were lucky, though, in that the British were already pushing the Germans back from the borders of Egypt.

What happened to Rommel at the Battle of el-Alamein?

Many things contributed to the British victory at el-Alamein, but the simplest was that Rommel ran out of gas. He was attempting to deprive the British of their petrol supplies in Egypt, but, in the height of irony, *his* tanks ran out of gas just as they crossed the border.

General Bernard Law Montgomery has assembled a large British, Canadian, and Australian force. At first the Commonwealth and Empire troops fought on the defensive, but as the telltale signs of Rommel's weakness emerged, they went on the offensive. By the beginning of November, they had Rommel on the run, and he had just learned that the Americans had landed behind him.

Who commanded the Allied landings in North Africa?

General Dwight David Eisenhower was a farm boy from the Midwest who had made good. His performance in World War I was minimal, but he had risen, through skill, diplomacy, and tact, to become the choice of FDR and General George C. Marshall. Eisenhower was not always loved by his subordinate generals, who believed their battle and tactical skills superior to his. To the average American infantryman, however, Eisenhower was the symbol of the U.S. military: patient, tolerant, and ever gaining in strength.

Another oddity involved with the Allied landings was that the U.S. Navy had a top historian involved. Samuel Eliot Morison was already known as the best of the "Boston Brahmin" historians: a writer of elegant prose, often about colonial and maritime subjects. In 1942, he was with the troops that landed in North Africa and was able to draw on his own experiences to compile his monumental fifteen-volume history of the naval war. Morison was the only American to have been a private in one war (World War I) and a rear admiral in another (World War II).

How did the Allies fare in North Africa?

The Americans and Canadians lost only 2,000 men in the initial landings, but they suffered almost 6,000 killed, wounded, and missing in their first tank battles with the Germans. Rommel's Afrika Korps was on its last legs, but its experienced tank commanders still had some lessons to teach the Americans. Inexorably, however, Montgomery's Eighth Army pressed from the east, and the Americans approached from the west. In March 1942, Rommel was airlifted from North Africa, never to return.

Five Star General Dwight D. Eisenhower was supreme commander of the Allied Forces in Europe during World War II and, from 1953 to 1961, was America's thirty-fourth president.

Rommel pleaded with Hitler to recognize the futility of the situation in North Africa, but Hitler, preoccupied with the Eastern Front, paid no attention. This led to the greatest surrender of German forces in the war. In May 1943, almost 250,000 Germans and Italians laid down their arms in North Africa.

What, meanwhile, had happened in Russia?

In some ways the story was the same as in North Africa. Safe from the battle scenes, Hitler made the absurd decision that no soldier should retreat or yield an inch of hard-won Russian soil. As a result, the Russians had plenty of time to complete their encirclement and send in their best troops to battle the Germans in the streets of Stalingrad.

The horror of that six-week battle has often been told, but something is always lost in the telling. Only 5,000 of the Germans who eventually surrendered ever made it home, and very few wrote memoirs of the worst experience of their lives. The fighting was house by house, street by street, and sometimes yard by yard. If Hitler had shown an irresistible will in his desire to take Stalingrad, then Stalin displayed a supreme sense of irony by making it the Germans' grave. By late January, the German Sixth Army was a mere shell of its former self. Field Marshal Von Paulus radioed Berlin, asking permission to surrender.

How did Hitler respond?

He promoted Von Paulus from general to field marshal. He knew, as did Von Paulus, that no German field marshal had ever been taken prisoner since the time of Frederick the Great. Von Paulus understood perfectly: he was expected to commit suicide.

Von Paulus chose otherwise, however. On the last day of January, 1943, he surrendered to the Russians, and within two days all of his men had given up. The Germans lost roughly 120,000 men in the fight for Stalingrad and another 90,000 taken prisoner. This was the single greatest catastrophe of the war for Germany, and coupled with the surrender in North Africa three months later, it meant that Hitler had completely lost the initiative.

What did the Axis empire look like in the middle of 1943?

On the map it still looked very impressive, with red markers indicating German and Italian possession of nearly all of Western Europe, all of Italy and Sicily, and large sections of the Soviet Union. This map view is quite deceptive, however. The Germans and Italians were on the verge of losing confidence in their leaders.

During the summer of 1943, British and American bomber squadrons made their first significant "runs" across northern Germany. They took off from British bases at twilight, dropped their bombs at around midnight, and returned by way of the English Channel around daybreak. Songs and poems that spoke of the "White Cliffs of Dover" took on a new meaning for the pilots that survived. These bombing runs were a major reason for the weakening of German morale.

JAPANESE HIGH TIDE

What did the Imperial Japanese map look like in 1942?

Similar to the Nazi German map, Japan's influence peaked sometime in 1942. And in a fashion similar to that of Germany, the black markers (those indicating Japanese possession) were soon to recede.

Where did Japan turn after its stunning victory at Pearl Harbor?

In retrospect, it seems Japan might have been wiser to follow up on Pearl Harbor immediately, pressing the Americans. But in the winter and spring of 1942, Japanese policy paid high dividends.

In January, Japan attacked both the Philippines and Dutch Indonesia. Flush with high morale, the Japanese pushed the Philippine and American defenders down the islands. In February 1942, General Douglas MacArthur (1880–1964)—whose father had been a Civil War lieutenant—gave a radio broadcast to the Philippinos, vowing that "I shall return." MacArthur left command of the skeleton U.S. forces to Major General Jonathan Wainwright, who was forced to surrender a few weeks later. More Americans (7,000) laid down their arms than in any previous contest, and many of them died on the terrible "Bataan Death March" that followed.

How did the Japanese fare in Dutch Indonesia?

They were after the oil, which would make their war machine run smoothly. But first they had to progress down the Malay Peninsula, which was defended by native Malays, Dutch, and a large British garrison at the fortress of Singapore.

The defensive works and fortress cannon of Singapore were justly famous, but they were intended for a different kind of enemy. The siege guns did little to defend against the Japanese infantry, accustomed to jungle fighting, and in February 1942, Singapore surrendered. Over 100,000 British and Malay were taken prisoner in what is considered the greatest disaster of British arms in the twentieth century. The Japanese, meanwhile, pressed their advantage, seizing the oil fields of Indonesia, and even moving against Papua New Guinea. If that colony fell, the way to Australia was open for the Japanese.

How difficult, or desperate, was the situation for the Americans and their allies?

Australia could have fallen, and Japan would have gained an immense land space, but in strategic terms the loss of Singapore was probably greater. The American and British high command were in constant touch over the situation in Southeast Asia, with the latter more concerned than the former. If Australia fell, Japan's reach would be enormous, but the distance from Hawaii to Tokyo remained the same. In other words, the United States' military situation would not have been impacted to the same extent as Britain.

Were there tensions between Australia and the motherland?

There were many, some of which dated back to World War I. Australians and New Zealanders were, naturally, proud of what their fathers had accomplished in the Great War, but there was a lingering suspicion that the British had used them as cannon fodder. It did not help that Churchill, the mastermind of the Gallipoli Campaign, was now in charge of the entire British and Imperial war effort.

How important were the naval codes?

Both the Japanese and their enemies worked feverishly to break each other's naval codes, which would allow them to predict their enemy's movements. The Americans were the first to succeed in doing so.

In the months following the attack on Pearl Harbor, Captain Joseph Rochefort, U.S. Navy, spent many sixteen-hour days working in a basement at the naval base. Rochefort had a special gift for the work, and, assisted by a tiny staff, he broke the Japanese naval code by April 1942. Therefore, when the Japanese sent a naval task force to attack Papua New Guinea, the Americans were able to get their naval units just in time for the Battle of the Coral Sea.

What was so different about the Battle of the Coral Sea?

Fought between April 4 and April 8, 1942, the battle was the first in naval history where two major fleets fought without having visual contact. The distance between the U.S. and Japanese fleets was sometimes more than twenty miles, with all sorts of planes scrambling from the decks of both fleets. The naval commanders aboard never saw their opponents, however.

In strictly technical terms, the battle was a standoff, with a slight advantage to the Japanese, but in strategic terms it represented something far greater. The relentless tide of Japanese advances in the Pacific halted for the first time, and the Americans bought time to analyze the Japanese intentions. That was where the radio codes made all the difference.

Why was Jimmy Doolittle's raid so important?

In February 1942, Captain James Doolittle led six small American planes, taking off from U.S.S. *Hornet*. They flew 650 miles to Tokyo and dropped a handful of bombs, the first the Japanese capital had felt. Doolittle, whose actions were later celebrated in the film *Thirty Seconds Over Tokyo*, had accomplished something truly great. Though he knew it not, he panicked some high-level Japanese officials. Believing that the homeland, and the sacred person of the emperor, was in danger, these officials began planning the largest strike of the war, one that would dwarf the attack on Pearl Harbor.

Admiral Isoroku Yamamoto commanded Japan's Combined Fleet at the time of the Battle of the Coral Sea.

How much materiel did the Japanese commit?

Admiral Isoroku Yamamoto (1884–1943) planned the massive strike, which committed four aircraft carriers, four battleships, and an immense number of support craft. Yamomoto's plan, which was approved by the Japanese high command, was to seize Midway Island and use it as an air base from which to bomb Hawaii. If Japan could take the Hawaiian Islands, they would, quite likely, prevent any further American air raids against the home islands.

Yamamoto was more confident than he had been in 1941. While he still doubted Japan could win the war, it seemed possible Japan could force a standoff, restricting the United States to the western part of the Pacific. Given time, Japan could overrun Australia, leaving the Americans and their allies nowhere to go.

MIRACLE AT MIDWAY

Why do we so frequently characterize the Battle of Midway as a miracle?

When one assesses the relative strength of the Japanese and U.S. navies—as of June 1942—and when one calculates how terrible the situation would have been for the United States had it lost, the Battle of Midway can characterized as a miracle. This was one of those occasions when everything went wrong for hours, when a great deal hung in the balance, and when the balance suddenly corrected itself (from the American point of view).

Why did Admiral Yamamoto stake so much on this one campaign?

The Doolittle air raid over Tokyo had deeply upset Yamamoto and many other Japanese. Throughout the war, one of their main goals was to ensure that Emperor Hirohito—who they saw as semidivine—be protected from any American air strikes. Admiral Yamamoto, therefore, decided on a second incredibly bold venture. Having succeeded at Pearl Harbor, he determined on another enormous task force, this time in order to lure the American battle fleet out to its destruction.

Much of Yamamoto's plan was sound, but, as at Pearl Harbor, it depended on great efficiency and secrecy. What the Japanese admiral did not know was that the Americans had broken most of Japan's naval codes (this heroic activity was undertaken by a handful of men working in a basement at Pearl Harbor). Admiral Chester Nimitz (1885–1966) knew, therefore, that a major Japanese offensive was in the making; what he could not be certain of was "where."

How important was Midway Island?

An atoll only six miles in circumference, Midway Island did not look like much until one assessed its position as the easternmost point of American air power. There was a small naval base on Midway and about 3,000 men ready to defend it. That was all the U.S. could spare in May 1942.

Admiral Nimitz trusted his intelligence officers and the code-breakers, who correctly ascertained that Midway would be the principal Japanese target; there would be a diversionary strike against the Aleutian Islands of Alaska. Nimitz, therefore, concentrated all the strength he had at Pearl Harbor and then sent his main force to be stationed to the northwest side of Midway Island.

How great of a risk did Nimitz take?

If the intelligence was correct, it was surely the right move to make; if the intelligence proved faulty, it was possible that the Japanese would sneak through on Midway's south side and attack Hawaii for a second time. Gambles like this are a necessary thing at times, but one has to applaud Nimitz for his planning *and* his resolution.

Who commanded the Imperial Japanese fleet?

Admiral Nagumo, who had led the attack on Pearl Harbor, was in operational command, but Admiral Yamamoto—the only Japanese naval officer to have been present at the Battle of Tsushima in 1905—was only a few hundred miles behind, aboard the immense, super-battleship *Yamato*. The Japanese did not realize that the Americans had cracked their codes, and both Nagumo and Yamamoto expected a quick victory at Midway Island. They were, however, puzzled at the lack of sign of U.S. aircraft carriers.

Both in Japan and the mainland United States, there were still naval planners who believed that the battleship was the key to success, but anyone who had been present at Pearl Harbor or the Coral Sea knew different: the aircraft carrier had become the key to success at sea. Battleships still mattered, but they could be hit from the air with relative impunity.

When did the Battle of Midway commence?

At 5:20 A.M. on June 4, Admiral Nagumo sent a first wave of Japanese planes to attack Midway Island. The Japanese bombers caused plenty of damage but killed rather few Americans, and, most importantly, they did not make the runway on Midway inoperational.

Admiral Raymond A. Spruance was in position northwest of Midway when he learned of the Japanese planes; he immediately gave the order for his fighters and

Japanese Admiral Chuichi Nagumo led the Imperial Navy at Midway.

bombers to launch. Spruance was a fine fighting admiral, but he had never been in charge of an aerial operation such as this: he was to prove both resolute and determined.

What were the first bombing runs like?

The Americans descended from 20,000 feet to attack the main body of the Japanese fleet. Admiral Nagumo was astonished that the Americans—of whom he had no sign or sight—had found him, but the cover provided by his fighters proved first-rate. Of the first American bombing run, nearly three quarters of the planes were brought down either by Japanese fighters or anti-aircraft fire. One American pilot survived landing in the water and spent the next few hours observing the ferocious battle that ensued.

The second American attack was made by planes carrying torpedoes, and this time the Japanese air cover was insufficient. Nagumo correctly perceived that his only hope was to zigzag the movement of his ships, and none of the American torpedoes hit home. To this point, at about 9 A.M., the Japanese were clearly ahead. Nagumo remained nervous, but that was to be expected. At this moment, he turned to his number-one naval tactician to ask whether he should now launch his own second assault or whether he should wait until his returning planes had refueled.

Was this the moment? Was this the decision that cost Japan the Battle of Midway?

This was the decision, and the moment came forty minutes later. The Americans had tried twice and failed. There was a third row of bombers, but they were not in great condition, and many of the pilots were young and untested. Admiral Spruance went right ahead, however, sending out his last wave of bombers. If they missed their target, Spruance and the U.S. fleet would be a sitting duck for the Japanese, who were still refueling.

When did the decisive moment come?

At about 9:50 A.M. on June 4, 1942, 150 American planes descended from the sky to find Admiral Nagumo's ships without adequate air cover. The Japanese had zigzagged so many times that they had shaken off some of their own planes. The Americans dropped to a few hundred feet and began bombing the decks of Japan's four most prestigious aircraft carriers. The damage would have been bad, but it was much worse because there were almost 300 planes lined up on those decks, ready to take off. One explosion led to another; one American bomb fell right through the midsection of carrier *Akagi* and practically destroyed it. In about ten minutes, three Japanese aircraft carriers were damaged to the point that they later sank; a fourth struggled on for a few hours more.

Admiral Nagumo almost had a mental breakdown. Admiral Yamamoto, operating from 200 miles back, relieved Nagumo of command, replacing him with another man on the scene.

Why didn't the Japanese come on for a fight to the finish?

Yamamoto had lots of ships and planes in reserve, but he—and virtually all his officers— was utterly dismayed by the loss of the four aircraft carriers: this was one-third of the entire carrier capacity of the Imperial Japanese Navy. Then, too, the Japanese morale was quite different from that of the Americans. Knowing that their foe had greater material resources, the Japanese depended on sensational victories to keep their spirits high; the sudden experience of a major failure, or defeat, cast them down accordingly.

Yamamoto, therefore, pulled back all his forces, including those which had made a diversionary attack on the Aleutian Islands. He knew—though he did not declare it—that Japan could no longer win the war in the Pacific. She could make a good fight of it, and delay the Americans for long periods, but with the loss of four aircraft carriers in one morning, she could not mount another major offensive.

The U.S.S. *Yorktown* is hit by a Japanese torpedo during the heat of the action at the Battle of Midway.

Did the Americans realize the magnitude of their victory?

Ensign George H. Gay had been in one of the planes that carried torpedoes; he had been forced to crash his plane into the Pacific. He watched the battle of June 4 unfold, and when—of all miracles—he was sighted and picked up by a Catalina plane, he related what he'd seen to the U.S. commanders They then knew that they had prevailed. Not only was Midway Island safe, but they had delivered an enormous blow to the Japanese.

What was the strategy of "island hopping"?

In the summer of 1942, the United States went on the offensive in the Pacific and never relinquished it. One of the key concepts involved was that of "island hopping," meaning that the Americans did not commit themselves to capturing each and every island occupied by Imperial Japan. The Japanese had shown themselves fearsome fighters, and the casualties would, quite likely, be overwhelming. Instead, the Americans resolved to capture one island, jump over two, three, or even four, before capturing another. Given the enormous American strength at sea, these Japanese islands could do nothing to hinder their progress, and the garrisons would eventually be starved out.

This was one of the most intelligent, farsighted, and best executed decisions that the United States high command made during the entire war.

Why was Guadalcanal so important?

One of the Solomon Islands, Guadalcanal was vital because of its tiny airport strip in the midst of the jungle. The Americans got there first, chasing out the small Japanese garrison, but the Japanese kept coming and coming: their nighttime reinforcement runs were known as the "Tokyo Express."

The U.S. Marines were involved from the beginning, and their training and determination proved vital. Over the next several months, over 10,000 Japanese died in the fight for Guadalcanal, while the Americans lost about 1,500. The numbers do not tell the entire story, however, because most of the Japanese who died there were the elite fighters, the shock troops who had paved the way for so many past successes. By the time Guadalcanal fell entirely into American hands early in 1943, Japan was restricted entirely to the defensive.

Was there any moment when the GIs and naval personnel in the Pacific realized that they could not lose the war, that time was on their side?

Among the U.S. servicemen of 1941 to 1945, there was a grim but confident belief that the democratic nations could not and would not fail. America and its allies were up against an evil so great, so malicious, that they simply had to prevail.

This is not to say that life was ever easy, or jovial, for the U.S. serviceman.

Was Japan a defeated power?

By no means. The Japanese were expert defensive fighters, and they expected to contest every piece of ground and every section of air space. Many of their troops were tied down in China, however, and they did not realize the vast air power America was about to release.

THE ALLIED INVASIONS

Who used the expression the "soft underbelly of Europe"?

In 1943, Britain and the United States were under increasing pressure from Joseph Stalin, who wanted them to open a second front on land against Nazi Germany. No one could argue against the idea—it was obvious that Russia had endured the most—but neither the American nor the British war planners were keen on meeting German tanks in Northern Europe. The plan, therefore, called for Britain and America to invade by way of Italy, which Churchill labeled Europe's soft underbelly.

On paper, the plan made good sense. The Italians were much less enthusiastic than the Germans where the war was concerned, and knocking out Mussolini's Fascist regime would be an excellent opening step. Other factors were involved, however, not the least of which was the geography of Italy.

When did Operation Husky commence?

Early in July 1943, thousands of British and American troops landed on the beaches of southern Sicily. They came by a traditional invasion route—one that had been used since ancient times—but their motorized columns found the going difficult, especially in mountainous terrain. The Sicilians put up no resistance, the Italians very little, and it was therefore up to the Germans to be the ones to fight.

American General George S. Patton—an eccentric and brilliant leader—commanded the American Third Army, which stormed all the way to Palermo. The British Eighth Army, commanded by Bernard Law Montgomery, meanwhile traveled a shorter distance along the east coast. This was the beginning of a long, mutual dislike between Patton and Montgomery, two men of great abilities and great prejudices. For a brief few weeks, it seemed as if Montgomery would have the field all to himself.

What did General George Patton do wrong?

While celebrating the victory in Sicily, Patton visited an Allied hospital. Coming across two American GIs who were hospitalized for shell shock, Patton began berating them. One soldier received verbal insults, and the other was slapped. Newspapers picked up the story, and pressure built for Patton to be cashiered.

General Dwight D. Eisenhower was not a complete admirer of Patton, but he knew who his best field general was. Eisenhower, therefore, removed Patton from field command for a few months, waiting for the right time to bring him back to the front.

How did the invasion of Italy begin?

The Germans had escaped across the Strait of Messina with a good amount of guns and equipment. The Allies pursued them in September and met almost no resistance in what is called the "toe" of the Italian boot. Many Italians practically rushed to American lines to surrender, and it seemed that the entire invasion would be a lark. This was not the case, however. Nazi Germany could not allow for the collapse of Fascist Italy.

Field Marshal Albert Von Kesselring hastened south with many German units and established a defensive line, anchored on the Abbey of Monte Cassino, ninety miles south of Rome. Von Kesselring was a specialist in defensive warfare. The Allies had it all their way in the air and were able to bomb at will, but they could not break Kesselring's defensive line.

What happened to Mussolini?

Almost as soon as the Allies landed in southern Italy, King Victor Emmanuel told Benito Mussolini that it was time for him to depart the political scene. Mussolini, whose confidence was badly rattled, agreed, and it seemed as if he would tamely surrender power, allowing for a smooth takeover by the Allies. Mussolini, instead, was rescued by Hitler, who did not wish to see his fellow dictator fall from power.

In a truly daring move, German paratroopers glided onto the mountain where Mussolini was being held and freed him. Brought north to Milan, Mussolini became a symbol for Italian defiance of the Allies, but he was, in fact, a finished and ruined man. He had little strength other than for his weekly radio addresses, and few Italians paid attention to him after the winter of 1944.

Why were the landings at Anzio so hard-fought?

Anzio, on Italy's west coast, was thirty miles ahead of the foremost American lines and less than fifty miles from Rome; once ashore, the Americans expected to make a major push on Rome and perhaps succeed right away. Instead, they arrived on the beaches at the very moment when a crack German panzer division had just been moved to that general area (there was no tip-off; the Germans just got lucky). Therefore, when the Americans and British came ashore, they advanced no more than five miles before running into heavy enemy resistance.

Anzio could have been the breakout that made the Italian campaign; instead, it slowly became the nightmare which characterized just how hard-fought the war in Italy was. Thousands of Americans were killed and wounded for a rather small advance in the overall Allied strategy. By the end of 1943, many planners and strategists believed that Winston Churchill had been quite mistaken about Italy and the Mediterranean being the "soft underbelly" of the Axis Powers.

When did the planning for D-Day begin?

More than a year prior to the actual landings. All the top military men involved—from Churchill to Dwight Eisenhower—concurred that the invasion had to be an unqualified success: anything less would be a propaganda coup for the Germans. Millions of men and an unprecedented amount of materiel had to be assembled.

D–DAY

Was D-Day the actual name for the invasion?

No, the technical term was Operation Overlord. But with so many people—from planners to soldiers on the ground—involved, it was almost inevitable that there would be nicknames for the grand invasion, and D-Day is the name that stuck.

For how long did the Allies prepare?

The planning began early in 1943, with British and American chiefs of staff meeting on a frequent basis. One thing on which almost all the planners agreed was that a failure would be nearly fatal; if the Allies should stumble and be repulsed, the result would be an enormous boost in morale for the Nazis. It was therefore essential that everything be planned.

D-Day was a joint operation, with British and Canadians alongside the Americans, but no one could doubt which nation supplied the most men and the greatest amount of materiel. Nearly three million American soldiers were in England by the spring of 1944, and the number of

(Left to right) American Generals George Patton and Omar Bradley, with British General Sir Bernard Montgomery meeting during the Normandy invasion in 1944.

tanks, jeeps, and personnel carriers was almost beyond count. One rather big surprise was that by that spring the man in charge was not General George C. Marshall.

How badly did George C. Marshall want to be commander-in-chief?

No man could have wanted it more. Marshall was a brilliant staff officer who had risen to Army chief of staff thanks to his meticulous performance in World War I, during which he organized the Meuse-Argonne Offensive in 1918. Beyond that, however, Marshall was truly a soldier without peer: liked, trusted, and with absolutely no doubts as to his integrity. Marshall wanted desperately to command the D-Day invasion and thereby cap his already remarkable career.

The decision was not made until around Christmas Day of 1943. Tradition has it that FDR and General Marshall were in an automobile when the president told the Army chief of staff that he simply couldn't do without him. Dwight D. Eisenhower (1890–1969) would be commander-in-chief of the Allied invasion forces. Marshall was deeply disappointed, but like the soldier he was, he accepted the decision. His moment of glory came at the war's conclusion, when Secretary of Defense Henry Stimson told him: "I have known a great many soldiers in my life, and you, sir, are the finest soldier I have ever known."

Was Eisenhower as genial as he usually appears in the photographs?

Born in Kansas in 1890, Eisenhower was the third eldest in a farming family of seven children. Throughout life, he acted like a farm boy because that is what he was down deep. Like the Midwesterner he was, Eisenhower found it easy to smile and get along with people. Members of his staff, however, knew that the grin concealed a powerful temper and that "the boss" was not to be trifled with. Eisenhower was not a first-rate

The colossal scale of the Normandy invasion by Allied troops is captured by this photograph. There had never before in history been a seaborne invasion of such an epic scope.

general in terms of day-to-day tactics, but he was a fine long-range strategic planner; more important, he was the only top-ranking U.S. general humble enough—at least for the camera—to get along with the British military brass. No one—from FDR down to the lowest private—ever regretted that Eisenhower was chosen for the great role.

For his part, Eisenhower was nervous throughout April and May. He had an immense force built up, most of it right on the southern coast of England, but there were sections of the Channel where one hundred miles lay between those men and their objectives. He did not know—could not know—whether the Luftwaffe might make a surprise appearance or if the Germans still had enough U-Boats to dent the invasion force. And, he could not predict the weather.

Why was the weather so important?

The English Channel is known for choppy waves but also for sudden squalls. The latter could wreak havoc on an invasion force, especially if the tide ran counter to the flow of men and materiel. It was essential, therefore, to have some foreknowledge of the weather, and Eisenhower consulted the meteorologists almost as frequently as his top generals.

On the afternoon of June 5, 1944, Eisenhower and his generals heard the weather report. The next morning might be choppy, they were told, but the afternoon would be rather good. Following that, another front could move in, and no one could predict what would happen. Everyone sat silent for a time, and Eisenhower finally stood and uttered those well-remembered words, "OK, let's go." Hundreds, even thousands, of commands quickly went over the wires as hundreds of thousands of men moved into position for what would be the biggest moment of their careers, perhaps even their lives.

How well prepared were the parachutists?

Eisenhower had taken special care of them, visiting them frequently. He told them that they were the vanguard of a real crusade and that much depended on their ability to land behind the Germans and cut their radio and telephone lines. The paratroopers, about 24,000 in all, jumped during the night of June 5–6, 1944.

Were the Germans ready for the Americans?

Not behind the lines. The parachute drop was a major success, with the men cutting lines all night long. It was a different matter on the beaches, however.

A massive aerial bombardment took place during the night, and at about 0500 hours—or 5 A.M.—a massive naval bombardment followed. The Germans in their defensive positions must have had no doubt that this was the main Allied assault, but they could not get the information back to their superiors: neither the phones nor the wires worked. One can only pity the Germans in their pillboxes and fortifications who, after receiving an enormous artillery bombardment, witnessed literally hundreds of ships a mile out to sea and thousands of small boats bringing U.S., British, and Canadian troops ashore.

What was the Higgins landing craft?

Named for Andrew J. Higgins of New Orleans—whose 20,000 employees built all the craft—the Higgins was a flat-bottomed boat with minimal draft, meaning that the Allied soldiers could get very close to the beach. Eisenhower later called Higgins "the man who won the war for us," and it is true that without that kind of craft, the Allies would have needed access to a major harbor to land their men. Instead, they were able to make a "soft" landing on the beaches of Normandy, where they then faced something else: withering machine-gun fire from the German defenders.

Has anyone ever done a good analysis of what it was like to be on the German, or receiving, end?

The Germans, of course, did not know where the attack would come, but they knew that it would be a battle of men against materiel; the Allies simply had far more tanks, jeeps, planes, and explosives. As it turned out, however, some of the best German units were at Omaha Beach, just waiting for the moment to open fire.

It turned out that all the bombardment from above and from sea had not done the job; thousands of Germans were still in their fortified positions, and they rained down fire on the first Americans to come ashore at Omaha Beach. The landing was supposed to be made easier by the arrival of fifty tanks, which had mixed propulsion systems, enabling them to move through sand. But many of the tanks arrived at the wrong location, and most of those that got to Omaha sank in the heavy surf.

What was the arrangement of the five beaches?

From the German perspective, which means standing in Normandy and looking out to sea, Utah Beach was the last part of an indentation in the coastline (this was to be taken by the U.S. VII Corps). Omaha Beach, one major step to the right, or east, was the target of the U.S. V Corps, with a group of U.S. Rangers especially chosen to take the guns at Pointe de Hoc. Gold Beach, the third as one moved from left to right, was the target of the British XXX Corps, and Juno Beach was assailed by the Canadians. Sword Beach, last of the five, was the target of the British I Corps. In all more than 125,000 men were to land in the opening hours, making D-Day by far the most ambitious of all amphibious landings—before or since.

An aerial view of Omaha Beach taken on June 6, 1944.

With that uncanny intuition he sometimes displayed, Hitler had predicted the Allies would come to Normandy. He was no longer as able to back up his hunches, however, and his generals persuaded him that the main Allied assault would take place at the Pas-de-Calais, the narrowest part of the English Channel. To make sure Hitler believed this, the Allies had built up dummy forces in that area.

Where did things go the most wrong?

One can almost say that they went wrong all over the place. Eisenhower had predicted this, declaring that the plans meant nothing once action had commenced but that the planning was invaluable, if only because the soldiers got used to improvising. Even so, we can say that Omaha Beach is where the largest number of elements went awry, and there were moments, at about 1300 hours, when General Omar Bradley considered pulling his men back. What changed his mind was the sudden passing of an alert: men who had previously been pinned down were now advancing and capturing German fortified positions.

Many of the heroes on those beaches are anonymous—American, British, and Canadian soldiers who simply did their jobs—but a handful of known heroes emerged. One was Major General Theodore Roosevelt junior, son of the former American president. Another was Brigadier-General Norman Cota, of the U.S. 29th Division, who practically led his men by hand on Omaha Beach. None of the truly senior generals—Eisenhower, Patton, Montgomery, and others—were on the beaches that first day.

Why did the Germans not make better use of their tank division twenty miles back?

That panzer division had just arrived a few days before, and its tank commanders were eager for a confrontation. Hitler had made it abundantly clear, however, that this—his

If that is so, then how do we account for the tank actions in *Saving Private Ryan*?

No one wishes to criticize *Saving Private Ryan*, which is surely one of the finest military movies ever brought to the wide screen. The beach scenes are quite accurate, especially the manner in which U.S. soldiers finally take the heights and storm the German pillboxes. But when *Saving Private Ryan* takes the viewer to the interior and shows a handful of U.S. soldiers blasting their way through sections of German infantry, it goes too far. Anyone who ever fought the Germans admitted that they were fantastic fighters and were seldom taken by surprise. Then, too, *Saving Private Ryan* takes place in the days and weeks after the D-Day landings, when in fact it was not until mid-July that the Allies engineered their breakout from Normandy.

only mobile reserve—was not to be used without his express permission, and the Führer—who had taken pills to help him sleep—was not fully conscious until early on the afternoon of June 6, 1944. Hitler immediately gave his permission, but the panzer division was halted by furious fighting from the British who had come ashore at Gold Beach.

Once that panzer division was held in place and forced on to the defensive, there was little, if anything, the Germans could do. Their commanders—Erwin Rommel most especially—had argued long and hard that they must hit the Allies hard on the opening day in order to have any chance of success. Late that afternoon, one of Rommel's aides asked if there was now any chance. Rommel put on a brave front, saying that he had usually succeeded in the past. Even he did not realize the magnitude of the landing, however, or the immense force that was now about to descend.

How many men got ashore on the opening day?

Between 125,000 and 130,000 men got safely ashore by nightfall, and that number virtually doubled the following day. From that point on, there really was no hope for the German defenders. A quarter of a million men who received regular reinforcements simply could not be dislodged, especially while the Allies controlled the skies.

Hitler, typically, put too much trust in Hermann Goering. The Luftwaffe had made virtually no resistance to the Allied landings, but Goering continued to declare that his planes would make life miserable for the Allied troops. The German planes accomplished very little, but the German tanks—the Tiger tank most especially—made the going hard. Even so, most Allied soldiers in Normandy concluded that geography, rather than men, created the most difficulty.

How could hedgerows make so much trouble?

Anyone who has strolled either the countryside of southern England or western France knows that hedgerows can be formidable; many of them are centuries old, and they require regular cutbacks just to make ordinary movement possible. The hedgerows of Normandy were especially thick, however, and the Germans made excellent use of them; one well-placed Tiger tank could keep back an entire infantry regiment for hours, just as long as its flanks were secured by hedgerows.

Then, too, the Germans fought extremely well. They knew the Allies were coming and were determined to sell their lives dearly. They also did not fear, as did their comrades on the Eastern Front, that they would be tortured or brutalized if captured. Throughout World War II, the Germans routinely caused 1.5 to 2 times as many casualties as they themselves suffered; perhaps the ratio was not as formidable at Normandy, but it still was in their favor.

BREAKOUT

How long did it take the Allies to secure all of Normandy?

It took about six weeks, and there was plenty of hard fighting along the way. Not until the Allies seized the town of Cherbourg, with its fine natural harbor, were they able to bring in all the men and materiel they desired; within days of that accomplishment, the Allies were close to having one million men in Normandy, most of them supplied by air. The German defenders were, at this point, about 300,000 in number, but their morale was greatly lessened; among other things, they lost their much loved general when Erwin Rommel was hit in his motorcar. Rommel went to hospital in Berlin, while the hopes of his men dropped even further.

When did the breakout begin?

George Patton and the Third Army were chafing at the bit, and when, in mid-July, they sensed a weakness in the southwestern sector, they pushed with all their might. Achieving a breakthrough, Patton charged ahead of his men, much as Rommel had done during the Battle of France in 1940. Hitler, all too typically, asserted that this was the time for a counterattack; the effort he demanded led to thousands of Germans being trapped in the "Falaise Gap." By then, Hitler had much more serious problems, however.

Why did it take so long for someone to make a serious attempt to kill the Führer?

Numerous attempts by Germans had already been made: all had come to nothing. In July 1944, however, a large group of German leaders—military and civilian—formed a serious group and planned to take over the entire government. Their man, Colonel Claus von Stauffenberg (1907–1944), was at the Wolf's Lair, in Bavaria, on the afternoon of July 20, 1944. Pretending to listen to the reports of one military disaster after another, Von Stauffenberg placed his briefcase, which contained a bomb, underneath the desk where Hitler stood. Von Stauffenberg made an excuse, made his exit, and minutes later, as his car drove away, he saw a blinding flash and heard the explosion which, he was quite sure, had killed Adolf Hitler.

Claus Von Stauffenberg's office is now a museum dedicated to the July 20, 1944, plot to assassinate Hitler.

What happened the evening of the assassination attempt on Hitler?

All went well from the conspirators' point of view. Thousands of SS and Gestapo soldiers were rounded up in Berlin with a provisional government, headed by General Ludwig Beck, calling the shots. The success was breathtaking, until the comedown.

Sometime that evening, Hitler went on the air to announce, in slurred tones, that he was very much alive. So great was the spell he cast over his countrymen that the men who had tamely surrendered to the provisional government now turned on it. By 10 P.M., most of the conspirators, including Von Stauffenberg, had been rounded up or killed. Hitler's vengeance, as one would expect, was terrible. Over 5,000 people were given swift trials that ended with executions.

How did Hitler escape being killed?

We will never know the complete details, because the key players, including Von Stauffenberg, were not in the room when the bomb exploded. Quite likely, a German staff officer found Von Stauffenberg's briefcase and moved it, perhaps only a matter of six inches or so. Those inches made all the difference, and when the bomb blew up, it threw the desk upward, hitting Hitler in the face and stunning him, but not killing him. Hitler, all too typically, declared he had been saved by God.

What happened to Erwin Rommel?

If he was involved in the attempt to assassinate Hitler, it was in a very tangential way. Rommel was not a rebel against Hitler; he was, just possibly, more realistic than many of his fellow German generals. But in the aftermath of the failed assassination at-

How accurate, or inaccurate, is the 2008 film *Valkyrie*?

Valkyrie, which starred Tom Cruise as Colonel Von Stauffenberg, was one of the most accurate of all World War II films; it depicts the tense four weeks leading to the attempted coup and then the desperate twelve-hour struggle for Berlin. Unlike many other World War II films, *Valkyrie* displays many of the honorable, even admirable, aspects of the German military. Once a man, either a private or a general, has given his word, he must deliver.

The tension builds remarkably, and at thirty minutes before the film's end, it still seems possible that the rebels will succeed and that Hitler's regime will be toppled. When everything goes wrong and Hitler's twisted voice is once more heard on the radio, the viewer knows that the efforts of tens of thousands of people—men and women—have failed. When all is lost and men go before the firing squad, one is inclined to weep. Brought before the firing squad, Tom Cruise shouts "Long live sacred Germany!" before collapsing from repeated rifle shots. The antihero, General Frohm, is magnificently portrayed by veteran actor Tom Wilkinson.

tempt, Rommel, who was recovering from a wound suffered on the Western Front, was visited by two SS leaders. They told him he had a choice between suicide and an honorable state funeral or execution and the persecution of his family. He chose the former, and most Germans did not suspect he had been involved in the attempt to assassinate the Führer.

When was Paris liberated?

The British and French were in a position to enter, but they waited until August 26, when a small number of Free French troops, led by General Charles de Gaulle, could have the honor. Paris, which had witnessed much deprivation during four years of occupation, went wild with joy.

Not all reunions were pleasant, however. Of all the countries defeated and occupied by the Nazis, France was torn apart the worst, meaning that there were many people who had collaborated with the Nazis. Public humiliation of those collaborators followed, and revenge killings were not unknown. It took France many years to recover from the World War II experience.

What was Operation Market Garden?

General Eisenhower and his advisors were divided between those who urged a full press all along the line and others who claimed that the direct, northern route through Belgium and Holland was the simplest way to strike at Germany. In an attempt to assuage hard feelings between British and American leaders, Eisenhower allowed British General Bernard Montgomery to develop his plan for a sudden attack in Holland, led by paratroopers.

Operation Market Garden might well have succeeded if two SS divisions had not been close at hand. When the Allied paratroopers jumped, they saw enormous stakes pointed from the ground in their direction. Many paratroopers were killed or captured on the first day, and within a week Market Garden was called off.

THE RUSSIAN ONSLAUGHT

Why did the Russians take so long to free their entire country from Germans?

Two factors were involved. First, European Russia is so vast a place that pockets of Germans could hide and later become behind-the-line fighters. The second, perhaps more important, reason is that Joseph Stalin wished to use this opportunity to "cleanse" Russia of all domestic opposition.

Stalin knew in July 1944 that he and his Western allies would win the war. He was looking ahead to a time when the Soviet Union could completely dominate Eastern Europe and perhaps influence, or threaten, Western Europe. One of Stalin's high priorities, therefore, was to rub out all opposition in Russia, Poland, and other nations he invaded.

Could the Nazis have stopped the Soviet drive to the west?

It would have taken something like a miracle to stop the Russian juggernaut. No matter how many men Stalin lost, he could always find and feed more into the battles. But in terms of sheer equipment, too, the Russians were gaining the ascendancy. The T-54 Tank was just as good, and in some ways even better than, the famous German Tiger. Then, too, the Germans were spread over far too large a front.

Of all the German generals, only Rommel might have found a solution, and his talents were being employed on the Western Front. Throughout the war, the Germans had maintained a technical superiority—major for major, colonel for colonel, and general for general—but even this was disappearing fast.

How many men did Hitler lose in the battles of 1944?

He lost perhaps 200,000 fighting the Allies in France and perhaps three times that number fighting the Russians. The previous year, 1943, had been bad enough, especially the defeat at Kursk, but 1944 was simply catastrophic.

What did the Poles think of the Russian advance?

To put it in a nutshell, they were thrilled. Poland had been the first victim of Nazi oppression, and in some ways it suffered the most of all the occupied nations. In September 1944, the liberation movement rose against the Germans. Centered on the capital of Warsaw, the Polish movement had a real chance of success and in its opening days seized most of the capital and much of the surrounding area. Given that the Russian advance units were only seventy-five to a hundred miles off, it seemed certain they would succeed. But that was when the hammer fell.

Stalin ordered his tank columns to stop at the River Vistula. Historians have ever since mulled over the action, inquiring whether it was as cynical as it seemed. The answer, almost certainly, is that it was entirely cynical, a naked desire to see the Polish rebels crushed. When questioned in later years, Stalin never gave a complete or satisfactory answer, but anyone on the Russian–Polish border in 1944 sensed the truth.

How thoroughly did the Nazis squelch the Polish Revolt of 1944?

Squelch is a good term but does not fully convey the ferocious behavior of the Nazis. Between 20,000 and 30,000 Poles were killed, and nearly all the leaders of the rebellion perished. There were machine-gun squads, hangings, and very likely some torture involved. What this indicates to us today is that even in its waning hours, the Nazi regime was incapable of merciful practices. Each and every attempt at defiance was handled the same way.

BATTLE OF THE BULGE

When did George Patton come fully into his own?

He had already shown moments of surpassing skill, but his true brilliance as a tank commander was showcased in the Liberation of France in the summer of 1944. Breaking out from the Normandy peninsula, Patton practically raced across Midwestern France, liberating towns and cities along the way. He did not get to enjoy the liberation of Paris, because that was given to another American commander, who, along with a division of Free French fighters, entered the capital on August 24, 1944.

Typically, Hitler had ordered that Paris be razed to the ground and the precious works of art destroyed, rather than allow the garrison to surrender. For once, an important German commander defied the Führer, and the city on the Seine was turned over in decent shape.

How did the rivalry between George Patton and Bernard Montgomery progress?

One can almost see it in the numerous still photographs: Patton, with his hands on his hips, looks like a Western cowboy, and Montgomery, inclining his trademark beret, looking like a British Imperial aristocrat (he was actually from the middle class). But the third, most important, figure also shows up in the photographs: Dwight D. Eisenhower.

Plagued by requests, demands, and constant mini-emergencies, Eisenhower was equally annoyed with Patton and Montgomery: sometimes even his relations with Omar

Soldiers from the 630th Tank Destroyer Battalion, Company "B," dig in near Bastogne, Belgium, during the December 1944 Battle of the Bulge.

Bradley were strained. Eisenhower, of all these men, had a great capacity for keeping things on an even keel, however. While acknowledging Eisenhower's occasional mistakes, most military historians concur that no one else could have held the Western Alliance together as well for so long.

Could the war have ended in 1944?

Many people, especially those who admire George Patton, believe so. What they overlook, however, is the sheer stubbornness as well as creativity of the Germans on the defense. Operating on his own hook, Patton could very likely have reached the Rhine in central France: whether he could have forced the bridge and entered Germany is altogether uncertain. To have advanced that far that fast would also have meant extended supply lines.

In truth, the war could only have ended if the Russians, British, and Americans had all agreed to a relentless, day-by-day series of attacks. Given that no one feared losing the war at this point, such an aggressive policy seemed unnecessary. As autumn waned, some American and British units felt it would be a quiet winter and that they would wait until spring to assail the Third Reich.

How did Hitler manage to launch a counteroffensive?

The German military had always been best while on the offense, and Hitler gambled that just enough of the former skill and drive remained. On December 16, 1944, German infantry and panzer units poured across a fifty-mile front in the Ardennes Forest. Some of the Germans were coming the same way they had in May 1940, during the Battle for France.

Hitler's attack took the Allies completely by surprise. No one expected an attack at all, but for the Germans to come through the Ardennes Forest seemed most improba-

---

Where did Hitler ever get the expression "The Third Reich"?

To get the full flavor, one has to listen to the rest of the sentence. Hitler often spoke, shouted, or screamed about the "Third Reich … which shall last 1,000 years!"

Hitler meant that his Reich (or Empire) was the third of German history. First, in order of succession, was the Holy Roman Empire established by Charlemagne and then King Otto the Great. Technically that Reich did last a thousand years, from the coronation of Charlemagne on Christmas Day of 800 to 1806, when it was abolished by Napoleon. The second Reich was Imperial Germany, established by Otto von Bismarck and Kaiser Wilhelm I in 1871. And the third Reich was, very clearly, Hitler's own creation, which he intended to last virtually forever.

ble. In the opening twelve hours, Hitler's men cut through Allied—mostly American—defenses and opened a whole new front in the war. Things got even better, from the German point of view, in the next twelve hours, and Hitler celebrated in his Berlin bunker, exulting that he had again pulled the wool over his enemy's eyes. To some extent he had, but the main difference was that Hitler needed the weather to remain precisely what it was: heavy, dull conditions with cloud cover.

What prevented the Germans from making a larger breakthrough?

Credit goes to those few Americans on the ground who fought so stubbornly that the German front did not widen beyond a certain point. The Germans took the town of Malmedy, with its railroad connections, but they came up short at Bastogne, the town with as many as eight roads running through. This was the key to the entire "Bulge," and General McAuliffe knew it. When summoned to surrender, he replied with a single word: "Nuts."

As long as Bastogne held, the Germans could not expand beyond their initial indentation. Hitler's original aim had been to reach Antwerp, where the Allies' supply depots were. Failing that, his men had to keep at it, plugging away each day, until the skies cleared. The weather change came on Christmas Day and with it the opportunity for the Allied planes to attack the German tank columns. Within forty-eight hours, most of Hitler's remaining armored units were wrecks on the battlefield.

Was the Battle of the Bulge worth it from the German point of view?

In terms of morale, it probably was. The Germans were thrilled to go from defense to offense. They also showed—if anyone still doubted—that they were one of the finest militaries ever seen. But the price was very high. Perhaps 200,000 Germans went killed, wounded, or missing, and the lost tanks could not be replaced.

What was the situation on New Year's Day of 1945?

Any doubt of eventual Allied victory had been erased: everyone knew it was only a matter of time. Some Allied generals pled for a massive assault on Germany, while others argued for a slow approach. Concerns were raised as to whether the British, Americans, or Russians would reach Berlin first, and which group would hold the largest share of the city, once occupied.

On the German side, pessimism and fatalism worked together to create a uniquely German approach: some men would fight to the end, while others were eager to surrender. A subtle shift in the German population was observed, with individuals and families moving from east to west Germany. They did not like any of the Allies, but they much preferred the Americans and the British to the Russians.

When did the Russians commence their great offensive?

The Red Army had been quiet for several months, but it struck with devastating effectiveness on January 12, 1945. No fewer than seven different army groups, with as many as three million men in total, hit the Germans on a front extending from the Baltic Sea to central Hungary. Some German units fought with skill and fatalism, while others simply melted away.

That Stalin wished his men to take Berlin was beyond dispute, but it remains an interesting debate as to whether the British and Americans could have gotten there first. For his part, Eisenhower eschewed any such race; to him, it was far more important to mop up the remaining German resistance in the field. Montgomery was for an aggressive move toward Berlin, and his chief, Winston Churchill, wanted to be sure that the eventual "handshake" with the Red Army be conducted as far to the east as possible.

U.S. President Franklin D. Roosevelt (left) with British Prime Minister Winston Churchill at the Yalta Conference. The other important participant not pictured here is the Soviet Union's Joseph Stalin.

How did FDR get to the great summit meeting at Yalta?

In January 1945, FDR—who was a very sick man—went aboard the U.S.S. *Quincy* which took him to Yalta. There he met Churchill, and the two men flew to the Crimea to meet "Uncle Joe," as Stalin then was known.

Even before the Big Three sat at conference tables, it was evident that the Great Alliance was beginning to fragment. Hitler and the Third Reich would soon be part of the dustbin of history, but what kind of new world would emerge? Would Poland, which had so long been denied its place among the world nations, be given true freedom? Would the Eastern European nations which had fought with Nazi Germany be punished? And what would Germany look like in the future?

What were the "non-negotiable" parts of each Allied leader's program?

To FDR, it was most important, by far, that a new world government be established. He knew as well as anyone of the failure of the League of Nations, but he spoke passionately of the need for a new "World Instrument of Peace." For Churchill, maintenance and retention of the British Empire was number one. A true Victorian, Churchill wished to see the Union Jack fly over the parts of the world which had been "stolen" by the Germans and Japanese.

Because the Red Army was so large (and potentially menacing) Stalin held strong cards at Yalta, but he was masterful at concealing some of them. Unfailingly courteous in public, Stalin maneuvered to ensure that Eastern Europe would fall under Russian domination. Poland was his true area of non-negotiability; he intended it to serve as a buffer zone for the Soviet Union, defending it from attacks from central and Western Europe.

FDR, beyond any doubt. But Churchill, who drank liquor two to three times a day, was not in good health either, and Stalin's hair had turned completely white during the previous three years. None of the Big Three expected to live very long, and each was consequently keen to shape the new world about to emerge before he lost his chance.

When did the British and Americans commence their spring campaign?

One can call it "winter," because it began on February 8, 1945. One thousand and thirty-four guns laid down half a million shells over the course of a mere six hours, the heaviest bombardment seen on the Western Front during the entire war. Following this barrage, the British and Americans began to move and encountered little opposition. As usual, George Patton's Third Army covered ground the fastest, and some of his tank commanders expressed the opinion that they could get to Berlin ahead of the Russians. Patton, for once, kept his mouth shut on the subject.

What was the single most condemned Allied bombardment of the war?

Throughout 1944, many journalists had raised questions over the continued escalation of Allied aerial bombings. The greatest questions emerged in the aftermath of the destruction of the German city of Dresden. On the evening of February 13, 1945, over 1,000 British and American bombers pounded the beautiful city, leaving roughly 135,000 people dead. Whether this was merely another pounding of an enemy city or if it had been selected for vengeful purposes remains debated to this day. What was taking place in the Pacific War, however, had the potential to eclipse even the Allied bombings of Germany.

WAR IN THE PACIFIC

When did General MacArthur get the number-one photo opportunity of World War II?

When he departed the Philippines in 1942, MacArthur had vowed, simply, "I shall return." In October 1944, he got the opportunity, but this time he came with almost 200,000 Americans at his back.

MacArthur and a group of aides splashed ashore on October 12, 1944, to much fanfare and the click of many cameras. MacArthur purposely wore his favorite military hat—he had always disdained helmets—and this was his supreme moment during the war, when he honored his pledge to return, and did so in a blaze of glory.

Douglas MacArthur (center), U.S. five star general and field marshal of the Philippine Army, made good on his promise by returning to the Philippines, landing in Leyte in October 1944.

By that point, how much willingness did the Japanese still possess?

Much more than we might expect. Time and again, when asked if they would continue to fight under the conditions the Japanese of 1944 experienced, the typical American responds with a negative. To the Japanese, however, it did not seem a matter of choice. Their society was so different from the Americans, and their belief in the sanctity of the emperor was so strong that they were ready to fight on.

During the Battle for the Philippines, a handful of Japanese leaders developed the idea for the Kamikaze planes and pilots. Japanese fighters had committed suicide before this, but they had never done so in such a dramatic and public way. On October 22, 1944, beginning with an attack on an Australian battle cruiser, Japanese pilots began coming out of the sky with both themselves and their planes strapped with explosives. Crashing into the flight deck of an enemy warship, they often caused great damage, and on some occasions they sank the ship.

Where did the Pacific War stand on January 1, 1945?

From the American point of view, things were progressing very well. One island after another had fallen to the U.S. Army and Marines. The disturbing aspect of the situation was

419

the increasingly high casualties. On some islands, as many as 10,000 Japanese fought to the death, with the Americans taking only 250 prisoners. On each occasion, the Americans took fewer casualties than they caused, but if the ratios continued in this direction, the final conquest of Japan would be very bloody indeed.

From the Japanese point of view, things were grim and getting worse, but they maintained an unshakable resolve. Regardless of how many men were killed, they would fight to the last. Even the regular U.S. bombings, some of which produced genuine firestorms, did not shake the Japanese belief. Japan, too, had a new weapon.

When were kamikaze pilots first deployed?

During the Battle for the Philippines, toward the end of 1944. One thing Americans did not expect was that Japanese pilots would aim their planes straight at the decks of American ships and blast in to immediate death. Under the Japanese code of Bushido, however, an honorable death was one of the best things a person could ask for.

The first few kamikaze attacks were successful, but over time the American anti-aircraft gunners became expert at picking out the lone plane, headed for their decks. What they could not contend with was a mass of kamikaze planes at once, and this happened during the Battle for Okinawa.

What was so important about Okinawa and Iwo Jima?

American military planners determined that these islands had to be conquered before any approach could be made against the main islands of Japan. Iwo Jima, especially, was needed as an airport for the American aircraft.

Iwo Jima was a volcanic island which had emerged from the sea only fifty years previous. Roughly 21,000 Japanese defenders were subjected to an intense aerial and naval bombardment that lasted for three days, but when the Americans came ashore they discovered the Japanese had remained largely safe in their defenses. As a result, the fighting for Iwo Jima was intense, often hand to hand. The Japanese fought with fanatical determination; the Americans responded with the grim determination that they would prevail. And so they did. Only 216 Japanese were taken prisoner; all the rest perished. American casualties were even higher: about 26,000 killed, wounded, or gone missing.

Which island came next?

The island of Okinawa is sixty miles long and five miles wide, and it is about halfway between Formosa (today's Taiwan) and Japan. Okinawa would have to be taken, the war planners declared, in order for a U.S. invasion force to gather before striking the Japanese home islands. Therefore, an immense army of close to half a million men and naval forces with roughly eight battleships and eight aircraft carriers were assembled for the assault. As at Iwo Jima, the Japanese did not contest the landings; they concentrated their forces in the island's middle and fought ferociously.

The U.S.S. *Okinawa* burns after being hit by two Japanese kamakaze pilots during the battle for Okinawa.

Iwo Jima had been terrible: Okinawa resembled people's private images of hell. The Japanese fought for every yard. On April 6, 1945, 355 Japanese kamikaze pilots climbed into their planes parked on one mainland airfield. Nearly half of these planes were taken down before they reached Okinawa, but those that arrived did terrible damage to the U.S. fleet. On that same day, Battleship *Yamato*—the last major Japanese warship— sailed on a suicidal run. It was sunk before it reached Okinawa, and nearly all 1,500 sailors were lost.

How many people died on Okinawa?

When one includes the sailors on both sides and the kamikaze pilots, the death total comes to about 120,000 Japanese and 25,000 Americans. This was, quite likely, the single worst cauldron of the war, surpassing even Stalingrad in terms of sheer misery. When the battle for Okinawa was over, no neutral observer could fail to comment on the heroism of both sides. But the end for Imperial Japan seemed very close.

The Japanese high command was in what might call a schizoid state. The top military men declared they would fight to the bitter end, while the top diplomats looked everywhere for a solution. One sad, forlorn hope was that the Russians might mediate between the U.S. and Japan. Russia, however, had its eye on a much bigger prize: the takeover of Eastern Europe.

421

HITLER'S FALL

Did Hitler still, somewhere in his mind, think he could win?

He alternated, during his final days, between abject despair and sudden, short-lived rallies. Some miracle might still occur, he said. The British and Americans, he said, would wake up to the terrible danger posed by Russian communism and join him in a war against Stalin. As fantastical and as ridiculous as these ideas seem, there was one solitary moment when Hitler's luck did seem to change. That was when FDR died.

What were FDR's last moments?

The morning of April 12, 1945, found FDR in Warm Springs, Georgia, taking a short holiday at the home of two of his female cousins. A portrait painter came that morning and fussed over her work to such an extent that the Roosevelt cousins branded her a batterer of an elderly, sick man. Indeed, FDR looked old and frail, but there was plenty of inner strength remaining. It was his body that was about to implode.

Early that afternoon, FDR complained of a terrible headache, put his hands to his head, and soon went unconscious. Doctors were summoned from all directions, but the first one pronounced the president dead at 3:55 P.M. The immediate cause of death was a cerebral hemorrhage, perhaps the result of long-lasting effects of polio and overwork.

Who became president after FDR died?

Just three hours later, Harry S. Truman (1884–1972), the sitting vice president, was sworn in as president of the United States. Just ten months earlier, Truman had been a little-known senator from Missouri, well liked by his colleagues but not held in high regard. A forceful, often loud, and sometimes impatient person, he seemed like a poor replacement for the fallen FDR.

America went into mourning. FDR had become—to the common person—the emblem of a fuller, fairer, and friendlier nation. Those who remembered what life had been like in January 1933, when he was sworn into office, claimed that their lives were divided into two sections: "before" and "after" FDR. To be sure, FDR had made many enemies, but even they were quiet at the time of his death.

Did FDR's death change anything on the front lines?

Not a thing. There were those—many Britons especially—who feared Harry Truman would prove a weak, indecisive president. Within days they admitted their mistake: the man from Missouri knew his mind and kept to his own decisions, regardless of the political cost. The Allies, meanwhile, pressed their invasion of Germany.

How did the Russians get to Berlin first?

Even today it is arguable whether the British and Americans could have reached Hitler's capital before the Red Army. What is not arguable is that most British and American troops would not have wished the dreadful task of fighting for each street and building (the Russians lost 200,000 men in this, their final offensive).

Hitler and a handful of stalwart Nazis remained in the bunker, while many others, including Herman Goering, fled for other parts of the Reich. Hitler grew weaker and less decisive by the day, and on April 29, 1945—with the sound of Russian guns clearly audible—he married his longtime mistress, Eva Braun (1912–1945), and said farewell to his staff.

Is there any chance Hitler faked his own death and escaped to live in exile?

About one chance in 100,000. Hitler and his wife killed each other on April 30, 1945, and, pursuant to his instructions, their bodies were taken out of the bunker and dowsed in petrol. They were set afire, ensuring that Hitler's body would never be exhibited in an Allied victory celebration.

Thus perished the greatest evil genius of the twentieth century and perhaps the greatest of all human history. Blessed with a mediocre intellect but superb intuition, Hitler had risen from the lower middle-class to become the most powerful man in the world. Had he known how to stop—perhaps in 1937 and 1938—he would have gone down as a reasonably good political and military leader. Instead, he plunged the world into the cauldron of World War II and attempted to eliminate an entire group of people.

Hitler with Eva Braun in 1942. They married in 1945, not long before they both committed suicide.

Did any fighting continue after Hitler's death?

Yes. Not only were some German soldiers fanatical to the point where they did not believe the Führer was dead, but there was also a handful of leaders who mistakenly believed they could continue the Third Reich, even in much reduced circumstances. The leader of these was Admiral Karl Von Doenitz, Hitler's closest confidante toward the end. As long as Doenitz and even a few German divisions held out, the war continued.

Roughly around the time that Hitler's body was consumed by the flames, the Russians raised the Soviet flag over the Reichstag, home of the German legislature. By May 1, 1945, most of Berlin was in Russian hands, albeit at a terrible cost. For Stalin, too, the war was not over. He directed his southernmost army groups to seize Vienna and as much of Czechoslovakia as possible.

What were the celebrations like?

On May 5, 1945, Admiral Doenitz signed the document of unconditional surrender. Even though some German units, especially in mountainous terrain, continued to fight, the European War was clearly over.

The Americans celebrated with gusto; a famous photograph shows a GI kissing a woman on a New York street (whether they are married, friends, or strangers remains unknown). The Australians went wild with joy. Quite likely, the palm goes, however, to the British, who had been in the war the longest. England and Scotland had lost nearly 400,000 men, and their economies and merchant marines were in tatters. This did not prevent the English, Welsh, and Scots from giving full throat to their jubilation. The Irish Republic, by contrast, had never declared war on Hitler's Germany, and the response there was muted.

Can one people or nation truly claim to have won the European War?

The British claimed they had done it, and one can argue that they stood alone for a time. The Russians claimed they had fought the hardest and suffered the most (both were probably true). The Americans shrugged and pointed both to the performance of their men and the enormous contributions they made in terms of war materiel. Even the Free French, led by Charles de Gaulle, made claims.

The truth is that *all* the efforts—of *all* of these people—were required. Monstrous as Hitler's regime was, one can only admire the skill and determination with which its people fought. If Britain had *not* stood alone in 1940–1941, there might have been no Great Alliance. If Russia had not stopped Hitler *just shy of Moscow*, the Nazis might have gained tremendous reserves of manpower and materiel. And if the United States had not thrown its *immense weight* into the war effort, the contest might have dragged on for years.

What did the former Third Reich look like in the summer of 1945?

There was tremendous confusion, especially among the millions of displaced persons. There were Poles living in western Germany, and Germans surviving in eastern Poland.

There were great Allied armies occupying most of the former Third Reich. What prevented the confused, unhappy scene from becoming truly tragic was the attitude of the Western Allies, the United States most especially.

No other soldier had as much food, money, and time to spare as the American GI. Sometimes he was angry; sometimes he went over the line in berating former Nazis; but for the most part, the GI understood that Hitler's crimes were not those of the German people as a whole. When one compares GI Joe of 1945 to his Red Army counterpart, there is no question that the Germans, Austrians, and others would much prefer to have been governed by the United States than the Soviet Union.

Did many former Nazis suffer for their crimes?

Not in the immediate aftermath of the war. The Nuremberg Trials of 1947–1948 accomplished that work. For the moment, however, the United States had to look to another front. Imperial Japan had not yet surrendered.

SURRENDER OF JAPAN

Were the kamikaze flights enjoying any success?

Very little. Japan still had plenty of pilots willing to make the ultimate sacrifice, but it had very few planes for them to fly.

Could the U.S. Navy and U.S. Air Force simply have pounded the Japanese into submission?

Very likely, but it would have taken a long time. The Americans, from President Harry Truman to the newest recruit, wanted to end the war quickly. Therefore, although preparations for an invasion of the home islands began, most of the top planners put their hope in the newly created atom bomb.

Who had built this bomb that was called "Destroyer of Worlds"?

Slightly more than 100,000 Americans were involved in the Manhattan Project. Despite its name, the operation was conducted in places like Chicago and Oak Ridge, Tennessee rather than New York City.

General Leslie Groves (1896–1970) was leader of the Manhattan Project, which brought together soldiers, sailors, Marines, and civilians. By July 1945, the project had developed some weapons to the point where they could be tested, and President Truman, in Potsdam, Germany, learned that the first test, in the New Mexico desert, had been successful.

How did Harry Truman fare in his first "Big Three" meeting?

Truman was very conscious of being the newest member of the Big Three. He was impressed with Churchill and somewhat irritated by Stalin, who seemed utterly sure of himself. Truman tried to steer a middle course between the other two leaders but found them relentless. Hard lines were being drawn, with Churchill's British imperialism and Stalin's Russian communism dictating their actions. More than once, Truman threatened to go home if the Big Three did not get down to business. What they did agree upon was a four-part division of Germany for the foreseeable future, with Russian, British, American, and Free French zones of control. On learning of the successful test of the atom bomb, Truman brought it up obliquely in a conversation with Stalin, who appeared uninterested. Truman, therefore, felt he had a free hand in deciding whether or not to use the bomb.

At what precise moment did Harry Truman make the decision to drop the bomb?

We don't know. Several leading members of the Truman administration worked with the president in making the decision, and though Truman later claimed that the decision was his and his alone, history suggests there were several players who offered their input. General Eisenhower, upon learning of the bomb, voted against using it, as did a number of other military men. In general, the American civilian leaders were the keenest on using the bomb against Japan.

Would the United States truly have lost one million men in an invasion of the Japanese islands?

This is one of the most keenly debated of questions, but it is very difficult to come up with a firm, defensible answer. To those Americans who had attacked at Iwo Jima and Okinawa, it was patently obvious that the Japanese would fight to the death and cause a huge number of casualties. To the war planners who observed the implosion of Imperial Japan, which had almost no planes or petrol remaining, it seemed obvious that the Americans, with their materiel, would triumph. No one could be certain, however, of the fighting level that remained in Japan.

President Truman made his decision based on many factors, but at the root was a desire to end the conflict quickly *and* to teach the Japanese a severe lesson. If we could interview Truman today, he would likely reply that the atom bomb was merciful because it brought the fighting to an end.

When was the first atom bomb dropped?

At 8:16 A.M. local time on Monday, August 6, 1945, "Little Boy," as the bomb was called, was dropped from the Boeing B-29 *Enola Gay* and obliterated Hiroshima, Japan. An American crew of twelve were on board the plane that carried the bomb. After locating the city of Hiroshima, the crew dropped the bomb, then watched as an enormous mushroom cloud rose from the point one hundred yards above ground, where the detonation occurred. The crew returned to base, confident they had accomplished their mission, yet not knowing what had happened.

We know, of course, that the bomb was the most ferocious, destructive weapon ever unleashed, and we believe that around 75,000 Japanese died in a matter of minutes; almost an equal number of people died later due to leukemia or other diseases related to long-term effects resulting from the radiation. We know that Hiroshima ceased to exist in the normal sense and that an entirely new era had opened in military affairs. For the first time in human history, it seemed possible that man might destroy all of civilization.

Did Japan surrender?

Almost total radio silence prevailed. Even the entry of Russia into the Pacific War two days later did not bring about an immediate surrender.

Americans of 1945—who learned of the event two days after—assumed that the Japanese were too stubborn to face reality, but the likelihood is that the Japanese leaders were simply stunned. More men and women had died in the firestorm over Tokyo in June 1945, but never had so many people perished so quickly. The Japanese said nothing, communicated nothing, and President Truman gave the go-ahead for a second atom bomb to be dropped.

Originally built in 1915 and called the Hiroshima Prefectural Commercial Exhibition, the Genbaku Dome, or Hiroshima Peace Memorial, was the only building left standing at the point where the Americans dropped the first atomic bomb in 1945.

When was the second atom bomb dropped?

"Fat Man" was dropped (again from the *Enola Gay*) on the city of Nagasaki on August 9, 1945. The crew of ten had a difficult time finding its target, and the bomb killed fewer people—perhaps 45,000—on first impact. How many later died from diseases related to the bombing remains in question.

Now, and only now, did the Japanese consider surrender. The top military leaders were tied in their vote, which was broken by Emperor Hirohito. Not only would the country surrender without condition, he declared, but he would make a radio broadcast to his subjects, asking them to "endure the unendurable." There was plenty of resistance; some troops even attacked the imperial palace, hoping to stop the radio address. All went off as planned, however, and millions of Japanese heard their emperor's voice for the first time.

When did the surrender ceremony take place?

General Douglas MacArthur had already landed in Japan and was setting up a provisional government, but the actual ceremony was held aboard battleship U.S.S. *Missouri*, on September 3, 1945. The Japanese dignitaries were held waiting for some time—as a final act of humiliation—and when they signed, General MacArthur gave a short speech about the need to bring the blessings of peace to a troubled world. Six years and two days after it began with the Nazi invasion of Poland, World War II was over.

How many people died in World War II?

At least fifty million died. Some scholars believe the number to be considerably higher. One only has to go through a short list of the major combatants.

The Soviet Union lost in the neighborhood of twenty million, when one adds the civilian and military deaths together. Germany lost at least five million, but perhaps as many as seven million. Poland lost only 150,000 men in the original fighting, but it had at least six million people taken during the war (many to death camps). Japan lost at least three million soldiers and perhaps as many as one million civilians. China, which was fighting throughout the war, may have lost as many as ten million. The British (390,000) and American (406,000) losses seem much more bearable, but there were plenty of war widows for the ensuing decade.

Can all of this terrible destruction really be laid at the feet of one man?

A great deal of it can. Hitler made the choice to A) invade Poland; B) conquer France; C) bomb the British Isles; D) attack the Soviet Union; and E) attempt to exterminate the Jews. That he was the single greatest destructive force of human history thus far seems inarguable.

Of course, other factors were involved. The Russian animus toward Poland was long-standing. The Franco-German enmity was almost seventy years old. The Japanese way of war had been developed centuries earlier. Even so, when Hitler is removed from the equation, the situation would qualify as a great conflict but probably not be labeled a "World War."

THE COLD WAR: 1945 TO 1980

Was the Cold War inevitable?

Yes. Two economic systems as thoroughly divergent as democratic capitalism and communistic dictatorship—personified by the United States and Soviet Union—were bound to conflict. Whether the Cold War could have been "easier" or "softer" with fewer direct confrontations is another question entirely.

When did the Cold War begin?

Though no one said so at the time, the Cold War began in the days and weeks following the fall of Hitler's Third Reich. Soviet troops advanced into almost half a dozen nations in Eastern Europe, removing nascent political groups and asserting Russian dominance. If Franklin D. Roosevelt had still been alive and the "Big Three" of earlier days been in place, some of this might have been averted.

FDR had died of natural causes in April 1945, and Churchill was booted from office by the British voters in July. As a result, Joseph Stalin was the only remaining member of the former "Big Three." Stalin took advantage of this, pressing his foreign policy goals in Eastern Europe; given enough time, he might have taken much of Western Europe as well. He was thwarted by two things: American possession of the atomic bomb and the surprising willpower shown by President Harry S. Truman.

What was the relative strength of the two sides when the Cold War began?

The Soviet Union, or U.S.S.R. (Union of Soviet Socialist Republics), possessed an amazing lead in all the conventional means of war: five million men in uniform, at least 10,000 tanks, and more airplanes than anyone could count. The United States possessed two antidotes to this, however. First and foremost, America had the atomic bomb, which could neutralize almost any Russian offensive. Second, and almost as important, the

U.S. Navy was far superior to its Russian counterpart, allowing the United States to deploy its much smaller forces more effectively.

Even with this measure of superiority, the United States was concerned by some of Stalin's moves. The Russian leader was a gambler, and he believed he could bluff his way past Truman and the new British prime minister, Clement Atlee. On occasion, he succeeded, but by mid-1947, the British and Americans had taken the full measure of Stalin.

When did the United States become the undisputed leader of the free world?

It had, in numerous ways, already played the role, but when Truman declared in March 1947 that his country would resist communist insurgency anywhere it took place, America became, beyond any doubt, the bulwark and bastion of freedom. Today, this claim sounds boastful, but to millions, perhaps hundreds of millions, of people around the globe, it was absolutely clear in 1947 that only the United States could, and would, stand up to the bully in the Kremlin.

Britain had, until 1947, defended Greece and Turkey against communist insurgency, but it announced that it was unable to continue. Truman stepped into the gap, asserting the Truman Doctrine. At almost the same time, however, Truman also announced the rollout of the European Aid Program, known ever since as the Marshall Plan.

Which European nations accepted the economic assistance offered by the Marshall Plan?

Virtually all the nations of Western Europe accepted; almost all the nations of Eastern Europe rejected. The difference was quite simple: Russian coercion.

U.S. President Harry S. Truman had to tie up the loose ends of World War II after FDR died, but, even more challenging, he was tasked with the advent of the Cold War against the Soviet Union.

How important was George Marshall to the winning of the early phase of the Cold War?

George C. Marshall (1880–1959) was one of those truly remarkable public servants without whom governments cannot achieve great things. When he entered the U.S. Army, the horse and wagon were still as well known as the car and jeep; when he retired, the world saw nuclear submarines and atomic bombs. Marshall bridged the gap between these eras with a career distinguished by honesty, integrity, and clear thinking.

Stalin made it plain that acceptance of American economic aid was tantamount to betrayal of the Soviet Union. All the nations of Eastern Europe, therefore, declined to participate, with disastrous results for their economies. One can, of course, argue that the United States was acting in its self-interest, but it was an enlightened self-interest. The Russian position, on the other hand, was akin to cutting off one's nose in order to spite one's face.

What was the geographic flash point for the Cold War?

Almost from the beginning up to the very end, the city of Berlin was the place where Russian and American, communist and capitalist, interests clashed the most. In the months following the end of the Third Reich, Berlin was divided into four zones of occupation: Britain, France, America, and Russia each had control of one. Berlin itself, however, lay within the Russian zone of occupation of Germany as a whole, and there was a real concern that it would be blockaded or starved out.

Stalin attempted this in 1947–1948. When Russian tanks and troops prevented the resupply of the three other zones, the United States announced an airlift of food and medicine to the desperate people of West Berlin. In the fourteen months that followed, American technical proficiency was demonstrated as planes dropped the food and medicine from the air, but American moral superiority was showcased to an even higher degree. Perhaps at no other time in the twentieth century did the United States stand so high in the eyes of the world as during the Berlin Airlift.

How did Stalin respond to the American bloodless victories?

The cynical man in the Kremlin had more of a sense of humor than one might suppose. He acknowledged the Americans had boxed him in and made him look bad, but he genuinely believed that these were mere setbacks. Like Lenin before him, Stalin was 100 percent convinced that communism and the Soviet Union would, in the end, prevail. And the events of 1949 suggested that he, and his nation, were on the right track.

431

CHINA, KOREA, AND VIETNAM

When did the Soviet Union explode its first atomic bomb?

Late in August 1949, which just happened to be the tenth anniversary of the notorious Anti-Aggression Pact, the Soviet Union exploded its first atomic bomb in the desert of Kazakhstan. Russian scientists had been helped by information stolen from the United States, but there is little doubt they would have gotten there sooner or later.

President Truman released the news to the American people on September 23, 1949, and the Soviet Union promptly confirmed that it had, indeed, passed the atomic threshold. Americans, who thought of the Russians as inferior technicians, were appalled.

What was the second major shock of that season?

The autumn of 1949 was long remembered as the season in which the Cold War entered its second phase. The Americans, and their allies, had won nearly all the "battles" of the first phase, and morally they stood much taller than their Russian opponents. News of the Russian atom bomb was bad, so far as Americans were concerned, but the news from China was even worse.

On October 1, 1949, one week after Truman revealed that Russia had the atomic bomb, Chairman Mao Zedong stood atop a pavilion in Tiananmen Square to announce the establishment of the People's Republic of China. Looking as confident as he sounded, Mao declared that the people of China had accomplished this and that their goals—synonymous with his own—would eventually result in the creation of a new, socialist world. Television was not yet a fixture in American homes; had it been, Mao's declaration would have been even more frightening to the American public.

What was meant by the expression "Who lost China"?

China, of course, was not a province of the United States, and the expression makes little sense from our present-day perspective. But to millions of Americans in 1949, it seemed as if Nationalist China, which had been an ally of the United States in World War II, had indeed been "lost" to the Communists.

Americans are, by and large, a practical people, and they do not usually indulge in fantasies about who lost what. In the aftermath of the Russian atomic bomb and the declaration of the Peoples Republic of China, however, many Americans succumbed to fear, loathing, and even self-persecution. Millions of Americans suspected treason on some level, and when a junior senator from Wisconsin declared there were 200 known Communists in the U.S. State Department, they tended to agree.

Was Joseph McCarthy as important as we have been led to believe?

Only in that he exposed and exploited the ugliest side of the American character. Joseph McCarthy (1908–1957) was a shrewd political manipulator who made it appear as if he had all the answers and that the press and the people should pay great attention to him. McCarthy would never have succeeded in his outlandish claims in other times: it required the vitriol and fear of the Cold War to thrust him into national prominence.

Would McCarthy ever be humbled?

Yes, in 1954, but until then he rode the wave of paranoia rather like a tiger. His star might have faded had the Korean War not begun in June of 1950. The beginning of that conflict made McCarthy seem like a prophet.

Senator Joseph McCarthy (R-Wisconsin) chaired the House Un-American Activities Committee, which was a witch hunt for supposed American communists plotting to undermine the United States.

On June 25, 1950, North Korean tanks and troops streamed across the 38th parallel, the dividing line between North and South Korea since the end of World War II. North Korea achieved almost complete surprise, and its weaponry, provided primarily by the Soviet Union, was more than enough to secure early victories. Within weeks, the North Koreans had taken the capital of South Korea and were pressing the remaining forces to the bottom of the Korean peninsula. By then, however, South Korea had a powerful new ally: American troops fighting under the blue flag of the United Nations.

How long did Truman take to make his decision?

He probably decided within minutes, but many photographs were taken that day of the president huddling with his advisors. Should America go it alone or do it under the umbrella of the United Nations? Should troops be sent from occupied Japan or from the mainland of the United States? Something quite different had emerged. Thanks to the ubiquitous television camera, a chief executive and his advisors could be seen as they conferred on the momentous decision of whether to go to war.

The United Nations Security Council voted in favor, and by July 1950, hundreds of thousands of troops—the great majority of them American—were on their way to South Korea. The choice for supreme UN commander was an easy one, because General Douglas MacArthur, the liberator of the Philippines in 1944, was in Japan.

433

How high did MacArthur stand in the aftermath of the landings at Inchon?

One historian later called him the "American Caesar." No previous American leader since Ulysses Grant in 1865 had stood so high in the opinion of his countrymen. Some people who knew MacArthur more closely were less flattering: they considered him a publicity hound and a crowd pleaser. In the immediate aftermath of Inchon, however, Americans had their hero in the fatigue-clad, cigar-puffing general who seemed to know no fear. He even refused to wear a helmet.

How close did the North Koreans come to total victory?

By late August, they had taken eighty percent of all of South Korea and had the UN forces pinned down to a very small area on the southeastern side of the peninsula. The sheer success of the North Korean onslaught took its toll, however; the North Koreans were weary, and when General MacArthur unleashed a counteroffensive, they had to yield all the ground they had gained.

On September 15, 1950, the UN Forces went ashore at Inchon, on the central-west part of the Korean Peninsula. No one expected them to come at this point, where the tidal waves were so high; that was precisely why MacArthur chose that point. Not only was it dismaying to learn that the Americans had landed behind them, but the North Koreans were badly positioned. Within days, they commenced a retreat that soon had them back at the 38th parallel, where they had started three months earlier. The landings at Inchon were another clear-cut American victory, a demonstration of technical competence as well as sheer guts and determination.

Who decided to prevent the Americans from taking all of North Korea?

Whether it was completely Stalin's decision or a shared decision taken with Mao remains difficult to determine. What is clear, however, is that the major Communist powers could not afford a complete loss in Korea: it would undermine their status worldwide.

While MacArthur's blue-helmeted troops crossed into North Korea, roughly 300,000 Chinese crossed the border into that country and set a trap for the invading Americans. MacArthur was usually on top of matters such as these, but he suffered from overconfidence in 1950, and when the Chinese "volunteers" attacked in November 1950, he was taken completely by surprise. Within days, he telegrammed Washington, D.C., that he, and the United States, now faced a much broader and more difficult war.

How bad was it for the men on the ground?

Surprised, even stunned, by the Chinese counterattack, the Americans fell back slowly, determined to make the communists pay for every inch of ground. Several units, including a Marine division, took terrible losses that December, and it was known among many American units as the worst of times, the worst of seasons. MacArthur, meanwhile, practically begged his superiors for authority to drop atomic bombs on the advancing Chinese.

President Truman was a true Cold War leader; he had no illusions about the Soviets and the threat they posed. Right now, however, he was faced with the prospect of having to fight the Red Chinese on the ground and the Red Russians in the air, with the possibility of a true atomic war. The United States had far more atomic bombs (365) than the Russians (6) but the chance of even one atomic bomb being dropped on an American city was more than the president could contemplate. This would be, as he later declared, "the wrong war with the wrong enemy at the wrong time."

Why did Truman fire MacArthur?

The two men were at odds personally and politically. MacArthur showed too much independence as a military leader and not enough respect for civilian authority. Twice, the president ignored MacArthur's pandering to the press, but on the third occasion he simply fired the general.

MacArthur came home to celebrations and parties and thoughts of one day running for president. He gave a memorable address to both Houses of Congress before heading off into retirement. The truth is that he was a fine military leader who had little sense of politics. His great days had already come and gone.

Where did the Korean War stand as the election of 1952 approached?

Eisenhower ran for president on the Republican ticket; his Democratic opponent was Adlai E. Stevenson. Eisenhower made the most of his military credentials, declaring that if elected, he would "go to Korea" to determine a workable solution. Stevenson had no answer to this, and Eisenhower rode handily to victory in November.

Making good on his promise, Eisenhower toured the UN lines in South Korea that December and came away with the impression that the situation had stabilized. More important, Eisenhower wanted the freedom to act on a larger scale because he feared the growing power of Communist China. Outgoing President Harry Truman quietly predicted that Eisenhower would

American marines in Seoul, Korea. The Korean War was the first major military conflict of the struggle for power between the communist East and democratic West.

make a poor chief executive because things would not run smoothly, as they tended to do in the military. In terms of the situation, he was quite correct; in terms of Eisenhower's temperament, he could hardly have been more mistaken.

What was the bombshell of March 1953?

Eisenhower had been in office for only six weeks when Joseph Stalin died on March 6, 1953. The death was from natural causes—not poison or any other nefarious instrument—but the reaction across the world was one of undisguised relief. No matter who stepped into Stalin's shoes, Westerners believed, he could not be worse than the tyrant who had ruled the Soviet Union for so long.

Eisenhower correctly saw Stalin's death as an opportunity. During the power struggles that followed, the Soviet Union did not have a number-one leader, while the United States did. Eisenhower, therefore, had more freedom to act, and he announced the end of active operations in Korea in the summer of 1953. Just as soon as he was finished with one international problem, however, Eisenhower was confronted by yet another.

For how long had France been involved in Vietnam?

Today we call it Vietnam, but for almost a century it was known as French Indochina. This area included all of what we now call Vietnam, plus Cambodia and Laos. France had colonized the area during the empire of Napoleon III and hung on to it long after it failed to provide much economic return. Prestige, as well as national pride, was concerned.

The insurgent movement in Vietnam was led by Ho Chi Minh, a communist and nationalist, who had long conspired to throw out the French. Back in 1919, he had appeared at the Versailles Peace conference, asking its leaders to consider the needs and interests of the Vietnamese people. Rebuffed and ignored, Ho continued to work for Vietnamese independence, and in 1954 he was the spirit behind the Vietnamese insurgency. The actual military operations were conducted by General Vo Nguyen Giap.

Why was Dien Bien Phu so important?

It was a forward military base for the French army, which was fighting for its life against the Vietnamese insurgents. Very likely, it was an error for the French to spend so many

---

Did the American people know how close Eisenhower's "brinksmanship" sometimes brought them to nuclear war?

Not really. Assuaged by belief in the superiority of its nuclear arsenal, Americans were confident their nation would prevail in any conflict. They did fear there would be casualties, however, and the mid-1950s saw the fullest expression of that fear in the numerous defensive drills conducted in schools across the country, where children practiced hiding underneath desks in their classrooms.

men and so much materiel in support of this city, but during the winter of 1954 the situation became a crisis. The French government—known as the Fourth Republic—appealed to the United States for aid.

President Eisenhower was much more volatile behind the scenes than when in front of a television camera. In private, he excoriated the French for making a bad decision and then asking to be bailed out. In public, however, Eisenhower declared that the United States would employ all methods and means to rescue its ally.

Did American parents and teachers truly believe that hiding beneath the desk would help?

They really seem to have believed it. The absurdity of the precaution was not made 100 percent clear until the autumn of 1983 with the debut of the television film *The Day After*. Only after seeing that program—frightening in all manner of ways—did most Americans realize that nuclear war would be an enormous calamity and that it might be just as well to stand outside and watch the bombs fall as to hide in a room or under a desk.

How close to nuclear war did the world come in 1954?

Eisenhower contemplated the use of nuclear weapons and privately rejected the idea, but in public his tough stance caused some fear in communist headquarters, including the

During the Cold War, American children were told to "duck and cover" under their desks in case of a nuclear attack. The notion that a school desk could protect you from nuclear explosions and fallout was, however, patently absurd.

Kremlin. Sensing this, Eisenhower became more—not less—willing to employ the nuclear possibility. Though he did not rescue the French, and though Dien Bien Phu fell in May 1954, Eisenhower strengthened in his belief that nuclear deterrence was the best option on the table. From that season forward, the Eisenhower administration drew up increasingly detailed plans for future nuclear attacks, including the idea of sending nuclear warheads against all communist nations.

Wasn't Eisenhower a grandfatherly figure?

He was indeed, to those who watched him on television. Those who knew him in the flesh knew that he combined a gentle appearance with an enormous will. Eisenhower was one of the most resolute of all the Cold War warriors, a man who would take great risks to do what he believed would make his nation more secure. No other leader during the Cold War—from Ronald Reagan to Joseph Stalin or Mikhail Gorbachev—had as much personal knowledge of war. Eisenhower acted accordingly. He was seldom intimidated by anyone, and his own calculating personality led him to employ what one historian has aptly called "Ike's Bluff."

Knowing that the United States possessed a dramatic lead in nuclear weapons, Eisenhower was willing to use this advantage to intimidate his foes. By 1954, the United States possessed the hydrogen or "H" bomb as well as the atomic bomb.

INDIA, ISRAEL, AND EGYPT

What was India's status at the end of World War II?

In 1945, India was still, just barely, under British control. The British pulled out completely in the spring of 1947, however, but not before they partitioned India into two countries: primarily Hindu India and primarily Muslim Pakistan.

The two countries fought each other right away, first in a bloodbath over the status of refugees and then in a declared war. The contest was frightful and the stakes were high, because both India and Pakistan wished to be "non-aligned" nations, meaning they did not wish to join either the capitalist or communist camp. The ethnic violence that erupted following the partition was a tragedy for the people of India and Pakistan. The deep divisions caused by partition remain to this day, as evidenced in several books on the subject, including *From Amritsar to Lahore*.

How was the State of Israel created?

This was accomplished by the United Nations. Both the General Assembly and the Security Council agreed that the Holocaust must never happen again and that the best solution for the millions of displaced Jews could be resolved by the creation of a Jewish state. On May 15, 1948, the state of Israel came into being, alongside the nation of Palestine.

Which is the better, more accurate, term: Israelis or Jews?

It really depends on one's audience. By and large, people who had moved to Israel before the partition of 1948 prefer *Jews*, and those who came later prefer Israelis. This is not a hundred percent rule, however.

Israel was carved from land that belonged to Palestine, and the Palestinians rightly claimed they were being made to suffer for the wrongs done by Hitler's Third Reich. What harmed the Palestinian cause, in the court of world opinion, was that many Palestinians had sympathized with the Nazis during World War II. Making matters worse, the four Arab nations bordering Israel all declared war on the Jewish state the very day it was established. Egypt, Iraq, Syria, and Jordan were all aligned against Israel, but world opinion favored the Israelis.

How did Israel win the first Arab–Israeli War, that of 1948–1949?

Through sheer guts and willpower. For at least a thousand years, the Jews had been derided as a non-military people who could not defend themselves, and this notion was given further credence because so many were killed during the Holocaust. The Israelis were determined to defend themselves once the nation of Israel was established.

In the later Arab–Israeli Wars (1956, 1967, and 1973), Israel benefitted greatly from arms and ammunition sent by the United States. This was not the case in 1948–1949, however. The Israelis fought with whatever means were closest to hand, and their Arab foes, who were not fighting for survival, did not care as deeply. By the spring of 1949, Israel had prevailed, and it was on its way to becoming a genuine nation.

Where did that leave the Arab nations?

In 1949, the Arab world was not far behind the new Jewish state, but each subsequent year demonstrated the economic superiority of Israel to its neighbors. In part, this is because so many Jews came from Europe and were exposed to a hypercapitalism that almost none of the Arabs had experienced. The Arabs did not make their own cause better, however. They continued to fulminate hostility toward Israel, ignoring their own economic needs. The Palestinians, needless to say, suffered the most. It was during this period (1949–1951) that the refugee camps in the Gaza Strip were established.

Was it inevitable that Israel would become aligned with America and that the Arabs would turn to the Soviet Union?

It was not. In the early days of the Arab–Israeli conflict, the United States approached many of the Arab states with generous offers of economic aid; most of these were spurned. Over the succeeding decade, America became so closely aligned with Israel that the Arab nations turned to Russia for military hardware.

How important was the price of oil, and gas, at this point?

Any policy or military analyst would quickly declare that the price of oil was one of the most important of all factors having to do with geopolitics; the average American citizen, however, was shielded from this information. To the average consumer, it was perfectly acceptable to drive a large car that yielded twelve miles per gallon, especially because gasoline only cost thirty cents per gallon.

When was the second Arab–Israeli War?

It came in the autumn of 1956 but was actually part of something even larger: the Suez Canal Crisis of that year.

Egypt took full possession of the Suez Canal in 1953, but Britain and France had long memories: both the leaders and their peoples remembered that the canal had been dug and consecrated through first

Israelis taking cover in a trench in Negba, Israel, during the 1948 Arab–Israeli War.

French and then British efforts. And when the leaders of Britain and France decided that Egypt was too volatile, or unsettled, a nation to assume control of the canal, they concocted a plan to retake the canal, with Israel doing most of the dirty work.

How long was the actual fighting?

Israeli tanks and troops swept through the Sinai Desert, taking much of the peninsula in one week. British and French paratroopers, meanwhile, landed, seizing key sections of the Suez Canal. But although their military success was swift, the British, French, and Israelis did not anticipate how world opinion would turn against them or how their "grab" would be perceived in the United States.

The man on the spot, as so often, was President Eisenhower. He knew the British and French leaders all too well and might have been expected to side with them. Eisenhower was a realist, however, and he lambasted his former allies, declaring he could not support an action which would cause the United States to lose "the whole Arab world." Eisenhower excoriated the British and French in public and forced the leaders to withdraw their forces. Egypt had suffered a military loss but a geostrategic victory.

SUMMIT MEETINGS

When was the first face-to-face meeting between leaders of the two superpowers?

The idea of a sit-down meeting between Stalin and Truman had hardly been considered; both men were too blunt and sure of themselves to agree to anything. Eisenhower and Khrushchev were a bit different, to be sure, but Eisenhower was not sure until 1959 that anything could be accomplished. Only in September of that year did a massive Russian plane descend at Washington and Soviet Premier Nikita Khrushchev (1894–1971) step off and onto the runway.

Television had, by now, entered almost two-thirds of all American homes, and millions of viewers watched, fascinated, as the rotund and sometimes comical Khrushchev engaged in verbal combat with the dignified but sometimes petulant Eisenhower. Neither man was really at his best during the two weeks that followed.

What did Khrushchev mean when he declared, "We will bury you!"

Of all the unfortunate things Khrushchev ever said, this was probably the most ill-timed: he spent years attempting to explain it. Quite likely, Khrushchev meant that Soviet communism was superior to American capitalism and that over time the former would witness the collapse and destruction of the latter (as it turned out, he had it precisely backward). But in 1959, it seemed as if Khrushchev meant that his country would use nuclear weapons to "bury" the United States.

Without attempting it, Khrushchev gave verbal ammunition to the Democratic Party, which would win the general election of 1960, in part thanks to the idea that a "missile gap" existed between the U.S.A. and U.S.S.R. A missile gap did exist, but it was clearly in favor of the United States.

Was Khrushchev really as uncouth and outspoken as he seemed?

It does not appear to have been an act. Khrushchev was poorly educated, and years of command with little need to worry about consequences had made him both a risk taker and a risky proposition. The Soviet premier had plenty of native intelligence, but he lacked the smoothness and diplomatic finesse to engage in a successful summit meeting. When he flew back to Moscow, Khrushchev left a series of divided opinions in the United States. He had, at least, displayed a very human face, one quite unlike that of Joseph Stalin, but whether it was an improvement was difficult to say.

Eisenhower, for his part, was weary of the Cold War and of his office. Two terms was enough, he told friends in private. Eisenhower did wish his vice president, Richard Nixon (1913–1994), to succeed him in office, but he was not about to go all-out on Nixon's behalf.

What was the U-2 Incident?

On May Day of 1960 (May Day was a major holiday in the U.S.S.R.) an American plane, a U-2, was shot down over Russian air space. The pilot, Gary Francis Powers, was captured.

East meets West in 1959, with (left to right) Nina Khrushchev (wife of Nikita), First Lady Mamie Eisenhower, Soviet Premier Nikita Khrushchev, and U.S. President Dwight D. Eisenhower attending a state dinner.

Khrushchev made the most of this propaganda opportunity. He announced to the press that the pilot was "quite alive and kicking" and asserted that any future American flights over Soviet airspace would be treated in the same fashion. What Khrushchev did not reveal was that American planes had, for the past two years, been making these flights and that the aerial photography they provided had shown the American military the relative weakness of Russia's antiballistic system.

Eisenhower was embarrassed by the U-2 incident; it spoiled the end of his presidency. The information he and his advisers had gained over the previous two years was more than enough, however. Then, too, Eisenhower was ready to leave the White House. When Democrat John F. Kennedy (1917–1963)—hereafter referred to as JFK—won the general election of 1960, Eisenhower made a point of briefing the younger man on the status of U.S.-U.S.S.R. military strength. One area that Eisenhower marked for special consideration was the island of Cuba, which had recently experienced a change in government, and which seemed on the road to becoming a socialist country.

Who coined the term "military-industrial complex"?

On January 17, 1961, three days before leaving the White House, Eisenhower delivered a memorable farewell address on television (it was also carried on radio). He knew quite well that no previous American president other than George Washington had ever been in such an in an enviable position. Having led his nation to victory in World War II, Eisenhower left the presidency at a time when the United States was doing reasonably well in the Cold War. The outgoing president said little about his many successes, however; he knew that if these turned out to have negative consequences, he would be blamed. Instead, Eisenhower warned his countrymen about the implications of the growth of the "military-industrial complex," which, ironically, had grown exponentially during his administration.

Few Americans paid much attention in 1961, because it was so obvious that the M-I complex" had done good, if not great, things by them during the previous decade. But a decade later, in 1971, the "military-industrial complex" came in for a great deal of censure, especially because of its role in the War in Vietnam.

What was so different about JFK?

In two words: *almost everything*. If Eisenhower had been grandfatherly, then JFK was everyone's handsome young uncle. Where Eisenhower had been old-fashioned, JFK was decidedly "hip." Eisenhower had treated the press corps with quiet respect; JFK almost pampered the press, which, in turn, showered him with adulation. In one important respect, however, JFK was very much like Eisenhower: both men were genuine Cold War warriors.

Born in Boston and educated at Harvard, JFK had been the commander of a PT-Boat in World War II. His dramatic escape from the wreck of that ship had become nearly legendary, and his attitude toward all foes—the Russians especially—remained that of a man who had served in combat. Perhaps he was wittier and more fun than Eisenhower; that did not mean he would go "softly" toward the Russians.

Where did JFK make his first major foreign policy move?

In what was also his first major blunder, JFK authorized an attack to assist a group of Cuban exiles on the north side of Cuba. These men had been trained by the CIA, and the intent was for them to overthrow the new regime of Fidel Castro (1926–). The attack, which took place on April 17, 1961, was a fiasco, with Castro's army pinning the insurgents down on the beaches. American air power might have made the difference, but JFK decided not to employ it. As a result, the exiles were killed or captured, and Castro exulted in a propaganda coup even larger than the one celebrated by Nikita Khrushchev a year before.

JFK grimly asserted that it was all his responsibility and therefore his fault. Privately, he cursed the CIA and the Eisenhower administration, which had drawn up the plan in the first place. Known as the Bay of Pigs incident, the fiasco made JFK even

When was the CIA (Central Intelligence Agency) founded?

It was established in 1947 and led by a handful of men who had performed dare-devil operations during World War II. It was not, initially, expected that the CIA would become so large or play so important a role.

more determined to overthrow Fidel Castro, and his administration devoted an inordinate amount of time and energy in that direction over the next two years.

Why were the Kennedy brothers so obsessed with Castro and Cuba?

JFK was generally a smooth operator, but Castro and the Communist regime in Cuba really got under his skin. His younger brother Robert, who was attorney-general of the United States, was generally prickly and ill-tempered, and Castro practically made him see red. Between them, the Kennedy brothers planned and overplanned where Castro and Cuba were concerned.

When was the first summit meeting of the new decade, the 1960s?

On June 3, 1961, JFK met with Nikita Khrushchev behind closed doors in Vienna. Until that moment, Kennedy's European trip had been a stellar success, with crowds exclaiming their liking for the young American president and his attractive wife, Jacqueline Bouvier Kennedy. Behind closed doors, however, almost everything went awry.

Khrushchev actively bullied the younger man, demanding that he secure access between East and West Berlin. Whether Khrushchev actually threatened to use nuclear weapons remains unknown (in part because JFK died before writing a memoir). Practically everyone JFK spoke to in the next few days echoed the same idea, however: Khrushchev had ranted, railed, and seems to have intimidated JFK.

Why was Khrushchev so concerned about Berlin, which was still divided into "East" and "West"?

In the three years that preceded the summit meeting, at least half a million East Berliners had left their homes and moved to West Berlin. After a short stay with relatives, they typically immigrated to West Germany, increasing its population while denuding that of East Germany. The reason for their migration is not complicated.

West Berlin and West Germany had established a capitalistic system which, if not flourishing, was at least showing signs of real progress. East Berlin and East Germany were grim, socialist economies, with almost no motivation for the worker or industrialist to improve his or her lot. As a result, the "West" looked much better than the "East." Khrushchev was appalled by the numbers, and he wanted to corral the people of East Germany to keep them where they were.

When did the Berlin Wall—soon known simply as "The Wall"—go up?

During the night of August 16–17, 1961, Russian and East German police and military put up a section of barbed wire about twelve feet high. It took some weeks for them to make the full circumference, dividing East and West Berlin completely, but when they were done, a truly ugly situation was the result: a nasty-looking fence of barbed wire, with numerous machine-gun nests and command towers. Over the next year, much of The Wall was turned into reinforced concrete.

The first response of many people in the West was of alarm, even horror, but JFK, in private, expressed it best, saying that a wall was an ugly thing but it was much better than a war. Indeed, The Wall may have reduced tensions in East and West Berlin, even while it angered people on both sides (physical and ideological). That the U.S.S.R. and East Germany had to go to this extreme showed, quite clearly, the relative failure of the communist system in their societies, even as it also displayed their military might.

If Berlin—East and West—was the flash point of Cold War tension, where else did the superpowers experience confrontation?

A battle in and around Berlin could have meant a fight for all the marbles and the use of all the weapons available to both sides. It made much better sense, therefore, for the two sides to probe each other in other areas.

The Berlin Wall—shown here in 1974—was a grim, tangible reminder of the Cold War separation between the communist East and democratic West. Between 1961 and 1989, when the wall came down, over 130 people died trying to cross into West Berlin.

The Middle East was relatively quiet in the early 1960s, but Cuba, and the possibility of new socialist regimes in South America, was not. Then, too, the space race between the Russians and Americans began early in the decade.

Who was ahead in the space race?

Up until about 1964, the U.S.S.R. was firmly in the lead. The Russians put the first satellite in orbit (1957), and a Russian was the first man to orbit the earth (1961). The Russians managed to place four men in one space capsule long before the Americans could do so. What was not known was the enormous sacrifice required to accomplish these things.

The Russian space program was woefully underfunded compared to the American, and numerous cosmonauts—as they were known—were injured or killed in various tests. Although no one could be quite certain in the mid-1960s, the Russian space program suffered when compared to its American counterpart. Much of the success of West Berlin mocked East Berlin's failure; so did the continued American string of successes demonstrate the greater technical competence of the Americans. They had the first man to walk in space (1965), the first space-effected rendezvous (1966), and by 1969 they were well on their way to the moon.

THE CUBAN MISSILE CRISIS

How did the Cuban Missile Crisis begin?

Sometime in 1962—the date is uncertain—Khrushchev took another of the gambles for which he was famous: he allowed Russian missiles to be shipped to the island of Cuba. The first missiles transported were not tipped with nuclear warheads, but the potential was there.

Khrushchev did this in order to bolster the new regime of Fidel Castro and to strike fear into the hearts of the Americans. He, and the Russian public, had long lived with a similar experience: American missiles in Turkey were aimed straight at his country. American ballistic and guidance systems were far superior to Russians, and it was therefore necessary for Khrushchev to place his missiles very close to the United States. The whole arrangement made perfect sense to the leaders in the Kremlin, especially because Khrushchev believed he had taken the full measure of JFK in their summit meeting in Vienna in 1961.

It seems so daring. Was there any chance that the U.S. would stand by?

Almost none. Ever since 1898, when it won the Spanish–American War, the United States had viewed Cuba as a semi-protectorate. Then, too, Cuba was only ninety miles from Key West, Florida. No American president could allow a threat from that island and keep his job.

More important, however, Khrushchev had underestimated JFK. The American president was as resolute a Cold Warrior as Eisenhower, and he was about to demonstrate it to the world.

What was Kennedy's first action in Cuba?

On October 16, 1961, JFK and his advisers learned that overflights of U.S. planes had produced photographs of Russian missiles in Cuba; whether they were "tipped" was at this point irrelevant. Ambassador Adlai E. Stevenson took the case to the United Nations. The photographs were displayed, earning sympathy for the Americans.

No "hotline" between the White House and the Kremlin existed at that time, and all communication took place over international channels. JFK demanded that Khrushchev remove the missiles. When no answer was given, Kennedy went on television and put the case to the American people. He did not "ask" their permission to act; rather, he asserted that he would employ all means necessary to remove the threat. JFK also announced a "quarantine" of the island of Cuba, asserting that the ships of all nations—Russians most especially—stay away from Cuba.

How alarmed did the world become?

There was, quite likely, no precedent in all of human history. Humankind had faced many threats and dangers during its existence, but never had there been the type of rapid communications that allowed the people of virtually all nations to track the progress, or lack thereof, in a situation. Hundreds of millions of people around the globe held their breath.

At first, there was no answer from the Kremlin. The Cuban socialists, led by Castro and Che Guevara, readied for an American invasion. Only the hardiest of the Soviet technicians wanted a confrontation; most of them believed it would be better to avert a showdown. At the same time, a handful of Russian ships, carrying plenty of military hardware, made their way toward Cuba.

Later, in 1964, Che went to the United Nations, where he addressed the General Assembly. Wearing his trademark green fatigues and beret, he looked every inch the Communist rebel. That day, Che was more conciliatory than usual, but he emphasized that a genuine socialist state had been created in Cuba and that he and his followers would never back down because of intimidation by the capitalist powers. From the day he gave that speech—December 11, 1964—Che became a hero to many young Americans, and they passed along not his message but his personality, embedded on the front of T-shirts.

What did Eisenhower say to JFK about the crisis?

On October 22, 1963, JFK called former president Dwight Eisenhower, someone who knew a great deal about international crisis because of his firsthand experience in 1954, 1956, and 1960. The conversation began with JFK posing a question: "General, what about if the Soviet Union—Khrushchev—announces tomorrow, which I think he will, that if we attack Cuba that it's going to be nuclear war? And what's your judgment as to the chances they'll fire these things off if we invade Cuba?"

Eisenhower: Oh, I don't believe that they will.

JFK: You don't think they will?

Eisenhower: No.

JFK: In other words, you would take that risk if the situation seemed desirable?

Eisenhower: Well, as a matter of fact, what can you do?

JFK: Yeah.

Eisenhower: If this thing is such a serious thing, here on our flank, that we're going to be uneasy and we know what thing is happening now, all right, you've got to use something.

JFK: Yeah.

Eisenhower: Something may make these people shoot them off. I just don't believe this will.

(Source: *Ted Widmer, Listening In: The Secret White House Recordings of John F. Kennedy.* New York: Hyperion, 2012.)

Had Eisenhower made JFK's task easier or even more difficult?

Eisenhower often spoke cryptically, making it difficult for his listener to get his full drift, but here he expressed his confidence that "these people" (by whom he meant the Russians, the Cubans, or both) would not go so far as to fire missiles in this particular crisis. Although JFK was relieved that Eisenhower, the former Supreme Commander of Allied Forces in Europe, believed that the Cubans and Soviets would not attack, the president knew full well that if he made the wrong choice, he, not Eisenhower, would be blamed.

Who would have "won" in a full-scale confrontation?

In technical terms, the U.S. would surely have won because of the proximity to Cuba and the superiority of its nuclear arsenal. In the court of public opinion, the U.S. would have lost, because it acted like a bully. And in sheer human terms, there would have been no winner, only losers to one degree or another.

Fortunately, it did not come to that. On October 26, 1961, the leading Russian ships headed away from the confrontation with the U.S. quarantine. Planes continued to overfly Cuba, and tensions remained

U.S. President John F. Kennedy (far right) meets with Soviet Foreign Minister Andrei Gromyko (on couch, far right), who is not aware that Kennedy knows about the Cuban missiles in this October 18, 1962 White House photo.

448

high for weeks, but the main crisis had passed. The American public praised JFK for having prevailed, but the Americans did not know that Kennedy had privately agreed that the missiles in Turkey would be removed within six months. The "this for that" allowed Khrushchev to save some face.

CHINA AND VIETNAM

Who was the first major world leader to speak of a reduction in nuclear weapons?

The credit goes to JFK, who, in a major speech at the University of Washington in June 1963, spoke of the growing danger posed by nuclear weapons. Kennedy seems to have evolved in the weeks and months following the Cuban Missile Crisis; perhaps more than most, he realized how close to disaster the crisis had taken the world.

Kennedy had little time to act on his new intention, however, because he was assassinated on November 22, 1963. Whether the assasin was aided and abetted by others and whether Fidel Castro had anything to do with it remains a matter of some controversy, but in all the years that have passed, no piece of documentary evidence has yet emerged to support a conspiracy theory. The most important thing at the time was that leadership of the United States passed from JFK to the new president, Lyndon B. Johnson (1908–1973), hereafter referred to as LBJ.

Was LBJ substantially different from JFK?

In personal circumstances, there was a large difference. LBJ grew up poor and had forged his way in life, while JFK was the quintessential rich man's son. In style, too, JFK was much smoother and more gracious than LBJ, who sometimes acted like a man out of control. But in terms of the Cold War, they were very much alike.

Where LBJ was especially vulnerable was the concept of the "domino theory." First articulated by Dwight Eisenhower a decade earlier, the domino theory asserted that if one capitalist nation fell into the communist camp, others would surely follow. That this thinking was in error could be shown by looking at South America. Cuba's transition to communism did not lead other South American nations that way. But LBJ, and his advisers, who were later ridiculed as the "best and the brightest," clung to their theory, and it led them to place American troops in Southeast Asia.

Why was Vietnam such a special case?

After France gave up the fight to keep its empire in Indochina, the Geneva peace accords divided Vietnam into "North" and "South," with the 17th parallel of north latitude as the dividing line. The North Vietnamese, who had embraced Maoist Communism, did not find this satisfactory, and by the summer of 1964, they attacked South Vietnam with relative impunity. Clearly, South Vietnam might fall.

President Johnson was determined that this would not be the case, and when the North Vietnamese fired on an American destroyer in the Gulf of Tonkin in August 1964, LBJ took his case to the American Congress. The Gulf of Tonkin resolution was not a formal declaration of war, but it allowed the president great latitude as to how to defend South Vietnam from the North Vietnamese aggressor. Americans did not doubt their president or the wisdom of his actions; then, too, the sudden change in China alarmed many of them.

When did the Peoples Republic of China enter the nuclear club?

In October 1964, Communist China exploded its first atomic bomb in the desert of Central Asia. This was alarming, but events in Russia were even more traumatic. In that same month, a quiet coup took place, and Nikita Khrushchev was removed from power (he was allowed to retire). Americans had not loved Khrushchev, but he was a clear case of "the devil you know" being better than "the devil you don't."

The new Soviet premier, Leonid Brezhnev, was relatively unknown, but over time he revealed himself as a rather bland functionary, fond of good living and expensive means. Though they liked him no better than his predecessors, many American policymakers found Brezhnev both more predictable and easier to deal with than Khrushchev. What was surprising, and what developed over the next five years, was a crack in the former "Communist Bloc" of Russia and China.

How did Mao Zedong change during the 1960s?

Mao was the same as ever: a ruthless, down-to-earth cynic who believed that he knew what was best for the Chinese and perhaps everyone else as well. While Stalin was in power, Mao had played the number-two role; while Khrushchev was in the Kremlin, Mao was close to an equal. But with the departure of Khrushchev, Mao truly became his own man, able and willing to direct the Peoples Republic of China. He had in mind something quite different from the Russian model of Communism. Mao foresaw a day when the Chinese peasants would perform all the functions of an industrial proletariat. Then, too, his possession of the atomic bomb in 1964 allowed him to chart a different course.

How much did the average American know about what happened in China during the 1960s?

Almost nothing. The United States and China had severed diplomatic relations in 1949, and no American journalists were allowed in China during the 1960s; the average American reader, therefore, mistakenly believed that China and its people were much as they had been described in Pearl Buck's novel *The Good Earth*, published in 1931. Quite a few Chinese actually wished they were back in those times, because every step Mao took seemed to lead them to greater disasters. The great famine of 1961–1964 was followed by the Cultural Revolution, beginning in 1966. Almost every innovation undertaken by "the Great Helmsman," as Mao was called, led to the same result: increased suffering for the poor, accompanied by even greater success on the grand political scale for Mao.

THE SIX-DAY WAR

Who was most ready for war in the spring of 1967?

The Arab nations, most notably Egypt and Syria, seemed ready. Egyptian President Gamal Nasser ordered the United Nations forces to leave the Sinai and Suez Canal area by May 1, 1967. At the same time, the loudspeakers in Arab capitals bellowed for war and the annihilation of the Jewish state.

Observing the situation from afar, both the United States and the Soviet Union thought Israel's chances were small. The four Arab nations on Israel's borders—Egypt, Syria, Jordan, and Iraq—had almost twice as many tanks and planes and perhaps five times as many men in uniform. These numerical calculations did not take into effect the importance of the first strike, however.

When did Israel attack?

Early in the morning of June 5, 1967, Israeli warplanes screeched in the air, crossed the borders, and destroyed half of the Egyptian air force on the ground. The Israelis hit the Syrian air force at the same time, with an equal level of success. Even when the Arab pilots scrambled and rose to meet the Israelis, the dogfights that followed mostly went the Israeli way. It was a matter of better weapons systems and of pilots who enjoyed a higher level of motivation and morale.

Having won control of the skies, Israel then put its tanks and soldiers into operation, with results that were much the same. In the first two days, Israel seized half of the Sinai Desert and most of the Golan Heights. The Arabs sometimes fought fiercely, but they did not understand how to use all the weaponry they had received from the Soviet Union; the Israelis, by contrast, were in full operational control of the equipment they had received from the United States.

Where was the contest the toughest?

The Egyptians fought poorly, and the Syrians fought stubbornly but were defeated. Only the Jordanians, whose center was the Arab Legion, fought on a par with the Israelis. The battle for the Holy City of Jerusalem was especially tough, but Israeli paratroopers succeeded by June 9, 1967. When a ceasefire was arranged, the world stood amazed at what Israel had accomplished. One of the world's smallest states, geographically speaking, Israel had thrashed four foes, and in so doing it had more than doubled the size of its territory.

One of the last actions of the war was Israel's seizure of Mount Hebron. Located at the northwest corner of the Golan Heights, Mount Hebron had a magnificent observatory, from which almost everything that Syria might do could be seen. Mount Hebron became known as the "eyes" of the state of Israel.

Who was more humiliated by the Six-Day War: the Arabs or the Russians?

In the court of public opinion, the Arabs were painfully humiliated. They had provoked the crisis and suffered terrible losses as the result. But in the world of geostrategic politics, the Russians looked very bad indeed. The tanks the Arabs drove to war were Russian-made, and Russian advisers had guided the Arabs in their strategy, all to no avail.

Israel had won an outstanding victory, but over the next few years it was seen—for the first time—as the overdog and even the bully in Middle East politics. The United Nations passed Resolution 242, calling for Israel to return to the borders that existed before the Six-Day War: Israel refused.

VIETNAM

What was the height of American involvement in Vietnam?

When JFK entered the White House in 1961, there were 2,000 Americans in Vietnam, serving as military advisors to the South Vietnamese regime, based in Saigon. When JFK died in November 1963, there were over 14,000 Americans. But after the Gulf of Tonkin incident in August 1964, American involvement surged, and by 1966 there were about 450,000 U.S. troops in South Vietnam. When one compares this to the later American involvement in the First Persian Gulf War of 1990–1991, it is obvious that America sent a far greater percentage of its soldiers to Vietnam.

What did LBJ and his advisers believe?

President Johnson kept most of the Kennedy administration men in their positions. Known as the "Best and the Brightest," these policymakers believed that the United States could not lose the conflict in Vietnam (they were careful not to dignify it with the title of "war"). Jointly, the Johnson advisors believed that America would win in Vietnam though air power as well as a large presence on the ground.

The air power was expensive, but it was as nothing compared to the emotional sacrifice required of millions of American families. Unlike World War II—in which they saw themselves as unquestionably the "good guys"—or Korea, where they operated under a United Nations mandate, the American soldiers in Vietnam felt very much on their own. If truth be told, many of them were not certain why the Johnson administration sent them to that East Asian nation. But if all other aspects failed, things would still be all right so long as the United States achieved victory. And that, it seemed, was on the way in 1965 and 1966.

President Lyndon Johnson meets with South Vietnam's Vice President Nguyen Cao Ky in this February 1966 photo.

Who was William Westmoreland?

The captain of the West Point cadets in the class of 1935, Westmoreland (1914–2005) was now a four-star general and perhaps the most popular general America had seen since World War II. He had done his part, and more, in World War II—had landed with the troops at Normandy—and he now was called upon to lead what would be his most difficult assignment: the achievement of victory in Vietnam.

"Chesty," as some called him thanks to his magnificent posture, had no doubts as to victory; he would achieve it as long as the Pentagon sent him enough soldiers. By the end of 1965, there were 200,000-plus Americans in South Vietnam; a year later, the number rose to 360,000. At the all-time high in 1968, there would be 530,000-plus. Westmoreland was confident that his well-trained men, backed by American air power, could not lose.

What was operating against Westmoreland?

The American public was staunchly behind Lyndon Johnson in 1964, and it stuck with him through some doubts in 1965. But by the middle of 1966, it was apparent that the nation was drifting into an ever larger commitment of troops, with no real guarantee of victory. Complicating matters was the manner in which world opinion began to tilt away from the United States.

One of the worst moments for America came in 1968, when a photographer for *Life* magazine captured a devastating photo of a young Vietnamese girl. Her upper body cov-

453

ered with napalm, she was running as fast as she could, perhaps to escape bullets or rockets from helicopters. Americans were appalled. Virtually all of the major World War II photographs, most especially the one that showed five Marines lifting the flag at Iwo Jima, had shown the Americans as heroes. Now they were the bad guys.

THE EXPLOSIONS OF 1968

In what way was 1968 a "year like no other"?

No other year in the twentieth century can compare to 1968 in terms of the immense changes it brought and the potential for terrible conflicts that might wreck everything. The explosions of 1968, which occurred in the United States, Vietnam, France, Czechoslovakia, and elsewhere, were the result of disillusionment with "politics as usual."

The Baby Boom that commenced in 1946 was not solely an American phenomenon; people around the world started having more children in the wake of World War II's conclusion. As a result, many millions of young people came to maturity at about the time the Vietnam War began, and in 1968 they were ready to take action: either in favor or against.

What was the percentage of Americans who still backed the War in Vietnam?

American youth was split almost directly down the middle, with 50 percent in favor and 50 against. The energy, or momentum, was with the antiwar youth, however, because of their enthusiasm and because they spoke of truly American ideals which, they declared, had been tainted when America became an imperialist power. Precisely when that had occurred remained highly debatable, but it was clear to millions that Vietnam was the wrong place for America to be.

What was the so-called "Tet Offensive"?

Vietnamese celebrated "Tet," or the beginning of the New Year, at the end of February 1968. On the day of the festivities, North Vietnam struck at virtually all the provincial capitals of South Vietnam; some North Vietnamese soldiers even got into the compound of the U.S. Embassy in Saigon before being ejected twelve hours later. Americans—both at home and in Vietnam—were stunned by the success of the enemy's guerrilla actions.

That America recovered, and that the North Vietnamese suffered nearly 24,000 casualties during the Tet Offensive, mattered little, if at all. The Viet Cong had clearly shown a gritty determination which, over time, would lead to victory. And morale in the American forces in Vietnam sank to an all-time low.

U.S. Marines watch for enemies in the destroyed village of Dai Do during the Tet Offensive in Vietnam.

Who was the first casualty of the Tet Offensive?

General William Westmoreland was quietly relieved as commander on the ground in Vietnam and brought home as chief of staff for the U.S. Army. This had seldom, if ever, happened to an American commander in a foreign war; about the closest parallel that could be found was Patton's temporarily being relieved of command in 1943.

Westmoreland would later sue CBS (Columbia Broadcasting System) for having defamed his character. The suit, which took place in the mid-1980s, did nothing for the reputation of either the general or the broadcast company. But if Westmoreland was the first major casualty of the Tet Offensive, then President Lyndon B. Johnson was the second.

How low had LBJ sunk during the winter of 1968?

There were rumors—some later confirmed—that the president acted like a man sleepwalking, and that when he was fully awake, his misery knew no bounds. LBJ had wanted, from the very beginning, to be known as the president who led America into becoming the "Great Society," meaning the eradication of poverty and the establishment of racial equality.

The news from Vietnam was bad and getting worse, and LBJ's advisors, who had assured him all would be well, were deserting the administration like rats from a sinking ship. LBJ hung tough as long as he could, but when liberal Senator Eugene McCarthy challenged and nearly defeated him in the New Hampshire primary, the president could take no more.

When did LBJ make his announcement?

On March 31, 1968, precisely two months after the Tet Offensive and just four days after the New Hampshire primary, LBJ went on television to announce he would not seek another term: he would not run in any more Democratic primaries. The news was received with unfeigned rejoicing by millions of Americans, but this only compounds the tragedy. Many Americans—then and now—never understood that LBJ was one of the best friends they ever had in the Oval Office. No president—before or since—worked for the common man, the "little guy," as powerfully as LBJ.

The tragedy of Lyndon B. Johnson has been examined by numerous biographers, but no one has ever been able to plumb the hole, to explain how a man of such obvious good intentions and such a good heart could be lured—by his own errors and his advisors— into a war that brought him low and which made the United States look like the "bad guy" for the first time in its history. What was clear was that LBJ was on his way out.

How did the troops in Vietnam take the news of LBJ's fall?

The reports are anecdotal, not scientific, but they suggest that the troops never censured LBJ in the way that the general public did. LBJ had visited the wounded in hospitals and done all he could to lift their spirits.

But by the time Americans began to respond to the news, they learned that Czechoslovakia had risen against Soviet rule, and there was a possibility, however slim, that the Iron Curtain might suffer a major tear.

Why did the Czechs choose the spring of 1968 to rise against their Soviet masters?

The Czech Revolt was against two entities: the Communist government in Prague and the Communist power in the Kremlin that was backing them. In the early days, it seemed possible that everything would fall. Communist officials were chased from their offices by defiant young people who planted trees in the center of the capital, declaring that this was "Prague's Spring." There was an eerie similarity to the beginning of the Thirty Years' War, which had commenced with the "Defenestration of Prague" in 1618.

The Soviets made their move in October. The Russians were reluctant to reveal their full force, knowing that world opinion would turn against them. Once Brezhnev made the decision, however, thousands of tanks and over 250,000 Russian soldiers crossed into Czechoslovakia, and the matter was decided in just days. The Prague Spring was crushed in its infancy. Whether the Russians would have acted with such force had the United States not been preoccupied is another matter, however.

Soldiers from the communist Polish army occupy Czechoslovakia, supporting the Soviet Union to put down the rebellion in Prague.

What happened in the United States in the spring of 1968?

Everything—that was how it seemed. On April 4, just five days after LBJ backed away from seeking another term, Martin Luther King Jr.—who had done more for the advancement of civil rights than anyone—was shot and killed in Memphis, Tennessee. The African-American communities did erupt in anger and rage, but these feelings were at least equaled by the sentiment of shock. Then, on June 6, 1968, minutes after having won the Democratic primary in California, Robert F. Kennedy—the younger brother of JFK—was shot and killed in a hotel.

Robert Kennedy had often been on the "wrong" side, so far as American liberals were concerned, but he had made an abrupt about-turn in 1968, and when he was killed, he was seen as the hope for the Democratic Party. Democrats from all walks of life mourned Kennedy's death, and when the Democratic National Convention convened in August, it seemed that it, and the city of Chicago, would never recover from the violence and rage that was shown. The late summer of 1968 was, arguably, one of the lowest points for the United States thus far. Much of the world saw it either as the oppressor of North Vietnam or as a paper tiger when compared with the virile Soviet Union. Many Americans had lost faith in their government. They were not alone, however.

When did Charles de Gaulle finally exit the political scene?

Thanks to personal longevity and to incredible tenacity, de Gaulle was still on the scene long after Eisenhower, Churchill, FDR, and his other great contemporaries. De Gaulle continued to sell himself as the savior of France until the late 1960s, when he suddenly appeared to be passé. De Gaulle attempted to declare that he was the only person who could lead France through and out of the quagmire of the student youth revolt of 1968 (student protests against capitalism that eventually spread to France's working class), but the French public no longer believed in him.

Were the youth rebellions of 1968 a complete failure?

They were, indeed. Of course, some good things came out of them, and many radicals would later emerge from the closet to boast proudly about what they had done in '68. At the time, however, it was clear that the Establishment—in Prague, in America, and in France—had prevailed, albeit at a great cost. Almost none of the major powers came out of 1968 looking better than when they entered it.

The greatest surprise of all came in November, when Richard M. Nixon, the true-blue conservative who had narrowly lost to JFK and who had been trounced when he tried to win the governorship of California, came back as the Republican nominee to narrowly win the presidential election of 1968. Truly, it was a remarkable comeback, but it also showcased the weakness of American politics. A year which saw the passing of giants like Martin Luther King and Robert Kennedy ended with a throwback winning the White House.

VIETNAM AGAIN

Was Richard Nixon able to end the conflict in Vietnam?

He proved nearly as inept as his predecessor in that regard. Nixon made headlines in the summer of 1969, when he announced that 25,000 soldiers would be withdrawn from North Vietnam. This was a beginning, even a good one, but it obscured the fact that slightly more than half a million young Americans were still in Vietnam. Even the most hard-line military families were now on the verge of admitting that the conflict in Vietnam could not be won, at least not by the use of conventional means.

Could the United States have won the conflict in Vietnam?

Only by employing all of its conventional war methods, and that included using everything short of nuclear warheads. Studies conducted since have shown that thousands of rounds of American ammunition were used to kill each North Vietnamese soldier. The performance of the U.S. Air Force, too, was much less sensational than expected.

As bad as the Vietnam War was—57,000 Americans were killed—it could have been much worse. Had Richard Nixon, or LBJ, truly gone for broke, employing everything short of nuclear means, the United States might have won in Vietnam, but the cost— both human and psychological—would have truly been unbearable. Vietnam would have emerged not as a nation but as a shattered ghost of its former self, and everyone would know who to blame. America, too, might have gone through even worse social convulsions than in 1968. The answer, therefore, is that the United States could indeed have won in Vietnam and that it could, quite likely, have destroyed itself in the process.

When did a real pull-back from Vietnam begin?

President Nixon and his longtime national security adviser, Henry M. Kissinger (1923–), began the process in 1970. By 1971, the number of troops in Vietnam had been cut by a third, and in 1972 peace talks began in Paris.

The Paris accords, signed in February 1973, gave North Vietnam much, but not all, that it had ever desired. North Vietnam clearly emerged as the winner, and the United States was the loser that managed to retain its face. A dramatic scale-down of U.S. soldiers began right away, and by the end of 1973, there were fewer than 100,000 Americans in South Vietnam. It was, quite likely, fortunate for America that so many of its soldiers were back home when yet another crisis came in the autumn of 1973.

YOM KIPPUR WAR

For how long had Israel been the bully on the block?

Until the Six-Day War, Israel was generally perceived as the underdog, and its victories— in 1948 and 1956—were seen as little short of miraculous. After the Six-Day War, Israel was seen as the predominant military power in the Middle East, and though Israel would neither confirm nor deny its possession of nuclear weapons, most world powers suspected that the real answer was "yes." It came as quite a surprise, therefore, when the Arabs launched the Yom Kippur War, which began on the Jewish holy day on October 6, 1973.

Egyptian forces crossed the Suez Canal, routing the few Israeli defenders in a matter of hours. At precisely the same time, thousands of Syrian tanks rumbled into the Golan Heights to contest that territory which Israel had gained in 1967.

Was there any chance Israel would have lost the Yom Kippur War?

Almost none. The Israeli Air Force was dramatically superior to the Arabs, and only the SAM-6 missile sites, stationed just behind the fighting, allowed the Egyptians and Syrians to keep the matter close. But there were some frightening moments in the first two days, when it seemed that the Syrians might achieve a complete breakthrough on the Golan Heights.

The turnaround came in three parts. First, Israel stopped the Syrians, who lost about 1,400 tanks. Second, the United States, led by President Nixon, undertook a major resupply of Israel, sending an immense number of tanks, jeeps, and military hardware. The third, and final, part came when Israel's elite tank commander, General Ariel ("Arik") Sharon (1928–2014), broke through the Egyptians on the Sinai, crossed the Suez Canal,

A destroyed Israeli M60 tank sits immobilized by Egyptian military during the Yom Kippur War.

and began knocking out the Sam-6 missile batteries. From that moment forward, Israeli victory was a certainty.

Who suffered the worst losses in the Yom Kippur War?

Egypt and Syria (Jordan had wisely kept out) took a bad beating. Between them, they had 15,000 men killed and at least as many wounded. The loss of materiel, too, was something the Arab states could not afford. Even so, the Arab nations held their heads high after the Yom Kippur War, and most historians believe that the war was essential for the rebuilding of Arab pride, which allowed the first state—Egypt—to formally recognize Israel and begin a process of negotiation that led to the return of most of the Sinai Peninsula.

Israel came through with an increased sense of its strength—which was so well-demonstrated in the battles—and a new knowledge of its vulnerability. No nation—not even Israel—could forever keep its enemies at bay: some type of negotiations were needed. Israel lost about 2,200 men killed and an equal number wounded. Its losses in war materiel, however, were quickly made good by the United States.

Given that everyone seems to have gained something, who was the real loser of the Yom Kippur War?

The Soviet Union. Its T-72 tanks failed to deliver the Golan Heights to Syria, and its Sam-6 missile batteries were eventually rendered useless by the Israeli ground forces. Even Soviet diplomacy, toward the end of the war, was seen as less effective than that of the United States. Secretary of State Henry Kissinger (1923–) shuttled endlessly back and forth between Washington, Tel Aviv, and Cairo, and he, not his Soviet counterparts, emerged with a much enhanced reputation.

No one was ready to pronounce the U.S.S.R. a paper tiger, but its military reputation suffered as a result of the Yom Kippur War. The United States, by contrast, was applauded both for its resupply of Israel and for the manner in which President Nixon put the U.S. Sixth Fleet on high alert; in the crisis of October 1973, American air and carrier power seemed considerably stronger than its Russian equivalent.

Had the United States emerged from its malaise, which was so apparent in 1968–1971?

Not quite. But President Nixon was making a strong comeback, and U.S. military power looked better than previously, not least because Nixon had penetrated into what was supposed to be the heart of the Communist alliance. He had seized on the differences between Brezhnev's Russia and Mao's China.

NIXON IN CHINA

Has posterity been unfair to President Richard M. Nixon?

In one area only. Nixon was a terrible chief executive, suspicious to the point of paranoia. He authorized the break-in at the headquarters of the Democratic Party in order to gain a leg up on his political opponents. In one area, however, Nixon showed true skill, even brilliance, and that was in the development of U.S. foreign policy.

Nixon and his right-hand foreign policy analyst, Henry Kissinger, saw no quick or easy answer to the problem of Vietnam, but they kept their eyes on East Asia and decided that an initiative in the direction of Red China was in order. The United States had had no diplomatic relations with Beijing—none whatsoever—since 1949, back when Nixon was a junior member of the U.S. House of Representatives. Back then, he had been an outspoken opponent of the Peoples Republic of China; Nixon now performed a complete about-face.

How was Nixon's visit to China arranged?

In 1971, Henry Kissinger feigned illness while in Pakistan and flew clandestinely to Beijing in order to meet with several high-level Communist leaders (he did not meet with Chairman Mao Zedong). Kissinger expressed President Nixon's interest, and he received an unqualified "yes," but no promises were made; in other words, it was entirely possi-

U.S. President Richard Nixon toasts Chinese Premier Zhou Enlai during his historic visit to China in 1972.

461

ble that Nixon could fly all the way to China and have the Chinese leaders decline to meet with him. Nixon decided that the possible benefit was worth the risk, and in February 1972, his fellow Americans were astonished to see their tough, hard-line chief executive in China courtesy of television.

Nixon, Chairman Mao, and Premier Zhou Enlai (1898–1976) were all on their best behavior during the three-day visit, which was a triumph for Nixon and the United States. In one shrewd move, he increased the distance between Red Russia and Red China, and made war between any of the superpowers even riskier than before.

What was the relative strength of the U.S. and U.S.S.R. in 1973?

The United States had a commanding lead in missiles and overall number of bombs, but Russia had nearly caught up in naval terms: its navy was even larger than the Americans'. Then, too, the Soviet Union had more men in uniform and soldiers ready to shoot than the United States. American power was about to come in for a severe test, however, one which arrived in the autumn of 1973.

OIL AND THE ARABS

Why is the Yom Kippur War of 1973 remembered so much more than any of the other Arab-Israeli conflicts?

The war was memorable on its own, involving several shifts of momentum, but Americans, and Europeans and Japanese too, long remembered 1973, because it was the time of the great oil embargo, carried out by the nations of OPEC.

Until October 1973, most Western nations fed their increasing need for petroleum at very cheap prices. This was because Western companies had won the concession for many of the oil-exporting nations. Ever since 1960, the year it was formed, OPEC had attempted to elevate the price of oil: nearly all those efforts ended in failure. But in the wake of yet another Israeli victory over the Arabs, the Arab oil-producing nations nearly doubled the price of oil in a few weeks, from five dollars per barrel to roughly ten. At the same time, the leading oil producers cut production, leading to genuine shortages.

Which nation(s) was most hard-hit by the Embargo of 1973?

Japan's vulnerability to oil supplies and the price of oil had been shown in World War II; the Japanese government practically reversed its policy toward the Arab world in 1973 in order to gain better treatment. But it was the United States, the great technical and automated giant, which suffered the most.

In 1973 and 1974, there were many Americans who had driven for their entire lives—some as long as half a century—and had never known an oil shortage. Now they faced long lines, occasional closings of gas stations, and tempers rose accordingly. Americans realized, for the first time, the vulnerability exposed by their fondness for large automobiles and trucks, and a movement toward energy self-sufficiency began in 1973–1974.

When did things start to return to "normal"?

The Arab nations brought their export of oil back to where it had been by the middle of 1974, and long lines at gas pumps disappeared. A true return to normal never took place, however, because the Achilles heel of the American system had been revealed. Subsequent oil shortages, in 1979 especially, continued to demonstrate that the American way of life, including its military, had a short lease on life.

Did other nations feel the same pinch?

In economic terms, they felt it even worse than the United States. Britain, France, Germany, and Italy all suffered from the dramatic rise in the cost of petroleum. All these nations, however, were better positioned to weather shortages, or even outright deprivation. This is because their towns and cities, largely rebuilt after 1945, maximized the use of bicycles and human feet as well as cars and trucks.

THE END OF THE VIETNAM WAR

Did the North Vietnamese take American political events into account?

They were shrewd strategists, and it made perfect sense that they launched their final, culminating offensive during the autumn of 1974; Richard Nixon had resigned the U.S.

Why did the promise of energy self-sufficiency fail to deliver?

For Americans, it was a bitter irony that their supplies, primarily in Texas, began to decline at the very time when the Arab nations put on the squeeze. But Americans can also blame themselves, because each attempt to find and develop new sources of energy (including solar and wind power) has been followed by yet more purchases of large vehicles and a continued reliance on the oil barons whether they are from Texas or Saudi Arabia.

presidency in August of that year. Even if Nixon had remained in office, it is difficult to see how he could have influenced events in Vietnam, however.

The late winter and early spring of 1975 witnessed devastating attacks by the Viet Cong, whose confidence grew with each passing day. The South Vietnamese, by contrast, were low in spirit and could not see how surrender would materially affect their lives (actually it would). The collapse became evident in mid-April, and the U.S. Navy and Air Force embarked on a massive program to evacuate all U.S. personnel—and as many of their allies as possible—from Saigon.

How bad was the scene in Saigon on the last day?

On April 30, 1975, there were still thousands of people in and around the U.S. Embassy, all of them begging to be permitted an exit. One helicopter after another took off from the roof of the Embassy, sometimes with desperate South Vietnamese civilians hanging on to the gunwales of the chopper. Americans back home watched with pain and disbelief as the helicopter runs came to an end and the U.S. Embassy was taken by the Viet Cong.

That day—April 30, 1975—long remained in the consciousness of most Americans. Some Americans were furious with their government for having prolonged the war, while others were angry that all means—including nuclear weapons—had not been employed in the search for victory. One thing was—and remains—certain: the Vietnam War scarred the American public.

When did Post-Traumatic Stress Disorder enter the American lexicon?

The expression was used soon after 1975; it probably originated in the Veterans Administration Hospitals that provided medical and psychiatric care to the returning soldiers. Post-Traumatic Stress Disorder was the new form of Shell Shock—the expression employed during World War I and World War II—but it seemed substantially worse in many respects. Numerous veterans complained of staying awake night after night, hearing helicopters that did not exist; others recounted with horror the atrocities they had seen.

What emerged between 1975 and 1980 was a profound distaste on the part of many Americans for war. This is especially evident in the number of movies that highlight the worst, most painful aspects of the Vietnam experience. *Coming Home* was among the first; *Platoon* was next; and by 1980, there was a powerful segment of the U.S. public that was strongly opposed to any war, anywhere, at any time.

DÉTENTE AND THE DICTATORS

What is détente?

Richard Nixon and Henry Kissinger popularized the term in the early 1970s, using it to characterize their approach toward the Soviet Union. Nixon and Kissinger did not love the U.S.S.R. or its leaders—far from it—but they saw them as human and as business-men with whom rational dealings could be effected. Nixon and Kissinger both deserve praise for this, and U.S.-Soviet tensions eased considerably during the mid-1970s mak-ing that era a far cry from the mid-1950s, for example.

One reason détente seemed possible is that Leonid Brezhnev, premier of the U.S.S.R., was not a hard-line communist in the Stalin model; fond of good food and high living, Brezhnev seemed, at times, rather like a capitalist. This does not mean that he was a pop-ulist, however; dissident nationalities within the Soviet Union came in for harsh treat-ment during his long tenure.

Why do historians sometimes call this period the Age of the Dictators?

Dictators have long been with us, but the mid-1970s was a time when there were more dictators in power than ever before. Fidel Castro, whatever his original economic poli-cies, was quite dictatorial in the mid-1970s. But the mid-1970s was also known for the "passing of the dictators."

General Francisco Franco, who had ruled Spain since 1939, passed away in 1975. The transition was peaceful, because Franco had long since named Carlos, grandson of Spain's last king, as the successor. But Franco's death was small potatoes when compared to the passing of Chairman Mao in October 1976. Officially, China mourned the passing of its Great Helmsman. Privately, many Chinese were pleased to see the end of a career

---

Is it true that Jimmy Carter is the best of all "former presidents"?

Beyond a doubt. Though his years in the White House left him open to much criticism, Carter accomplished more in his retirement years than nearly all his contemporary ex-Pres-idents combined. He monitored elections in other countries, working for the United Nations; he lent his wisdom to numer-ous international organizations; at home, he participated in the building of houses for the poor. In all this, he was far more ac-tively involved than other ex-Presidents such as Gerald Ford, Ronald Reagan (1911–2004), and Bill Clinton (1946–). The trouble was that he often provoked resentment by seeming holier than others.

What was Israel's birthday gift to the United States in 1976?

Americans awoke on July 4, 1976, prepared to celebrate the 200th anniversary of their nation's birth. They learned, just hours later, that Israel had pulled off one of the truly sensational coups of the decade, if not the century. An Israeli airliner had been hijacked and forced to land in Entebbe, capital of Idi Amin's Ethiopia. Israeli commandos landed, freed the hostages, and headed home, with the loss of precisely one man.

that had brutalized them and their nation. As a result of Mao's policies, at least fifty million Chinese perished from starvation between 1955 and 1976.

If the dictators were passing away, who was in charge in the Free World?

After Richard M. Nixon resigned the U.S. presidency in 1974, Gerald Ford (1913–2006) was the caretaker for two years. He lost his own election bid, however, to Jimmy Carter (1924–), one of the most unlikely people to win the American presidency.

Born in rural Georgia, Carter was a typical "New Southern" leader, meaning that he rejected race politics and race baiting. He was, however, a complicated mixture of technocrat and populist. Carter had served in the U.S. Navy during the period of its expansion and transformation into the nuclear navy; he probably knew more about Cold War technology and military systems than any other leader worldwide. But because he intended to reverse the failed policies of Richard Nixon, Carter postured as a populist, a man of the people.

Was Carter "soft" on communism?

Yes. Though he understood the mechanics of Cold War policy better than almost anyone, Carter seemed blind to the monstrosities that still existed behind the Iron Curtain. He viewed the loathing that many Americans still felt for the Soviet Union as anachronistic, and he seemed willing to deal with the Russians on terms of cordiality. At the same time, however, Carter excoriated smaller regimes, especially in Latin America and Africa, declaring that the United States would not negotiate with them.

Carter was a complex person. Had he been better advised, or if he had listened more attentively, he might have been an outstanding president. He stumbled badly, however, as a result of his lack of knowledge in some areas and his stubborn refusal to accept the facts in others.

THE PERSIAN GULF

For how long had the United States been allied with Iran?

The alliance between the United States and the government, or regime, of the Shah of Iran dated to the 1953 coup, which had toppled the nationalist liberal leader Mohammad Mosaddeq. Though no policymaker ever phrased it precisely this way, there was a clear understanding that Iran would provide relatively cheap petroleum to America in exchange for American military assistance. Over the next twenty-five years that aid amounted to billions of dollars, and in 1972, when he celebrated the 2500th anniversary of the reign of Cyrus the Great, the Shah of Iran was in a very strong position. His armed forces, about half a million strong, were the best in his part of the Middle East, and his secret police were second to none. Iran looked, to all the world, like the most successful Middle Eastern state with the exception of Israel.

Of course this was not the whole, or entire, story. Millions of Iranians chafed under the Shah's regime, which appeared to invalidate many Muslim customs and beliefs: wearing of the veil, for example, almost disappeared among Iran's elite during the Shah's tenure. Other Iranians disliked the relatively pro-Israel attitude of the Shah; still others loathed the use of the secret police to keep the population under control.

President Eisenhower gave the go-ahead for two coups, both backed by the CIA and monitored with great interest by the U.S. government.

How did the United States become so identified with a regime on the point of failure?

Photographs taken of Jimmy Carter meeting with the Shah suggested that American backing for the Iranian regime was as strong as ever. Carter went out of his way to declare that access to the Persian Gulf was vital to U.S. national security; he called it "our jugular vein." What Carter—who was usually acutely aware of dissident sentiment—overlooked was the anger which had built against the Shah and therefore against his American sponsors.

How did the CIA become involved in Iran and Guatemala?

In the case of both of these nations, profit was the overriding motive. By 1953, Guatemala had a socialist president and Iran had a nationalist one. Guatemala had long been under the quasi control of the United Fruit Company, and British Petroleum had for some time been the dominant economic force in Iran. In both cases, the CIA intervened.

President Eisenhower gave the go-ahead for two coups, both backed by the CIA and monitored with great interest by the U.S. government.

The Iranian Revolution, which began in late 1977, was not aimed at the United States, but the more they dug into the apparatus of the Shah's regime, the more the revolutionaries became convinced that it was America that held the keys to the Shah's power. And who could blame them? The secret police were trained by the CIA; the tanks and planes were mostly American made. As a result, the anger which initially focused on the Shah turned against Jimmy Carter and the United States.

The United States supported the Shah of Iran, Mohammad Reza Shah Pahlavi (1919–1980), whom many Iranians considered a tyrant. He was overthrown in the 1979 Iranian Revolution.

When was the Shah of Iran forced from power and ousted from the country?

In January 1979. The Shah, who was in poor physical health, asked for asylum in the United States. Carter's first response was a qualified "yes," but enough dissidents in the United States objected that the Shah eventually went to Mexico. His departure was the biggest change in Middle East politics in more than two decades.

Weeks after the Shah departed, Ayatollah Ruhollah Khomeini (1902–1989) returned to Iran. His place in Iranian society is difficult to describe because he was such a mixture of political and religious belief. Khomeini had been in exile in France for many years, but the Iranians never forgot him, and when he returned in 1979, he was greeted as something akin to a Shi'ite saint. It is, of course, only coincidence that Khomeini became such a legend at the same time that another man of God—Pope John Paul II (1920–2005)—began to rise to prominence. In both cases, however, the man was identified with the nation of his youth: Poland for the Pope and Iran for the Ayatollah.

What was so different about Pope John Paul II?

Almost everything. He was the first Pole ever to become Pope, and he was the first non-Italian to become Pope in more than 450 years. John Paul II was handsome, virile, and utterly fearless, qualities which would earn him the love of millions. On top of all that, he was a fervent anti-Communist.

Having grown up in the 1930s and witnessed the worst of World War II, Pope John Paul II was against all forms of dictatorship and tyranny. This does not mean that he was blind to the errors of democratic and socialist states, but he viewed them as the lesser of two evils. When John Paul returned to Poland in June 1979 as the new Pope, he was welcomed in a manner quite similar to the way Khomeini was received in Iran. There the similarity ended, however.

When did the protest movement in Iran come to a boil?

It simmered all during the summer of 1979 and then burst forth, like a flame, in the mid-autumn of that year. The first that Americans knew about trouble was on November 4, 1979, when thousands of Iranian students broke into the U.S. Embassy in Tehran, seizing fifty-four Americans as hostages. The news was so incredible that many people refused to believe it, but over the next few weeks it became evident that Iran, which had cast off the Shah and his government, intended to take on the United States.

Day after day the major television networks—CBS, ABC, and NBC—broadcast film of Iranians chanting "Death to America," "The Great Satan," and other such slogans. Whether the Iranian students fully understood what they declared is impossible to say, but Americans slowly became aware of the anger that their nation's policies had created in Iran. Some Americans denounced their own government, saying that it was to blame, while others touted their patriotism and said America should use its nuclear power to flatten Iran into a parking lot.

Was that nuclear option ever on the table?

No. Jimmy Carter was not a pacifist, but he knew far too much about nuclear technology to even consider its use. Even when Ronald Reagan succeeded him in office, the United States did not consider a nuclear response. There was, however, a demand on the part of the public that some type of rescue mission be implemented; some people lamented that the American military did not perform an Entebbe-like "miracle" to rescue the hostages, similar to what the Israelis had done in 1976.

What was the absolute low point of the Cold War, so far as most Americans were concerned?

Although Vietnam had been devastating, and though the 1950s had involved many crises, the lowest point for the American public came at the end of 1979 and the beginning of 1980. Never, it seemed, had America and its allies been besieged on so many fronts.

How influential was the hostage crisis in terms of changing American news coverage?

Throughout the whole of the Cold War—including Vietnam—American news networks had treated the public to a mere half hour of news, usually commencing at 6:30 each evening. Those thirty minutes seemed sufficient to treat the news of the day. The hostage crisis entirely changed that, with NBC leading the way, promoting *Nightline* which aired at 11:30 P.M. As a result, the American public became accustomed to late-night news and commentary, and when the Cable Network News (CNN) debuted in 1981, Americans were ready for it. The twenty-four-hour news cycle had begun.

The Soviet invasion into Afghanistan ended in failure and embarassment for the U.S.S.R. The occupation lasted from 1979 to 1989, at which point the Russians left so quickly that artillery like this was simply abandoned.

Another gasoline shortage had inflamed tempers throughout the summer of 1979. Americans had not done enough to curb their reliance on foreign oil. Then Iranian students—students!—had seized the embassy in Tehran. As bad as all these events were, the Soviet invasion of Afghanistan in December 1979 eclipsed all of them. To many foreign observers—and to some at home—it seemed as if the United States had indeed become the "paper tiger."

When did the Soviet Union invade Afghanistan?

The tanks and planes moved on December 23–24, but Americans learned the news on Christmas Day of 1979. This was perhaps the least welcome Christmas "present" the American public ever received.

The leaders in the Kremlin had had their eyes on Afghanistan for some time. They relished the idea of using that country as a conduit for their oil and natural gas resources, and they also feared that it might, otherwise, become a haven for Muslim militants determined to bring down the Soviet Union. Given that the United States was preoccupied with Iran, this seemed like the perfect moment for the U.S.S.R. to flex its muscles.

Was there any saving grace, anything to make Christmas of 1979 seem more like Christmas?

There was not. This was one of the few times in the American experience when all the news seemed bad and when there was no saving grace to be seen. The 1970s had begun with America mired in Vietnam, and the midpoint of the decade—1975—had seen helicopters take off from the U.S. Embassy in Saigon. The decade's end witnessed Americans in captivity and the U.S. Embassy in Tehran in ruins. Just to make the misery complete, the U.S.S.R. had shown its comparative strength by seizing much of Afghanistan.

Gloom prevailed throughout the United States. *Very* few journalists or policymakers would have predicted in December 1979 that December of 1989 would witness the success, indeed the triumph, of free-market capitalism or that the U.S.S.R. would no longer be a threat to the Free World.

RESOURCE WARS AND RELIGIOUS CONFLICTS: 1980 TO 2014

When does the Cold War end and the Resource Wars begin?

There is a ten-year overlap between the two. The Cold War lasted until 1989, but during its last ten years (1979–1989) the brand-new Resource Wars coexisted alongside it and some-times stole all the headlines from it. Of course, there is a connection between the Cold War and the Resource Wars, but there is enough difference to justify a separate chapter.

THE HOSTAGE CRISIS

How did the Iranian hostage crisis commence?

On November 4, 1979, several thousand college students broke through the gates of the U.S. Embassy in Tehran; in short order, they seized and made prisoner fifty-four Americans within the building. This was the beginning of a crisis that would have long-lasting effects, both in the Middle East and the United States.

President Jimmy Carter is a fine person in many respects, but he was not the right person for an emergency such as this. Carter had long deplored the tendency of the United States to back foreign dictators, and though he had been on friendly relations with the Shah, he had not done much to prevent his fall. When the hostage crisis hit in November and December of 1979, Carter seemed vacillating, even weak. There were few, if any, words of threat or suggestions of retaliation; rather, Carter seemed to believe that Americans must weather the crisis, however long it took. As bad as things were, they were soon to become even worse.

When did the Soviet Union invade Afghanistan?

Plans for this move had already existed, but the Iran hostage crisis may have prompted the leaders in the Kremlin to act sooner, rather than later. On December 23, 1979, just seven weeks after the takeover of the U.S. Embassy in Tehran, the Soviet Union invaded Afghanistan with roughly 100,000 men and a huge number of tanks, planes, and helicopters. Given the closeness of the two events—both in geography and chronology—it is safe to say that the Christmas holiday season of 1979–1980 was the gloomiest the United States had experienced in years, perhaps even decades.

The Red Army swarmed all over the "floor" of Afghanistan—meaning the lower levels of altitude—within the first three months, capturing the capital city and eliminating the Afghani army as a threat. Much more difficult was the attempt to control the "roof" of Afghanistan, meaning the areas above about 8,000 feet in altitude. These mountain ranges had seldom, if ever, been conquered in human history, and the Russians seemed oblivious to the old expression that Afghanistan was the "graveyard of empires."

How did the United States respond in the year 1980?

One can almost say that it did not respond. President Carter authorized one rescue mission in April 1980, but when it failed—with a humiliating crash of helicopters in the Iranian desert—all future thoughts were put aside. Carter went from weakness to weakness, and it was the American public, the news media most especially, that stepped into the breach.

NBC Nightly News began to run a special program, *Nightline*, at 11:30 P.M. Plans for the development of the Cable News Network (CNN) were already underway but were spurred by the Iranian hostage crisis. As a result, the United States had its first twenty-four-hour news cycle as early as the summer of 1981, with the hostage crisis being the main precipitator.

Is this how Ronald Reagan became president of the United States?

The American public was disenchanted with President Jimmy Carter by 1979, but his handling of the hostage crisis tipped the scales against Carter even more. Carter ran a good re-election campaign, but he was perceived as weak, while his Republican challenger, Ronald Reagan, was perceived as a "cowboy" who would put some fright into those who had brought America low. Reagan won the election of 1980 handsomely, and

474

President Reagan and First Lady Nancy Reagan met with Pope John Paul II at the Vatican in 1982. The United States has had a strong alliance with the Catholic Church.

when he was sworn into office at noon on January 20, 1981, he looked like a new presence, one who would make America's enemies think twice. As it turned out, Reagan benefitted enormously from what happened ten minutes later.

Iran freed the fifty-four hostages at the same time Reagan was sworn into office. The news broke on all American television stations as the president finished his inaugural address, and the Reagan presidency was off to a remarkable beginning. No one has ever definitively proven whether Iran freed the hostages in order to humiliate Jimmy Carter or to ward off retaliation from the incoming president. All that people could say was that it was a marvelous change.

How did Ronald Reagan and Pope John Paul II become such strong allies?

The two had much in common, including humble origins and a profound belief that the U.S.S.R. represented the greatest evil in the twentieth-century world. What really brought the president and the Pope together, however, were two failed assassination attempts. An American, John Hinckley, tried to kill Ronald Reagan in March 1981, and a Turkish anarchist tried to kill Pope John Paul II in May that same year. Both attempts failed, and both leaders emerged with enhanced admiration and authority.

475

By 1983, President Reagan was employing terms such as the "evil empire" to describe the U.S.S.R. Pope John Paul II was usually less strident, but his commitment to anti-communism was even stronger. Because John Paul II was the first non-Italian Pope in 450 years (he was Polish), he spoke with great authority on Eastern European matters. To the old men in the Kremlin, it was clear that the Pope and the American president were their greatest foes.

Just how old were the men who ran the Kremlin?

Between about 1970 and 1985, the average age of the top Soviet leaders was about seventy-five, with some men in their eighties. They looked the part. On May Day parades, when Soviet missiles and tanks slowly paraded by the Kremlin, the old men who looked out from the balconies, receiving the salutes and cheers, looked—for the most part—as if they belonged in retirement homes. This made them no less scary: their age may even have prompted more fears and concerns.

Is this when Ronald Reagan and Margaret Thatcher became so cozy, politically speaking?

In person they were never the great friends that they appeared in public, but they did have similar views of the world. Both saw Communism as the great enemy; both also viewed economic inflation and liberal programs as the death of capitalism at home. By 1985, Reagan and British Prime Minister Margaret Thatcher (1925–2013) had become firmly melded in the public eye. Their alliance helped persuade some members of the Kremlin bureaucracy that the Western, capitalistic powers would outlast the Soviet Union.

Meanwhile, how did the United States become so embroiled in the Caribbean?

For nearly twenty-five years, Cuba was the great enemy in the Caribbean; nearly every American administration attempted to undermine Fidel Castro's regime. In the 1980s, however, President Reagan picked out other targets, and in 1984, the U.S. military invaded the island of Grenada, conquering it in less than twenty-four hours. At the same time, President Reagan's administration worked to destabilize the regime of the Sandinista government

Margaret Thatcher served as British Prime Minister from 1979 to 1990. Known as the "Iron Lady," she recaptured the British Falkland Islands after the Argentinian invasion there in 1982.

in Nicaragua, going as far as sending clandestine CIA observers and advisors. Reagan's fear, which was shared throughout the Republican Party, was that any communist or socialist government in the Caribbean would harm U.S. interests in that region.

LEBANON WAR

What was Israel's goal in invading Lebanon?

Israel had been to war again in the spring of 1982, invading southern Lebanon, from where numerous rockets had been fired into Israeli territory. The goal was to remove the Palestinian Liberation Organization (PLO) from that country and install an Israel-friendly government.

Led by General Ariel Sharon (1928–2008), who would later be prime minister of Israel, the Israelis penetrated fifty miles north of the border, and in so doing they provoked the entry of the Syrian air force. Even when allowance for exaggeration is made, it seems clear that the Israelis shot down ten Syrian planes for every one of theirs that was lost or damaged. The idea that the IDF (Israeli Defense Forces) had lost its technical superiority over the Arabs was laid to rest. At the same time, the Israelis went further north to besiege Beirut, which had become the home of the PLO (Palestine Liberation Organization).

How important had Yasser Arafat become?

He was a very poor tactician, often allowing the PLO to be drawn into all sorts of uncertain situations, but Arafat did possess a certain strategic genius. When the IDF pounded Beirut, Yasser Arafat (1929–2004) negotiated a surrender under which he and the PLO would evacuate and be free to move elsewhere. The Israeli government agreed, and Arafat soon won the attention of the world media and the sympathy of some world leaders. He even had an audience with Pope John Paul II.

The Israelis had, largely, won the war but lost the peace. Even their success against the Syrians led to claims that Israel had become the bully of the Middle East. Israelis did not often make a good case for themselves; some of their more militant leaders, including Ariel Sharon, spoke of evicting all their Arab neighbors.

Yasser Arafat was president of the Palestinian Liberation Organization from 1994 to 2004.

Was Ariel Sharon the George Patton of Israel?

The similarities are striking. Both were self-made men, who brushed off criticism and advice with equal disdain. Both were supreme nationalists, who believed, respectively, that Israel and the U.S.A. were the greatest of countries. Both men also had unattractive sides to their personalities: Patton slapped U.S. soldiers in a military hospital, and Sharon provoked a conflict with the Palestinians by visiting the Temple Mount in 2000.

REAGAN AND GORBACHEV

How did a younger man finally come to power in the U.S.S.R.?

Soviet Premier Yuri Andropov died in March 1985 and was quickly succeeded by Mikhail Gorbachev (1931–). A vigorous man of fifty-three, Gorbachev was feared in the U.S.A. at the time of his succession, but he soon extended his hand to Reagan, offering to meet in person (their first summit meeting took place in Iceland in 1986). Reagan's admirers—of whom there were many—forever claimed that it was their man who brought the Russian leader to the table and that he did so by increasing the U.S. national budget for defense. During Reagan's eight years in the White House (1981–1989) U.S. defense depending nearly tripled, leading to a consequent rise in the federal debt.

Mikhail Gorbachev never revealed all of his motives, but it seems quite likely that Russia's failing corn and wheat crops had a lot to do with his willingness to negotiate. Then, too, President Reagan was talking—to anyone who would listen—about his new Strategic Defense Initiative. This, Reagan believed, would be a missile system that would shoot down any Soviet rocket, bomb, or plane in American airspace, allowing the U.S.A. to prevail in any nuclear encounter.

Was there anything to the "Star Wars" concept?

Star Wars was a very popular movie which debuted in 1977 and led to several sequels. Most of the truly dramatic moments of the *Star Wars* films revolved around daring pilots bringing rockets and fighter planes into the enemy areas and detonating explosives, which destroyed them. Always, it seemed, that the heroes escaped without consequence. Although President Reagan was highly intelligent, he sometimes exhibited a primitive trust in technology.

President Reagan (left) and Soviet Union General Secretary Mikhail Gorbachev at the Geneva Summit in 1985.

What was the Nuclear Freeze Movement?

Founded by a handful of members of the group Physicians for Social Responsibility, the Nuclear Freeze Movement was a bottom-to-top social movement of the 1980s. Persuaded that nuclear war represented the greatest of all possible evils, numerous civic leaders, in different parts of the U.S.A., encouraged their fellow citizens to vote to create their town or city as a "Nuclear-Free Zone." Critics had a lot of fun at their expense, laughing at their methods, but the Nuclear Freeze volunteers were in earnest, and they found many counterparts and peers in Western Europe.

Though a "Star Wars" system might have defended sections of the U.S.A., it could never have prevented all incoming bombs and planes.

How fast, or slowly, did the nuclear arms talks proceed?

At glacial speed. Reagan and Gorbachev were equally sincere in their desire to limit the number of weapons produced, but both men stood atop military-industrial complexes that lived or died by contracts between industry and the government. Quite a few new nuclear weapons were made during the mid-1980s, but a look at the total in the field showed some slight decrease.

At the same time, the Nuclear Freeze Movement in the United States and Western Europe reached its apogee, with millions of young people protesting the way in which their world had become so militarized. The MX Mobile Defense and the Pershing Missile—both of which were developed during the early 1980s—proved especially controversial. All the protests in the world did not convince as many people as one nuclear disaster, however.

What happened at Chernobyl?

In late April 1986, a Russian nuclear plant melted down following an accident. The Chernobyl nuclear plant was in poor condition, and some Soviet technicians had quietly voiced their belief that it should be closed. The meltdown came as a great shock to the Soviet government, however; this was the first time that a major disaster could not—in any way—be covered up. The first estimates were exaggerated, but there is no doubt that hundreds of square miles of land became essentially uninhabitable and that many thousands of Russians and Ukrainians suffered from birth defects in the years that followed.

Americans, it turned out, were especially attuned to the possibilities of nuclear disaster. The Nuclear Freeze movement was astute in its education efforts, but the nonpartisan film *The Day After* convinced far more people than any other means or technique. Aired on CBS in October 1983, *The Day After* graphically depicted what the American heartland—where many U.S. missile silos were stationed—would look like in the aftermath of a nuclear attack. The short answer—in the answer of the filmmakers and many weapons experts—was that no one would really want to live in that postapocalyptic world.

Was there a Russian equivalent to the Nuclear Freeze movement?

No. The Soviet bureaucracy and secret police were still powerful enough that the Russian citizenry could not express its sentiments openly. News of the Chernobyl disaster did spread through the U.S.S.R., however, with a consequent decline in Russian morale. For almost two generations, the Russian people had been promised that economic reforms and improvements would follow victory over the capitalist West; given that victory seemed further away than ever, many Russians began to demand changes.

Mikhail Gorbachev was not the great humanitarian that he is sometimes described as; he was, however, a realist who saw that the Soviet economy was on the verge of collapse. Each year, Russia imported large quantities of wheat from Canada and the U.S.A.; each year, military defense spending strained the overall Russian budget more tightly. And the demand on the part of many consumers for a better lifestyle pushed him as well. Even so, with all of these pressures, it is unlikely that the Soviet system would have "melted down" if not for pressure from outside. As it turned out, that pressure came both from the eastern and western directions.

TIANANMEN SQUARE

How did the protests develop inside Peking, so close to the major government buildings?

Late in May of 1989, a group of Chinese dissidents initiated protests within the capital city of Peking (also known as Beijing). The initial protests were small but were, over the course of a handful of days, swelled by others who spontaneously joined. The rioters did not desire to topple the government—they did not believe it possible to do so—but they wanted the government to release political prisoners and commence a dialogue within the nation about the future. For several days, the Chinese government held its hand, and the protests grew. On the first of June 1989, the government began its crack-

How much congruence was there between Tiananmen Square and the death of Khomeini?

These two major events happened in the same week, forcing news networks to perform at greater speeds than ever before. When Khomeini died, four million people gathered in Tehran for his funeral. Tiananmen Square had the potential to involve even more people because of China's vast population.

down; the most visible symbol of the protests was the confrontation between one un-armed Chinese protestor and a fully equipped army tank.

By the time the protests fizzled around June 5, 1989, several dozen people had been killed and several thousand arrested. The crackdown was complete, and the iron determination of the government of the Peoples Republic seemed greater than ever. Those who observed and watched, however, noticed that the government did receive a message of some kind. The PRC began, shortly thereafter, to move toward a form of semicapitalism.

FALL OF THE SOVIET BLOC

How many nations, in 1989, were still part of the Soviet Bloc?

Roughly ten nations were part of the "bloc" which had been formed in the weeks and months that followed the end of World War II. Some people called it Soviet Eastern Europe while others labeled it Communist Europe. Whatever the name, it was clear that the Russians were in charge. Revolts in Hungary in 1956 and Czechoslovakia in 1968 had been brutally crushed, and the number of Russian tanks and troops—in 1989—was, if anything, even greater than before. Despite this, and against many odds, a student protest movement began in October of 1989.

Precisely what the original intent was remains uncertain, but within days the student protestors found the East German regime weaker than expected. Plenty of troops stood on the barricades and atop the Berlin Wall, but they showed little inclination to fire on their countrymen. This type of holding back had never before been seen, and the protestors, taking heart, pushed the matter further. At first, the major news networks did not take the story seriously. When anecdotal reports spread throughout Western Europe, the news cameras were rushed to the scene.

Which week was decisive for the success of the German revolution of 1989?

Observers made much of the fact that it was the two hundredth anniversary of the French Revolution, which started with the fall of the Bastille. The Berlin Wall was hated at least as much as the Bastille, and in the first week of November 1989, hundreds of thousands of Germans—on *both* sides—began pressing the police and military. By November 10, 1989, the Wall had, in some sections at least, ceased to exist.

The success of the German revolution led other countries of the Soviet Bloc to rise in rebellion, and by November 20, nearly every nation in Eastern Europe witnessed people on the streets, confronting the military and police forces. What was so amazing to observers was the heavy equipment possessed by the military and how little it seemed to matter. In city after city, and capital after capital, the revolutionaries succeeded.

Why did Gorbachev choose not to intervene?

This is, perhaps, the sixty-four-million-dollar question. Gorbachev had a very powerful Russian military, in some cases positioned less than a hundred miles back from the "front." In almost every nation that saw revolts, the Russians possessed enough tanks and planes to overcome the protestors, but they did not intervene in a single case.

Gorbachev has, naturally, received a great deal of credit for forbearance, but the fact may be that he simply knew it was impossible to restore order. Two generations of communism had depleted the economies and even the landscape of the Eastern European countries; very few people really wanted to fight for a system that had performed so poorly. The Russians stayed out, and all the revolutions succeeded.

Was there any place where the resistance was strong?

Only in Romania. Dictator Nicolae Ceaucescu (1918–1989) and his wife had created a regime nearly unparalleled in its violence toward the people and even the environment. Suspecting there would be no mercy for them, the husband and wife fought to the death: perhaps 15,000 people were killed and wounded in the fighting which ended right about Christmas Day of 1989.

What did the situation look like on New Year's Day of 1990?

Never—in the lifetime of anyone alive on that day—had so much change taken place in a matter of two months. On November 1, 1989, there was still a Soviet Bloc; by New Year's Day of 1990, the Soviet Bloc no longer existed. The U.S.S.R. still existed, but it looked rather shaky, and the strength of its military, which had previously been taken on faith, was now questioned by many. Just a decade earlier, the U.S.S.R. had invaded Afghanistan, making the U.S.A. look like a "paper tiger." That situation had almost completely flipped around.

As early as January 1990, commentators began to speak about the "peace dividend" which, they believed, would soon descend on the American people. The Cold War had ended with a whimper, and the U.S.A. was now the world's only superpower. The administration of President George H. W. Bush (1924–) was expected to divert money from defense spending to infrastructure projects. As if to complete the rosy scenario, the system of apartheid in South Africa was suddenly jeopardized.

Romanian dictator Nicolae Ceaucescu ruled his country with an iron fist until his overthrow and execution in 1989.

How long had Nelson Mandela languished in South African prison?

He had been sentenced to life imprisonment in 1965 and was still in prison twenty-seven years later when the administration of F. W. De Klerk announced that Mandela would be freed. He walked out of prison on February 12, 1990, and to millions of observers on television, it seemed as if a new era had surely begun. The Soviet Bloc was gone; the U.S.S.R. was weak; and South Africa was clearly moving, however slowly, toward the dismantlement of apartheid.

How different did the world look in the spring of 1990?

Problems still existed: it was not a time of peace and perfection. But the possibility of world peace suddenly seemed more real, even imminent, than ever before. Millions, perhaps even hundreds of millions, of people had believed that the Berlin Wall would never disappear in their lifetimes; it was now gone, after 28.5 years.

The Cold War still existed, but only in the barest of terms. The U.S.S.R. was clearly headed toward a breakup, and it seemed that the Western democratic powers would have the upper hand for decades to come. Just as people celebrated the appearance of a new age, however, they were reminded of their Achilles' heel: their need for oil.

END OF THE COLD WAR

When did the Soviet Union cease to exist?

Right around Christmas Day of 1991. Americans were still preoccupied with their internal issues, including the return of veterans from the First Gulf War. Americans, therefore, were amazed to turn on CNN to see Gorbachev preside over a short ceremony that declared the end of the Soviet Union: from here on, there would be a number of separate nations, with the Russian Republic, led by Boris Yeltsin, being the largest. At a crucial moment in the ceremony, documents were handed to Gorbachev, and, right there on TV, it was discovered that he had no pen. The former leader of an enormous military and political system was reduced to borrowing a pen from a CNN reporter. When the signatures were affixed, there was no U.S.S.R.

Seldom if ever in human history had a nation loomed so large and powerfully as the U.S.S.R. during the 1940s through 1970s. What most people, including the best and the brightest journalists and pundits, missed was that Russia never designed a solid economic system and never managed to feed all its people. Such a system was doomed to fail, and we might today inquire how it ever managed to hold together for so long!

What happened in the Soviet Union in 1991?

The nation—if one can still call it such—was treading on very thin ice. The demise of the Communist empire in Eastern Europe was the first blow that shook the U.S.S.R.

Others, primarily economic in nature, followed. The more that the fall of the Iron Curtain revealed, the more disgusted many Russians became with their own government. Mikhail Gorbachev had led the U.S.S.R. into a new era, and had won great popularity abroad, but he was thoroughly unpopular at home.

In August 1991, during the late summer vacation season, a coup was carried out. Gorbachev was arrested and held at his vacation spot in the Crimea, while leaders of the Soviet military attempted to bring back what some of them regarded as the "good old days" of Communism. They were thwarted by Boris Yeltsin, an ambitious politician who had long been at loggerheads with Gorbachev but who displayed great mettle on this occasion. Yeltsin remained in the Kremlin, sometimes brandishing a rifle and acting as if he alone would prevent the collapse of the U.S.S.R. To some extent, he succeeded. The coup leaders backed down, and Gorbachev was released from custody. He was never quite the same afterward, however, and in any future confrontation, it was clear that Yeltsin would have the upper hand.

FIRST GULF WAR

How did Saddam Hussein come to be such a prominent—and scary—Middle Eastern figure?

Hussein had been the leader of Iraq for a decade and a half, and his detractors were fond of pointing out his blunders. He had bragged about his nuclear weapons, for example, and this led to the Israelis bombing his would-be reactor in the summer of 1981. He had started the Iran–Iraq War in 1982 and bitten off more than he could chew. But in the summer of 1990, Hussein looked very strong. Major American news magazines ran essays and covers, describing him as the world's most dangerous man (thanks to the one-million-strong army he commanded).

On August 1, 1990, Hussein sent thousands of men and hundreds of tanks across the border, invading the tiny neighboring country of Kuwait. The resistance was overcome in less than two days, and Hussein suddenly stood atop a supply of oil

Saddam Hussein was president of Iraq from 1979 until he was overthrown in 2003; he went into hiding but was captured the next year by U.S. troops. He was tried and convicted of crimes against humanity in 2006 in Iraqi court, which executed him by hanging.

that came close to doubling his total. The sheer effrontery of the move caught many people by surprise, and it seemed that Hussein was now much stronger. One person stood against the tumult. American President George H. W. Bush declared, simply, that "This will not stand."

How large was the coalition that was built to combat Hussein's aggression?

Between August and December 1990, President George H. W. Bush brokered agreements between almost thirty nations, some of them Arab, to create an enormous "coalition of the willing" to fight Iraq. During those months, the United States built up its military and naval presence in the Persian Gulf to where there were over half a million Americans in the region. Over time, these were joined by perhaps 100,000 soldiers from other coalition nations, meaning that President Bush had assembled the largest joint force seen since World War II.

At several times during those months, offers were made to Hussein, asking him to evacuate Kuwait. Had Hussein truly understood the force that was headed in his direction, he would have backed off, but the idea of the United States being a "paper tiger"—a holdover from the 1970s—lingered in his mind and those of his advisers. Hussein also failed to realize that the United States and its allies were coming at him with massive technological superiority: the most prominent of this was the Americans' superiority in fighting at night.

What brought about the first Persian Gulf War?

American planners, especially those who concentrated on the geopolitics of oil, had been jittery for more than a decade, but the situation seemed fairly calm in the midsummer of 1990. Then, on August 2, 1990, three divisions of the Iraqi army crossed the border into Kuwait.

Saddam Hussein and his government claimed Kuwait on historical, geographical terms, saying it had once belonged to Iraq. Beyond that, however, it was obvious that he desired the oil revenues of Kuwait. In 1990, Kuwait produced 1.7 million barrels of oil per day, not far behind Iraq's 2.6 million. By adding Kuwait's oil to his own, Hussein would become the second largest producer of petroleum in the entire world, after Saudi Arabia, which then produced 5.3 million barrels per day. Saudi Arabia was very much on the minds of American strategists, because it was possible that the Iraqi army would continue to move south.

What was President George H. W. Bush's reaction?

The American president was in Aspen, Colorado, at a meeting with British Prime Minister Margaret Thatcher, when the news came out. Thatcher made a rather long speech about the necessity of ejecting Iraq from its illegal conquest, while Bush simply said, "This will not stand." Critics of President Bush—and there were many—would later point out the rather cozy ties between the Bush family, which had made its fortune in the Texas oil business, and many leaders around the Arab world, but in the summer of

1990, George H. W. Bush stood tall: he looked, to all the world, like a World War II-style leader, resisting aggression.

Bush took immediate action deploying the first 20,000 American troops (they arrived by plane on August 6) and sending the *Independence* and *Missouri* aircraft carrier groups: they arrived in the Persian Gulf on August 8. Another tense ten days followed, but by about August 20, it was apparent that Hussein was not about to invade Saudi Arabia and that the United States would have the time necessary to build up its forces.

What was meant by "human shields" in the First Gulf War?

Days after his invasion of Kuwait, Saddam Hussein blandly "invited" all foreigners, especially Americans, to remain in Iraq. Days later, it was announced that these people would be employed as human shields in the event of any American invasion. If Hussein still had any credibility in the international community, it was sacrificed by this propaganda move, and sympathy began to swing in favor of the Kuwaitis who had been invaded and to the Americans who promised some type of deliverance.

President Bush, meanwhile, decided that the United States would be on shaky ground if it invaded an Arab nation without the assistance of others. He, therefore, began the job of assembling a large coalition of allies to operate under the umbrella of the United Nations. Bush was a former U.S. ambassador to the UN, and he played his cards so skillfully that over thirty nations eventually joined the coalition. At the same time, Bush continued to increase the U.S. military presence in Saudi Arabia.

How did the Saudi Arabians feel about the presence of so many U.S. military personnel?

They were distinctly uneasy. Not only was Saudi Arabia the world's largest producer of oil, but it was also the guardian and protector of the holy cities of Mecca and Medina. Many Saudi people protested the appearance of U.S. tanks, planes, and military personnel, but the Saudi government, led by King Fahd stuck by its decision.

The United Nations heard from both sides, and on November 29, 1990, the Security Council authorized the use of force if Iraq did not evacuate Kuwait by January 15, 1991. At the time this resolution was passed, there was still some hope that the situation could be resolved without armed conflict, but Saddam Hussein proved obdurate. Not realizing the size of the coalition that was built against him, he continued to declare that Iraq was sovereign over Kuwait and that his army would remain in place. One wonders—and cannot be certain—whether he would have acted differently had he possessed better knowledge of the facts.

How did Americans feel as armed conflict neared?

A good deal of apprehension prevailed. Those who examined the military situation on its own merits concluded that America and its allies would prevail, while those who harkened back to Vietnam believed that Iraq might prove yet another quagmire. President Bush, who was so articulate and even charming when speaking to international leaders, proved the opposite when speaking to his own countrymen; a World War II bomber pilot, he kept his cards close to the chest.

By January 1991, the size of the coalition buildup was startling. Over 630,000 troops were in Saudi Arabia, about 470,000 of them American. The coalition forces had 3,449 tanks, of which 1,900 were American. Numbers do not tell the whole story, however. The U.S. forces employed the M1 Tank, far superior to the T-72s used by the Iraqi military. Then, too, the coalition forces had a great advantage in aircraft as well as materiel on the ground. One of the "smallest" yet most important articles were the night glasses employed by many U.S. soldiers; these gave them a distinct advantage in what followed.

How could Saddam Hussein have been so foolish? Did he not know that there were thirty nations against one?

Hussein was blinded by arrogance and pride. He had "won" the long Iraq–Iran War by hanging tough, and he thought he could do it again. His troops were well-entrenched, and he seems to have had little idea of how powerful the coalition air forces would be. Just before the war began, he spoke of "the mother of battles," predicting that it would be the graveyard of many Americans.

A last-ditch effort to avoid combat took place on January 9, 1991, when U.S. Secretary of State James Baker met with Iraqi Foreign Minister Tarik Aziz in Geneva. The two men spoke for more than an hour, but it was obvious that Aziz would do nothing to change the scenario; he refused even to accept a letter to Saddam Hussein, written by President Bush.

When and how did the war begin?

On January 17, 1991, two days after the UN resolution deadline expired, coalition forces began a massive, dramatic aerial bombardment of the Iraqi positions in Kuwait. Roughly 2,800 aerial sorties were made that day, and this remained the average for the next thirty-seven days of the bombardment. No one could say for certain how much damage was done, but Americans who watched CNN (Cable Network News) were treated, each night, to a series of photographs which suggested that the bombs were indeed falling on their targets.

The Bush administration rightly feared that hundreds of thousands of protesters would turn out in the United States, but the protests of 1991 were tame compared to those of 1967 and 1968. Many of the people who had been young protesters in 1968 were now college administrators and high-level businessmen, and they proved adept at "managing" the dissent. It must be said, too, that the protesters made a clear division—as they had not in 1967 and 1968—of excoriating the policy while supporting the soldiers in the field.

What kind of resistance was made by the Iraqi air force?

There was virtually no resistance. Iraq had almost 700 planes, but they were no match for the coalition opponents. Most of the Iraqi pilots, therefore, flew to Iran—their for-

The 4th Fighter Wing flies near Kuwait as oil fires set by the Iraqi army burn below during Operation Desert Storm.

mer foe—when the war began. They were, indeed, safe from American attacks, but those planes never returned to Iraq: they remained in Iran.

Both in the skies and on the decks of their ships, the coalition forces reigned supreme. Over one hundred Tomahawk cruise missiles were fired on the first day alone, and the coalition forces kept up the pressure. The Iraqis could do nothing other than sit through the bombardment; the chances are that many of their soldiers longed for the air war to end and the ground war to begin because they would at least have a chance to inflict punishment on the enemy.

Did Saddam have an ace up his sleeve?

Many observers feared that he had it in the SCUD missiles, which he threatened to use against Israel. The Jewish state had stayed out of the war, in part because President Bush argued long and hard against any Israeli intervention (it would necessarily drive the Arab forces from the coalition, he declared). But Israel made no promises where SCUDs were concerned, and when the first one landed in Tel Aviv, Israel readied for action.

President Bush had an ace up his sleeve, however, and he persuaded Israel to stay its hand by sending PATRIOT missile batteries to Israel and Saudi Arabia. During the entire conflict, eighty-eight SCUDs were fired, forty-eight of them against Saudi Arabia and forty against Israel.

Did anyone make peace proposals during the aerial bombardment?

The Soviet Union made a few proposals, but its status was so weakened by the Revolutions of 1989 that it could not make the difference. Aside from the U.S.S.R., almost all countries that were not part of the coalition chose to stand aside.

When did the ground war begin?

On February 24, 1991, hundreds of thousands of coalition soldiers went into action. Their tactics were described as those of "distraction and outflanking," but in truth little disguise was necessary. The Iraqi soldiers that were still alive put up a fight until the coalition forces rained artillery on them; from that moment forward, they began to surrender. One of the most surprising photographs was of an Iraqi soldier captured by U.S. Marines; upon realizing that he would not only be spared but would actually be fed, he kissed the hands of the marines who held him.

How long did it take to liberate Kuwait City?

That was the question posed by *Time* Magazine, which highlighted the success of Operation Desert Storm with a cover photograph of U.S. soldiers in Kuwait City. The photograph was revealing, both of the joy felt by the liberated and by the panorama of U.S. soldiers who took part in the operation. Of the ten U.S. soldiers shown, five were African-American, and one looked Asian. This revealed a startling change in the racial and ethnic demographics of the U.S. Armed Forces. What the photograph did not reveal, and what became apparent only later, is that 7 percent of the U.S. forces in the Persian Gulf were female. A major social and gender revolution was happening quietly, behind the scenes, and would become much more evident during the Second Gulf War.

What happened to the Republican Guard?

When the war began, many observers warned the coalition troops about the fierce quality of the Republican Guard soldiers, Saddam Hussein's key soldiers. In battle, however, the Republican Guards seemed little different from other Iraqis; like almost all their countrymen, the Guards wanted to get out of Kuwait and on the highway to Baghdad.

In the few armored clashes that took place, a group of U.S. tanks destroyed over one hundred Republican Guard tanks in less than one hour. It was a matter of superior equipment, but also of morale. Virtually all the Iraqis were demoralized from being pounded from the air for thirty-eight days.

Who made the decision to call the war at "100 Hours"?

The ground war began on February 24 and ended on February 28. Because of the different time zones, reporters used slightly different "numbers," but most accounts concur that the war lasted approximately 100 Hours. The decision to call the war quits came from President Bush.

Almost at the very hour that the war officially ended, some American servicemen reported seeing strange dark clouds, and when it rained that night some of the personnel went out to get a nice soaking. Instead of refreshing rain, they encountered a heavy mist that they later learned was residue from oil refineries which Hussein's men had set afire. The Persian Gulf War was over, but the conflict with Saddam Hussein lingered, and festered, a very long time.

How much worse could the First Gulf War have been?

One shudders to think. If Israel had responded to the SCUD attacks, it is quite possible that both Iraq and Iran may have retaliated against the Jewish state. Neither country possessed long-range missiles, but their actions could have been enough to shatter the American-led coalition and even to spread war to the entire Middle East. While we rightly praise the soldiers, sailors, marines, and aircraft pilots, we have to save some of our kudos for the diplomats who kept Israel cool and prevented a much wider war.

Why did Bush, and the other coalition leaders, not push on to Baghdad?

President Bush was criticized for this on many occasions, but it must be remembered that the UN resolution did not call for Hussein's overthrow, just the liberation of Kuwait. Bush and his top advisers, too, feared that advancing further might result in chaos that would be even worse than what Iraq currently experienced. On balance, most thoughtful analyses come to the same conclusion: it was wise for the coalition to liberate Kuwait but *not* to push on to Baghdad.

Anyone looking from an airplane or at aerial reconnaissance photos would have concluded that the end of Hussein was near. He had lost perhaps 100,000 men in the war, and those who survived looked shell-shocked and dismayed. The Road of Death, as it was called, ran nearly one hundred miles from Kuwait City to the north, and it was simply littered with destroyed cars, tanks, and personnel carriers. No one knows how many people perished on that terrible highway, but it was surely the single greatest infliction of punishment from the air that ever had been seen in war. About the only means of revenge Hussein could employ was to set the oil refineries ablaze.

What were the terms of the truce?

Hussein's regime had to disavow any claims to Kuwait. More important, it had to agree to a series of "no-fly" zones, over which only coalition airplanes could fly. This was meant, quite intentionally, to prevent Hussein from punishing anyone who rose in revolt against him, and many coalition leaders believed that the Shi'ite minority in southern Iraq as well as the Kurdish minority in the north would rise very shortly. They did, but with disastrous consequences.

The truce also stipulated that Hussein must allow UN weapons inspectors in Iraq, who were to be given free access to all his major munitions plants in order to determine whether Iraq was stockpiling chemical weapons: nerve gas was especially feared. To all these terms, Saddam Hussein agreed.

What was the immediate aftermath of the war like?

Americans were completely jubilant. Their military, which had endured a stalemate in Korea and a real loss in Vietnam, had now been vindicated. The all-volunteer army instituted after Vietnam had achieved stunning success. And in terms of weapons technology, the United States was clearly number one. The nation that expressed the second-greatest admiration for what transpired was Israel. The Jewish state had, atypically, held back from retaliation, and for once that technique had been useful.

Coalition countries also expressed relief that Saddam Hussein's regime had been emasculated, but the firing of the oil wells—and the subsequent revolt of the Kurds in northern Iraq—led to deep feelings of insecurity. If Hussein no longer had an army, he could still arm and equip terrorists, and as long as he was in power, Iraq would be regarded as dangerous.

What was the 1991 homecoming like?

It was of a type never seen before. When America demobilized after World War II, the men came home in stages, and most were anxious just to get back in civilian clothing and resume normal lives. After the Persian Gulf War, the homecomings were swift, and they included the return of many thousands of women veterans. As a result, major family celebrations and a celebration of a new type of family—where the woman was sometimes the major moneymaker—took place. There was also a sense that the United States in 1991 was so powerful that no other nation would give it trouble for a long time. The celebrations of 1991, therefore, had a different look and feel from any previous ones.

9/11

What exactly happened on 9/11?

On the morning of September 11, 2001, a handful of air traffic controllers noticed that two planes, which had taken off from Boston, had deviated from their normal flight patterns. There was no reason to believe that anything really untoward had taken place, but alerts were sent to Air Force command and control, and jets were readied for take-off. Whether any of those planes could have arrived in time to make a vital difference is difficult to say.

At 8:40 A.M., the first of the two planes—which had been hijacked—slammed into the tower of 1 World Trade Center in New York City. Minutes later, another plane slammed into 2 World Trade Center. But that wasn't the end of the attacks. A third plane that had taken off from Washington, D.C., crashed into the Pentagon; a fourth plane, which had left from New Jersey, was also hijacked. Before it could reach its target, the passengers of the fourth plane tried to stop the terrorists, and the plane crashed into an open field near Shanksville, Pennsylvania.

What was the scene below and in the streets?

It was a terrible day, made even worse by the seemingly surrealistic weather. September 11, 2001 was one of those truly cloudless days with magnificent but not overpowering sunshine that remain in people's minds as the "perfect" day. On average, Manhattan

In the most shocking attack on U.S. soil since Pearl Harbor in 1941, the World Trade Center in New York City gushes smoke and flames after two passenger planes that were hijacked by al-Qaeda terrorists smashed into the towers. More than 2,600 people died there, as well as 125 at the Pentagon and forty passengers and crew aboard United Airlines Flight 93, which crashed in Pennsylvania.

probably has about twenty of those days each calendar year. The combination of smoke, flame, and terror on people's faces contrasted with the magnificent weather to produce a truly unusual experience, one that was long remembered.

Many New York firefighters performed acts of great bravery that day and in subsequent days as they sifted through rubble for survivors. Mayor Rudolph Giuliani feared that the death toll would be too much for New Yorkers to bear, but in the end it was calculated at slightly less than 3,000. That simple number, however, does not convey how deeply the United States was shocked by the events of 9/11.

What was the international response to the September 11 attacks?

For days, weeks, and even months, the international community was 100 percent behind the United States. The terrorists were condemned as cowards—and the United States was held up as the shining example of freedom. That initial response did not last more than a year, however, as it became increasingly evident that the United States would go to war to punish the people responsible for 9/11.

> ## Were other planes also involved in the 9/11 terrorist attacks?
>
> Two other planes were hijacked. One flew into the lower levels of the Pentagon, causing significant damage, but the other was recaptured by the passengers. They heroically fought the terrorists and forced a crash landing in Pennsylvania.

Did George W. Bush and his staff decide to attack Iraq right away?

No. Defense Secretary Donald Rumsfeld (1932–) and Vice President Richard Cheney (1941–), as well as National Security Adviser Rice, all had it in for Saddam Hussein (1937–2006), but they could not make a case for him in the days immediately following the terrorist attacks on New York City on September 11, 2001. They decided, therefore, to invade Afghanistan to punish the Taliban sect of Islam, which had initiated the September 11 attacks.

How different was President George W. Bush from his father?

George W. Bush was the product of the same prep schools and Ivy League colleges as his father, and, like his father, he had worked in the oil industry. On a gut level, however—and this was a phrase that the second President Bush frequently employed—he was quite different: bolder and more likely to strike back at his foes. Where his father had been the quintessential Ivy League gentleman, a person well-attuned to diplomatic concerns, the son embodied a cowboy approach to the world. As people sometimes say, "It was his way or the highway."

Wasn't Bush served by the same group of advisers as his father, Bush?

In about seventy percent of the cases, this was true. George Bush appointed many of the same people who had served his father and sometimes even moved them to positions of higher authority. For example, General Colin Powell (1937–), who had been head of the joint chiefs of staff for George H. W. Bush, was now secretary of state. Richard Cheney, who had been secretary of defense, was now vice president. And Donald Rumsfeld, whose connection to the Bush family went back three decades, was secretary of defense. About the only new face was that of Condoleezza Rice (1954–), the national security adviser, and she was, if anything, even more hawkish than those who had been around a longer period of time.

Was there any chance that the United States would take the attacks of September 11 "on the chin"?

There was almost no chance of that happening. Within two days of the terrorist attacks, Secretary of Defense Ronald Rumsfeld was grilling subordinates about possible areas of attack. When first told about the connection between the terrorist hijackers and the Taliban regime in Afghanistan, he brushed it off, saying that there were no "good targets" in Afghanistan for the U.S. Air Force to hit. President Bush was not as vehement as his top advisers—at least not at first—but when he went to the United Nations to speak on the subject, he made it plain that the United States reserved all its options.

President Bush also spoke to the American public by television, and in his address he described an "Axis of Evil," consisting of the regimes in Iran, Iraq, and North Korea (the last of these was well along in its development of a nuclear bomb). Bush made a forthright declaration to all nations of the world, stating that he would make no distinction between those that actively sponsored terrorism and those who merely harbored terrorists. This was a strong case of "those who are not with us are against us" (this quote is general, not from President Bush's lips).

How and when did the United States hit back?

Having ascertained that the 9/11 terrorist attacks were planned by Osama bin Laden (1957–2011), Bush authorized covert U.S. operations in Afghanistan, which had long been the terrorist leader's hideout. U.S. Special Forces were in Afghanistan by mid-October 2001, and a major buildup of U.S. forces came by December. President Bush did

Americans figured out that part of winning the war against terrorism in Asia and the Middle East was making friends. In this photo, soldiers of Bravo Company, 1st Battalion, 4th Infantry Regiment, and the U.S. Army Europe meet with village leaders in Afghanistan.

not seek an outright declaration of war; instead, he secured a congressional resolution allowing him to employ force.

Although various Taliban groups fought with skill and desperation, the power of the U.S. military was soon made obvious; American helicopters ruled the skies, and American Special Forces won most of their battles on the ground. Whether the United States could "hold" Afghanistan as effectively as it had conquered it was, of course, another question.

How many Americans were in Afghanistan? Why couldn't they capture Osama bin Laden?

Perhaps 50,000 Americans were in Afghanistan by 2002, and they soon demonstrated that they were not the U.S. military of Vietnam; moving fast and hitting hard, they demoralized the enemy and toppled the Taliban government in short order. Public opinion in the United States was strongly supportive and when it was declared that a new, democratically elected government would be instituted in Afghanistan, Americans were full of praise for the Bush administration. As one television commentator expressed it, "If he [Bush] succeeds in bringing democracy to the Middle East, then he belongs on top of Mount Rushmore."

Osama bin Laden was an adept escape artist, but he would not have survived so long without the assistance of some of the Pashtun tribes of northwest Pakistan. These peoples enjoyed semi-autonomy from the national government, and they had a fierce sense of right and wrong, especially where hospitality was concerned. Once a man invited a guest into his home, he had to provide for his safety, regardless of the personal cost.

Could the U.S. success against the Taliban have been sufficient? Would it have satisfied those Americans who were furious over the 9/11 attacks?

Americans are the most polled people in the world, yet they remain difficult to understand. There were, to be sure, many flags displayed and many demands for revenge, but there was a counter-trend as well, one that articulated the notion that revenge would inevitably be followed by revenge. The American military, therefore, made a point of de-

How accurate was the film *Lone Survivor*?

The film came out in 2014, as the Afghanistan and Iraq wars were winding down, but it was, perhaps, the most dramatic and successful of all the films connected to those conflicts. The hero—a U.S. Navy Seal—survives after the loss of his team, and he is briefly taken in by an Afghani family. Stunned and surprised, he asks why, and his host replies—more in sign language than in words—that the code of hospitality requires it.

claring that it intended to win the "hearts and minds" of Afghanis, in addition to destroying the Taliban regime.

Regardless, however, of whether the man in the street was satisfied, the Bush administration had already decided to go after Iraq. Beginning in the summer of 2002, leading Bush administration officials sounded a steady drumbeat toward war. Saddam Hussein was connected—in some way—with the terrorist attacks of 9/11, the administration declared, and he must be chastised. The expression "regime change" already existed in the political lexicon, but it was used much more frequently after 2002.

Who made the most persuasive arguments regarding war with Iraq?

Vice President Cheney was respected because of his previous service as secretary of defense, but he seemed—in 2002—to go too far, asserting that the administration knew for certain that Hussein possessed "weapons of mass destruction" (hereafter referred to as "WMD"). Secretary of Defense Donald Rumsfeld seemed much more interested in the techniques of the war to come rather than explaining why it was necessary, and the task, therefore, fell to Colin Powell, the Secretary of State. Much like Adlai Stevenson in 1962, Powell went to the United Nations and employed maps, charts, and photographs to assert that WMDs existed and that they posed a significant threat.

A long litany of Saddam Hussein's human rights violations was recited, and almost no one outside of Iraq supported the man or his regime. By March of 2003, the Bush administration had won enough public support at home and assembled a small coalition of allies (known as the "coalition of the willing") to bring about Hussein's downfall.

What was the last chance for peace?

Given the enormous amount of men and materiel that had been assembled, it was difficult to see anything but armed combat as the result, but President Bush made a televised speech on March 17, 2003. He made a number of demands, primary among them

---

Was Donald Rumsfeld as oblivious to human suffering as he sometimes appeared?

A filmmaker interviewed Rumsfeld for hundreds of hours in 2014. The filmmaker concluded that Rumsfeld had no doubt as to the rightness of his cause or the necessity of the American actions against Iraq. What can be said is that Rumsfeld had a capricious and self-serving response to many of the questions leveled at him during the course of the Iraq War. Had terrible things happened, reporters asked? Was it true there was looting of some of the most important of antiquities? "Stuff happens!" That was the opening sentence of Rumsfeld's reply.

being that Hussein and his sons leave the country within twenty-four hours. When these demands were not met, Bush declared war on Iraq.

Operation Iraqi Freedom—named by the Pentagon—began on March 19, 2003. Hundreds of American planes flew over Baghdad, dropping bombs, and scores of Tomahawk cruise missiles were fired from warships in the Persian Gulf. As developed by Secretary of Defense Donald Rumsfeld, the Second Gulf War was to be a campaign of "shock and awe" rather than a ponderous collection of forces.

How did the American invasion progress?

It moved with astonishing speed. The war began on March 19, and by April 4, U.S. troops were already in Baghdad. An enormous statue of Saddam Hussein, placed in the heart of the city, was toppled by Iraqis who appeared jubilant about the fall of the tyrant. Hussein himself disappeared during the war and did not resurface for some time.

American troops—of whom almost 15 percent were female—were delighted by the positive response they received from many Iraqis. Sunni, Shi'ite, and Kurds, they all seemed pleased by Hussein's removal. Within a matter of weeks, however, the victorious Americans discovered that Iraq's economy was on the verge of collapse. People had been hungry for months, even years, and were quick to demand that the conquering Americans establish new electricity lines and provide food.

Was anything missing from the American success in 2003?

Only one thing: WMDs. During the months that followed the American conquest, weapons inspectors fanned out through the countryside, examining bomb shelters and supply depots. While they found many weapons, including some nerve gas and chemical agents, they found no evidence of nuclear capabilities.

As a result, American public opinion—which had been about 60 percent in favor of the war—fell to a point where Americans were equally divided between those who favored and those who opposed the war. This shift took place during the summer of 2003.

A major reason for the shift was that Americans did not experience the joyous homecomings that had been the case in 1991. Relatively few soldiers came home during 2003, and those who were killed were not shown on the evening news. This, in retrospect, was a major error of the Bush administration, because it led many American families to believe that their leaders did not respect, or honor, the sacrifices their sons and daughters had made.

How large was the female presence in the U.S. Armed Forces?

To someone who had soldiered in Vietnam, or even in Grenada, the change was stunning. Roughly fifteen percent of all U.S. military personnel in Iraq were female, and many performed at high levels of technical efficiency. The single best case, showcased in *Time* magazine, was that of Colonel Laura Richardson (thirty-nine years old) and her husband Colonel Jim Richardson. She was the leader of the 5th battalion of Black Hawk fighters; he commanded the Apache helicopters of the 3rd Battalion (they were both part of the 101st Airborne). One thing on which most Americans in 2003 agreed was the pride they took in the participation of American women. The Armed Forces were a far cry from those of 1945 or even 1975.

How did the situation look as 2003 changed to 2004?

The American public was the single biggest factor. No one knew how long public opinion would support the administration, and the first major casualty reports were dismaying. Not only did more Americans die in the war's aftermath than the war itself, but the wounded men and women suffered terribly. Concealed explosive devices were placed near American compounds by Iraqi insurgents, and the IED became a commonplace horror of the occupation of Iraq.

The Bush administration pressed its case ever more strongly, and when the Democratic Party nominated Massachusetts Senator John F. Kerry (1943–), the presidential election of 2004 became a showdown over the events in Iraq, with more than a touch of the Vietnam War in the background. Kerry was a decorated U.S. war hero from Vietnam, but he had since displayed significant antiwar tendencies. The Bush administration was quick to seize upon these, turning the election of 2004 into a referendum on American involvement overseas.

What was the first major comment on the state of the U.S. Armed Forces?

One of the most brilliant, as well as trenchant, commentaries came from Evan Wright, a journalist who penned a number of *Rolling Stone* essays that turned into *Generation Kill*, his exposé of the young Americans in Iraq. Unlike many fellow commentators, Wright said little, if anything, about the female presence in the U.S. military; rather, he commented at length about how different the young men were from their grandfathers. Comparing them to the "Greatest Generation," the men who had won World War II, Wright had this to say: "Since the 9/11 attacks, the weight of America's 'War on Terrorism' has fallen on their shoulders.... They are the first generation of young Americans since Vietnam to be sent into an open-ended conflict." Wright went on to say that these young men—or at least fifty percent of them—were from broken homes and had never known two parents at the same time. They were, in his mind, raised on video games, violent movies, and were filled with latent aggression that made them excellent soldiers. Whether they would successfully make the transition to civilian life was another question.

What was Abu Ghraib, and why was it so important?

In 2003 Abu Ghraib was an industrial plant twenty miles west of Baghdad, which the Bush administration claimed was being used for the development of chemical weapons. Whether there was any truth to this claim or not, the victorious American forces seized Abu Ghraib and turned the 260-acre complex into a prison for Iraqi detainees. Right from the beginning, there were Americans—both at home and in Iraq—who claimed that many people were detained under flimsy evidence at best, but the real scandal broke early in 2004.

Because the Internet had become so ubiquitous and because so many people had digital cameras, it was not too surprising that photographic images from inside Abu Ghraib were disseminated; what was shocking was the content of those images. Some of the most extraordinary and horrifying were those showing American soldiers torturing Iraqi captives.

Are there different standards of torture? Do they vary from one nation to another?

Not in this case. One photograph showed an Iraqi prisoner, naked and hooded, standing in front of a fellow prisoner simulating oral sex. Another, perhaps even more disturbing, showed a female American soldier holding a leash, at the end of which was an Iraqi prisoner, cringing at her feet. As *Time* magazine expressed it on the cover: "IRAQ: How has it come to this?"

Did Americans not do things like this to German or Japanese prisoners during World War II?

They may have. The dearth of photographic images from that time makes it impossible to prove that such things did not happen. Americans, however, simply were not used to thinking of themselves in this way. To detain people was one thing; to humiliate them was another; but to torture them was going entirely too far.

Secretary of Defense Donald Rumsfeld proved especially obtuse on the issue. He did not even discuss it with President Bush until it became necessary, and when confronted by the press, Rumsfeld used highly inappropriate language. When he was told that some of the interrogation techniques involved keeping prisoners standing for long periods, Rumsfeld curtly answered that he stood at his desk eight hours a day (it was true: he had long been known for physical fitness).

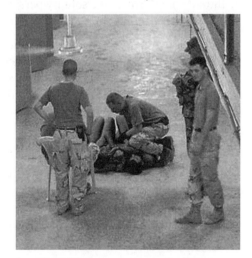

How badly did the Abu Ghraib incident(s) sour or stain American leadership in the Middle East?

Some Arabs doubtless knew that their own governments performed similar activities and then dismissed the fact that the Americans did, too. But for an impressionable generation of Arab youngsters—Sunni and Shi'ite alike—the scenes from Abu Ghraib

American soldiers are seen apparently abusing prisoners in Abu Ghraib. The international community was incensed by photos like these that seemed to defy the Geneva Convention's rules against torture.

Many Americans—then and since—have declared it to be so, but the better, more accurate, answer is that the Bush administration was truly imperial. Once a vote was taken by the U.S. Congress or by the people at large, the Bush officials took it as a mandate, regardless of the slimness of their victory. George W. Bush had made this plain while running for president in 2000. He told the delegates of the Republican national convention: "Give me a mandate, I will use it."

put the lie to the idea that the Americans had come to bring freedom and liberty to the Middle East.

Why was Donald Rumsfeld not fired?

He should have been. Any major government official who has things like this occur "on his watch" is accountable for the actions of his subordinates. President Bush kept Rumsfeld in his position another two years, however, before replacing him in November 2006.

Who was Cindy Sheehan?

She was the mother of a twenty-one-year-old who lost his life in Iraq, and during the summer of 2004, she staked out President Bush's Texas ranch. Day after day, she stood by the side of the road, one solitary person amid a sea of Secret Service agents and the press. Day after day she implored President Bush to meet with her: he steadfastly refused.

Millions of Americans sympathized with Cindy Sheehan and excoriated the president for his unwillingness to meet with her. Never, not even during Vietnam, had one person had such an effect on Americans' sentiments about war, pro or con. As the summer wore on, Cindy Sheehan was joined by numerous other protestors. One was Senator Max Cleland, a decorated Vietnam War hero who had lost both legs in that conflict.

Who won the election of 2004?

George Bush defeated John Kerry by fifty-two to forty-eight percent of the popular vote. As so often, Ohio was the key swing state; had it gone to the Kerry column, the Massachusetts senator would have won in the Electoral College. One major reason why Bush won the election of 2004 is that the "surge" in American combat personnel seemed to be working.

Months earlier, President Bush had declared that more troops were needed to pacify Iraq and to make it safe for the democracy that he expected to take hold. Roughly 20,000 of the best to be found in the U.S. Armed Forces were dispatched to Iraq, and they made the difference in the bitter fighting for the city of Fallujah.

U.S. Marines are shown here in Fallujah, Iraq, searching for members of al-Qaeda.

What was the fighting in Fallujah like?

Only the U.S. personnel who fought there could give a complete answer, and they—for the most part—would say that it was a confusing, bloody mess and that it was sometimes difficult to tell friend from foe. Many Iraqis were deeply sympathetic to the Americans. Little children would sometimes ask to run errands for them. On most occasions, these children turned out to be harmless do-gooders, but sometimes they carried explosive devices, with deadly results.

When was Saddam Hussein finally found?

In December 2004, almost two years after the war began, Hussein was found hiding in the cellar of an Iraqi house. He was in desperate condition, had gone unshaved for months, and he looked terrible, but he had nearly one million dollars in cash on his person.

Paul Bremmer, leader of the U.S. occupation, declared, "Ladies and gentlemen, we've got him." Hussein was turned over to the provisional Iraqi government. After a lengthy trial, he was found guilty of crimes against the nation and executed in May 2006.

Was the Iraq War finally over?

Not by a long shot. One would think that the execution of the tyrant might bring peace, but Iraq was bitterly divided between Sunni, Shi'ite, and Kurd. As well, many Iraqis had turned against the American occupiers, saying that had brought neither democracy nor

501

running water. As a result, the Iraq War—which still was not an officially "declared" conflict—dragged on.

One naturally wonders how U.S. personnel were able to maintain their morale, and the short answer is that they did not do so. Many continued to serve, heroically, and to receive the appreciation of their fellow Americans, but the trials were severe for nearly all of them. Military suicides began to increase as early as 2004, and by 2010 they had exceeded all previous records. The Bush administration continued to stand firm in Iraq and maintained that democracy would be the result.

What happened in the elections of 2008?

George W. Bush had served two terms and was not eligible to run again. Senator John McCain, a U.S. veteran of Vietnam, became the Republican standard bearer. McCain had not only served: he had been a prisoner of war for nearly four years, during which he had been extensively tortured by the North Vietnamese.

McCain was an American military man of the old school: his father had been an admiral and his grandfather a general. McCain did not promise victory in Iraq, but he made it plain that he would honor all commitments to U.S. personnel and to allies of the American cause. Democratic nominee Barack Obama was a member of the Vietnam generation; he and his family had been touched by the soul-searching quality of the late 1960s. Obama cautiously asserted that American troops would be withdrawn but that no precise timetable would be given. His vice presidential nominee, Senator Joe Biden, spoke with authority on the matter, declaring that even if the new administration wished, it could not bring the troops home sooner than eighteen months after such a decision had been made.

How important was the financial and economic crisis of 2008?

In the months leading up to the American presidential election, a wave of financial crises rocked the U.S. economy and therefore sent reverberations around the globe. Numerous U.S. financial institutions were found either insolvent or on the verge of becoming so. Though the wars in Iraq and Afghanistan had cost the nation perhaps three trillion dollars, the immediate outcry was not against the Defense Department, but the reckless way in which lending institutions had encouraged borrowers to take on debt.

How did military families fare during the stock market drop and the real estate implosion of 2008 to 2011?

Many military families, a solid majority in fact, either had Armed Forces housing or were renters when the financial crisis began, and their wallets were not as fiercely hit as was their overall morale. Very few military families, however, declared that their financial position improved during the crisis of 2008 to 2011.

At almost every level—from the humble renter to the wealthiest homeowner—Americans had steadily added mortgage and consumer debt during the 1990s and 2000s. There were, of course, exceptions to the rule, people who stayed within the economic safety margin, but these were often derided for their foolishness in not jumping on the real-estate bandwagon (real estate prices grew by ten percent each year). As a result, during the autumn of 2008, Americans looked at their depleted finances—caused by a significant stock market drop—and at the moral exhaustion brought on by nearly seven years of war.

By what margin did Barack Obama win the election of 2008?

It was a relatively narrow margin—fifty-two to forty-eight percent—but people around the globe were astonished that the United States, which had long been known as one of the most racist of nations, had elected a black president. To President Barack Obama's (1961–) supporters, especially those who had believed in him since the very beginning, his election was the culmination of a process of vindication for American ideals and beliefs.

This is not to say that Obama lacked critics, however. While he was transparently intelligent and cerebral, Obama was sometimes too "cool," meaning that he did not feel the pain of the common American. This criticism was made many times, but it was most convincing when made by military families, who complained that the chief executive did not understand the sacrifices they made during the wars in Iraq and Afghanistan.

Did Obama fulfill his pledge to close down the detention camp at Guantanamo in Cuba?

Obama dragged his feet. The torture which had been endemic during the Bush administration swiftly came to an end, but American prestige did not return in full measure, perhaps because Obama kept the camp at Guantanamo open.

Did the Obama administration bring clarity to the situation in Iraq?

Not right away. Obama was elected by a slim margin, and unlike George W. Bush, he proceeded cautiously. Obama had promised, for example, to close the detention center at Guantanamo Bay immediately, but this did not happen. He began a slow reduction of U.S. forces in Iraq, but at the same time he kept a sharp eye on

U.S. President Barack Obama has disappointed some Democrats by continuing wars in Afghanistan and Iraq and has also dragged his feet about closing the camp at Guantanamo in Cuba.

> ## Is there a difference between "enhanced interrogation techniques" and torture?
>
> **N**ot to the person who experiences the two: they are, to him, synonymous. One way of showing how negative, or deleterious, torture was is to compare the moral standing of the United States in, say, 1945 with its standing in, say, 2010. In both cases, the vast majority of people around the world sympathized with the Americans, not their foes, but the actions of America where torture was concerned cost the United States dearly.

Afghanistan. Many of those who voted for him expressed their disappointment with Obama during his first year in office. The major change took place in 2010.

When did President Obama declare combat operations had ceased?

The magic date was assigned to September 1, 2010. A symbolic handover from American officials to Iraqis took place in Baghdad. It was announced that 50,000 uniformed Americans would remain in Iraq, but that they would be in support positions and would only be used in combat when the situation was dire.

Time magazine noted that the troops scheduled to go home were exhausted, but held their heads high. What had they accomplished? They had defeated Saddam Hussein's army in 2004, then taken down the Sunni insurgency in Fallujah, and finally they had defeated the Shi'ite Mahdi army. To what extent the troops—men and women—had changed because of their experience was more difficult to say. Many went home with metal legs and arms or with synthetic compounds inside their bones, but there were internal changes as well. It was unlikely that anyone who served in Iraq for a long time would ever be completely the same.

For how long was Osama bin Laden able to evade the U.S. military?

President Bush had declared in 2001 that Osama bin Laden was wanted "dead or alive," but it took until the spring of 2011 for the terrorist leader to be tracked down. U.S. Special Forces acted on tips that led them to a hideout in northwest Pakistan. That country was a U.S. ally, making the matter more difficult, but President Obama gave the go-ahead, and he, Secretary of State Hillary Clinton, and other officials waited and watched as a Special Forces unit attacked the compound where Bin Laden was hiding. Osama bin Laden was killed in the firefight, and the American military chose to drop his body into the Indian Ocean rather than deliver it to any earthly burial.

Bin Laden's death closed a chapter in American foreign policy, but he had accomplished more than he knew. The United States, in the spring of 2011, was tangibly different from the nation of September 2001. Some of the changes were technical in nature—the country was awash in cell phones, for example—but there were psychological and social scars as well. Few Americans trusted their government to the same extent as ten years earlier, and a significant majority were pessimistic about the future. Some of this sentiment stemmed from the economic situation; the rest came from the ten-year war.

Was that it for the war in Iraq?

So far as the majority of Americans went, that was it. Weary of hearing about either Iraq or Afghanistan, many Americans simply closed their ears to the news reports of the next three years, which suggested that both the Taliban and Iraqi insurgents were once more on the rise. Even a terrible civil war in Syria—beginning in 2012—could not rouse Americans from their slumber, and it was difficult to blame them. President Obama swayed first one way and then the next on Syria: he was unable to develop a coherent foreign policy toward that nation.

Where did the neoconservatives turn their attention next?

Ever since about 2006, the neoconservatives had waxed about the need to take on Iran, which was slowly building toward nuclear capacity. The danger seemed greater during the presidency of Mahmoud Ahmadinejad; Israel, too, frequently warned that it would not stand by while Iran gained nuclear capabilities. But the big surprise took place not in Iran, but in Iraq!

What was the Arab Spring?

In the early winter of 2010–2011, there was a marked rise in tension throughout the Arab World. Veteran observers, including those in the U.S. State Department, brushed off the early indicators of something really big because they had seen similar signs before. This time, however, both the leading Arab regimes and the United States were about to reap a whirlwind of discontent.

The fighting began in Tunisia, one of the smaller Arab nations. Eight demonstrators were killed in early January of 2011; their deaths led to a full-fledged revolution in that country. Within three weeks, President Ibn Saud, who had been in power for twenty-seven years, was forced to step down from office. By then, the student uprisings had spread to Cairo.

Were the Arab Spring protestors mainly students?

Students were at the vanguard, but it is fair to say that many other young people, and quite a few middle-aged protesters as well, were ready to join the movements spreading throughout the Arab world. Discontent had built and simmered for more than a generation, with millions of young people seeking the right moment to chastise their dictators. The key difference in 2011, as opposed to, say, 1991, was that the young people had modern technology, including cell phones and computers, with which to coordinate their actions.

The results were stunning. The leader of Tunisia fell first and was followed by Egypt's Hosni Mubarak (governed 1981–2011), who had been in power ever since the death of Anwar Sadat in 1981. Bashar al-Assad managed to hang on in Syria, but that nation soon degenerated into a terrible civil war that practically ruined the country. About the only Arab regime that remained truly unaffected was Saudi Arabia, and this is because the state-controlled police turned out early enough to thwart the protestors.

What was the situation in the Middle East in 2014?

Americans, on the whole, were utterly tired of hearing about Iraq and Afghanistan. Even so, they were shocked, in the early summer of 2014, to learn that a new movement which seemed to combine all the worst aspects of their Middle Eastern foes had arisen. Known as the Syria-Iraq movement, this appeared to be a spontaneous uprising of those who wanted to combine the Arab regimes in Syria and Iraq.

Acting with speed and astonishing ease, the militia of this new group practically put the newly formed Iraqi army out of business in June and July 2014. Entire regiments of the Iraqi army simply folded when matched up against the militia, and it seemed for a time that Baghdad itself might fall to the insurgents. President Obama declared that Iraq had to win this war, and he approved the sending of thousands of Americans to act as military advisers.

What is ISIS/ISIL?

The rise of ISIL (Islamic State of Iraq and the Levant), or ISIS (Islamic State of Iraq and Syria), was little short of amazing. In 2013, most Americans had heard neither the name

Ukrainian citizens protest against the Russian invasion of the Crimean peninsula in a March 2014 rally.

nor the goals of the movement; during the late summer of 2014, however, Americans became alarmed as they heard of beheadings and mass executions. At one point it seemed possible that the ISIL forces would capture Baghdad; this was thwarted by the use of American air power. Whether ISIL would continue to be a major power in the region was open to question, but as of the autumn of 2014, its forces controlled one-sixth of Syria and one-quarter of Iraq.

ISIL was the original name of this group of extremists, with the name ISIS coming shortly afterward. In either case, the aims and goals of the leaders are the same: the creation of a pan-Islamic state where Sharia law—a fundamentalist version of that taught by the Prophet Mohammad—would prevail.

Where else was American, or Western, power threatened?

In the early spring of 2014, Russian leader Vladimir Putin stunned the world by quickly invading and overrunning the Crimean Peninsula. That Russia had some interests in the Crimea was obvious, but that it presently belonged to the Ukraine was inarguable. U.S. President Barack Obama cautioned the Russians several times, gently pointing out, on American television, the disparity between his armed forces and theirs.

THE FUTURE OF WAR

Is there any recurring pattern in military history, one that can perhaps guide us to a new future?

Many patterns have developed and asserted themselves, but one of the axioms of combat is that the generals, and even the nations, prepare for the last war. This does not mean the final conflict, something such as Armageddon, but rather that they assume that war in the future will resemble war in the past. As a result, strategists and tacticians are often taken off balance by what does happen.

One pattern that seems likely to continue—long into the future—is the long battle between light and heavy equipment. On numerous occasions, the tribe or nation that uses the heavier equipment—armor on the men, for example—has prevailed; on at least as many occasions, the side that employs the lighter equipment—the longbow versus the crossbow, for example—has won the victory. The two militaries that have shown the greatest skill in mixing light and heavy armaments are those of the United States and Israel, but this does not mean they will continue to do so.

Is there any chance that peoples, the world over, will grow so weary of war that it will be outdated?

The chances are about ninety-five percent against. Even if all the developed and industrialized nations—those that have the most to lose—decided tomorrow to outlaw war, they would still need a certain minimum of armaments to keep themselves safe from the less fortunate, less developed ones. Then, too, having a great deal to lose has never proven a foolproof means of avoiding war. Numerous societies—France in 1660 and Russia in 1914 for example—have been doing fine internally, with many fine things to their credit, but have still been led to lasting combat, partly as the result of recklessness shown by their leaders.

What role will technology like the Internet play in warfare?

Many nations have already been using computers to spy on both enemies and friends. Experts in programming learn how to hack into business and government databases to extract information on everything from new weapons to where personnel are stationed. Countries like China, for instance, also conduct espionage using computers and can also track the activities of dissidents. In the United States, the National Security Agency (NSA) has been a concern to American citizens who believe they are being spied on even when they are not suspected terrorists or foreign agents.

Who is Edward Snowden?

In the early summer of 2013, Americans were stunned and dismayed to learn that many government secrets had been leaked to international organizations, much of the work being done by twenty-nine-year-old Edward Snowden (1983–). Born in New Jersey, he enjoyed a normal middle-class life and education, and he joined the Central Intelligence Agency in 2006. In 2012 to 2013, while working as a contractor for the National Security Agency (NSA), Snowden chose to leak hundreds of thousands of classified documents. When questioned, he replied that he and his generation of young Americans believed that surveillance was both illegal and immoral and that he was pleased to use the most modern technology to thwart his former employers. Whether Snowden is a hero (as some claim), a villain (as others assert), or simply a misguided person depends very much on the worldview of the person making the pronouncement. As of this printing, Snowden is currently hiding in Russia from American authorities.

How dominant was the U.S., militarily speaking, in the year 2014?

American defense spending—in the neighborhood of 600 billion annually—slightly exceeded that of all other nations in the world combined. The U.S. active military—including all sections of the Armed Forces—came to slightly more than 1.5 million. And to take a special case, that of naval power, the United States possessed nineteen aircraft carriers—most of them state of the art—compared to twelve for the rest of the world combined.

Was there a number two?

No. In 2014, the United States stood ahead of all friends and foes by such a margin that no one could really count as an effective second. Some people might point to the British,

French, and Russian militaries, but all of them combined would not even come close to equaling American military power. Others might look to the People's Republic of China, which certainly had performed amazing economic feats, but which still lagged the United States by a long way, militarily speaking. America's world position in 2014 was rather like that of the doleful answer given to Queen Victoria. In 1852, while her royal yacht was positioned to observe the America's Cup sailing race, Queen Victoria commented that she saw that the United States was first. And who was second, she inquired? "Madam, there is no second" was the sad answer.

What was the state of guerrilla or insurgency actions around the world in 2014?

The world seemed quieter in 2014 than usual, but it was the calm that comes after many years of covert actions, insurgencies, and counterinsurgencies. Experts pointed to certain areas of success, such as the Democratic Republic of the Congo, which was more peaceful than at any time in the previous decade.

Will the world ever see a calamitous, enormous war along the lines of what we saw in 1914–1918 and in 1939–1945?

Many experts bet against it, arguing that warfare has changed so much that a repeat is unlikely. This author is not so certain. Human nature has not changed that much since

U.S. Army Gen. Martin E. Dempsey, chairman of the Joint Chiefs of Staff, greets Chinese Army General Fang Fenghui, chief of the general staff, at a 2014 ceremony at the Pentagon. Could the Chinese one day take America's place as the number one world power?

the enormous twentieth-century wars. Certainly, we—the billions of people knit together by the Information Age—can often see dangers when they are still far off, but there is no way to ensure that a Hitler, a Stalin, or a Mussolini will not emerge.

For how long will the United States remain the one great superpower?

This one is so tricky that almost no one can answer and feel confident of his response. But the overall suggestion is: not as long as we Americans would like to think. Consider, for example, the state of the British Empire in the year 1910. To the average Briton, it seemed nearly impossible that any other country would arise to challenge the greatness of England and its overseas empire. Yet merely a decade later, in 1920, Britain had suffered nearly one million war dead, and it was being overtaken, in an economic sense, by the United States.

Economic and military power often go hand in hand. The American technological superiority over all enemies—at the time of this writing—is based on an entrepreneurial society, where new ideas and talents are constantly rising to the top. So long as that economic style continues, it is possible that the United States will remain "number one."

How significant—to the United States—is the rise in China's military power?

One of the long-standing continuities of Chinese history is that its leaders do not go about forecasting their intentions. Some scholars believe that China has already assigned itself a Fifty Year Plan, according to which it will take that long for China to rise to number one in the world. If China can devote its great resources and the energies of its people to that goal, it may well attain the top position. China has some special difficulties, however, that may make its rise especially difficult.

First and foremost, China has a population problem. It is well known that there are 1.54 billion Chinese and that the country constantly struggles with keeping them fed. Less known is that China has a population dearth of young people—between the ages of about ten and thirty. These young people are needed to perform all sorts of tasks, including the care of the elderly, and from the current perspective it is difficult to see how China will accomplish this. Then, too, China has an environmental problem. The Gobi Desert grows a little larger every year, and it is possible that China will run out of water before it runs out of food.

If China does run into snags, and if the United States declines, what other nation, or group of nations, might step in to fill the void?

Many people predict that the European Union will take over as the amalgamated nation of choice: the arbiter of other people's affairs. While this is possible, the attitude of many Europeans—East, West, and Central—argues against this possibility; even today, in 2014, the Europeans are deeply affected by World War II.

Further Reading

Bard, Mitchell G. *The Complete Idiot's Guide to World War*. New York: Penguin Group, 2010.

Baxter, John. *Paris at the End of the World: The City of Light during the Great War, 1914-1918*. New York: HarperCollins, 2014.

Blum, Howard. *The Eve of Destruction: The Untold Story of the Yom Kippur War*. New York: HarperCollins, 2003. Blum, Harold.

Blunt, Wilfrid. *The Golden Road to Samarkand*. New York: The Viking Press, 1973.

Boot, Max. *Invisible Armies: An Epic History of Guerrilla Warfare from Ancient Times to the Present*. New York: W.W. Norton, 2013.

Borneman, Walter R. *The Admirals: Nimitz, Halsey, Leahy, and King: The Five-Star Admirals Who Won the War at Sea*. New York: Back Bay Books, 2012.

———. *American Spring: Lexington, Concord, and the Road to Revolution*. Boston: Little, Brown, 2014.

Bowman, John S., ed. *Facts about the American Wars*. New York: H.W. Wilson, 1997.

Burlingame, Michael. *The Inner World of Abraham Lincoln*. Champaign, IL: University of Illinois Press, 1994.

Carter, Miranda. *George, Nicholas and Wilhelm: Three Royal Cousins and the Road to World War I*. New York: Vintage Books, 2011.

Cline, Eric H. *1177 BC: The Year Civilization Collapsed*. Princeton, NJ: Princeton University Press, 2014.

Cordingly, David. *Under the Black Flag: The Romance and the Reality of Life among the Pirates*. New York: Random House, 1998.

Crompton, Samuel Willard. *Illustrated Atlas of Native American History*. New York: Chartwell, 1999.

———. *The Cheyenne*. New York: Chelsea House, 2011

Crowley, Roger. *1453: The Holy War for Constantinople and the Clash of Islam and the West*. New York: Hyperion, 2005.

———. *Empires of the Sea: The Siege of Malta, the Battle of Lepanto, and the Contest for the Center of the World*. New York: Random House, 2008.

Dando-Collins, Stephen. *Caesar's Legion: The Epic Saga of Julius Caesar's Elite Tenth Legion and the Armies of Rome*. Hoboken, NJ: John Wiley & Sons, 2002.

Darwin, John. *After Tamerlane: The Global History of Empire since 1405*. New York: Bloomsbury Books, 2008.

Dijked, Ruud van, ed. *Encyclopedia of the Cold War*, 3 vols. New York: Routledge, 1998.

Fenby, Jonathan. *The General: Charles De Gaulle and the France He Saved*. New York: Skyhorse Publishing, 2013.

Fox, William F. *Regimental Losses in the American Civil War*. Albany, NY: Albany Publishing Company, 1889.

Furtado, Peter. ed. *1001 Days That Shaped the World*. Hauppauge, NY: Barrons Educational, 2012.

Gaddis, John Lewis. *The Cold War: A New History*. New York: Penguin Books, 2005.

Gall, Carlotta. *The Wrong Enemy: America in Afghanistan, 2001–2014*. Boston: Houghton Mifflin Harcourt, 2014.

Gardner, Brian. *The Year That Changed the World: 1945*. New York: Coward-McCann, 1963.

Goldstein, Joshua S. *Winning the War on War: The Decline of Armed Conflict Worldwide*. New York: Penguin, 2011.

Goldsworthy, Adrian. *How Rome Fell: Death of a Superpower*. New Haven, CT: Yale University Press, 2009.

———. *Augustus: First Emperor of Rome*. New Haven, CT: Yale University Press, 2014.

Greenblatt, Mark Lee. *Valor: Unsung Heroes from Iraq, Afghanistan, and the Home Front*. Lanham, MD: Taylor Trade, 2014.

Hamilton, Nigel. *The Mantle of Command: FDR at War, 1941–1942*. Boston: Houghton Mifflin Harcourt, 2014.

Hanson, Neil. *The Confident Hope of a Miracle: The True History of the Spanish Armada*. New York: Alfred A. Knopf, 2005.

Hanson, Victor Davis. *The Western Way of War: Infantry Battle in Classical Greece*. Oakland, CA: University of California Press, 2009.

Hastings, Max. *Inferno: The World at War, 1939–1945*. New York: Vintage Books, 2011.

Heather, Peter. *Empires and Barbarians: The Fall of Rome and the Birth of Europe*. New York: Oxford University Press, 2009.

Herring, George C. *From Colony to Superpower: U.S. Foreign Relations since 1776*. New York: Oxford University Press, 2008.

Holzer, Harold, and the New York Historical Society. *The Civil War in 50 Objects*. New York: Viking, 2013.

Jenkins, Philip. *The Great and Holy War: How World War I Became a Religious Crusade*. New York: Harper One, 2014.

Kahaner, Larry. *AK-47: The Weapon That Changed the Face of War*. Hoboken, NJ: John Wiley & Sons, 2007.

Kwarteng, Kwasi. *War and Gold: A 500-Year History of Empires, Adventures, and Debt*. New York: Public Affairs, 2014.

Leepson, Marc. *What So Proudly We Hailed: Francis Scott Key, A Life*. London, New York: Palgrave Macmillan, 2014.

Lieven, Dominic. *Russia against Napoleon: The True Story of the Campaigns of War and Peace*. New York: Penguin, 2009.

Listening In: The Secret White House Recordings of John F. Kennedy, selected and introduced by Ted Widmer. New York: Hyperion, 2012.

Lloyd, Nick. *Hundred Days: The Campaign that Ended World War I*. New York: Basic Books, 2014.

Lucks, Daniel S. *Selma to Saigon: The Civil Rights Movement and the Vietnam War*. University Press of Kentucky, 2014.

Macdonald Publishers. *Japanese Aircraft Carriers and Destroyers*. London: Macdonald, 1964.

Mearns, David, and Rob White. *Hood and Bismarck: The Deep-Sea Discovery of an Epic Battle*. London, England: Channel 4 Books, 2001.

Morris, Ian. *War! What Is It Good For?: Conflict and the Progress of Civilization from Primates to Robots*. New York: Farrar, Srauss, & Giroux, 2014.

Morton, W. Scott, and J. Kenneth Olenik. *Japan: Its History and Culture*. New York: McGraw Hill, 2005.

Reynolds, David. *The Long Shadow: The Legacies of the Great War in the Twentieth Century*. New York: W.W. Norton, 2014.

Ricks, Thomas E. *The Generals: American Military Command from World War II to Today*. New York: Penguin Books, 2012.

Rostker, Bernard. *Providing for the Casualties of War: The American Experience through World War II*. Santa Monica, CA: The RAND Corporation, 2013.

Ryder, Roland. *Edith Cavell*. New York: Stein & Day, 1975.

Scahill, Jeremy. *Dirty Wars: The World Is a Battlefield*. New York: Nation Books, 2013.

Sheehy, Gail. *The Man Who Changed the World: The Lives of Mikhail S. Gorbachev*. New York: Harper Collins, 1990.

Smith, Dennis Mack, ed. *Garibaldi: Great Lives Observed*. Englewood Cliffs, NJ: Prentice-Hall, 1969.

Strachan, Hew. *The First World War*. New York: Penguin Books, 2003.

Vogel, Steve. *Through the Perilous Fight: Six Weeks That Saved the Nation*. New York: Random House, 2013.

Winston, Robert A. *Aircraft Carrier* New York: Harper & Brothers, 1942.

Worthington, Ian. *By the Spear: Philip II, Alexander the Great, and the Rise and Fall of the Macedonian Empire*. New York: Oxford University Press, 2014.

Wright, Evan. *Generation Kill: Devil Dogs, Iceman, Captain America, and the New Face of American War*. New York: Berkley Caliber, 2004.

Zabdecki, David T. ed. *World War II in Europe: An Encyclopedia*, 2 vols. New York: Garland Publishing, 1999.

Timeline

3000 B.C.E.	Egypt and Sumer emerge as nations
2200 B.C.E.	Babylonia begins its rise to empire
1700 B.C.E.	Both Egypt and Babylon enter period of decline
1300 B.C.E.	The Late Bronze Age reaches the peak of development
1177 B.C.E.	This year has been somewhat arbitrarily chosen as the time when the Late Bronze Age countries and empires experienced great difficulty
c. 1000 B.C.E.	Kingdom of Israel approaches peak of its success
c. 900 B.C.E.	Kingdom of Assyria begins its rise as the number-one military power in the Middle East
732 B.C.E.	Kingdom of Israel destroyed by Assyria
587 B.C.E.	Kingdom of Judah attacked; thousands of Jews taken as captives to Babylon
539 B.C.E.	Cyrus the Great—leader of the Persians—captures Babylon
529 B.C.E.	Cyrus dies on campaign in Central Asia
494 B.C.E.	Ionian Revolt against the Persians begins
490 B.C.E.	Battle of Marathon fought north of Athens
480 B.C.E.	Battles of Thermopylae and Salamis
479 B.C.E.	Battle of Plataea; end of Greco–Persian Wars
475–432 B.C.E.	Golden Age of Greece
432–402 B.C.E.	Peloponnesian War
c. 350 B.C.E.	Thebes becomes the number-one Greek state
334 B.C.E.	Alexander the Great departs Greece
333 B.C.E.	Alexander wins the Battle of Issus
331 B.C.E.	Alexander wins the Battle of Gaugamela
323 B.C.E.	Alexander dies in Babylon
262 B.C.E.	The First Punic War begins over conflicts in Sicily
218 B.C.E.	The Second Punic War begins; Hannibal crosses the Aps

216 B.C.E.	Battle of Cannae; bloodiest day of Ancient World
202 B.C.E.	Scipio Africanus defeats Hannibal at Battle of Zama
149 B.C.E.	Third Punic War begins
146 B.C.E.	Carthage is conquered and destroyed; Corinth, Greece, is conquered and destroyed
100 B.C.E.	Julius Caesar born in Rome
61 B.C.E.	Caesar becomes proconsul of The Province
55 B.C.E.	Caesar invades Britain
55 B.C.E.	Caesar builds a bridge across the Rhine
53 B.C.E.	Gallic "Revolt" begins under leadership of Vercingetorix
52 B.C.E.	Caesar captures Gallic city of Alesia
49 B.C.E.	Roman Civil War begins
48 B.C.E.	Gaius Pompey defeated at Battle of Pharsalus
44 C.E.	Julius Caesar assassinated in Rome
69 C.E.	"Year of Four Emperors" in Rome
70 C.E.	Jewish Revolt is suppressed
100 C.E.	The *Pax Romana* begins
196 C.E.	Era of the Good Emperors and the *Pax Romana* goes into decline
260 C.E.	Emperor Valerian captured and killed by Parthians in Iraq
281 C.E.	The new wall—the Aurelian Wall—is built around Rome
305 C.E.	Constantine becomes Emperor
350 C.E.	Constantinople and Rome are of equal size and importance
380s	The Huns make their first appearance in Eastern Europe
410	Rome is sacked for the first time—by Goths under Alaric
476	Rome is sacked; the last Emperor is dethroned
530s	Byzantine Empire approaches peak of its military power
610	Battles between Persians and Byzantines approach a climax
632	Death of The Prophet Mohammed; beginning of Arab wars of conquest
711	Arabs/Berbers cross Strait of Gibraltar and invade Spain
717–718	Major Arab siege of Constantinople fails
732	Christian Frankish cavalry wins Battle of Tours in France
778	Charlemagne's rear guard is ambushed by the Basques in northern Spain
800	Charlemagne is crowned by Pope Leo on Christmas Day, marking the beginning of the Holy Roman Empire
c. 801	Viking raids in France and Ireland begin

814	Death of Charlemagne
842	Treaty of Verdun divides Charlemagne's empire into three kingdoms
c. 875	Magyars arrive in present-day Hungary
955	Otto the Great wins Battle of Lechfeld
c. 1000	Vikings arrive in Newfoundland
1014	Battle of Clontarf in Ireland
1066	January: King Edward the Confessor dies
	March: William of Normandy asserts English throne is his
	September: Battle of Stamford Bridge
	October 14: Battle of Hastings
	December: William the Conqueror crowned King William I of England
1071	Seljuk Turks win Battle of Manzikert
1095	Pope Urban II preaches the First Crusade
1096	Failure of Peasants' Crusade, start of Knights' Crusade
1098	Siege of Antioch
1099	Crusaders capture Jerusalem
1140s	Second Crusade is ineffective
1187	Saladin wins Battle of Hattin, takes Jerusalem
1188	The Third Crusade is proclaimed
1190	Frederick Barbarossa dies near Syrian-Turkish border; Richard and Philip winter in Sicily before proceeding to Holy Land
1191	Richard conquers Cyprus; Richard and Philip complete the conquest of Acre; Richard wins the Battle of Arsulf
1192	Richard and Saladin agree to three-year truce
1193	Saladin dies in Damascus; Richard is captive of Emperor Henry IV
1199	Richard dies while besieging French castle
1206	Genghis Khan proclaimed leader of all the Mongols
1211	Genghis Khan invades northern China
1214	Philip II wins Battle of Bouvines
1215	King John agrees to the Magna Carta
1215	Beijing falls to Mongols
1215	King John signs the Magna Carta
1238	Mongols enter Western Russia
1240	City of Kiev falls to the Mongols
1241	Mongols invade Hungary and Poland

1258	Mongols sack Baghdad
1260	Mamelukes win Battle of Ain Jalut
1274	Kublai Khan conquers southern China
1277	Mongol fleet fails to conquer Japan
1306	William Wallace is captured and executed
1314	Scots win Battle of Bannockburn
1334	Hundred Years' War begins
1346	England wins the Battle of Crecy
1347	King Edward III captures Calais
1356	England wins Battle of Poitiers
1415	England wins Battle of Agincourt
1429	Joan of Arc leads the Dauphin Charles to Rheims to be crowned
1431	Joan of Arc is sentenced to burn after an ecclesiastical trial
1453	Hundred Years' War ends with French victory in Gascony; Ottoman Turks capture Constantinople and rename it Istanbul
1492	Columbus sails west, arrives in the Bahamas
1494	Charles VIII of France invades Italy
1519–1522	Magellan and El Cano complete first circumnavigation of the earth
1522	England and France go to war
1525	King Francis I captured at Battle of Pavia
1555	Peace of Augsburg temporarily ends religious wars
1556	Emperor Charles V abdicates his many thrones
1568	Dutch revolt against Spanish rule begins
1577–1580	Francis Drake completes second circumnavigation
1587	Mary, Queen of Scots, is executed
1588	Spanish Armada fails to conquer England
1598	King Philip II dies
1603	Queen Elizabeth I dies
1607	English settlers arrive in Jamestown
1608	French settlers arrive at Quebec
1609	Spanish settlers arrive at St. Augustine
1609	Twelve Years' Truce between Holland and Spain begins
1618	The Defenestration of Prague leads to war between Austria and Bohemia
1620	Austria wins the Battle of White Mountain; Pilgrim Fathers land at Plymouth
1621	Holland and Spain resume war

1625	High point of Spanish success in Thirty Years' War
1630	Puritan settlers establish Boston; King Gustavus Adolphus brings Sweden into Thirty Years' War
1632	Gustavus Adolphus killed at Battle of Lutzen
1635	France declares war on Spain
1638	Holland wins the Battle of the Downs against Spanish fleet
1642	King Charles of England goes to war against Parliament
1644	Oliver Cromwell emerges as Parliament's major champion
1645	Parliamentary forces win the Battle of Naseby
1648	Thirty Years' War ends with treaties signed at Westphalia
1661	King Louis IV embarks on military adventures
1675	King Philip's War begins in New England
1676	Bacon's Rebellion takes place in Virginia
1688	William of Orange dethrones his father-in-law, James II
1689	The War of the League of Augsburg begins
1690	Massachusetts militiamen fail to capture Quebec City
1697	Peace of Ryswick ends the War of the League of Augsburg
1701	War of the Spanish Succession begins
1704	Duke of Marlborough wins Battle of Blenheim
1712	Peace comes to Europe
1739	War of Jenkins' Ear between Britain and Spain begins
1740	War of the Austrian Succession begins
1744	Britain and France exchange declarations of war
1745	New England militiamen take Louisburg on Cape Breton Island
1746	Bonnie Prince Charlie defeated at Battle of Culloden
1748	Peace comes with the Treaty of Aix-la-Chapelle
1754	George Washington's wilderness actions spark the French and Indian War
1755	Braddock defeated in Pennsylvania
1756	The Seven Years' War officially begins; Marquis de Montcalm captures Oswego
1757	Montcalm captures Fort William Henry and a massacre takes place
1757	William Pitt becomes secretary of state in England
1758	Jeffrey Amherst captures Louisburg; James Abercromby fails miserably at Ticonderoga; Edward Forbes captures Fort Duquesne
1775	April: Battles of Lexington and Concord
	June: George Washington becomes commander-in-chief

	December: Americans nearly capture Quebec City
1776	March: Washington forces British evacuation of Boston
	August: Battle of Long Island
	September: British capture Manhattan
	December: Washington down to 4,000 men
	December: Washington captures the Hessians at Trenton
1777	January: Washington outmaneuvers Cornwallis at Princeton
	July: Burgoyne captures Ticonderoga
	August: Battle of Oriskany
	September: Battles of Bemis Heights and Freemans Farm
	October: Burgoyne surrenders with 7,000 men
1778	March: Treaty of alliance between France and the United States
	July: Battle of Monmouth
	August: Failed siege of Newport, Rhode Island
1780	May: British capture Charleston and 5,000 men
1789	July: Fall of the Bastille in France
	October: King and Queen of France taken from Versailles to Paris
1792	Austria and Prussia declare war on France
1793	January: Louis XVI of France executed
	February: France declares war on Britain
	June: United States declares neutrality in the Anglo-French War
1795	July: Napoleon dismisses the Paris crowd with artillery
1798	June: Napoleon wins the Battle of the Nile
	July: Admiral Nelson wins the Battle of Aboukir
1804	Napoleon readies an invasion force
1805	September: Nelson wins Battle of Trafalgar
	December: Napoleon wins Battle of Austerlitz
1806	Napoleon crushes Prussia in six-week campaign
1807	Napoleon and Czar Alexander come to (private) agreement
1808	Napoleon invades Spain, places his brother Joseph on throne
1809	Britain lands expeditionary force in Portugal
1812	British capture Badajoz, Spain; Napoleon invades Russia; America declares war on Britain; USS *Constitution* meets and captures HMS *Guerriere*
1813	Perry wins Battle of Lake Erie; Harrison wins Battle of the Thames
1814	Napoleon abdicates his throne(s); Britain sends troops to America; British capture Washington, D.C.; British are repulsed at Baltimore; peace treaty signed at Ghent, Belgium

1815	Andrew Jackson wins Battle of New Orleans; Napoleon escapes exile on Elba; The Hundred Days; Wellington defeats Napoleon at Waterloo; Napoleon abdicates and is sent to Saint Helena
1830	Paris overturns King Charles X; Belgium rises in power
1831	Neutrality of Belgium guaranteed by all major powers
1846	U.S.–Mexican War begins
1847	Battle of Buena Vista; capture of Vera Cruz; capture of Mexico City
1848	Treaty of Guadeloupe Hidalgo; revolution in France overthrows Louis-Philippe; subsequent revolutions throughout Europe
1851	Taiping Rebellion begins in China
1854	Taiping Rebels capture Nanking, make it their capital
1855	Crimean War begins
1856	Siege of Sevastopol
1860	Garibaldi's Red Shirts land in Sicily; Italian unification achieved
1861	Confederates attack and take Fort Sumter; Lincoln calls for 75,000 volunteers; fighting begins in Western states; Battle of Bull Run
1862	Battle of Shiloh; Farragut takes New Orleans; McClellan comes within 10 miles of Richmond; Seven Days' Battle; Second Battle of Bull Run; Battle of Antietam; Emancipation Proclamation
1863	Grant moves to besiege Vicksburg; Lee moves north; three-day Battle of Gettysburg; Vicksburg surrenders (July 4); Battle of Chickamauga; Battle of Lookout Mountain; Confederates flee from Chattanooga
1864	Battle of the Wilderness; Sherman advances toward Atlanta; Battle of Cold Harbor; siege of Richmond and Petersburg; Battle of the Crater; Sherman captures Atlanta; Sherman takes Savannah
	Huang dies in Nanking of natural causes; Huag's son is captured by Chinese Manchus
1865	Sherman marches north from Georgia; Lee breaks free from Siege of Richmond; Lee surrenders to Grant at Appomattox; Lincoln assassinated in Washington, D.C.
1870	Franco–Prussian War begins
1871	Paris surrenders; Bismarck proclaims new German Empire
1876	Custer and troopers wiped out at Little Bighorn
1877	Chief Joseph and Nez Perce surrender at Bear Paw
1888	Wilhelm II becomes German Kaiser
1895	Cuban revolt against Spain intensifies
1898	USS *Maine* blows up in Havana Harbor; U.S. captures Cuba and Puerto Rico
1899	Mafeking surrenders to Boers

1900	The Boxer Rebellion begins with a siege of the foreign legations in the city of Beijing
1901	Queen Victoria celebrates Golden Jubilee
1904	Japan attacks Port Arthur in sneak attack
1905	Japan wins Battle of Tshushima; Russo–Japanese War ends
1911	First Balkan War begins
1914	June 28: Archduke Ferdinand is assassinated in Sarajevo
	July 28: Austria declares war on Serbia
	August 1: Russia and Germany exchange declarations of war
	August 2–3: France and Britain declare war on Germany
	August: President Woodrow Wilson declares U.S. neutrality
	August 16: Belgian fortress of Liege falls to Germans
	August 20: British Expeditionary Force is now in Belgium and northern France
	September 3–11: First Battle of the Marne
1918	November 11: End of World War I
1918–1919	The German Revolution results in establishment of the Weimar Republic
1933	Adolf Hitler becomes Chancellor of Germany
1939	August 23: Non-Aggression Pact signed
	September 1: Germany invades Poland
	September 23: U.S.S.R. invades eastern Poland
1940	May 5: Germany attacks France in the Ardennes Forest
	May 10: Winston Churchill becomes Prime Minister of Britain
	May 25–June 24: Successful evacuation of troops from Dunkirk
	July: The Battle for Britain begins
	August: After coming close to success, Hitler redirects Luftwaffe attacks from British airfields to British cities
	October: Hitler calls off Operation Sea Lion
1941	April 17: St. Paul's Cathedral sustains a direct bomb hit
	June: Battleship *Bismarck* sunk in Atlantic
	June 22: Hitler invades the Soviet Union
	July: FDR cuts off oil sales to Imperial Japan
	July: Germans advance 500 miles, taking one million prisoners
	August: Germans capture Kiev, including 400,000 Russians
	August: FDR and Churchill met at sea; draw up the Atlantic Charter
	November 25: Japanese task force departs, maintains radio silence

December 5: German invasion grinds to a halt

December 6: Russian counter-attack begins

December 7: Japan attacks Pearl Harbor; seven battleships sunk or damaged; 2,400 Americans killed

December 8: U.S.A. declares war on Japan

December 11: Germany declares war on U.S.A.

December: Joint British-American planning begins

1942   May: Germany starts new invasion of southern Russia; Battle of Coral Sea is fought to a draw

June: Afrika Korps captures Tobruk

June 4: Battle of Midway ends with four Japanese carriers sunk

September: First German troops enter Stalingrad; first German troops reach Egyptian border

October: Allied troops come ashore at Algeria during Operation Torch; Battle of el-Alemain begins

November: Soviet Union launches huge counterattack outside Stalingrad

1943   February 1: Field Marshal von Paulus surrenders

June: Battle of Kursk begins

July: U.S.S.R. wins Battle of Kursk

July: British and Americans invade Sicily

1944   June 6: Operation Overlord, better known as D-Day, begins

June 8: Roughly 250,000 Allies troops are now ashore in Normandy

July 20: Unsuccessful attempt to assassinate Hitler and end Third Reich

July 27: Allied liberation of Paris

December 16: Battle of the Bulge—named for the way it looks on a map—begins

December 16–22: Germans make unexpected gains; fail to capture Bastogne

December 26: Bastogne relieved by Patton

December 31: End of the year finds Germans where they were prior to Battle of the Bulge

1945   February: FDR, Churchill, and Stalin meet at Yalta

April 12: FDR dies in Warm Springs, Georgia

April 18: Battle for Berlin begins

April 30: Hitler and wife commit suicide in a bunker

May 4: Admiral Doenitz signs surrender document

May 5: Victory in Europe Day; immense celebrations

		August 6: A-Bomb dropped on Hiroshima
		August 8: U.S.S.R. enters Pacific War, invades Manchuria
		August 9: A-Bomb dropped on Nagasaki
		August 15: Internal struggles in Japan
		September 2: Japan officially surrenders during ceremonies aboard battleship *Missouri*
	1947	March: President Truman declares U.S.A. will assist countries that fight against communist infiltration
		June: Blockade of Berlin begins
	1948	June: Blockade of Berlin ends
	1949	August: U.S.S.R. explodes its first A-Bomb
		September: Americans learn of Russian successful bomb test
		October 1: Mao Zedong proclaims the new People's Republic of China
	1950	February: Senator Joseph McCarthy denounces communists in U.S. State Department; he is short on specifics
		June 25: Korean War begins with invasion of the South by the North
		September 15: United Nations troops land at Inchon
		November 27: Chinese troops begin massive assault on U.N. forces
	1953	March: Josef Stalin dies
	1954	May: Eisenhower contemplates use of nuclear weapons to prevent French defeat in Indochina
	1956	October: Suez War, also known as Arab-Israeli War of 1956, begins
	1957	October: U.S.S.R. launches *Sputnik*, world's first artificial satellite
	1960	May 1: U.S. pilot and U-2 plane shot down in Russia
	1961	January: Eisenhower warns of "military industrial complex"
		April: American failure at the Bay of Pigs
		June: John F. Kennedy and Khrushchev meet in Vienna
		August: Building of the Berlin Wall begins
	1962	October: Cuban Missile Crisis
	1963	June: Kennedy speaks of scaling back nuclear arms; Diem assassinated in South Vietnam; Kennedy assassinated in Dallas
	1964	March: People's Republic of China detonates nuclear bomb
		May: Gulf of Tonkin incident
		October: Khrushchev ousted as Soviet leader
	1967	June 5–11: The Six-Day War in the Middle East
524	1968	January 30: Tet Offensive is launched by Viet Cong

March 30: Lyndon Johnson declares he will not seek reelection

April 4: Martin Luther King, Jr. assassinated in Memphis

June 4: Robert Kennedy assassinated in Los Angeles

August: Democratic National Convention nearly tears Chicago apart

1969 January: Richard Nixon inaugurated in Washington, D.C.

July 20: American astronauts land on the Moon

1970 May 5: Students shot and killed by National Guard at Kent State University

1972 February: Richard Nixon makes surprise visit to Beijing

1973 October 3–16: Yom Kippur War in the Middle East

October 20: Arab oil boycott begins

1974 August 8: Richard Nixon resigns presidency

August 9: Gerald Ford begins caretaker administration

1975 April 30: Last U.S. servicemen depart Vietnam

September: General Franco dies; Juan Carlos becomes King of Spain

1976 September: Mao Zedong, China's Great Helmsman, dies

1979 January: Shah departs Iran

February: Ayatollah Khomeini returns to Iran

June: Jimmy Carter gives incoherent speech about malaise in U.S. national spirit

November 4: Iranian students seize U.S. Embassy in Tehran

December 23: U.S.S.R. invades Afghanistan

1980 April: U.S. rescue effort of hostages fails in Iran

1981 January 20: Ronald Reagan inaugurated; American hostages in Iran are released

spring: Reagan and Pope John Paul II both survive assassination attempts

1982 winter: Falklands War between Britain and Argentina

1983 March: Reagan uses words "evil empire" in speech about Soviet Union; Reagan addresses fellow Americans on subject of his Strategic Defense Initiative, which his critics quickly label "Star Wars"

October: U.S. invades and occupies Caribbean Island of Grenada; 100 million viewers watch "The Day After" on American television

1985 March: Mikhail Gorbachev becomes leader of U.S.S.R.

November: Reagan and Gorbachev meet in Geneva

1986 December: Reagan and Gorbachev meet in Iceland

1989 June: Funeral of Ayatollah Khomeini in Iran; Tiananmen Square protests in China

October–November: Fall of the Berlin Wall

December: Communist regime in Romania is ousted

1990   August: Saddam Hussein invades Kuwait

fall: Build-up of Coalition forces in Saudi Arabia

1991   January: Air assault on Hussein's army begins

February: U.S. Operation Desert Storm routs Hussein's army from Kuwait

December: U.S.S.R. ceases to exist; replaced by Russian Republic

2001   September 11: al Qaeda terrorists hit and destroy the World Trade Center in New York City

October: U.S. covert actions in Afghanistan begin

2003   March: Second Gulf War begins

April: Saddam Hussein's regime is toppled

May: President George W. Bush declares "Mission Accomplished"

2004   December: Saddam Hussein found and captured; he is executed in 2006

2011   Al Qaeda leader Osama bin Laden found and killed by U.S. troops

2014   Ukrainian Revolution overthrows President Viktor Yanukovych; Russia invades the Crimean Peninsula; China overtakes the United States as the world's largest economy

Index

Note: (ill.) indicates photos and illustrations.

528

N